Lecture Notes in Computer Science   16100

Founding Editors

Gerhard Goos
Juris Hartmanis

Editorial Board Members

Elisa Bertino, USA
Wen Gao, China

Bernhard Steffen, Germany
Moti Yung, USA

Advanced Research in Computing and Software Science

Subline of Lecture Notes in Computer Science

Subline Series Editors

Giorgio Ausiello, *University of Rome 'La Sapienza', Italy*
Vladimiro Sassone, *University of Southampton, UK*

Subline Advisory Board

Susanne Albers, *TU Munich, Germany*
Benjamin C. Pierce, *University of Pennsylvania, USA*
Bernhard Steffen, *University of Dortmund, Germany*
Deng Xiaotie, *Peking University, Beijing, China*
Jeannette M. Wing, *Microsoft Research, Redmond, WA, USA*

The series Lecture Notes in Computer Science (LNCS), including its subseries Lecture Notes in Artificial Intelligence (LNAI) and Lecture Notes in Bioinformatics (LNBI), has established itself as a medium for the publication of new developments in computer science and information technology research, teaching, and education.

LNCS enjoys close cooperation with the computer science R & D community, the series counts many renowned academics among its volume editors and paper authors, and collaborates with prestigious societies. Its mission is to serve this international community by providing an invaluable service, mainly focused on the publication of conference and workshop proceedings and postproceedings. LNCS commenced publication in 1973.

Hakjoo Oh · Yulei Siu
Editors

Static Analysis

32nd International Symposium, SAS 2025
Singapore, Singapore, October 13–14, 2025
Proceedings

Editors
Hakjoo Oh
Korea University
Seoul, Korea (Republic of)

Yulei Siu
UNSW Sydney
Sydney, NSW, Australia

ISSN 0302-9743   ISSN 1611-3349 (electronic)
Lecture Notes in Computer Science
ISBN 978-3-032-07105-7   ISBN 978-3-032-07106-4 (eBook)
https://doi.org/10.1007/978-3-032-07106-4

© The Editor(s) (if applicable) and The Author(s), under exclusive license
to Springer Nature Switzerland AG 2026

This work is subject to copyright. All rights are solely and exclusively licensed by the Publisher, whether the whole or part of the material is concerned, specifically the rights of translation, reprinting, reuse of illustrations, recitation, broadcasting, reproduction on microfilms or in any other physical way, and transmission or information storage and retrieval, electronic adaptation, computer software, or by similar or dissimilar methodology now known or hereafter developed.
The use of general descriptive names, registered names, trademarks, service marks, etc. in this publication does not imply, even in the absence of a specific statement, that such names are exempt from the relevant protective laws and regulations and therefore free for general use.
The publisher, the authors and the editors are safe to assume that the advice and information in this book are believed to be true and accurate at the date of publication. Neither the publisher nor the authors or the editors give a warranty, expressed or implied, with respect to the material contained herein or for any errors or omissions that may have been made. The publisher remains neutral with regard to jurisdictional claims in published maps and institutional affiliations.

This Springer imprint is published by the registered company Springer Nature Switzerland AG
The registered company address is: Gewerbestrasse 11, 6330 Cham, Switzerland

If disposing of this product, please recycle the paper.

Preface

This volume contains the proceedings of the 32nd edition of the International Static Analysis Symposium, SAS 2025, held on October 13–14, 2025, in Singapore. Following the most recent tradition, the conference was a co-located event of SPLASH, the ACM SIGPLAN conference on Systems, Programming, Languages, and Applications: Software for Humanity. Static analysis is widely recognized as a fundamental tool for program verification, bug detection, compiler optimization, program understanding, and software maintenance. The series of Static Analysis Symposia serves as the primary venue for the presentation of theoretical, practical, and applied advances in the area. Previous symposia were held in Pasadena, Cascais, Auckland, Chicago, Porto, Freiburg, New York, Edinburgh, Saint-Malo, Munich, Seattle, Deauville, Venice, Perpignan, Los Angeles, Valencia, Kongens Lyngby, Seoul, London, Verona, San Diego, Madrid, Paris, Santa Barbara, Venice, Pisa, Paris, Aachen, Glasgow, and Namur.

SAS 2025 called for papers on topics including, but not limited to, abstract interpretation, automated deduction, data flow analysis, debugging techniques, deductive methods, emerging applications, model checking, data science, program optimizations and transformations, program synthesis, program verification, machine learning and verification, security analysis, tool environments and architectures, theoretical frameworks, type checking, distributed or networked systems, and LLM for static analysis and static analysis for LLM. Besides the regular papers, authors were encouraged to submit submissions in the NEAT category to discuss visions, challenges, experiences, problems, and impactful solutions in the field of static analysis from both a research and applications perspective. Authors were encouraged to submit artifacts accompanying their papers to strengthen evaluations and the reproducibility of results.

The conference employed a double-blind reviewing process supported by HotCRP, including an author response period. This year, SAS received 32 full-paper submissions, including 5 NEAT papers. Each paper underwent at least three first-round reviews, after which authors were given the opportunity to respond. Following the author-response period, the Program Committee held a thorough discussion to assess each submission's quality and relevance, ultimately reaching consensus on acceptance decisions. Overall, 15 papers (12 regular and 3 NEAT) were accepted and appear in this volume.

We consider artifacts essential to the success and development of static analysis as making artifacts available enables independent reproduction of experiments, significantly enhancing the transparency and impact of the research. Kihong Heo and Yue Li served as chairs of the Artifact Evaluation Committee (AEC) and coordinated the artifact evaluation process. Following the practice established at SAS 2024, authors could submit artifacts either as Docker or Virtual Machine images. Accepted artifacts are publicly archived on Zenodo at https://zenodo.org/communities/sas-2025. The committee awarded badges to artifacts at three levels: Validated (correct functionality), Extensible (easy addition of new capabilities), and Available (on Zenodo). The badge artwork was designed by Arpita Biswas (Rutgers University) and Suvam Mukherjee (Microsoft). This year, SAS 2025 received 9 artifact submissions. Similarly to paper submissions, each artifact underwent review by three AEC members, and 7 out of 9 submissions earned the Validated badge.

In addition to the contributed papers, SAS 2025 featured four invited talks by distinguished researchers: Olivier Danvy (National University of Singapore), Xavier Rival (INRIA & CNRS & ENS Paris), Ilya Sergey (National University of Singapore), and Qirun Zhang (Georgia Institute of Technology). The Program Committee also selected the recipient of the Radhia Cousot Young Researcher Best Paper Award, recognizing a paper with a significant student contribution. The winner was announced during the conference. This award honors the memory of Radhia Cousot for her foundational contributions to static analysis and her instrumental role in promoting and organizing the SAS conference series.

The SAS 2025 program would not have been possible without the dedicated efforts of many people. We sincerely thank them all. Members of the Program Committee, the Artifact Evaluation Committee, and external reviewers worked tirelessly to assemble a strong technical program, providing authors with thoughtful and constructive feedback. We are also grateful to the SPLASH 2025 Organizing Committee, chaired by Charles Zhang (Hong Kong University of Science and Technology), for their invaluable efforts toward the success of the conference. Special thanks go to the SAS 2024 chairs, Roberto Giacobazzi and Alessandra Gorla, as well as the entire SAS Steering Committee for their guidance and support. We also thank our sponsors for their generous support of the conference. Finally, we thank Springer for publishing these proceedings.

August 2025

Hakjoo Oh
Yulei Sui

Organization

Program Committee Chairs

Hakjoo Oh	Korea University, South Korea
Yulei Sui	University of New South Wales, Australia

Steering Committee

Bor-Yuh Evan Chang	University of Colorado & Amazon, USA
Patrick Cousot	New York University, USA
Cezara Dragoi	Amazon Web Services, France
Roberto Giacobazzi	University of Arizona, USA
Alessandra Gorla	IMDEA Software Institute, Spain
Manuel Hermenegildo	UPM and IMDEA Software Institute, Spain
José F. Morales	UPM and IMDEA Software Institute, Spain
Kedar Namjoshi	Nokia Bell Labs, USA
David Pichardie	Meta and University of Rennes, ENS Rennes, IRISA, France
Mihaela Sighireanu	LSV, ENS Paris-Saclay, France
Gagandeep Singh	UIUC and VMware Research, USA
Caterina Urban	Inria and École Normale Supérieure, France

Program Committee

Karim Ali	NYU Abu Dhabi, UAE
Kyungmin Bae	POSTECH, South Korea
Sébastien Bardin	CEA LIST, Université Paris-Saclay, France
Roberto Bruni	University of Pisa, Italy
Liqian Chen	NUDT, China
Lucas C. Cordeiro	University of Manchester, UK
Mila Dalla Preda	University of Verona, Italy
Pierre Ganty	IMDEA Software Institute, Spain
Samir Genaim	Universidad Complutense de Madrid, Spain
Ningyu He	Hong Kong Polytechnic University, Hong Kong SAR China
Quang Loc Le	University College London, UK

Pedro López-García   CSIC and IMDEA Software Institute, Spain
Antoine Miné   Sorbonne Université, France
Ashish Mishra   IIT Hyderabad, India
Sidi Mohamed Beillahi   University of Toronto, Canada
Raphaël Monat   Inria & University of Lille, France
Jorge A. Navas   Certora, USA
Jihyeok Park   Korea University, South Korea
Goran Piskachev   Amazon Web Services, Germany
Xiaokang Qiu   Purdue University, USA
Xavier Rival   Inria & CNRS & ENS Paris, France
Xujie Si   University of Toronto, Canada
Gagandeep Singh   UIUC & VMware Research, USA
Sunbeom So   GIST, South Korea
Fu Song   Institute of Software, Chinese Academy of Sciences, China
Tian Tan   Nanjing University, China
Mohit Tekriwal   Lawrence Livermore National Laboratory, USA
Manas Thakur   IIT Bombay, India
Caterina Urban   Inria & École Normale Supérieure, France
Yuepeng Wang   Simon Fraser University, Canada
Peisen Yao   Zhejiang University, China
Jooyong Yi   UNIST, South Korea
Enea Zaffanella   University of Parma, Italy
Qirun Zhang   Georgia Institute of Technology, USA
Xin Zhang   Peking University, China

Artifact Evaluation Committee Chairs

Kihong Heo   KAIST, South Korea
Yue Li   Nanjing University, China

Artifact Evaluation Committee

Giacomo Boldini   Ca' Foscari University of Venice, Italy
Menglong Chen   Nanjing University, China
Pierre Goutagny   Inria & University of Lille, France
Sujin Jang   KAIST, South Korea
Danya Lette   University of Toronto, Canada
Teodors Lisovenko   Ca' Foscari University of Venice, Italy
Jie Liu   ByteDance, China

Amirmohammad Nazari	University of Southern California, USA
Wonseok Oh	Korea University, South Korea
Jyoti Prakash	University of Passau, Germany
Milla Valnet	Sorbonne Université, France
Xiangzhe Xu	Purdue University, USA
Zhenyu Yan	Peking University, China
Shengyuan Yang	University of Wisconsin–Madison, USA
Giacomo Zanatta	Ca' Foscari University of Venice, Italy
Teng Zhang	Nanjing University, China
Charles de Haro	École Normale Supérieure/Université PSL, France

Additional Reviewers

Xiao Cheng
Daniela Ferreiro
Fabio Gadducci
Daniel Jurjo

Jiawei Ren
Louis Rustenholz
Francesco Tiezzi
Qin Wang

Invited Talks

Towards Static Analyses and Abstract Domains for Hyperproperties

Xavier Rival

Inria & CNRS & ENS Paris, France
Xavier.Rival@ens.fr

Abstract. Abstract interpretation-based static analysis aims at computing program properties such as absence of runtime errors, (non)-termination, security properties, and more. Semantic properties of interest may generally be classified into families such as trace properties (including safety and liveness) or hyperproperties. Since the former are simpler to express and prove as they feature sound and complete proof methods, they are also addressed by a comprehensive body of works in static analysis techniques and abstract domains. By comparison, hyperproperties are more difficult to analyse in a precise manner. In this presentation, we recall the main distinctions between each of these classes of properties. We cite several examples of hyperproperties, and illustrate the difficulties to compute them. Finally, we compare several static analysis techniques to infer specific families of hyperproperties.

Multi-Modal Verification of Distributed Systems in Lean

Ilya Sergey

National University of Singapore
ilya@nus.edu.sg

Abstract. In this talk, I will present Veil, a framework for automated and interactive verification of transition systems, aimed specifically at conducting machine-assisted proofs about concurrent and distributed algorithms. Veil is implemented on top of the Lean proof assistant. It allows one to describe a transition system and its specification in a simple imperative language, producing verification conditions in first-order logic, to be discharged automatically via a range of SMT solvers. In case automated verification fails or if the system's description requires statements in a higher-order logic, Veil provides an interactive verification mode, by virtue of being embedded in a general-purpose proof assistant. Veil's automated verification performance is acceptable for practical verification tasks, while it also allows for seamless automated/interactive verification of system specifications beyond the reach of existing automated provers.

From Within: Compiler Testing and Validation via Compilers

Qirun Zhang

Georgia Institute of Technology
qrzhang@gatech.edu

Abstract. Ensuring compiler correctness is fundamental to computing. Compiler testing and translation validation are two popular techniques to improve compiler correctness. In this talk, we revisit these traditional tasks from a compiler-centric perspective, showing how internal compiler information can be harnessed to strengthen both testing and validation. We will present two case studies, highlight their advantages, and outline open challenges and future directions toward a unified compiler-centric analysis framework.

Contents

On a Simple Problem Due to Yves Bertot 1
    Olivier Danvy

Verifying Neural Networks with PyRAT 11
    Augustin Lemesle, Julien Lehmann, Tristan Le Gall, and Zakaria Chihani

Contextual Equality Saturation 34
    Alexandre Drewery, Thomas P. Jensen, and David Pichardie

A Programming Language for Feasible Solutions 62
    Weijun Chen, Yuxi Fu, and Huan Long

Specifying and Verifying Future Conditions 90
    Yahui Song, Darius Foo, and Wei-Ngan Chin

AURA: Precise Abstract Interpretation of Probabilistic Programs
with Interval Data Uncertainty 113
    Zixin Huang, Jacob Laurel, Saikat Dutta, and Sasa Misailovic

Comparing the Precision of Abstract Operators in the eBPF Verifier Using
Differential Synthesis 142
    *Matan Shachnai, Harishankar Vishwanathan, Srinivas Narayana,
    and Santosh Nagarakatte*

Bounded-Exhaustive Subspace Diversification for SMT Solver Testing 167
    Junda Zheng and Peisen Yao

Abstracting Concolic Execution for Soft Contract Verification 190
    Bram Vandenbogaerde, Quentin Stiévenart, and Coen De Roover

Enhancing Neural Network Robustness via Synthesis of Repair Programs 221
    Tom Yuviler and Dana Drachsler-Cohen

Relating Distances and Abstractions: An Abstract Interpretation
Perspective 249
    Marco Campion, Isabella Mastroeni, and Caterina Urban

DUCTAPE: Optimizing Dynamically Typed Programs Using Ahead-of-Time
Compilation and Data-Flow Analysis 278
    Adi Harif and Shachar Itzhaky

Automated Catamorphism Synthesis for Solving Constrained Horn
Clauses over Algebraic Data Types 305
    Hiroyuki Katsura, Naoki Kobayashi, Ken Sakayori, and Ryosuke Sato

Formal Analysis of Networked PLC Controllers Interacting with Physical
Environments 328
    Jaeseo Lee and Kyungmin Bae

Monarch: A Modular Framework for Abstract Definitional Interpreters
in Haskell 357
    *Bram Vandenbogaerde, Sarah Verbelen, Noah Van Es,
    and Coen De Roover*

Delta Store Semantics: Abstract Garbage Collection for Abstract
Definitional Interpreters 386
    Noah Van Es, Bram Vandenbogaerde, and Coen De Roover

Author Index 423

On a Simple Problem Due to Yves Bertot

Olivier Danvy[✉]

School of Computing, National University of Singapore, Singapore, Singapore
danvy@acm.org

Abstract. Yves Bertot, in his pedagogical wisdom, gives the following simple problem in his introduction to the Rocq Proof Assistant: "Is the product of two consecutive natural numbers even?" This simple problem is a classical exercise in elementary mathematics, but tackling it mobilizes all the growing cognitive faculties of the learner, from decomposing this informal mathematical statement into its components – from what it means for two natural numbers to be consecutive to the nature of even numbers – to formalizing these components, composing the results of these formalizations into a suitably quantified formal mathematical statement, and then proving this statement formally. The problem can be fruitfully generalized to investigating the divisibility properties of the product of three (or four, or five, ...) consecutive natural numbers. Overall, Yves Bertot's simple problem gives rise to an engaging adventure of mathematical and computational discovery (as well as to one of self-discovery), which the present article describes.

Keywords: The Rocq Proof Assistant · divisibility of the product of consecutive natural numbers · nested induction · binomial coefficients

1 Introduction and Motivation

Mathematics and computing are not just for counting and for calculating.
They are for reasoning and for reflecting.
Therein lies their lasting value.

What makes the Rocq Proof Assistant [1] appealing to connect mathematics and computing is that its core language of tactics seems directly inspired by the way proofs are written in the Bourbaki school of mathematics, which is implicit in undergraduate courses about calculus, discrete mathematics, and linear algebra. And so computer-science students feel welcome in a world where they can write proofs as rigorously as when they write programs in a functional programming language, where they state theorems and auxiliary lemmas with the same rationale as when they declare main functions and auxiliary functions, and where lexical scope rules too. Another advantage of using a proof assistant is that it offers a safe playground to learn how to state theorems and lemmas, which undergraduate students have zero experience with.

This article describes a lab activity in Week 6 of a semester-long introduction to functional programming and proving at Yale-NUS College, where Week 1 is dedicated to functional programming, Week 2 to proving logical propositions and algebraic properties, Week 3 to specifications and structural induction, Week 4 to reasoning equationally about recursive programs, and Week 5 to mystery functions [2]. This lab activity is inspired by Yves Bertot's simple problem that he also presents early in his introduction to the Rocq Proof Assistant: "Is the product of two consecutive natural numbers even?" – a classical exercise in elementary mathematics. Prior to Week 6, the students – who work in groups – have been exposed to implementing parity predicates recursively and to proving their soundness and their completeness inductively:

```
Fixpoint evenp (n : nat) : bool :=
  match n with 0    => true
             | S n' => oddp n'
  end
with oddp (n : nat) : bool :=
       match n with 0    => false
                  | S n' => evenp n'
       end.

Theorem soundness_and_completeness_of_evenp_and_oddp :
  forall n : nat,
    (evenp n = true <-> exists m : nat, n = 2 * m)
    /\
    ( oddp n = true <-> exists m : nat, n = S (2 * m)).
```

(A side note: Students blindly accept this statement of soundness and completeness. To sharpen their critical sense, a teacher can playfully ask them about "the other cases." Indeed, what about the cases where `evenp` and `oddp` return `false`? Shouldn't one also prove that `evenp` returns `false` if and only if it is applied to an odd number, and that `oddp` returns `false` if and only if it is applied to an even number? The students acquiesce that yes, this is an issue. They can then be made to realize that these other cases actually follow from the theorem as stated (and vice-versa, actually). Eventually, they mutter to themselves that this all makes sense. (Eliciting this kind of understanding is a Holy Grail for a reflective teacher, and in the author's experience, a progressive and `simpl`-free introduction to Rocq delivers this kind of reflective understanding in spades.))

Later on in the semester, the students learn how to reason about accumulator-based functions, which provides them with an opportunity to reflect on the computational nature of accumulators. They are also exposed to strong induction.

1.1 Prerequisites and Notation

The target audience of this article includes readers who enjoy seeing how a simple property generalizes simply into an unexpected result; readers who are curious about formalizing such a simple property as well as its generalization; students who wish to acquire more insight about induction and nested induction; teachers

on the lookout for a fun lab activity with their students; and more generally
(static or dynamic) analytical readers who – to use Rota's classification [3] –
appreciate theorizing as well as problem solving.

The reader is expected to be minimally familiar with functional programming
(e.g., the earlier declaration of evenp and oddp), with reading elementary logical
statements (e.g., the earlier statement of soundness_and_completeness_of_evenp_
and_oddp) and with mathematical induction. For example, Theorem soundness_
and_completeness_of_evenp_and_oddp is proved by induction over n, and so are
the following properties:

```
Property even_or_odd :
  forall n : nat,
    (exists q : nat, n = 2 * q) \/ (exists q : nat, n = S (2 * q)).

Property evenp_or_oddp :
  forall n : nat,
    evenp n = true \/ oddp n = true.
```

In words, a number is either even or odd. (Each of these properties is also a
corollary of the other and of the soundness and completeness of evenp and oddp.)

1.2 Roadmap

The rest of this paper is structured as follows. [1] Sect. 2 states the simple problem
and analyzes how the students tackle it. Section 3 generalizes the simple problem
from two consecutive numbers to three consecutive numbers. Section 4 generalizes the simple problem to arbitrarily many consecutive numbers. Section 5 puts
the simple problem into perspective.

2 The Simple Problem and How the Students Tackle It

> *Consider the product of two consecutive natural numbers.*
> *Is this product an even number?*

The first step for tackling the problem is to remind oneself what it means for a
number to be even, the second is to understand the meaning of "two consecutive
natural numbers," and the third is to assess whether the product of two such
numbers is even or not. The soundness theorem mentioned in Sect. 1 notwithstanding, most of the students say that a number is even if it is divisible by 2.
Next, all by themselves, the students consider $2 \cdot 3$, $3 \cdot 4$, etc., and then they
observe that $2 \cdot 3 = 6$ and 6 is even, that $3 \cdot 4 = 12$ and 12 is even, etc. They can
then gently be asked (a) why – which forces them to articulate that multiplying

---

[1] Factoid: This sentence is a French alexandrine (it has twelve syllables), like *Attention
à la marche en descendant du train* in the Parisian RER. Poetry is everywhere.

two numbers yields an even number when at least one of the two numbers is even – and (b) whether the property also holds for smaller numbers. They explore $1 \cdot 2$ and then even $0 \cdot 1$, and conclude affirmatively, an elementary instance of the scientific method.

For students with no experience in stating theorems, it is not obvious at all that the simplest way to write the product of two consecutive numbers is $n \cdot (n+1)$, for any given n, instead of, e.g., quantifying two numbers and then qualifying them. Often, they need to be gently encouraged to simplify the first versions of their formal statement until the point where they will have meaningfully stated their very first theorem in a way that ends with the approval of their teacher. This first theorem has profound implications for their ability to state Eureka lemmas when reasoning about accumulator-based functions later on in the semester.

What happens next depends on the mindset of each student, and in the author's experience, it is a good idea to preface the simple problem with the warning that the way each will solve it (implicitly leaving no doubt about the fact that they *will* solve it) will reveal something about the way they primarily think: like a mathematician or like a computer scientist (in that a mathematician tends to consider what is being computed whereas a computer scientist tends to consider how things are computed). This simple warning induces a lot more reflection in the classroom, because the problem has stopped to be "just another exercise" – it has become a mini-journey of self-discovery.

Each student has their own understanding of what it means for a number to be even: It may be independent and involve the "modulo" operator (that we have not seen at all, and therefore that induces a stressful exploration of unknown material that is explained in unknown terms); it may be intensional and involve `evenp`; or it may be extensional and involve an existential quantifier. (The intensional understanding and the extensional understanding are the two sides of the theorem about soundness and completeness, but these two understandings are typically not reflective enough for the students to make the connection, their personal tree of knowledge still being a disconnected graph.)

The classroom then splits into individual explorations that are federated by the group in which each student solves the weekly exercises, while the lecturer goes from student to student, listening to the rendition of their exploration and encouraging them to simplify their formal statement.

Nowadays, nearly no students have a pen and a paper in their bag. Some students have a graphics tablet, though, and nearly all students have their laptop with them. So the lecturer brings pens and sheets of paper as well as whiteboard markers in his own bag, just in case, and invariably they end up being used for sketching informal proofs.

Some students embark on an economical exploration that relies on the resident parity predicate in the `Nat` library:

```
Theorem the_product_of_two_consecutive_nats_is_even_economically :
  forall n : nat,
    Nat.even (n * (n + 1)) = true.
```

They use the Rocq search facility to locate relevant lemmas about even numbers, and they prove their theorem quite rapidly. They are then encouraged to devise a more stand-alone proof, and if that does not appeal to them, to move on to the later exercises about the product of three consecutive numbers, where they typically get stuck, lacking library support, which prompts them to backtrack in their investigation and find another tack.

Some students embark into an intensional exploration that relies on evenp:

```
Theorem the_product_of_two_consecutive_nats_is_even_intensionally :
  forall n : nat,
    evenp (n * (n + 1)) = true.
```

They rapidly discover that they need more general properties about the parity of the product of two numbers depending on the parity of each of these numbers. They start to state and prove these more general properties, and are very receptive to the breadth-first value of stating auxiliary lemmas lazily, admitting them first to see whether they do the job, and only proving these auxiliary lemmas if they do the job.

Some students embark into an extensional exploration that relies on an existential quantification:

```
Theorem the_product_of_two_consecutive_nats_is_even_extensionally :
  forall n : nat,
    exists q : nat,
      n * (n + 1) = 2 * q.
```

They all start with an induction proof. Most give up in the induction step and seek Eureka lemmas, e.g., one to the effect that either a number is even or its successor is even – a sensible take considering the statement of the simple problem:

```
Lemma a_number_is_even_or_its_successor_is_even :
  forall n : nat,
    exists q : nat,
      n = 2 * q \/ S n = 2 * q.
```

A few do not give up, complete the induction step, and move on to the later exercises about the product of three consecutive numbers, wondering a little bit about all the activity in the rest of the classroom.

In the course of the lab session, many realize that writing S n instead of n + 1 in their theorem simplifies both the proof of this theorem and the proofs that use it, since one constructs a value – and therefore requires no proof steps – whereas the other carries out a computation – and therefore requires proof steps.

Once they have completed their first proof, the students are encouraged to come back to their initial analysis of the simple problem, where they articulated that multiplying two numbers yields an even number when at least one of the two numbers is even. They formalize this articulation as a lemma, they see how this lemma enables them to prove their theorem, and they prove this lemma.

To wrap up, the lecturer highlights the various proof strategies elaborated in the classroom, broadly classifies them as inspired by mathematics or by computing, and stresses that backtracking is an integral part of devising proofs. Numerous are the students who then animatedly explain how they started one strategy, gave up for no good reason, moved on to another, and in retrospect should have trusted themselves more and pursued their first strategy. Ditto for how the strategy they picked reveals an inclination towards mathematics or towards computing, how intuitive this strategy feels, etc. They have started to reflect about what they do, how they do it, and who they are.

> *C'est avec la logique que l'on prouve et avec l'intuition que l'on trouve.*
> *(We find intuitively and we prove logically.)*
> – Henri Poincaré

3 Generalizing the Simple Problem to the Product of Three Consecutive Numbers

The next two exercises are about proving (a) that the product of three consecutive numbers is divisible by 2, and (b) that it is divisible by 3:

```
Theorem the_product_of_three_consecutive_nats_is_divisible_by_2 :
  forall n : nat,
    exists q : nat,
      n * (n + 1) * (n + 2) = 2 * q.
```

```
Theorem the_product_of_three_consecutive_nats_is_divisible_by_3 :
  forall n : nat,
    exists q : nat,
      n * (n + 1) * (n + 2) = 3 * q.
```

The point of the first exercise is to make the students realize that this property is a corollary of the one they just proved, since the product of three consecutive numbers contains the product of two consecutive numbers. But this realization is not obvious, and many students need a gentle push towards it so that they can make this realization and then own the concept of a corollary.

The point of the second exercise is to make the students generalize the property that a number n is even (there exists a number q such that $n = 2 \cdot q$) or it is odd (there exists a number q such that $n = 2 \cdot q + 1$) – or equivalently that either a number is even or its successor is even. (Proving this equivalence is independently rewarding, e.g., at an oral exam.) This generalization is that a number is either ternary (there exists a number q such that $n = 3 \cdot q$), post-ternary (there exists a number q such that $n = 3 \cdot q + 1$), or pre-ternary (there exists a number q such that $n = 3 \cdot q + 2$) – or equivalently that either a number is ternary, or its successor is ternary, or the successor of its successor is ternary. (This equivalence can also be proved at an oral exam.)

```
Lemma a_number_is_ternary_or_one_of_its_two_successors_is_ternary :
  forall n : nat,
    exists q : nat,
      n = 3 * q \/ S n = 3 * q \/ S (S n) = 3 * q.
```

This generalization, however, is even less obvious, and most students start from scratch and look for something else, e.g., the modulo operator. They need to be encouraged to reflect on what they know rather than to ceaselessly seek new things with the tacit admission that what they know is useless since they are not reusing it. [2]

The next exercise hints at a more general property: proving that the product of three consecutive numbers is divisible by 6:

```
Proposition the_product_of_three_consecutive_nats_is_divisible_by_6 :
  forall n : nat,
    exists q : nat,
      n * (n + 1) * (n + 2) = 6 * q.
```

The mathematically inclined students point out that if a number is divisible by 2 and by 3, it is divisible by 6, but proving this property requires a slightly stronger form of induction than ordinary mathematical induction, and they accept that we will revisit this property and prove it a bit later in the semester. For practice, though, they are encouraged to state this property. And again for practice, they are also asked about its converse (a number divisible by 6 is divisible by 2 and by 3), which they then prove, exercising their muscle memory as well as expanding their comfort zone.

Meanwhile, most other students realize that the earlier generalization (either n is divisible by 6, or $n + 1$ is divisible by 6, or $n + 2$ is divisible by 6, or $n + 3$ is divisible by 6, or $n + 4$ is divisible by 6, or $n + 5$ is divisible by 6), is not sustainable, as it requires bigger and bigger proofs. They are made to discover that in contrast, the size of an ordinary induction proof is unchanging and therefore unproblematic.

4 Generalizing the Simple Problem to the Product of More Consecutive Numbers

The next series of exercises is about the product of four consecutive numbers, which are divisible by 2 as well as by 3, 4, 6, 8, 12, and 24:

```
Proposition the_product_of_four_consecutive_nats_is_divisible_by_24 :
  forall n : nat,
    exists q : nat,
      n * (n + 1) * (n + 2) * (n + 3) = 24 * q.
```

The next exercise is about the product of five consecutive numbers, which – to cut the chase – is divisible by 120 (and thus by any of the divisors of 120).

---

[2] Actually, this admission is not tacit, it is unstated, and either way it nurtures their insecurity. In contrast, a reinforcing strategy makes the learner secure in the knowledge that their knowledge is actionable, and it makes them rejoice in learning something genuinely new because of all the ways they can both use and reuse this new thing. At Yale-NUS College, this reinforcing strategy changed Computer Science from not being for everybody to being for everyone, without fuss.

Proposition the_product_of_five_consecutive_nats_is_divisible_by_120 :
  forall n : nat,
    exists q : nat,
      n * (n + 1) * (n + 2) * (n + 3) * (n + 4) = 120 * q.

The next exercise is about the product of six consecutive numbers, which – to also cut the chase – is divisible by 720.

At that point, the students realize that they have seen 2, 6, 24, 120, and 720 before, namely when writing unit tests for the factorial function, and they are made to conjecture that the product of seven consecutive numbers is divisible by 7!, i.e., 5040, which is challenging for Rocq due to its representation of natural numbers as Peano numbers (all bets are off for numbers larger than 5000, or so a warning says).

So the students are made to revisit each of the previous proofs – that the product of two consecutive numbers is divisible by 2!, that the product of three consecutive numbers is divisible by 3!, that the product of four consecutive numbers is divisible by 4!, etc.:

Proposition the_product_of_two_consecutive_nats_is_divisible_by_fac_2 :
  forall n : nat,
    exists q : nat,
      n * (n + 1) = fac 2 * q.

Proposition the_product_of_three_consecutive_nats_is_divisible_by_fac_3 :
  forall n : nat,
    exists q : nat,
      n * (n + 1) * (n + 2) = fac 3 * q.

Proposition the_product_of_four_consecutive_nats_is_divisible_by_fac_4 :
  forall n : nat,
    exists q : nat,
      n * (n + 1) * (n + 2) * (n + 3) = fac 4 * q.

And they are made to realize that the proof about three consecutive numbers uses the property about two consecutive numbers, that the proof about four consecutive numbers uses the property about three consecutive numbers, etc. and that these proofs can be written with the very same structure.

So the students are made to program a product function that, given a natural number i strictly greater than 1 and a natural number n, computes the product of i consecutive numbers, starting from n, i.e., $n \times (n+1) \times \cdots \times (n+i-1)$, or equivalently $1 \times (n+0) \times (n+1) \times \cdots \times (n+i-1)$:

Fixpoint product_of_successive_nats (i n : nat) : nat :=
  match i with
    0   => 1
  | S i' => product_of_successive_nats i' n * (n + i')
  end.

They are made to prove that this product is divisible by $i!$, after writing unit tests (a) for the product function and (b) for the divisibility property:

Lemma the_product_of_SSi_consecutive_nats_is_divisible_by_fac_SSi :
  forall i n : nat,
    exists q : nat,
      product_of_successive_nats (S (S i)) n = fac (S (S i)) * q.

The proof is by induction on i: its base case is the simple problem they first solved (since the smallest i strictly greater than 1 is 2), and the induction step is proved by induction on n and embodies the structure that is common to the proofs above (where the proof about $n + 1$ consecutive numbers uses the property about n consecutive numbers, a.k.a. the induction hypothesis here), which requires stating and proving two properties of the product function:

Lemma about_product_of_successive_nats_0 :
  forall i : nat,
    product_of_successive_nats (S (S i)) 0 = 0.

Lemma about_product_of_successive_nats_S :
  forall i n : nat,
    n * product_of_successive_nats (S (S i)) (S n) =
    product_of_successive_nats (S (S (S i))) n.

Finally, the students are made to generalize the property to the cases where i is 0 or 1:

Theorem the_product_of_i_consecutive_nats_is_divisible_by_fac_i :
  forall i n : nat,
    exists q : nat,
      product_of_successive_nats i n = fac i * q.

And as a punchline, they are made to realize that since the product of consecutive numbers is divisible by a factorial number, the result of these divisions by a factorial number is not a rational number, but an integer, as pointed out by Leonhard Euler in the first published proof of Fermat's Little Theorem [4]:

> "quamvis habeat fraction speciem dabit numerum integrum"
> (despite its specification as a fraction, it gives an integer)

Question: What is this integer?

Alternatively, suppose that product_of_successive_nats, given a natural number n and a natural number k that is smaller than n, computes $n \times (n - 1) \times \cdots \times (n - k + 1)$, i.e., the product of k consecutive natural numbers, the largest of which is n instead of the product of k consecutive natural numbers, the smallest of which is n. This alternative definition gives rise to an alternative theorem with the same punchline: This alternative product is divisible by $k!$, and therefore the result of this division is an integer. Alternative question: What is this integer?

Answering these two questions provides a new vantage point that makes the students appreciate how for any given natural numbers n and i, $(i \times n)!$ is divisible by $n!^i$ (when $i = 3$, this divisibility property is exploited in Dixon's formula) and how the factorial of a sum is divisible by the product of the factorial of the summands. They then grow an appreciation of the divisibility property that underlies, e.g., multinomial coefficients.

This appreciation gives rise to an understanding that is documented in a written report – on the ground that what one understands, one can explain – and that is tested in individual oral exams.

All in all, Yves Bertot's simple problem gives rise to a lab session where an insightful time is had by all – even more so if a student or three have independently consulted a generative AI about the simple problem and its derivatives.

5 Reflection

Throughout, the students mobilize their knowledge to tackle the simple problem, analyzing its informal statement and synthesizing the formal statement of their first theorem. They then apply their understanding to prove this theorem and they come up with several proofs, which they compare, contrast, and reflect upon. Finally, they tackle successive generalizations of the simple problem, they generalize their solutions, and they identify the punchline of the generalizations, connecting it with something they had independently been exposed to in another course. All in all, they score a run by touching the six bases of Bloom's taxonomy of educational objectives [5] – namely knowledge, comprehension, application, analysis, synthesis, and evaluation – and their personal tree of knowledge evolves from being a disconnected graph to becoming a directed acyclic graph.

Acknowledgments. The author is grateful to Yves Bertot for his simple problem as well as for his eagle eye. Thanks are also due to Julia Lawall for her grounded comments and to Hakjoo Oh and Yulei Sui for their invitation to present this material at SAS 2025.

References

1. Bertot, Y., Castéran, P.: Interactive Theorem Proving and Program Development. Springer (2004)
2. Danvy, O.: Mystery functions: making specifications, unit tests, and implementations coexist in the mind of undergraduate students. In: Stutterheim, J., Chin, W.N., eds.: IFL '19: Proceedings of the 31st Symposium on Implementation and Application of Functional Languages, pp. 1–9, Article No. 2, Singapore, ACM Press (2019)
3. Rota, G.C.: Problem solvers and theorizers. In: Indiscrete Thoughts. Birkhaüser (1996)
4. Euler, L.: Theorematum quorundam ad numeros primos spectantium demonstratio (a proof of certain theorems regarding prime numbers). Commentarii academiae scientiarum Petropolitanae **8** (1741) 141–146 https://scholarlycommons.pacific.edu/euler-works/54/
5. Anderson, L.W., Krathwohl, D.R.: A taxonomy for learning, teaching, and assessing: a revision of Bloom's taxonomy of educational objectives. Longman, New York (2001) ISBN 978-0-8013-1903-7

Verifying Neural Networks with PyRAT

Augustin Lemesle, Julien Lehmann, Tristan Le Gall[(✉)], and Zakaria Chihani

University Paris-Saclay, CEA, LIST, Orsay, France
{tristan.le-gall,Zakaria.CHIHANI}@cea.fr

Abstract. We present PYRAT, a tool based on abstract interpretation to verify the safety and robustness of neural networks. PYRAT uses multiple abstractions to find the reachable states of a neural network starting from its input. Its analysis is fast and accurate. PYRAT has already been used in several industrial and academic collaborations, to ensure safety guarantees, with its second place at the VNN-Comp 2024 showcasing its performance.

1 Introduction

There is no doubt that Artificial Intelligence (AI) has taken over an important part of our lives, now reaching new sectors such as health, aeronautics, energy, etc., where it can bring tremendous benefits but could also cause environmental, economic, or human damage in critical or high-risk systems. Indeed, similarly to a classical software, deep neural networks (NN), when implemented in critical systems, should be tested and validated in order to provide strong guarantees regarding their safety. For this, PYRAT (**Py**thon **R**eachability **A**ssessment **T**ool), a verification tool under development at CEA since 2019, relies on *abstract interpretation* techniques [13,14] to prove safety properties on NN and combines them with fully parallel data representation and optimisation methods to perform efficient analysis. Through its extended support of common AI frameworks (ONNX, PyTorch, Keras, etc.), and multiple interfaces, PYRAT provides formal methods techniques accessible to everyone to formally verify NN on practical use-cases and foster their industrial use.

Outline. Figure 1 represents the architecture of PYRAT. Preprocessing of the different input formats for NN along with the given specification are presented in Sect. 2. Section 3 details the key elements of the reachability analysis, its abstract domains and implementation details as well as the branch and bound mechanisms while Sect. 4 documents the use of PYRAT highlighting its different APIs and logging features. In Sect. 5, we also show some experiments to illustrate how PYRAT work on some benchmarks with different abstract domains and techniques. Finally, PYRAT has been time-tested in several national and international projects involving industrial partners (see Sect. 6).

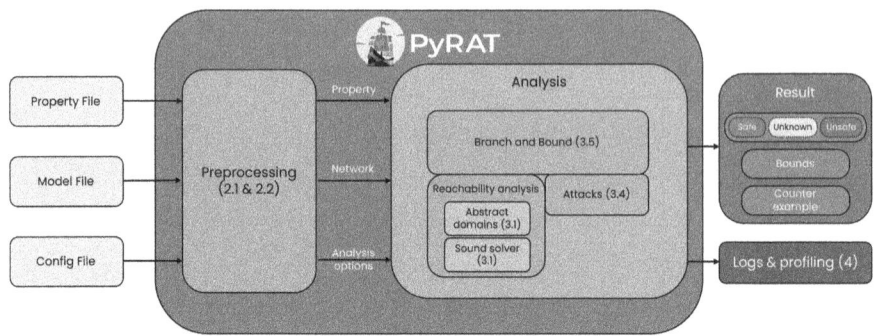

Fig. 1. High-level architecture of PyRAT; the numbers refer to the (sub)sections of this paper in which the features are explained

Related Tools. Many verification techniques used for AI were initially developed to increase trust in (classical) software, including *model-checking* [9,10], Satisfiability Modulo Theory (SMT) [3], or *abstract interpretation*. These methods were later adapted to the verification of NN with specific modifications, *e.g.* no loops, no memory to allocate, but instead linear and non-linear operations on tensors. The first tools developed for this purpose were SMT-based methods [17,30,34,49] and Mixed Integer Programming (MIP) based tools [19,55]. However, both of these techniques are known to be computationally expensive.

PyRAT uses Abstract Interpretation-based methods which have been developed to avoid these costly computations [22,60]. We briefly present a non-exhaustive list of those tools and we refer to [59] for a more comprehensive survey. Many of these tools, including PyRAT, accept the Open Neural Network Exchange (ONNX) format to describe the NN and the VNN-LIB format (based on SMT-LIB) to describe the properties to be verified.

- α, β–CROWN [61,63,65], winner of VNN-Comp 2021 to 2024, uses the CROWN-domain, mathematically equivalent to the polytope domain, with a tailored abstraction for the Rectified Linear Unit (ReLU) and other non-linear functions combined with branch and bound verification strategy (BaB).
- MN-BaB [20] is a dual solver built on the DeepPoly domain [54] leveraging multi-neural relaxation of the ReLU along BaB.
- NNV [39,56] and NNENUM [1,2] use the star set domain that uses linear programming to optimise ReLU abstractions.
- CORA [35] performs a reachability analysis using polynomial zonotopes. It can do both open-loop verification (like all the other tools presented here) but also closed-loop verification[1].
- LIBRA [42] also uses abstract interpretation, although for checking fairness properties. Like PyRAT, LIBRA can combine several abstract domains to increase the precision of its analysis. Its domains include intervals, as well

---

[1] Open-loop verification means that CORA verifies the NN alone. Closed-loop verification means that the NN is used as a *controller* of a dynamic system, and that CORA verifies the closed loop, NN and dynamic system, as a whole.

as domains from the APRON [31] library or domains reimplemented from SYMBOLIC [38], DEEPPOLY [54], and NEURIFY [58].

2 Parsing and Preprocessing

2.1 Network and Property Parsing

Representation of a NN. There are several standards to represent a neural network N, with $x \in \mathbb{R}^n$ as the input and $y = N(x) \in \mathbb{R}^m$ as the output. PYRAT supports the ONNX standard as its main input but it can also parse, though with a more limited support, Keras/Tensorflow or PyTorch models. A NN, represented by a directed graph of layers, is parsed as such into PYRAT's own internal representation with a *Layer* object corresponding to each layer and storing its specific information. PYRAT can handle simple feedforward neural networks with different activation functions σ between layers (Fig. 2) as well as more complex architectures that can include some residual connections between layers to represent more complex behaviours (Fig. 3).

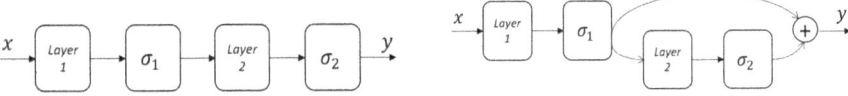

Fig. 2. Feedforward neural network.   **Fig. 3.** Residual neural network.

PYRAT supports the most commonly used activation functions including the ReLU, LeakyReLU, Sigmoid, SiLU, Tanh or Softmax, and about 40 types of layers including matrix multiplication, convolution or pooling layers, as well as concatenation, split, reshape or resize layers.

Properties. A specification can be seen as a set of formal *properties* that can be defined by a set of logical constraints on the inputs and outputs of N, or equivalently as two sets $X \subseteq \mathbb{R}^n$ and $Y \subseteq \mathbb{R}^m$, such that the *property* is satisfied if and only if $N(X) \subseteq Y$. We consider two kinds of properties. The first are specific relations between inputs and outputs (*e.g.* "if the altitude is greater than a and the speed is less than b, then the inclination signal of the aircraft should be lower than c"). These are often found in the context of control-command systems such as ACAS-Xu [41] (see [33] for examples of properties).

The second form of properties is more general and are often conducted around a selected representative set of inputs (*e.g.* "for a neighbourhood ϵ around entry x, the decision should not vary"). This type of properties (often called local robustness) is usually the main focus of validation for use-cases with unstructured, high-dimensional data such as images or sound. *Local robustness* properties are formally defined as follows: given an input $x_0 \in \mathbb{R}^n$ and a modification size $\epsilon > 0$, we want to prove or invalidate the following property

$$\forall x' \in \mathbb{R}^n, \ \|x_0 - x'\|_\infty \leq \epsilon \implies N(x_0) = N(x').$$

Both kinds of properties can be specified either in VNN-LIB, by our own textual format, or through a Python API as shown in Fig. 4. The simplest way to define properties in PYRAT is to define two scalar constraints on each input, i.e. an interval for each input, and a condition to be respected on the outputs. This condition can contain conjunctions, disjunctions or negations between the different outputs of the NN. To do so, PYRAT relies on the pyparsing library to parse the properties and separate inputs' and outputs' constraints.

```
input = Box(lower=[1, 3],        x0 >= 1
            upper=[5, 10])       x0 <= 5
output = "y0 >= 3"               x1 >= 3
                                 x1 <= 10
                                 y0 >= 3
```

Fig. 4. Equivalent properties for PYRAT in Python (left) and in a text file (right).

The VNN-LIB format also allows more complex properties to be defined with logical constraints including both input and output. On the other hand, the simpler text format providing by PYRAT allows for a quick definition of small property when the VNN-LIB format can be heavy. On top of that, to facilitate usage, PYRAT provides special options to directly verify *local robustness* properties for classification tasks by only providing the expected label of the input and the perturbation ϵ.

2.2 Preprocessing

PYRAT first performs a simplification of the network by relying partly on the onnx-simplifier library to remove unneeded dynamical parts of an ONNX model. Further simplifications are made by PYRAT to facilitate the verification. These may include removing unnecessary softmax, fusing matmul and add, etc. Some patterns from exported neural networks are also recognized and simplified, *e.g.* the SiLU is often split into a multiplication and a sigmoid by export libraries is transformed into a unique *SiLU* layer. These operations remain conservative and do not alter the result of the network inference w.r.t. the property.

Some rewriting is also performed to simplify the properties for the verification as in the works of [54,62]. For example, PYRAT will rewrite comparisons between variables in the given property, *i.e.* $y_0 \leq y_1$ will become $z_0 = y_0 - y_1 \leq 0$, introducing a new variable and adding a subtraction between variables with a new layer in the network. This will improve the precision of the analysis performed by PYRAT when using relational abstract domains.

Maxpool to ReLU. A critical obstacle to most verification techniques is the non-linearity of some operations. As such, the maxpool operation, *i.e.* returning the maximum of a set of variables, is often a source of imprecision. The precision of their verification was improved in DNNV [51] by relying on the formula:

$$\max(a, b) = \mathrm{ReLU}(a - b) + \mathrm{ReLU}(b) - \mathrm{ReLU}(-b)$$

Thus any maxpool layer can be transformed in a succession of Convolution (to extract the $a-b$, b and $-b$) and ReLU. For a maxpool of kernel size k this results in approximately $2log_2(k)$ convolutions followed by ReLU layers. However, while this simplification has the potential for a notable improvement in the precision as opposed to a direct abstraction of the maximum, it is not without cost. Indeed, one needs to compute additional convolutions and the abstraction of three new non-linear ReLU functions each time. Instead of this simplification, PYRAT implements the following:

$$\max(a, b) = \mathrm{ReLU}(a - b) + b$$

transforming the maxpool into a convolution and only one ReLU as shown in 5. This *reduces the convolution size by a third* and avoids unnecessary abstraction of the ReLU making it faster and more precise than DNNV's abstraction.

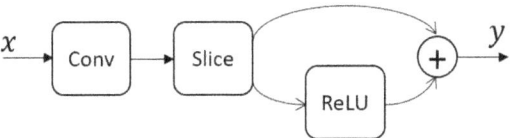

Fig. 5. Maxpool layer transformed in PYRAT.

3 Core Components of PYRAT

3.1 Reachability Analysis in PYRAT

PYRAT computes an over-approximation of the reachability set $N(X)$ for any given input set $X \subseteq \mathbb{R}^n$. Indeed, as computing exactly $N(X)$ is NP-complete [34], PYRAT uses *abstract interpretation* to compute an over-approximation of the reachable set $N(X)$. To do this, PYRAT will follow the graph execution order to compute it *layer by layer*. An abstract domain is used to abstract the semantic of each layer and each domain possesses its own characteristics. In PYRAT, abstract domains are objects implementing their respective arithmetic and can be called with a specific *Layer* object to compute the result of this layer.

For each analysis, the user is able to select multiple abstract domains with PYRAT to benefit from their respective strengths and complement their approaches. However, rather than a true reduced product of the abstract domains [13], their interaction is limited to a simple intersection of the concretisation of each abstraction.

We now present some of these domains.

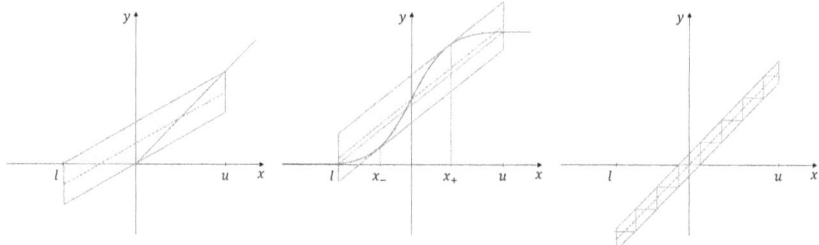

Fig. 6. ReLU, Sigmoid and Floor functions and their *zonotope* abstraction (from left to right).

Boxes and Interval Arithmetic. One of the easiest ways to abstract any set $X \in \mathcal{P}(\mathbb{R}^d)$ is to abstract each dimension individually (we consider the projection of X on dimension i: $X_i = \mathrm{proj}_i(X)$). We thus obtain a *box* $\alpha(X) = (x_1, \ldots, x_d)$ where, for each dimension i, $x_i = [\underline{x}_i, \overline{x}_i]$ is an interval with $\underline{x}_i = \min X_i$ and $\overline{x}_i = \max X_i$. This is the first abstract domain implemented in PyRAT.

For each dimension, we can then do interval arithmetic to compute the result of different operations[2] [44]. We can combine three operations (addition, opposite and scalar multiplication) to compute the multiplication of an abstraction $X \in \mathcal{P}(\mathbb{R}^d)$ by a weight matrix $W \in \mathbb{R}^{p \times d}$ by decomposing $W = W^+ + W^-$ between positive and negative weights and then computing $WX = W^+X + W^-X$. In PyRAT, this is used to optimise the computation done on the Box domain for large matrix multiplication, often found in neural networks.

Moreover, note that the abstraction of any increasing function (resp. decreasing function) f is simply $f([a,b]) = [f(a), f(b)]$ (resp. $f([a,b]) = [f(b), f(a)]$). For example, the ReLU function defined as $f(x) = \max(0, x)$ is increasing, therefore its abstraction for an interval [a,b] is:

$$\mathrm{ReLU}([a,b]) = \max(0, [a,b]) = [\max(0, a), \max(0, b)]$$

Overall, the Box domain is very efficient as it allows to compute reachable bounds for any operation with the same complexity as that operation (on average only 2 operations are needed, one for the lower bound and one for the upper bound of the interval). However, this domain often lacks precision, *e.g.* if $x \in [-1, 1]$ then a simple operation like $x - x = [-1, 1] - [-1, 1] = [-2, 2] \neq 0$ will produce a wider result than expected. Due to the nature of the Box domain, they do not capture the relations between the different variables or inputs of a problem and so may fail to simplify such equations. In the context of neural networks, there are numerous relations between the inputs due to the fully connected or convolutional layers. Therefore, more complex abstract domains that capture the relations between variables such as zonotopes will be presented.

---

[2] In this section, we only present intervals with finite (real number) bounds and refer to [16, 29] for the extension to intervals with floating-point or infinite bounds.

Zonotopes [27]. A *zonotope* z in $\mathbb{R}^d$ is formally defined as the weighted *Minkwoski sum* over a set of m *noise symbols* $(\epsilon_1, \ldots \epsilon_m) \in [-1, 1]^m$, *i.e.*, let $\alpha \in \mathbb{R}^{d \times m}$ and $\beta \in \mathbb{R}^d$, for every dimension $1 \leq i \leq d$ we have

$$z_i := \left\{ \sum_{j=1}^{m} \alpha_{i,j} \epsilon_j + \beta_i \,\middle|\, \epsilon \in [-1, 1]^m \right\}.$$

where $\alpha_{i,j}$ and β_i are real numbers. The *zonotope* z can be represented in vector form $\alpha \epsilon + \beta$ where α is a matrix of dimension $d \times m$, ϵ is a vector of dimension m taking value in $[-1, 1]$ and β is a vector of dimension d.

To represent the input set X as a *zonotope*, PYRAT considers its box representation $a(X)$ which is equivalently represented by the *zonotope* $\frac{x + \overline{x}}{2} \epsilon + \frac{x + \overline{x}}{2}$ with $\epsilon \in [-1, 1]^d$.

For the affine layers, the arithmetic of zonotopes relies on affine arithmetic [11] to compute the layers' output. For non-linear operations, such as ReLU, Sigmoid or cast to integer, PYRAT constructs a linear abstraction as shown in Fig. 6. For the ReLU it relies on the abstraction presented in DeepZono [53] while PYRAT builds on the work of Uewichitrapochana and Surarerks (2013) [57] for the Sigmoid abstraction. These abstractions require the introduction of at least one new noise symbol for each node where it is used. As the number of abstractions tends to grow in large networks, the number of noise symbols introduced can also grow significantly during the analysis, and in turn slow it down.

Complexity Reduction for Zonotopes. To alleviate this, PYRAT implements multiple heuristics to reduce the number of noise symbols. Criteria such as the one presented in [32] can be used to choose the noise symbols to remove. An overapproximation of their values is performed so that the analysis with PYRAT remains sound although it does lose some precision. Different parameters allow the user to tune this reduction efficiently depending on the network used.

Constrained Zonotopes. Building on the work of Scott et al. (2016) [50], we extend our *zonotope* domain by adding linear constraints shared over the d dimensions of the *zonotope*. These constraints allow for more precise abstractions of non-linear functions, reducing the over-approximation introduced. At the same time, they can be used in a branch and bound approach for increased precision (see Sect. 3.5).

More formally a *constrained zonotope* $x = (x_1, \ldots, x_d) \in \mathbb{R}^d$ with K constraints and m *noise symbols* is defined by:

$$x_i = \left\{ \sum_{j=1}^{m} \alpha_{i,j} \epsilon_j + \beta_i \,\middle|\, \begin{array}{c} \epsilon \in [-1, 1]^m \\ \forall k \in \{1, \ldots, K\}, \sum_{j=1}^{m} A_{k,j} \epsilon_j + b_k \geq 0 \end{array} \right\}$$

where $A_{k,j}$ and b_k are real numbers. Note that A and b are not indexed by i, implying that the constraints are shared for all i. At the start of the analysis, the *constrained zonotope* is unconstrained ($K = 0$) and constraints are added at different layers.

An example is shown in Fig. 7 with the ReLU abstraction when using the *constrained zonotope* domain. The linear abstraction remains unchanged (in green) but two constraints (half-plane in purple) are added, $y \geq x$ and $y \geq 0$, reducing the approximation introduced. These two constraints are added for each unstable ReLU neuron (*i.e.* a neuron that can be active or not) and shared by all neurons and accross all layers.

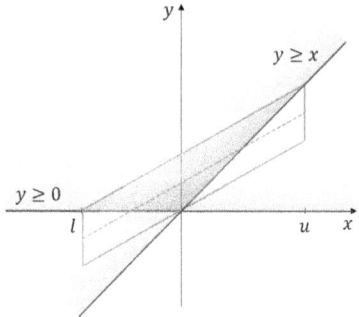

Fig. 7. Abstraction of the ReLU with the *constrained zonotope* domain

Thus, *constrained zonotopes* are more precise, but their concretisation requires to solve a system of linear equations with linear inequality constraints. To efficiently solve these equations, PYRAT integrates an in-house linear solver that computes simple yet precise conservative bounds. More particularly, the soundness of the solver is guaranteed by computing dual bounds while its efficiency comes from cheap gradient descent iterations (see [37] for more details). PYRAT also implements ways to limit the number of constraints introduced, as the more constraints there are, the slower the concretisation.

Hybrid Zonotopes. Introduced in the field of closed loop dynamical systems by Bird et al. (2023) [4] and then extended to neural networks by Zhang et al. (2023) [66] and Ortiz et al. (2023) [46], an *hybrid zonotope* can be seen as the union of *constrained zonotopes*. Over d dimensions, we define an *hybrid zonotope* x_i for all dimension $i \in \{1, ..., d\}$ with K constraints similarly to other *zonotopes* with m_c continuous noise symbols and m_b binary noise symbols:

$$x_i = \left\{ \sum_{j=1}^{m_c} \alpha_{i,j} \epsilon_j^c + \sum_{j=1}^{m_b} \gamma_{i,j} \epsilon_j^b + \beta_i \;\middle|\; \begin{array}{c} \epsilon^c \in [-1,1]^{m_c},\; \epsilon^b \in \{-1,1\}^{m_b}, \\ \forall k \in \{1, ..., K\}: \\ \sum_{j=1}^{m_c} a_{k,j} \epsilon_j^c + \sum_{j=1}^{m_b} b_{k,j} \epsilon_j^b + c_k = 0 \end{array} \right\}$$

where $\gamma_{i,j} \in \mathbb{R}$ is called binary generators and $a_{k,j}, b_{k,j}, c_k \in \mathbb{R}$.

The union of *constrained zonotopes* is here defined through the binary noise symbols that can only take the discrete values of -1 or 1. The *hybrid zonotope* is thus the union of 2^{m_b} *constrained zonotopes*. The constraints used here are equality constraints. The arithmetic is the same as classical *zonotope*. Nevertheless, an *hybrid zonotope* has the advantage of being able to exactly represent any piece-wise linear function such as the ReLU activation. With them, PYRAT can thus obtain an exact representation of any neural network for which the activation functions are piece-wise linear. For example, Fig. 8 shows how to get an exact representation of the ReLU operation.

This exact representation of the network can then be used for any analysis on the network. Then, to check whether the property is verified on the reachable set constructed by an *hybrid zonotope*, a mixed integer linear programming (MILP) problem has to be solved, *i.e.* the verification query has been transferred to a MILP solver. However, considering the number of variables in large neural networks, this can be very expensive. Therefore, the use of *hybrid zonotopes* is currently limited to small networks. Techniques like the reformulation-linearization in [24] can help to improve the sharpness of the MILP representation possibly leading to a better scalability through a linear relaxation. This will be the subject of future work in PYRAT to scale *hybrid zonotopes* to larger models and improve their overall usability.

Other Domains. Additionally, PYRAT implements a variety of other domains such as Polytopes [54] or Polynomial Zonotopes [36]. PYRAT also provides clear interfaces to add new domains.

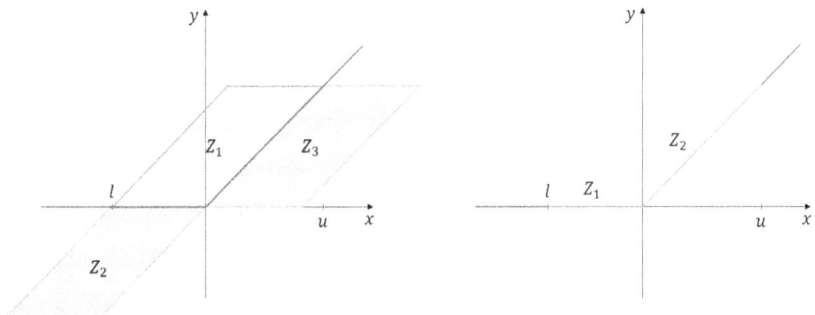

Fig. 8. *Hybrid zonotope* abstraction of the ReLU function. $H = Z_1 \cap (Z_2 \cup Z_3)$ from [46] on the left. $H = Z_1 \cup Z_2$ from [66] on the right.

Soundness. At the end of its analysis, PYRAT obtains an over-approximation of the achievable outputs of the network on which it evaluates the given property. In that sense, PYRAT is **sound** but the abstraction may be too rough and the reachability analysis alone may not be able to conclude on the property. This incompleteness is a common characteristic of abstract interpretation.

3.2 Data Representation

As NN rely on high-dimensional tensors, it is essential for PYRAT to scale to large architectures. For this, PYRAT implements the various matrices and vectors of its abstract domains using NumPy arrays [28] or PyTorch tensors [47]. More precisely for zonotopic domains, the coefficients associated to noise symbols are divided according to their origin into arrays or tensors of smaller size; either from the initial noise symbols or the non-linear layer at which they were introduced. This allows PYRAT to retain information on the noise symbols while keeping efficient arrays operations. PYRAT can then automatically optimise some computation by modulating this size.

While a choice between NumPy or PyTorch can be done manually by the user, PYRAT can automatically select the best library. Experimentally, we see that NumPy is faster on smaller size matrices than PyTorch. On large networks, it can also leverage GPU computation through PyTorch, thus scaling to much larger networks. For example, PYRAT is more than 10 times faster with GPU on the cifar100 benchmark from the VNN-Comp. The abstract domains in PYRAT are designed to be agnostic of the computation library used and additional computation libraries can be implemented easily through predefined APIs.

3.3 Soundness w.r.t. Real Arithmetic

PYRAT considers the mathematical definition of the NN operations, *i.e.* a semantic based on real numbers. However, computers use floating-point arithmetic, which usually introduces rounding errors. In order for its abstract domains to be sound *w.r.t.* real arithmetic, PYRAT captures the rounding errors caused by the computation of each of their abstract operators by choosing the most pessimistic rounding mode. This means that if the result of a real number computation is x, then PYRAT will compute a range $[\underline{x}, \overline{x}]$ where $\underline{x}$ and $\overline{x}$ are floating-point numbers such that $\underline{x} \leq x \leq \overline{x}$. We refer to [26] (resp. [8]) for a presentation of an abstract domain sound w.r.t real arithmetic based on Zonotope (resp. Polyhedra). This soundness is only limited to CPU in PYRAT.

3.4 Counterexample Check

While the primary objective of PYRAT remains to prove that the property holds, it can happen that the property does not hold. Such cases tend to be hard to handle with abstract interpretation alone as it over-approximates the outputs. Thus, complementary to reachability analysis, PYRAT will look for counterexamples. Random points and adversarial attacks will be generated before the analysis to try to falsify the property through inferences on the model. If a counterexample is found, PYRAT will return it and conclude the analysis as the property is falsified. This counterexample search is optional and tunable with the adversarial attack parameters. Using the foolbox library on top of in-house adversarial attacks, PYRAT can use a large scope of attacks such as FGSM [25], PGD [40], DeepFool [45], etc.

3.5 Branch and Bound

When the reachability analysis does not allow PYRAT to conclude due to a lack of precision of the abstractions, PYRAT can perform multiple analyses to provide more accurate results by partitioning the verification problem. This method is called Branch and Bound (BaB) [7,64]. PYRAT implements both BaB on inputs and BaB on ReLU nodes. While not implemented in PYRAT it is worth noting that BaB can be performed on any non-linear or even linear layers.

BaB on Inputs. It splits the input space of the property recursively until every subspace is proven safe or until one of the subspaces invalidates the property. The core of the method lies in the choice of the dimension to split and how to split it. To this end, PYRAT implements multiple heuristics including its own: ReCIPH [18]. For each input dimension, PYRAT computes a score combining the width of the associated input and its influence on the output property. The influence is extracted from the output abstract domains of the parent analysis and does not require additional computation.

By default, the input dimension with the highest score is then divided equally in half and two new reachability analyses are performed from the two resulting subspaces; both inheriting the parameters and results of the parent analysis. Additionally, PYRAT provides a booster mechanism to customized the way the split is done allowing to split inputs in more than two, multiple inputs at the same time, or in unequal parts. This booster mechanism allows PYRAT to directly analyse smaller input spaces and bypass intermediate analyses.

This BaB approach performs well on low dimensional inputs but struggles when the input space gets bigger, *e.g.* for images. Indeed, with higher dimensions, the number of divisions needed to achieve an increase in precision grows exponentially as inputs are often very interconnected. To resolve this issue, BaB on ReLU has been developed, directly dividing the intermediate network space.

BaB on ReLU. Initially presented in RELUPLEX [34], BaB on ReLU is now present in most state-of-the-art verifiers [20,61]. Through it we can force the input of a specific ReLU to be either positive or negative which transforms the ReLU in a linear operation: the 0-function if the input is negative and the identity if the input is positive. Thus, using BaB on ReLU allows PYRAT to be **complete** given an infinite timeout for ReLU-only networks. Conceptually, the algorithm for splitting on ReLU is similar to the one for input splitting: it chooses an unstable ReLU in the neural network, it forces the aforementioned ReLU to be negative in one branch and positive in the other before performing a reachability analysis. On each branch, these constraints are enforced on the current abstract domains and are soundly handled by our solver. The *constrained zonotope* domain is by default the domain used in this case as it can natively support these constraints.

Similarly to BaB on input and after each reachability analysis, PYRAT computes a score determining which ReLU to split next. Multiple heuristics are implemented, combining the influence of a given ReLU on the outputs and the expected gains of constraining that ReLU. Additionally, by reusing parent bounds and abstract domains until the latest split added, PYRAT can speed up the analysis and increase the precision.

Using the `multiprocessing` library, PYRAT is able to parallelise the BaB on CPU for a better

4 Usage

PYRAT is packaged as a Python 3 module and, once downloaded, can be installed with `pip` on any system with a Python version superior to 3.10. And while PYRAT is closed-source, it can be made freely available under an academic licence for research and teaching purposes.

As a Python module, PYRAT can be used directly in Python or from command line. Using `ConfigArgParse`, it can take arguments from the command line using specific keywords or with a configuration file containing the different parameters. During the analysis, PYRAT displays information such as the current time taken by the analysis along with the percentage of completion for BaB. Without BaB the output bounds of the analysis will be shown at the end. The Python usage allows one to investigate the results more in details, fetching the values of the different abstract domains used for different layers or the decisions taken during a BaB analysis. Some information can also be logged in files and the BaB decisions can be saved and visualised as a split tree using `networkx` (see Fig. 9).

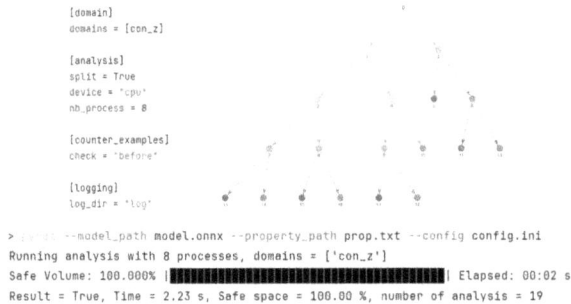

Fig. 9. Example of configuration file (top left), command line execution (bottom) and output split tree (top right)

Using the Trace Event Format and the `trace-events` library, PYRAT is also able to provide some profiling of the analysis (see Fig. 10). This profiling can include the time taken for the analysis of each layer, the current domain width, but also the number of constraints or noise symbols at any given point of the analysis. More information can be added manually in the profiling. This profiling can allow either a user to analyse where his analysis takes time or where precision is lost to improve PYRAT parameters or the network itself. It can also allow developers in PYRAT to optimise the analysis and its implemntation.

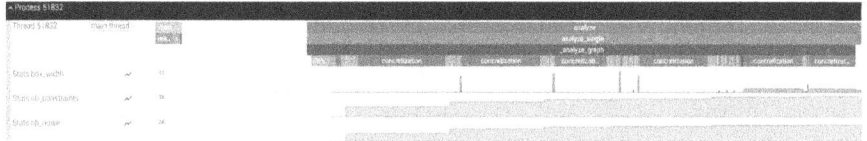

Fig. 10. Profiling in PYRAT.

Following an analysis, PYRAT will provide four possible outputs: "True", the property is verified; "False", the property is false and a counterexample is provided; "Unknown", it could not be verified nor falsified with the given options; "Timeout", the analysis stops when the (optional) timeout is reached.

5 Experiments

This section details some experiments to assess the different domains implemented in PYRAT, *i.e.* their strengths and weakness on different benchmarks. These experiments were run on an Intel Core i9-11950H 2.60GHz CPU as well as an NVIDIA RTX A3000 GPU. For reproductibility, we used a single thread, even when using BaB.

Most of our experiments are performed on benchmarks used in the VNN-Comp. For every benchmark in the VNN-Comp, properties are randomly perturbed with an unknown seed. This explains the slight differences between our experiments and the one in the competition.

We have published an artifact to reproduce these experiments. It is available here: https://doi.org/10.5281/zenodo.15746759.

5.1 Mooring Line Failure Detection

We first consider a small example with four safety properties on a single model. The model is a neural network with 7 inputs and 5 outputs performing a classification task. It consists of 3 hidden fully connected layers of 25 neurons each. This network was developed for mooring line failure detection on offshore platforms [52] and has already been used in [18] to compare BaB on input heuristics in PYRAT. The safety properties considered here are functional properties on the network with large possible input variations.

Table 1 shows the results of PYRAT's analysis with different domains and options. As a baseline, we indicate the time and the result of the analysis without any BaB for *zonotopes* and *constrained zonotopes*. These analyses are inconclusive because the properties have a large input space and have from 60% to 100%

of unstable ReLU. With both BaB approaches, all properties are proved with similar time for *zonotopes* with BaB on input and *constrained zonotopes* with BaB on ReLU. Through Table 2, we see the number of reachability analyses performed by PyRAT for all approaches. For input BaB, we see that the number of split required for *constrained zonotope* is significantly less than for *zonotope* as we are more precise, but the overhead in computation time makes the overall analysis slower. The average analysis time on these networks is around 0.006 s for *zonotope* and 0.03 s for *constrained zonotope*.

BaB on ReLU further reduces the number of analyses needed, which compensates for the time overhead. Our heuristics for choosing the best ReLU to split on allow us to reduce the number of split by prioritizing the correct ReLU nodes. Finally, *hybrid zonotope* are able to prove the four properties in only 6.28 s with most of the time spent in the MILP solver (here we use the `cvxpy` library with the `Gurobi` solver). This is more than ten times faster than BaB approaches. As the network is small and the number of neurons is low, the MILP solver are able to solve this problem very quickly with our exact representation thus outperforming the other methods that need to over-approximate the network.

5.2 LinearizeNN and ACAS-Xu

We then compare our domains on both the `LinearizeNN` and the `ACAS-Xu` benchmarks from the VNN-Comp 2024 and we refer the reader to the competition report [5] for the full details of these benchmarks. Both benchmarks have a small number of inputs: 4 for `LinearizeNN` and 5 for `ACAS-Xu`. The models are fully connected models with varying depth and from 100 to 256 neurons on each

Table 1. Results of different analysis on the 'Mooring line' example.

	Unknown	Proven	Time
Zonotopes	4	0	0.13
Constrained zonotopes	4	0	0.19
Zonotopes w/ BaB input	0	4	94.88
Const. zono. w/ BaB input	0	4	140.49
Const. zono. w/ BaB ReLU	0	4	95.25
Hybrid zonotopes	0	4	6.28

Table 2. Number of analysis for BaB approaches on the same example.

Property	Zono. BaB input	Constr. zono. BaB input	Constr. zono. BaB ReLU
1	879	445	323
2	10113	2967	1067
3	1369	607	253
4	1763	557	657

hidden layer. We compare our abstract domains on the 60 and 186 safety properties of `LinearizeNN` and `ACAS-Xu`. The timeout for `LinearizeNN` is at 60 s and at 116 s for `ACAS-Xu`.

These benchmarks are more difficult to verify than the previous example, as shown in Table 3 and Table 4. The baseline with only *zonotope* or *constrained zonotope* proves or falsifies (by finding a counterexample) a small number of properties of the benchmark and we can see the increase in precision of *constrained zonotope* as compared to simple *zonotope*. The tables clearly show a better performance for the methods based on BaB on input rather than BaB on ReLU. In fact, the number of inputs is much smaller than the number of unstable ReLU to split (up to 500 unstable ReLU on `LinearizeNN`). While on `LinearizeNN` *zonotopes* have a slight edge in speed, on `ACAS-Xu`, where the properties are longer to prove, *constrained zonotopes* are faster overall because their increased precision outweighs the overhead. Additionally, we observe that *hybrid zonotopes* barely prove more properties than *constrained zonotopes* on `LinearizeNN` while performing even worse on `ACAS-Xu`. As the number of unstable ReLU grows, the generated MILP problem becomes too large to solve within the given timeout. The number of properties falsified in Table 3 and 4 varies in function of the domain used and the BaB approach. Indeed, the property can be falsified if the entire output set of the reachability analysis does not satisfy the property. Thus, the precision of the abstract domain used plays an important role. During BaB multiple analyses are done on smaller input sets leading to more precision and more search for counter examples. In turn, the number of falsified properties is higher with BaB approaches and may vary depending on the number of analyses done.

Table 3. Results of different analysis on the `LinearizeNN` benchmark.

	Falsified	Proven	Unknown	Time
Zonotopes	0	3	57	11.67
Const. zono.	0	10	50	51.58
Zonotopes w/ BaB input	2	58	0	123.34
Const. zono. w/ BaB input	2	58	0	191.89
Const. zono. w/ BaB ReLU	0	19	41	2520.74
Hybrid Zonotopes	0	11	49	3181.84

5.3 Cifar100

Finally, the `cifar100` benchmark (also from the VNN-Comp) is used to illustrate PyRAT's domains on a larger model and with higher input dimensionality. We limit the experiment here to the medium size network of the benchmark with 2.5 million parameters including convolutional layers, residual connections and

Table 4. Results of different analysis on the ACAS-Xu benchmark.

	Falsified	Proven	Unknown	Time
Zonotopes	13	4	169	27.16
Const. zono.	13	42	131	137.13
Zonotopes w/ BaB input	45	133	8	3376.74
Const. zono. w/ BaB input	47	138	1	2921.28
Const. zono. w/ BaB ReLU	42	83	61	11022.07
Hybrid Zonotopes	14	22	150	18184.11

ReLU activations. There are 100 safety properties to check, corresponding to a local robustness property on 100 images from the CIFAR-100 dataset (32x32 pixels and 100 output classes). The experiments here are run using GPU with a timeout of 100 s.

As seen in Table 5, the counterexample search using adversarial attacks finds 12 counterexamples while the *zonotope* analysis does not prove any property. Using *constrained zonotope*, we can directly prove 8 properties without BaB and 32 out of 100 with BaB on ReLU. Due to the high dimensionality of the input, the BaB on inputs with *constrained zonotopes* does not prove any additional property. On this benchmark, *hybrid zonotopes* fail to scale and are therefore not included in these results as they timeout on all properties. Overall, we only prove less than half of the 100 properties of this benchmark; future work will aim to increase this number by improving the speed of analysis to perform more BaB but also improving BaB heuristics as BaB on ReLU is highly dependant on the chosen ReLU nodes.

6 Applications

Functional Properties. The first application of PYRAT is the verification of functional properties on structured data. On top of the usual ACAS-Xu application and the properties defined by RELUPLEX [33], PYRAT was used in a collaboration with Technip Energies to verify artificial neural networks for mooring line failure detection [52] on which formal safety properties were defined and verified.

Table 5. Results of different analysis on the cifar100 benchmark.

	Falsified	Proven	Unknown	Time
Zonotopes	12	0	88	100.05
Const. zono.	12	8	80	261.72
Const. zono. w/ BaB input	12	8	80	8216.16
Const. zono. w/ BaB ReLU	12	32	56	6277.12

These small applications mainly rely on PyRAT's input splitting technique due to their low dimensionality and large input space to prove (Fig. 5).

Local Robustness. Through several projects such as the Confiance.ai program[3], PyRAT has been used in industrial use cases, including large image classification neural networks. These projects were an opportunity to confront formal methods with industrial use cases where inputs of 224x224 pixels can be considered small. To be able to provide local robustness guarantees with PyRAT on such use cases, improvements had to be made (use of GPU, reduction of RAM usage, ...). Additionally, training techniques using abstract interpretation techniques [43] were used to train models that are easier to verify on 224x224 pixel dataset. On these models, which achieved 95% accuracy, PyRAT was able to prove more than 90% of the test set to be locally robust to small perturbation [12]. PyRAT is also being used in the TRUMPET project [48] to verify local robustness properties on privacy-enhanced NN for medical applications.

Embedded AI and Quantized Networks. PyRAT was used to verify embedded NNs and their Operational Design Domain (ODD) on the ACAS-Xu use case in a collaboration with Airbus [21]. Following the methodology described in [15], the verification was performed on quantized neural networks in int8. Although these networks use quantized operators such as QLinearMatmul from the ONNX library, these operators still rely in part on floating point numbers. In this sense, PyRAT had to implement a new abstraction for conversion from float to integer datatype. In fact, since most of the MatMul operator is done with integer, the network is less prone to floating point errors and PyRAT is able to be correct *w.r.t.* floating points by correctly representing this floating point error for the remaining float operations. In addition, splitting mechanisms [18] were also used by PyRAT to improve the ODD verification. Through this work, Airbus was able to produce a hybrid system using neural networks when the ODD is verified by PyRAT and present a certification approach according to the ED-324/ARP6983 standard. While initially used in embedded environments, quantized neural networks are not limited to this as quantification approaches are becoming a mainstream practice to reduce the size and footprint of the models in all environments. The need for safety of quantized networks and the potential use of PyRAT is therefore not limited to embedded AI systems.

CAISAR [23] is an open-source platform for evaluating the trustworthiness of AI through a unified entry point and high-level specification language using WhyML. In addition to its standalone use, PyRAT is closely integrated with CAISAR in order to provide a wider range of properties beyond classical safety or local robustness.

VNN-Comp. PyRAT participated in 2023 and 2024 in the international neural network verification competition on a wide variety of benchmarks [5,6] reaching respectively the 3rd and 2nd place. From these participations, we

---
[3] https://confiance.ai/.

can see the improvements made in PYRAT with new supported benchmarks, *e.g.* `ml4acopf` or `cifar100`, and overall verification improvements. Figure 11 shows that PYRAT can verify small instances quickly, while for more complex instances is only second to $\alpha, \beta-$CROWN. Its wide support of layers and architecture allows PYRAT to prove more properties than others.

Yet, PYRAT has approximately 500 more timeout than $\alpha, \beta-$CROWN. 400 of them happen on "Safe" properties that PYRAT could not verified. Digging into the detailed results of the report, we found that PYRAT falls behind on larger input space problems such as `cifar100`. It highlights some shortcomings of PYRAT's BaB methods on ReLU, and the need to improve and generalize the heuristics and BaB methods in PYRAT on non-linear activation functions. On the contrary, we found that PYRAT performs particularly well on problems with small input spaces which can be explained by the cheapness of the *zonotope* domain combined with a well-calibrated BaB on input.

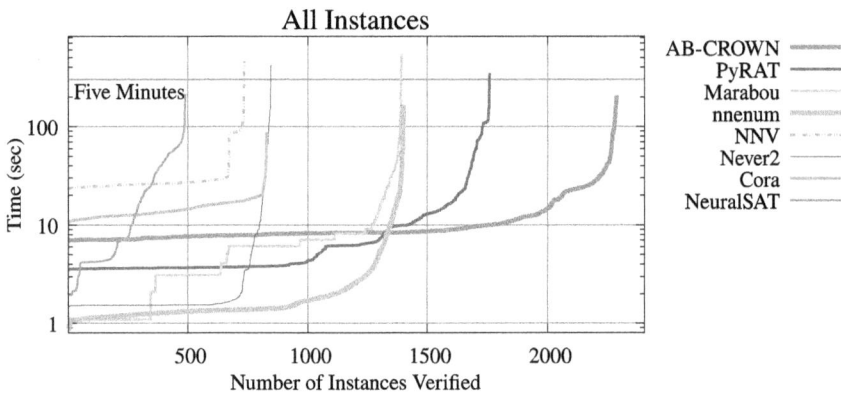

Fig. 11. VNN-Comp 2024 results on all instances (from [5])

Soundness Benchmark. [67] is a benchmark to assess the correction of neural network verifiers. They propose a training procedure to hide counterexamples from verifiers and evaluate the state-of-the-art verifiers on different architecture. PYRAT is one of the two tools that are assessed as correct on this benchmark.

7 Future Works

As the AI landscape evolves, new architectures and activations are developed, bringing new verification challenges to tackle. The development in PYRAT and the strong basis we built with our reachability techniques will be the key to adapt and scale to these new architectures without starting from scratch. Current works in PYRAT already focus on generalising our approaches for non-linear functions as well as more precise abstraction. Efforts to verify architectures such as RNN and Transformers have also started and will be the subject of future works. Additionally, with the development of edge AI and the proliferation of IoT devices, PyRAT will strive to address embedded AI systems with their specific problems (integer mixed with floating points, new operations, ...). This work will be the subject of collaboration with the `Aidge` platform[4]. Finally, PyRAT will extend its BaB techniques to new layers under a unified framework for both input and ReLU splitting as well as other non-linear layers.

Acknowledgment. This work has been supported by the French government under the "France 2030" program, as part of Confiance.ai program, the SAIF project with grant ANR-23-PEIA-0006, and as part of the DeepGreen project with grant ANR-23-DEGR-0001. PyRAT has also been funded under the Horizon Europe SPARTA project grant no. 830892 and TRUMPET project grant no. 101070038 as well as the European Defence Fund AINCEPTION project grant no. 101103385.

Main Contributors. (current) Augustin Lemesle, Julien Lehmann, Tristan Le Gall; (past) Serge Durand, Samuel Akinwande.

References

1. Bak, S.: nnenum: verification of relu neural networks with optimized abstraction refinement. In: NASA Formal Methods Symposium, pp. 19–36. Springer (2021)
2. Bak, S., Tran, H.D., Hobbs, K., Johnson, T.T.: Improved geometric path enumeration for verifying ReLU neural networks. In: 32nd International Conference on Computer-Aided Verification (CAV) (2020)
3. Barrett, C., Fontaine, P., Tinelli, C.: The Satisfiability Modulo Theories Library (SMT-LIB) (2016). www.SMT-LIB.org
4. Bird, T.J., Pangborn, H.C., Jain, N., Koeln, J.P.: Hybrid zonotopes: a new set representation for reachability analysis of mixed logical dynamical systems. Automatica **154**, 111107 (2023)
5. Brix, C., Bak, S., Johnson, T.T., Wu, H.: The fifth international verification of neural networks competition (vnn-comp 2024): summary and results (2024). https://arxiv.org/abs/2412.19985
6. Brix, C., Bak, S., Liu, C., Johnson, T.T.: The fourth international verification of neural networks competition (vnn-comp 2023): Summary and results. arXiv preprint arXiv:2312.16760 (2023)
7. Bunel, R., Lu, J., Turkaslan, I., Torr, P.H., Kohli, P., Kumar, M.P.: Branch and bound for piecewise linear neural network verification. J. Mach. Learn. Res. **21**(42), 1–39 (2020)
8. Chen, L., Miné, A., Cousot, P.: A sound floating-point polyhedra abstract domain. In: Ramalingam, G. (ed.) Programming Languages and Systems, pp. 3–18. Springer, Berlin Heidelberg, Berlin, Heidelberg (2008)
9. Clarke, E.M., Emerson, E.A.: Design and synthesis of synchronization skeletons using branching time temporal logic. In: Kozen, D. (ed.) Logic of Programs 1981. LNCS, vol. 131, pp. 52–71. Springer, Heidelberg (1982). https://doi.org/10.1007/BFb0025774

---

[4] https://eclipse.dev/aidge/.

10. Clarke, E.M., Emerson, E.A., Sifakis, J.: Model checking: algorithmic verification and debugging. Commun. ACM **52**(11), 74–84 (2009). https://doi.org/10.1145/1592761.1592781, https://doi.org/10.1145/1592761.1592781
11. Comba, J.L.D., Stol, J.: Affine arithmetic and its applications to computer graphics. In: Proceedings of VI SIBGRAPI (Brazilian Symposium on Computer Graphics and Image Processing), pp. 9–18 (1993)
12. Confiance.ai: Benchmark for abstract interpretation training (2024)
13. Cousot, P.: Principles of Abstract Interpretation. MIT Press (2022)
14. Cousot, Patrick, R.: Abstract interpretation: a unified lattice model for static analysis of programs by construction or approximation of fixpoints. In: Proceedings of the 4th ACM SIGACT-SIGPLAN Symposium on Principles of Programming Languages. POPL '77 (1977)
15. Damour, M., et al.: Towards certification of a reduced footprint ACAS-Xu system: a hybrid ML-based solution. In: SAFECOMP 2021: Computer Safety, Reliability, and Security, pp. 34–48 (2021). https://doi.org/10.1007/978-3-030-83903-1_3, https://hal.science/hal-03355299
16. Dawood, H.: Theories of interval arithmetic: mathematical foundations and applications. LAP Lambert Academic Publishing (2011)
17. Duong, H., Xu, D., Nguyen, T., Dwyer, M.B.: Harnessing neuron stability to improve DNN verification. Proc. ACM Softw. Eng. **1**(FSE), 859–881 (2024). https://doi.org/10.1145/3643765
18. Durand, S., Lemesle, A., Chihani, Z., Urban, C., Terrier, F.: Reciph: relational coefficients for input partitioning heuristic. In: 1st Workshop on Formal Verification of Machine Learning (WFVML 2022) (2022)
19. Dutta, S., Jha, S., Sanakaranarayanan, S., Tiwari, A.: Output range analysis for deep neural networks. arXiv preprint arXiv:1709.09130 (2017)
20. Ferrari, C., Muller, M.N., Jovanovic, N., Vechev, M.: Complete verification via multi-neuron relaxation guided branch-and-bound. arXiv preprint arXiv:2205.00263 (2022)
21. Gabreau, C., et al.: A study of an ACAS-Xu exact implementation using ED-324/ARP6983. In: 12th European Congress Embedded Real Time Systems - ERTS 2024. Toulouse (31000), France (2024). https://hal.science/hal-04584782
22. Gehr, T., Mirman, M., Drachsler-Cohen, D., Tsankov, P., Chaudhuri, S., Vechev, M.: Ai2: safety and robustness certification of neural networks with abstract interpretation. In: 2018 IEEE Symposium on Security and Privacy (SP), pp. 3–18. IEEE (2018)
23. Girard-Satabin, J., Alberti, M., Bobot, F., Chihani, Z., Lemesle, A.: CAISAR: a platform for characterizing artificial intelligence safety and robustness. In: AISafety. CEUR-Workshop Proceedings, Vienne, Austria (2022). https://hal.science/hal-03687211
24. Glunt, J.J., Robbins, J.A., Silvestre, D., Pangborn, H.C.: Sharp hybrid zonotopes: Set operations and the reformulation-linearization technique (2025). https://arxiv.org/abs/2503.17483
25. Goodfellow, I.J., Shlens, J., Szegedy, C.: Explaining and harnessing adversarial examples (2015). https://arxiv.org/abs/1412.6572
26. Goubault, E.: Static analyses of the precision of floating-point operations. In: Cousot, P. (ed.) Static Analysis, 8th International Symposium, SAS 2001, Paris, France, July 16-18, 2001, Proceedings. Lecture Notes in Computer Science, vol. 2126, pp. 234–259. Springer (2001). https://doi.org/10.1007/3-540-47764-0_14

27. Goubault, E., Putot, S.: A zonotopic framework for functional abstractions (2009). https://arxiv.org/abs/0910.1763
28. Harris, C.R., et al.: Array programming with NumPy. Nature **585**(7825), 357–362 (2020). https://doi.org/10.1038/s41586-020-2649-2
29. Hickey, T., Ju, Q., Van Emden, M.H.: Interval arithmetic: from principles to implementation. J. ACM **48**(5), 1038–1068 (2001). https://doi.org/10.1145/502102.502106
30. Huang, X., Kwiatkowska, M., Wang, S., Wu, M.: Safety Verification of Deep Neural Networks. In: Majumdar, R., Kunčak, V. (eds.) CAV 2017. LNCS, vol. 10426, pp. 3–29. Springer, Cham (2017). https://doi.org/10.1007/978-3-319-63387-9_1
31. Jeannet, B., Miné, A.: Apron: a library of numerical abstract domains for static analysis. In: Bouajjani, A., Maler, O. (eds.) Computer Aided Verification, 21st International Conference, CAV 2009, Grenoble, France, June 26 - July 2, 2009. Proceedings. Lecture Notes in Computer Science, vol. 5643, pp. 661–667. Springer (2009). https://doi.org/10.1007/978-3-642-02658-4_52
32. Kashiwagi, M.: An algorithm to reduce the number of dummy variables in affine arithmetic. Scientific Computing, Computer Arithmetic and Verified Numerical Computations (SCAN) (2012)
33. Katz, G., Barrett, C., Dill, D., Julian, K., Kochenderfer, M.: Reluplex: an efficient SMT solver for verifying deep neural networks (2017). https://arxiv.org/abs/1702.01135
34. Katz, G., Barrett, C., Dill, D.L., Julian, K., Kochenderfer, M.J.: Reluplex: An Efficient SMT Solver for Verifying Deep Neural Networks. In: Majumdar, R., Kunčak, V. (eds.) CAV 2017. LNCS, vol. 10426, pp. 97–117. Springer, Cham (2017). https://doi.org/10.1007/978-3-319-63387-9_5
35. Kochdumper, N., Schilling, C., Althoff, M., Bak, S.: Open- and closed-loop neural network verification using polynomial zonotopes. In: Rozier, K.Y., Chaudhuri, S. (eds.) NASA Formal Methods - 15th International Symposium, NFM 2023, Houston, TX, USA, May 16-18, 2023, Proceedings. Lecture Notes in Computer Science, vol. 13903, pp. 16–36. Springer (2023). https://doi.org/10.1007/978-3-031-33170-1_2
36. Kochdumper, N., Schilling, C., Althoff, M., Bak, S.: Open- and closed-Loop neural network verification using polynomial zonotopes, p. 16–36. Springer Nature Switzerland (2023). https://doi.org/10.1007/978-3-031-33170-1_2
37. Lemesle, A., Lehmann, J., Gall, T.L.: Neural network verification with pyrat (2024). https://arxiv.org/abs/2410.23903
38. Li, J., Liu, J., Yang, P., Chen, L., Huang, X., Zhang, L.: Analyzing deep neural networks with symbolic propagation: towards higher precision and faster verification. In: Chang, B.Y.E. (ed.) Static Analysis, pp. 296–319. Springer International Publishing, Cham (2019)
39. Lopez, D.M., Choi, S.W., Tran, H.D., Johnson, T.T.: NNV 2.0: The neural network verification tool. In: 35th International Conference on Computer-Aided Verification (CAV) (2023)
40. Madry, A., Makelov, A., Schmidt, L., Tsipras, D., Vladu, A.: Towards deep learning models resistant to adversarial attacks (2019). https://arxiv.org/abs/1706.06083
41. Manfredi, G., Jestin, Y.: An introduction to ACAS Xu and the challenges Ahead. In: DASC, 2016 IEEE/AIAA 35th Digital Avionics Systems Conference. Digital Avionics Systems Conference (DASC), 2016 IEEE/AIAA 35th, Sacramento, United States (2016). https://enac.hal.science/hal-01638049. ISBN: 978-1-5090-2524-4

42. Mazzucato, D., Urban, C.: Reduced products of abstract domains for fairness certification of neural networks. In: Drăgoi, C., Mukherjee, S., Namjoshi, K. (eds.) Static Analysis, pp. 308–322. Springer International Publishing, Cham (2021)
43. Mirman, M., Singh, G., Vechev, M.: A provable defense for deep residual networks (2020). https://arxiv.org/abs/1903.12519
44. Moore, R.E.: Interval analysis, vol. 4. prentice-Hall Englewood Cliffs (1966)
45. Moosavi-Dezfooli, S.M., Fawzi, A., Frossard, P.: Deepfool: a simple and accurate method to fool deep neural networks (2016). https://arxiv.org/abs/1511.04599
46. Ortiz, J., Vellucci, A., Koeln, J., Ruths, J.: Hybrid zonotopes exactly represent relu neural networks. In: 2023 62nd IEEE Conference on Decision and Control (CDC), pp. 5351–5357. IEEE (2023)
47. Paszke, A., et al.: Pytorch: an imperative style, high-performance deep learning library (2019). https://arxiv.org/abs/1912.01703
48. Pedrouzo-Ulloa, A., et al.: Introducing the trumpet project: trustworthy multi-site privacy enhancing technologies. In: 2023 IEEE International Conference on Cyber Security and Resilience (CSR), pp. 604–611 (2023). https://doi.org/10.1109/CSR57506.2023.10224961
49. Pulina, L., Tacchella, A.: Challenging SMT solvers to verify neural networks. AI Commun. **25**(2), 117–135 (2012)
50. Scott, J.K., Raimondo, D.M., Marseglia, G.R., Braatz, R.D.: Constrained zonotopes: a new tool for set-based estimation and fault detection. Automatica **69**, 126–136 (2016). https://doi.org/10.1016/j.automatica.2016.02.036, https://linkinghub.elsevier.com/retrieve/pii/S0005109816300772
51. Shriver, D., Elbaum, S., Dwyer, M.B.: DNNV: a framework for deep neural network verification, pp. 137–150. Springer International Publishing (2021). https://doi.org/10.1007/978-3-030-81685-8_6
52. Sidarta, D.E., O'Sullivan, J., Lim, H.J.: Damage detection of offshore platform mooring line using artificial neural network. In: International Conference on Offshore Mechanics and Arctic Engineering. vol. Volume 1: Offshore Technology, p. V001T01A058 (2018). https://doi.org/10.1115/OMAE2018-77084
53. Singh, G., Gehr, T., Mirman, M., Püschel, M., Vechev, M.: Fast and effective robustness certification. In: Proceedings of the 32nd International Conference on Neural Information Processing Systems, pp. 10825–10836. NIPS'18, Curran Associates Inc., Red Hook, NY, USA (2018)
54. Singh, G., Gehr, T., Püschel, M., Vechev, M.: An abstract domain for certifying neural networks. In: Proceedings of the ACM on Programming Languages **3**(POPL), 1–30 (2019)
55. Tjeng, V., Xiao, K., Tedrake, R.: Evaluating robustness of neural networks with mixed integer programming. arXiv preprint arXiv:1711.07356 (2017)
56. Tran, H.D., et al.: NNV: the neural network verification tool for deep neural networks and learning-enabled cyber-physical systems. In: 32nd International Conference on Computer-Aided Verification (CAV) (2020)
57. Uewichitrapochana, P., Surarerks, A.: Signed-symmetric function approximation in affine arithmetic. In: 2013 10th International Conference on Electrical Engineering/Electronics, Computer, Telecommunications and Information Technology, pp. 1–6 (2013). https://doi.org/10.1109/ECTICon.2013.6559630
58. Urban, C., Christakis, M., Wüstholz, V., Zhang, F.: Perfectly parallel fairness certification of neural networks. Proc. ACM Program. Lang. **4**(OOPSLA) (2020). https://doi.org/10.1145/3428253
59. Urban, C., Miné, A.: A review of formal methods applied to machine learning (2021). https://arxiv.org/abs/2104.02466

60. Wang, S., Pei, K., Whitehouse, J., Yang, J., Jana, S.: Formal security analysis of neural networks using symbolic intervals. In: 27th USENIX Security Symposium (USENIX Security 18), pp. 1599–1614 (2018)
61. Wang, S., et al.: Beta-CROWN: efficient bound propagation with per-neuron split constraints for complete and incomplete neural network verification. arXiv preprint arXiv:2103.06624 (2021)
62. Weng, L., et al.: Towards fast computation of certified robustness for relu networks. In: International Conference on Machine Learning, pp. 5276–5285. PMLR (2018)
63. Xu, K., et al.: Fast and complete: enabling complete neural network verification with rapid and massively parallel incomplete verifiers. In: International Conference on Learning Representations (2021). https://openreview.net/forum?id=nVZtXBI6LNn
64. Yin, B., Chen, L., Liu, J., Wang, J.: Efficient complete verification of neural networks via layerwised splitting and refinement. Trans. Comp.-Aided Des. Integ. Cir. Sys. **41**(11), 3898–3909 (2022). https://doi.org/10.1109/TCAD.2022.3197534
65. Zhang, H., Weng, T.W., Chen, P.Y., Hsieh, C.J., Daniel, L.: Efficient neural network robustness certification with general activation functions. Adv. Neural Inf. Process. Syst. **31**, 4939–4948 (2018). https://arxiv.org/pdf/1811.00866.pdf
66. Zhang, Y., Zhang, H., Xu, X.: Backward reachability analysis of neural feedback systems using hybrid zonotopes. IEEE Control Syst. Lett. (2023)
67. Zhou, X., Xu, H., Xu, A., Shi, Z., Hsieh, C.J., Zhang, H.: Testing neural network verifiers: a soundness benchmark with hidden counterexamples (2024). https://arxiv.org/abs/2412.03154

Contextual Equality Saturation

Alexandre Drewery[1(✉)], Thomas P. Jensen[1,3], and David Pichardie[2]

[1] Inria, Université de Rennes, Rennes, France
alexandre.drewery@inria.fr
[2] Meta, Paris, France
[3] Department of Computer Science, University of Copenhagen,
Copenhagen, Denmark

Abstract. Equality saturation is a semantics-based technique for automatically and efficiently proving that two programs are equivalent modulo a fixed set of equality axioms. In this paper, we extend the equality saturation technique with contextual reasoning in order to perform rewriting under assumptions that are locally valid inside a conditional branch. This is based on a new notion of cyclic e-graphs with contextual annotations. We experimentally validate the efficiency and scalability of this new technique by proving equivalence of several families of programs where contextual reasoning is required.

1 Introduction

Equality saturation [22] is a semantics-based technique for proving equivalence of programs based on efficient term rewriting. It has successfully been used to validate program optimisations [20]. In order to compare programs and prove that a given source program has been optimised into a target program, the technique first convert both programs into a term representation of their semantics called a PEG (Program Expression Graph) [22]. A PEG can be loaded in an *e-graphs*, a data structure originally developed for proving term equivalence in SMT solvers and recently crafted into a high-performance Rust library named *egg* [26]. Equality saturation then consists in applying a series of rewriting rules on e-graphs in order to prove that the two programs have equivalent semantics.

There is, however, a fundamental limitation to Equality Saturation: it does not perform *contextual reasoning*. To illustrate this limitation, consider proving equivalence between the two tests `i+1>n` and `i==n`. These two tests are in general

---

This work was partially funded by the France 2030 project ANR-22-PECY-0005 "Secureval".

© The Author(s), under exclusive license to Springer Nature Switzerland AG 2026
H. Oh and Y. Sui (Eds.): SAS 2025, LNCS 16100, pp. 34–61, 2026.
https://doi.org/10.1007/978-3-032-07106-4_3

not equivalent but they will be in certain contexts, *e.g.* if we also know that
(i<=n)==true holds. For example, two terms if (i<=n) then T[i+1>n] else
U and if (i<=n) then T[i==n] else U are equivalent, for any term T[·] which
contain a contextual hole [·]. The inability of equality saturation to perform
contextual reasoning prohibits certain program transformations. For example, a
compiler might produce this loop construction

```
var x = 1; if (1 <= n) {
    x = 2*x; for (int i = 1; i != n; i++) { x = 2*x; }
}
```

from the following for-loop

```
int x = 1; for (int i = 1; i <= n; i++) { x = 2*x; }
```

but, without context reasoning, equality saturation cannot prove that the resulting programs are equivalent.

The purpose of this paper is to extend the equality saturation approach with such contextual reasoning. Equality saturation is an otherwise efficient program equivalence technique. Its main strength is the ability to reduce intricate equality deductions as a local calculation on terms. Our goal is to keep this philosophy in our contextual extension via a system of incremental bookkeeping.

In this paper:

- we extend the notion of e-graph with a new mechanism of *contextual annotation* that can be efficiently queried to detect potential contextual reasoning;
- we also introduce a new notion of *contextual rewriting rule* to implement this contextual reasoning. We design the algorithmic framework needed to e-match[1] and apply these rules;
- we provide an experimental evaluation of the efficiency of EQUIMATCH, a new OCaml library for contextual equality saturation that implements these algorithms.

2 Equality Saturation and E-graphs

Equality saturation aims to produce a set of equivalent terms given an initial term and some term rewriting rules that preserve equivalence. The general idea is to keep track of the set of all encountered terms and all equivalences between them. The rewriting rules are applied to sub-terms whenever possible, which enrich this set with new terms and new equivalences. To represent the equivalence classes of terms, equality saturation uses an efficient data structure called **equality graphs (e-graphs)** [8], a union-find data structure [21] enriched with a congruence closure [9] reasoning. Whenever a new equality between two terms t_1 and t_2 is discovered, the structure is also able to prove efficiently that $f(t_1)$

---

[1] Detecting an occurrence of a left hand side rewriting rule in en e-graph is called *e-matching* [6].

and $f(t_2)$ are equal, for any function symbol f. This data structure is the backbone of many SMT solvers [7].

Intuitively, an e-graph can be seen as a mix between term graphs and an union-find structure, representing both a sub-term relation and an equivalence relation. Whereas in a term graph a node represents a term, in an e-graph, an **e-node** represents a set of terms. E-nodes do not directly point towards other children e-nodes but rather towards **e-classes**, equivalence classes of e-nodes.

Figure 1 is an example of a small e-graph for the two arithmetic expression terms $(a\times 2)/2$ and $(2\times a)/2$: e-classes are represented in dotted lines. The e-class C_2 contains two $\times$ e-nodes: it indicates that they represent sets of equivalent terms. The e-node in e-class C_1 represents all terms with function symbol $/$ and sub-terms obtained by picking in the children e-classes. All instances of the term 2 as a sub-term are represented by the same e-class C_4 containing the 2 e-node: this **sharing** improves the memory performances of the structure.

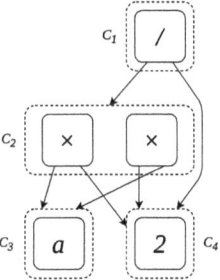

Fig. 1. A simple e-graph.

Definition 1. *An **e-graph** is a defined by a set of e-nodes $\mathcal{N}$ and a set of e-classes $\mathcal{C}$:*

- *each e-class $C \in \mathcal{C}$ is a subset of e-nodes and the set $\mathcal{C}$ of all e-classes forms a disjoint set partition of all e-nodes $\mathcal{N}$;*
- *each e-node $n \in \mathcal{N}$ is characterized by a function symbol f from the term language and some (potentially zero) ordered children e-classes $C_1, \ldots, C_k \in \mathcal{C}$.*

More formally, an e-class represents the set of terms represented by its e-nodes. An e-node of symbol f and children e-classes $C_1, \ldots, C_n$ represents all terms of root term symbol f and direct subterms picked respectively from terms represented by $C_1, \ldots, C_n$. We use $rep(C)$ and $rep(n)$ to denote these **sets of represented terms**:

$$rep(C) = \bigcup_{n \in C} rep(n)$$

$$rep(f(C_1, \ldots, C_n)) = \{f(t_1, \ldots, t_n) \mid t_1 \in rep(C_1), \ldots, t_n \in rep(C_n)\}$$

The e-graph data structure supports the following operations:

- **adding new e-node** to the e-graph in a fresh e-class and connecting its children to the proper e-classes (the process can be iterated to add a complete new term),
- **merging two e-classes** to incorporate new equalities (it can start a cascade of merging because of the congruence closure reasoning)
- and **e-matching a term pattern** in the e-graph. A **pattern** is a term p built from term function symbols and variables from a set of pattern variables $\mathcal{X}$. E-matching such a pattern is used to identify a left hand-side of a rewriting rules before applying this rule to the e-graph.

An **occurrence** of a pattern p is a pair (C, σ) of an e-class C and a substitution $\sigma \in \mathcal{S}$ such that e-node $\sigma(p)$ is in C, which we denote $p \in_\sigma C$. **E-matching** is the operation that looks for all occurrences of a pattern in an e-graph. For instance, e-matching the pattern $X \times Y$ in Fig. 1 will yield two occurrences in C_2: one with substitution $X \rightarrow C_3$, $Y \rightarrow C_4$ and one with substitution $X \rightarrow C_4$, $Y \rightarrow C_3$.

A **rewriting rule** takes the form of two patterns $p_1 \leadsto p_2$, with the restriction that all variables that appear in p_2 also appear in p_1. Intuitively such a rule states that for any substitution σ, the e-node $\sigma(p_1)$ is equivalent to the e-node $\sigma(p_2)$. For instance, the rule $X \times 2 \leadsto X + X$ makes the term $a \times 2$ and $a + a$ equivalent.

Equality saturation exploits these mechanisms by iteratively **applying** rewriting rules to the e-graph: e-match for occurrences of the rules, add the rewritten term and indicate equivalence by merging the two e-classes. The e-graph is saturated when no rule application can yield a new term: for instance, the e-graph of Fig. 1 is saturated for rule $X \times Y \leadsto Y \times X$. Equality saturation terminates when the e-graph is saturated for the whole rule set or when a timeout condition is reached.

3 Program Equivalence Proof by Equality Saturation

Equality saturation has been used to perform program equivalence checking efficiently, as demonstrated by Tate et al. [22]. The technique is based on an advanced intermediate representation of program, called PEG for Program Expression Graph, which is a variant of e-graphs and which share similarities with advanced intermediate representations used in the modern compilers (like Gated-SSA [12] or Sea-of-nodes [17]). It has been successfully used to validate difficult translation validation challenges [20] posed by advanced compiler optimizations techniques (dead code elimination, global value numbering, partial redundancy elimination, sparse conditional constant propagation, loop-invariant code motion, loop deletion, loop unswitching, dead store elimination, loop-induction variables). Their approach is composed of 3 distinct steps:

1. Building a term representation of programs
2. Identifying a fixed set of equivalence axioms

3. Run a custom saturation solver

Each program is converted into a term representation name PEG that is a pure functional representation of a program. If the two terms are equivalent according to a fixed set of equivalence axioms (rewriting rules) then the two initial program are observably equivalent. Such a term encoding is not trivial. Several specific reserved function symbols are introduced to reason on control flow (conditionals, loops) and also memory. Because we are mainly interested in contextual reasoning that is possible inside a if-then-else branch, we will focus on the Φ operator that they introduce for this specific construction. Φ is a ternary symbol that represents a conditional. The first child sub-term is the conditional, the second child is a term that represents the *then*-branch and the third child represents the *else*-branch. For instance, the term $\Phi(eq(x,0),2,5)$ represents the conditional that evaluates to 2 is x is equal to 0 and 5 otherwise. This operator is similar to the Φ operator used in Gated-SSA [12].

Tate *et al.* provides rewriting rules for standard arithmetic expressions as well as rules that manipulate the various control flow operators, including the Φ operator. Figure 2 shows the rewriting rules that interact with Φ. Rule [PHI-NEG] switches the branches of a conditional by negating its condition. Rules [PHI-TRUE] and [PHI-FALSE] simplify a conditional with trivial condition. Rule [PHI-SAME] removes a condition if both branches are equivalent. Rules [PHI-BOOL] and [PHI-BOOL-NEG] turn a condition into a simpler boolean expression when both branches are equivalent to boolean literals. Rules [PHI-DEAD-THEN] and [PHI-DEAD-ELSE] remove dead branches when two nested conditional test equivalent conditions. Rule [PHI-DEAD-DEEP] simplifies a nested conditional at depth 3 when an equivalent test is performed at depth 1. The fact that this last rule only applies to conditionals of fixed depth and structure demonstrates the lack of contextual reasoning that motivates the current paper.

$$[\text{PHI-NEG}] : \Phi(neg(X), Y, Z) \rightsquigarrow \Phi(X, Z, Y)$$
$$[\text{PHI-TRUE}] : \Phi(true, X, Y) \rightsquigarrow X$$
$$[\text{PHI-FALSE}] : \Phi(false, X, Y) \rightsquigarrow Y$$
$$[\text{PHI-SAME}] : \Phi(X, Y, Y) \rightsquigarrow Y$$
$$[\text{PHI-BOOL}] : \Phi(X, true, false) \rightsquigarrow X$$
$$[\text{PHI-BOOL-NEG}] : \Phi(X, false, true) \rightsquigarrow neg(X)$$
$$[\text{PHI-DEAD-THEN}] : \Phi(X, \Phi(X, T, D), E) \rightsquigarrow \Phi(X, T, E)$$
$$[\text{PHI-DEAD-ELSE}] : \Phi(X, T, \Phi(X, D, E)) \rightsquigarrow \Phi(X, T, E)$$
$$[\text{PHI-DEAD-DEEP}] : \Phi(X_1, \Phi(X_2, \Phi(X_1, T, D), E_2), E_1) \rightsquigarrow \Phi(X_1, \Phi(X_2, T, E_2), E_1)$$

Fig. 2. Rewriting rules on Φ-terms used in PEGGY [22].

Tate *et al.* designed their own saturation solver, specialized for reasoning on equivalences classes of PEGs. The most notable difference with standard e-graph solvers used in SMT (like Z3) is the special treatment of cyclic expressions. Once the two initial terms have been loaded into the solver, the equality saturation process starts applying rules and merging classes. New merged classes may generate new rewriting opportunities. The iterative process can be stopped as soon as the two classes representing the returned value of each program are merged. If no more rules can be applied or a timeout is reached, the checking is inconclusive.

They showed that the custom saturation engine is capable of performing successful program reasoning using equality saturation, by doing translation validation of Soot optimizations on Java program, and translation validation of LLVM optimizations on LLVM programs. The set of rules must be chosen carefully, though, taking into account the expected differences and similarities between inputs. Adding too many rules may increase the number of rewriting steps and hence the risk of timeout before merging the two classes representing the return value of each compared programs.

In general, equality saturation comes with potential weaknesses that must be taken into account when engineering a tool with it. Some rulesets may lead to an unbounded number of rewritings. The search exploration must be kept bounded because of a risk of memory overflow, or even non-termination and well-chosen heuristics are necessary. Finally, there is a fundamental limitation that we have illustrated with the previous set of rewriting rules on Φ-patterns: equality saturation does not represent well the scope of a Φ-test and misses opportunities to merge equivalent program fragments. The rest of the paper presents a novel technique that remove this limitation.

4 Contextual Equality Saturation

We want our rewriting rules to be able to exploit information gained in the conditionals. A basic example of such a rule is given in Fig. 3: the Φ-node checks if X and Y are different and this information can be used as a context in the *then*-child to change a greater-or-equal check to a greater-than check.

However, as written, the rule of Fig. 3 can only be used if e-node $gte(X, Y)$ is in the immediate *then*-child e-class of the Φ-node. In practice this will rarely be the case in a term obtained from a real program: $gte(X, Y)$ will often appear as a subcomputation in a bigger term, not right under the Φ-node. We are more often in the situation of Fig. 4 where the instance of $gte(X, Y)$ is further along the *then*-branch of the term. The dotted edge notation denotes the same term structure in both terms, except for the instance of X replaced by Y.

The main subtlety of the transition from the conditional rule of Fig. 3 to the contextual rule of Fig. 4 is that the two equivalent classes **are not those of** $gte(X, Y)$ **and** $gt(X, Y)$ but rather the classes of the Φ-nodes (the checks are equivalent but only **under the condition that** $neq(X, Y)$ **holds**). The rule must therefore encompass the Φ-nodes. The pattern of the rule of Fig. 4 cannot be explicitly specified using the standard pattern language since it must allow branches from Φ to $gte(X, Y)$ that are of arbitrary length.

We introduce the new notation $neq(X, Y) \vdash gte(X, Y) \rightsquigarrow gt(X, Y)$ for the rule of Fig. 4. This can be read as *the rewriting of $gte(X, Y)$ into $gt(X, Y)$ where*

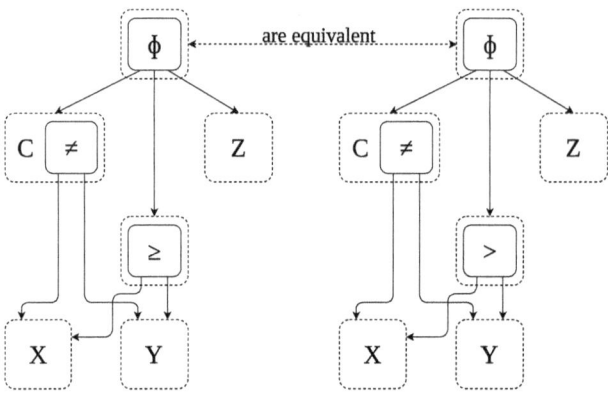

[GTE-TO-GT]: $\Phi(neq(X,Y), gte(X,Y), Z) \rightsquigarrow \Phi(neq(X,Y), gt(X,Y), Z))$

Fig. 3. A conditional rewriting rule that exploits an inequality in a condition.

the context $neq(X,Y)$ is known to be true. We call this new kind of rules that works on arbitrary Φ-terms for **contextual rewriting rules**.

Definition 2. *A **contextual rewriting rule** has the form*

$$p_c \vdash p_1 \rightsquigarrow p_2$$

*The pattern p_c is called the **contextual requirement** of the rule and the $p_1 \rightsquigarrow p_2$ part is a standard rewriting rule. We call p_1 the **structural requirement** of the rule.*

Intuitively, a contextual rule can be applied whenever we find an e-class C that matches the structural requirement p_1, in the *then*-branch of a Φ-node $\Phi(C_c, C_t, C_e)$ such that C_c matches the contextual requirement p_c. The fact that C is *found* in the *then*-branch denoted by C_t is formally defined below.

Definition 3. *A e-class C_1 is a **subclass** of an e-class C_2 (written $C_1 \preceq C_2$) if and only if there exists a term $t_1 \in rep(C_1)$ and a subterm $t_2 \in rep(C_2)$ such that t_1 is a subterm of t_2 (written $t_1 \preceq t_2$).*

For example, on Fig. 5, both $C_{\geq} \preceq C_{\wedge}$ and $C_x \preceq C_{\wedge}$ hold.

Definition 4. *Given a contextual rule $p_c \vdash p_1 \rightsquigarrow p_2$, a **contextual occurrence** is a pair (C, σ) of an e-class C and a substitution $\sigma \in S$ such that:*

- *the pair (C, σ) is an occurrence of p_1 (written $p_1 \in_\sigma C$ in Sect. 2);*
- *there exists an e-node $\Phi(C_c, C_t, C_e)$ such that $p_c \in_\sigma C_c$ and $C \preceq C_t$.*

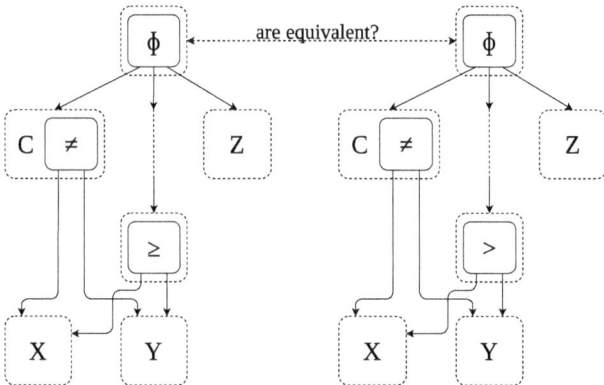

[CONTEXTUAL-GTE-TO-GT]: $neq(X,Y) \vdash gte(X,Y) \rightsquigarrow gt(X,Y)$

Fig. 4. Contextual version of the rule [GTE-TO-GT].

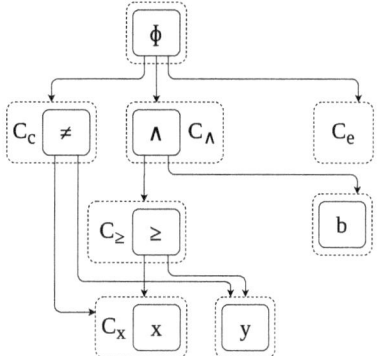

Fig. 5. E-graph where the rule [CONTEXTUAL-GTE-TO-GT] can be used.

For instance, on Fig. 5, there is a contextual occurrence in e-class $C_\geq$. This e-class represents the term $gte(x,y)$ and is in the *then*-branch of a conditional of condition $neq(x,y)$.

In the following subsections, we describe algorithms that use the notion of context to determine when a contextual rewriting rule can be applied and how the rule updates the e-graph. We first describe naive versions of the algorithms, before defining the efficient algorithms as optimized versions of the naive counterparts.

4.1 Naive Contextual Rewriting

The simplest way of looking for contextual occurrences of a contextual rule $p_c \vdash p_1 \rightsquigarrow p_2$ is to search for all Φ-terms which condition matches p_c and then explore the entire *then*-branch of these term in search for a match for p_1. We propose a pseudo-code for this process in Algorithm 1.

Algorithm 1. Pseudo-code for a naive contextual e-matching procedure.

1: **function** CONTEMATCHINGNAIVE(contextual requirement p_c, structural requirement p_1)
2:     **for** all e-nodes $\Phi(C_c, C_t, C_e)$ such that $\exists \sigma_c.\ p_c \in_\sigma C_c$ **do**
3:         traverse downward the e-graph starting from C_t
4:         **for** all met e-classes C such that $C \preceq C_t$ and $\exists \sigma_1.\ p_1 \in_{\sigma_1 \circ \sigma_c} C$ **do**
5:             $(C, \sigma_1 \circ \sigma_c)$ is an occurrence
6:         **end for**
7:     **end for**
8: **end function**

Once this algorithm finds occurrences for the contextual rule, they can be passed to the procedure of Algorithm 2 that will perform the rewriting.

The intuitive idea of this algorithm is, given an occurrence (C, σ), to build a node n' similar to $n = \Phi(C_c, C_t, C_e)$ (which is also passed as an argument), except that instances of e-class C in e-nodes of the *then*-branch C_t are replaced with a rewritten e-class. The e-classes of n' and n are then merged. The result of this procedure can be seen in Fig. 6, in which the entire *then*-branch of the Φ-node has been copied under a new Φ-node, but with the e-class $C_\geq$ replaced by a new e-class for term $gt(x, y)$.

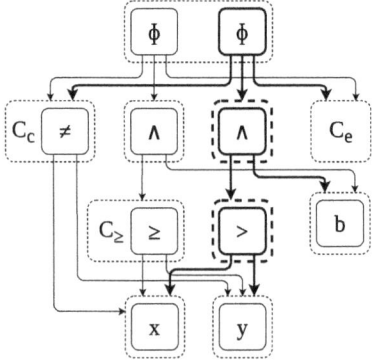

Fig. 6. E-graph of Fig. 5 after contextual rewriting with [CONTEXTUAL-GTE-TO-GT].

In this naive approach, we explicitly enumerate (and build) the new terms $t_t[t_1 \to t_2]^2$, which is unrealistic but explains the objective of this section. Another problem is that the naive e-matching algorithm performs exploratory e-graph traversals in search of occurrences. In practice, this is too inefficient for the process of contextual rewriting that may be run frequently. In the following subsections, we design a more efficient framework for contextual rewriting using these naive algorithms as a specification.

Algorithm 2. Pseudo-code for a naive contextual rewriting procedure.

1: **function** CONTREWRITINGNAIVE(contextual rule $p_c \vdash p_1 \rightsquigarrow p_2$, occurrence (C, σ), e-node $n = \Phi(C_c, C_t, C_e)$ in its e-class C_n)
2:     add e-node $\sigma(p_2)$ to the e-graph
3:     let t_2 be a term of $rep(\sigma(p_2))$
4:     **for** all terms $\Phi(t_c, t_t, t_e) \in rep(n)$ **do**
5:         **if** t_t has a subterm $t_1 \preccurlyeq t_t$ in $rep(\sigma(p_1))$ **then**
6:             add term $t'_t = t_t[t_1 \to t_2]$ to the e-graph in an e-class C'_t
7:             add e-node $n' = \Phi(C_c, C'_t, C_e)$ to e-graph and merge its e-class with C_n
8:         **end if**
9:     **end for**
10: **end function**

4.2 Context Annotations

One way to improve the complexity of this process is to **annotate** all subclasses in the *then*-branch C_t of an e-node $\Phi(C_c, C_t, C_e)$ with the information that they are in the context of C_c being true. This allows for a local check of which *then*-branches a term is in, rather than having to do an exploration every time.

The kind of annotations we want is shown on a basic e-graph in the square boxes in Fig. 7. Annotations are attached to e-classes and an e-class can have multiple annotations. All annotations are pairs (C_c, e) with C_c an e-class of boolean terms (the **context**) and e an edge of the e-graph (the **source information**). Such a pair intuitively means that further upward edge e, there is at least one Φ-node with condition C_c. An annotation for an e-class C can contain several pairs for the same context C_c if different paths lead to C from Φ-nodes with condition C_c. For example, in Fig. 7, the e-graph represents a program with two conditionals with the same condition in two *then*-branches arranged sequentially. These multiple instances of the *then*-branch are associated with different paths in the e-graph, hence there are two annotations for the e-class of the +-node.

Definition 5. *Let C_c be an e-class (the **context**) and e an edge (the **source information**) in an e-graph. The pair (C_c, e) is an **annotation** for e-class C_k if the e-graph represents a term $\Phi(t_c, t_t, t_e)$ such that:*

---

[2] This notation means that all occurrences of t_1 in t_t have been simultaneously replaced by t_2.

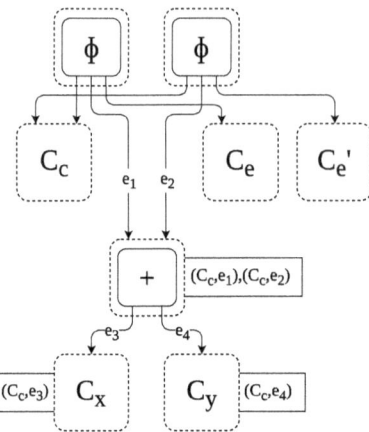

Fig. 7. E-graph annotation with different sources.

- $t_c \in rep(C_c)$ (i.e. C_c represents t_c);
- e is an edge from a node n to the class C_k (i.e. n is of the form $f(C_1, \ldots, C_k, \ldots)$);
- for some $t_k \in rep(C)$, there exists a subterm $f(t_1, \ldots, t_k, \ldots) \in rep(n)$ of t_t.

Annotations allow to check locally the context of an e-class. The source information in annotations allow to find the parents Φ-nodes that generates these contexts. In the following subsections, we present how more efficient contextual rewriting is done in a fully annotated e-graph. We delay the description of the incremental annotation process until Sect. 4.5.

4.3 Efficient Contextual E-matching

Assuming an e-graph that is properly annotated, it is possible to efficiently e-match for occurrences of a contextual rule $p_c \vdash p_1 \leadsto p_2$ by e-matching (with a regular e-matching procedure) for the structural requirement p_1 and then, for each occurrence (C, σ), use the annotation associated with C to get some e-class candidates that we can try to match with the contextual requirement p_c. For instance, in Fig. 8a, when trying to activate the rule [CONTEXTUAL-GTE-TO-GT], the naive approach would first e-match for $neq(X, Y)$ and then naively traverse the full *then*-branch of the Φ-node, searching for pattern $gte(X, Y)$. Instead, we can now immediately identify that the only possible occurrence of our structural pattern is in $C_\geq$ and immediately after, check that $C_\geq$ indeed have C_c as a context in its annotations.

Algorithm 3 describes this procedure. A strength of Algorithm 3 is that it can rely on a regular, optimized e-matching procedure to identify matches for the structural requirement.

Algorithm 3. Contextual e-matching algorithm that exploits the annotations.

1: **function** CONTEMATCHING(contextual requirement p_c, structural requirement p_1)
2:    e-match for occurrences of p_1
3:    **for** all such occurrences (C, σ_1) **do**
4:      **if** C has an annotation (C_c, e) such that $\exists \sigma_c.\ p_c \in_{\sigma_c \circ \sigma_1} C_c$ **then**
5:         $(C, \sigma_c \circ \sigma_1)$ is an occurrence
6:      **end if**
7:    **end for**
8: **end function**

In comparison with Algorithm 1, both algorithms have the same worst-case complexity: quadratic in e-graph size. Note that in general, e-graph algorithms suffer from similar limitations: the optimized algorithm often do not improve the worst case complexities of naives versions. On an average e-graph, Algorithm 3 has the advantage on focusing immediately on structural occurrences of p_1 without a need to explore irrelevant parts of the *then*-branch.

4.4 Contextual Rewriting

Contextual rewriting can also exploit the annotations. The intuition is the same as in Sect. 4.1 but the path that connects a source e-node $\Phi(C_c, C_t, C_e)$ to an occurrence (C, σ) can be built starting from C and moving upwards using the clues provided by the annotations e-class encountered.

This process is illustrated in Fig. 8. Starting from the initial configuration of Fig. 8a, the structural part of the rewriting is performed to get to Fig. 8b with a new >-node. The path information of the annotation of $C_\geq$ indicates to copy the structure above e_2: a ∧-node. We add a new ∧-node above the e-class of the >-node in Fig. 8c. The same process then copies a Φ-node to get to Fig. 8d. Since this Φ-node has condition C_c, the process ends here and the two e-classes of Φ-nodes are merged (Fig. 8e).

Algorithm 4 describes the procedure for this contextual rewriting. It is split in two: CONTEMATCHING will perform the structural part of the rewriting (creating a new e-node $\sigma(p_2)$), while REBUILDPATH iteratively inserts copies above the new e-node $\sigma(p_2)$ of the paths that lead from Φ-nodes to $\sigma(p_1)$.

A subtlety of this algorithm is what happens when several possible parents propagate context C_c to e-class C. For instance, this happens in the e-class of the +-node in Fig. 7. In that case the rewriting process splits into two distinct rewritings on the fly: all rewritings associated with all paths are performed.

The contextual rewriting process may need to travel upward along an arbitrary path in the e-graph, so it is more costly than a standard rewriting: linear in the length of this path. Thanks to the path informations of annotations, it visits exactly the e-nodes it needs to in order to rebuild a path from the Φ-node to the occurrence. This linear complexity is the same as Algorithm 2.

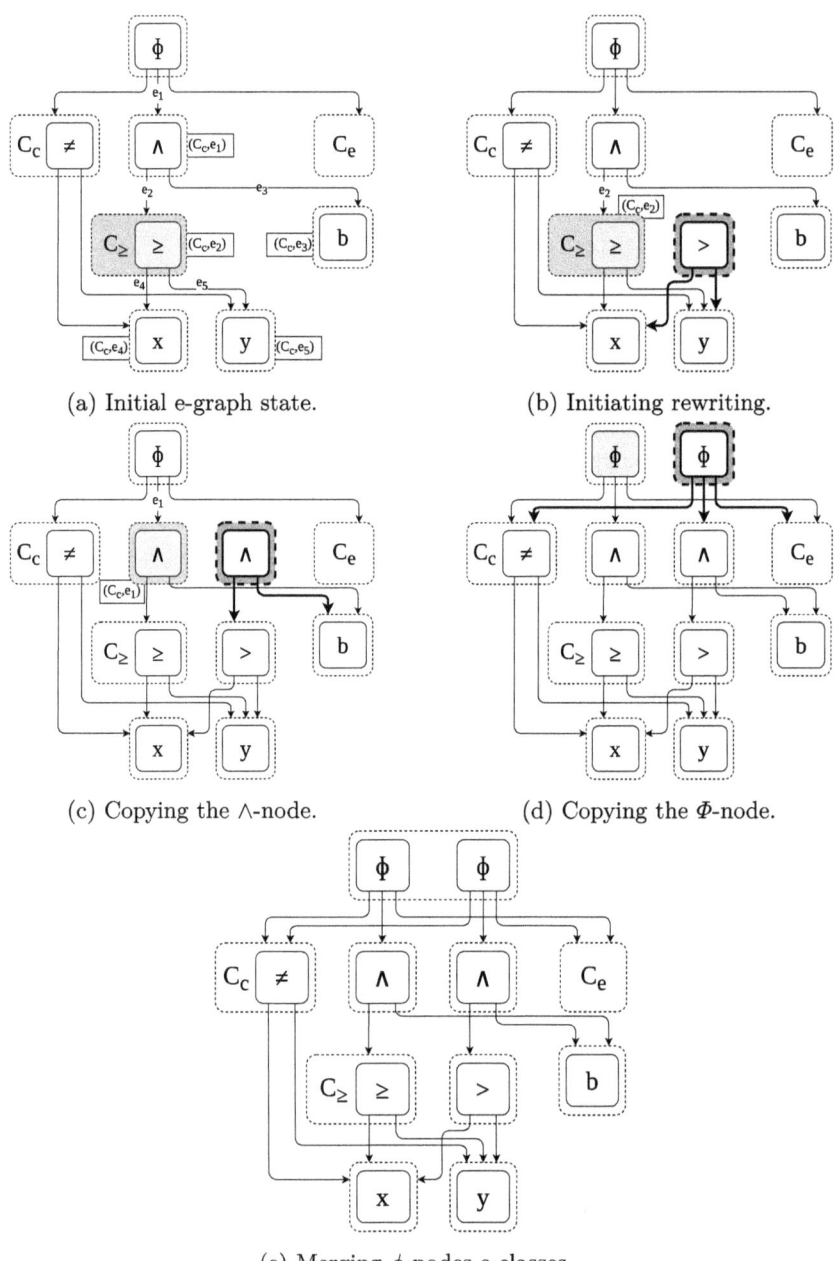

Fig. 8. Step-by-step contextual rewriting.

Algorithm 4. Contextual rewriting algorithm that exploits the annotations.

1: **function** CONTEMATCHING(contextual rule $p_c \vdash p_1 \leadsto p_2$, occurrence (C, σ))
2:     add e-node $\sigma(p_2)$ to the e-graph, let C' be its e-class
3:     let C_c be the e-class of $\sigma(p_c)$
4:     call procedure RebuildPath(C,C',C_c)
5: **end function**

1: **function** REBUILDPATH(C,C',C_c)
2:     **for** all annotations (C_c, e) of C **do**
3:         let e-node $n = f(\ldots, C, \ldots)$ be the source of e and C_n the e-class of n
4:         add e-node $n' = f(\ldots, C', \ldots)$ to the e-graph, let C'_n be its e-class
5:         **if** $n = \Phi(C_c, C, C_e)$ **then**
6:             merge C_n and C'_n
7:         **else**
8:             call RebuildPath(C_n,C'_n,C_c)
9:         **end if**
10:     **end for**
11: **end function**

4.5 Incremental E-graph Annotation

We have explained how the contextual annotations can be used to perform contextual rewriting. We will now explain how to compute these annotations. Because e-graph are progressively built by alternating the e-graph operations *add* and *merge*, we redefine these operations to incrementally build an annotated e-graph.

The general intuition of the annotation process is a downward propagation of context annotations along the edges of the e-graph whenever a new context appears. Both annotation-update procedures take the form of *maintenance functions* that must be called immediately after a *add* or *merge* has been performed.

The procedure for adding a new e-node n is described in Algorithm 5. If n is not a Φ-node, it does not add any new context. Otherwise, if n is a Φ-node $\Phi(C_c, C_t, C_e)$ then a new context C_c is iteratively propagated to its *then*-child e-class C_t.

Algorithm 5. Updating annotations whenever an e-node is added.

1: **function** UPDATEONADD(added e-node n, its e-class C)
2:     **if** n has the form $\Phi(C_c, C_t, C_e)$ **then**
3:         let e be the edge outgoing of n to C_t
4:         Propagate($C_t, \{C_c\}, e$)
5:     **end if**
6: **end function**

When merging two e-classes C_1 and C_2, the context annotations must also be merged. This is done with Algorithm 6. The paths leading to C_1 now also lead to C_2 and vice versa so contexts are now shared. Since all e-nodes of the new merged e-class have potentially new possible contexts, the propagation process must be invoked on their children as well.

Algorithm 6. Updating annotations whenever e-classes are merged.

1: **function** UPDATEONMERGE(merged e-classes C_1 and C_2, resulting e-class C)
2:     let A_1 and A_2 be the sets of annotations of C_1 and C_2
3:     annotate C with $A_1 \cup A_2$
4:     let the set of contexts $\mathcal{C}$ be $\{C_c|(C_c, e) \in A_1 \cup A_2$
5:     **for** all e-nodes $n \in C$ **do**
6:         **for** all outgoing edges e' (pointing towards C') of n **do**
7:             Propagate($C', \mathcal{C}, e'$)
8:         **end for**
9:     **end for**
10: **end function**

The propagation procedure is an e-graph traversal described in Algorithm 7. This traversal uses the incoming edges in order to annotate e-classes with the correct path information. This propagation plays a role similar to the e-graph traversal in the naive e-matching algorithm of Sect. 4.1, but it is called only once when needed, it is only performed on e-classes of the e-graph whose annotations must be updated, and the process only uses information **local** to these e-classes.

Algorithm 7. Propagation of annotations.

1: **function** PROPAGATE(e-class C, set of contexts $\mathcal{C}$, incoming edge e)
2:     let $\mathcal{A}$ be the annotations of C
3:     **if** $\{(C_c, e)|C_c \in \mathcal{C}\} \subseteq \mathcal{A}$ **then**
4:         do nothing
5:     **else**
6:         $\mathcal{A} \leftarrow \{(C_c, e)|C_c \in \mathcal{C}\} \cup \mathcal{A}$
7:         **for** all e-nodes $n \in C$ **do**
8:             **for** all outgoing edges e' (pointing towards C') of n **do**
9:                 Propagate($C', \mathcal{C}, e'$)
10:            **end for**
11:        **end for**
12:    **end if**
13: **end function**

The PROPAGATE procedure holds most of the maintenance cost of the annotation framework. In the worst case, PROPAGATE is linear in the number of edges of the e-graph. This implementation is however minimal in the sense that it only visits the edges that propagate new contextual annotations. Some additional work could further improve the performance of contextual rewriting such as delaying the annotation maintenance, similar to the performance-improving approach of *egg* of delaying invariants maintenance in the e-graph [26].

In terms of complexity, this bookkeeping do not worsen the already linear in e-graph size complexity of e-graph maintenance. The only exception is the addition of a Φ-node. This operation does not require much maintenance on a standard e-graph, but with our framework it now has a linear complexity. Note that this corresponds exactly to the e-graph traversal complexity of Algorithm 1 if it were performed exactly once rather than every time the e-matching procedure is called.

The program term representation we use involves cyclic terms to represent loops. Although all definitions hold on cyclic terms, using a contextual rewriting rule on such a term may lead to rewritings inside the loop bodies that makes no sense regarding the initial program. We choose not to propagate context through loops operators to prevent this behaviour.

5 Evaluation

We aim to evaluate the scalability of the contextual equality saturation framework we propose, as the size of the e-graphs increases. To this end, we have generated three collections of pairs of equivalent programs. Proving their equivalence is based on the use of the contextual rule of Sect. 4:

$$[\text{Contextual-Gte-To-Gt}]: neq(X,Y) \vdash gte(X,Y) \rightsquigarrow gt(X,Y)$$

We task the equality saturation engine described in this paper, EQUIMATCH[3], with solving these problems. We compare its performances with three other rewriting strategies described in Sect. 5.1.

5.1 Experimental Settings

Naive Swap-Based Non-contextual Engine: The first setting represents how state-of-the-art equality-saturation tools would simulate contextual rewriting at the cost of introducing extra *swapping* rules. In this setting we force EQUIMATCH to only perform regular non-contextual rewritings, but we feed the solver with the rule:

$$[\text{Gte-To-Gt}]: \vdash \Phi(neq(X,Y), gte(X,Y), Z) \rightsquigarrow \Phi(neq(X,Y), gt(X,Y), Z)$$

This rule encodes the same reasoning as the contextual one, but only for contextual requirement at distance 1 of the structural requirement. We complement this rule with swapping rules between Φ-nodes and other types of nodes that appear in the problems, *e.g.* f-nodes:

$$\vdash \Phi(X_c, f(X_t^1, X_t^2), f(X_e^1, X_e^2)) \rightsquigarrow f(\Phi(X_c, X_t^1, X_e^1), \Phi(X_c, X_t^2, X_e^2))$$

These rules (one for each operator f) help recover the lack of specific contextual reasoning by pushing down the context-bearing Φ-term or pushing up the

---
[3] Repository of development of the prototype can be found at https://framagit.org/adrew108/equality-saturation-ocaml.

structural point of application closer to each other. However, depending on the operator f, they can usually only be used in limited situations since f has to appear on both sides of the Φ operator.

Naive Traversal-Based Contextual Engine: The second setting implements contextual equality saturation but using naive algorithmic approach. In this setting, we force EQUIMATCH to perform the expensive graph traversal presented in Algorithm 1 and 2 in Sect. 4.1, and we do not use the efficient incremental context annotation algorithms presented in Sects. 4.2, 4.3, 4.4 and 4.5.

EquiMatch Annotation-Based Contextual Engine: The third setting implements full contextual equality saturation based on the contextual annotation bookkeeping system of the current paper.

Unsound Rewriting Setting: The last setting is a non-contextual rewriting strategy that quickly solves the problems using the (unsound) rule:

$$\vdash gte(X, Y) \rightsquigarrow gt(X, Y)$$

We introduce this setting to have a kind of baseline with respect to the e-matching phase. However this approach does not provide a strict baseline since it does not produce the exact same terms as the three sound previous settings. As an example, the two terms $\Phi(neq(X,Y), f_1(f_2(f_3(gte(X,Y)))), Z)$ and $\Phi(neq(X,Y), f_1(f_2(f_3(gt(X,Y)))), Z)$ will be merged by all four strategies but the unsound setting will also merge each pair of subterms $f_i(\ldots(gte(X,Y)))$ and $f_i(\ldots(gt(X,Y)))$ in specific classes.

Still this setting can be used as an estimate for the time EQUIMATCH takes to load the two PEG and to perform an ideal e-matching procedure.

5.2 Source-Pattern Distance Benchmark

The first benchmark consists of pairs of programs that measure each method performance when the distance N between a context source and a structural pattern increases. All pairs have the following structure and vary only in the number N:

```
if (x != y) {                        if (x != y) {
    if (x >= y) {                        if (x > y) {
        z = z + 1;                           z = z + 1;
    };                                   };
    <N buffer instructions>              <N buffer instructions>
};                                   };
return z;                            return z;
```

For a given number N, the only difference between the left and right programs is the condition of the inner conditional. Notice that, due to the way that the

PEG is built, the buffer of size N that is added **after** the inner conditional will increase the distance between Φ-terms of the inner and the outer conditionals in the PEG associated with these programs as shown in Fig. 13 in the Appendix B.

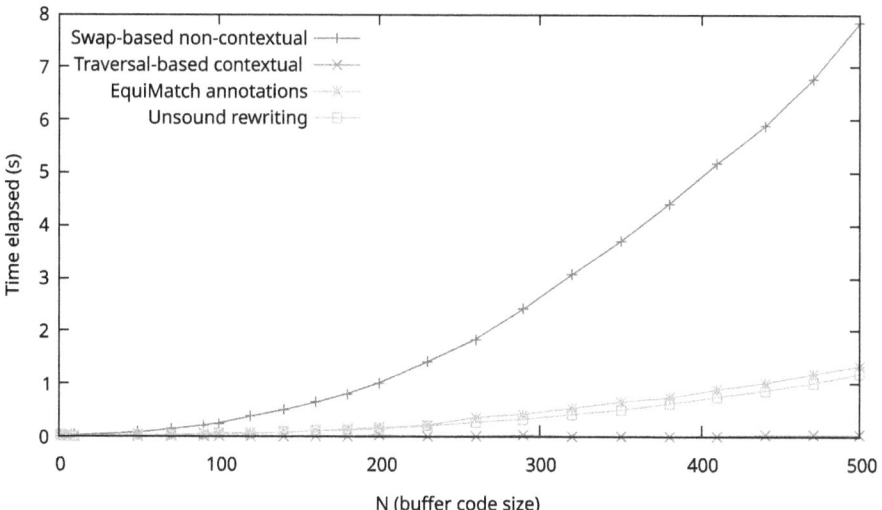

Fig. 9. Results for the Source-pattern distance benchmarks

Experimental Results: Figure 9 shows the time elapsed for equivalence proving with each experimental setting, for values of N up to 500.

This benchmark is very favorable to the naive traversal-based approach, which outperforms even the unsound rewriting. Indeed, contextual e-matching is called exactly once, performs a singular traversal of the (linear) *then*-branch of the left program. This traversal is light in memory-write accesses, and will result in the merging of the outer Φ-terms. In comparison, the unsound proof requires N recursive e-class merging from the bottom of the e-graph.

Still the annotation-based approach behaves as well as the unsound rewriting. The difference in performance with the naive traversal-based approach is explained by the amount of memory-write accesses needed to setup the annotations. Note that this benchmark does not play to the strengths of the annotation framework as every problem is solved in one single contextual rewriting rule application.

Both contextual approaches perform better than the swap-based approach, validating the relevance of contextual reasoning.

5.3 Number of Sources Benchmark

Experimental Setup: We evaluate how contextual equality saturation performs on programs with multiple contextual sources. This benchmark tests the path information part of the annotation framework: multiple paths from multiple sources lead to the structural pattern. We study a new family of pairs of programs that combines N conditionals sharing some calculations in a large *then*-branch containing the structural pattern for the contextual rewriting rule:

```
if (x != y) {
    if (x >= y) {
        z = z + 1;
    };
    <fixed buffer code>
};
a = a + z;
<... above code is copied N times>
return a;
```

```
if (x != y) {
    if (x > y) {
        z = z + 1;
    };
    <fixed buffer code>
};
a = a + z;
<... above code is copied N times>
return a;
```

The associated PEG structure of the left program can be found in Fig. 14 in the Appendix B.

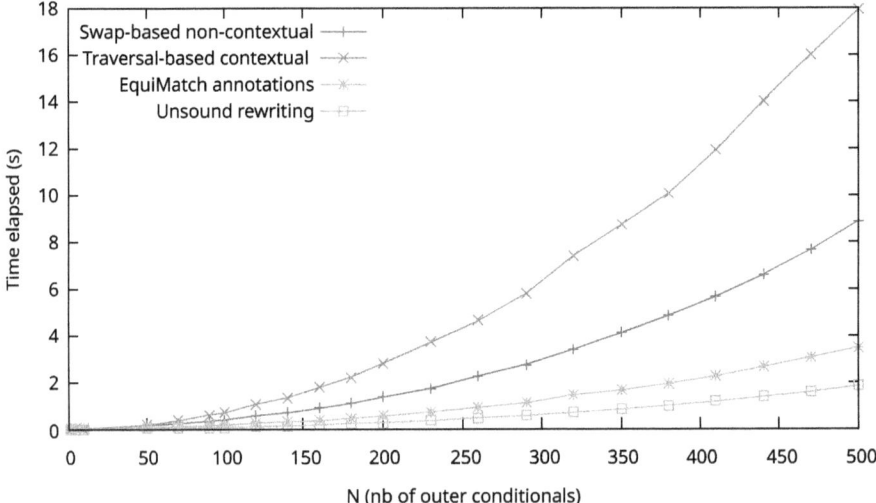

Fig. 10. Results for the number of sources benchmarks

Experimental Results: Figure 10 shows the time elapsed for equivalence proving with each experimental setting, for values of N up to 500.

The naive traversal-based contextual approach has the worst performance on these benchmark. Each contextual source leads to another *then*-branch traversal during contextual e-matching which naturally lowers the performances of the approach.

Annotation-based contextual equality saturation performs better than all other sound approaches. The annotation bookkeeping framework is efficient here, as it is only computed once on shared parts of an e-graph.

5.4 Complex Equivalence Task Benchmark

Experimental Setup: In this last benchmark we propose a last family of pairs of programs where N rewriting rules must be performed in the *then*-branch before the contextual pattern appears. This benchmark tests the contextual e-matching and the incremental annotation parts of the annotation framework: it requires detecting when the contextual pattern appears, and updating annotations when rewriting are performed in a *then*-branch. The family we study is similar to the previous one, except that N now controls both the number of conditionals and the complexity of some patterns <p1(N)> and <p2(N)> in the condition of the conditionals:

```
if (x != <p2(N)>) {              if (x != <p2(N)>) {
    if (x >= <p1(N)>) {              if (x > <p1(N)>) {
        z = z + 1;                       z = z + 1;
    };                               };
    <fixed buffer code>              <fixed buffer code>
};                               };
a = a + z;                       a = a + z;
<... above code is copied N times>   <... above code is copied N times>
return a;                        return a;
```

The pattern <p1(N)> can be shown equivalent to <p2(N)> in N standard rule applications. As N grows, these programs simulate increasingly complex equivalence tasks in both number of conditionals in the program and proof substeps. The associated PEG structure of the left program can be found in Fig. 15 in the Appendix B.

Experimental Results: Figure 11 shows the time elapsed for equivalence proving with each experimental setting, for values of N up to 120 (due to quadratic size of associated PEG).

The ranking of approach remains the same as for the previous task. Annotation-based contextual rewriting performs around 30% better than the non-contextual approach.

The naive traversal-based contextual approach performs worse than on the previous task. Some traversals will be performed despite the contextual pattern not being present in the e-graph prior to the rewriting of <p1(N)> to <p2(N)>.

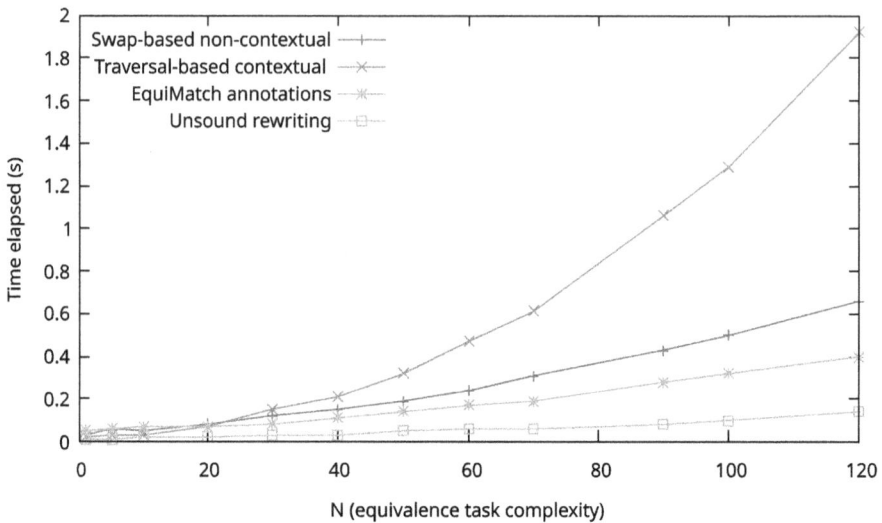

Fig. 11. Results for the complex equivalence task benchmark

As a conclusion, we observe that the swap-based approach is not practical when the size of e-graph grows and it is always outperformed by the annotation-based contextual rewriting we propose. The naive traversal-based rewriting is doing well only on the first benchmark and behaves badly on the others, which validates the pertinence of the incremental annotation we propose. Overall, in the three experiments the incremental annotation-based contextual rewriting has the best scalability properties.

6 Related Work

Equality saturation was initially introduced [22] as an optimization technique: the program to be optimized is turned into a PEG and a collection of rewriting rules is applied on the resulting e-graph to obtain an implicit representation of multiple optimized version of the original input. Heuristics pick the optimized candidate and decompile it from PEG to a real program. The approach was later used to perform translation of advanced compiler optimizations techniques for the LLVM compiler [20]. Premtoon et al. [18] later showed how to adapt the equality saturation technique to perform semantic search of programming pattern. Semantic search has many applications, including bugfinding and program simplification (for example by detecting opportunities to use calls to library functions). The open-source Rust project Egg [26] represents the state-of-the-art in equality saturation. Is has been used recently in several application areas [16, 23, 25, 27].

Relational Hoare logic [3] is an axiomatic approach to program comparison. It is a variant of Hoare logic that aims to reason about two programs at once. As it studies two programs rather than one, it needs to track and compare the states of two executions. It comes with an extensible proof system of inference rules. Building an automatic verifier with this approach requires to design a good proof system together with a strategy for applying them. Benton [4] has built such an automated semantic difference finder in order to compare the code produced by two compilers for the Hack programming language [11], a typed PHP variant. Both compilers generate HHVM bytecode[4]. The semantic core of the tool uses relational Hoare logic and performs a semantic comparison of the instructions at intraprocedural level for functions of the same name.

In [14], Lahiri et al. present SymDiff, a tool capable of checking equivalence and displaying semantic differences between imperative programs regardless of the programming language used. They rely on the Boogie intermediate verification language, which can be obtained via translations from multiple source languages such as C, C#, and x86. The tool works by first composing versions of the two programs to be compared, then building a *product program* [2,28], and generating verification conditions to be discharged by the Z3 SMT solver. Barthe et al. explores a similar approach [1] in the context of the CompCert verified compiler project [15] where they use a custom solver to increase control over the expected differences between the two program inputs. Another custom program equivalence verifier was also introduced by Rideau and Leroy [19] in order to validate register allocation algorithms in CompCert. Building a suitable product program is not an easy task. To make sure the companion program verifier succeeds, the product needs to be properly *aligned*. Churchill et al. [5] proposed advanced techniques to perform such a product.

Some work focuses on equivalence checking technique for translation validation of advanced loop transformations on affine programs [10,24]. The proof is performed by combining the dependence graphs of both input programs and infer an *equivalence tree* of the product by abstract interpretation. Such a tree explores the various possible alignments between loop bodies on each side.

7 Conclusion

In this paper we introduce *contextual* equality saturation, a novel extension to equality saturation that adds support for contextual rewriting rules. Contextual equality saturation makes it possible to propagate information obtained from the boolean test in conditional statements when proving the equivalence of programs. This extends the capability of equality saturation beyond existing non-contextual techniques. We present a new annotation system for e-graphs which can be incrementally updated after each standard e-graph updates. These annotations are an essential part in the design of algorithms for efficient equality saturation of contextual rules. We have implemented a prototype tool for evaluating the effectiveness of our contextual equality saturation algorithms, using a set of

---

[4] HHVM [13] is an open-source virtual machine designed for executing programs written in Hack.

benchmark programs which confirm the added precision and the scalability of the method.

One promising application of contextual equality saturation is as a general technique for the validation of code re-factoring and code migration. We intend to develop and evaluate a validator for the Java-to-Kotlin code migrator, as implemented in the IntelliJ tool, which transforms a Java program into its Kotlin equivalent. Both programs can be compiled into Java bytecode representations and be semantically compared with equality saturation. Our first experiments show that state-of-the-art equivalence checkers based on equality saturation cannot handle some common loops patterns while our approach makes this checking feasible. This is a strong indication that contextual equality saturation is an important step towards building a full-fledged validation tool.

Another avenue for further work is to investigate how information coming from other program analyses can be integrated into the e-graph framework, so as to help proving more program equivalences. The annotations that we have defined in this paper represent information that comes from boolean tests in the program. Other sources of data flow information can provide complementary information which would enable more rules to apply, and our annotations provides the infrastructure for integrating such data flow information.

Finally, in order to address the migration of larger code bases, it is also necessary to design a methodology for modularising the use of equality saturation, so that local equivalences can be extended to more global equivalences without having to build e-graphs for an entire procedure (which is likely to be prohibitive in terms of computational complexity). For this strand of research, the techniques presented by of Churchill *et al.* [5] on semantic program alignment seem especially pertinent.

A   Symbols Used in the Text

(See Fig. 12).

Function symbols for our terms	$\mathcal{F} \ni f \mid g \mid h \mid ...$
Constant symbols for our terms	$a \mid x \mid y \mid ...$
Variable placeholders for terms	$\mathcal{V} \ni X \mid Y \mid Z \mid ...$
Terms	$\mathcal{T} \ni t \mid t' \mid ...$
Patterns	$p \mid p' \mid ...$
Substitutions	$\mathcal{S} \ni \sigma \mid \sigma' \mid ...$
E-nodes	$\mathcal{N} \ni m \mid n \mid n' \mid ...$
Edges	$\mathcal{E} \ni e \mid e' \mid ...$
E-classes	$\mathcal{C} \ni C \mid C_1 \mid C_2 \mid ...$

Fig. 12. Notation used in this paper.

B Benchmarks PEG Structures

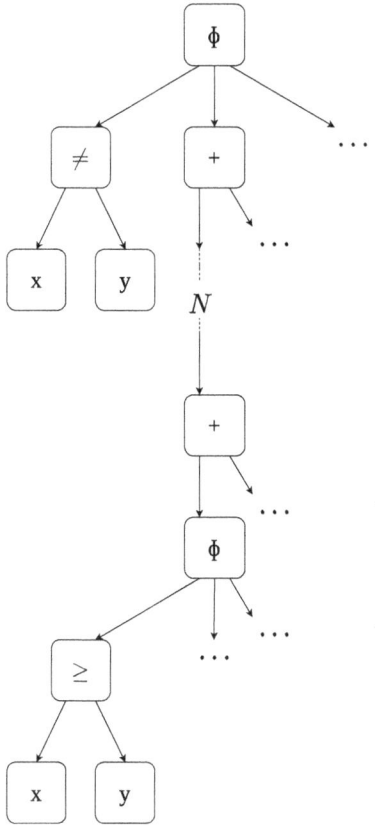

Fig. 13. PEG structure of the left programs of the source-pattern distance benchmark

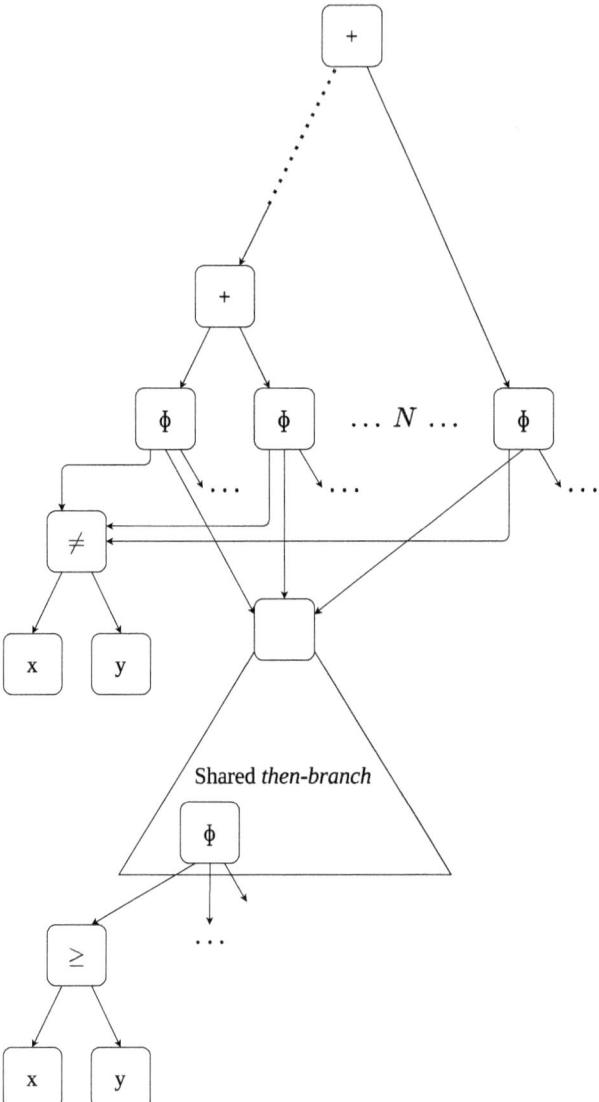

Fig. 14. PEG structure of the left programs of the number of sources benchmark

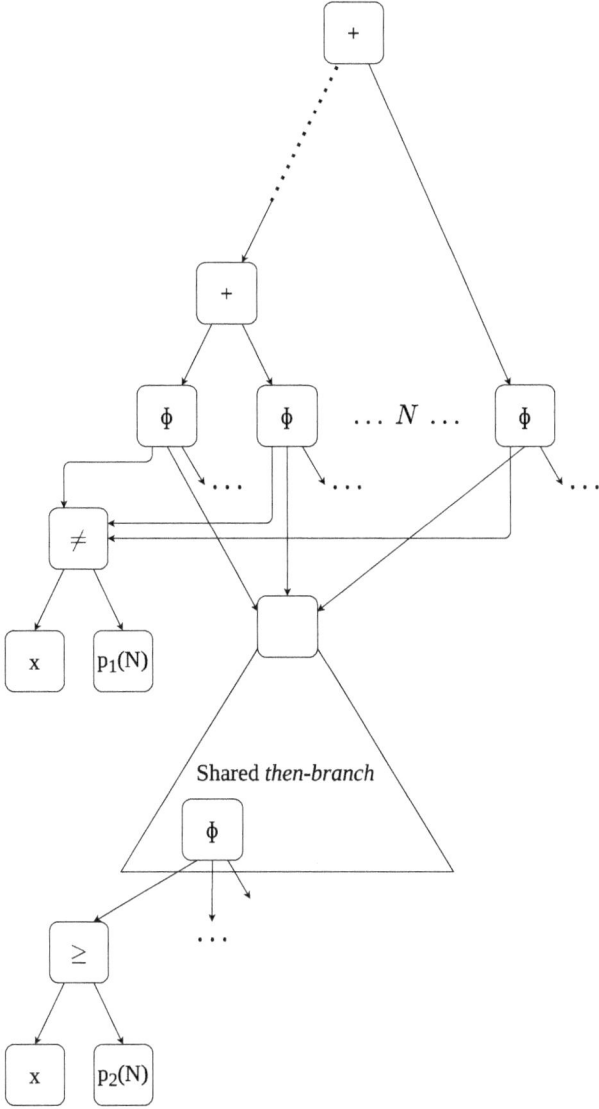

Fig. 15. PEG structure of the left programs of the complex equivalence task benchmark

References

1. Barthe, G., Blazy, S., Laporte, V., Pichardie, D., Trieu, A.: Verified translation validation of static analyses. In: Proceedings of the CSF'2017 IEEE 30th CSF. IEEE Computer Society (2017)
2. Barthe, G., Crespo, J.M., Kunz, C.: Product programs and relational program logics. J. Log. Algebraic Meth. Program. **85**(5) (2016)

3. Benton, N.: Simple relational correctness proofs for static analyses and program transformations. In: Proceedings of the POPL'2004. ACM (2004)
4. Benton, N.: Semantic equivalence checking for HHVM bytecode. In: Proceedings of the PPDP'2018. ACM (2018)
5. Churchill, B.R., Padon, O., Sharma, R., Aiken, A.: Semantic program alignment for equivalence checking. In: Proceedings of the PLDI'2019. ACM (2019)
6. De Moura, L.M., Bjørner, N.S.: Efficient e-matching for SMT solvers. In: Proceedings of the CADE'2021. LNCS, vol. 4603. Springer (2007)
7. Moura, L., Bjørner, N.: Z3: an efficient SMT solver. In: Ramakrishnan, C.R., Rehof, J. (eds.) TACAS 2008. LNCS, vol. 4963, pp. 337–340. Springer, Heidelberg (2008). https://doi.org/10.1007/978-3-540-78800-3_24
8. Detlefs, D., Nelson, G., Saxe, J.B.: Simplify: a theorem prover for program checking. J. ACM **52**(3) (2005)
9. Downey, P.J., Sethi, R., Tarjan, R.E.: Variations on the common subexpression problem. J. ACM **27**(4) (1980)
10. Dutta, S., Sarkar, D., Rawat, A., Singh, K.: Validation of loop parallelization and loop vectorization transformations. In: Proceedings of the ENASE'2016. SciTePress (2016)
11. Hack documentation. https://hacklang.org. Accessed 01 Apr 2024
12. Havlak, P.: Construction of thinned gated single-assignment form. In: Proceedings of the LCPC'1993. LNCS, vol. 768. Springer (1993)
13. HHVM documentation. https://hhvm.com. Accessed 01 Apr 2024
14. Lahiri, S.K., Hawblitzel, C., Kawaguchi, M., Rebêlo, H.: SymDiff: a language-agnostic semantic diff tool for imperative programs. In: Madhusudan, P., Seshia, S.A. (eds.) CAV 2012. LNCS, vol. 7358, pp. 712–717. Springer, Heidelberg (2012). https://doi.org/10.1007/978-3-642-31424-7_54
15. Leroy, X.: Formal verification of a realistic compiler. Commun. ACM **52**(7) (2009)
16. Nandi, C., et al.: Synthesizing structured CAD models with equality saturation and inverse transformations. In: Proceedings of the PLDI'2020, pp. 31–44. ACM (2020)
17. Paleczny, M., Vick, C.A., Click, C.: The Java hotspot server compiler. In: Proceedings of the Java Virtual Machine Research and Technology Symposium. USENIX (2001)
18. Premtoon, V., Koppel, J., Solar-Lezama, A.: Semantic code search via equational reasoning. In: Proceedings of the PLDI'2020. ACM (2020)
19. Rideau, S., Leroy, X.: Validating register allocation and spilling. In: Gupta, R. (ed.) CC 2010. LNCS, vol. 6011, pp. 224–243. Springer, Heidelberg (2010). https://doi.org/10.1007/978-3-642-11970-5_13
20. Stepp, M., Tate, R., Lerner, S.: Equality-based translation validator for LLVM. In: Gopalakrishnan, G., Qadeer, S. (eds.) CAV 2011. LNCS, vol. 6806, pp. 737–742. Springer, Heidelberg (2011). https://doi.org/10.1007/978-3-642-22110-1_59
21. Tarjan, R.E.: Efficiency of a good but not linear set union algorithm. J. ACM **22**(2) (1975)
22. Tate, R., Stepp, M., Tatlock, Z., Lerner, S.: Equality saturation: a new approach to optimization. Log. Methods Comput. Sci. **7**(1) (2011)
23. VanHattum, A., Nigam, R., Lee, V.T., Bornholt, J., Sampson, A.: Vectorization for digital signal processors via equality saturation. In: Proceedings of the ASPLOS'2021, pp. 874–886. ACM (2021)
24. Verdoolaege, S., Janssens, G., Bruynooghe, M.: Equivalence checking of static affine programs using widening to handle recurrences. ACM Trans. Program. Lang. Syst. **34**(3) (2012)

25. Wang, Y.R., Hutchison, S., Suciu, D., Howe, B., Leang, J.: SPORES: sum-product optimization via relational equality saturation for large scale linear algebra. Proc. VLDB Endow. **13**(11) (2020)
26. Willsey, M., Nandi, C., Wang, Y., Flatt, O., Tatlock, Z., Panchekha, P.: EGG: fast and extensible equality saturation. In: Proceedings of the POPL'2021. ACM (2021)
27. Yang, Y., Phothilimthana, P.M., Wang, Y.R., Willsey, M., Roy, S., Pienaar, J.: Equality saturation for tensor graph superoptimization. In: Proceedings of the MLSys 2021 (2021)
28. Zaks, A., Pnueli, A.: CoVaC: compiler validation by program analysis of the cross-product. In: Cuellar, J., Maibaum, T., Sere, K. (eds.) FM 2008. LNCS, vol. 5014, pp. 35–51. Springer, Heidelberg (2008). https://doi.org/10.1007/978-3-540-68237-0_5

A Programming Language for Feasible Solutions

Weijun Chen, Yuxi Fu(✉), and Huan Long

BASICS, Shanghai Jiao Tong University, Shanghai, China
{cwj2018,longhuan}@sjtu.edu.cn, fu-yx@cs.sjtu.edu.cn

Abstract. Runtime efficiency and termination are crucial properties in the studies of program verification. Instead of dealing with these issues in an ad hoc manner, it would be useful to develop a robust framework in which such properties are guaranteed by design. This paper introduces a new imperative programming language whose design is grounded in a static type system that ensures the following equivalence property: All definable programs are guaranteed to run in polynomial time; Conversely, all problems solvable in polynomial time can be solved by some programs of the language. The contribution of this work is twofold. On the theoretical side, the foundational equivalence property is established, and the proof of the equivalence theorem is non-trivial. On the practical side, a programming approach is proposed that can streamline program analysis and verification for feasible computations. An interpreter for the language has been implemented, demonstrating the feasibility of the approach in practice.

Keywords: Feasible Computation · Polynomial Time · Imperative Programming Language · Static Type System · Efficient Verification

1 Introduction

Program verification and analysis depend heavily on programming languages. From the early days of programming in assembly languages to recent experiments in applying deep learning techniques to verification and analysis [31], different programming languages have been proposed to address the increasingly demanding concerns from industry on software correctness and safety. A lot of tools and theoretical frameworks (Hoare logic, symbolic execution, theorem prover, to name a few) [1,2,5,28] that have been developed in the field are based on program logics and program semantics. The fundamental barrier to program verification and analysis is the undecidability. One of the basic program properties is the termination issue, which is well-known to be undecidable. Even if a program property is decidable, it is often computationally infeasible. Exponential blowup is more a rule than an exception.

Modern software systems are composed of many components with complex interconnections. Different parts of the system may well be designed at different times, in different locations, by different people using different programming languages. Most components of a software system do not require the full Turing computability. A good strategy to reduce the burden of verification is to impose strong constraints on the power of the programming language used to develop a particular component, thereby making some properties hold *a priori*. In many real-world cases, program executions should be feasible, meaning they can run within bounded resources, with running time being the most critical resource. If we can design a programming language that admits only feasible programs, the issue of program efficiency effectively disappears, placing us in a far better position to pursue program verification and analysis. To achieve this goal, we must first determine what constitutes *practical efficiency*, on which it is difficult for the industry to reach a clear consensus.

Meanwhile, modeling feasible computation is also a central theme in theoretical research [21]. The thesis promoted by Cobham [8] and Edmonds [14] is widely accepted among theoretical researchers: an algorithm is considered *theoretically feasible* if it can be computed within polynomial time. The complexity classes **P** (the class of the problems solvable in polynomial time) for decision problems and **FP** for functions were introduced to capture the theoretically feasible problems. Strictly speaking, theoretical feasibility cannot fully predict a program's practical performance, with the Coppersmith-Winograd algorithm [11] and the simplex algorithm [23] for linear programming serving as famous counterexamples. Nonetheless, the Cobham-Edmonds Thesis still provides a solid explanation for practical efficiency and has inspired extensive related research [9,10]. Based on this, designing a simple and elegant programming language that precisely characterizes the class **FP** is a crucial step toward implementing our strategy.

The original characterization of **FP** is in terms of polynomial-time Turing machines that involve low-level manipulations and incur undecidability issues. A different research avenue is to design light-weight models that characterize **FP** in a direct manner. The seminal work of Bellantoni and Cook [4] has laid down the foundation for this line of research and has inspired a wide range of subsequent developments [18,20,29]. This line of thinking has led to the implicit computational complexity (ICC) theory [12], whose goal is to characterize complexity classes without imposing explicit restrictions on resources. Various research, such as linear logic systems [15,25], bounded arithmetic [6,7,16,17], and the soft lambda calculus [3], also falls within this line of work.

With the strong connection to application contexts, programming languages are well-suited to bridge theoretical foundations and practical concerns. In this light, a program for **FP** represents both a continuation of ICC research and a further exploration of program verification. The challenge of designing such a language is twofold. Firstly, does it exist? Secondly, does such a language look natural? Studies in ICC [19,22,27] only partially affirm the first question. For the language to look natural, the loop statements are preferred over recursion. The problem now is that one has to settle for the loop statements without any bounds. Such programs may not terminate, which brings us back to square one.

To design a language that is both intuitive to use and formally guarantees polynomial-time complexity is inherently challenging. This creates a trade-off, and in this paper, we aim to strike a balance between soundness and naturalness. We propose a novel programming approach based on an imperative programming language called PolyC that captures precisely the problems in **FP**. The design of PolyC enables pre-verified efficient programming by embedding verification guarantees into the language. This contrasts to the practice in which implementation comes first and safety verification comes afterwords, often incurring significant overhead. In safety-critical scenarios such as aviation, PolyC, which guarantees termination and low time complexity, offers inherent advantages.

Several programming languages [19,22] and type systems [27] have been designed to characterize complexity classes. It has become a consensus that restrictions on the usage of variables in these languages are necessary. Despite sharing this common mechanism with the prior works, our design differs in some critical dimensions.

1. Our priority is to design a practical programming language for **FP**, rather than proposing yet another model. In PolyC, termination and polynomial-time execution are guaranteed for all well-typed programs. Previous models [19,27] may admit non-terminating programs, necessitating termination verification techniques [24,26] to ensure polynomial-time termination.
2. Most previous works rely on flow analysis [33] to ensure non-interference that prohibits information flow across types. In contrast, PolyC restricts the use of variables in different program blocks.
3. We provide a deterministic static type-checker accompanied by an interpreter to validate practical feasibility. The implementation issue of the type system is rarely discussed in the literature.

Contribution. The goal of this paper is to lay down the foundation for the proposed approach. We shall confine our attention to PolyC, focusing on the formal semantics of the language and the equivalence property we have explained in the above. The main contributions of the paper are summarized as follows:

1. We present a formal description of CorePolyC, an imperative programming language with simple syntax, operational semantics, and a type system. We demonstrate that well-typed CorePolyC programs always terminate. Additionally, we show that the set **FPC** of the CorePolyC computable functions is precisely **FP** (Theorem 2).
2. We extend CorePolyC to a more user-friendly programming language, PolyC, and demonstrate that they are equally expressive (Theorem 5). We have developed an interpreter for PolyC, allowing users to write and run PolyC programs for problem-solving. The details are available online.
3. We have pointed out that the verification problem for PolyC programs is relatively easy (Proposition 4), and our type system can be further extended as a tool for time-complexity analysis of other programming languages.

```
Types      t ::= iint | int | bool
Operator   op ::= + | - | / | % | size |
                  >= | <= | > | < | == | != | ! | && | ||
Expressions e ::= x | c | op(ẽ) | (e)
Statements  s ::= t x; | x=e; | { s̃ } | if(e) s₁ else s₂ | for(x<size(e)) s
Programs    p ::= int main(int x₁,...,int xₘ){ s̃ return e; }
```

Fig. 1. The syntax of CorePolyC.

Organization. Section 2 defines CorePolyC. Some key properties of PolyC are stated. Section 3 proves that CorePolyC characterizes **FP**. Formal proofs are presented in the full version. Section 4 formally introduces PolyC and establishes its equivalence to CorePolyC in terms of expressive power. Section 5 concludes.

2 CorePolyC

CorePolyC is a strongly typed programming language. A CorePolyC program outputs an integer upon termination. The semantics and the type system guarantee that all well-typed CorePolyC programs terminate.

2.1 Syntax

The syntax of CorePolyC is defined in Fig. 1. CorePolyC is a strongly typed language requiring explicit type annotations. There are three *fundamental data types*: iint (for iterable int), int and bool. The difference between an iint variable and an int variable is that the former must abide by specific rules given in Sect. 2.3. Notably, in CorePolyC, integers (both iint and int) are unbounded, which aligns with standard models of computation used in complexity theory. Let $\mathsf{Int} := \{\mathtt{int}, \mathtt{iint}\}$ and $\mathsf{Bool} := \{\mathtt{bool}\}$. We write t for an element of $\mathsf{T} := \mathsf{Int} \cup \mathsf{Bool}$. The set of variables is denoted by L, and we typically use $x, y, z, \ldots$ to range over L. A variable is *iterable* if it is declared as iint.

Let $\mathsf{D} := \{0, \ldots, 9\}$ and $\mathsf{C} := \mathsf{D}^+ \cup \{\mathtt{true}, \mathtt{false}\}$ represent all the literals. The set of all operators in CorePolyC is denoted by O. It is important to note that the multiplication $*$ is not present in our language, even though it is a fundamental operator in almost all programming languages. An intuitive explanation of this design will be provided at the end of this section. All operators and their precedence and associativity are standard except for size, which is defined as the bit-size of $\mathrm{abs}(x)$, i.e., $\mathrm{size}(x) = |x| = \lceil \log(\mathrm{abs}(x) + 1) \rceil$.

Expressions are constructed from variables $x \in \mathsf{L}$, constants $c \in \mathsf{C}$, and operators $\mathrm{op} \in \mathsf{O}$. We abbreviate a sequence of expressions $e_1, \ldots, e_m$ to $\tilde{e}$, where the meta notation m ranges over the set $\mathbb{N}$ of natural numbers. An expression is *iterable* if it contains only iterable variables; it is *non-iterable* otherwise.

Remark 1. In the syntax, all expressions are generated in prefix form. However, for readability, the examples presented later will typically use *infix notation* for binary operators. For instance, we write 1==1 instead of ==(1,1).

The statements are standard except for the loop statement. The notation $\widetilde{s}$ is for a sequence of statements. A loop statement includes a *loop counter* and an explicit *loop bound* on the number of iterations, which must be a size expression. A simple example is for(i<size(x)){y=y+1;}, where the loop counter is i and the loop bound is size(x). Note that the counter i should be a new variable implicitly declared here. When executing the loop statement, the counter i is automatically assigned the initial value 0, and at the same time, the loop bound is evaluated. The value of i will be increased by 1 upon the completion of an execution. Furthermore, a loop statement must meet two restrictions.

1. It is not allowed to declare any iterable variables within any loop body.
2. No assignment to any iterable variables may occur within the loop body.

The semantics and constraints mentioned above will be ensured, respectively, by the semantic rules and typing rules in the following sections.

We call a string generated by the non-terminal program a *well-formed program*, denoted by p. Note that *all* parameters are of type int. Since boolean values can be encoded within integers, for simplicity, we do not introduce bool parameters for CorePolyC. The number of its inputs is denoted by ary(p). The set of the variables appearing in p is denoted by L(p). The set of all well-formed programs is denoted by P. Similarly the set of all well-formed expressions e (resp. statements s) is denoted by E (resp. S). Unless otherwise stated, the syntactic entities in the following text are all well-formed.

Remark 2. We now provide some intuitions behind the design of CorePolyC.

1. **Loop bound.** In CorePolyC, we completely prohibit unbounded loop statements, such as while(true){...}, which run the risk of non-termination. Such a trade-off is acceptable, since the bounded loops together with the size operation mirror widespread programming practices: loops with explicit iteration ranges (e.g., for(auto i: vec){...} and for i in range(n){...}) dominate array/matrix algorithms and dynamic programming. They also fit well within some programming practices, where explicit resource parameterization, such as specifying security parameters, is standard.
2. **The size operator.** The loop bound must be a size expression. Without this constraint, we would be able to write a loop statement for(i<x){...}. The loop body can be executed $\Theta(2^{|x|})$ times (exponential in the bit-size of x), which defeats the polynomial time computability restriction we set out.
3. **Absence of multiplication.** If the multiplication operator * is admitted in CorePolyC, one can design the following code snippet.

```
1   x=2;
2   for(i<size(z))  x=x*x;
```

It effectively implements the function $z \mapsto 2^{2^{|z|}}$, which takes exponential time to output this number. Therefore, the multiplication operator must be prohibited in our language. As a comparison, Example 1 provides a valid implementation of multiplication in CorePolyC. A more general discussion of operations will be presented in Sect. 4.1.

4. **Iterable variables and expressions.** If we do not impose these distinctions between the iterable and the non-iterable variables, the following code would be legitimate.

```
1    for(i<size(z)){
2        y=x;
3        for(i<size(y)) x=x+x;
4    }
```

The program calculates the function $(x, z) \mapsto 2^{|x|(2^{|z|}-1)}x$ whose size grows exponentially. In this work, we employ a specialized type system (iterable types) to avoid this problematic scenario.

2.2 Semantics

Let $\mathcal{A}$ denote the set of ASCII characters and $\mathcal{A}^*$ the set of all finite-length strings over $\mathcal{A}$. Let $\mathbb{Z}$ be the set of integers $i, j, k, \ldots$, $\mathbb{N}$ the set of natural numbers $m, n, \cdots$, and $\mathbb{B} = \{\text{\#t}, \text{\#f}\}$ the set of boolean values b. We denote by $\mathbb{V} := \mathbb{Z} \cup \mathbb{B}$ the set of all possible values v that variables can be assigned during execution. A tuple of values $(v_1, \ldots, v_m)$ is abbreviated to $\tilde{v}$ with its size $|\tilde{v}| := \sum_{i=1}^{m} |v_i|$. Accordingly, the input variables of program p are often abbreviated to $\tilde{x}$.

The *auxiliary interpretation operator* $[\![\cdot]\!]_m$ is defined partially on $\mathcal{A}^*$. Given an operator op and its arity ary(op), we can interpret it as an ary(op)-ary total function $[\![\text{op}]\!]_{\text{ary(op)}}$. For all operators given in Fig. 1, the interpretation is straightforward. Recall that $[\![-]\!]_1$ is defined as negation function, and $[\![-]\!]_2$ is the subtraction function. For maintaining the totality of functions, $[\![/]\!]_2$ and $[\![\%]\!]_2$ are defined to return 0 when the divisor is 0. Conventional language implementations typically handle such situations by throwing a runtime error. A constant can be treated as a 0-ary operator as follows.

$$[\![\text{true}]\!]_0 = \text{\#t}, \quad [\![\text{false}]\!]_0 = \text{\#f}, \tag{1}$$

$$[\![0]\!]_0 = 0, \ldots, [\![9]\!]_0 = 9, \quad [\![w\alpha]\!]_0 = 10[\![w]\!]_0 + [\![\alpha]\!]_0 \text{ for } w \in \mathsf{D}^+ \text{ and } \alpha \in \mathsf{D}. \tag{2}$$

When applied to an element #t of $\mathsf{T} \subseteq \mathcal{A}^*$, the function $[\![\cdot]\!]_0$ is defined as:

$$[\![t]\!]_0 = \begin{cases} 0, & \text{if } t \in \mathsf{Int}, \\ \text{\#f}, & \text{if } t \in \mathsf{Bool}, \end{cases} \tag{3}$$

which gives the initial values for variables of these types. From now on, we will omit the subscript of $[\![\cdot]\!]_m$ whenever there is no ambiguity.

A *store environment* Σ is essentially a mapping from L to $\mathbb{V}$ with a finite domain $\text{dom}(\Sigma)$. It is a snapshot of the variable values at a certain moment during program execution. An environment Σ can be spelt out as $[x_1 \mapsto v_1][x_2 \mapsto v_2]\cdots[x_m \mapsto v_m]$ where $\text{dom}(\Sigma) = \{x_1,\ldots,x_m\}$. The empty store environment is denoted by $\emptyset$, and $\Sigma[x \mapsto v]$ is an *update* of Σ defined as follows:

$$\emptyset(x) = \uparrow, \quad \Sigma[x \mapsto v](y) = \begin{cases} \Sigma(y), & \text{if } y \not\equiv x, \\ v, & \text{if } y \equiv x, \end{cases} \tag{4}$$

where $\uparrow$ indicates undefinedness and $\equiv$ is the syntactic equality. For m-tuples $\widetilde{x}$ and $\widetilde{v}$, the update $\Sigma[x_1 \mapsto v_1]\cdots[x_m \mapsto v_m]$ is abbreviated to $\Sigma[\widetilde{x} \mapsto \widetilde{v}]$.

$$\frac{x \in \text{dom}(\Sigma)}{\langle \Sigma, x \rangle \Downarrow \Sigma(x)}[\Sigma\text{-Var}] \qquad \frac{c \in \mathsf{C}}{\langle \Sigma, c \rangle \Downarrow [\![c]\!]}[\Sigma\text{-Const}] \qquad \frac{\langle \Sigma, e \rangle \Downarrow v}{\langle \Sigma, (e) \rangle \Downarrow v}[\Sigma\text{-Paren}]$$

$$\frac{\langle \Sigma, \widetilde{e} \rangle \Downarrow \widetilde{v} \quad \text{op} \in \mathsf{O}}{\langle \Sigma, \text{op}(\widetilde{e}) \rangle \Downarrow [\![\text{op}]\!](\widetilde{v})}[\Sigma\text{-Op}] \qquad \frac{}{\langle \Sigma, \mathsf{t}\ x; \rangle \Downarrow \Sigma[x \mapsto [\![\mathsf{t}]\!]]}[\Sigma\text{-Decl}]$$

$$\frac{\langle \Sigma, \widetilde{\mathsf{s}} \rangle \Downarrow \Sigma'}{\langle \Sigma, \{\ \widetilde{\mathsf{s}}\ \} \rangle \Downarrow \Sigma'}[\Sigma\text{-Block}] \qquad \frac{x \in \text{dom}(\Sigma) \quad \langle \Sigma, e \rangle \Downarrow v}{\langle \Sigma, x\mathtt{=}e; \rangle \Downarrow \Sigma[x \mapsto v]}[\Sigma\text{-Asgmt}]$$

$$\frac{\Sigma_0 := \Sigma \quad \langle \Sigma_{i-1}, \mathsf{s}_i \rangle \Downarrow \Sigma_i, \quad \text{for } 1 \leq i \leq m.}{\langle \Sigma, \widetilde{\mathsf{s}} \rangle \Downarrow \Sigma_m}[\Sigma\text{-Seq}]$$

$$\frac{\langle \Sigma, e \rangle \Downarrow b \quad \Sigma' := \begin{cases} \Sigma_1, & \text{if } b \wedge \langle \Sigma, \mathsf{s}_1 \rangle \Downarrow \Sigma_1, \\ \Sigma_2, & \text{if } \neg b \wedge \langle \Sigma, \mathsf{s}_2 \rangle \Downarrow \Sigma_2. \end{cases}}{\langle \Sigma, \mathtt{if(e)\ s}_1\ \mathtt{else\ s}_2 \rangle \Downarrow \Sigma'}[\Sigma\text{-Cond}]$$

$$\frac{\langle \Sigma, e \rangle \Downarrow i \quad \Sigma_0 := \Sigma \quad \langle \Sigma_j[x \mapsto j], \mathsf{s} \rangle \Downarrow \Sigma_{j+1}, \text{ for } 0 \leq j < i.}{\langle \Sigma, \mathtt{for(}x\mathtt{<}e\mathtt{)\ s} \rangle \Downarrow \Sigma_i}[\Sigma\text{-Loop}]$$

$$\frac{\langle \Sigma, \widetilde{\mathsf{s}} \rangle \Downarrow \Sigma' \quad \langle \Sigma', e \rangle \Downarrow i}{\langle \Sigma, \mathtt{int\ main(}\widetilde{\mathsf{t}\ x}\mathtt{)\{\ \widetilde{s}\ return\ }e\mathtt{;\}} \rangle \Downarrow i}[\Sigma\text{-Prog}]$$

Fig. 2. Semantics of CorePolyC.

Once we know the current store environment, we can evaluate an expression to a value. The *semantics* of CorePolyC is defined by the structural operational rules in Fig. 2. The judgments $\langle \Sigma, e \rangle \Downarrow v$ specifies that the evaluation of e terminates with value v under the store environment Σ. The judgement $\langle \Sigma, \widetilde{e} \rangle \Downarrow \widetilde{v}$ is an abbreviation for $\langle \Sigma, e_i \rangle \Downarrow v_i$ for $1 \leq i \leq m$, assuming that the length m of the tuple is known. Similarly, the judgment $\langle \Sigma, \mathsf{s} \rangle \Downarrow \Sigma'$ states that under the store environment Σ, the execution of s terminates with the effect that updates Σ to Σ'. The judgement $\langle \Sigma, \mathsf{p} \rangle \Downarrow v$ indicates that the execution of program p terminates with output v under Σ.

For $w \in \mathsf{E} \cup \mathsf{S} \cup \mathsf{P}$, if $\langle \Sigma, w \rangle \Downarrow \cdot$, let the derivation tree of rule instances that lead to this conclusion be denoted by $\mathscr{E}_{\Sigma, w}$. It is well-defined and unique since the semantics rules are all deterministic.

2.3 Termination-Guarantee Typing System

In this part, we present the typing rules of CorePolyC, which enforce the special restrictions on iterable variables. It is expected that the execution of every well-typed CorePolyC program terminates and produces the correct output.

Typing Rules. A *typing environment* $\Gamma : \mathsf{L} \to \mathsf{T}$ is a partial map from variable names to types such that the domain $\mathrm{dom}(\Gamma)$ is finite. The operations of Γ are defined similarly as those of Σ. The empty typing environment is also denoted by $\emptyset$. The equivalence relation $\sim_\mathsf{T}$ is induced by the partition of T by $\mathsf{Int}, \mathsf{Bool}$. In other words, $\mathsf{t}_1 \sim_\mathsf{T} \mathsf{t}_2$ if $\mathsf{t}_1, \mathsf{t}_2 \in \mathsf{Int}$ or $\mathsf{t}_1, \mathsf{t}_2 \in \mathsf{Bool}$.

Let $(\mathsf{Int}, \preccurlyeq)$ be a total order relation determined by $\mathtt{iint} \preccurlyeq \mathtt{int}$. For m-tuple $\tilde{\mathsf{t}} \in \mathsf{Int}^m$, we write $\bigvee_{i=1}^{m} \mathsf{t}_i$ for the supremum under the order relation $\preccurlyeq$. By definition, $\bigvee_{i=1}^{m} \mathsf{t}_i \equiv \mathtt{iint}$ if and only if $\mathsf{t}_i \equiv \mathtt{iint}$ for $1 \le i \le m$. The type of an expression is the supremum of the types of the variables in the expression.

The *auxiliary typing operator* $\{\!|\cdot|\!\}_m$ is defined partially on $\mathcal{A}^*$. For $\mathsf{c} \in \mathsf{C}$, $\{\!|\mathsf{c}|\!\}_0 \in \mathsf{T}$ is defined as the type of c. Thus,

$$\{\!|\mathtt{true}|\!\}_0 = \{\!|\mathtt{false}|\!\}_0 = \mathtt{bool}, \qquad \{\!|\mathsf{c}|\!\}_0 = \mathtt{iint}, \quad \text{for } \mathsf{c} \in \mathsf{D}^+. \tag{5}$$

For an m-ary operator $\mathtt{op} \in \mathsf{O}$, $\{\!|\mathtt{op}|\!\}_m$ is a partial map from T^m to T:

- $\{\!|\mathtt{op}|\!\}_m(\mathtt{bool}^m) = \mathtt{bool}$ if $\mathtt{op} \in \{\mathtt{\&\&}, \mathtt{||}, \mathtt{!}\}$;
- $\{\!|\mathtt{op}|\!\}_m(\tilde{\mathsf{t}}) = \mathtt{bool}$ if $\mathtt{op} \in \{\mathtt{>=}, \mathtt{<=}, \mathtt{>}, \mathtt{<}, \mathtt{==}, \mathtt{!=}\}$ and $\tilde{\mathsf{t}} \in \mathsf{Int}^m$;
- $\{\!|\mathtt{op}|\!\}_m(\tilde{\mathsf{t}}) = \bigvee_{i=1}^{m} \mathsf{t}_i$ if $\mathtt{op} \in \{\mathtt{+}, \mathtt{-}, \mathtt{*}, \mathtt{/}, \mathtt{\%}\}$ and $\tilde{\mathsf{t}} \in \mathsf{Int}^m$;
- $\{\!|\mathtt{op}|\!\}_1(\mathtt{iint}) = \mathtt{iint}$ if $\mathtt{op} \equiv \mathtt{size}$.

The subscript m in $\{\!|\cdot|\!\}_m$ is often omitted.

A *loop indicator* ℓ is a boolean variable indicating whether the current statement is inside any loop body. The predicate Asg is defined on $\mathbb{B} \times \mathsf{T}$ by $\mathsf{Asg}(\ell, \mathsf{t}) = \neg(\ell \wedge \mathsf{t} \equiv \mathtt{iint})$, meaning that an assignment can be performed whenever it is not inside a loop or the variable being assigned is not of iterable type.

The typing judgment of the form $\Gamma, \ell \vdash \mathsf{e} : \mathsf{t}$ states that under the typing environment Γ and the loop indicator ℓ, the expression e has type t. Similarly, we use typing judgments of the form $\Gamma, \ell \vdash \mathsf{s} : \Gamma'$ and $\Gamma, \ell \vdash \mathsf{p} : \mathsf{t}$ for statements and programs, respectively. Figure 3 gives the typing rules for CorePolyC.

We can now formally state that an expression e is iterable under the typing environment Γ if $\Gamma, \mathtt{\#f} \vdash \mathsf{e} : \mathtt{iint}$ holds. The definition of $\{\!|\cdot|\!\}$, together with the rule Γ–Op ensure that the operand of the $\mathtt{size}$ operation must be iterable. Note that among these rules, the only place where ℓ is modified is in the premise of Γ–Loop. Setting ℓ to $\mathtt{\#t}$ indicates that type checking is performed within a loop body. On the other hand, ℓ is used in rules Γ–Decl and Γ–Asgmt, which formalizes the restrictions on the iterable variables by Asg (See Example 2 and Example 3 for an intuitive explanation). Proposition 1 in the next section provides a formal statement of these observations.

We end this part with some examples to explain our type system.

$$\frac{x \in \operatorname{dom}(\Gamma)}{\Gamma, \ell \vdash x : \Gamma(x)}[\Gamma\text{-Var}] \qquad \frac{c \in C}{\Gamma, \ell \vdash c : \{|c|\}}[\Gamma\text{-Const}] \qquad \frac{\Gamma, \ell \vdash e : t}{\Gamma, \ell \vdash (e) : t}[\Gamma\text{-Paren}]$$

$$\frac{\Gamma, \ell \vdash \widetilde{e} : \widetilde{t} \quad \widetilde{t} \in \operatorname{dom}(\{|op|\}) \quad op \in O}{\Gamma, \ell \vdash op(\widetilde{e}) : \{|op|\}(\widetilde{t})}[\Gamma\text{-Op}] \qquad \frac{\operatorname{Asg}(\ell, t) \quad x \notin \operatorname{dom}(\Gamma)}{\Gamma, \ell \vdash t\, x; \; : \Gamma[x \mapsto t]}[\Gamma\text{-Decl}]$$

$$\frac{\Gamma, \ell \vdash \widetilde{s} : \Gamma'}{\Gamma, \ell \vdash \{\,\widetilde{s}\,\} : \Gamma}[\Gamma\text{-Block}] \qquad \frac{\operatorname{Asg}(\ell, \Gamma(x)) \quad \Gamma, \ell \vdash e : t \quad \Gamma(x) \sim_T t}{\Gamma, \ell \vdash x{=}e; \; : \Gamma}[\Gamma\text{-Asgmt}]$$

$$\frac{\Gamma_0 := \Gamma \quad \Gamma_{i-1}, \ell \vdash s_i : \Gamma_i, \quad \text{for } 1 \le i \le m.}{\Gamma, \ell \vdash \widetilde{s} : \Gamma_m}[\Gamma\text{-Seq}]$$

$$\frac{\Gamma, \ell \vdash e : \mathsf{bool} \quad \Gamma, \ell \vdash s_1 : \Gamma_1 \quad \Gamma, \ell \vdash s_2 : \Gamma_2}{\Gamma, \ell \vdash \mathtt{if(e)}\; s_1\; \mathtt{else}\; s_2 : \Gamma}[\Gamma\text{-Cond}]$$

$$\frac{\Gamma, \ell \vdash e : \mathsf{iint} \quad x \notin \operatorname{dom}(\Gamma) \quad \Gamma[x \mapsto t], \#\mathsf{t} \vdash s : \Gamma'}{\Gamma, \ell \vdash \mathtt{for}(x{<}e)\; s : \Gamma}[\Gamma\text{-Loop}]$$

$$\frac{\Gamma[\widetilde{x} \mapsto \widetilde{t}\,], \ell \vdash \widetilde{s} : \Gamma' \quad \Gamma', \ell \vdash e : t' \in \mathsf{Int}}{\Gamma, \ell \vdash \mathtt{int\ main}(\widetilde{t\,x})\{\;\widetilde{s}\; \mathtt{return}\; e;\}: \mathtt{int}}[\Gamma\text{-Prog}]$$

Fig. 3. The typing rules of CorePolyC.

Example 1 (Fast multiplication). Figure 4 gives two programs in the style of CorePolyC that intend to implement the fast multiplication of two positive integer variables x, y. Both programs are well-formed but only the right one is well-typed. The left program violates the rules Γ–Loop and Γ–Asgmt, because the non-iterable variable y appears as the parameter of size operation, and the iterable variable o is modified in the loop body.

```
1   int main(int x,int y){
2       iint o;
3       for(i<size(y)){
4           if(y%2!=0){
5               o=o+x;
6           } else {}
7           x=x+x;
8           y=y/2;
9       }
10      return o;
11  }
```

```
1   int main(int x,int y){
2       int o; iint z; z=y;
3       for(i<size(z)){
4           if(y%2!=0){
5               o=o+x;
6           } else {}
7           x=x+x;
8           y=y/2;
9       }
10      return o;
11  }
```

Fig. 4. Two CorePolyC implementations of fast multiplication. The left one violates the rules Γ–Loop and Γ–Asgmt, while the right one is well-typed.

Note that the program on the right declares an iterable variable z. Therefore, this part of the code cannot be placed inside a loop to achieve the effect of `for(i<size(z)) x=x*x;`, which, as we have explained earlier, should be prohibited. This is also equivalent to defining a function `mul(x, y)` and attempting

to invoke it within a loop. In Sect. 4.1, we will discuss how to introduce function calls in PolyC to prevent such constructions.

Example 2 (Typing derivation). Considering the statement $s_1 \equiv $ x=x+x; and $\Gamma_1 = [x \mapsto \text{int}]$, we may derive that $\Gamma_1, \#t \vdash s_1 : \Gamma_1$. The corresponding typing derivation is shown as follows:

$$\text{Asg}(\#t, \text{int}) \quad \frac{\dfrac{x \in \text{dom}(\Gamma_1)}{\Gamma_1, \#t \vdash x : \text{int}} \quad (\text{int}, \text{int}) \in \text{dom}(\{|+|\})}{\dfrac{\Gamma_1, \#t \vdash \text{x+x} : \{|+|\}(\text{int}, \text{int}) = \text{int}}{\Gamma_1, \#t \vdash s_1 : \Gamma_1}} \quad \text{int} \sim_T \text{int}$$

where $\{|+|\}(t_1, t_2) = t_1 \vee t_2$. The above results indicate that if the variable x is of type int, then assignment statements like s_1 can appear within a loop body. However, if we let $\Gamma_1' = [x \mapsto \text{iint}]$, the similar type inference cannot be completed because the predicate $\text{Asg}(\#t, \Gamma_1'(x))$ evaluates to false. This implies that if the variable x is of type iint, then assignments to it cannot occur within any loop body. The situation with declaration statements is similar.

Furthermore, both $\Gamma_1, \#f \vdash s_1 : \Gamma_1$ and $\Gamma_1', \#f \vdash s_1 : \Gamma_1'$ hold because $\ell = \#f$ indicates that the current check is carried out in the scenario where s_1 is not within any loop. In this case, there are no restrictions on assignment or declaration statements. This example elucidates how ℓ and Asg ensure that the program complies with the requirements during type checking.

Example 3 (Loop). Let $s_2 := $ for(i<size(z)) s_1; and $\Gamma_2 = \Gamma_1[z \mapsto \text{iint}]$, with Γ_1 and s_1 defined in Example 2. Now, we have $\Gamma_2, \#f \vdash s_2 : \Gamma_2$ as follows:

$$\dfrac{\dfrac{z \in \text{dom}(\Gamma_2)}{\Gamma_2, \#f \vdash z : \text{iint}} \quad \text{iint} \in \text{dom}(\{|\text{size}|\})}{\Gamma_2, \#f \vdash \text{size(z)} : \text{iint}} \quad i \notin \text{dom}(\Gamma_2) \quad \dfrac{\ldots}{\Gamma_2', \#t \vdash s_1 : \Gamma_2'}$$
$$\Gamma_2, \#f \vdash s_2 : \Gamma_2$$

where $\Gamma_2' = \Gamma_2[i \mapsto \text{iint}]$. Since $\Gamma_2'(x) = \Gamma_1(x)$, we can obtain $\Gamma_2', \#t \vdash s_1 : \Gamma_2'$ similar to Example 2. Therefore, we have omitted the corresponding part here.

Termination-Guarantee of Well-Typed Programs. The *well-typedness* of syntactical entities with regards to the type system is defined as follows.

1. An expression e is *well-typed* if $\Gamma, \ell \vdash e : t$ for some Γ, ℓ and t.
2. A statement s is *well-typed* if $\Gamma, \ell \vdash s : \Gamma'$ for some Γ, ℓ and Γ'.
3. A program p is *well-typed* if there exists a type t such that $\emptyset, \#f \vdash p : t$.

It follows from the structural definition that if p is well-typed, all syntactically well-formed components within p are also well-typed.

Now, we establish the connection between types and semantics. We say that value v is *consistent* with type t if $(v, t) \in \mathbb{Z} \times \text{Int} \cup \mathbb{B} \times \text{Bool}$. A store environment Σ and a typing environment Γ are consistent if $\text{dom}(\Gamma) \subseteq \text{dom}(\Sigma)$, and for any

$x \in \text{dom}(\Gamma)$, $\Sigma(x)$ and $\Gamma(x)$ are consistent. We also say that these two environments (Γ, Σ) form a consistent pair. Lemma 1 formalizes that, in CorePolyC, all constants and operators have consistent types and semantics.

Lemma 1. *The following statements are valid.*

1. *For each* $c \in C$, $[\![c]\!]$ *and* $\{\!|c|\!\}$ *are consistent.*
2. *For each* $t \in T$, $[\![t]\!]$ *and* t *are consistent.*
3. *For* $op \in O$, $\tilde{v} \in \text{dom}([\![op]\!])$ *and* $\tilde{t} \in \text{dom}(\{\!|op|\!\})$, *if* $\tilde{v}$ *are consistent with* $\tilde{t}$, *then* $[\![op]\!](\tilde{v})$ *are consistent with* $\{\!|op|\!\}(\tilde{t})$.

Let $(\text{dom}(\Gamma_1) \subseteq \text{dom}(\Gamma_2)) \wedge (\forall x \in \text{dom}(\Gamma_1).\Gamma_1(x) = \Gamma_2(x))$ be abbreviated to $\Gamma_1 \subseteq \Gamma_2$. That is, all variables in Γ_1 are also contained in Γ_2 with the same types. It can be proved that the consistency described above is preserved throughout the type-checking and evaluation processes of expressions and statements.

Lemma 2. *Suppose* (Γ, Σ) *is a consistent pair and* ℓ *is a loop indicator.*

1. *For each expression* e, *if* $\Gamma, \ell \vdash e : t$ *for some* t, *there exists a unique value* $v \in V$ *such that* $\langle \Sigma, e \rangle \Downarrow v$ *and* v *is consistent with* t.
2. *For each statement* s, *if* $\Gamma, \ell \vdash s : \Gamma'$ *for some* Γ', *then* $\Gamma \subseteq \Gamma'$ *and there exists a unique store* Σ' *consistent with* Γ' *such that* $\langle \Sigma, s \rangle \Downarrow \Sigma'$.

Recall that all programs have only integer inputs. We now present the main theorem of this section, which states that, given a set of inputs, any CorePolyC program will terminate and produce a unique integer output.

Theorem 1 (Type Safety). *Given a program* p *whose input is an m-tuple* $\tilde{x}$, *for any* $\tilde{v} \in \mathbb{Z}^m$, *there exists a unique integer* i *such that* $\langle \emptyset[\tilde{x} \mapsto \tilde{v}], p \rangle \Downarrow i$.

Given two consistent store and typing environments Σ and Γ, let $\text{dom}_I(\Gamma)$ denote the set $\{x \in \text{dom}(\Gamma) : \Gamma(x) \equiv \text{iint}\}$. The *iterable restriction* of Σ on Γ is defined as $(\Sigma)_{\restriction \Gamma} := \Sigma \restriction \text{dom}_I(\Gamma)$. Two store environments Σ_1 and Σ_2 are equivalent, denoted as $\Sigma_1 \sim \Sigma_2$, if $\text{dom}(\Sigma_1) = \text{dom}(\Sigma_2)$, and $\Sigma_1(x) = \Sigma_2(x)$ for every $x \in \text{dom}(\Sigma_1)$. The behaviors of the iterable variables are made predictable by the strong constraints imposed on their usage. Proposition 1 shows that our type system ensures that the iterable variables are well-behaved.

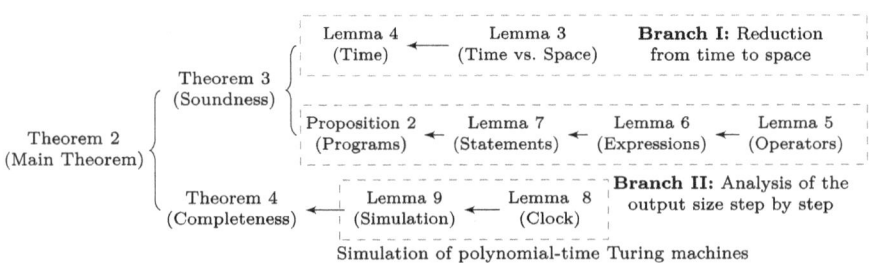

Fig. 5. The dependency graph for the proof of Theorem 2.

Proposition 1 (Loop Invariant). *Given a statement s and a consistent pair (Σ, Γ), if there exists Γ' such that $\Gamma, \#\mathsf{t} \vdash \mathsf{s} : \Gamma'$, then*

1. $\mathrm{dom}_\mathrm{I}(\Gamma') = \mathrm{dom}_\mathrm{I}(\Gamma)$, *and*
2. *there exists Σ' such that $\langle \Sigma, \mathsf{s} \rangle \Downarrow \Sigma'$ and $(\Sigma')_{\upharpoonright \Gamma'} \sim (\Sigma')_{\upharpoonright \Gamma} \sim (\Sigma)_{\upharpoonright \Gamma}$.*

These two conclusions above correspond respectively to i) no new iterable variables are declared, and ii) no existing iterable variables have their values changed.

3 Core PolyC Is a Model of FP

This section substantiates our claim that CorePolyC captures precisely the polynomial time computability. Unless otherwise stated, all programs will be well-typed CorePolyC programs. The set of all finite-arity total functions is denoted by $\mathscr{F}$. Given an m-ary program p with input variables $\widetilde{x}$, for any $\widetilde{v} \in \mathbb{Z}^m$, we define $[\![\mathsf{p}]\!](\widetilde{v})$ as the value v' such that $\langle \emptyset[\widetilde{x} \mapsto \widetilde{v}], \mathsf{p} \rangle \Downarrow v'$. By Theorem 1, $[\![\mathsf{p}]\!]$ is a well-defined total function from $\mathbb{Z}^m$ to $\mathbb{Z}$, i.e., $[\![\mathsf{p}]\!] \in \mathscr{F}$. We call an $f \in \mathscr{F}$ to be *CorePolyC Computable* if there is a CorePolyC program p such that $[\![\mathsf{p}]\!] = f$. Let **FPC** denote the set of all CorePolyC computable functions. The following theorem is the main result of the paper.

Theorem 2 (Main Theorem). **FPC = FP**.

This section is devoted to the proof of Theorem 2. The overall proof is divided into two main parts, as illustrated in Fig. 5. For readability, we present only the key and concise proofs; details can be found in the full version.

1. In Sect. 3.1, we establish the soundness direction **FPC ⊆ FP** (Theorem 3), i.e., all CorePolyC programs run in polynomial time. Since all operators are interpreted as polynomial-time computable functions, it suffices to show that (i) every well-typed CorePolyC program performs only a polynomial number of operations, and (ii) each operation is applied to operands whose sizes are polynomially bounded. Interestingly, due to the well-structured nature of CorePolyC programs, (i) can be reduced to the proof of (ii) (Branch I). Therefore, it is sufficient to analyze how variable sizes grow step by step, from operators to expressions, statements, and finally programs (Branch II).
2. In Sect. 3.2, we prove the completeness direction **FP ⊆ FPC** (Theorem 4). We show that CorePolyC programs can construct a "hard-wired clock" for any polynomial, enabling them to simulate each step of a polynomial-time Turing machine, and ultimately produce a consistent output.

3.1 Soundness

To analyze programs' running time, we introduce the cost semantics for CorePolyC. The judgments are in the form $\langle \Sigma, \cdot \rangle \Downarrow_k \cdot$, where k bounds the number of steps of evaluation. For example, the cost semantic rule for iteration statements is defined as follows.

$$\frac{\langle \Sigma, \mathsf{e} \rangle \Downarrow_k i \quad \Sigma_0 := \Sigma \quad \langle \Sigma_j[x \mapsto j], \mathsf{s} \rangle \Downarrow_{k_j} \Sigma_{j+1}, \text{ for } 0 \le j < i.}{\langle \Sigma, \mathtt{for(x<e)\ s} \rangle \Downarrow_{k+\sum_{j=0}^{i-1} k_j} \Sigma_i} [\Sigma\text{-Loop}]$$

This rule intuitively means that the running time of executing a loop is the sum of the running time of each iteration. The complete set of rules can be found in the full version. Given a program p, there is a unique k such that $\langle \emptyset[\ \tilde{x} \mapsto \tilde{v}\ ], \mathsf{p} \rangle \Downarrow_k v'$. We define the *instruction count* of p under input $\tilde{v}$ as $\mathrm{ic}(\mathsf{p}, \tilde{v}) := k$, which is essentially the running time of p.

Time Versus Space in CorePolyC. The function $|\cdot|$ can be extended from $\mathbb{Z}$ to $\mathbb{V}$ by defining $|\mathtt{\#t}| = |\mathtt{\#f}| = 1$. Given a store environment Σ, the notation $|\Sigma|$ stands for $\max_{x \in \mathrm{dom}(\Sigma)} |\Sigma(x)|$, that is, the maximum length of the values currently stored in Σ. Given a derivation tree $\mathscr{E}_{\Sigma, p}$, the size $|\mathscr{E}_{\Sigma, p}|$ is defined as $\max\{|\Sigma'| : \Sigma' \text{ appears in } \mathscr{E}_{\Sigma, p}\}$. Let $T : \mathbb{N} \to \mathbb{N}$ denote a time function with $T(n) \ge n$. Suppose the size of an input $\tilde{v}$ to a program p is n. Given a function $f : \mathbb{V}^m \to \mathbb{V}$, we say that $f = O(T(n))$ if for any $\tilde{v} \in \mathbb{V}^m$, $f(\tilde{v}) \le g(|\tilde{v}|)$ for some $g : \mathbb{N} \to \mathbb{N}$ such that $g(n) = O(T(n))$. Then the following are well-defined.

1. p *has an instruction count of* $O(T(n))$ if $\mathrm{ic}(\mathsf{p}, \tilde{v}) = O(T(n))$,
2. p *produces output of size* $O(T(n))$ if $|[\![\mathsf{p}]\!](\tilde{v})| = O(T(n))$, and
3. p *generates (intermediate) values of size* $O(T(n))$ if $|\mathscr{E}_{\emptyset[\ \tilde{x} \mapsto \tilde{v}\ ], \mathsf{p}}| = O(T(n))$.

These concepts measure the time/space resources consumed by p. The following crucial lemma of Branch I in Fig. 5 demonstrates that the time complexity and space complexity of CorePolyC programs are strongly correlated.

Lemma 3. *Let $T(n) \ge n$ be a time function. The following three are equivalent:*

1. *All CorePolyC programs have an instruction count of $O(T(n))$.*
2. *All CorePolyC programs only produce outputs of size $O(T(n))$.*
3. *All CorePolyC programs only generate values of size $O(T(n))$.*

It should be clear that Lemma 3 still holds if we replace $T(n)$ by a family of functions $\mathtt{poly}(n)$, say the family of polynomials. Lemma 4 reveals the relationship between the space complexity and the soundness of CorePolyC.

Lemma 4. $\mathbf{FPC} \subseteq \mathbf{FP}$ *if and only if* $\forall f \in \mathbf{FPC}. |f(\tilde{v})| = O(\mathtt{poly}(n))$.

Proof. Assume that each $f \in \mathbf{FPC}$ can be computed in polynomial time by a Turing machine. Then its output size can only be polynomial. Hence, the "$\Longrightarrow$" holds. As for the "$\Longleftarrow$" direction, assume that $\forall f \in \mathbf{FPC}. |f(\tilde{v})| = O(\mathtt{poly}(n))$ holds. Then the lengths of values generated by the CorePolyC programs and the instruction counts are all polynomial according to Lemma 3. Thus, there exists a program p computing f, and p can be evaluated in polynomial steps. We simulate p instruction by instruction using a Turing machine M. Since p has only a polynomial number of polynomial-time computable operations, and each operation only involves operands of polynomial size, the simulation can be done in polynomial time. Therefore $f \in \mathbf{FP}$, from which $\mathbf{FPC} \subseteq \mathbf{FP}$ follows. □

Polynomial Bounds for Output. Lemma 4 reveals that if CorePolyC can only produce output of polynomial size, the soundness must be valid. Therefore, we need to examine the size of all outputs produced by CorePolyC programs. The most fundamental task is to examine the growth rate of values under the operators provided by CorePolyC. Given an operator op $\in$ O, we observe that

1. $|[\![\mathrm{op}]\!](\tilde{v})| = 1$, if op $\in \{\texttt{\&\&}, \texttt{||}, \texttt{!}\} \cup \{\texttt{>=}, \texttt{<=}, \texttt{>}, \texttt{<}, \texttt{==}, \texttt{!=}\}$,
2. $|[\![\mathrm{op}]\!](\tilde{v})| \leq \max_{i=1}^{m} |v_i| + 1$, if op $\in \{\texttt{+}, \texttt{-}, \texttt{/}, \texttt{\%}\}$, and
3. $|[\![\texttt{size}]\!](v)| = ||v|| \leq |v|$, where $||v||$ is the size of $|v|$.

A parameter is said to be a *constant* if it is independent of any input and any store environment. With this remark, the next lemma should be clear.

Lemma 5. *For any* op $\in$ O, $|[\![\mathrm{op}]\!](\tilde{v})| \leq \max_{i=1}^{m} |v_i| + k$, *where k is a constant.*

An expression can only contain a constant number of operators. Intuitively, the value of an expression should also have a similar upper bound. Lemma 6 formalizes these ideas. Note that statement (2) corresponds to the cases of iterable expressions, whose size depends only on iterable variables in the environment.

Lemma 6. *Given an expression* e *and a consistent pair* (Γ, Σ), *if there exist v and* t *such that* $\langle \Sigma, \mathrm{e} \rangle \Downarrow v$ *and* $\Gamma, \#\mathrm{f} \vdash \mathrm{e} : \mathrm{t}$, *then the following statements hold.*

1. $|v| \leq |\Sigma| + k$, *where k is a constant.*
2. *If* e *is iterable, i.e.,* t = iint, *then* $|v| \leq |(\Sigma)_{\restriction \Gamma}| + k$, *where k is a constant.*

Moreover, let $a \dot{-} b = \max(a - b, 0)$. Then Lemma 7 is convenient in upper bound estimation of values after executing a statement. Particularly, if a statement is inside a loop ($\ell = \#\mathrm{t}$), then the growth of all values during execution of this statement depends only on the iterable variables.

Lemma 7. *Given a statement* s *and a consistent pair* (Γ, Σ) *such that* $\Gamma, \ell \vdash \mathrm{s} : \Gamma'$ *and* $\langle \Sigma, \mathrm{s} \rangle \Downarrow \Sigma'$ *for some* ℓ, Γ' *and* Σ', *then the following statements hold.*

1. *If* $\ell = \#\mathrm{t}$, *then* $|\Sigma'| \dot{-} |\Sigma| = O(|(\Sigma)_{\restriction \Gamma}|^d)$, *where d is a constant.*
2. *If* $\ell = \#\mathrm{f}$, *then* $|\Sigma'| \dot{-} |\Sigma| = O(|\Sigma|^{d^k})$, *where d and k are constants.*

Intuitively, in Lemma 7, d represents the maximum depth of the nested loops in the statements, and k represents the number of the sequential loop statements in s, i.e., the number of maximal subtrees induced by Γ–Loop in the derivation tree. We are now able to bound the output produced by any programs and deduce the soundness of CorePolyC.

Proposition 2. *Given a program* p, *it holds that* $|[\![\mathrm{p}]\!](\tilde{v})| = O(\texttt{poly}(n))$.

Proof. Assume that $\mathrm{p} \equiv \texttt{int main(}_1 \texttt{x}_1, \ldots,_m \texttt{x}_m\texttt{)\{ }\tilde{\mathrm{s}}\texttt{ return e;\}}$. There exists a store Σ' such that $\langle \emptyset[\tilde{x} \mapsto \tilde{v}], \tilde{\mathrm{s}} \rangle \Downarrow \Sigma'$ and $\langle \Sigma', \mathrm{e} \rangle \Downarrow [\![\mathrm{p}]\!](\tilde{v})$. Since $|\emptyset[\tilde{x} \mapsto \tilde{v}]| \leq |\tilde{v}|$, by Lemma 7 and Lemma 6, there exists constants k and k' such that $|[\![\mathrm{p}]\!](\tilde{v})| \leq |\Sigma'| + k' \leq |\tilde{v}| + |\tilde{v}|^{d^k} + k' = O(\texttt{poly}(n))$. □

Theorem 3 (Soundness). **FPC** $\subseteq$ **FP**.

Proof. For any $f \in$ **FPC**, there exists a program p computing f. By Proposition 2, we have $|f(\tilde{v})| = |[\![\mathrm{p}]\!](\tilde{v})| = O(\texttt{poly}(n))$. The result follows from Lemma 4. □

3.2 Completeness

We now prove that every function computable in polynomial time by a Turing machine is also CorePolyC computable, or equivalently, every polynomial-time Turing machine M can be simulated by a CorePolyC program. During this process, it is standard to construct a variable to indicate the current step of the execution. Since the running time of M is always bounded by a polynomial p, we must prove that CorePolyC programs can generate a value v such that $p(n)$ can be bounded by $|v|$. Lemma 8 is sufficient to address the above issue.

Lemma 8. *For each $d \geq 1$, there exists an $O(d \log d)$-size program p such that $|[\![\mathsf{p}]\!](v)| = d|v|^d$.*

We say that a CorePolyC program p simulates a Turing machine M if for each binary number α, $M(\alpha) = \beta$ if and only if $\mathsf{p}(\hat{\alpha}) = \hat{\beta}$, where $\hat{\alpha}$ for example is an efficient encoding of α. Then the following simulation lemma holds.

Lemma 9. *Every polynomial-time Turing machine can be simulated by a CorePolyC program, and such a program can be constructed in polynomial time.*

Proof. We start by recalling the definition of Turing machines. A *Turing machine* M is a 6-tuple $(Q, \{\mathtt{0},\mathtt{1}\}, \Lambda, \delta, q_0, q_{halt})$, where

1. Q is a finite set of states,
2. $\Lambda = \{\mathtt{0},\mathtt{1},\square\}$ where $\square$ is the blank symbol,
3. $q_0, q_{halt} \in Q$ are the start state and the halt state, respectively.
4. $\delta : Q \times \Lambda \to Q \times \Lambda \times \{\mathtt{L},\mathtt{R}\}$ is the transition function of M.

The Turing machine M has a single, one-way infinite tape and behaves in a standard manner. Its configuration is represented by uqw, where q is the current state, $uw \in \Lambda^*$ is the current tape content, and the head points at the first symbol of w. When M halts, the head will return to the leftmost position, and the content on the tape represents the computation result.

Given $M = (Q, \{\mathtt{0},\mathtt{1}\}, \Lambda, \delta, q_0, q_{halt})$ whose running time is given by a polynomial $T(n)$. There is a constant d such that $T(n) \leq dn^d$. We construct a program p with input variable $\mathtt{x}$ as follows:

Configuration. We use an `int` variable $\mathtt{y}$ and the input variable $\mathtt{x}$ to present the contents of the tape in ternary representation, where the symbols 0, 1, and $\square$ are represented by the digits 0, 1, and 2, respectively. The value of $\mathtt{y}$ represents the contents to the left of the head, while the value of $\mathtt{x}$ represents the contents to the right of the head. For convenience, the digits of $\mathtt{x}$ are in reverse order so that the least significant digit of $\mathtt{x}$ represents the content under the tape head. To ensure the most significant digit is nonzero, we prepend a digit 2 to $\mathtt{x}$ and $\mathtt{y}$. Additionally, we declare an `int` variable $\mathtt{q}$ to simulate the state of M. W.l.o.g., we assume that $Q = \{q_0, q_1, q_2, \cdots, q_{|Q|-1}\}$, where $q_1 = q_{halt}$.

Input and Initialization. Assume that the input on the tape are $w \in \{0,1\}^*$. Let $w' = 2 \circ w^r$, where w^r represents the reverse of w. Interpret w' as a ternary number and convert it to the corresponding decimal number v, which will serve as the input to p. We declare an int variable y and assign it the value 2. For example, if the input of M is $w = $10010, then $w' = (201001)_3$ and $v = (514)_{10}$.

Timer. We utilize the method presented in the proof of Lemma 8 to generate a value whose length grows to $d|v|^d$, and assign it to an iterable variable cnt. Then we design a statement of the form for(i<size(cnt)){ ... } such that every Turing machine operation is simulated in an iteration of the loop.

Simulation. Inside the loop body, we simulate δ by a sequence of conditional statements. M will only modify its state once in each step. Therefore, we declare a boolean variable flag at the beginning of the loop body to indicate whether q has been updated. Given a constant m, we introduce the syntax sugar m*a, which means a+...+a (m occurrences of a).

1. *Read.* For any transition $\delta(q_i, \alpha)$, where $i \neq 1$, we use the following conditions to simulate the tape's reading and state recognition. If they match, the statement inside {} simulates the instructions to be executed.

    if(!flag && q==i && x%3==α) {...}.

2. *Write.* If M needs to change the content to $\beta \in \Lambda$ and update the state to q_j, it can be done by executing

    x=x-α+β'; q=j; flag=true;,

    where β' is corresponding to β, i.e., if $\beta \in \{0,1\}$, then $\beta' = \beta$; otherwise $\beta' = 2$. Set flag to #t to skip the remaining conditional statements.
3. *Leftward Movement.* If the head of M needs to move left, the last digit of y is appended to the end of x. However, it is important to note that if the tape head is already at the leftmost position, no movement is performed. This process can be simulated as follows:

    if(y>2) {x=3*x+y%3; y=y/3;} else {}

    In base three, the value of y always begins with 2, representing the leftmost end of the tape ($\square$).
4. *Rightward Movement.* The rightward movement is simulated by appending the last digit of x to the end of y. If the head is in the rightmost position, it can still move right. In this case, the head will point to a blank symbol $\square$, so we should append digit 2 to the end of y.

    if(x>2) {y=3*y+x%3; x=x/3;} else {y=3*y+2;}

5. *Halt and Output.* We do not add any statements for q_1. Once the program enters this state, it performs no operations until the loop terminates. Add `return x;` at the end of p to return the encoded output.

For example, assuming $\delta(q_0, 0) = (q_1, 1, \text{L})$ and $\delta(q_0, 1) = (q_3, 0, \text{R})$, the corresponding simulation statements are shown in Fig. 6. Since δ is defined on $Q \times \Lambda$, the number of conditional statements is at most $3|Q|$. Hence, the entire simulation process can be constructed in polynomial time.

```
1  for(i<size(cnt)){
2      bool flag;
3      // ...
4      if(!flag&&q==0&&x%3==0){
5          x=x-0+1;
6          q=1;
7          flag=true;
8          if(y>2){
9              x=3*x+y%3;
10             y=y/3;
11         } else {}
12     } else {}
13     // other transitions...
14 }
```

```
1  for(i<size(cnt)){
2      bool flag;
3      // ...
4      if(!flag&&q==0&&x%3==1){
5          x=x-1+0;
6          q=3;
7          flag=true;
8          if(x>2){
9              y=3*y+x%3;
10             x=x/3;
11         } else y=3*y+2;
12     } else {}
13     // other transitions...
14 }
```

Fig. 6. Examples of the simulation process. The left program simulates the transition $\delta(q_0, 0) = (q_1, 1, \text{L})$, while the right one simulates the transition $\delta(q_0, 1) = (q_3, 0, \text{R})$.

The program p fully simulates the computation of M. Since the tape head of M eventually returns to the leftmost position, the reversed ternary representation of the output without the last digit corresponds to the output of M. □

The completeness result is now immediate.

Theorem 4 (Completeness). FP $\subseteq$ FPC.

4 PolyC

As noted in Sect. 3, the set of CorePolyC computable functions corresponds precisely to **FP**. Important verification properties such as efficient termination are intrinsic to CorePolyC programs, eliminating the need for additional verification. Once the theoretical foundation has been laid down, we look for a greater level of programming convenience. In this section, we extend CorePolyC with additional syntactic sugars while maintaining the expressive power of CorePolyC. The extension is not done in a simple-minded way since it is easy to break the polynomial computability barrier. We shall call the extended language PolyC.

4.1 The Language

We outline how to embed in PolyC a few familiar programming constructs. Some programming examples of PolyC are provided in Sect. 4.3. We emphasize that we view PolyC as an open and extensible language: features can be introduced, and some design choices can also be modified, as long as such changes do not violate the core design goal: to faithfully characterize **FP**.

Data Types. For convenience, we introduce the new data types array and string. The elements in a multi-dimensional array are initialized to 0 or #f. The size of an array is defined as the maximum length among all elements. As for strings, there is an iterable version of the string type, i.e., the istring type, such that the operator size is applicable to istring variables. In addition, the parameters of the main function are not restricted to be only int.

Functions. We are free to use those statements and expressions that can be translated into CorePolyC, such as +=, ++, etc. We can also introduce function declarations and function applications. The syntax is as follows.

$$\text{Statement} \quad s ::= \ldots \mid \text{\#t } f(t_1 \ x_1, \ldots \ t_m \ x_m)\{ \ \tilde{s} \text{ return e;}\}$$
$$\text{Expression } e ::= \ldots \mid f(\tilde{e})$$

The type of a function is an arrow type $\tilde{t} \to t$. If we do not care about the output of a function, then it can output any value, or we can use the syntax sugar void to declare the return type. A function value is actually a closure $(\Sigma, \tilde{x}, \tilde{s}, e)$. The typing rules and the operational semantics of functions are defined as follows.

$$\frac{\Gamma[\tilde{x} \mapsto \tilde{t}], \text{\#t} \vdash \tilde{s} : \Gamma' \quad \Gamma', \text{\#t} \vdash e : t \quad f \notin \text{dom}(\Gamma)}{\Gamma, \ell \vdash \text{t } f(\widetilde{t \ x})\{ \ \tilde{s} \text{ return e;}\} : \Gamma[f \mapsto (\tilde{t} \to t)]} [\Gamma\text{-Fun}]$$

$$\frac{\Gamma, \ell \vdash \tilde{e} : \tilde{t}_1 \quad \tilde{t}_1 \preccurlyeq \tilde{t}_2 \quad \Gamma(f) = \tilde{t}_2 \to t}{\Gamma, \ell \vdash f(\tilde{e}) : t} [\Gamma\text{-App}]$$

$$\frac{}{\langle \Sigma, \text{t } f(\widetilde{t \ x})\{ \ \tilde{s} \text{ return e;}\}\rangle \Downarrow \Sigma[f \mapsto (\Sigma, \tilde{x}, \tilde{s}, e)]} [\Sigma\text{-Fun}]$$

$$\frac{\Sigma(f) = (\Sigma_f, \tilde{x}, \tilde{s}, e) \quad \langle \Sigma, \tilde{e}\rangle \Downarrow \tilde{v} \quad \langle \Sigma_f[\tilde{x} \mapsto \tilde{v}], \tilde{s}\rangle \Downarrow \Sigma' \quad \langle \Sigma', e\rangle \Downarrow v'}{\langle \Sigma, f(\tilde{e})\rangle \Downarrow v'} [\Sigma\text{-App}]$$

The partial order relation $(\mathsf{T}^m_+, \preccurlyeq)$ is a pairwise extension of $(\mathsf{Int}, \preccurlyeq)$ on m-tuples, where iint $\preccurlyeq$ int. This indicates that a parameter specified as a non-iterable type in the definition of a function can also be supplied with an iterable value.

It is clear that recursion is not definable in this version of PolyC. However, this restriction does not significantly impact the expressive power of functions. The constraints on the iterable variables are also imposed on the body of a function, with the loop indicators ℓ set to #t. Otherwise, it would be easy to write a function mul(a,b) similar to Example 1 to simulate general multiplication and then invoke x=mul(x,x) in a loop, leading to an exponential explosion of variable lengths. Therefore, when defining a function, it is necessary to consider that the function may be used within a loop body, and the typing rules above provide a solution to this issue.

Some form of recursion can be incorporated into PolyC, as long as it does not destroy the polynomial computability. For instance, simple tail recursion can be incorporated. More generally, to prevent divergence, we would need to ensure that the size of function parameters strictly decreases under some well-founded ordering (i.e., a termination metric). However, since this must be determined statically, defining recursive functions becomes more complex; for instance, some form of decreasing proof must be provided. In the simplest case, if we restrict recursion to only allow predefined monotonically decreasing metrics, then recursion would resemble loops in both structure and expressiveness. For simplicity, we have not discussed the issues raised by recursion.

Operators. PolyC is compatible with a variety of atomic operators. Instead of specifying all the operators of PolyC, we would like to clarify what kinds of operators can be included in the operator set. It is easy to verify that any polynomial-time computable operator satisfying the bound given in Lemma 5 is harmless to PolyC, which falls into the category of *positive operators*, as defined in [19]. However, this condition can be relaxed. The principle of adding an operator op to PolyC is to make sure that it is polynomial-time computable and renders true the following predicate.

If $\Gamma, \#f \vdash \mathtt{op}(\widetilde{x}) : \mathtt{t}$ and $\langle \Sigma, \mathtt{op}(\widetilde{x}) \rangle \Downarrow v$, then $|v| \dot{-} |\Sigma| = O(\mathtt{poly}(|(\Sigma)_{\restriction \Gamma}|))$.

We can now explore why some operations are unsuitable for PolyC and how such operations can be restricted to meet the aforementioned conditions. For example, since $|s_1 \circ s_2| = |s_1| + |s_2|$, the general string concatenation must be prohibited, unless we restrict its type to $\mathtt{string} \times \mathtt{istring} \to \mathtt{string}$. Similarly, scalar multiplication has the type $\mathtt{iint} \times \mathtt{int} \to \mathtt{int}$, and is therefore safe. We already introduced this syntactic sugar earlier in the proof of Lemma 9. The sensitivity highlights the fact that we must be very careful when extending PolyC.

4.2 Coincidence with FP

We shall use the subscript "+" to annotate the PolyC counterparts of what is defined for CorePolyC. For clarity, we only consider the PolyC computable functions of type $\mathbb{Z}^m \to \mathbb{Z}$ and denote the corresponding set by **FPC**$_+$. Clearly, by Theorem 4, one has $\mathbf{FP} \subseteq \mathbf{FPC} \subseteq \mathbf{FPC}_+$. We only need to show that $\mathbf{FPC}_+ \subseteq \mathbf{FP}$, whose intuition resembles the roadmap shown in Fig. 5. Note that the proof of Branch I relies solely on the structure of the program and is unaffected by newly introduced data types or syntactic sugar. We can derive the following lemma, whose proof elaborates on the proof of Lemma 4.

Lemma 10. $\mathbf{FPC}_+ \subseteq \mathbf{FP}$ *if and only if* $\forall f \in \mathbf{FPC}_+.\ |f(\widetilde{v})| = O(\mathtt{poly}(n))$.

For Branch II, the introduction of functions and function calls in PolyC enhances the growth rate of variable lengths in expressions. Since functions may have parameters and can be invoked in a nested fashion, the size of return values can grow polynomially. Lemma 11 can be seen as an analog of Lemma 6, with the constant k replaced by a polynomial overhead $\text{poly}(|(\Sigma)_{\upharpoonright \Gamma}|)$.

Lemma 11. *Given a PolyC expression* e *and a consistent pair* (Γ, Σ), *if there exist* v *and* t *such that* $\langle \Sigma, \mathsf{e} \rangle \Downarrow v$ *and* $\Gamma, \#\mathsf{f} \vdash \mathsf{e} : \mathsf{t}$, *then*

1. $|v| = |\Sigma| + O(|(\Sigma)_{\upharpoonright \Gamma}|^d)$ *where d is a constant.*
2. *if* $\mathsf{t} \in \{\mathtt{iint}, \mathtt{istring}\}$, *then* $|v| = O(|(\Sigma)_{\upharpoonright \Gamma}|^d)$.

However, it should be clear that there is no essential difference between a constant and a polynomial $\text{poly}(|(\Sigma)_{\upharpoonright \Gamma}|)$. Hence, Lemma 7 remains applicable for PolyC. Moreover, it follows that Proposition 2 also holds for PolyC, which illustrates that PolyC can only construct outputs of polynomial size. By Lemma 10, one has that $\mathbf{FPC}_+ \subseteq \mathbf{FP}$. We can now conclude the expressive power of PolyC.

Theorem 5. $\mathbf{FPC}_+ = \mathbf{FP}$.

Using arrays, the simulation of Turing machines is more straightforward. However, the completeness proof for CorePolyC does have the virtue in revealing that the four arithmetic operations (+, -, %, and /), and the `size` operator, in combination with the loop and the conditional statements, are already sufficient to simulate every polynomial-time Turing machine.

4.3 Implementation and Examples

To demonstrate the practical feasibility of PolyC, we focus on its implementation and present several non-trivial examples in this part.

Implementation. We have implemented an interpreter for PolyC, making use of the tool ANTLR (ANother Tool for Language Recognition) [30] to generate a syntax tree from the PolyC grammar. Special attention is given to the handling of the iterable variables. The source code and the implementation details can be accessed through the supplemental materials. This tool allows us to do problem-solving in a polynomial time programming paradigm, leveraging its advantages in various programming tasks. It is our hope that the experiments with this implementation of PolyC will guide the future development of the language.

It is interesting to understand the complexity of the interpreter. Here again, we see the advantage of PolyC. In most models for $\mathbf{FP}$, the termination property is not available, rendering meaningless the complexity issue of any interpreter. Formally let $\mathscr{I}_m : \mathsf{P}_+ \times \mathbb{V}_+{}^m \to \mathbb{V}_+$ denote the abstract interpreter function for programs of arity m, i.e., $\mathscr{I}_m(\mathsf{p}, \widetilde{v}) = [\![\mathsf{p}]\!](\widetilde{v})$. When considering only the decision version of this problem, i.e., $\{(\mathsf{p}, \overline{v}, i) : \mathsf{p}(\overline{v}) = i\}$, there is already an intrinsic difficulty in interpreting such programs.

Proposition 3. $\mathscr{I}_0$ *is* 2-**EXP**-*complete.*

Note that the upper bound does not increase as m grows, so we easily obtain the following corollary.

Corollary 1. *For all $m \geq 0$, $\mathscr{I}_m$ is 2-**EXP**-complete.*

Intuitively, The double exponential in Corollary 1 arises from the $O(|\Sigma|^{d^k})$ form in Lemma 7. The complexity of the interpreter characterizes the simplicity of PolyC, since the more concise the language, the less efficient the interpreter tends to be. Another way to understand this is that Proposition 3 concerns the fact that, for any PolyC program, the length of its execution paths is at most double-exponential; whereas Theorem 5 characterizes the case where, for a fixed program, the length of its execution paths is guaranteed to be polynomial. These two should not be conflated. Moreover, in general-purpose programming languages, both scenarios are unbounded, which is one of the reasons why PolyC can simplify the program verification process.

From the theoretical perspective, there remains an open question: for any language characterizing **FP**, what is the lower bound for the complexity of the interpreter of the language? By diagonalization, the complexity of any such interpreter is strictly beyond **P**. It is extremely unlikely that such an interpreter is inside **NP** or **PSPACE** since that would separate **NP** or **PSPACE** from **P**.

More Examples. Next, we shall present several PolyC program examples that make use of the newly added features.

Example 4 (Knapsack Problem). In the Knapsack problem, given m items with positive integer weights $w_1, \ldots, w_m$ and positive integer values $c_1, \ldots, c_m$, it is asked to find a subset of items such that the sum of their weights does not exceed a given positive integer W, and the total value is maximized. The most straightforward way to compute the value is by using the dynamic programming algorithm in $O(mW)$-time. Note that a pseudo-polynomial $O(mW)$ of input length, which rules out any implementation in PolyC. But if we use the unary representation of W, the classic dynamic programming algorithm for knapsack can be implemented in PolyC.

```
1  int max(int x, int y){
2      if(x>y) return x;
3      return y;
4  }
5
6  int knapsack(array<int> w, array<int> v, iint W, iint n){
7      array<array<int>> dp=array(size(n));
8      for(i<size(n)) dp[i]=array(size(W)+1);
9      for(i<size(n)){
10         for(j<size(W+W)){
11             if(i==0){
12                 if(j>=w[0]) dp[i][j]=v[0];
13                 else dp[i][j]=0;
14                 continue;
```

```
15            }
16            if(j<w[i]) dp[i][j]=dp[i-1][j];
17            else dp[i][j]=max(dp[i-1][j],dp[i-1][j-w[i
                  ]]+v[i]);
18        }
19    }
20    return dp[size(n)-1][size(W)];
21 }
```

Note that the parameters W and n in the function knapsack appear in the size function. Both must be of iint type. For example, when $w = [1, 2, 2, 3, 1]$, $v = [1, 2, 3, 4, 5]$, $W = 5$, and $n = 5$, one may invoke knapsack(w, v, 0b11111, 0b11111) to get the answer.

Example 5 (Graph Reachability Problem). The PATH problem asks whether there exists a path from a given source node s to a target node t in a directed graph $G = (V, E)$. The problem can be solved by an $O(|V| + |E|)$-time Depth-First Search algorithm (DFS). Assuming $|V| = m$, using an adjacency matrix to record information about a directed graph and encoding it as a string adjacent, we get a boolean representation of the answer by invoking path(m, s, t, adjacent) as follows.

```
1  bool path(int m,int s, int t,istring adjacent){
2      array<bool> visited=array(size(adjacent));
3      for(i<size(adjacent)) visited[i]=false;
4      array<int> stack=array(size(adjacent));
5      stack[0]=s;
6      int top=1;
7      int current;
8      for(i<size(adjacent)){
9          if(top!=0){
10             top-=1;
11             current=stack[top];
12             visited[current]=true;
13             int row=0;
14             for(j<size(adjacent)){
15                 if(j/m==current){
16                     if(adjacent[j]=="1"&&visited[j%m]==
                            false)
17                     {
18                         stack[top]=j%m;
19                         top+=1;
20                     }
21                 }
22             }
23         } else break;
24     }
25     return visited[t];
26 }
```

We remark that designing a correct PolyC program for a problem is essentially a proof that the problem is in **FP**. Therefore, we have proved that **NL** ⊆ **P** by this program, since the PATH problem is **NL**-complete.

The interesting aspect in Example 5 lies not only in representing the adjacency matrix of the graph using strings but also in using a loop with the assistance of a stack to replace the original recursive algorithm of DFS. In fact, it is possible to write a library in PolyC, allowing us to freely use stacks. This demonstrates that even though PolyC does not admit recursively defined functions, it is possible to convert a polynomial recursive algorithm into an equivalent iterative form. Below, we consider a slightly more complex yet very common problem in real life, the sorting problem.

Example 6 (Sorting Problem). The input for sorting algorithms is an array A, and the goal is to rearrange the elements' positions so that they are sorted in non-decreasing or non-increasing order. There are various sorting algorithms, and typically, their average time complexity is $\Theta(n \log n)$, where n is the number of elements in the array. Although the size of individual elements is not explicitly considered, overall it is still a polynomial-time algorithm and can be easily addressed using PolyC.

```
void merge(array<int> arr,int left,int mid,
        int right,array<int> tmp,iint m){
    int index=left,p1=left,p2=mid;
    for(i<size(m)){
        if(p1<mid&&p2<right){
            if(arr[p1]<arr[p2]){
                tmp[index]=arr[p1];index++;p1++;
            } else {
                tmp[index]=arr[p2];index++;p2++;
            }
            continue;
        }
        if(p1<mid){
            tmp[index]=arr[p1];index++;p1++;
            continue;
        }
        if(p2<right) {
            tmp[index]=arr[p2];index++;p2++;
            continue;
        }
        break;
    }
}

void sort(array<int> arr,iint m){
    array<int> tmp=array(size(m));
    int gap=1;
    for(i<size(m)){
```

```
                int left=0,mid=min(left+gap,size(m));
                int right=min(mid+gap,size(m));
                for(j<size(m)){
                    if(left<size(m)){
                        merge(arr,left,mid,right,tmp,m);
                        left+=gap+gap;
                        mid=min(left+gap,size(m));
                        right=min(mid+gap,size(m));
                    } else break;
                }
                for(j<size(m)) arr[j]=tmp[j];
                gap=gap+gap;
                if(gap>size(m)) break;
            }
}
```

Since the loop statement breaks when the array is sorted, the complexity remains $O(n \log n)$. The function sort requires an additional parameter specifying the length of the array in unary. For instance, if there is an array arr of length 5, we can invoke sort(arr, 0b11111) to sort it.

4.4 Application

In this part, we explore the potential applications of PolyC within the field of formal methods. Indeed, the impacts of PolyC are at least two-fold.

Verification of PolyC Programs. Most verification problems of PolyC programs have an exact algebraic characterization. Since all well-typed PolyC programs are well-structured, the loops in PolyC can be unrolled such that any nested structures can ultimately be transformed into a form with at most one loop. Formally, we say that a program is *simple* if its main function consists of three parts: i) declaration of variables, ii) a loop for(i<size(y)) s, where s does not contain any loops or function calls, and iii) a return statement. Proposition 4 demonstrates that any program can be reduced to a simple one.

Proposition 4. *For any m-ary PolyC program* p *with inputs* $\tilde{x}$*, there exists a bound* $t_0(n) = O(n^{|p|^{|p|}})$ *and a* $O(\text{poly}(|p|))$*-size* $(m+1)$*-ary simple program* p_0 *with inputs* $(\tilde{x}, y)$ *such that*

1. *the loop bound in the main function of* p_0 *is* y*, and*
2. *for any inputs* $\tilde{v} \in \mathbb{V}^m$ *and* $t \geq t_0(|\tilde{v}|)$*,* $[\![p_0]\!](\tilde{v}, t) = [\![p]\!](\tilde{v})$.

The idea behind this proposition is simple: since any program implements a function in **FP**, they have the normal form as shown in the proof of Lemma 9. A constructive proof is given in the full version.

By Proposition 4, for any program p, we can construct efficiently the corresponding p_0 and t_0, where t_0 is bounded by a doubly-exponential function of the program size. Assume that there are k variables declared in the first part of p_0, including the inputs. Then the effect of the loop body can be viewed as a function loop : $\mathbb{V}^k \to \mathbb{V}^k$, and the expression in the return statement can be viewed as ret : $\mathbb{V}^k \to \mathbb{Z}$. The input stage can be viewed as a function init : $\mathbb{V}^m \to \mathbb{V}^k$, where any newly declared variables are initialized to their default values. Finally, the effect of p can be characterized as $[\![\mathsf{p}]\!] = \mathsf{ret} \circ \mathsf{loop}^{[t_0]} \circ \mathsf{init}$, where the superscript $[t_0]$ denotes the t_0-fold composition of the loop body's effect. Some semantic properties, for example, the equivalence of two programs p_1 and p_2 can be precisely reduced to a boolean statement of the form

$$\varphi_{\mathsf{equiv}}(\mathsf{p}_1, \mathsf{p}_2) := \forall \widetilde{v}.\ (\mathsf{ret}_1 \circ \mathsf{loop}_1^{[t_1]} \circ \mathsf{init}_1)(\widetilde{v}) = (\mathsf{ret}_2 \circ \mathsf{loop}_2^{[t_2]} \circ \mathsf{init}_2)(\widetilde{v}). \quad (6)$$

Note that a general Turing-complete language cannot provide such algebraic characterizations. Moreover, in daily life, we only consider bounded inputs. Then such formulas can be viewed as instances of co-**NP** problem **TAUTOLOGY**. Furthermore, by considering over-approximations or restricting to subclasses of programs, more lightweight analysis methods may be achieved.

Impact on Other Programming Languages. Our type system can also serve as a complexity analysis tool for other programming languages. A straightforward approach would involve the following steps, as shown in Algorithm 1.

Algorithm 1. A simple complexity analysis procedure

1: Assign iterable types to all variables;
2: **repeat**
3:    Perform type checking;
4:    **if** type checking succeeds **then**
5:       **output** "poly";
6:       **return**
7:    **else**
8:       Update some types to non-iterable types accordingly;
9:    **end if**
10: **until** all involved types cannot be adjusted
11: **output** "unknown";

This algorithm is sound but not complete. Consider the left program in Fig. 4 as an example. In the first step, y is assigned the type iint. Since y is modified within the loop body, its type must eventually be updated to int. However, because y also serves as the operand of the size operator, it must retain the type iint. As a result, the program fails to pass the polynomial check. Nevertheless, this does not imply that its running time is non-polynomial. A key challenge in enhancing this method lies in inferring whether loop bounds are dominated by the bit-size of an iterable expression. For instance, y can easily be replaced by a newly declared iterable variable z. If such substitutions can be effectively detected, the class of programs for which the tool can soundly determine the "poly" status would be significantly extended.

5 Remark

What have we achieved? We have designed a simple imperative programming language, provided a rigorous definition of its syntax, semantics, and type system, and shown the consistency of the type system. We have proved that PolyC captures precisely the class **FP** of the polynomial time computable functions, and thus have laid down a firm foundation for a programming methodology. The design of PolyC has successfully addressed the problems that appeared in the previous models and languages. It is discussed in the supplementary materials how to introduce more features in PolyC.

What can PolyC offer? It is clear that PolyC forces a particular programming methodology on programmers. Designing a correct program for a problem is itself a proof that the problem is polynomial time computable (See Example 5). Programming in PolyC calls for more low-level algorithmic thinking. Programmers may spend more time in the design phase, trying to understand the problem better before programming. The language's built-in complexity boundaries create a natural simplification to theorem provers and model checkers: By eliminating infinite state space inherent to general-purpose languages, PolyC reduces verification overhead and may even enable lightweight verification strategies.

What more can we do with PolyC? Some software systems implement algorithms for **NP**-complete problems. In reality, their performance is just fine. The reason is that among all the input parameters of any one such system, the algorithm depends only on some input exponentially, and the size of the input tends to be small in applications. The problems solved by these systems are studied in the theory of parameterized complexity [13]. There is more than one way to implement such systems in PolyC. Either a constant upper bound is placed on an input parameter, or the input is coded up in unary. The dynamic algorithm of the knapsack problem, for example, can be implemented in PolyC using the unary encoding of the parameters (Example 4). Thus PolyC is far more useful than it appears at first sight. Further development of the type system is also a promising future work. As discussed in Sect. 4.4, we can slim down programs designed in other languages to a PolyC-like form to certify their theoretical efficiency, where the inference of the loop bound is crucial.

Randomization is becoming more and more useful in algorithm design. It is shown in [32] and the follow-up works that the simplex method has randomized algorithms whose average running time is polynomial. It means that we may design with a randomized PolyC a program for the linear programming problem that has a great success rate. In the setting of randomized computation, a polynomial-time algorithm is all we need. PolyC can, of course, be extended in different manners in different application scenarios.

Acknowledgements. This work is supported by the National Natural Science Foundation of China (No. 62072299, 62020106005) and the Science and Technology Commission of Shanghai Municipality (No. 24BC3200500).

References

1. Ali, N.A.: A survey of verification tools based on Hoare logic. Int. J. Softw. Eng. Appl. **8**, 87–100 (2017)
2. Baier, C., Katoen, J.P.: Principles of Model Checking. MIT Press (2008)
3. Baillot, P., Mogbil, V.: Soft lambda-calculus: a language for polynomial time computation. In: International Conference on Foundations of Software Science and Computation Structures, pp. 27–41. Springer (2004)
4. Bellantoni, S., Cook, S.: A new recursion-theoretic characterization of the polytime functions (extended abstract). In: Proceedings of the Twenty-Fourth Annual ACM Symposium on Theory of Computing, STOC '92, pp. 283–293. Association for Computing Machinery, New York, NY, USA (1992). https://doi.org/10.1145/129712.129740
5. Bertot, Y., Castéran, P.: Interactive Theorem Proving and Program Development: Coq'Art: The Calculus of Inductive Constructions. Springer (2013)
6. Buss, S.R.: Bounded arithmetic. Princeton University (1985)
7. Buss, S.R.: The polynomial hierarchy and intuitionistic bounded arithmetic. In: Structure in Complexity Theory: Proceedings of the Conference held at the University of California, Berkeley, California, 2–5 June 1986, pp. 77–103. Springer (1986)
8. Cobham, A.: The intrinsic computational difficulty of functions. In: Bar-Hillel, Y. (ed.) Logic, Methodology and Philosophy of Science, pp. 24–30. North-Holland Pub. Co. (1965)
9. Cook, S., Urquhart, A.: Functional interpretations of feasibly constructive arithmetic. In: Proceedings of the Twenty-First Annual ACM Symposium on Theory of Computing, pp. 107–112 (1989)
10. Cook, S.A.: Feasibly constructive proofs and the propositional calculus (preliminary version). In: Proceedings of the Seventh Annual ACM Symposium on Theory of Computing, STOC '75, pp. 83–97. Association for Computing Machinery, New York, NY, USA (1975). https://doi.org/10.1145/800116.803756
11. Coppersmith, D., Winograd, S.: Matrix multiplication via arithmetic progressions. J. Symb. Comput. **9**(3), 251–280 (1990). https://doi.org/10.1016/S0747-7171(08)80013-2, https://www.sciencedirect.com/science/article/pii/S0747717108800132, computational algebraic complexity editorial
12. Dal Lago, U.: A short introduction to implicit computational complexity. In: European Summer School in Logic, Language and Information, pp. 89–109. Springer (2010)
13. Downey, R.G., Fellows, M.R.: Parameterized Complexity. Springer (2012)
14. Edmonds, J.: Paths, trees, and flowers. Can. J. Math. **17**, 449–467 (1965)
15. Girard, J.Y.: Linear logic. Theoret. Comput. Sci. **50**(1), 1–101 (1987)
16. Gurevich, Y.: Algebras of feasible functions. In: 24th Annual Symposium on Foundations of Computer Science (SFCS 1983), pp. 210–214. IEEE (1983)
17. Hainry, E., Jeandel, E., Péchoux, R., Zeyen, O.: COMPLEXITYPARSER: an automatic tool for certifying poly-time complexity of Java programs. In: Cerone, A., Ölveczky, P.C. (eds.) ICTAC 2021. LNCS, vol. 12819, pp. 357–365. Springer, Cham (2021). https://doi.org/10.1007/978-3-030-85315-0_20
18. Hainry, E., Kapron, B.M., Marion, J.Y., Péchoux, R.: A tier-based typed programming language characterizing feasible functionals. In: Proceedings of the 35th Annual ACM/IEEE Symposium on Logic in Computer Science, pp. 535–549 (2020)

19. Hainry, E., Péchoux, R.: A general noninterference policy for polynomial time. Proceedings of the ACM on Programming Languages **7**(POPL), 806–832 (2023)
20. Hainry, E., Péchoux, R., Silva, M.: A programming language characterizing quantum polynomial time. In: Foundations of Software Science and Computation Structures. LNCS, vol. 13992, p. 156 (2023)
21. Hartmanis, J., Stearns, R.E.: On the computational complexity of algorithms. Trans. Am. Math. Soc. **117**, 285–306 (1965)
22. Jones, N.D.: LOGSPACE and PTIME characterized by programming languages. Theoret. Comput. Sci. **228**(1–2), 151–174 (1999)
23. Klee, V., Minty, G.J.: How good is the simplex algorithm. Inequalities **3**(3), 159–175 (1972)
24. Kuwahara, T., Terauchi, T., Unno, H., Kobayashi, N.: Automatic termination verification for higher-order functional programs. In: European Symposium on Programming Languages and Systems. pp. 392–411. Springer (2014)
25. Lafont, Y.: Soft linear logic and polynomial time. Theoret. Comput. Sci. **318**(1–2), 163–180 (2004)
26. Lee, C.S., Jones, N.D., Ben-Amram, A.M.: The size-change principle for program termination. In: Proceedings of the 28th ACM SIGPLAN-SIGACT Symposium on Principles of Programming Languages, pp. 81–92 (2001)
27. Marion, J.Y.: A type system for complexity flow analysis. In: 2011 IEEE 26th Annual Symposium on Logic in Computer Science, pp. 123–132. IEEE (2011)
28. Moura, L., Ullrich, S.: The Lean 4 theorem prover and programming language. In: Platzer, A., Sutcliffe, G. (eds.) CADE 2021. LNCS (LNAI), vol. 12699, pp. 625–635. Springer, Cham (2021). https://doi.org/10.1007/978-3-030-79876-5_37
29. Oitavem, I.: The polynomial hierarchy of functions and its levels. Theoret. Comput. Sci. **900**, 25–34 (2022)
30. Parr, T.J., Quong, R.W.: ANTLR: A predicated-LL(k) parser generator. Softw. Pract. Exp. **25**(7), 789–810 (1995)
31. Si, X., Naik, A., Dai, H., Naik, M., Song, L.: Code2Inv: a deep learning framework for program verification. In: Lahiri, S.K., Wang, C. (eds.) CAV 2020. LNCS, vol. 12225, pp. 151–164. Springer, Cham (2020). https://doi.org/10.1007/978-3-030-53291-8_9
32. Spielman, D., Teng, S.H.: Smoothed analysis of algorithms: why the simplex algorithm usually takes polynomial time. In: Proceedings of the Thirty-Third Annual ACM Symposium on Theory of Computing, STOC '01, pp. 296–305. Association for Computing Machinery, New York, NY, USA (2001). https://doi.org/10.1145/380752.380813
33. Volpano, D., Smith, G., Irvine, C.: A sound type system for secure flow analysis. J. Comput. Secur. **4** (2000). https://doi.org/10.3233/JCS-1996-42-304

Specifying and Verifying Future Conditions

Yahui Song(✉), Darius Foo, and Wei-Ngan Chin

School of Computing, National University of Singapore, Singapore, Singapore
{yahui.song,dariusf}@u.nus.edu, chinwn@nus.edu.sg

Abstract. This paper formalizes *future conditions*, which complement traditional pre- and post-conditions to provide a more comprehensive specification of each function's *behaviour* and *expectation*. Pre-conditions govern the required states before each function call, while post-conditions define the immediate outcomes (post-states) upon completion. Future conditions extend this paradigm by specifying expected temporal behaviors and states that manifest after the function call has finished, potentially affecting subsequent operations or program states. Together, these three types of conditions form a robust specification mechanism for reasoning about API behaviors across various temporal contexts. However, existing techniques for reasoning about future conditions have three key limitations: inefficient entailment checking, under-approximation of program behaviors, and bounded loop unrolling. To address these challenges, we propose a set of over-approximating Hoare-style forward rules that accommodate future conditions that are processed once per method declaration. Moreover, we propose a novel solution for modelling recursive behaviors via a *bag* of future conditions, which can be heuristically synthesized and verified in the verification system. We formally prove the soundness of our proposal in Coq and use experimental results to demonstrate its effectiveness in detecting non-trivial, real-world API misuses.

Keywords: Future Conditions · Hoare Logic · Linear Temporal Logic · Separation Logic · Coq Proof Assistant

1 Introduction

Pre-conditions and post-conditions are fundamental concepts in formal methods of software engineering, particularly in the context of *design by contract* [15]. Considering function definitions as the smallest software components, classic pre- and post-conditions provide constraints for behaviors before the function call and expected outcomes from the current function execution, respectively. However, they are inflexible in expressing constraints on program behavior after the function call has completed. This limitation becomes particularly apparent when modeling complex API behaviors, where the impact of a function call may extend beyond its immediate execution context. For instance, they struggle to capture requirements such as: "Opening a read-only file should not be followed by any writing operations"; "Memory allocated by *malloc* must be finally freed before exiting the program"; or "If loading a certificate returns an error code, the program must exit in the next step", etc. These examples illustrate the need for a mechanism to specify and reason about program behavior beyond the immediate scope of a function call, highlighting a limitation in the expressiveness of traditional pre- and post-conditions.

Prior work [23] proposes *future conditions* to express the aforementioned constraints on program behavior after function calls have been completed. When combined with pre- and post-conditions, this triplet-style specification effectively encapsulates a usage protocol for each function and the key APIs involved. For example, the specification for `malloc` is written in Fig. 1[1]. Its pre/post-condition state that the input value should be positive and when a pointer is successfully allocated, i.e., $res \neq null$, it triggers an event $malloc(res)$, where res denotes the return value. We use ϵ for empty traces and $\_^*$ for permitting any traces. Its future-condition enforces that the allocated pointer should be finally freed ($\mathcal{F}$ denotes the temporal operator *finally*), which effectively prevents a memory-leak. The *free* function triggers an event $free(ptr)$ and its future condition ensures that after the deallocation, the input pointer cannot be accessed throughout its lifetime ($\mathcal{G}$ denotes the temporal operator *globally*), which effectively prevents double-free or use-after-free violations.

```
void *malloc (size_t size);
// pre:    size>0 ∧ _*
// post:   (res=null ∧ ε) ∨ (res≠null ∧ malloc(res))
// future: (res=null ∧ _*) ∨ (res≠null ∧ F free(res))

void free (void *ptr);
// pre:    true
// post:   true ∧ free(ptr)
// future: true ∧ G !_(ptr)
```

Fig. 1. Triplet specifications for *malloc* and *free* APIs, taken from [23].

Future conditions provide a general mechanism for specifying both safety and liveness properties through linear temporal logic (LTL) formulas, including resource usage, null-pointer dereferences or unchecked return values, etc.

---
[1] The specifications are in the form of $\bigvee(\pi \wedge \theta)$, i.e., a disjunctive set of conjunctions between pure arithmetic constraints (π) and trace constraints (θ).

However, prior work [23] for detecting violations of future conditions suffers from several limitations. First, it uses an inefficient entailment checking strategy, where each future condition must be independently verified against all subsequent code. This leads to redundant checks – particularly when processing sequences of function calls, each with its own future conditions. Second, it prioritises bug-finding (no incorrectly flagged safe code) over soundness (no missed violations), which under-approximates program behavior. This involves arbitrarily discarding paths and handling loops via bounded unrolling, risking unsoundness by omitting critical behaviors. Lastly, a major open question is how to effectively represent the future conditions produced by the recursive execution of recursive data structures.

To address the aforementioned challenges, this paper utilizes a set of Hoare-style verification rules to enable sound reasoning about future conditions. For effectful loops working with recursive data structures, we introduce predicates that represent a bag of items for both traces and future conditions, where the commutative law applies. To enhance automation, we employ a lightweight loop invariant synthesis procedure, whose output is constructed using such predicates and can be reliably verified by the proposed verification system. Overall, our approach aims to establish a verification framework based on over-approximation, designed to soundly prove the absence of violations of future conditions.

1. We introduce a set of sound forward reasoning rules to propagate future conditions efficiently. These rules employ over-approximation of behaviors, guaranteeing the absence of false negatives (missed violations) when verifying future conditions. The formal definition and proof of soundness for these rules are presented in Theorem 3.
2. To facilitate the forward reasoning process, we formalize a set of *trace inclusion checking* rules and a set of *trace subtraction* rules. We define and prove their soundness in Theorem 1 and Theorem 2, respectively.
3. We utilize predicates to represent collections of traces and future conditions and implement a trace invariant synthesis procedure that generates these predicates, which our verification rules can then reliably verify.
4. We demonstrate the effectiveness of the proposed verification framework through experimental results and case studies. All lemmas and theorems presented have been proven in Coq. Our artifact is publicly available [18].

2 Overview and Motivating Examples

This section outlines the current solution and challenges for reasoning about future conditions, highlighting our contributions through examples.

2.1 The Current Solution

The essence of reasoning future conditions in [23] can be captured by the following rule for function calls, where proof obligations are highlighted:

$$\frac{f\,(\overline{x})\,[\Phi_{pre},\Phi_{post},\Phi_{future}] \in \mathcal{E} \quad \Phi \sqsubseteq \Phi_{pre} \quad \{\Phi \circ \Phi_{post}\}\; e\; \{\Phi_e\} \quad \Phi_e \sqsubseteq \Phi_{future}}{\{\Phi\}\, f(\overline{x})\,;\, e\, \{\Phi_{post} \circ \Phi_e\}} \; [FV\text{-}Call\text{-}Inefficient]$$

A traditional Hoare-style verification rule for function calls works roughly as follows: it retrieves the callee f's specification from the environment $\mathcal{E}$, and if the current program state Φ entails ($\sqsubseteq$) the callee's pre-condition Φ_{pre}, it extends the program state with the callee's post-condition. Here "$\Phi \circ \Phi_{post}$"[2] means to sequentially compose two specifications. Now, having Φ_{future}, [23] extends the rule with one more proof obligation: the behavior of e (where e denotes the rest of code following the call to $f(\overline{x})$), as captured by Φ_e, entails the callee's future condition, effectively imposing constraints on the code e after the call.

```
1.  int main(int argc, char **argv){
2.      char *buf1, *buf2, *buf3;
3.      buf1 = malloc(1);
// malloc(buf2)·free(buf2)·malloc(buf3)·strncpy(buf2)·free(buf1)·free(buf3)⊑F(free(buf1))
4.      buf2 = malloc(1);
// free(buf2)·malloc(buf3)·strncpy(buf2)·free(buf1)·free(buf3)⊑ F(free(buf2))
5.      free(buf2);
// malloc(buf3)·strncpy(buf2)·free(buf1)·free(buf3) ⋢ G(!_(buf2))  ⇐ Bug Detected!
6.      buf3 = malloc(1);
// strncpy(buf2)·free(buf1)·free(buf3) ⊑ F(free(buf3))
7.      strncpy(buf2,argv[1],1); //A UAF bug here!
8.      free(buf1);
// free(buf3) ⊑ G(!_(buf1))
9.      free(buf3);}
// ϵ ⊑ G(!_(buf3))
```

Fig. 2. Detecting a UAF bug from CWE-416 [7]

While this solution is correct, it suffers from repeated invocation(s) of entailment checking, as demonstrated in Fig. 2. The example includes multiple memory operations, with a use-after-free (UAF) bug at line 7. According to the specifications in Fig. 1, every call to *malloc* or *free* necessitates checking the subsequent code against the specified future conditions. We mark all triggered trace entailment checks in blue, and the UAF bug is detected when an entailment failure occurs at line 5. This approach introduces redundant checks – for example, events *free(buf2)* (generated from line 5) and *free(buf1)* (generated from line 8) are checked at least two and four times, respectively. The inefficiency escalates further when future conditions are applied to operations like *strncpy*. In

---

[2] The interpretation of ∘ depends on the specific logic employed in Φ: for pure arithmetic: $\circ \equiv \wedge$ (logical conjunction); for separation logic: $\circ \equiv *$ (separating conjunction); for linear temporal logic: $\circ \equiv \cdot$ (temporal concatenation), etc.

the worst case, the checking process exhibits (informally) quadratic complexity relative to program length. To overcome this limitation, we propose an improved specification method for future conditions that efficiently detects the UAF bug while eliminating redundant re-analysis.

2.2 Towards Efficient Propagation for Future Conditions

We propose a simplified specification syntax that reduces redundancy by associating future conditions with post-conditions, thereby eliminating unnecessary arithmetic constraints. As shown in Fig. 3, each specification comprises a precondition (**req** clause), and a *post summary* (**ens** clause) structured as "**req**: π **ens**: $\bigvee (\pi\,;\theta\,;F)$". Here, π is the precondition, and each disjunctive case in the post summary includes: a post-state pure constraint π, a trace formula θ recording triggered events and an associated future condition F. We use _* for the default future condition, which imposes no constraints on future executions.

```
void *malloc (size_t size);
//req: size > 0  ens: (res = null ; ϵ ; _*) ∨ (res ≠ null ; malloc(res) ; F(free(res)))
void free (void *ptr);
//req: true  ens: (res = () ; free(ptr) ; G(!_(ptr)))
char *strncpy (char *dest, const char *src, size_t n)
//req: true  ens: (res = dest ; strncpy(dest) ; _*)
```

Fig. 3. An improved way for specifying future conditions for memory usage APIs.

The new specifications of *malloc* and *free* are semantically equivalent to their original version shown in Fig. 1. For *strncpy*, it triggers an event involving its first argument. We show in Fig. 4 how the revised specification achieves both conciseness and linear-complexity propagation of future conditions.

Program states are captured in the form of $\{\bigvee (\pi\,;\theta\,;F)\}$. By associating future conditions with program states, we can conjunctively combine different future conditions and compute the next states through *trace subtraction*. Figure 4 highlights these incremental updates to future conditions. In particular, at line 5, subtracting the event "*free(buf2)*" from "$\mathcal{F}(free(buf2))$" yields _*, indicating the fulfillment of the deallocation obligation. At line 7, the UAF bug is detected when we subtract the event "*strncpy(buf2)*" from "$\mathcal{G}(!\_(buf2))$", producing $\bot$ (*false*) – a contradiction that indicates the invalid usage of "*buf2*".

Our approach processes future conditions once per method declaration, requiring only a single analysis pass per event. The key idea is to embed future conditions into program states and support logical operations – such as conjunctive obligations and trace subtraction – over these future conditions. We formalize this approach through a set of novel forward rules and prove their soundness in Sect. 4. Next, we illustrate how to specify and verify future conditions for loops.

2. `char *buf1, *buf2, *buf3;`
$\{(\exists \mathit{buf1}, \mathit{buf2}, \mathit{buf3}. \mathit{true} \, ; \, \epsilon \, ; \, \_^*)\}$

3. `buf1 = malloc(1);`
$\{(\exists \mathit{buf1}, \mathit{buf2}, \mathit{buf3}. \mathit{buf1} \neq \mathit{null} \, ; \, \mathit{malloc}(\mathit{buf1}) \, ; \, \mathcal{F}(\mathit{free}(\mathit{buf1})))\}$

4. `buf2 = malloc(1);`
$\{(\exists \mathit{buf1}, \mathit{buf2}, \mathit{buf3}. \mathit{buf1} \neq \mathit{null} \wedge \mathit{buf2} \neq \mathit{null} \, ; \, \mathit{malloc}(\mathit{buf1}) \cdot \mathit{malloc}(\mathit{buf2}) \, ; \,$
$\mathcal{F}(\mathit{free}(\mathit{buf1})) \wedge \mathcal{F}(\mathit{free}(\mathit{buf2})))\}$

5. `free(buf2);`
$\{(\exists \mathit{buf1}, \mathit{buf2}, \mathit{buf3}. \mathit{buf1} \neq \mathit{null} \wedge \mathit{buf2} \neq \mathit{null} \, ; \, \mathit{malloc}(\mathit{buf1}) \cdot \mathit{malloc}(\mathit{buf2}) \cdot \mathit{free}(\mathit{buf2}) \, ; \,$
$\mathcal{F}(\mathit{free}(\mathit{buf1})) \wedge \_^* \wedge \mathcal{G}(!\_(\mathit{buf2}))))\}$

6. `buf3 = malloc(1);`
$\{(\exists \mathit{buf1}, \mathit{buf2}, \mathit{buf3}. \mathit{buf1} \neq \mathit{null} \wedge \mathit{buf2} \neq \mathit{null} \wedge \mathit{buf3} \neq \mathit{null} \, ; \, \mathit{malloc}(\mathit{buf1}) \cdot \mathit{malloc}(\mathit{buf2})$
$\cdot \mathit{free}(\mathit{buf2}) \cdot \mathit{malloc}(\mathit{buf3}) \, ; \, \mathcal{F}(\mathit{free}(\mathit{buf1})) \wedge \mathcal{G}(!\_(\mathit{buf2})) \wedge \mathcal{F}(\mathit{free}(\mathit{buf3})))\}$

7. `strncpy(buf2,argv[1],1);`
$\{(\exists \mathit{buf1}, \mathit{buf2}, \mathit{buf3}. \mathit{buf1} \neq \mathit{null} \wedge \mathit{buf2} \neq \mathit{null} \wedge \mathit{buf3} \neq \mathit{null} \, ; \, \mathit{malloc}(\mathit{buf1}) \cdot \mathit{malloc}(\mathit{buf2})$
$\cdot \mathit{free}(\mathit{buf2}) \cdot \mathit{malloc}(\mathit{buf3}) \cdot \mathit{strncpy}(\mathit{buf2}) \, ; \, \mathcal{F}(\mathit{free}(\mathit{buf1})) \wedge \bot \wedge \mathcal{F}(\mathit{free}(\mathit{buf3}))) \Leftarrow \text{✗}\}$
FC Violation Found: subtracting "strncpy(buf2)" from "$\mathcal{G}(!\_(\mathit{buf2}))$" leads to false!

Fig. 4. Detecting the UAF bug in Fig. 2 in a more efficient way.

2.3 Predicates for Bags of Traces and Future Conditions

The program in Fig. 5 creates an array of length n and iteratively invokes *malloc* for each element. The specification for *mallocN*, given in Fig. 6, comprises two predicates: "$\mathit{pred}_t(B, i)$" for triggered traces, and "$\mathit{pred}_f(B, i)$" for the future conditions. Predicates are in the form of "$\Lambda_i^B(\bigvee(\pi \wedge \theta))$", where i

```
1  void* mallocN(int n,void **arr,){
2      int i = 0;
3      while (i < n) {
4          arr[i] = malloc(4); i = i+1;}
5      return *arr;}
6
7  void main () {
8      void *arr[5]; mallocN (5, arr);
9      free(arr[0]);/* memory leak */}
```

Fig. 5. Iteratively malloc n times

denotes the iterator and B denotes the bag of elements that satisfies the specification $\bigvee(\pi \wedge \theta)$, allowing flexible specification under different arithmetic constraints. Predicates enforce commutativity, discarding trace order sensitivity among each element in the bag.

In Fig. 7, we demonstrate the forward reasoning for *main*. After the function call to *mallocN(5, arr)*, the predicates are instantiated with the concrete bag, i.e., [0..5). At line 9, when the first element is freed, the future condition predicate updates to a new bag [1..5), reflecting the removal of *arr[0]*. By the end, the memory leak is detected via a failed entailment checking, that the empty trace is not always permitted in the future condition "$\mathit{pred}_f([1..5), i)$". To automate this process, we introduce a heuristic-based synthesis for predicate generation, and enable the predicate propagation in the trace subtraction rules.

$$mallocN(n, arr) \equiv \textbf{req}: length(arr) {\geq} n$$
$$\textbf{ens}: (\exists i.\ true\ ;\ pred_t([0..n), i)\ ;\ pred_f([0..n), i))$$
$$pred_t(B, i) \equiv \Lambda_i^B (arr[i] {\neq} null \wedge malloc(arr[i])) \vee (arr[i] {=} null \wedge \epsilon)$$
$$pred_f(B, i) \equiv \Lambda_i^B (arr[i] {\neq} null \wedge \mathcal{F}(free(arr[i])))$$

Fig. 6. Specification for $mallocN$.

```
8. void *arr[5]; mallocN (5, arr);
```
$\{(\exists arr, i.\ length(arr){=}5\ ;\ pred_t([0..5), i)\ ;\ \underwave{pred_f([0..5), i))}\}$

```
9. free(arr[0]);
```
$\{(\exists arr, i.\ length(arr){=}5\ ;\ pred_t([0..5), i) \cdot free(arr[0])\ ;\ \underwave{pred_f([1..5), i) \wedge \mathcal{G}(!\_(arr[0]))})\}$

FC Violation Found: empty trace "ϵ" does not satisfy the obligation "$pred_f([1..5), arr)$"!

Fig. 7. Forward reasoning for $main$ and detecting the memory leak in Fig. 5.

Remark. Such memory usage violations can also be detected by static analyzers such as Pulse (a memory safety checker in Infer [14]), which relies on separation logic. However, Pulse requires an additional side check upon function exit to account for residual footprints when detecting memory leaks. In contrast, our approach employs a lightweight, general-purpose temporal logic to explicitly define obligations, avoiding the need for implicit checks. This not only simplifies verification but also extends applicability beyond memory safety, enabling the verification of both safety and liveness properties. We showcase the variety of bug types that can be handled by specifying future conditions in Table 2.

3 Target Language and Specifications

We target an imperative, first-order, call-by-value core language, defined in Fig. 8. A program $\mathcal{P}$ comprises a list of function declarations $\overline{Func}$. Here, we use the $\overline{overline}$ to denote a finite list of items, for example, $\overline{x}$ refers to a list of variables, $x_1, \ldots, x_n$. Each function has a name f, formal arguments $\overline{x}$, and an expression-oriented body e. Function specifications contains a pre-condition π, and a post summary Δ, which is a set of disjunctive tuples. Each three-element tuple contains: a pure formula π, a trace formula θ, and a future condition F.

We utilize π as the basic logical formula, capturing the Presburger arithmetic conditions on program inputs and local variables. Values include variables and constants ranging from integers, Boolean, unit, null, and * for non-deterministic values. Expressions include sequencing, function calls, conditionals, assignments, while loops, etc. Furthermore, we use "$ev(A)$" for explicitly raising events, and "$\textbf{assert}_f\ F$" for asserting constraints for future behaviors.

Traces are regular expressions, comprising $false$ ($\bot$); empty traces ϵ; singleton events A; sequential concatenations $\theta_1 \cdot \theta_2$; disjunctions $\theta_1 \vee \theta_2$; conjunctions $\theta_1 \wedge \theta_2$; and finite time (zero or many) repetition of a trace, constructed by a

(Program)	$\mathcal{P}$ ::=	$\overline{Func}$	(Function Decl.) $Func$ ::=	$f(\overline{x})\{e\}$
(Post Summary)	Δ ::=	$\bigvee(\pi\,;\theta\,;F)$	(Specification)	[req: π ens: Δ]
(Expressions)	e ::=	\multicolumn{3}{l	}{$v \mid x:=e \mid local\ x \mid e_1\,;\,e_2 \mid ev(A) \mid$}
		\multicolumn{3}{l	}{if $b\ e_1\ e_2$ $\mid$ while π do e $\mid f(\overline{x}) \mid$ assert$_f$ F}
(Trace)	θ ::=	\multicolumn{3}{l	}{$\bot \mid \epsilon \mid A \mid \theta_1 \vee \theta_2 \mid \theta_1 \wedge \theta_2 \mid \theta_1 \cdot \theta_2 \mid \theta^*$}
(Single Events)	A ::=	\multicolumn{3}{l	}{$ev(t) \mid \neg ev(t) \mid \neg\_(t) \mid \_ \mid pred(B,i)$}
(Future Cond.)	F ::=	θ	$pred(B,i)$ ::=	$\Lambda_i^B(\bigvee(\pi \wedge \theta))$
(Pure)	π ::=	\multicolumn{3}{l	}{$T \mid F \mid bop(t_1,t_2) \mid \pi_1 \wedge \pi_2 \mid \pi_1 \vee \pi_2 \mid \neg\pi \mid \exists x.\,\pi \mid \forall x.\,\pi$}
(Terms)	t ::=	$v \mid t_1{+}t_2 \mid {-}t$	(Values) v ::=	$x \mid i \mid b \mid () \mid null \mid *$
(Bag)	B ::=	\multicolumn{3}{l	}{$\emptyset \mid \{v\} \mid B_1\text{-}B_2 \mid B_1 \cup B_2 \mid B_1 \cap B_2$}

Fig. 8. Syntax of the core language and the specification language

Kleene star θ^*. In this paper, we use LTL operators $\mathcal{F}(A)$, $\mathcal{G}(A)$ and $\backslash(A)$ as short hands for regular expressions "$(\neg A)^* \cdot A \cdot \_^*$", "$(A)^*$" and "$\_ \cdot A \cdot \_^*$", respectively. Singleton events include: parameterized events $ev(t)$; negated parameterized events $\neg ev(t)$; forbid argument $\neg\_(t)$; wildcards $\_$ matching any event; predicates that capture a bag of disjunctive traces. Future conditions constraint temporal behaviors in the future and are essentially trace constructs; we use "F" to denote them for clarity and to avoid ambiguity.

We use "$\_^*$" to represent the default future condition, which permits any possible future executions. The Boolean values of T and F are respectively indicated by *true* and *false*. The binary operators bop are from $\{<,\leq,=,\geq,>\}$. A term can be a simple value v or simple computations of terms, $t_1{+}t_2$ and ${-}t$. A bag ia a set of unique elements, and we use $[0..n]$ as a shorthand for $\{0..(n-1)\}$.

3.1 Instrumented Semantics for the Target Language

To facilitate the soundness proof for the forward rules, we present an instrumented reduction $[s,\rho,F,e] \longrightarrow [s',\rho',F',v]$ for the core language, shown in Fig. 9. Each reduction rule operates on a concrete program state on the left hand side, where an expression e is associated with a concrete stack s; a sequence of events triggered in the course of its execution ρ, and a future condition F. Given Var is a set of variables, and Val denotes all the concrete values, s and ρ are from the following concrete domains: $s \triangleq Var \rightarrow Val$ and $\rho \triangleq list\ A$. The big-step semantics reduce any given program e to a resulting value v, and when the e terminates, the state is transformed from (s,ρ,F) to (s',ρ',F'). We use $[\![\pi]\!]_s$ to denote that validity of the constraint π with respect to a concrete stack. In particular, when triggering an event $ev(t)$, [OP-Ev] subtracts the event from the current future condition. We use $Pure(s)$ to convert a concrete stack into a pure constraint which contains all the equalities between variables and values. Intuitively, $F \ominus_{lin} \theta \hookrightarrow_\pi F'$ subtracts a trace θ from the given future condition F, resulting in a next state future condition F'. For instance, $\mathcal{F}(free(x)) \ominus_{lin} free(x) \hookrightarrow_{true} \_^*$, and $\mathcal{G}(!\_(x)) \ominus_{lin} free(x) \hookrightarrow_{true} \bot$. Trace subtraction is detailed in Sect. 4.3.

$$\frac{}{[s, \rho, F', \mathbf{assert}_f \, F] \longrightarrow [s, \rho, F' \wedge F, ()]} \, [\text{OP-Assume}] \qquad \frac{A = ev(t) \quad F \ominus_{lin} A \hookrightarrow_{Pure(s)} F'}{[s, \rho, F, ev(t)] \longrightarrow [s, \rho ++ [A], F', ()]} \, [\text{OP-Ev}]$$

$$\frac{}{[s, \rho, F, v] \longrightarrow [s, \rho, F, v]} \, [\text{OP-Val}] \qquad \frac{}{[s, \rho, F, \mathbf{local} \, x] \longrightarrow [s ++ [x], \rho, F, ()]} \, [\text{OP-Local}]$$

$$\frac{[s, \rho, F, e_1] \longrightarrow [s_1, \rho_1, F_1, v_1] \quad [s_1, \rho_1, F_1, e_2] \longrightarrow [s_2, \rho_2, F_2, v_2]}{[s, \rho, F, e_1\,;\,e_2] \longrightarrow [s_2, \rho_2, F_2, v_2]} \, [\text{OP-Let}] \qquad \frac{x \in dom(s) \quad [s, \rho, F, e] \longrightarrow [s_1, \rho_1, F_1, v]}{[s, \rho, F, x := e] \longrightarrow [s_1[x := v], \rho_1, F_1, ()]} \, [\text{OP-Assign}]$$

$$\frac{[s, \rho, F, e_1] \longrightarrow [s', \rho', F', v]}{[s, \rho, F, \mathbf{if} \, true \, e_1 \, e_2] \longrightarrow [s', \rho', F', v]} \, [\text{OP-Cond-T}] \qquad \frac{[s, \rho, F, e_2] \longrightarrow [s', \rho', F', v]}{[s, \rho, F, \mathbf{if} \, false \, e_1 \, e_2] \longrightarrow [s', \rho', F', v]} \, [\text{OP-Cond-F}]$$

$$\frac{[\![\pi]\!]_s = true \quad e' = (e\,;\,\mathbf{while} \, \pi \, \mathbf{do} \, e) \quad [s, \rho, F, e'] \longrightarrow [s', \rho', F', v]}{[s, \rho, F, \mathbf{while} \, \pi \, \mathbf{do} \, e] \longrightarrow [s', \rho', F', v]} \, [\text{OP-While-T}]$$

$$\frac{[\![\pi]\!]_s = false}{[s, \rho, F, \mathbf{while} \, \pi \, \mathbf{do} \, e] \longrightarrow [s, \rho, F, ()]} \, [\text{OP-While-F}] \qquad \frac{f(\overline{y})\{e\} \in \mathcal{P} \quad [s, \rho, F, e\,[\overline{x}/\overline{y}]] \longrightarrow [s', \rho', F', v]}{[s, \rho, F, f(\overline{x})] \longrightarrow [s', \rho', F', v]} \, [\text{OP-Call}]$$

Fig. 9. Big-step instrumented semantic model for the core language

3.2 Semantic Model for Logical Assertions

We define the semantic model for program assertions in Fig. 10. Let $s, \rho \models \pi \wedge \theta$ denote the *models* relation, i.e., the concrete stack s and a concrete sequence of events ρ satisfy the logical state π and the temporal specification θ. Here, [] is an empty sequence and ++ appends two trace sequences. A concrete state s, ρ models a trace predicate if for every element j in the bag B, there exists an instantiated disjunctive case that can be modelled by s, ρ.

$$
\begin{aligned}
s, \rho &\models \pi \wedge \epsilon & \Leftrightarrow \quad & \rho = [] \text{ and } [\![\pi]\!]_s = true \\
s, \rho &\models \pi \wedge (\theta_1 \vee \theta_2) & \Leftrightarrow \quad & s, \rho \models \pi \wedge \theta_1 \text{ or } s, \rho \models \pi \wedge \theta_2 \\
s, \rho &\models \pi \wedge (\theta_1 \wedge \theta_2) & \Leftrightarrow \quad & s, \rho \models \pi \wedge \theta_1 \text{ and } s, \rho \models \pi \wedge \theta_2 \\
s, \rho &\models \pi \wedge (\theta_1 \cdot \theta_2) & \Leftrightarrow \quad & \text{exists } \rho_1 \, \rho_2 \text{ such that } \rho_1 ++ \rho_2 = \rho \text{ and} \\
& & & s, \rho_1 \models \pi \wedge \theta_1, s, \rho_2 \models \pi \wedge \theta_2 \\
s, \rho &\models \pi \wedge \theta^* & \Leftrightarrow \quad & s, \rho \models \pi \wedge \epsilon \text{ or } s, \rho \models \pi \wedge \theta \cdot \theta^* \\
s, \rho &\models \pi \wedge ev(t) & \Leftrightarrow \quad & \text{exists } t' \text{ such that } \rho = [ev(t')] \text{ and } [\![\pi \wedge (t = t')]\!]_s = true \\
s, \rho &\models \pi \wedge \neg ev(t) & \Leftrightarrow \quad & \text{exists } ev', t' \text{ such that } \rho = [ev'(t')] \text{ and} \\
& & & \text{either } ev \neq ev' \text{ or } [\![\pi \wedge (t = t')]\!]_s = false \\
s, \rho &\models \pi \wedge \neg\_(t) & \Leftrightarrow \quad & \text{exists } ev, t' \text{ such that } \rho = [ev(t')] \text{ and } [\![\pi \wedge (t = t')]\!]_s = false \\
s, \rho &\models \pi \wedge \_ & \Leftrightarrow \quad & \text{exists } ev, t \text{ such that } \rho = [ev(t)] \text{ and } [\![\pi]\!]_s = true \\
s, \rho &\models \Lambda_i^B (\bigvee(\pi \wedge \theta)) & \Leftrightarrow \quad & \text{forall } j \in B \text{ such that } s, \rho \models (\bigvee(\pi \wedge \theta))[j/i]
\end{aligned}
$$

Fig. 10. Semantic model of trace specifications.

4 Forward Reasoning

We formalize a set of syntax-directed forward rules in Fig. 11, in the form of Hoare-style triples: $\{\pi\}\ e\ \{\Delta\}$, i.e., a shorthand for $\mathcal{E} \vdash \{(\pi\,;\epsilon\,;\_^*)\}\ e\ \{\Delta\}$, where $\mathcal{E}$ is an environment mapping from functions to their specifications, ϵ represents an empty history trace and $\_^*$ is the default future condition. Under a partial correctness interpretation, which we adopt in this paper, the triple means that if π describes the state before executing e, if e terminates, Δ describes the resulting post-summary.

Rule [FV-Assume-F] interpolates future conditions into program states, thereby constraining subsequent execution behaviors. Rule [FV-Ev] generates one event into the triggered trace, leaving a default future condition, $\_^*$. Rule [FV-Value] updates the result value in the post state, where we use the reserved variable res to denote the (temporarily) result values, leaving a default future condition. Rule [FV-Seq] reasons about e_1 and e_2 in sequence, and implicitly relies on [FV-Disj] to distribute the disjunctions introduced by e_1, and [FV-Struct] to propagate traces and future conditions structurally. Rule [FV-Local] introduces an existential variable x into the state. Rule [FV-Cond] computes the post-summaries from both branches by extending the state with b being true and false, respectively; then, it disjunctively unions the results. Rule [FV-Call] retrieves the verified specification of the callee function, checks the entailment between the current state and the callee's pre-condition, then concludes the instantiated post-summary.

$$\frac{}{\{\pi\}\ \mathbf{assert}_f\ F\ \{(\pi\,;\epsilon\,;F)\}}\ [\text{FV-Assume-F}] \qquad \frac{}{\{\pi\}\ ev(t)\ \{(\pi\,;ev(t)\,;\_^*)\}}\ [\text{FV-Ev}]$$

$$\frac{\pi'=\pi \wedge (res\!=\!v)}{\{\pi\}\ v\ \{(\pi'\,;\epsilon\,;\_^*)\}}\ [\text{FV-Value}] \qquad \frac{\{\pi\}\ e_1\ \{\Delta_1\} \quad \{\Delta_1\}\ e_2\ \{\Delta_2\}}{\{\pi\}\ e_1\,;e_2\ \{\Delta_2\}}\ [\text{FV-Seq}]$$

$$[\text{FV-Local}]\ \frac{\text{fresh}\ x}{\{\pi\}\ local\ x\ \{(\exists x.\,\pi\,;\epsilon\,;F)\}} \qquad \frac{\{\pi \wedge b\}\ e_1\ \{\Delta_1\} \quad \{\pi \wedge \neg b\}\ e_1\ \{\Delta_2\}}{\{\pi\}\ \mathbf{if}\ b\ e_1\ e_2\ \{\Delta_1 \vee \Delta_2\}}\ [\text{FV-Cond}]$$

$$\frac{\text{fresh}\ r \quad f(\overline{y})[\mathbf{req}\!:\pi'\ \mathbf{ens}\!:\Delta] \in \mathcal{E} \quad \pi \leq \pi'[\overline{x}/\overline{y}]}{\{\pi\}\ f(\overline{x})\ \{\exists r.\,\Delta[\overline{x}/\overline{y},r/res]\}}\ [\text{FV-Call}]$$

$$[\text{FV-Assign}]\ \frac{\text{fresh}\ r \quad \{\pi\}\ e\ \{\Delta_1\}}{\{\pi\}\ x:=e\ \{\Delta_1[r/res] \wedge (x\!=\!r)\}} \qquad [\text{FV-While}]\ \frac{\{(\pi \wedge \pi_g\,;\theta\,;F)\}\ e\ \{(\pi\,;\theta\,;F)\}}{\{(\pi\,;\theta\,;F)\}\ \mathbf{while}\ \pi_g\ \mathbf{do}\ e\ \{(\pi \wedge \neg \pi_g\,;\theta\,;F)\}}$$

$$[\text{FV-Disj}]\ \frac{\forall (\pi\,;\theta\,;F) \in \Delta.\ \{(\pi\,;\theta\,;F)\}\ e\ \{\Delta_i\}}{\{\Delta\}\ e\ \{\bigvee \Delta_i\}} \qquad [\text{FV-Struct}]\ \frac{\{\pi\}\ e\ \{\Delta\} \quad \forall (\pi'\,;\theta_1\,;F_1) \in \Delta.\ F \ominus \theta_1 \hookrightarrow_{\pi'} F'}{\{(\pi\,;\theta\,;F)\}\ e\ \{\bigvee (\pi'\,;(\theta \cdot \theta_1)\,;(F' \wedge F_1))\}}$$

$$\frac{\{\pi_3\}\ e\ \{(\pi_4\,;\theta'\,;F')\} \quad \pi_1 \leq \pi_3 \quad \pi_4 \leq \pi_2 \quad \theta' \sqsubseteq_{\pi_4} \theta \quad F \sqsubseteq_{\pi_4} F'}{\{\pi_1\}\ e\ \{(\pi_2\,;\theta\,;F)\}}\ [\text{FV-Conseq}]$$

Fig. 11. Forward verification and inference rules.

Rule [FV-Assign] derives the post-summary Δ_1 for e by introducing a fresh variable r to represent Δ_1's return values, substituting all occurrences of res with r, and binding x and r in the final post-summary. In [FV-While], the initial state $(\pi \,;\, \theta \,;\, F)$ serves as a loop invariant, and executing the loop body must re-establish the loop invariant under the same trace and future conditions. We present a trace invariant synthesis procedure in Sect. 4.1.

Furthermore, [FV-Disj] distributes the disjunctive tuples from the left-hand side and unions their independent reasoning results. Rule [FV-Struct] is a structural rule designed to handle arbitrary tuples from the left-hand side. Given any history traces θ and context future conditions F, [FV-Struct] performs two key operations: it concatenates the extended traces to the history trace $(\theta \cdot \theta_1)$; and propagates the subtracted F, represented as $F \ominus \theta_1 \hookrightarrow_\pi F'$, to be part of the post-summary. Intuitively, this rule concludes a conjunctive future condition, i.e., $F' \wedge F_1$, which encompasses both the future condition F_1 obtained by executing e and the future condition propagated from the context F_1. Lastly, Rule [FV-Conseq] soundly weakens the post-summaries by weakening postconditions (the covariant) and strengthening pre/future-conditions (the contravariants).

Entailment Checking and Trace Subtraction. Pure constraints entailment $(\pi \leq \pi')$ are discharged by the Z3 [8] solver. Trace inclusions $(\theta_1 \sqsubseteq_\pi \theta_2)$ are discharged by a term rewriting system (TRS), which is extended from a known solution [5] for solving inequalities between regular expressions, detailed in Sect. 4.2. Trace subtraction from future conditions $(F \ominus \theta \hookrightarrow_\pi F')$ propagates the context future condition concerning specific execution traces, detailed in Sect. 4.3. Overall, our main technical contributions are: extending the TRS to accommodate our new event types, and developing novel trace subtraction rules.

Specification Inference for Function Definition. Given a set of primitive specifications, our goal is to develop a verification system that is *as automated as possible*, where the specification for each function definition is inferred compositionally. The top-level inference process is illustrated in [FV-Func]. The environment $\mathcal{E}$ includes both primitive specifications and the specifications inferred so far. For each function definition $f(\overline{x}) \, \{e\}$ in the given program, we derive the specification for e using the forward rules in Fig. 11 and then reason the rest of the program with the extended environment $\mathcal{E}'$.

$$\frac{\mathcal{E} \vdash \{\pi'\} \; e \; \{\Delta\} \quad \forall (\pi \,;\, \theta \,;\, F) \in \Delta. \quad \delta(F_\exists) = true}{\mathcal{E} \vdash f(\overline{x}) \, \{e\} \,;\, \mathcal{P}} \quad \text{[FV-Func]}$$

For each tuple in e's post-summary Δ, we check whether the empty trace satisfy the future conditions involving existential variables, i.e., $F_\exists$, as the lifetime of existential variables ends when the function concludes. The $F_\exists$ is computed from F by replacing all events related to universally quantified variables – including the formal arguments $\overline{x}$ and the return value res – into wildcards "_", and the resulting future condition thus retains only the constraints on existential variables. For example, in Fig. 5, the memory leak error upon the usage of *arr* is detected in *main* instead of *mallocN*, as *arr* is universally quantified in *mallocN*, but existential quantified in *main*. The Nullable function (cf. Definition 1) returns a Boolean value indicating if θ permits the empty trace.

Definition 1 (Nullable). *Given any sequence θ, we recursively define $\delta(\theta)$:*

$$\delta(\theta_1 \cdot \theta_2) = \delta(\theta_1) \wedge \delta(\theta_2) \qquad \delta(\theta_1 \vee \theta_2) = \delta(\theta_1) \vee \delta(\theta_2) \qquad \delta(\theta_1 \wedge \theta_2) = \delta(\theta_1) \wedge \delta(\theta_2)$$

$$\delta(\Lambda_i^B(\bigvee(\pi \wedge \theta))) = \exists \theta. \ (\delta(\theta) = true) \qquad \delta(\epsilon) = \delta(\theta^\star) = true \qquad \delta(\bot) = \delta(A) = false$$

4.1 Trace Invariant Synthesis

A key challenge in automating the verification lies in inferring trace invariants – specifically, given a loop expression "**while** π_g **do** e", determining the initial state $(\pi\,;\theta\,;F)$, deployed in [FV-While]. The trace invariant synthesis process is outlined in Algorithm 1. It takes a loop statement as input and either outputs a valid invariant or triggers a verification failure – indicating that the loop invariants must be provided manually.

At lines 1–2, it derives the specification for e and obtains a fresh iterator i. Then deploys the bag bounds generation function (Definition 2) to produce a set of candidate bags. For each candidate bag B, lines 4-5 construct the trace and future condition predicates respectively. If there exists an invariant that can be re-established after one iteration of the loop body (line 6), it is deemed valid. Otherwise, the synthesis fails and the verification could not proceed due to the absence of trace invariants.

Algorithm 1. Loop Invariant Synthesis

Require: A loop: **while** π_g **do** e
Ensure: A Loop Invariants or Failure
1: $\{\pi'\}\ e\ \{\bigvee(\pi\,;\theta\,;F)\}$
2: **fresh** i
3: **for all** $B \in \mathcal{BB}(\pi_g)$ **do**
4: $\quad \theta \leftarrow \Lambda_i^B(\bigvee(\pi \wedge \theta))$
5: $\quad F \leftarrow \Lambda_i^B(\bigvee(\pi \wedge F))$
6: $\quad$ **if** $\{(\pi' \wedge \pi_g\,;\theta\,;F)\}\ e\ \{(\pi'\,;\theta\,;F)\}$
7: $\quad$ **then return** $(\pi'\,;\theta\,;F)$
8: **end for**
9: **return** Unknown Loop Invariant

Definition 2 (Bag Bounds Generation). *For any loop guard π, we propagate a set of candidate bag bounds using $\mathcal{BB}(\pi)$, for constructing the trace predicates:*

$$\mathcal{BB}(t_1 < t_2) = \{[0..t_1), \ldots\} \qquad \mathcal{BB}(\pi_1 \wedge \pi_2) = \mathcal{BB}(\pi_1) \cup \mathcal{BB}(\pi_2)$$
$$\mathcal{BB}(t_1 \leq t_2) = \mathcal{BB}(t_1 < (t_2+1)) \qquad \mathcal{BB}(t_1 > t_2) = \mathcal{BB}(t_2 < t_1) \qquad \mathcal{BB}(t_1 \geq t_2) = \mathcal{BB}(t_2 \leq t_1)$$

In Definition 2, the base case is generating the candidate bags for $t_1 < t_2$ while the remaining cases are derived by reduction to the base case. For example,

Fig. 12 demonstrates the verification process for the loop in *mallocN* (Fig. 5). At line 3, Algorithm 1 generates an invariant where i serves as the iterator and "$[0..i)$" denotes the bag representation. The verification then establishes that this invariant holds through each loop iteration specifically, the program states after lines 3 and 5 are isomorphic with respect to the iterator's value. The final program state is derived by conjoining with the negated loop guard, i.e., $(i=n)$.

This process employs heuristics and is inherently incomplete: it may fail to capture the complete bag range or the precise iterator (which can be improved by incorporating the loop iterator's initial value). Nevertheless, the verification remains sound, as [FV-While] only succeeds when valid invariants are provided.

```
      3. while (i < n){
```
$\{(\exists i.\ true\ ;\ pred_t([0..i), i)\ ;\ pred_f([0..i), i))\}$
```
      4.    arr[i] = malloc(4);
```
$\{(\exists i.\ true\ ;\ pred_t([0..i+1), i)\ ;\ pred_f([0..i+1), i))\}$
```
      5.    i = i+1;
```
$\{(\exists i.\ true\ ;\ pred_t([0..i+1), i+1)\ ;\ pred_f([0..i+1), i+1))\}$
```
      6. }
```
$\{(\exists i.\ i\!=\!n\ ;\ pred_t([0..i))\ ;\ pred_f([0..i)))\} \rightsquigarrow \{(\exists i.\ true\ ;\ pred_t([0..n))\ ;\ pred_f([0..n)))\}$

Fig. 12. Outlining the reasoning for the loop in Fig. 5.

4.2 Trace Inclusion

As shown in Fig. 13, we use $(\mathcal{H} \vdash \theta_1 \sqsubseteq_\pi \theta_2)$ to denote the inclusion between two traces, where $\mathcal{H}$ contains a set of proof hypotheses, and when omitted it is initialized with $\{\}$. [Inc-Disprove] disproves the inclusions when the antecedent is nullable (containing the empty trace ϵ), while the consequent is not. [Inc-Reoccur] proves an inclusion by leveraging existing hypotheses in the proof context $\mathcal{H}$ that soundly justify the current goal. [Inc-Unfold] serves as the inductive step, unfolding inclusions – proof of the original inclusion succeeds if all derivative inclusions succeed. Termination of the rewriting is guaranteed because the set of derivatives to be considered is finite, and possible cycles are detected via memorization ([Inc-Reoccur]). We define the soundness of these rules in Theorem 1.

$$[\text{Inc-Disprove}] \quad \frac{\delta(\theta_1) \wedge \neg\delta(\theta_2)}{\mathcal{H} \vdash \theta_1 \not\sqsubseteq_\pi \theta_2} \qquad [\text{Inc-Reoccur}] \quad \frac{(\theta_1 \sqsubseteq_\pi \theta_2) \in \mathcal{H}}{\mathcal{H} \vdash \theta_1 \sqsubseteq_\pi \theta_2} \qquad [\text{Inc-Unfold}] \quad \frac{\forall A \in \mathit{fst}(\theta_1).\ (\theta_1 \sqsubseteq_\pi \theta_2) ,\!+\!\!+ \mathcal{H} \vdash \mathcal{D}_A^\pi(\theta_1) \sqsubseteq_\pi \mathcal{D}_A^\pi(\theta_2)}{\mathcal{H} \vdash \theta_1 \sqsubseteq_\pi \theta_2}$$

Fig. 13. Trace inclusion checking rules.

To facilitate these inclusion rules, we provide the definitions of the deployed auxiliary functions: *Nullable* (δ) at Definition 1, *First* (*fst*) at Definition 3, and

Derivative ($\mathcal{D}_A^\pi(\theta)$) at Definition 4. Informally, the First function $fst(\theta)$ computes a set of possible initial events from θ. The Derivative function $\mathcal{D}_A^\pi(\theta)$ eliminates an event A from the head of θ and returns what remains.

Definition 3 (First). *Let $fst(\theta)$ be the set of initial events derivable from θ.*

$$fst(\bot) = fst(\epsilon) = \{\} \quad fst(A) = \{A\} \quad fst(\theta_1 \vee \theta_2) = fst(\theta_1) \cup fst(\theta_2) \quad fst(\theta^\star) = fst(\theta)$$

$$fst(\theta_1 \wedge \theta_2) = fst(\theta_1) \cap fst(\theta_2) \quad fst(\theta_1 \cdot \theta_2) = \begin{cases} fst(\theta_1) \cup fst(\theta_2) & \text{if } \delta(\theta_1) = true \\ fst(\theta_1) & \text{if } \delta(\theta_1) = false \end{cases}$$

Definition 4 (Derivative). *The partial derivative $\mathcal{D}_A^\pi(\theta)$ eliminates an event A from the head of a trace θ, defined as follows:*

$$\mathcal{D}_A^\pi(\bot) = \mathcal{D}_A^\pi(\epsilon) = \bot \quad \mathcal{D}_A^\pi(\theta_1 \wedge \theta_2) = \mathcal{D}_A^\pi(\theta_1) \wedge \mathcal{D}_A^\pi(\theta_2) \quad \mathcal{D}_A^\pi(\theta_1 \vee \theta_2) = \mathcal{D}_A^\pi(\theta_1) \vee \mathcal{D}_A^\pi(\theta_2)$$

$$\mathcal{D}_A^\pi(\theta^\star) = \mathcal{D}_A^\pi(\theta) \cdot \theta^\star \quad \mathcal{D}_A^\pi(\theta_1 \cdot \theta_2) = \begin{cases} (\mathcal{D}_A^\pi(\theta_1) \cdot \theta_2) \vee \mathcal{D}_A^\pi(\theta_2) & \text{if } \delta(\theta_1) = true \\ \mathcal{D}_A^\pi(\theta_1) \cdot \theta_2 & \text{if } \delta(\theta_1) = false \end{cases}$$

Definition 5 serves as the base case for Definition 4, computing the derivatives between two events. While these auxiliary functions were originally designed to solve inequalities between regular expressions, they only supported cases where events were simple alphabets [5], with derivatives computed via lexical comparison. In our work, events could be trace predicates or parameterized with program variables. To handle such cases, we thus extend the Derivative function with pure constraints. In Definition 5, the definition of event derivatives adheres strictly to the semantic model (cf. Figure 10). Notice that A takes one of two forms: a positive event "$ev(t)$", or a trace predicate, as they are the only cases that are derivable from the program executions. When both A and B are trace predicates, they must first be normalized into the same bag "B" and then processed using the trace subtraction operator (detailed in Sect. 4.3).

Definition 5 (Derivative for Events). *Given any two events A, B, the derivative of B with respect to A, i.e., $\mathcal{D}_A^\pi(B)$ is defined as follows: ($\bot$ for the unmentioned scenarios)*

$$\mathcal{D}_{ev(t)}^\pi(ev(t')) = \begin{cases} \epsilon & \text{if } \pi \Rightarrow (t=t') \\ \bot & \text{otherwise} \end{cases} \quad \mathcal{D}_{ev(t)}^\pi(\neg\_(t')) = \begin{cases} \epsilon & \text{if } \pi \not\Rightarrow (t=t') \\ \bot & \text{otherwise} \end{cases}$$

$$\mathcal{D}_{ev(t)}^\pi(\neg ev'(t')) = \begin{cases} \bot & \text{if } ev = ev' \text{ and } \pi \leq (t=t') \\ \epsilon & \text{otherwise} \end{cases}$$

$$\mathcal{D}_{ev(t)}^\pi(\_) = \epsilon \quad \mathcal{D}_{ev(t)}^{\pi'}(\Lambda_i^B(\ldots)) = \Lambda_i^B(\ldots)$$

$$\mathcal{D}_{\Lambda_i^B(\bigvee(\pi_2 \wedge \theta_2))}^{\pi'}(\Lambda_i^B(\bigvee(\pi_1 \wedge \theta_1))) = \Lambda_i^B(\bigvee(\pi_1 \wedge \pi_2 \wedge \theta')) \text{ where } \theta_1 \ominus \theta_2 \hookrightarrow_{\pi'} \theta'$$

Theorem 1 (Soundness of Trace Inclusion). *For all π, θ_1, θ_2, s and ρ, given $\theta_1 \sqsubseteq_\pi \theta_2$, it means that if $s, \rho \models \pi \wedge \theta_1$, then $s, \rho \models \pi \wedge \theta_2$.*
Proof. By induction on the derivation of $\theta_1 \sqsubseteq_\pi \theta_2$.

4.3 Subtracting Traces from Future Conditions

As shown in Fig. 14, we use $F \ominus \theta \hookrightarrow_\pi F'$ to denote the subtraction of the trace θ from the given future condition F, resulting in a "left-over" future condition F', which we call a *residue*. Rule [TS-Base] captures the base case where the trace to subtract is an empty trace, leaving the future condition unchanged. Rule [TS-Bot] handles the case where the subtracted trace is $\bot$, leading to false future conditions. Rule [TS-Ind] disjunctively unions all the subtraction results from the derivatives. Rule [TS-Conseq] allows for strengthening the subtraction residues and weakening the input future conditions. Rule [TS-Trans] captures the case where we can strengthen the subtracted trace. We define and prove the soundness of these rules in Theorem 2, which indicates that in a sound subtraction, the residue can only be strengthened.

$$[\text{TS-Base}] \quad \frac{}{F \ominus \epsilon \hookrightarrow_\pi \theta} \qquad [\text{TS-Bot}] \quad \frac{}{F \ominus \bot \hookrightarrow_\pi \bot} \qquad \frac{\forall A \in \mathit{fst}(\theta_2). \; \mathcal{D}_A^\pi(\theta_1) \ominus \mathcal{D}_A^\pi(\theta_2) \hookrightarrow_\pi \theta_i}{\theta_1 \ominus \theta_2 \hookrightarrow_\pi \bigvee \theta_i} \; [\text{TS-Ind}]$$

$$\frac{F_3 \ominus \theta \hookrightarrow_\pi F_4 \quad F_3 \sqsubseteq_\pi F_1 \quad F_2 \sqsubseteq_\pi F_4}{F_1 \ominus \theta \hookrightarrow_\pi F_2} \; [\text{TS-Conseq}] \qquad \frac{F_1 \ominus \theta \hookrightarrow_\pi F_2 \quad \theta' \sqsubseteq_\pi \theta}{F_1 \ominus \theta' \hookrightarrow_\pi F_2} \; [\text{TS-Trans}]$$

Fig. 14. Trace subtraction rules.

Theorem 2 (Soundness of Trace Subtraction). *For all π, F, F', θ, s and ρ, given $F \ominus \theta \hookrightarrow_\pi F'$ it means that if $s, \rho \models \pi \wedge (\theta \cdot F')$ then $s, \rho \models \pi \wedge F$.*

Proof. By induction on the derivation of $F \ominus \theta \hookrightarrow_\pi F'$.

4.4 Soundness of Forward Reasoning

We here define the soundness of the forward rules and highlight the key lemmas. Theorem 3 presents the soundness for the generalized forward rules, where rules like $\{\pi\} \; e \; \{\Delta\}$ are generalized into the form of $\{(\pi \,;\, \epsilon \,;\, \_^*)\} \; e \; \{\Delta\}$. The soundness states that for any given expression e, starting from a concrete model which satisfies the pre-state, when e evaluates to a value v, the resulting concrete model satisfies one of the concluded post-summaries, which guarantees that all the forward rules soundly over-approximating e's behavior and strengthening the final future conditions.

Theorem 3 (Soundness of the Generalised Forward Rules). *For all e, π, θ_1, F, F', s_1, s_2, ρ_1, ρ_2, v, given $\{(\pi \,;\, \theta_1 \,;\, F)\} \; e \; \{\Delta\}$, $[s_1, \rho_1, F, e] \longrightarrow [s_2, \rho_2, F', v]$, and $s_1, \rho_1 \models \pi \wedge \theta_1$, there exists $(\pi' \,;\, \theta_2 \,;\, F'') \in \Delta$ such that $(s_2 \mathbin{{+}\mkern-10mu{+}} \mathit{res} = v)$, $\rho_2 \models \pi' \wedge \theta_2$ and $F'' \sqsubseteq_{\pi'} F'$.*

Proof. By induction on the structure of e, and applying Lemma 1 and Lemma 2 when proving the sequencing rule [FV-Seq] and the structural rule [FV-Struct].

Lemma 1 (Strengthening the Future Conditions from the Instrumented Semantics). For all, s_1, s_2, ρ_1, ρ_2, F_1, F_2, F_3, v, given $[s_1, \rho_1, F_1, e] \longrightarrow [s_2, \rho_2, F_2, v]$ and $F_3 \sqsubseteq_{Pure(s_1)} F_1$, there exists F_4, such that, $[s_1, \rho_1, F_3, e] \longrightarrow [s_2, \rho_2, F_4, v]$ and $F_4 \sqsubseteq_{Pure(s_2)} F_2$.

Proof. By induction on $[s_1, \rho_1, F_1, e] \longrightarrow [s_2, \rho_2, F_2, v]$.

Lemma 2 (Approximating the Concrete Trace Subtraction). For all F_1, θ, F_2, s, ρ, given $F_1 \ominus \theta \hookrightarrow_\pi F_2$ and $s, \rho \models \pi \wedge \theta$, then exists F_3 such that $F_1 \ominus_{lin} \rho \hookrightarrow_{Pure(s)} F_3$ and $F_2 \sqsubseteq_{Pure(s)} F_3$.

Proof. By induction on $F_1 \ominus \theta \hookrightarrow_\pi F_2$.

Lemma 1 states that in the instrumented semantics, starting with a stronger future condition leads to stronger resulting future conditions. In Lemma 2, we use $\ominus_{lin}$ to denote subtracting a linear sequence of events ρ from a given future condition without any approximation. It states that the trace subtraction $\ominus$ introduces approximation and results in stronger residues.

Table 1. Selected propositions for reasoning future conditions

$$\theta_1 \wedge \theta_2 \leftrightarrow \theta_2 \wedge \theta_1 \quad (1) \qquad \theta_1 \wedge (\theta_2 \wedge \theta_3) \leftrightarrow (\theta_1 \wedge \theta_2) \wedge \theta_3 \quad (2)$$
$$\bot \cdot \theta = \theta \cdot \bot \rightarrow \bot \quad (3) \qquad (\theta_1 \cdot \theta_2 \neq \bot) \rightarrow (\theta_1 \neq \bot) \wedge (\theta_2 \neq \bot) \quad (4)$$
$$\_^* \sqsubseteq_\pi \theta \rightarrow (\theta = \_^*) \quad (5) \qquad (\theta_1 \wedge \theta_2 \neq \bot) \rightarrow (\theta_1 \neq \bot) \wedge (\theta_2 \neq \bot) \quad (6)$$
$$(\_^* \ominus A \hookrightarrow_\pi \theta) \rightarrow (\theta = \_^*) \quad (7) \qquad \theta_1 \sqsubseteq_\pi \theta_2 \rightarrow (\theta_2 \sqsubseteq_\pi \theta_3 \rightarrow \theta_1 \sqsubseteq_\pi \theta_3) \quad (8)$$
$$(\_^* \ominus_{lin} A \hookrightarrow_\pi \theta) \rightarrow (\theta = \_^*) \quad (9) \qquad \Lambda_i^{B_1 \cup B_2}(\ldots) \leftrightarrow \Lambda_i^{B_1}(\ldots) \wedge \Lambda_i^{B_2}(\ldots) \quad (10)$$
$$\Lambda_i^B(\bigvee(\pi \wedge \_^*)) \rightarrow \_^* \quad (11) \qquad \Lambda_i^{\{v\}}(\bigvee(\pi \wedge \theta)) \rightarrow (\bigvee(\pi \wedge \theta))[v/i] \quad (12)$$

Additionally, Table 1 presents a set of propositions essential for improving completeness. For example, the trace subtraction for the predicate in Fig. 7 is performed after applying propositions (10) and (12), detailed in Fig. 15.

$$pred_f([0..5), arr) \ominus free(arr[0]) \qquad (Table\,1\text{-}10)$$
$$\hookrightarrow_{true} (pred_f(0, arr) \wedge pred_f([1..5), arr)) \ominus free(arr[0]) \qquad (Table\,1\text{-}11)$$
$$\hookrightarrow_{true} (\mathcal{F}(free(arr[0])) \ominus free(arr[0])) \wedge pred_f([1..5), arr) \qquad (Definition\,4, 5)$$
$$\hookrightarrow_{true} \_^* \wedge pred_f([1..5), arr) \quad \hookrightarrow_{true} \quad pred_f([1..5), arr)$$

Fig. 15. Trace subtraction example for predicates.

5 Evaluation and Case Studies

We formalize the soundness proofs presented in this work using Coq, publicly available from our artifact [18]. The Coq development comprises approximately 2,300 lines of code (LoC). We also prototype our system into an automated verification tool, implemented in 3,600 LoC of OCaml, demonstrating its applicability in verifying real-world programs. Experiments were done on a MacBook with a 2.6 GHz 6-Core Intel i7 processor. The source code and the evaluation benchmark are openly accessible [18].

Experiment Setup. Table 2 categorizes APIs by functionality and specifies the future conditions required for their safe usage. The table organizes these APIs into six categories (1–6), covering operations such as file I/O, thread synchronization, memory management, and more. These conditions were manually derived from official documentation and common usage patterns. In particular, we treat the *unchecked return value* (URV) and *null-pointer dereference* (NPD) vulnerabilities to be a critical use case for future conditions. URVs and NPDs occur when a program fails to validate the return value of a function, potentially leading to crashes or undefined behavior. To mitigate such risks, developers must ensure that all function return values are checked and handled appropriately.

Table 2. Selected APIs with their specifications in different usage contexts

Category	Example APIs	Future Conditions
1. File Ops	fopen, open fclose, close	Finally to close the file descriptor Globally do not access the file descriptor Read-only files cannot be written to
2. Threads	pthread_create pthread_mutex_lock	Finally to pthread_join or detach the thread Finally to pthread_mutex_unlock
3. Memory	free malloc realloc	Globally do not access the pointer Finally free the new pointer Globally the old pointer is not accessed & finally free the new pointer
4. Sockets	socket	Finally to close the socket
5. Database	sqlite3_open	Finally to sqlite3_close the connection
6. URV/NPD	fgets, gethostbyaddr	Check the return value immediately after calls

Experimental Results. Our evaluation uses real-world C programs sourced from: (i) the CWE database (containing diverse vulnerability types); (ii) API usage tutorials (demonstrating correct practices); and (iii) GitHub repositories (featuring real-world usage of critical APIs). The benchmark contains 51

Table 3. Experimental Results

Category	LoC	PrimS	InferredS	InferredInv	Report/Exp.	Time(s)
1	675	8	30	7	14/12	13.66
2	330	4	25	1	4/4	0.49
3	409	6	30	12	26/24	6.60
4	103	2	6	1	3/3	0.50
5	109	4	6	0	4/4	0.50
6	95	10	4	0	4/4	0.03
Total	1721	34	101	21	55/51	21.78

manually verified API misuse violations, serving as ground truth for evaluation. Results are summarized in Table 3, with the following metrics: **PrimS** is the number of primitive specifications (manually provided, avg. 4.5 LoC/spec), **InferredS** is the number of inferred specifications (equals to the number of analyzed function declarations), **InferredInv** is the number of inferred trace invariants, **Report/Exp.** stands for reported violations/ground truth violations, and **Time** records the total verification time in seconds. Our evaluation spans 1721 LoC across six distinct categories, with verification and inference applied to 101 functions. The tool reports 55 violations, including all 51 manually verified true positives and 4 false positives (incorrectly flagged safe code). Total verification time is 21.78 s, with processing time scaling proportionally to the program length and the number of primitive specifications.

```
1 void false_positive1() {
2   int** ptr1= malloc(4);
3   int*  ptr2= malloc(4);
4   *ptr1 = ptr2;
5   free(*ptr1);
6   free(ptr1); }
7 False positive: Memory Leak!
```

```
1 void false_positive2
2       (const char* filename) {
3   int r = unlink(filename);
4   if (r == 0) {
5     int fd=fopen(filename,"r");
6     assert(fd == NULL);}}
7 False positive: Unclosed File!
```

Fig. 16. False positive example for (ii).

Fig. 17. False positive example for (iii).

Expressiveness Limitations. The observed false positives arise from three limitations: (i) trace invariant inference fails under non-structured control flow, e.g., goto statements; (ii) incomplete modeling for memory usage; and (iii) limited to the local view of the file system. We next illustrate (ii) and (iii) with concrete examples. As shown in Fig. 16, the pointer ptr1 points to the address of ptr2 (assigned at line 4). In this code, freeing *ptr1 (the content of ptr1) and then ptr1 itself is safe and correctly avoids memory leaks. However, the deployed pure arithmetic logic fails to recognize the *points-to* relationship established at line 4. As a result, it incorrectly reports a memory leak, suggesting that ptr2 is never freed – even though it is freed via *ptr1. This can be mitigated by extending the basic logic with *points-to* relations. As demonstrated in Fig. 17, the unlink function removes a file from the filesystem when it returns 0. Consequently, the subsequent call to fopen at line 5 will always fail (returning NULL), making the code correct – the assertion at line 6 will always succeeds. However, because our tool does not model unlink's side effects – specifically, that future fopen calls on the same filename must fail – it incorrectly reports a file descriptor leak. Tracking external system for file states would resolve this limitation. Despite these limitations, our framework remains the first *sound* verification system capable of detecting a broad range of violations via temporal logic encoding – providing a foundation for these aforementioned extensions.

```
1. int *foo(struct st *p){
2.    int *q;
```
$\{\exists q.\ true\ ;\ \epsilon\ ;\ \_^*\}$
```
3.    if (p->flag) q = malloc(1);     [FV-Call][FV-Assign][FV-Cond][FV-Struct]
```
$\{\exists q,l.\ (p{\rightarrow}\mathit{flag}) \wedge q{=}l\ ;\ \mathit{malloc}(l)\ ;\ \mathcal{F}\,(\mathit{free}(l))\}$
```
4.    else q = p->f;                  [FV-Assign][FV-Cond][FV-Struct]
```
$\{\exists q.\ \neg(p{\rightarrow}\mathit{flag}) \wedge q{=}(p{\rightarrow}f)\ ;\ \epsilon\ ;\ \_^*\}$
```
5.    return q;}                      [FV-Value][FV-Cond][FV-Struct][FV-Seq]
```
$\{\exists l.\ (p{\rightarrow}\mathit{flag}) \wedge \mathit{res}{=}l\ ;\ \mathit{malloc}(l)\ ;\ \mathcal{F}\,(\mathit{free}(l))\ \vee\ \neg(p{\rightarrow}\mathit{flag}) \wedge \mathit{res}{=}(p{\rightarrow}f)\ ;\ \epsilon\ ;\ \_^*\ \}$

```
6. int main(){
7.    struct st p; int *q;
```
$\{\exists p,q.\ true\ ;\ \epsilon\ ;\ \_^*\}$
```
8.    p.f = malloc(1);                [FV-Call][FV-Assign][FV-Struct]
```
$\{\exists p,q,l.\ p.f{=}l\ ;\ \mathit{malloc}(l)\ ;\ \mathcal{F}\,(\mathit{free}(l))\}$
```
9.    q = foo(&p);                    [FV-Call][FV-Assign][FV-Struct][FV-Seq]
```
$\{\exists p,q,l,l_1.\ (p.\mathit{flag}) \wedge p.f{=}l \wedge q{=}l_1\ ;\ \mathit{malloc}(l) \cdot \mathit{malloc}(l_1)\ ;\ \mathcal{F}\,(\mathit{free}(l)) \wedge \mathcal{F}\,(\mathit{free}(l_1))$
$\vee\ \exists p,q,l.\ \neg(p.\mathit{flag}) \wedge q{=}p.f \wedge p.f{=}l\ ;\ \mathit{malloc}(l)\ ;\ \mathcal{F}\,(\mathit{free}(l))\}$
```
10.   free(q);                        [FV-Call][FV-Struct][FV-Seq]
```
$\{\exists p,q,l,l_1.\ (p.\mathit{flag}) \wedge p.f{=}l \wedge q{=}l_1\ ;\ \mathit{malloc}(l) \cdot \mathit{malloc}(l_1) \cdot \mathit{free}(l_1)\ ;\ \mathcal{F}\,(\mathit{free}(l)) \wedge \mathcal{G}\,(!\_(l_1))$
$\vee\ \exists p,q,l.\ \neg(p.\mathit{flag}) \wedge q{=}p.f \wedge p.f{=}l\ ;\ \mathit{malloc}(l) \cdot \mathit{free}(l)\ ;\ \mathcal{G}\,(!\_(l))\}$
```
11.   free(p.f); }                    [FV-Call][FV-Struct][FV-Seq]
```
$\{\exists p,q,l,l_1.\ (p.\mathit{flag}) \wedge p.f{=}l\ ;\ \mathit{malloc}(l) \cdot \mathit{malloc}(l_1) \cdot \mathit{free}(l_1) \cdot \mathit{free}(l)\ ;\ \mathcal{G}\,(!\_(l)) \wedge \mathcal{G}\,(!\_(l_1))$
$\vee\ \exists p,q,l.\ \neg(p.\mathit{flag}) \wedge q{=}p.f \wedge p.f{=}l\ ;\ \mathit{malloc}(l) \cdot \mathit{free}(l) \cdot \mathit{free}(l)\ ;\ \bot\quad \Longleftarrow\ \text{\ding{55}}\}$

Fig. 18. Inter-procedural analysis for detecting a conditional double free violation.

Case Study: Inter-procedural Analysis and Conditional Violation. Figure 18 presents a non-trivial double-free example, drawn from prior works [13,23]. The *foo* function takes a pointer p and returns either a newly allocated pointer or the existing pointer $p{\rightarrow}f$, based on the value of $p{\rightarrow}\mathit{flag}$. In *main* function, a local *st* structure is created, memory is allocated for $p.f$, and foo is called. The potential double-free occurs because: if $p.\mathit{flag}$ is false, q and $p.f$ point to the same memory (line 4). Both q and $p.f$ are then freed (lines 10, 11), causing a double-free when $p.flag$ was false (line 11). This example is non-trivial because it requires a precise inter-procedural analysis and path sensitivity.

The verification proceeds as follows: Lines 2 and 7 initialize the program states using existentially quantified variables. Lines 3 and 4 reason about the two branches of the conditional and creates the existential variable l for the newly allocated heap address. By integrating the results, line 5 leads to a disjunctive post-summary which says that when $p{\to}flag$ is true, the program returns a newly allocated heap location l, and there is a future condition to finally free l; when $p{\to}flag$ is false, it returns $p{\to}f$ and have no meaningful future conditions.

When calling the function foo, line 9 retrieves its specification (obtained after line 5), renames all its existential variables using fresh variables, and composes the instantiated specification into the current summaries. In line 10, under the condition $\neg(p.flag)$, freeing q updates the propagated future conditions from $\mathcal{F}(free(l))$ to $\mathcal{G}(!\_(l))$. Subsequently, in line 11, when freeing $p.f$, it detects the double free under the pure constraint $\pi = (\exists p, q, l.\, \neg(p.flag) \wedge q = p.f \wedge p.f = l)$—the following trace subtraction step results in $false$: $\mathcal{G}(!\_(l)) \ominus free(p.f) \hookrightarrow_\pi \bot$.

6 Related Work

Statically Checked Contracts. Typestate systems [24], recently revisited in various forms [2,10,17,26], may also be used to a similar outcome as future conditions. These systems associate an object's state with its type, enforcing valid operation sequences based on that state, which is useful in object-oriented programming. Both typestates and future conditions model the correct execution order of operations on entities. However, typestates operate on objects, while future conditions operate on program variables. Additionally, implementing typestate systems often requires extensive boilerplate code. For instance, developers must meticulously define state transitions in a global view and manage associated types, increasing complexity in code maintenance and readability. In contrast, future conditions offer a more concise and modular way to specify and verify temporal properties without requiring explicit global state transitions. Their modularity stems from the fact that each future condition encapsulates temporal constraints specific to its associated function, independent of any global state.

Rust's type system [1] primarily enforces memory safety (ownership, borrowing, lifetimes), while the *typestate pattern* extends this by encoding state transitions into the type system, ensuring operations are only valid in certain states (e.g., a File<Open> can be read, but a File<Closed> cannot). However, typestates do not explicitly handle temporal properties (e.g., "eventually, this operation must happen"). Such properties must instead be verified separately against the global state transitions. Our approach unifies and extends both typestate systems and Rust's type system by: encoding memory safety using LTL formulas and enabling temporal reasoning (e.g., "this resource remains valid until condition π holds") alongside memory safety. Lastly, effect systems are also closely related, as they constrain which effects can be performed. While ordinary effect systems do not consider the order of effects, sequential effect systems [12,22,25] do. However, they follow the form of pre-/post-conditions, which is inadequate for describing future conditions in a modular style.

Dynamically Checked Contracts. Trace contracts [16] are for specifying and verifying properties of sequences of function calls and returns in the Racket programming language. They allow developers to define predicates over the sequence of values that flow through function calls, enabling the detection of violations of expected behaviors across multiple function invocations. By monitoring programs at run time, trace contracts are able to take advantage of the precision that run-time checking offers, which possibly goes beyond statically decidable properties. Similar to typestate systems, trace contracts describes a global view of the protocols, while future conditions provide a more modular and local view of each effectful operation. Moreover, apart from the run-time overhead and increased resource consumption, trace contracts has limited expressiveness for imperative assignments and effectful loops, which are now supported in our verification framework.

Term Rewriting Regular Expressions. Given two regular expressions θ_1 and θ_2, inclusion ($\theta_1 \sqsubseteq \theta_2$) is typically decided using a term rewriting system (TRS), which iteratively checks derivatives [4]. This process terminates because the set of derivatives is finite, and cycles are efficiently detected using memorization (Γ). Prior works [3,6,9,11,19–22] show that TRSs can be more efficient than automata-based techniques, as it avoids costly translations and enables early rejection of invalid inclusions. In this work, we extend derivative-based techniques to trace subtraction. Rather than checking for inclusion, our approach focuses on computing the future condition obligations for the next states.

Bug Finding at Scale. While Pulse [14] (based entirely on separation logic) and ProveNFix [23] (grounded in temporal logic) both use specification inference to detect memory and resource violations, our work generalizes both solution and yields a more comprehensive solution. Unlike Pulse, we eliminate the need for implicit side-checks, and compared to ProveNFix, we avoid repeated analysis while maintaining full temporal violation detection capabilities.

7 Conclusion

Future conditions extend traditional pre- and post-conditions by specifying temporal behaviors and states that emerge after a function call completes. This work tackles the central question: *"How can we efficiently and soundly reason about future conditions using temporal logic?"* We propose a compositional verification framework that propagates future conditions independently of contextual code. Our solution introduces novel trace inclusion and trace subtraction mechanisms to facilitate a more efficient propagation of future conditions, where they are processed once per method declaration. Additionally, we present a approach for verifying effectful loops using trace and future condition predicates. The soundness of our system is formally proven, and its practicality is demonstrated through experimental results and non-trivial case studies.

Acknowledgments. This research is supported by the Ministry of Education, Singapore, under its MOE Academic Research Fund Tier 3 (RIE2025) (MOE Award No: MOET-MOET32021-0001), and by the Ministry of Education, Singapore, under the Academic Research Fund Tier 1 (FY2023). We thank anonymous reviewers for their insightful comments, which led to improvements in the paper presentation.

Data Availability. The source code of the tool, the dataset, proofs, are available from [18].

References

1. The Rust Programming Language (2017). http://rust-lang.org
2. Aldrich, J., Sunshine, J., Saini, D., Sparks, Z.: Typestate-oriented programming. In: Arora, S., Leavens, G.T. (eds.) Companion to the 24th Annual ACM SIGPLAN Conference on Object-Oriented Programming, Systems, Languages, and Applications, OOPSLA 2009, October 25-29, 2009, Orlando, Florida, USA, pp. 1015–1022. ACM (2009)
3. Almeida, M., Moreira, N., Reis, R.: Antimirov and Mosses's rewrite system revisited. Int. J. Found. Comput. Sci. **20**(4), 669–684 (2009)
4. Antimirov, V.: Partial derivatives of regular expressions and finite automata constructions. In: Mayr, E.W., Puech, C. (eds.) STACS 1995. LNCS, vol. 900, pp. 455–466. Springer, Heidelberg (1995). https://doi.org/10.1007/3-540-59042-0_96
5. Antimirov, V.: Partial derivatives of regular expressions and finite automaton constructions. Theoret. Comput. Sci. **155**(2), 291–319 (1996)
6. Antimirov, V.M., Mosses, P.D.: Rewriting extended regular expressions. Theor. Comput. Sci. **143**(1), 51–72 (1995)
7. CWE. Cwe-416: Use after free. https://cwe.mitre.org/data/definitions/416.html
8. Moura, L., Bjørner, N.: Z3: an efficient SMT solver. In: Ramakrishnan, C.R., Rehof, J. (eds.) TACAS 2008. LNCS, vol. 4963, pp. 337–340. Springer, Heidelberg (2008). https://doi.org/10.1007/978-3-540-78800-3_24
9. Hovland, D.: The inclusion problem for regular expressions. J. Comput. Syst. Sci. **78**(6), 1795–1813 (2012)
10. Jaspan, C., Aldrich, J.: Checking framework interactions with relationships. In: Drossopoulou, S. (ed.) ECOOP 2009. LNCS, vol. 5653, pp. 27–51. Springer, Heidelberg (2009). https://doi.org/10.1007/978-3-642-03013-0_3
11. Keil, M., Thiemann, P.: Symbolic solving of extended regular expression inequalities. In: Raman, V., Suresh, S.P. (eds.) 34th International Conference on Foundation of Software Technology and Theoretical Computer Science, FSTTCS 2014, December 15-17, 2014, New Delhi, India, volume 29 of *LIPIcs*, pp. 175–186. Schloss Dagstuhl - Leibniz-Zentrum für Informatik (2014)

12. Koskinen, E., Terauchi, T.: Local temporal reasoning. In: Henzinger, T.A., Miller, D. (eds.) Joint Meeting of the Twenty-Third EACSL Annual Conference on Computer Science Logic (CSL) and the Twenty-Ninth Annual ACM/IEEE Symposium on Logic in Computer Science (LICS), CSL-LICS '14, Vienna, Austria, July 14 - 18, 2014, pp. 59:1–59:10. ACM (2014)
13. Lee, J., Hong, S., Oh, H.: Memfix: static analysis-based repair of memory deallocation errors for C. In: Leavens, G.T., Garcia, A., Pasareanu, C.S. (eds.) Proceedings of the 2018 ACM Joint Meeting on European Software Engineering Conference and Symposium on the Foundations of Software Engineering, ESEC/SIGSOFT FSE 2018, Lake Buena Vista, FL, USA, November 04-09, 2018, pp. 95–106. ACM (2018)
14. Meta. Infer static analyzer (2025). https://github.com/facebook/infer
15. Meyer, B.: Applying "design by contract". Computer **25**(10), 40–51 (1992)
16. Moy, C., Felleisen, M.: Trace contracts. J. Funct. Program. **33** (2023)
17. Pucella, R., Tov, J.A.: Haskell session types with (almost) no class. In: Gill, A. (ed.) Proceedings of the 1st ACM SIGPLAN Symposium on Haskell, Haskell 2008, Victoria, BC, Canada, 25 September 2008, pp. 25–36. ACM (2008)
18. Song, Y.: Benchmark and Source Code. https://zenodo.org/records/16690276 (2025)
19. Song, Y., Chin, W.-N.: Automated temporal verification of integrated dependent effects. In: Lin, S.-W., Hou, Z., Mahony, B. (eds.) ICFEM 2020. LNCS, vol. 12531, pp. 73–90. Springer, Cham (2020). https://doi.org/10.1007/978-3-030-63406-3_5
20. Song, Y., Chin, W.-N.: A synchronous effects logic for temporal verification of pure esterel. In: Henglein, F., Shoham, S., Vizel, Y. (eds.) VMCAI 2021. LNCS, vol. 12597, pp. 417–440. Springer, Cham (2021). https://doi.org/10.1007/978-3-030-67067-2_19
21. Song, Y., Chin, W.: Automated verification for real-time systems - via implicit clocks and an extended antimirov algorithm. In: Sankaranarayanan, S., Sharygina, N. (eds.) TACAS 2023, Part I. LNCS, vol. 13993, pp. 569–587. Springer, Cham (2023). https://doi.org/10.1007/978-3-031-30823-9_29
22. Song, Y., Foo, D., Chin, W.: Automated temporal verification for algebraic effects. In: Sergey, I. (eds.) APLAS 2022. LNCS, vol. 13658, pp. 88–109. Springer, Cham (2022). https://doi.org/10.1007/978-3-031-21037-2_5
23. Song, Y., Gao, X., Li, W., Chin, W., Roychoudhury, A.: ProveNFix: temporal property-guided program repair. Proc. ACM Softw. Eng. **1**(FSE):226–248 (2024)
24. Strom, R.E., Yemini, S.: Typestate: a programming language concept for enhancing software reliability. IEEE Trans. Software Eng. **12**(1), 157–171 (1986)
25. Tate, R.: The sequential semantics of producer effect systems. In: Giacobazzi, R., Cousot, R. (eds.) The 40th Annual ACM SIGPLAN-SIGACT Symposium on Principles of Programming Languages, POPL '13, Rome, Italy - January 23 - 25, 2013, pp. 15–26. ACM (2013)
26. Wolff, R., Garcia, R., Tanter, É., Aldrich, J.: Gradual Typestate. In: Mezini, M. (ed.) ECOOP 2011. LNCS, vol. 6813, pp. 459–483. Springer, Heidelberg (2011). https://doi.org/10.1007/978-3-642-22655-7_22

AURA: Precise Abstract Interpretation of Probabilistic Programs with Interval Data Uncertainty

Zixin Huang[1], Jacob Laurel[2](✉), Saikat Dutta[3], and Sasa Misailovic[1]

[1] University of Illinois Urbana-Champaign, Urbana, IL 61801, USA
{zixinh2,misailo}@illinois.edu
[2] Georgia Institute of Technology, Atlanta, GA 30332, USA
jlaurel6@gatech.edu
[3] Cornell University, Ithaca, NY 14853, USA
saikatd@cornell.edu

Abstract. We present AURA, a novel abstract interpretation for obtaining sound, precise bounds on the posterior distributions computed by probabilistic programs. AURA allows programmers to specify interval bounds that capture uncertainty or perturbations of the observed data. AURA abstractly computes the infinite set of posteriors that would result from performing inference for any possible data value in the specified perturbation range. AURA then certifies precise bounds on probabilistic queries over that set of posteriors. AURA's precision stems from a novel gradient-based optimization leveraging the structure of probabilistic programs. Our evaluation across 11 benchmarks with data perturbation shows that AURA improves precision by an order of magnitude (12.8x on average) over the interval-based abstract interpreter, within a run time of 3.1 s (geomean), using a GPU parallel implementation.

1 Introduction

Probabilistic programs (PPs) play an important role in many applications that make critical decisions such as security/privacy [13,38,47,69], computer networks [17,19,67], analyzing hardware errors [15,44], and pandemic modeling [6,39]. In these applications, one often requires formal guarantees on the posterior probability distribution [65,72]. Illustrating this critical need for formal assurances, prior work has shown Bayesian inference's fundamental susceptibility and brittleness to small perturbations [57], including adversarial perturbations to the observed data [24,35,57,77]. Moreover, while adversarial attacks on datasets have been studied for other ML models, verifying robustness to data perturbations has been far less explored in probabilistic programming.

Verifying robustness of probabilistic programs to dataset perturbations encounters several core issues. First, these programs often involve many continuous distributions, which require symbolically evaluating possibly intractable integrals and highly non-linear probability densities. Second, for verification, one needs the analysis to be scalable *and* precise. Third, to reason about robustness to data perturbations, one must obtain guarantees on a *set* of possible posterior distributions. Unlike bounds for a single posterior, the bounds must now enclose *any* possible posterior that could result from inference on perturbed data. Using these bounds, we can verify that an adversary making small perturbations to one or more observed data points can never change the posterior probability of an event by an unacceptable amount.

Our Work. AURA is a novel abstract interpretation of probabilistic programs that produces sound and precise bounds on the inferred posterior distributions. By evaluating a probabilistic program abstractly, the bounds AURA computes can be used to verify assertions over a program's posterior. Additionally, AURA is the first program analysis to efficiently compute precise and sound bounds on an *infinite set of possible posterior distributions* when the observed data is specified as bounds by the user. Lastly, AURA scales to data sizes that are an order of magnitude greater than the size handled in prior work [5,20,37].

AURA's key technical contribution is to reduce abstract interpretation to gradient-based optimization by leveraging a distribution-shape pattern commonly found in continuous PPs. Thus AURA constructs sound and optimally precise abstract transformers over the interval abstract domain. AURA's transformers are applicable to complex subprograms or even the entire program when their distributions are *pseudoconcave*. Pseudoconcavity [46] is a relaxation of the familiar notion of concavity, and many popular continuous distributions (e.g., Gaussian, Uniform, Exponential) and expressions over them satisfy this property. This insight helps AURA's abstract transformers achieve much higher precision than composing standard interval arithmetic operations for subexpressions. Moreover, we show how our abstraction can also be combined and composed with standard interval transformers to maintain the generality needed to analyze more complicated programs that may not be end-to-end pseudoconcave.

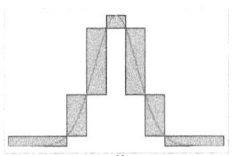
Fig. 1. Bound on a Single Posterior (no perturb.)

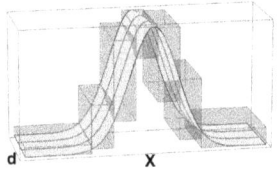
Fig. 2. Analysis of Data Perturbation (on 'd' axis)

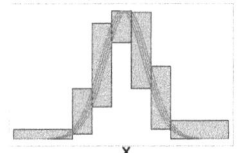
Fig. 3. Bound on the Set of Posteriors

In addition to precise and scalable abstract transformers, AURA allows programmers to specify interval bounds on the observed data which AURA then propagates through the program. These results can be used to certify bounds on probabilistic queries in order to bound the probability of an event. These bounds hold for *all* possible posterior distribution that could result from data perturbations. Thus AURA uses abstract interpretation to verify properties for infinitely many probabilistic programs simultaneously. AURA also makes integration of the over- and under-approximated densities tractable and efficient during marginalization, normalization, or expectation calculation. Figures 1, 2 and 3 illustrate AURA's abstraction for a *single posterior* and a *set of posteriors*.

Contributions. The paper presents the following core technical contributions:

- **Problem Formulation**. We introduce a novel formulation of the problem of certifying bounds on a set of posterior distributions resulting from (bounded) data perturbations.
- **Gradient-based Optimization**. We design a novel algorithm for obtaining precise abstract transformers for probabilistic programs that uses gradient-based optimization for tractably and optimally solving for precise bounds on the posterior distributions.
- **Soundness**. We show that our abstract interpretation can guarantee soundness for a broad class of probabilistic expressions and programs whose posteriors satisfy concavity or pseudoconcavity at each interval.
- **Evaluation**. We integrate AURA with PyTorch to leverage GPUs. Our evaluation of AURA across 11 programs with data perturbations shows that AURA improves precision by an order of magnitude (12.8x) over the interval-based abstract interpreter, within 3.1 s (geomean) on GPU. It also efficiently and precisely computes the probability of queries under perturbations.
  AURA is available at https://github.com/uiuc-arc/AURA.

2 Example

Probabilistic programming serves as a popular paradigm for encoding Bayesian probability models concisely as programs [26]. In addition, the probabilistic programming system automates Bayesian inference. Thus, the programmer only specifies the source program while the underlying inference details are abstracted away by the language. However, one may desire formal guarantees about the inference results. Hence our work aims to provide these guarantees with AURA.

Before describing AURA's approach, we first present our example probabilistic program, P in Fig. 4. This program infers the ground braking force. The latent parameter x represents the braking force exerted on the vehicle, while data[i] stores the observed deceleration (m/s^2) under experimental conditions. In this model, an engineer uses the observed variable data[i] to infer the value of latent x. As an assumption, they model x's prior distribution as a uniform (0,100). The model assumes the observed variables are normally distributed.

```
1  data = [....] # numerical values
2  x ~ uniform(0, 100)
3
4  for i in 1..100:
5     observe(
6        normal(0.1*x+1, 1),
7        data[i]
8     )
```

Fig. 4. Example Code.

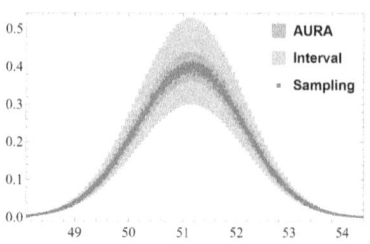

Fig. 5. Posterior x Result.

AURA's formalism allows one to express the scenario where the observed data values can suffer perturbations. We assume that multiple data observations can encounter sensor defects, potentially altering an observed value data[i] by up to 0.05. Here, we analyze the scenario where five observed points are simultaneously perturbed from sensor defects.

AURA's bounds are shown as blue boxes in Fig. 5 and soundly enclose the set of *all* possible posterior distributions that could arise from inference with perturbed data. The red dots in this figure represent a sampled histogram of x, based on different concrete observed data values data[i] within a specified interval $d^\sharp$, showing that AURA's bounds are precise. The orange boxes illustrate posterior bounds obtained by an analysis with standard interval abstract transformers and are much less precise than AURA at enclosing the sampled histograms. The reason for this trend is that composing over-approximate interval abstract transformers compounds imprecision. In contrast, AURA's abstraction improves precision by abstracting the entire unnormalized posterior at once. AURA can prove sound posterior bounds within just 0.115 s when using 200 partitions (i.e., subintervals) to represent the posterior.

Bounds on Probabilities of Queries. The certified bounds on the set of normalized posteriors can then be used for various queries. For instance, engineers may need to guarantee that the braking force x should not fall below a certain safety threshold, say 50 N. Hence AURA's posterior bounds can be used to bound the posterior's probability of the query $Q \equiv x < 50$.

AURA provides a probability range of $[0.11, 0.14]$ for the braking force falling below a critical threshold, which is twice as precise as the $[0.09, 0.17]$ range obtained from interval analysis. AURA's narrower bounds indicate a smaller effect from data perturbations, namely a better *robustness*, which is the ability to infer reliable results even in the face of data perturbations.

3 Preliminaries

Language. We present our probabilistic programming language in Fig. 6. Our syntax is similar to the syntax of Stan [21], separating the block with priors over the latent variables M and the observations in the data block D. The programmer can also specify models where the parameters of one distribution are an arithmetic expression E of other latent parameters. The priors in M must be continuous with compact (truncated) support. Our data perturbation formalism requires the observed distribution be continuous. While the implementation optionally permits discrete observed variables, this setting is limited to only regular inference and not analysis of data perturbations.

$$P ::= M \mid M; D$$
$$M ::= \mathtt{x}_i \sim Dist \mid M; M \mid \mathtt{if}\ \mathtt{flip}(p)\ M_1\ \mathtt{else}\ M_2 \mid \mathtt{for}\ \mathtt{j}=n_1\ \mathtt{to}\ n_2\ \mathtt{do}\ M \mid \mathtt{let}\ \mathtt{x}_i = E\ \mathtt{in}\ M$$
$$D ::= observe(Dist, d_i) \mid D; D \mid \mathtt{for}\ \mathtt{j}=n_1\ \mathtt{to}\ n_2\ \mathtt{do}\ D$$
$$E ::= \mathtt{x}_j \mid E+E \mid E-E \mid E*E \mid E/E \mid c \in \mathbb{R}$$
$$Dist ::= dist(E_1, \ldots, E_N),\ dist \in \{uniform, \ldots\}$$

Fig. 6. AURA Language

In the $\mathtt{flip}(p)$ primitive, p is a fixed constant between 0 and 1. The language is first-order (no recursion), however one can encode a broad class of popular probabilistic models such as Linear and Logistic Regressions, Time-Series Models, Hierarchical Bayesian models, and others. This language is constrained for the purpose of identifying and optimally analyzing pseudoconcave programs, however our language could be used to define other subprograms in general PPLs such as for nested inference (example in Appendix A.4 [36]).

Concavity and Convexity. A core component of AURA's abstraction relies upon concavity and concavity-like properties of posterior distributions. A set $\mathcal{X} \subseteq \mathbb{R}^d$ is *convex* if for all $\alpha \in [0, 1]$ and any $x_1, x_2 \in \mathcal{X}$, then $\alpha x_1 + (1-\alpha) x_2 \in \mathcal{X}$. A function f is **concave** over some convex domain $\mathcal{X}$ if for any $\alpha \in [0, 1]$ and any $x_1, x_2 \in \mathcal{X}$ the following inequality holds: $f(\alpha x_1 + (1-\alpha) x_2) \geq \alpha f(x_1) + (1-\alpha) f(x_2)$. The **Concave** functions remain closed under summation, which will be important for AURA's analysis. Additionally, we will see that AURA's analysis still supports weaker notions of concavity, which we describe next.

Definition 1. *Quasiconcavity. A function f is quasiconcave over some convex domain $\mathcal{X}$ if for any $\alpha \in [0,1]$ and any $x_1, x_2 \in \mathcal{X}$ the following holds: $f(\alpha x_1 + (1-\alpha) x_2) \geq \min(f(x_1), f(x_2))$.*

Definition 2. *Log-Concavity. A non-negative function f is logarithmically-concave over some convex domain $\mathcal{X}$ if for any $\alpha \in [0,1]$ and any $x_1, x_2 \in \mathcal{X}$ the following holds: $f(\alpha x_1 + (1-\alpha) x_2) \geq f(x_1)^\alpha \cdot f(x_2)^{1-\alpha}$.*

For a strictly positive function f (e.g., a probability density), the following implication holds: **Log-Concave** $f \implies$ **Concave** $\log(f)$. Many common probability densities are **Log-concave** (Appendix C; Table 6) and the **Log-concave** functions are closed under multiplication. Additionally, quasiconcavity is useful for defining pseudoconcavity.

Definition 3. Pseudoconcavity. *A function $f(x)$ is pseudoconcave if and only if $f(x)$ is quasiconcave and for any x^*, $\nabla f(x^*) = 0 \implies x^* = \arg\max f(x)$.*

Pseudoconcavity is similar to Quasiconcavity, however any stationary point of a pseudoconcave function

Fig. 7. Illustration of Different Notions of Concavity

is *necessarily* an optimum. Further, any quasiconcave function whose gradient is never zero is Pseudoconcave. Figure 7 shows example functions. One may notice the flat plateau of the quasiconcave function consists of stationary points which are *not* optimal. Hence in Sect. 6 we leverage pseudoconcavity to ensure a gradient ascent procedure does not become trapped in local extrema.

Abstract Interpretation. AURA's analysis builds upon abstract interpretation [10] with the interval domain. The interval abstract domain was chosen because it has found widespread success in many program analysis tasks [42,43,66] due to its scalability. In the interval domain each variable is abstracted by an interval $[a, b] \in \mathbb{IR}$ where a is the lower bound and b is the upper bound and $a \leq b$. The set of all m-dimensional intervals will be denoted as $\mathbb{IR}^m$, and a given element will be denoted as $x^\sharp \in \mathbb{IR}^m$ where $x^\sharp[i] = [a_i, b_i]$. The concretization $\gamma : \mathbb{IR}^m \to \mathcal{P}(\mathbb{R}^m)$ of a multidimensional interval is just the set of all points contained in that interval hence: $\gamma(x^\sharp) = \{(x_1, ..., x_m) : \forall i \in \{1, ..., m\}, a_i \leq x_i \leq b_i \text{ where } [a_i, b_i] = x^\sharp[i]\}$. For the interval domain, the basic abstract transformers are the standard interval arithmetic operations (we denote them as $+^\sharp$ and $\cdot^\sharp$), which can easily be composed [50], however we will later see how AURA obtains precise abstract transformers by solving optimization problems.

$[\![P]\!](x, d) = [\![M; D]\!](x, d)$ $\qquad$ $[\![M; D]\!](x, d) = [\![M]\!](x) \cdot [\![D]\!](x, d)$
$[\![\text{if flip}(p) \ P_1 \ \text{else} \ P_2]\!](x, d) =$ $\qquad$ $[\![M_1; M_2]\!](x) = [\![M_1]\!](x) \cdot [\![M_2]\!](x)$
$\qquad p[\![P_1]\!](x, d) + (1-p)[\![P_2]\!](x, d)$ $\qquad$ $[\![D_1; D_2]\!](x, d) = [\![D_1]\!](x, d) \cdot [\![D_2]\!](x, d)$
$[\![observe(Dist, d_i)]\!](x, d) = [\![Dist]\!](x, d) \circ d[i]$ $\qquad$ $[\![\mathbf{x}_i \sim Dist]\!](x, d) = [\![Dist]\!](x, d) \circ x[i]$
$[\![E_1 + E_2]\!](x, d) = [\![E_1]\!](x, d) + [\![E_2]\!](x, d)$ $\qquad$ $[\![E_1 - E_2]\!](x, d) = [\![E_1]\!](x, d) - [\![E_2]\!](x, d)$
$[\![E_1 * E_2]\!](x, d) = [\![E_1]\!](x, d) * [\![E_2]\!](x, d)$ $\qquad$ $[\![E_1/E_2]\!](x, d) \stackrel{\neq 0}{=} [\![E_1]\!](x, d)/[\![E_2]\!](x, d)$
$[\![\mathbf{x}_j]\!](x, d) = x[j]$ $\qquad$ $[\![cE]\!](x, d) = c \cdot [\![E]\!](x, d)$
$[\![dist(E_1, ..., E_N)]\!](x, d) = p_{dist}(u; [\![E_1]\!](x, d), ..., [\![E_N]\!](x, d)), \ dist \in \{uniform, ...\}$

Fig. 8. Key Rules of Unnormalized Concrete Semantics.

4 Concrete Semantics

We now formalize our concrete semantics of probabilistic programs. The semantic interpretation of a probabilistic program is the normalized posterior distribution, which corresponds to the unnormalized likelihood defined by the statements in the probabilistic program divided by a normalizing constant.

Preliminary Transformation. To simplify the formalism description, we do three source-to-source transformations. The first is moving conditionals upward hence the production for P becomes $P ::= M \mid M; D \mid \text{if flip}(p)\ P_1\ \text{else}\ P_2$. To move conditionals upward, it includes the code before and after the conditional into the branches. The second transformation is unrolling the for loops. Hence the productions for M becomes $M ::= \text{x}_i \sim Dist \mid M; M$ and the production for D becomes $D ::= observe(Dist, d_i) \mid D; D$ since loops can be unrolled to sequencing: $M; M$ and $D; D$. The third transformation replaces all occurrences of (fresh) variables introduced by the let bindings with their original expressions (using capture-avoiding substitution), so that all the expressions and subexpressions only contain variables corresponding to sampled distributions, x_k.

Unnormalized Concrete Semantics. We first formalize the concrete semantics of probabilistic programs in terms of their *unnormalized* likelihood. Because likelihoods are just density functions which map observations to scores, we formalize this mapping using a score-based functional semantics.

In the score-based semantics, the interpretation $[\![\cdot]\!]$ of a probabilistic program P is a function that scores the likelihood of a given trace $x \in \mathbb{R}^m$ (where m is the number of latents) and given data observations $d \in \mathbb{R}^n$. Hence $[\![\cdot]\!]$ is a function of both x and d. The semantic signature for interpreting a program P is $[\![P]\!] : \mathbb{R}^m \times \mathbb{R}^n \to \mathbb{R}$, and $[\![P]\!](x, d) : \mathbb{R}$. The full semantics are given in Fig. 8. For the distribution rule $[\![dist(E_1, \ldots, E_N)]\!](x, d)$, we take the probability density function (PDF) of that distribution, denoted as p_{dist}. Each statement multiplies the probability score by the corresponding probability density function of either the latent parameter or the observed data sample (see $[\![M; M]\!]$ and $[\![D; D]\!]$). For branches, we take the linear combination of the density functions.

Unnormalized Log-Likelihood Semantics, $[\![P]\!]_{\log}(x, d)$. For reasons of numerical stability it is often helpful to work with the logarithm of the likelihood instead of the original likelihood itself. Thus having defined the Unnormalized Concrete Semantics, we can now define the *log-likelihood* semantics by simply taking a logarithm. In particular: $[\![P]\!]_{\log}(x, d) = \log([\![P]\!](x, d))$ We can easily convert back to the original semantics: $[\![P]\!](x, d) = \exp([\![P]\!]_{\log}(x, d))$.

Normalized Concrete Semantics. We formalize the notion of a *normalized* probabilistic program, whose semantics is denoted $[\![\cdot]\!]_n$ and given by:

$$[\![P]\!]_n(x, d) = [\![P]\!](x, d) \Big/ \int_x [\![P]\!](x, d) dx,$$

where $\int_x [\![P]\!](x, d) dx$ is the normalizing constant. Generally, computing the normalizing constant and hence $[\![P]\!]_n$ can be intractable.

5   Abstract Semantics for Data Perturbation

We now define an abstract semantics for over-approximating *entire sets* of posterior distributions, which intuitively encode *all* posteriors obtainable when the data d could be perturbed. However if one wishes to only bound a *single* posterior, they can still use AURA, the data interval will just be degenerate.

5.1 Unnormalized Abstract Semantics for Data Perturbation

In the data perturbation setting, the observed dataset is given by some interval, $d^\sharp \in \mathbb{IR}^n$. Thus for abstractly interpreting program P we have the signature $[\![P]\!]^\sharp(x^\sharp, d^\sharp) : \mathbb{IR}^m \times \mathbb{IR}^n \to \mathbb{IR}$. In essence, we prove guaranteed bounds on all possible posteriors obtained after a bounded (adversarial) perturbation on the data. Hence AURA can analyze and verify properties for an infinite number of probabilistic programs, a task which has not been studied in any prior work.

Optimization. The core idea of AURA is to compute precise lower and upper bounds by respectively solving minimization and maximization problems. Hence instead of computing lower and upper bounds with interval arithmetic, AURA reduces abstract interpretation to continuous optimization. This optimization formulation is defined as:

$$[\![P]\!]^\sharp(x^\sharp, d^\sharp) = [l, u], \quad \text{where}$$

$$l = \min_{d \in \gamma(d^\sharp)} \min_{x \in \gamma(x^\sharp)} [\![P]\!](x, d), \quad \text{and} \quad u = \max_{d \in \gamma(d^\sharp)} \max_{x \in \gamma(x^\sharp)} [\![P]\!](x, d).$$

One can think of this formulation as defining an abstract transformer tailored for the *entire* program's (or subprogram's) expression instead of defining abstract transformers for individual primitive operations (as interval arithmetic does). Having an abstract transformer defined at this higher level of granularity allows AURA to improve precision greatly over interval arithmetic – and as we will show in Sect. 6, when the unnormalized likelihood $[\![P]\!](x, d)$ has a pseudo-concave structure, we can solve this optimization problem tractably.

However one can always use any $[l^*, u^*]$ where $l^* \leq l$ and $u \leq u^*$ as sound bounds. Hence, for programs which *lack* the necessary pseudoconcavity properties, one can always fallback to interval arithmetic to abstractly interpret the semantics of Fig. 8. This insight gives us the flexibility to analyze a (pseudo-concave) subprogram within P using AURA's precise optimization approach, while using interval arithmetic to bound other sub-expressions which may not be pseudoconcave and then compose the results. We can now state the following soundness result (the proofs are in Sect. 5.3):

Theorem 1. *The Unnormalized Abstract Semantics for data perturbation over-approximate the Unnormalized Concrete Semantics for fixed data observations. Equivalently for arbitrary program P, dataset $d^\sharp \in \mathbb{IR}^n$, and interval $x^\sharp \in \mathbb{IR}^m$, we have $\{[\![P]\!](x, d) : x \in \gamma(x^\sharp), d \in \gamma(d^\sharp)\} \subseteq \gamma([\![P]\!]^\sharp(x^\sharp, d^\sharp))$.*

Abstract Log-likelihood Semantics for Data Perturbations. We can take logarithmic transformations of the abstract unnormalized semantics, to define $[\![P]\!]^\sharp_{\log}(x^\sharp, d^\sharp) = [l', u']$, where $l' = \min_{d \in \gamma(d^\sharp)} \min_{x \in \gamma(x^\sharp)} [\![P]\!]_{\log}(x, d)$, and also $u' = \max_{d \in \gamma(d^\sharp)} \max_{x \in \gamma(x^\sharp)} [\![P]\!]_{\log}(x, d)$. Then, $[\![P]\!]^\sharp(x^\sharp, d^\sharp) = \exp([\![P]\!]^\sharp_{\log}(x^\sharp, d^\sharp))$.

5.2 Normalized Abstract Semantics for Data Perturbation

One of the most challenging parts of computing the abstract normalized semantics is performing the abstract integration $\int^\sharp$. The key intuition is that we partition the support of $[\![P]\!]$ into disjoint intervals and compute an interval bound of the unnormalized posterior over each partition. These bounds form lower and upper Riemann sums, which bound the value of the integral, and thus bound the integrating constant. Lastly, interval division of the previous bounds on the unnormalized posterior by the bounds on the integrating constant ultimately yields bounds on the normalized posterior, which we denote as $[\![P]\!]_n^\sharp$.

Definition 4 (Abstract Integral with Data Perturbation). *We let each $x_i^\sharp$ represent a multi-dimensional interval in $\mathbb{IR}^m$, such that $\mathrm{support}([\![P]\!]) = \cup_{i=1}^k \gamma(x_i^\sharp)$. Thus each $x_i^\sharp$ is a subset of the posterior distribution's support. Each $x_i^\sharp$ can be denoted as a Cartesian product (denoted as $\otimes$) of the intervals as $x_i^\sharp = \otimes_{j=1}^m [x_{l_{ij}}, x_{u_{ij}}]$. Here m represents the dimension of the latent variables, and for each dimension $j \in \{1,...,m\}$, the interval $[x_{l_{ij}}, x_{u_{ij}}] \in \mathbb{IR}$ corresponds to that dimension. The volume (or Lebesgue measure) of each $x_i^\sharp$ in the partition is $\mathrm{Vol}(x_i^\sharp) = \prod_{j=1}^k (x_{u_{ij}} - x_{l_{ij}})$. The abstract integral with data perturbation is:*

$$\int^\sharp [\![P]\!]^\sharp(x^\sharp, d^\sharp)\, dx = \left[\sum_{i=1}^k l_i \cdot \mathrm{Vol}(x_i^\sharp), \sum_{i=1}^k u_i \cdot \mathrm{Vol}(x_i^\sharp) \right]$$

The bounds $\mathrm{Vol}(x_i^\sharp) = \prod_{j=1}^m (x_{u_{ij}} - x_{l_{ij}})$ and $[\![P]\!]^\sharp(x_i^\sharp, d^\sharp) = [l_i, u_i]$ are defined in Sect. 5, however bounds obtained from *any* sound abstract transformer would also be valid. For distributions with compact support, there will be finitely many (non-zero) terms in the summation. We will see in Sect. 7 how this same idea can be used to abstractly integrate $[\![P]\!]_n^\sharp$ to formally bound probabilities of (measurable) events using the posterior bounds computed by $[\![P]\!]_n^\sharp$.

Lemma 1. *[Soundness of abstract integration for data perturbations] Given Theorem 1 and Definition 4, it follows that:*

$$\int [\![P]\!](x, d)\, dx \in \gamma \left(\int^\sharp [\![P]\!]^\sharp(x^\sharp, d^\sharp)\, dx \right).$$

We now formally define the normalized abstract semantics for programs where the support has been partitioned as $\cup_{j=1}^k x_j^\sharp$ and where $x_i^\sharp \in \mathbb{IR}^m$ is the partition of interest, Here $\div^\sharp$ represents interval division.

$$[\![P]\!]_n^\sharp(x_i^\sharp, d^\sharp) = \frac{[\![P]\!]^\sharp(x_i^\sharp, d^\sharp)}{\int^\sharp [\![P]\!]^\sharp(\cup_{j=1}^k x_j^\sharp, d^\sharp)}^\sharp$$

Theorem 2. *The Normalized Abstract Semantics for data perturbation overapproximates the Normalized Concrete Semantics for sets of data observations. Formally, for a program P, dataset $d^\sharp \in \mathbb{IR}^n$, and interval $x^\sharp \in \mathbb{IR}^m$, we have:*

$$\{[\![P]\!]_n(x, d) : x \in \gamma(x^\sharp), d \in \gamma(d^\sharp)\} \subseteq \gamma([\![P]\!]_n^\sharp(x^\sharp, d^\sharp)).$$

5.3 Soundness Proofs

Proof of Theorem 1. Since $[\![P]\!]^\sharp(x^\sharp, d^\sharp) = [l, u]$ is a 1D interval in $\mathbb{R}$, we have to show that

1. $l \leq \inf\{[\![P]\!](x, d) : x \in \gamma(x^\sharp), d \in \gamma(d^\sharp)\}$ and
2. $u \geq \sup\{[\![P]\!](x, d) : x \in \gamma(x^\sharp), d \in \gamma(d^\sharp)\}$.

However, by definition, $l = \min_{d \in \gamma(d^\sharp)} \min_{x \in \gamma(x^\sharp)} [\![P]\!](x, d)$ and

$$\min_{d \in \gamma(d^\sharp)} \min_{x \in \gamma(x^\sharp)} [\![P]\!](x, d) = \inf\{[\![P]\!](x, d) : x \in \gamma(x^\sharp), d \in \gamma(d^\sharp)\}$$

Similarly, $u = \max_{d \in \gamma(d^\sharp)} \max_{x \in \gamma(x^\sharp)} [\![P]\!](x, d)$ and

$$\max_{d \in \gamma(d^\sharp)} \max_{x \in \gamma(x^\sharp)} [\![P]\!](x, d) = \sup\{[\![P]\!](x, d) : x \in \gamma(x^\sharp), d \in \gamma(d^\sharp)\}$$

Hence soundness follows (by construction). □

Proof of Lemma 1. To prove $\int [\![P]\!](x, d)\, dx \in \gamma \left(\int^\sharp [\![P]\!]^\sharp(x^\sharp, d^\sharp)\, dx \right)$, we need to show that $\sum_{i=1}^{n} l_i \cdot \text{Vol}(x_i^\sharp) \leq \int [\![P]\!](x, d) dx \leq \sum_{i=1}^{n} u_i \cdot \text{Vol}(x_i^\sharp)$

However the left hand side is a lower Riemann sum which is always less than the true integral, and likewise the right hand side is an upper Riemann sum which is always greater than the true integral. □

Proof of Theorem 2. Since the unnormalized bounds are sound from Theorem 1, the bounds on the normalizing constant are sound from Lemma 1 and interval division is sound, the normalized bounds are sound too. □

6 AURA Optimization Algorithm

Having defined the abstract semantics $[\![P]\!]^\sharp(x^\sharp, d^\sharp)$ in terms of interval bounds where the lower and upper bounds come from solutions to optimization problems, we now describe how AURA can precisely solve these optimization problems.

Pseudoconcave Probabilistic Programs. A probabilistic program P is *pseudoconcave* if the unnormalized density function defined by $[\![P]\!](x, d)$ is a pseudoconcave function of both x and d (a condition satisfied by many distributions; see Appendix C). We also have the following implications:

$[\![P]\!](x, d)$ **Log-Concave** $\implies$ $[\![P]\!]_{\log}(x, d)$ **Concave** $\implies$ $[\![P]\!]_{\log}(x, d)$ **Pseudoconcave**

$[\![P]\!](x, d)$ **Pseudoconcave** $\implies$ $[\![P]\!]_{\log}(x, d)$ **Pseudoconcave**

We choose **Pseudoconcavity**, because to the best of our knowledge it is the weakest condition that ensures the lower and upper bounds from gradient-based optimizations remain sound. Pseudoconcave functions have derivatives which exist everywhere except a measure zero set. Hence, we can use these derivatives for Gradient Ascent to solve the optimization problems of Sect. 5.1.

6.1 Computing Lower Bounds with AURA

The first step in computing the abstract semantics $[\![P]\!]^\sharp(x^\sharp, d^\sharp)$ needed to soundly bound posteriors involves computing the interval's lower bound. In the case of data perturbations one must compute $l = \min_{d \in \gamma(d^\sharp)} \min_{x \in \gamma(x^\sharp)} [\![P]\!](x, d)$. However, because of the pseudoconcavity requirements on $[\![P]\!](x, d)$ this minimization problem becomes tractable. In particular we only have to check the corner points of $x^\sharp$ and $d^\sharp$, denoted as *Corners*. For numerical stability, we use logarithms, hence we can solve the optimization problem by computing:

$$l = \exp\left(\min_{d \in Corners(d^\sharp)} \min_{x \in Corners(x^\sharp)} [\![P]\!]_{\log}(x, d)\right) \quad (1)$$

Theorem 3. *(Soundness). The lower bounds l computed above in Eq. 1 are sound when the log-likelihood $[\![P]\!]_{\log}(x, d)$ is pseudoconcave.*

Proof. (Sketch) Any pseudoconcave function is also quasiconcave, and quasiconcave functions over compact convex sets are minimized at corner points [45]. □

A key benefit of using the Interval domain instead of the Polyhedral or Zonotope [22,23] domains is that checking extremal points of intervals is more scalable compared to checking extremal points of polyhedra or zonotopes. This lower bound is not just sound, it is **optimal**. We state this result below:

The lower bound computed in Eq. 1 is optimal – *the most precise bound possible*. Because $[\![P]\!]_{\log}(x, d)$ is continuous and the interval $d^\sharp \times x^\sharp$ is compact, the minimum will be attained on that interval. Since exp is monotonically increasing, the minimizer of $[\![P]\!]_{\log}(x, d)$ is also the minimizer of $\exp([\![P]\!]_{\log}(x, d))$.

6.2 Computing Upper Bounds with AURA

Similarly, to obtain sound enclosures, AURA computes the upper bound by solving the optimization problem $u = \max_{d \in \gamma(d^\sharp)} \max_{x \in \gamma(x^\sharp)} [\![P]\!](x, d)$. Our key technical insight is that this maximization can be solved directly by performing *Projected Gradient Ascent* on the log likelihood, $[\![P]\!]_{\log}(x, d)$. Our implementation uses automatic differentiation to efficiently compute the gradients. Further, since $x^\sharp$ and $d^\sharp$ define (multi-dimensional) intervals, they are convex sets, hence the constraints of this optimization problem are convex.

Definition 5. *Projected Gradient Ascent. Given a differentiable function $f(x) : \mathcal{X} \subset \mathbb{R}^m \to \mathbb{R}$, one iteratively computes:*

$$x_{n+1} = \Pi_\mathcal{X}(x_n + \eta \nabla_x f(x_n))$$

with learning rate $\eta \in \mathbb{R}_{>0}$ until convergence where $\|x_{n+1} - x_n\| \leq \epsilon$. Here $\Pi_\mathcal{X}$ is the projection operator that takes a x_{n+1} that may lie outside $\mathcal{X}$, and returns the closest point inside $\mathcal{X}$. If the constraints are intervals: $\mathcal{X} = \otimes_{i=1}^m [l_i, u_i] \subseteq \mathbb{R}^m$, the projection is $\Pi_\mathcal{X}(x) = \otimes_{i=1}^m \Pi_\mathcal{X}(x[i])$ where:

$$\Pi_{\mathcal{X}}(x[i]) = \begin{cases} l_i & \text{if } l_i > x[i] \text{ or} \\ x[i] & \text{if } x[i] \in [l_i, u_i] \text{ or} \\ u_i & \text{if } u_i < x[i] \end{cases} \quad (2)$$

AURA Gradient Optimization. AURA will run the following Gradient Ascent computations for the function $[\![P]\!]_{\log}(x,d) : \gamma(x^\sharp) \times \gamma(d^\sharp) \to \mathbb{R}_{\geq 0}$:

$$(x_{n+1}, d_{n+1}) = \Pi_{x^\sharp; d^\sharp}\big((x_n, d_n) + \eta \nabla [\![P]\!]_{\log}(x_n, d_n)\big) \quad (3)$$

until $x_{n+1} = x_n$ and $d_{n+1} = d_n$. The learning rate must satisfy $\eta \leq \frac{1}{\|\nabla [\![P]\!]_{\log}(x_n, d_n)\|}$ to ensure convergence. We further discuss the selection of the learning rate in Sect. 8. This optimization problem is constrained because the latent parameters x come from distributions with compact support (e.g., uniform). A key benefit of using the interval domain is that the projection function $\Pi_{x^\sharp; d^\sharp}$ in Eq. 3 reduces to the (efficiently computable) projection in Eq. 2 since $x^\sharp \times d^\sharp$ is just a multi-dimensional interval. Upon computing the $x_{n+1} = x_n$ and $d_{n+1} = d_n$ that the Projected Gradient Ascent converges to, we exponentiate the result to get:

$$u = \exp([\![P]\!]_{\log}(x_{n+1}, d_{n+1})) \quad (4)$$

Theorem 4. *(Soundness) The upper bounds u computed in Eq. 4 are sound when the log-likelihood $[\![P]\!]_{\log}(x,d)$ is pseudoconcave.*

Proof. (sketch) Projected gradient ascent/descent is guaranteed to converge to the *true* maxima (instead of a local one) for pseudoconcave/pseudoconvex functions [12,14,30]. Moreover, when projected gradient ascent applied to a pseudoconcave function finds a fixed point $x_{n+1} = x_n$, $d_{n+1} = d_n$, such a fixed point is guaranteed to the be the true optima ([14] Theorem 4.2) □

Corollary 1. *(Optimality) The upper bound computed in Eq. 4 is the most precise bound possible.*

Proof. (sketch) Since $[\![P]\!]_{\log}(x,d)$ is continuous and $d^\sharp \times x^\sharp$ is compact, the maximum is attained on that interval. Since exp is monotonically increasing, the maximizer of $[\![P]\!]_{\log}(x,d)$ is the maximizer of $\exp([\![P]\!]_{\log}(x,d))$ □

AURA runs the gradient ascent until a fixed point $(x_{n+1} = x_n)$ is found. Alternatively, AURA can run the gradient ascent for fewer iterations (before hitting a fixed point), and add an error bound to the result to account for the distance to the true optimum value. For instance, prior works [14,28] guaranteed for a pseudo-concave function $f(x) : \mathcal{X} \subset \mathbb{R}^m \to \mathbb{R}$, after T iterations of projected gradient ascent, the error between the true maximum and the current value will not exceed $E = \sqrt{\kappa^2 \|x_0 - x^*\|^2 / T}$, where x_0 denotes the starting point, x^* denotes the true maximum, and κ denotes the local Lipschitz constant over $\mathcal{X}$ that can be computed by AURA. Hence, even without a sufficient number of iterations to reach the fixed point, when adding tiny bound E, AURA still gives bounds which are sound. This strategy also applies if one wishes to account for numerical error, though prior work [2] shows that gradient ascent is already robust to floating point roundoff. Lastly, because of the optimality of the lower and upper bounds, *AURA achieves the most precise abstract transformer of pseudoconcave functions for the interval domain.*

6.3 Beyond Pseudoconcavity: Compositionality and Scaling

Supporting Branch Statements and Mixture Models. AURA supports mixture distributions that contain branches which can cause the likelihoods to no longer be pseudoconcave. The idea is that even if the entire posterior is multimodal and not pseudoconcave, each *component* when viewed in isolation could be pseudoconcave. For instance, we can define the abstraction of a branch as:

$$[\![\texttt{if flip}(p) \ P_1 \ \texttt{else} \ P_2]\!]^\sharp(x^\sharp, d^\sharp) = p \cdot^\sharp [\![P_1]\!]^\sharp(x^\sharp, d^\sharp) +^\sharp (1-p) \cdot^\sharp [\![P_2]\!]^\sharp(x^\sharp, d^\sharp) \quad (5)$$

Thus by applying AURA's abstract interpreter, $[\![\cdot]\!]^\sharp$, to each component (which are pseudoconcave) and combining the results with standard interval arithmetic, we can still obtain sound posterior bounds. We present the proof in Appendix A.1.

Pseudoconcave Subexpressions when Programs are not Pseudoconcave. We can generalize the previous case and fallback to interval arithmetic for *any* of the subexpressions in Fig. 8. Thus, even if the program P lacks a pseudoconcave posterior, we can compute optimized bounds on the largest subexpressions which *are* pseudoconcave, and then use standard interval arithmetic for the rest. Hence, Sects. 6.1 and 6.2 provide sound interval domain abstract transformers for *any* pseudoconcave function, including subexpressions within P. We state this property formally and prove it in Appendix A.2.

Optimizing Programs with High-Dimensional Latents. A common method for writing robust models is to add many *local* latent parameters [71,76], i.e., each observation depends on a fresh latent variable. Figure 9 gives an example model capturing this common pattern.

Line 5 encodes that each datapoint has its own i.i.d latent v_i, hence why there are $n+1$ latent variables. Given this pattern, we let u represent the *global* latent and v_i represent the *local* latents.

```
1  d = [1.3, 2.1, ... ]  #n data points
2  u ~ normal(...)
            #global latent variable
3  for i in range(n):
4      v_i ~ normal(u,1)
            #local latent variables
5      observe(d[i], normal(v_i,1))
```

Fig. 9. Robust Model with $n+1$ Latent Parameters

Thus the latent vector is $x = (u, v_1, ..., v_n)$ which means that naively, we would solve an $\mathcal{O}(n)$-dimensional optimization problem. However, AURA automatically reduces this problem to n easy $\mathcal{O}(1)$-dimensional subproblems since each local latent's respective optimization subproblem is $\mathcal{O}(1)$ dimension and they can be solved in parallel (full proof in Appendix A.3).

7 AURA Verification Algorithm

Having described AURA's optimization routine, we next describe how to use this routine for end-to-end robustness verification of probabilistic programs. In particular, Eqs. 1 and 4 provide a strategy to solve the optimization problems of Sect. 5.1, thus giving a way to compute $[\![P]\!]^\sharp(x^\sharp, d^\sharp)$. Hence we combine these insights together to give the full algorithm for AURA's abstract interpretation of normalized posterior distributions of probabilistic programs. The entire procedure is shown in Algorithm 1.

Algorithm 1. AURA Core Verification Algorithm

Input: Probabilistic Program P; Abstract dataset $d^\sharp$; The partition of P's support $\bigcup_{i=1}^m x_i^\sharp$ (from implementation heuristic); The query Q (optional)
Output: (1) Posterior Bounds $[\![P]\!]_n^\sharp(x, d^\sharp)$;
    (2) Query Bounds $[Q_l, Q_u]$ where $Pr(Q) \in [Q_l, Q_u]$ (only if Q provided)

1: **for** $x_i^\sharp$ in splits **do**
2:    $l_i, u_i = [\![P]\!]^\sharp(x_i^\sharp, d^\sharp)$ ▷ Unnormalized posterior bounds computed
                                                                        ▷ in Sections 6.1-6.3 (data parallel)
3: **end for**
4: $[c_l, c_u] = \int^\sharp [\![P]\!]^\sharp(x^\sharp, d^\sharp) dx$ ▷ Normalizing Constant bound computed
                                                                         ▷ in Def. 4 (reduction)
5: **for** $x_i^\sharp$ in splits **do**
6:    $[\![P]\!]_n^\sharp(x_i^\sharp, d^\sharp) = [l_i, u_i] \div^\sharp [c_l, c_u]$ ▷ Normalization (data parallel)
7: **end for**
8: **if** Query **then**
9:    $[Q_l, Q_u] = \int^\sharp \mathbf{1}_Q \cdot [\![P]\!]_n^\sharp(x^\sharp, d^\sharp) dx$ ▷ Abstract integration of posterior
                                                                                      ▷ from Def. 7 (reduction)
10: **end if**

Partitioning (Splits). As input, AURA requires a partition of the support of the latent variables. The core intuition is that we partition the support of P's distribution into disjoint interval "*splits*". If $x^\sharp$ is the interval containing the entire (compact) support of P's (unnormalized) likelihood, then we take partitions $x_i^\sharp$ such that $x^\sharp = \bigcup_i x_i^\sharp$. We use an equal-area splitting strategy but support other strategies (see Sect. 8). For each split $x_i^\sharp$, AURA computes $[\![P]\!]^\sharp(x_i^\sharp, d^\sharp)$ in lines 1-2. A key efficiency insight (inspired by DNN verification [80]) is that each split $x_i^\sharp$ can be processed in parallel on a GPU to compute $[\![P]\!]^\sharp(x_i^\sharp, d^\sharp)$.

Abstract Dataset. Another input to AURA is the abstract dataset $d^\sharp$ representing the observed data points's bounded range. A novelty of AURA is that we can verify bounds for both a single posterior, *and* an infinite set of posteriors. This set of posteriors is controlled by the width of $d^\sharp$, which represents the allowed dataset perturbation range.

Normalization. AURA finally outputs bounds on normalized posterior. To obtain bounds on the normalized posterior $[\![P]\!]_n^\sharp$ using unnormalized posterior bounds $[\![P]\!]^\sharp$, AURA performs abstract integration to bound the normalizing constant using the strategy in Definition 4. The partitions used in the previous step can be reused for lower and upper Riemann sums (line 4) as mentioned in Sect. 5.2. Upon computing the normalizing constant bound $[c_l, c_u]$, AURA performs interval division to normalize the posterior bound of each split (lines 5-6).

7.1 Certified Bounds on Probabilistic Queries

An optional input to AURA's algorithm is a query Q. AURA can use the normalized posterior bounds $[\![P]\!]_n^\sharp$ to certify bounds on the posterior probability of queries. In the data perturbation setting, the bounds computed by $[\![P]\!]_n^\sharp$ enclose not just a single posterior distribution (like in [5,73]) but an *infinite* number of posteriors. Hence, AURA's bounds on a query's probability hold for an infinite set of posteriors.

Definition 6. *Queries. A query Q is a logical formula over the variables of P given by the following grammar:* $Q ::= x_j \geq c \mid x_j \leq c \mid Q \wedge Q \mid Q \vee Q$

The queries formally define measurable events, hence we can define the posterior distribution's probability of a query Q. This probability is defined as:

$$Pr_{x \sim [\![P]\!]_n(\cdot, d)}(Q) = \int_x 1_Q \cdot [\![P]\!]_n(x, d)\, dx, \tag{6}$$

where 1_Q is the binary indicator function for the event Q. However, as in Sect. 4, in general this integral is not tractable, hence AURA *over-approximates* this probability. The over-approximation is computed using an abstract integration similar to Definition 4. The key difference is that we use the *normalized* posterior interval bounds, $[\![P]\!]_n^\sharp$, instead of the unnormalized bounds $[\![P]\!]^\sharp$ that Definition 4 uses. The new abstract integration is:

$$\int^\sharp 1_Q \cdot [\![P]\!]_n^\sharp(x, d^\sharp) dx = \sum_i [\![P]\!]_n^\sharp(x_i^\sharp, d^\sharp) \cdot Vol(x_i^\sharp \cap \{x : Q\}) = [l_Q, u_Q] \tag{7}$$

The summation ($\sum$) is interval addition and the $Vol(\cdot)$ function computes the Lebesgue measure of the input set. Since each $x_i^\sharp$ is an interval, and the set $\{x : Q\}$ is a union or intersection of finitely many intervals, the result of $x_i^\sharp \cap \{x : Q\}$ is itself a union or intersection of finitely many intervals and thus its Lebesgue measure can be computed easily. Hence Eq. 7 ultimately computes an interval that encloses the true integral. We can now state the soundness result:

Theorem 5. *(Soundness) For probabilistic program P, dataset $d \in \gamma(d^\sharp)$ and Query Q we have: $Pr_{x \sim [\![P]\!]_n(\cdot, d)}(Q) \in \int^\sharp 1_Q \cdot [\![P]\!]_n^\sharp(x, d^\sharp) dx$*

Proof.

$$\int^{\sharp} 1_Q \cdot [\![P]\!]_n^{\sharp}(x, d^{\sharp})dx = \sum_i [\![P]\!]_n^{\sharp}(x_i^{\sharp}, d^{\sharp}) \cdot Vol(x_i^{\sharp} \cap \{x : Q\})$$
$$= \sum_i [l_i, u_i] \cdot Vol(x_i^{\sharp} \cap \{x : Q\})$$
$$= \sum_i \left[l_i \cdot Vol(x_i^{\sharp} \cap \{x : Q\}), \ u_i \cdot Vol(x_i^{\sharp} \cap \{x : Q\}) \right]$$
$$= \left[\sum_i l_i \cdot Vol(x_i^{\sharp} \cap \{x : Q\}), \ \sum_i u_i \cdot Vol(x_i^{\sharp} \cap \{x : Q\}) \right]$$

Here the lower and upper bounds are just lower and upper Riemann sums, hence they enclose $\int 1_Q \cdot [\![P]\!]_n(x,d)dx$, which is exactly just $Pr_{x \sim [\![P]\!]_n(\cdot, d)}(Q)$. □

While the computational difficulty in evaluating this integral scales with the latent variable's dimension and the size of the query's predicate, the integration remains tractable for all our benchmarks.

7.2 Robustness

This soundness result directly implies the following proposition which relates soundness to a formal notion of robustness of probabilistic programs. Certification of this robustness property for a given program, is the most important output of AURA's verification approach.

Proposition 1 (Robustness). *For probabilistic program P, Query Q, data d_i and perturbation parameter ϵ_i then for any $d_i' \in [d_i - \epsilon_i, d_i + \epsilon_i]$*

$$Q_l \leq Pr_{x \sim [\![P]\!]_n(\cdot, d_i')}(Q) \leq Q_u$$

where Q_l and Q_u are the bounds computed by AURA in Algorithm 1

This proposition establishes that for a probabilistic program P, conditioning on observed data $d_i \in \mathbb{R}$, if an adversary can perturb each d_i within a range $[l_{d_i}, u_{d_i}]$, then the posterior probability of an event Q under *any such* adversarially perturbed posterior distribution of P is still guaranteed to lie between $[Q_l, Q_u]$ where Q_l, Q_u are the bounds computed by AURA. Thus AURA certifies the robustness of a posterior probability of a query subject to data perturbations.

7.3 Scope and Limitations

AURA only supports `for` loops with fixed number of iterations instead of `while` loops, since potentially unbounded loops can violate the pseudoconcavity properties. For data perturbations, AURA's support for discrete distributions remains limited to the `flip(p)` primitive which simulates a Bernoulli variable but is only used for encoding mixtures of continuous distributions. Similarly, AURA does not support conditioning on Boolean predicates (e.g., `observe(x>1)`).

While pseudo-concavity checks exists (e.g., using Hladik et al. [31]), AURA's implementation already assumes the probabilistic program is pseudoconcave and thus lacks such automated checks.

In addition, while it is theoretically possible to run projected gradient descent on zonotopes or polyhedra, our implementation requires the interval domain.

Lastly, our data perturbation specifications support *local* robustness guarantees and not global robustness guarantees since our intervals only cover a local range (e.g., $\pm\epsilon$) around a given data point, d_i. In contrast to reasoning about values in a local range (e.g., $[d_i - \epsilon, d_i + \epsilon]$), global robustness requires logical reasoning over *all* values in $\mathbb{R}$, a task which is not yet tractable.

8   Implementation

We implemented AURA to strike a balance between precision, efficiency and scalability. AURA supports a wide range of known distributions, including *normal, uniform, gamma, exponential, bernoulli, logistic, laplace, beta, bernoulli_logit,* and *bernoulli_probit*. For infinite support distributions (e.g., `normal`) AURA uses truncated versions in the priors to ensure compact support (as also done by GuBPI [5]), which we denote with a subscript t. The observed distributions need not be truncated. While AURA's implementation assumes ideal real arithmetic (as is common in ML verification [5,40,74]), our evaluation shows that numerical imprecision resulting from floating-point is negligible (Appendix E.3). Furthermore, our implementation can be directly extended to soundly account for floating-point roundoff error by using existing techniques [49] or by using arbitrary precision numerical libraries, e.g., NVIDIA XMP [79] for GPUs.

Parallelization. The steps of Algorithm 1 are parallelizable on CPU or GPU: the two for-loops are data-parallel, while abstract integration and computing bounds on queries are reductions. We implemented AURA using PyTorch, supporting both GPU and CPU backends. To scale to large datasets common in modern applications, which may exceed the memory of a single GPU, we used software tiling and sharding to distribute computations across multiple GPUs. We implemented a method for integration of local posterior tiles, eliminating the need to store and communicate all posterior tiles between devices.

Efficient Lipschitz Analysis for Learning Rate Selection. To determine the learning rate η, PyTorch's Automatic Differentiation allows us to compute the Lipschitz constant (LC) of the unnormalized posterior $[\![P]\!]$. The LC is bounded by the largest gradient norm (for the local region of the split), and for known distributions, this maximum gradient will occur at the boundaries. Furthermore, using the rules from [4], we aggregate the LCs of individual distributions and estimate the one for the unnormalized posteriors.

Precision-Enhancing Splitting. AURA performs partitions the parameter space into splits $x_i^\sharp$, which can be analyzed in parallel. However one question we ask is what is the *best* strategy for this splitting. While different splitting heuristics do not affect the soundness, they *do* affect the precision.

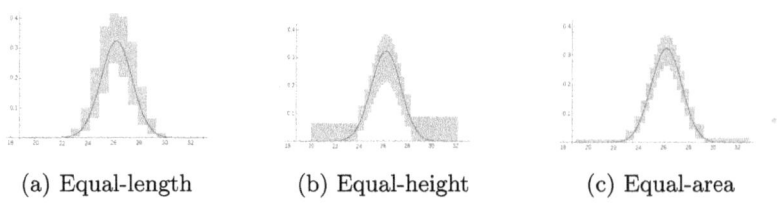

(a) Equal-length   (b) Equal-height   (c) Equal-area

Fig. 10. Example of the Analysis Results by Different Splitting Strategies.

As an illustration, Fig. 10 shows the resulting bounds obtained from three different heuristics each using 20 splits on a simple regression model (lightspeed). The blue line represents the ground truth and the bounds AURA found are the gray boxes. Figure 10a shows the result from the equal-length strategy, which divides the variable interval in equal-length sub-intervals. Due to its simplicity, this strategy is widely used, e.g. by the baseline GuBPI. However, as the plot shows, while the bounds at the tails are reasonably precise, the bounds around the mode (middle part) of the curve are imprecise.

Another strategy is the equal-height splits (Fig. 10b), which divides the intervals such that the resulting bounds have the same height. Without knowing the true bounds beforehand, AURA could run a separate analysis (like AQUA [34]) once with a small number of splits (e.g. 60 splits with equal-length) to estimate the shape of the curve, and then use those results to decide the splits with approximately equal height. Nevertheless, this strategy is imprecise for bounding the tails of the distribution.

Table 1. Benchmark program details. Symbols used: $\mathcal{B}$: Bernoulli, $\mathcal{U}$: Real Uniform, $\mathcal{N}$: Normal, $\mathcal{N}_t$: Truncated Normal, $\mathcal{S}$: Logistic. Operators: +: mix of distributions, ×: product of densities, $^\alpha$: number of priors/data.

Program	Prior	Lik	Description	PC
human_height	$\mathcal{B} \times (\mathcal{N}_t + \mathcal{N}_t)$	$\mathcal{N}^3$	Learning height with mixture prior [56]	✓$_{mix}$
reg_logistic	$\mathcal{N}_t$	$\mathcal{S}^{919}$	Linear regression with logistic likelihood [64]	✓$_{LC}$
lightspeed	$\mathcal{U}^2$	$\mathcal{N}^{40}$	Linear regression [68]	✓$_{PC}$
anova_radon_n	$\mathcal{U}^2$	$\mathcal{N}^{40}$	Hierarchical linear regression, non-predictive [68]	✓$_{PC}$
reg_laplace	$\mathcal{U}^2 \times \mathcal{L}_t^2$	$\mathcal{N}^{919}$	Linear regression with Laplace priors [78]	✓$_{LC}$
prior_mix	$\mathcal{B} \times (\mathcal{N}_t + \mathcal{N}_t)$	$\mathcal{N}^{10}$	Model with mixture prior [34]	✓$_{mix}$
IQStan	$\mathcal{U}^3$	$\mathcal{N}^3 \times \mathcal{N}^3$	Regression on 2 datasets w. shared variance [41]	✓$_{PC}$
timeseries	$\mathcal{U}^3$	$\mathcal{N}^{99}$	Timeseries model [68]	✓$_{LC}$
unemployment	$\mathcal{U}^3$	$\mathcal{N}^{40}$	Linear Regression [68]	✓$_{PC}$
altermu2	$\mathcal{U}^2$	$\mathcal{N}^{40}$	Model with param symmetry [34]	✓$_{LC}$
robust_model[†]	$\mathcal{N}^{101}$	$\mathcal{N}^{100}$	Robust model w. many local latent params. [71]	✓$_{mix}$

[†] This benchmark is evaluated separately as it requires more splits.

Therefore, we designed the third strategy to strike a balance between precisely bounding the tails and precisely bounding the mode. In Fig. 10c, we generate splits that results in similar the area for each bounding box. We estimate the shape of the curve, and use the results to generate splits with approximately equal area. We use this equal-area strategy as the default in AURA analysis, however AURA supports all three strategies and allows other customized splits.

9 Methodology

Benchmarks. We evaluated AURA on 11 benchmarks from existing literature including both PL works and real world end-user scientific applications with diverse program structure and distributions. We present the details of our selected benchmarks in Table 1. The studies of these models presented actionable insights to domain-experts across multiple communities (for discussion, see Appendix B). For each program, we manually verified its pseudoconcavity (the details of checking in Appendix C).

Baselines. We initially selected GuBPI [5], the start-of-the art tool for obtaining sound bounds on single posteriors and PSI [20], which leverages symbolic analysis to determine the exact posterior. However, our initial experiments for certifying bounds on *single posteriors* (without data perturbation) showed that: (1) GuBPI results in unacceptable imprecision even for simpler programs we studied here, is $> 70x$ slower than AURA on CPU, exhibits numerical instability, and the implementation does not support interval-valued data; (2) PSI can symbolically analyze programs with symbolic data noise, but its integration scales only to programs with a few observations. Hence, these tools cannot support computing bounds for *a set of posteriors*, which is needed for verifying robustness of complex probabilistic programs benchmarks we consider. This reason also rules out works derived from those tools such as PSense [37] and [73]. Nevertheless, to provide evidence for this choice we present a detailed comparison of AURA with GuBPI and PSI for *single posteriors* in Appendix E.

As the baseline, we instead implemented interval-based abstract transformers within AURA, akin to GuBPI's interval abstraction, but we carefully enhanced its numerical stability. Evaluating this interval analysis version on the benchmarks achieves much higher precision than GuBPI.

Precision Metric. We define the lower p_l and upper p_u bound functions for marginal posterior of the parameter x: $p_l(x) = l$ and $p_u(x) = u$ where $[l, u] = [\![P]\!]_n^\sharp(x_i^\sharp, d^\sharp)$ for $x \in \gamma(x_i^\sharp)$. Total Variation Distance (TVD) measures the discrepancy between the two bounds of a distribution: $\text{TVD}_x = \frac{1}{2} \int |p_l(x) - p_u(x)| \, dx$. For multiple parameters, TVD is averaged across each: $\text{TVD} = \frac{1}{M} \sum_{j=1}^{M} \text{TVD}_{x_j}$. Appendix D gives more detailed definitions of the metrics.

Setup for Adversarial Data Perturbation Analysis. We use AURA to find bounds on posteriors obtainable after data perturbations. We use 200 splits for the input domain. Perturbations involve 1–5 key data points per benchmark, identified by gradient magnitude $\frac{\partial}{\partial d}[\![P]\!](x,d)$. For datasets with <100 points, perturbations are capped at five points or 5% of the dataset. Perturbation intervals are computed by modifying the original data by $[0, 0.01\sigma]$ if $sign(\frac{\partial}{\partial d}[\![P]\!](x,d))$ is positive or $[-0.01\sigma, 0]$ if negative, where σ is the dataset's standard deviation. We adapt the adversarial data perturbation method from the Fast Gradient Signed Method (FGSM) [25], a prevalent method in machine learning, which is to add a small perturbation towards the direction increasing the loss (cf. decreasing likelihood). AURA and the baseline are enhanced with GPU acceleration and equal-area splits for efficiency.

Experimental Setup. We run AURA and all the other tools on a AMD 4.2 GHz machine with 32 cores and with 2 NVIDIA RTX A5000 GPUs.

10 Evaluation

We next describe the results that demonstrate AURA effectiveness and efficiency to compute posteriors under data perturbation and verify probabilistic queries.

10.1 Posteriors Under Data Perturbation

Precision of Bounds. We use AURA to find bounds for a set of posteriors when subjected to data perturbation. Table 2 presents the precision (in TVD) alongside the run time for both AURA and a baseline interval analysis. We run both using a GPU (CPU shows the same time trend).

On average (geo-mean), AURA achieves a precision 12.8× better than that of the interval analysis. We observed across all benchmarks that the data perturbation causing the maximum posterior error (TVD) almost never occurs at the extremes of the data perturbation interval, indicating that the sound bounds cannot be simulated just from data values at perturbation extremes.

Execution Time. AURA's run time averages at 3.14s (geometric mean). The increase in run time when compared to AURA analysing a single posterior without perturbation is due to the additional complexity of high-dimensional optimization across both the parameters and the data dimensions subjected to perturbation. Compared to the interval analysis, AURA has an additional cost of iteratively evaluating the unnormalized posterior during gradient ascent.

10.2 Analysis Examples

Figures 11 and 12 illustrate the bounds computed by AURA for two example models under data perturbation, compared with the results from the interval analysis and reference distributions generated via Stan sampling. To generate the reference distributions, we simulated at least three concrete perturbations for each perturbed data point and used Stan's NUTS to collect 400,000 samples for each concrete perturbation.

Table 2. AURA and Interval Analysis Results for Data Perturbation

Program	TVD		Time (s)	
	AURA	Interval	AURA (GPU)	Interval (GPU)
human_height	0.04	0.09 (2.3×)	0.25	0.02
reg_logistic	0.05	8.13 (175.8×)	3.49	1.39
lightspeed	0.07	0.56 (8.2×)	0.19	0.04
anova_radon_n	0.07	0.57 (8.2×)	1.52	0.05
reg_laplace	0.07	6.28 (87.6×)	10.44	1.18
prior_mix	0.07	0.23 (3.2×)	0.27	0.03
IQStan	0.07	0.20 (2.7×)	15.67	0.14
timeseries	0.18	1.04 (5.7×)	335.16	5.37
unemployment	0.23	4.10 (18.1×)	131.76	0.82
altermu2	0.28	16.43 (58.2×)	0.19	0.06
GeoMean	0.09	1.17 (12.8×)	3.14	0.19

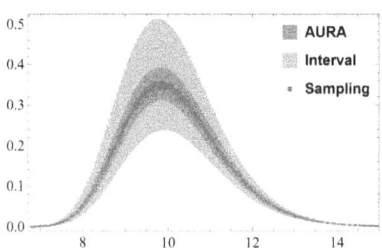

Fig. 11. lightspeed (param: σ)

Fig. 12. unemployment (param: β_1).

The plots show the parameter value on the x-axis against the posterior probability density on the y-axis, with red dots representing the sampled reference distributions and blue and orange rectangles representing the bounds computed by AURA and interval analysis, respectively. Consistent with the findings reported in Table 2, AURA shows significantly tighter bounds than those from interval analysis. Further, the AURA bounds are close to the envelope created by observed samples (red dots), which give an under-approximation. This precision of AURA's analysis stems from its optimization-based abstraction, which is designed to find the narrowest bounds before normalization.

Table 3. Results for Queries under Data Perturbation ("|" refers to the same benchmark as in the previous row)

Program	Query	Probability Bound		
		AURA	Interval	Improv.
human_height	$\mu > 165$	[0.93, 1.00]	[0.85, 1.00]	2.1×
		$170 < \mu < 172$	[0.11, 0.13]	[0.10, 0.14]	1.7×
reg_logistic	$\beta_0 \geq 1.35 \vee \beta_0 < 1.15$	[0.05, 0.07]	[0.00, 0.98]	63.6×
		$\beta_0 \geq 1.25$	[0.33, 0.40]	[0.02, 1.00]	14.0×
lightspeed	$20 \leq \beta_0 < 40$	[0.88, 1.00]	[0.47, 1.00]	4.4×
		$\beta_0 < 30 \wedge \sigma < 10$	[0.42, 0.55]	[0.21, 1.00]	6.1×
anova_radon_n	$0.9 \leq a_0 \leq 1$	[0.28, 0.34]	[0.14, 0.66]	7.6×
		$\sigma_y \leq 1 \vee a_0 > 1$	[0.86, 1.00]	[0.46, 1.00]	3.9×
reg_laplace	$1.3 \leq \beta_1 \leq 1.35$	[0.27, 0.36]	[0.02, 1.00]	11.5×
		$\beta_0 \geq -0.5$	[0.08, 0.11]	[0.01, 1.00]	34.1×
prior_mix	$\mu_0 \leq 0$	[0.74, 0.97]	[0.58, 1.00]	1.8×
		$\mu_0 > -2 \wedge \mu_0 < 2$	[0.08, 0.11]	[0.06, 0.12]	1.4×
IQStan	$\mu_1 \geq 85 \vee \mu_2 \geq 85$	[0.87, 1.00]	[0.71, 1.00]	2.2×
		$5 < \sigma < 10 \wedge \mu_1 > 95 \wedge \mu_2 > 95$	[0.25, 0.32]	[0.21, 0.38]	2.3×
timeseries	$\alpha < -1 \vee \beta < 1 \wedge lag < 0.8$	[0.69, 1.00]	[0.31, 1.00]	2.3×
		$\alpha > -0.5 \wedge lag > 0.5$	[0.02, 0.04]	[0.01, 0.09]	4.3×
unemployment	$\sigma < 1.2 \wedge \beta_0 < 3 \wedge \beta_1 < 0.7$	[0.19, 0.41]	[0.03, 1.00]	4.5×
		$0.95 < \beta_1 < 1$	[0.00, 0.01]	[0.00, 0.04]	10.4×
altermu2	$1 \leq \mu_0 \leq 1.1$	[0.02, 0.04]	[0.00, 0.84]	34.0×
		$\mu_0 < 1.5 \wedge \mu_1 < 1.5$	[0.47, 1.00]	[0.02, 1.00]	1.9×

10.3 Queries Under Data Perturbation

We demonstrate the use of AURA in evaluating the posterior probability of specific events when the input dataset is subject to perturbations. Intuitively, one provides a query, as described in Definition 6, and AURA then computes sound bounds on the posterior probability of the event defined by the query, where the probability bounds hold for *any* posterior that could result from the data perturbation.

Table 3 illustrates the results and the computation time AURA used to bound the posterior probability of each query. For each program amenable to data perturbation (i.e. those with continuous data), we formulated two distinct queries (shown in the **Query** column). The **Probability** columns show the bounds computed by AURA and the interval analysis we implemented as the baseline. The **Improv.** column shows the improvement by AURA, reflected in how many times smaller AURA's interval is compared to the results from interval analysis.

Across all programs with data perturbation, AURA's bounds on the queries are much more precise, being on geomean 5.35x narrower than the bounds from interval arithmetic. The time for each query is almost identical to the time for computing the posterior bounds under perturbation (geomean $\sim 3.1s$).

Table 4. AURA Scalability to Large Numbers of Local Latents.

#Local Latents	#Splits	W.o. Perturbation		W. Perturbation	
		Time (s)	TVD	Time (s)	TVD
20	1600	3.1	0.07	5.6	0.11
50	1600	7.7	0.19	14.4	0.33
50	5000	41.0	0.05	150.0	0.12
100	5000	82.1	0.11	303.9	0.26
100	10000	239.5	0.05	1017.4	0.16

10.4 Scaling to a Large Number of Local Latent Parameters

We evaluated the robust linear regression model in Fig. 9 by varying the number of latent parameters and splits. AURA's inference successfully scales to the large number of local latents in such a model. Table 4 presents the results for the model with up to 100 local latents/datapoints, with and without one datapoint subject to perturbation. This model requires more fine-grained splitting than our other benchmarks due to fine-grained integration of latents.

10.5 Ablation Studies

We performed several ablation studies of AURA's algorithm, detailed in Appendix E.3 and [33] and summarized next. (1) Increasing the number of observed data points to 5000 shows AURA's time increases linearly with data size. (2) AURA can extend computation across GPUs and obtian parallelization speeudp on CPU depends primarily on the size of the GPU memory. (3) Floating point imprecision vs double is small, with geomean error $\sim 10^{-7}$ and double taking only 10% more time on a GPU. (4) Increasing the number of splits increases the precision of the result, but also increases run time; for our benchmarks 200 splits (used in the evaluation) gives near-optimal point in this tradeoff space.

11 Related Work

Exact Probabilistic Programming Systems. Despite recent progress, exact inference systems are limited for continuous distributions: e.g., many support only discrete models (DICE [32]), only handle Sum-Product networks [62] or cannot solve many complicated integrals (PSI [20], Hakaru [55]). Exact inference also faces obstacles with scaling to large numbers of data observations.

Interval-Based Abstractions for Probabilistic Inference. Closest in spirit to our work is GuBPI [5] which computes interval bounds on a *single* posterior. While GuBPI supports recursion it is much less precise than AURA and cannot scale to the datasizes AURA supports. Subsequent work [73] offered improvements to GuBPI, however like GuBPI, [73] also restricts to analyzing bounds for only a single posterior distribution. They *do not* study nor evaluate the problem of certifying bounds for *all* possible posteriors obtainable from a data perturbation; neither [5,73] can be parallelized and thus suffer from scalability concerns. Furthermore, while [7] studies Bayesian inference, in contrast to AURA, their bounds are confidence-interval based and tailored to cumulative distribution functions instead of probability density functions.

Several existing works study probabilistic abstract interpretations [11,47] but they do not consider Bayesian inference and lack `observe` statements and distribution normalization, a limitation also present in other works [9,44,65]. Neither probability boxes [8,16] nor Dempster-Shafer structures [16] can be used in our setting since they do not have a mechanism to reason about Bayesian inference. Additionally, [41,51] compute heuristic bounds on likelihoods for fixed-point size selection, but they lack the formal verification guarantees that AURA provides and they do not study the data perturbation setting that AURA targets.

Sensitivity and Robustness Analysis of Probabilistic Programs. In addition, there are a few relevant works related to the sensitivity and robustness of probabilistic programs. PSense [37] performs sensitivity analysis on probabilistic programs but it builds directly on PSI [20] and thus inherits the same limitations regarding scalability. PSense also needs to analytically compute another integral characterizing the difference between the two normalized distributions with noise variables.

Additionally, AquaSense [81] is a tool that directly builds on Aqua [34], which provides only a weak asymptotic theorem that the computed distribution estimate converges to the true distribution when the number of splits is infinite (i.e., interval width tends to 0). Moreover, Aqua's distribution estimate provides a soundness guarantee only asymptotically – it has only a sound lower bound, which is equivalent to AURA's lower bound. In contrast, AURA provides both the sound lower and upper bounds for a finite number of splits.

Optimization-Based Abstract Interpretation. Using continuous optimization to perform abstract interpretation and sound bound computation has been extensively studied [1,18,40,52–54,61,63,66,72,75]. However these works target computations like DNNs [54,66], security properties [63], automatic differentiation [40], and non-probabilistic programs [1,18,53,75]. Unlike AURA, these applications do not typically obey the pseudoconcavity properties.

12 Conclusion

We presented AURA, a novel abstract interpretation of probabilistic programs that can certify bounds on posterior distributions under data perturbations, By designing custom, precise and scalable abstract transformers for probabilistic programming using optimization, AURA represents a first step towards making provably robust probabilistic programming a reality. We anticipate that AURA also opens the door to obtaining certified robustness for general probabilistic models (like Normalizing Flows and Probabilistic Circuits), and even abstracting other (non-probabilistic) pseudoconcave functions.

Acknowledgments. This research was supported in part by NSF Grants No. CCF-1846354, CCF-2008883, and CCF-2313028.

References

1. Adjé, A., Garoche, P.-L., Werey, A.: Quadratic zonotopes. In: Feng, X., Park, S. (eds.) APLAS 2015. LNCS, vol. 9458, pp. 127–145. Springer, Cham (2015). https://doi.org/10.1007/978-3-319-26529-2_8
2. Ahn, K., Jain, P., Ji, Z., Kale, S., Netrapalli, P., Shamir, G.I.: Reproducibility in optimization: theoretical framework and limits. Adv. Neural. Inf. Process. Syst. **35**, 18022–18033 (2022)
3. Bagnoli, M., Bergstrom, T.: Log-concave probability and its applications. In: Rationality and Equilibrium: A Symposium in Honor of Marcel K. Richter, pp. 217–241 (2006)
4. Barthe, G., Espitau, T., Grégoire, B., Hsu, J., Strub, P.Y.: Proving expected sensitivity of probabilistic programs, vol. 2 (2017)
5. Beutner, R., Ong, C.H.L., Zaiser, F.: Guaranteed bounds for posterior inference in universal probabilistic programming. In: Proceedings of the 43rd ACM SIGPLAN International Conference on Programming Language Design and Implementation, pp. 536–551 (2022)
6. Bherwani, H., et al.: Understanding COVID-19 transmission through Bayesian probabilistic modeling and GIS-based Voronoi approach: a policy perspective. Environ. Dev. Sustain. **23**(4), 5846–5864 (2021)
7. Boreale, M., Collodi, L.: Bayesian parameter estimation with guarantees via interval analysis and simulation. In: International Conference on Verification, Model Checking, and Abstract Interpretation (2023)
8. Bouissou, O., Goubault, E., Goubault-Larrecq, J., Putot, S.: A generalization of p-boxes to affine arithmetic. Computing **94**, 189–201 (2012)
9. Constantinides, G., Dahlqvist, F., Rakamarić, Z., Salvia, R.: Automated roundoff error analysis of probabilistic floating-point computations. ACM Trans. Probab. Mach, Learn (2024)
10. Cousot, P., Cousot, R.: Abstract interpretation: a unified lattice model for static analysis of programs by construction or approximation of fixpoints. In: POPL '77, pp. 238–252. ACM (1977)
11. Cousot, P., Monerau, M.: Probabilistic abstract interpretation. In: Programming Languages and Systems, pp. 169–193 (2012)

12. Cruz, J.B., Pérez, L.L.: Convergence of a projected gradient method variant for Quasiconvex objectives. Nonlinear Anal. Theory Meth. Appl. **73**(9), 2917–2922 (2010)
13. Darir, H., Dullerud, G.E., Borisov, N.: Probflow: using probabilistic programming in anonymous communication networks. In: NDSS (2023)
14. Dunn, J.C.: Global and asymptotic convergence rate estimates for a class of projected gradient processes. SIAM J. Control. Optim. **19**(3), 368–400 (1981)
15. Fernando, V., Joshi, K., Laurel, J., Misailovic, S.: Diamont: dynamic monitoring of uncertainty for distributed asynchronous programs. In: Feng, L., Fisman, D. (eds.) RV 2021. LNCS, vol. 12974, pp. 184–206. Springer, Cham (2021). https://doi.org/10.1007/978-3-030-88494-9_10
16. Ferson, S., Kreinovich, V., Ginzburg, L., Sentz, F.: Constructing probability boxes and dempster-shafer structures. Technical reprt, Sandia National Lab.(SNL-NM), Albuquerque, NM (United States); Sandia (2003)
17. Foster, N., Kozen, D., Mamouras, K., Reitblatt, M., Silva, A.: Probabilistic netkat. In: Programming Languages and Systems: 25th European Symposium on Programming, ESOP 2016, pp. 282–309 (2016)
18. Gawlitza, T.M., Seidl, H., Adjé, A., Gaubert, S., Goubault, É.: Abstract interpretation meets convex optimization. J. Symb. Comput. **47**(12), 1416–1446 (2012)
19. Gehr, T., Misailovic, S., Tsankov, P., Vanbever, L., Wiesmann, P., Vechev, M.: Bayonet: probabilistic inference for networks. In: Proceedings of the 39th ACM SIGPLAN Conference on Programming Language Design and Implementation, pp. 586–602. ACM (2018)
20. Gehr, T., Misailovic, S., Vechev, M.: PSI: exact symbolic inference for probabilistic programs. In: International Conference on Computer Aided Verification (2016)
21. Gelman, A., Lee, D., Guo, J.: Stan a probabilistic programming language for Bayesian inference and optimization. J. Educ. Beh. Statist. (2015)
22. Ghorbal, K., Goubault, E., Putot, S.: The zonotope abstract domain taylor1+. In: Computer Aided Verification: 21st International Conference, CAV 2009, pp. 627–633 (2009)
23. Ghorbal, K., Goubault, E., Putot, S.: A logical product approach to zonotope intersection. In: Computer Aided Verification: 22nd International Conference, CAV 2010, Edinburgh, UK, July 15-19, 2010. Proceedings 22, pp. 212–226 (2010)
24. Gloeckler, M., Deistler, M., Macke, J.H.: Adversarial robustness of amortized Bayesian inference. In: Proceedings of the 40th International Conference on Machine Learning, pp. 11493–11524 (2023)
25. Goodfellow, I.J., Shlens, J., Szegedy, C.: Explaining and harnessing adversarial examples. arXiv preprint arXiv:1412.6572 (2014)
26. Gordon, A.D., Henzinger, T.A., Nori, A.V., Rajamani, S.K.: Probabilistic programming. In: FoSE (2014)
27. GuBPI – An Analyzer for Probabilistic Programs to Compute Guaranteed Bounds on the Posterior (2022). https://github.com/gubpi-tool/gubpi
28. Hazan, E., Levy, K., Shalev-Shwartz, S.: Beyond convexity: stochastic quasi-convex optimization. In: Advances in Neural Information Processing Systems, vol. 28 (2015)
29. Heck, D.W., Thielmann, I., Moshagen, M., Hilbig, B.E.: Who lies? A large-scale reanalysis linking basic personality traits to unethical decision making. Judgm. Decis. Mak. **13**(4), 356–371 (2018)
30. Higgins, J.E., Polak, E.: Minimizing pseudoconvex functions on convex compact sets. J. Optim. Theory Appl. **65**(1), 1–27 (1990)

31. Hladík, M., Kolev, L.V., Skalna, I.: Linear interval parametric approach to testing pseudoconvexity. J. Global Optim. **79**, 351–368 (2021)
32. Holtzen, S., Van den Broeck, G., Millstein, T.: Scaling exact inference for discrete probabilistic programs. Proc. ACM Program. Lang. **4**(OOPSLA), 1–31 (2020)
33. Huang, Z.: Enhancing trustworthiness in probabilistic programming: systematic approaches for robust and accurate inference. Ph.D. thesis, University of Illinois at Urbana-Champaign (2024)
34. Huang, Z., Dutta, S., Misailovic, S.: Aqua: automated quantized inference for probabilistic programs. In: International Symposium on Automated Technology for Verification and Analysis (2021)
35. Huang, Z., Dutta, S., Misailovic, S.: Astra: understanding the practical impact of robustness for probabilistic programs. In: Uncertainty in Artificial Intelligence, pp. 900–910. PMLR (2023)
36. Huang, z., Laurel, J., Dutta, S., Misailovic, S.: Appendix for aura: precise abstract interpretation of probabilistic programs with interval uncertainty (2025). https://github.com/uiuc-arc/AURA/AURAappendix.pdf
37. Huang, Z., Wang, Z., Misailovic, S.: Psense: Automatic sensitivity analysis for probabilistic programs. In: 16th International Symposium on Automated Technology for Verification and Analysis. ATVA (2018)
38. Kučera, M., Tsankov, P., Gehr, T., Guarnieri, M., Vechev, M.: Synthesis of probabilistic privacy enforcement. In: Proceedings of the 2017 ACM SIGSAC Conference on Computer and Communications Security, pp. 391–408 (2017)
39. Laurel, J., Misailovic, S.: Continualization of probabilistic programs with correction. In: ESOP 2020. LNCS, vol. 12075, pp. 366–393. Springer, Cham (2020). https://doi.org/10.1007/978-3-030-44914-8_14
40. Laurel, J., Qian, S.B., Singh, G., Misailovic, S.: Synthesizing precise static analyzers for automatic differentiation. Proc. ACM Program. Langu. **7**(OOPSLA2) (2023)
41. Laurel, J., Yang, R., Sehgal, A., Ugare, S., Misailovic, S.: Statheros: compiler for efficient low-precision probabilistic programming. In: 58th ACM/IEEE Design Automation Conference (DAC). IEEE (2021)
42. Laurel, J., Yang, R., Singh, G., Misailovic, S.: A dual number abstraction for static analysis of Clarke Jacobians. Proc. ACM Program. Lang. **6**(POPL), 1–30 (2022)
43. Laurel, J., Yang, R., Ugare, S., Nagel, R., Singh, G., Misailovic, S.: A general construction for abstract interpretation of higher-order automatic differentiation. Proc. ACM Program. Lang. **6**(OOPSLA2), 1007–1035 (2022)
44. Lohar, D., Prokop, M., Darulova, E.: Sound probabilistic numerical error analysis. In: Ahrendt, W., Tapia Tarifa, S.L. (eds.) IFM 2019. LNCS, vol. 11918, pp. 322–340. Springer, Cham (2019). https://doi.org/10.1007/978-3-030-34968-4_18
45. Majthay, A., Whinston, A.: Quasi-concave minimization subject to linear constraints. Discret. Math. **9**(1), 35–59 (1974)
46. Mangasarian, O.L.: Pseudo-convex functions. In: Stochastic optimization models in finance, pp. 23–32. Elsevier (1975)
47. Mardziel, P., Magill, S., Hicks, M., Srivatsa, M.: Dynamic enforcement of knowledge-based security policies using probabilistic abstract interpretation. J. Comput. Secur. **21**(4), 463–532 (2013)
48. Wikipedia: Mean absolute error (2023). https://en.wikipedia.org/wiki/Mean_absolute_error
49. Miné, A.: Relational abstract domains for the detection of floating-point run-time errors. In: Schmidt, D. (ed.) ESOP 2004. LNCS, vol. 2986, pp. 3–17. Springer, Heidelberg (2004). https://doi.org/10.1007/978-3-540-24725-8_2

50. Miné, A., et al.: Tutorial on static inference of numeric invariants by abstract interpretation. Foundations and Trends in Prog. Lang. **4**(3-4) (2017)
51. Misra, A., Laurel, J., Misailovic, S.: VIX: analysis-driven compiler for efficient low-precision variational inference. In: 2023 Design, Automation & Test in Europe Conference & Exhibition (DATE), pp. 1–6. IEEE (2023)
52. Monniaux, D.: On using floating-point computations to help an exact linear arithmetic decision procedure. In: Bouajjani, A., Maler, O. (eds.) CAV 2009. LNCS, vol. 5643, pp. 570–583. Springer, Heidelberg (2009). https://doi.org/10.1007/978-3-642-02658-4_42
53. Monniaux, D.P.: Automatic modular abstractions for linear constraints. In: SIGPLAN Not, pp. 140–151 (2009)
54. Müller, M.N., Makarchuk, G., Singh, G., Püschel, M., Vechev, M.: Prima: general and precise neural network certification via scalable convex hull approximations. Proc. ACM Program. Lang. **6**(POPL) (2022)
55. Narayanan, P., Carette, J., Romano, W., Shan, C.C., Zinkov, R.: Probabilistic inference by program transformation in Hakaru (system description). In: FLOPS 2016 (2016)
56. Oberski, D.: Mixture models: latent profile and latent class analysis. Modern statistical methods for HCI, pp. 275–287 (2016)
57. Owhadi, H., Scovel, C., Sullivan, T.: On the brittleness of Bayesian inference. SIAM Rev. **57**(4), 566–582 (2015)
58. Pardo, R., Rafnsson, W., Probst, C.W., Wąsowski, A.: Privug: using probabilistic programming for quantifying leakage in privacy risk analysis. In: Bertino, E., Shulman, H., Waidner, M. (eds.) ESORICS 2021. LNCS, vol. 12973, pp. 417–438. Springer, Cham (2021). https://doi.org/10.1007/978-3-030-88428-4_21
59. PSI Solver (2019). https://github.com/eth-sri/psi/tree/e729dd7d68e23a4a75731b4bb800c95111a7a30b
60. Roberts, G.O., Rosenthal, J.S.: General state space Markov chains and MCMC algorithms. Probab. Surv. **1**, 20–71 (2004)
61. Rustenholz, L., López-García, P., Morales, J.F., Hermenegildo, M.V.: An order theory framework of recurrence equations for static cost analysis–dynamic inference of non-linear inequality invariants. In: International Static Analysis Symposium, pp. 352–385 (2024)
62. Saad, F.A., Rinard, M.C., Mansinghka, V.K.: SPPL: probabilistic programming with fast exact symbolic inference. In: PLDI (2021)
63. Saha, S., Ghentiyala, S., Lu, S., Bang, L., Bultan, T.: Obtaining information leakage bounds via approximate model counting. Proc. ACM Program. Lang. **7**(PLDI), 1488–1509 (2023)
64. Salimans, T., Karpathy, A., Chen, X., Kingma, D.P.: PixelCNN++: improving the PixelCNN with discretized logistic mixture likelihood and other modifications. arXiv preprint arXiv:1701.05517 (2017)
65. Sankaranarayanan, S., Chakarov, A., Gulwani, S.: Static analysis for probabilistic programs: inferring whole program properties from finitely many paths, pp. 447–458 (2013)
66. Singh, G., et al.: Safety and trust in artificial intelligence with abstract interpretation. Found. Trends Prog. Lang. **8**(3-4) (2025)
67. Smolka, S., et al.: Scalable verification of probabilistic networks. In: PLDI (2019)
68. Stan Examples (2018). https://github.com/stan-dev/example-models
69. Sweet, I., Trilla, J.M.C., Scherrer, C., Hicks, M., Magill, S.: What's the over/under? probabilistic bounds on information leakage. In: International Conference on Principles of Security and Trust (2018)

70. Thall, P.F., Ursino, M., Baudouin, V., Alberti, C., Zohar, S.: Bayesian treatment comparison using parametric mixture priors computed from elicited histograms. Stat. Methods Med. Res. **28**(2), 404–418 (2019)
71. Wang, C., Blei, D.M.: A general method for robust Bayesian modeling. Bayesian Anal. **13**(4), 1159–1187 (2018)
72. Wang, J., Sun, Y., Fu, H., Chatterjee, K., Goharshady, A.K.: Quantitative analysis of assertion violations in probabilistic programs. In: Proceedings of the 42nd ACM SIGPLAN International Conference on Programming Language Design and Implementation (2021)
73. Wang, P., Yang, T., Fu, H., Li, G., Ong, C.H.L.: Static posterior inference of Bayesian probabilistic programming via polynomial solving. In: Proceedings of the ACM on Programming Languages (PLDI) (2024)
74. Wang, S., et al.: Beta-crown: efficient bound propagation with per-neuron split constraints for neural network robustness verification. Adv. Neural. Inf. Process. Syst. **34**, 29909–29921 (2021)
75. Wang, T., Chen, L., Chen, T., Fan, G., Wang, J.: Making rigorous linear programming practical for program analysis. In: 27th International Conference on Principles and Practice of Constraint Programming (2021)
76. Wang, Y., Kucukelbir, A., Blei, D.M.: Robust probabilistic modeling with Bayesian data reweighting. In: Proceedings of the 34th International Conference on Machine Learning, pp. 3646–3655. ICML'17 (2017)
77. Wicker, M., Laurenti, L., Patane, A., Chen, Z., Zhang, Z., Kwiatkowska, M.: Bayesian inference with certifiable adversarial robustness. In: International Conference on Artificial Intelligence and Statistics. PMLR (2021)
78. Williams, P.M.: Bayesian regularization and pruning using a Laplace prior. Neural Comput. **7**(1), 117–143 (1995)
79. XMP Library (2016). https://github.com/NVlabs/xmp/tree/master
80. Yang, R., Laurel, J., Misailovic, S., Singh, G.: Provable defense against geometric transformations. In: 11th International Conference on Learning Representations (2023)
81. Zhou, Z., Huang, Z., Misailovic, S.: AquaSense: automated sensitivity analysis of probabilistic programs via quantized inference. In: International Symposium on Automated Technology for Verification and Analysis, pp. 288–301 (2023)

Comparing the Precision of Abstract Operators in the eBPF Verifier Using Differential Synthesis

Matan Shachnai[✉], Harishankar Vishwanathan, Srinivas Narayana, and Santosh Nagarakatte

Rutgers University, New Brunswick, USA
{m.shachnai,harishankar.vishwanathan,
srinivas.narayana,santosh.nagarakatte}@rutgers.edu

Abstract. The eBPF verifier ensures the safety of user-supplied programs before they are executed in the Linux kernel, relying on abstract interpretation. While the verifier's analysis must be sound, its utility hinges on precision. An overly conservative abstract operator can routinely cause the verifier to reject safe programs. In this paper, we introduce a framework for systematically comparing and validating the precision of competing abstract operator implementations used within the verifier. We provide a formal specification of the precision relationship between two abstract operators across all valid abstract inputs. However, reasoning about all valid abstract inputs over-approximates what is actually reachable in real verifier executions. This is because the eBPF verifier performs verification from a specific set of initial abstract states. Hence, many abstract inputs used in theoretical comparisons may never arise in practice. To address this gap, we propose SMT-based program synthesis to automatically generate concrete eBPF witness programs, explicitly demonstrating observable precision differences in actual verifier executions. Using these techniques and tools, we crafted a more precise multiplication abstract operator in the verifier, bpf_mul. Our multiplication patch has been upstreamed to the Linux kernel where the witness produced by our approach provided demonstration to the kernel developers. We have also used these techniques to check the precision of numerous kernel patches related to abstract operators in the eBPF verifier.

Keywords: Abstract interpretation · Kernel extensions · Program synthesis · eBPF

1 Introduction

The eBPF ecosystem has become the de facto approach for extending the functionality of the Linux kernel, enabling versatility, portability, and performance. It is used in a variety of contexts, such as load balancing [17], access control and DDoS mitigation [19,37], tracing [74], and memory optimization [47]. A key feature of the eBPF ecosystem is its safety guarantees; eBPF employs a static analyzer, the eBPF verifier, which serves as a bulwark to prevent incorrect eBPF programs from crashing or compromising the kernel once they are incorporated into the address space of the kernel. The eBPF verifier checks for safety properties such as program termination, safe memory access, and well-defined arithmetic operations. Once accepted by the verifier, eBPF programs are Just-in-time (JIT) compiled to the machine specific instruction set and implemented as efficiently as any other part of the kernel.

Under the hood, the eBPF verifier is designed using abstract interpretation [32]; it maintains multiple abstract domains that track eBPF register states for a given eBPF program. These abstract domains are then used to identify potential unsound behavior in the given program. It is crucial, therefore, that the analysis performed by the eBPF verifier is sound, rejecting unsafe programs and accepting only safe programs. However, logic bugs in the eBPF verifier can compromise the soundness of its analysis, leading to unsafe programs being accepted. Indeed, in recent years, the eBPF verifier has been shown to exhibit many vulnerabilities stemming from such bugs [2, 9–16, 23–26, 34, 39–41] and has also proved to be a ripe surface for attacks [50, 51, 59, 64].

Since the eBPF verifier has a direct impact on the integrity of the Linux kernel, verifying and testing the correctness of the eBPF verifier has been an ongoing effort [22, 38, 42, 46, 49, 54, 60, 65, 67, 68, 71, 73]. In our own research, we have focused on developing techniques and tools to formally reason about the value tracking performed by the verifier. Specifically, we formalized the tnum abstract domain, proved its soundness, and designed a sound and precise multiplication operator for the domain that has been upstreamed to the Linux kernel [20, 71]. More recently, we designed a tool, Agni [72, 73], which automatically checks the soundness of value tracking performed by the eBPF verifier by generating verification conditions for its abstract operators and proving their correctness. If no such proof can be attained, Agni generates a witness program that illustrates unsound behavior in the verifier using our differential synthesis approach [73]. Agni has since been used to patch unsound abstract operators in the verifier [4, 65]. While most of this prior work regarding the eBPF verifier pertains to its soundness, our primary focus in this paper is its precision.

Why Precision Matters in the eBPF Verifier? The eBPF verifier must ensure that its static analysis is not only sound but also sufficiently precise to allow practical use. A sound yet imprecise analysis can render the verifier ineffective by rejecting safe programs that should be accepted, simply because the analysis produces overly conservative approximations of program variables. Such imprecision arises when the verifier's abstract domains yield coarse bounds on the possible values of program variables, especially those used in memory accesses. The verifier employs five abstract domains, four interval domains and one bitwise domain [52, 55, 61, 71], and implements a collection of efficient abstract operators for these domains. It further uses cross-domain refinements to mutually improve the precision of each domain. The overall precision of the verifier is fundamentally limited by the precision of these abstract operators themselves. Imprecision in abstract operators can lead the eBPF verifier to reject programs that are in fact safe. Consider the following 4-bit example where a register r1 is tracked by an unsigned interval $[l, u]$:

```
1   ...
2   r1 = r1 & 0b0011;    // mask to keep only the low two bits
3   arr[r1];             // index into a 4-byte array
4   exit;
```

Suppose we wish to access an offset into an array arr which is 4 bytes large. Here the mask guarantees that r1 $\in \{0, 1, 2, 3\}$, so arr[r1] always stays within the 4-byte buffer and is therefore safe. For illustration purposes, let us assume the verifier's abstract AND operator is imprecise and results in the abstract interval $[0, 8]$, over-approximating the set of values r1 may take in a real execution. Unable to conclusively prove that the memory access is safe, the verifier conservatively rejects the program even though the memory access is safe and won't go out of bounds in any execution. Similar safe rejections have prompted several recent kernel patches that improve precision of various abstract operators [1,3,6–8,18].

Designing efficient yet precise operators is non-trivial. Although classical interval operators are well understood [32,53], bit-width constraints and performance requirements complicate their direct use in the verifier without modification. Bitwise operations are particularly tricky on fixed-width interval domains: interval endpoint reasoning is unsound, while exhaustive enumeration of operand pairs is impractical. For instance, consider the bitwise AND of two unsigned intervals: $x \in [142, 145]$, $y \in [13, 15]$. A naive abstraction might apply the AND operation only to the interval endpoints (e.g., 142 &13 = 12, 145 & 15 = 1), yielding the ill-formed interval $[12, 1]$. A less naive abstraction might try the operation on all combinations of the interval endpoints and take the minimum and maximum values, yielding the interval $[1, 14]$. However, enumerating all possible pairs (x, y) reveals that the actual set of outcomes is $\{0, 1, 12, 13, 14, 15\}$, meaning that both of these abstractions fail to capture all outputs that may result from this operation, hence they are neither sound nor precise. Importantly, an interval is not the ideal domain to represent this set since it is a sparse, non-contiguous set that cannot be tightly captured by a single interval alone. Correctly abstracting such operations requires reasoning about the bit-level structure of the operands, not just their numeric ranges. This difficulty is precisely why the eBPF verifier incorporates a dedicated bitwise domain (tnum) [71]. However, combining tnum and interval information precisely and efficiently in practice is not straight-forward and has required multiple fixes [3,4,6,57,65].

Overall, manual operator design in the verifier is labor-intensive and error-prone. Additionally, Linux developers who craft these operators generally rely on testcases to check them [5], which provides no formal guarantees of precision (i.e., is the new operator implementation at least as precise as the old one for all inputs). Hence, we develop approaches to prove precision relations between two competing implementations of abstract operators in the verifier.

Witness Generation for Comparing the Precision of Abstract Operators. While reviewing abstract operators in the verifier, we observed that some operators may be less precise for some ranges of inputs, which causes the eBPF verifier to reject safe programs. In particular, we noticed that when the multiplication operator is given negative values as inputs, it sets its abstract domains to their widest range, essentially nullifying any useful information from the operation. Hence, we focus on developing improved operators for the eBPF verifier and develop tools and techniques to show that the new operator is more precise than the existing operator. To accomplish this goal, we need a formal framework for comparing the precision of two operator implementations. This task entails expressing the behavior of these operators in first order logic and comparing them using a logical precision specification (*i.e.*, operator A is at least as precise as operator B for all inputs). However, comparing operators across the entire space of valid abstract inputs is insufficient for evaluating real-world benefit of the new operator. Evaluating over all abstract inputs can significantly over-approximate the values that actually arise during verifier execution, many of which are unreachable by any valid eBPF program (discussed in Sect. 4.1). This phenomenon happens with the eBPF verifier because the verifier starts every register in one of two legal abstract states, *known*-value or *fully unknown*, and each subsequent instruction must transform those states through the verifier's abstract semantics. Thus, even if a new operator is provably more precise, the gap may never manifest in real executions. To address this issue, we need to be able to generate real witness eBPF programs that illustrate precision improvements with the new operator. Our experience shows that such witnesses are rarely trivial to construct; they often cannot be hand-crafted with a single instruction or obvious inputs, but instead require multi-instruction sequences.

We propose an approach to compare the precision of two abstract operator implementations in the value tracking of the eBPF verifier. Our framework leverages our C-to-logic tool, designed in prior work [73], to express the behavior of two abstract operator implementations in logic. We develop a precision specification (Sect. 4.1) to formally prove the precision relationship between the two implementations (*e.g.*, one operator is more precise than another for some inputs). When our precision specification query shows one abstract operator is more precise for some abstract inputs, we invoke an enumerative SMT-based synthesizer (Sect. 4.2) that searches the space of bounded eBPF instruction sequences and produces a concrete eBPF program, a witness, whose analysis reaches the relevant abstract inputs. We build on Agni's sound, but incomplete, witness generation approach [73], adapting it to precision comparisons instead of soundness violations. Using our approach, we were able to show our latest bpf_mul patch (Sect. 3) is more precise than the former version and we generated a witness eBPF program that illustrates this improvement. Our patch has been upstreamed to the Linux kernel [7]. We evaluate our approach on prior patches to the kernel which aim to improve precision of abstract operators in the verifier and we were able to generate witness eBPF programs for all of them, demonstrating the practical value of the precision improvements (Sect. 5). Lastly, we also use our framework to show that the reduction operator in the verifier serves an important role in improving the precision of its abstract domains.

2 Background on Abstract Interpretation in the eBPF Verifier

In this section we describe how the eBPF verifier employs abstract interpretation. Specifically, we formally present how the verifier uses abstract domains and operators to perform value tracking. We then present notions of precision in the abstract interpretation literature, which will later be used to define our precision specification.

Path-Sensitive Analysis Without Joins. The eBPF verifier implements a path-sensitive abstract interpretation that diverges from classical join-based analyses. Instead of merging abstract states at control-flow joins using traditional join operations, it forks execution at each conditional branch and explores successor paths independently. Each execution path thus maintains its own set of abstract domains, updated by abstract operators at every instruction. This means that for every feasible execution path, the verifier maintains a separate abstract state, which allows it to retain path-specific precision that might otherwise be lost in merged (joined) states. To keep this analysis tractable, the verifier imposes strict bounds on instruction count, call stack depth, and loop unrolling.

2.1 Value Tracking in the eBPF Verifier

Abstract Domains for Value Tracking. The eBPF verifier uses multiple abstract domains to track register values. Specifically, it uses four signed and unsigned interval domains to track the upper and lower bounds of 64-bit and 32-bit registers (*i.e.*, A_{u64}, A_{u32}, A_{s64}, A_{s32}). In addition, it uses a bitwise domain, called the tnum domain (A_{tnum}) [58,71], to track individual bits across executions. The tnum domain represents possible register values using a pair of 64-bit unsigned integers: a value and a mask. The value encodes known bits, while the mask specifies which bits are unknown; any bit set to 1 in the mask is unconstrained (it may be 0 or 1), whereas bits set to 0 are known and must match the corresponding bits in the value. For example, a tnum with value 0b10 and mask 0b01 represents the set {0b10, 0b11}, since the low bit is unknown and the high bit is known to be 1. This representation efficiently captures uncertainty at the bit level and is structurally similar to the bitfield domain [52].

Signed Interval Domain. The signed interval domain, A_{s64}, models the range of values a 64-bit register can take during an execution of an eBPF program, using the signed interpretation. It captures these potential values as intervals, characterized by lower and upper bounds. Formally, the domain is defined as follows:

$$A_{s64} \triangleq \{[l, u] \mid l, u \in \mathbb{Z}_{64},\ l \leq_{s64} u\} \cup \{\bot\}.$$

Here, $\mathbb{Z}_{64}$ denotes the set of all 64-bit signed integers, $\leq_{s64}$ represents signed integer comparison for 64-bit integers, and $\bot$ represents the empty set. The C implementation within the eBPF verifier maintains these intervals using two signed 64-bit integers, `s64_min` and `s64_max`, which indicate the current minimum and maximum possible values for the register. The *concretization function* γ_{s64} translates the signed interval domain into the set of concrete values it represents, in this case:

$$\gamma_{s64}(a) \triangleq \begin{cases} \{z \in \mathbb{Z}_{64} \mid l \leq_{s64} z \leq_{s64} u\} & \text{if } a = [l, u] \\ \emptyset & \text{if } a = \bot \end{cases}$$

Conversely, the *abstraction function* α_{s64} converts a concrete set of values $c \subseteq \mathcal{P}(\mathbb{Z}_{64})$ into the interval containing all elements of c:

$$\alpha_{s64}(c) \triangleq \begin{cases} [\min_{s64}(c), \max_{s64}(c)] & \text{if } c \neq \emptyset \\ \bot & \text{if } c = \emptyset \end{cases}$$

where $min_{s64}(c)$ and $max_{s64}(c)$ calculate the minimum and maximum of the finite set c, respectively.

An *abstract operator* is the abstract interpretation counterpart of a concrete operation. Consider the subtraction abstract operator for this domain [31]. Let the subtraction operator $\ominus_{s64}$ on signed intervals be defined as follows; given two intervals $a_1 = [l_1, u_1]$ and $a_2 = [l_2, u_2]$ in the signed 64-bit integer domain, the abstract subtraction computes a resulting interval that approximates all possible concrete subtractions between elements from these intervals:

$$a_1 \ominus_{s64} a_2 \triangleq \begin{cases} [l_1 -_{s64} u_2, u_1 -_{s64} l_2] & \text{if no overflow} \\ [-2^{63}, 2^{63} - 1] & \text{otherwise} \end{cases}$$

Here, overflow is checked according to signed 64-bit arithmetic. If overflow occurs, the operation yields the maximal interval, ensuring soundness at the expense of precision. The eBPF verifier implements this abstract operator as defined above. Importantly, the other interval domains in the verifier follow the same formalism as the signed domain, adjusted according to their respective bit-width and signedness. Specifically, for the unsigned interval domains (e.g., A_{u64}), intervals similarly represent ranges of values using lower and upper bounds, but with arithmetic and comparisons interpreted according to unsigned integer semantics. Consequently, their minimal bound is always non-negative, and arithmetic overflow is checked using the corresponding unsigned arithmetic rules.

The Reduction Operator in the eBPF Verifier. The eBPF verifier does not combine information from multiple domains using traditional approaches, such as Cartesian or modular reduced products [33]. Instead, the verifier mixes abstraction and reduction [65,73] to improve precision of its abstract domains. For example, when computing interval results for bitwise operations (*e.g.*, `r1 = r1 & 0b10`), the verifier does not separately calculate interval and tnum domain values and then combine them via a formal product. Instead, it computes the abstract value in the tnum domain first (e.g., determining bits known to be fixed and unknown), and subsequently uses this information to derive an interval bound.

Beyond this strategy, the verifier also maintains a reduction operator which is shared by all abstract operators in the verifier [48] and is performed immediately after every abstract operator (arithmetic, logic, branch) is executed. The purpose of this operator is to systematically propagate information between domains to improve precision. Let each abstract domain $(A_i, \sqsubseteq_i)$ be equipped with an abstraction function $\alpha_i : \mathcal{P}(C_i) \to A_i$ and a concretization function $\gamma_i : A_i \to \mathcal{P}(C_i)$ defined over the same concrete domain $\mathcal{P}(C_i)$, where C_i denotes the set of concrete values associated with the ith abstract domain (e.g., signed 64-bit integers for A_{s64}, unsigned 64-bit integers for A_{u64}, etc.). Here, $\sqsubseteq_i$ denotes the partial order on the abstract domain A_i. The combined abstract domain is then the product lattice $A = A_1 \times \cdots \times A_k$ ordered component-wise:

$$(a_1, \ldots, a_k) \sqsubseteq (b_1, \ldots, b_k) \iff \forall i,\ a_i \sqsubseteq_i b_i.$$

The concretization of a product domain is commonly defined as the intersection of its component concretizations: $\gamma(a) = \bigcap_{i=1}^{k} \gamma_i(a_i)$. However, such a definition would be unsound in the context of the eBPF verifier's product domain; intersecting the concretizations of signed with unsigned interval domains would erroneously eliminate valid negative values, and intersecting concretizations of 32-bit and 64-bit domains would constrain values to 32-bit ranges. To avoid these issues, the verifier does not use an intersection-based concretization. Instead, it maintains domain-specific concretizations and refines them through its reduction operator. We define the product domain concretization γ^* as the tuple of its component concretizations:

$$\gamma^*(a) := (\gamma_1(a_1), \ldots, \gamma_k(a_k)), \quad \text{with each } \gamma_i(a_i) \subseteq C_i.$$

We write $\subseteq^*$, $\subset^*$, $\supseteq^*$, and $\supset^*$ to denote component-wise set inclusion between concretization tuples. For example, $\gamma^*(a) \subseteq^* \gamma^*(b) \iff \forall i,\ \gamma_i(a_i) \subseteq \gamma_i(b_i)$. Formally, the verifier's reduction operator is defined as a monotone function $\rho : A \to A$. Given an abstract state $a = (a_1, \ldots, a_k) \in A$, the reduction operator computes a refined abstract state $a' = \rho(a)$ satisfying

$$a' \sqsubseteq a \quad \text{and} \quad \gamma^*(a') \subseteq^* \gamma^*(a),$$

thereby locally refining each domain without enforcing an explicit intersection. The verifier strikes a balance between precision and performance by applying the reduction operator only a bounded number of times (usually two iterations), following a partially reduced products approach [53]. Informally, each invocation of the reduction operator consists of the following three sequential reduction steps:

1. **Bitwise-to-interval refinement**: Use known and unknown bits from the tnum domain to restrict possible values in each 64-bit signed and unsigned interval.

2. **Interval cross-domain propagation**: Propagate tightened bounds between 64-bit and 32-bit intervals, and between signed and unsigned intervals, ensuring consistency across width and signedness.
3. **Interval-to-bitwise refinement**: Use the updated intervals to detect newly fixed bits and mark them as known within the tnum domain.

Initially, the reduction operator was introduced without a formal soundness proof into the eBPF verifier. We proved the soundness of the verifier's reduction operator in prior work [65]. In this paper, we focus on its role in enhancing precision. In Sect. 5, we empirically evaluate it by comparing abstract operator precision with and without the reduction step.

2.2 Comparing the Precision of Abstract Operators

The eBPF verifier utilizes five non-relational abstract domains. We compare two abstract operators by ordering their results in the underlying abstract lattice, following the standard framework of abstract interpretation [32,53]. To compare the precision of two abstract operators, we assume sound abstractions, which we define next. Let $f : C \to C$ be a concrete operation over the set of all 64-bit machine values, and let $f^* : \mathcal{P}(C) \to \mathcal{P}(C)$ denote its collecting semantics. An abstract operator $F^\# : A \to A$ is *sound* with respect to f if, for every abstract state $a = (a_1, \ldots, a_k) \in A$ and for each component i, the following holds:

$$f^*(\gamma_i(a_i)) \subseteq \gamma_i(\pi_i(F^\#(a))),$$

where $\pi_i : A \to A_i$ denotes the projection onto the ith component of the product lattice A. This definition ensures that soundness is preserved individually within each component domain.

Definition 1 (Precision preorder, multi-domain). *Given two sound abstract operators $F_1^\#, F_2^\# : A \to A$, we say $F_1^\#$ is at least as precise as $F_2^\#$, denoted $F_1^\# \preceq F_2^\#$, if and only if:*

$$\forall a \in A : \quad F_1^\#(a) \sqsubseteq F_2^\#(a)$$

where $\sqsubseteq$ is the component-wise product order.

Intuitively, operator $F_1^\#$ is at least as precise as $F_2^\#$ if, for all inputs, the abstract states produced by $F_1^\#$ are component-wise at least as informative (i.e., smaller or equal in the lattice ordering) than those produced by $F_2^\#$. Equivalently, this implies $\gamma^*(F_1^\#(a)) \subseteq^* \gamma^*(F_2^\#(a))$ for every $a \in A$. If the opposite direction also holds ($F_2^\# \preceq F_1^\#$), then $F_1^\#$ and $F_2^\#$ are equally precise. If neither direction holds universally, the operators are incomparable.

3 Improving the Precision of Abstract Operators in the eBPF Verifier

While exploring abstract operators in the eBPF verifier, we observed that some abstract operators perform overly conservative approximations of their concrete counterparts, which resulted in loss of precision. Specifically, the eBPF verifier's multiplication operator seemed to exhibit this exact behavior (*i.e.*, returning loose bounds when given negative operands). To tackle this imprecision, we first needed to formalize how the verifier performs this operator to identify where imprecision stems from. Then, we wanted to craft a new operator that is at least as precise as the old operator for all abstract inputs, but also more precise for some inputs. This section presents these efforts. We first describe how the abstract operator for multiplication (bpf_mul) is performed by the eBPF verifier and where imprecision stems from. Then we propose an improved multiplication abstract operator and discuss proving its precision merits over the prior operator.

Beyond serving as a stand-alone improvement, this case study motivates the need for a more systematic approach to design and validate abstract operators. Crafting a more precise operator is only part of the challenge, ensuring that this improved precision is relevant to real-world eBPF programs is equally important. In particular, reasoning about all abstract inputs can over-approximate what is actually reachable in verifier executions, since the verifier begins analysis from constrained initial states and enforces strict invariants on how abstract states evolve. As such, many abstract inputs used in theoretical comparisons may never arise in practice. We present our techniques for comparing precision and witness generation in the following sections (Sect. 4).

How the eBPF Verifier Performs Abstract Multiplication (bpf_mul).
Formally, we represent the existing multiplication operator in the eBPF verifier as $F^{\#}_{\text{ebpf}-\text{mul}} : A \times A \to A$ where $A = A_{u64} \times A_{s64}$. While the verifier uses five abstract domains, we focus on these two domains for clarity and brevity as these two domains are enough to illustrate how imprecision manifests in this operator.

Operands. We define the operator's operands $a, b \in A$

$$a = ([\ell^a_{u64}, u^a_{u64}], [\ell^a_{s64}, u^a_{s64}]), \quad b = ([\ell^b_{u64}, u^b_{u64}], [\ell^b_{s64}, u^b_{s64}]),$$

where unsigned and signed interval invariants are maintained,
$0 \leq \ell^{(\cdot)}_{u64} \leq u^{(\cdot)}_{u64} \leq 2^{64} - 1$ and $-2^{63} \leq \ell^{(\cdot)}_{s64} \leq u^{(\cdot)}_{s64} \leq 2^{63} - 1$.

Bit-width constants. The following constants represent the minimum and maximum numeric values that can be represented using a fixed number of bits, as used by the verifier, when interpreted as signed or unsigned integers.

$$U64_{\min} = 0, \quad U64_{\max} = 2^{64} - 1,$$
$$S64_{\min} = -2^{63}, \quad S64_{\max} = 2^{63} - 1,$$
$$U32_{\max} = 2^{32} - 1.$$

Operator definition as represented by the eBPF verifier.

$$F^{\#}_{\text{ebpf}-\text{mul}}(a, b) = \begin{cases} \top, & \text{if } \ell^a_{s64} < 0 \lor \ell^b_{s64} < 0, \\ \top, & \text{if } u^a_{u64} > U32_{\max} \lor u^b_{u64} > U32_{\max}, \\ ([\ell^a_{u64} \cdot \ell^b_{u64}, u^a_{u64} \cdot u^b_{u64}], \Delta), & \text{otherwise} \end{cases}$$

where $\top := ([U64_{min}, U64_{max}], [S64_{min}, S64_{max}])$ is the greatest element of A and

$$\Delta = \begin{cases} [S64_{min}, S64_{max}], & u^a_{u64} \cdot u^b_{u64} > S64_{max} \\ [\ell^a_{u64} \cdot \ell^b_{u64}, u^a_{u64} \cdot u^b_{u64}], & \text{otherwise.} \end{cases}$$

$F^{\#}_{ebpf-mul}$ computes precise interval products under restrictive conditions; both operands must be non-negative and fit within 32-bit unsigned bounds, and the resulting product must not exceed the maximum representable 64-bit signed value, $S64_{max}$. Every other case is conservatively widened to the full 64-bit range. While this ensures soundness, it significantly limits the utility of the operator in practice, especially for signed computations, leading to overly conservative analyses and potential rejection of safe programs. As shown in Table 1, this behavior results in avoidable precision losses. To address this issue, we present an improved multiplication operator that retains soundness while computing tighter interval bounds in many of these previously imprecise cases.

Our More Precise eBPF Multiplication Abstract Operator. Our operator is grounded in interval arithmetic [56], which has become standard in abstract interpretation literature [32,53]. Specifically, we adapt interval multiplication to 64-bit fixed-width arithmetic, accounting for overflow as defined by the eBPF instruction set [45]. We formally define our abstract multiplication operator $F^{\#}_{our-mul} : A \times A \to A$ where $A = A_{u64} \times A_{s64}$. We use these two domains for brevity, but the operator is also directly extensible to the A_{u32} and A_{s32} domains. Our operator preserves the existing abstract multiplication for the tnum domain defined elsewhere [71]. Next, we define auxiliary products which we use to compute intervals:

$$U_{\ell\ell} = \ell^a_{u64} \cdot \ell^b_{u64}, \quad U_{uu} = u^a_{u64} \cdot u^b_{u64},$$
$$S_{\ell\ell} = \ell^a_{s64} \cdot \ell^b_{s64}, \quad S_{\ell u} = \ell^a_{s64} \cdot u^b_{s64},$$
$$S_{u\ell} = u^a_{s64} \cdot \ell^b_{s64}, \quad S_{uu} = u^a_{s64} \cdot u^b_{s64}.$$

Lastly, let $prod_{min} = \min\{S_{\ell\ell}, S_{\ell u}, S_{u\ell}, S_{uu}\}$ and $prod_{max} = \max\{S_{\ell\ell}, S_{\ell u}, S_{u\ell}, S_{uu}\}$. Our improved multiplication operator is defined as follows:

$$\boxed{F^{\#}_{our-mul}(a, b) = (\Delta_{u64}, \Delta_{s64})}$$

where

$$\Delta_{u64} = \begin{cases} [U64_{min}, U64_{max}], & \text{overflow in } U_{\ell\ell} \text{ or } U_{uu} \\ [U_{\ell\ell}, U_{uu}], & \text{otherwise} \end{cases}$$

$$\Delta_{s64} = \begin{cases} [S64_{min}, S64_{max}], & \text{overflow in } S_{\ell\ell} \text{ or } S_{\ell u} \text{ or } S_{u\ell} \text{ or } S_{uu} \\ [prod_{min}, prod_{max}], & \text{otherwise.} \end{cases}$$

Table 1. Precision gains in our abstract multiplication operator ($F^{\#}_{\text{our-mul}}$) compared to the verifier's operator ($F^{\#}_{\text{ebpf-mul}}$) where $a, b \in A_{u64} \times A_{s64}$. For instance, when any of the operands' signed intervals maintain negative values (second row), the verifier's operator will set its abstract values to $\top$, whereas ours will produce tight bounds when no overflow is possible.

Operands a, b	$F^{\#}_{\text{ebpf-mul}}(a,b)$	$F^{\#}_{\text{our-mul}}(a,b)$
$([2,3],[2,3])$, $([4,5],[4,5])$	$([8,15],[8,15])$	$([8,15],[8,15])$
$([1,1],[1,1])$, $([0,0],[-1,-1])$	$\top$	$([0,0],[-1,-1])$
$([2^{34},2^{34}],[2^{34},2^{34}])$, $([1,1],[1,1])$	$\top$	$([2^{34},2^{34}],[2^{34},2^{34}])$
$([0,5],[0,5])$, $([0,2],[-2,2])$	$\top$	$([0,10],[-10,10])$
$([2^{63},2^{63}],[0,2^{62}])$, $([2,8],[2,8])$	$\top$	$\top$

Our operator multiplies the operand intervals' bounds, returning precise unsigned and signed 64-bit product intervals when all auxiliary products do not overflow. If any product overflows, the operator conservatively widens the affected domain to the full 64-bit range. Table 1 exemplifies precision gains of our operator over the existing one.

Bridging Formal Precision and Real World Execution—Why We Need Automated Precision Comparison. The construction above guarantees that our operator $F^{\#}_{\text{our-mul}}$ is *never less precise* than the kernel's current operator $F^{\#}_{\text{ebpf-mul}}$, but we don't know if it is practically more precise in real eBPF executions since abstract inputs for which our operator is more precise may not be reachable under the verifier's strict constraints. Further, most of the verifier's operators are handcrafted by kernel developers and may involve subtle bit-level invariants, or interaction with multiple abstract domains in non-obvious ways (*i.e.*, bitwise operations for signed intervals). This means that we cannot rely on intuition or isolated examples to assess their precision. Hence, when a new abstract operator is proposed, in our case the multiplication operator, we argue it should achieve two goals: **(i)** *satisfy* the precision preorder $F^{\#}_{\text{our-mul}} \preceq F^{\#}_{\text{ebpf-mul}}$ for *all* abstract inputs (or a region of inputs that are of interest) and **(ii)** *demonstrate* concrete eBPF programs in which that improved precision is observable (*i.e.*, in the multiplication case, programs for which the old operator widens to $\top$ while the new one produces a tight bound).

Task (i) reduces to a lattice-theoretic proof obligation. Task (ii) amounts to searching the program space for witnesses where precision differences manifest. Performing this search by hand is error-prone and does not scale to the many arithmetic and branch operators maintained in the verifier. Hence we propose an *automated* pipeline that (a) encodes our precision specification as a logical formula, (b) systematically enumerates bounded eBPF instruction sequences, and (c) invokes an SMT solver to find a satisfying assignment that separates the two operators in terms of precision. The next section introduces our synthesis-driven framework for precision comparison.

4 Our Approach for Precision Comparison and Witness Synthesis

In this section, we describe how precision relationships between abstract operators can be formalized and checked via logical queries. To ground these formal guarantees in practice, we develop an automated pipeline that synthesizes concrete eBPF programs exposing true precision differences in the verifier. This two-part approach, proving precision formally and validating it empirically, ensures that abstract operator changes are both correct and meaningful in the context of real verifier executions.

4.1 Precision Specification for Comparing Abstract Operators

Let $F_1^\#, F_2^\# : A \times A \to A$ be two *sound* abstract operators over the domain $A = A_{u64} \times A_{u32} \times A_{s64} \times A_{s32} \times A_{tnum}$. To show that $F_1^\# \preceq F_2^\#$, we check the validity of the following query:

$$\forall t, u \in C, \quad a_t, a_u \in A :$$
$$mem_A(t, a_t) \wedge mem_A(u, a_u) \wedge$$
$$a_v = F_1^\#(a_t, a_u) \wedge a_v' = F_2^\#(a_t, a_u) \implies a_v \sqsubseteq a_v'. \qquad (1)$$

Here, $mem_A(x, a) \triangleq \bigwedge_{i=1}^{k} x \in \gamma_i(\pi_i(a))$ denotes that a concrete value x is a member of the abstract state $a \in A$ iff it lies in the concretization of every component of a. We use $a_v = F_1^\#(a_t, a_u)$ to represent an abstract operator and its input-output relationships as specified by the verifier's source code. Specifically, a_t and a_u represent the inputs to $F_1^\#$ and a_v the output. With this query, we compare each component (*i.e.*, A_{s64}, A_{u64}, etc.) of the abstract states produced by both abstract operators $F_1^\#$ and $F_2^\#$ and assert the precision relationship between them. For interval domains, checking whether $a_v \sqsubseteq a_v'$ amounts to verifying that $\ell' \leq \ell \wedge u \leq u'$, where $[\ell', u']$ and $[\ell, u]$ are the intervals represented by a_v' and a_v, respectively. For the tnum domain, where abstract values are represented as value-mask pairs (av', am') and (av, am), we check if $av = av' \wedge (am \mid am') = am'$.

We are also able to check the precision of individual components between the two operators. Let's assume we proved $F_1^\# \preceq F_2^\#$ for two operators we are comparing and we suspect that the A_{s64} component produced by $F_1^\#$ is not only at least as precise as the one produced by $F_2^\#$ for all inputs, but also more precise for some inputs. Using the previously defined projection function $\pi_i : A \to A_i$, which extracts the ith component of an abstract state, we express this query formally as:

$$\exists t, u \in C, \quad a_t, a_u \in A :$$
$$mem_A(t, a_t) \wedge mem_A(u, a_u) \wedge$$
$$a_v = F_1^\#(a_t, a_u) \wedge a_v' = F_2^\#(a_t, a_u) \implies \pi_{s64}(a_v) \sqsubset \pi_{s64}(a_v'). \qquad (2)$$

Table 2. Reachable and unreachable abstract states where $a \in A_{s64} \times A_{u64}$. R1 exhibits a case where both abstract values are aligned after reduction, representing the same values in their respective domains. R2 represents a reachable state where the signed interval cannot be used to inform the unsigned interval since $[-100, 200]$ cannot be represented soundly in an unsigned interval. U1 and U2 exemplify abstract states that have not been reduced which cannot happen in a real verifier execution, hence they are unreachable. After the reduction operation, U1 and U2 should be $([-10, -1], [2^{64} - 10, 2^{64} - 1])$ and $([5, 10], [5, 10])$, respectively.

Case	a	Reachable?
R1	$([-5, -1], [2^{64} - 5, 2^{64} - 1])$	✓
R2	$([-100, 200], [0, 2^{64} - 1])$	✓
U1	$([-10, -1], [0, 2^{64} - 1])$	✗
U2	$([5, 2^{32}], [5, 10])$	✗

We can adapt this query to reason about any of the other specific domains as well (*i.e.*, A_{s32}, A_{tnum}, etc.). Reasoning about precision of specific domains is useful because patches to the verifier's abstract operators may only improve the precision of a specific domain rather than all.

Reachability Constraints in the Verifier's Abstract State Space. While proving any of the above queries is useful for understanding the precision relations between two comparable operators, it may not reflect real-world precision improvements in the verifier. This is because the abstract states used in such specifications over-approximate the set of states that can arise during actual eBPF program analysis. In practice, the verifier initializes registers in either known or fully unknown states, and these states evolve only through a sequence of eBPF abstract operations and reduced by the reduction operator. As such, many abstract states used in the precision specification may never actually be realized during verifier execution. Table 2 illustrates examples of reachable and unreachable abstract states in the verifier, using only the 64-bit signed and unsigned domains for brevity. Consider the last row in the table; while it is a valid abstract state where each individual abstract value is sound, it is not reachable in a real verifier execution. This is because the reduction operator would tighten the signed interval such that the resulting state would become $([5, 10], [5, 10])$. Importantly, our precision specification considers all of these abstract states when comparing operators, regardless of reachability. If any unreachable states are used as inputs in our query to show precision improvements of one abstract operator over another, then that precision gain is impractical and no real eBPF program can illustrate it. Since we are interested in practical precision improvements that can manifest in a real verifier execution, we now present our witness generation approach for synthesizing eBPF programs that illustrates reachable precision improvements in one abstract operator over another.

4.2 Synthesizing Witness eBPF Programs for Precision Comparisons

Proving precision properties of abstract operators using our precision specification (Sect. 4.1) may not be enough to determine if one operator is truly more precise than another in any real eBPF program. This discrepancy underscores the need to test precision differences not just in theory, but through actual witness programs that drive the verifier into states where the two operators diverge. Our goal then is to automatically synthesize actual eBPF programs that illustrate an instance in which one abstract operator produces tighter bounds in one, or more, of its abstract domains compared to another operator as specified in Eq. 2.

To address this challenge, we adapt our differential synthesis approach [73], originally developed for soundness verification, to instead generate witness programs that highlight precision differences between abstract operators. We use bpf_add as our abstract operator under test to illustrate our witness generation in this section. Concretely, our approach aims to model the verifier's behavior when executed with two competing abstract operators. (*i.e.*, two different operators for bpf_add). This involves enumerating bounded length eBPF programs that exercise the abstract operators of interest. We use an SMT solver to determine when a program illustrates that one operator is more precise than the other. This method is sound–any synthesized program indeed demonstrates a precision improvement–but incomplete; failure to find a witness at a given bound does not preclude its existence.

Reaching Abstract States Starting from Initial States. The goal of our synthesis procedure is to produce an abstract state $a \in A$ which is the result of the verifier's analysis of a sequence of eBPF instructions. Importantly, the verifier begins all executions with an initial set of abstract states it allows. Formally, we use $init(b)$ to specify that abstract input $b \in A$ is an initial abstract state where b can be unknown ($b = \top$) or a singleton (*i.e.*, $b_{s64} = [\ell, \ell]$ where $\ell \in \mathbb{Z}_{64}$). Hence, a is reachable if there exists a sequence of eBPF instructions for which the verifier's analysis reaches a starting from the set of restricted abstract states such that $init(b)$ holds.

Witness Generation Procedure. Let $F_1^\#$ and $F_2^\#$ be two sound, comparable abstract operators that satisfy our precision specification (Eqs. 1 and 2). Our goal is to construct an executable eBPF program whose analysis in the verifier reaches an abstract state where the two operators diverge in precision. To generate a concrete witness program, we consider all instruction sequences up to a maximum length L. Each sequence includes a mix of arithmetic, logic, and branch instructions, with the final instruction reserved for the abstract operator under test. These programs are partially specified: instruction opcodes are fixed, but operands and data flow remain symbolic. For each such program, we construct a logical formula that (i) selects initial abstract states consistent with the verifier's start-state constraints (*e.g.*, known or fully unknown abstract states) using $init()$, (ii) models each instruction according to the verifier's abstract semantics, and (iii) ensures that the final instruction produces a strictly more precise abstract state under one abstract operator than the other. We emit every such program formula to an SMT solver and repeat this process until we reach our maximum bound length L or time limit.

To illustrate how this process begins, we first consider the case where the program consists of a single instruction, the abstract operator under test. In this case, we check whether the precision gap between $F^{\#}_{old\_add}$ and $F^{\#}_{new\_add}$ (modeling bpf_add) can be demonstrated using only initial abstract states. For illustration purposes, we test for precision differences in the A_{s64} domain, but this applies to any domain. This reduces to a satisfiability query over concrete and abstract inputs:

$$t, u \in C, \ a_t, a_u \in A :$$
$$init(a_t) \land init(a_u) \land mem_A(t, a_t) \land mem_A(u, a_u) \land$$
$$a_v = F^{\#}_{new\_add}(a_t, a_u) \land a'_v = F^{\#}_{old\_add}(a_t, a_u) \land \pi_{s64}(a_v) \sqsubset \pi_{s64}(a'_v) \quad (3)$$

Extending Witness Generation to Multiple Instructions. A single instruction may not be enough to elicit precision gaps between operators so we extend our synthesis to a larger program length. We explore all instruction sequences of length $L-1$ and reserve the Lth instruction for the operator under test. Operands are left symbolic. We assert that every operand must be either (i) an initial abstract state allowed by the verifier or (ii) the output produced by an earlier instruction. Extending Eq. 3, we illustrate a two-instruction (bpf_and followed by bpf_add) query:

$$p, q, r, t, u, v \in C, \ a_p, a_q, a_r, a_t, a_u, a_v \in A :$$
$$init(a_p) \land init(a_q) \land mem_A(p, a_p) \land mem_A(q, a_q) \land$$
$$r = conc_{and}(p, q) \land a_r = F^{\#}_{and}(a_p, a_q) \land mem_A(r, a_r) \land$$
$$(init(a_t) \lor assign(t, \{p, q, r\})) \land (init(a_u) \lor assign(u, \{p, q, r\})) \land$$
$$mem_A(t, a_t) \land mem_A(u, a_u) \land$$
$$a_v = F^{\#}_{new\_add}(a_t, a_u) \land a'_v = F^{\#}_{old\_add}(a_t, a_u) \land \pi_{s64}(a_v) \sqsubset \pi_{s64}(a'_v). \quad (4)$$

Here, variables $p, q, \ldots, v \in C$ denote concrete 64-bit values, and $a_p, a_q, \ldots, a_v \in A$ are their abstract counterparts. For the first instruction bpf_and, $r = conc_{and}(p, q)$ represents the concrete operator and $a_r = F^{\#}_{and}(a_p, a_q)$ represents its abstract counterpart. The abstract operator consumes initial abstract inputs a_p, a_q; its result a_r may later be used as an operand. For the second instruction, bpf_add, each abstract input may be *either* a fresh initial element $init(\cdot)$ or one of the earlier results $\{a_p, a_q, a_r\}$. We encode this choice with $assign(x, \{y_1, \ldots, y_m\}) = \bigvee_{i=1}^{m}(x = y_i \land a_x = a_{y_i})$, thereby linking concrete values and abstract states. Finally, the key precision-checking constraint is imposed: $\pi_{s64}(a_v) \sqsubset \pi_{s64}(a'_v)$, asserting that the new operator's output interval is strictly more precise than that of the old operator. If this formula is satisfiable, we get a model of a concrete two-instruction eBPF program which exposes a real precision advantage of the new operator over the old one. Otherwise we keep exploring the search space.

5 Experimental Evaluation

In this section, we evaluate our prototype which compares the precision of two abstract operator implementations in the eBPF verifier and produces witness eBPF programs to illustrate precision gaps between these operators in real eBPF programs. We test our framework on recent patches to the kernel that aim to improve precision of various abstract operators in range tracking. Additionally, we use our approach to evaluate the effectiveness of the verifier's reduction operator (called BPF_SYNC) which is called after every abstract operator executes. For brevity, we compare a limited set of arithmetic and logical abstract operators with and without reduction and present the results. Overall, with this evaluation we tackle the following questions:

1. **RQ1: Precision Comparison.** Can our formal framework determine whether a newly proposed abstract operator implementation is at least as precise, or strictly more precise, compared to an existing implementation, particularly in the kernel's precision-related patches?
2. **RQ2: Witness Generation.** Given identified precision gaps between operator implementations, can our automated framework reliably generate real eBPF programs as concrete witnesses that reveal these differences during verifier execution?
3. **RQ3: Impact of Reduction Operator.** Does the eBPF verifier's reduction operator (BPF_SYNC) tangibly improve the precision of abstract domains, and can our approach demonstrate these improvements through synthesized witness programs?

Experimental Setup. We conducted all experiments on a system running Ubuntu 20.04, equipped with an AMD Ryzen 5 3600 (6-core CPU) and 32GB RAM. Our prototype was implemented in Python 3.12, leveraging the Agni C-to-logic translation tool [73] to automatically convert abstract operator implementations from C into logical representations. For logical verification and witness synthesis tasks, we utilized the Z3 SMT solver [35], setting a query timeout of 10 min and synthesizing eBPF programs up to a length of 4 instructions.

Evaluating Kernel Precision Patches (RQ1 & RQ2). To evaluate the effectiveness of recent precision improvement efforts, we applied our precision comparison and witness generation framework to a set of kernel patches spanning Linux versions v5.7 to v6.8. These patches targeted various abstract operators, including the reduction operator (BPF_SYNC), to address overly conservative behavior in the verifier that resulted in rejection of safe programs. Table 3

Table 3. We show precision relation and witness generation results for selected eBPF abstract operator patches (Linux v5.7–v6.8). For each modified eBPF instruction we check the two-way precision preorder between the new and old abstract operators and indicate the abstract domains in which the patch demonstrably tightens results. We are able to generate real eBPF program as witnesses for all patches that are provably more precise for some inputs.

eBPF insn	Patch reference	$F_{new}^{\#} \preceq F_{old}^{\#}$	$F_{old}^{\#} \preceq F_{new}^{\#}$	Improved domains	Witness generated?
BPF_AND	[8]	✓	✗	A_{s64}, A_{s32}	✓
BPF_SYNC	[57]	✓	✗	All	✓
BPF_SYNC	[6]	✓	✗	A_{tnum}	✓
BPF_XOR	[1]	✓	✗	All	✓
BPF_MUL	[7]	✓	✗	$A_{u64}, A_{u32}, A_{s64}, A_{s32}$	✓

presents a summary of our evaluation. As shown in columns 2 and 3, our framework confirmed that all patched operators are *at least as precise* as their predecessors across all inputs and domains, and *strictly more precise* for some. Column 4 details the specific abstract domains where each patch demonstrably improved precision, ranging from individual domains like A_{s64} to improvements across all tracked domains. To assess the practical benefit of these precision improvements, we used our synthesis engine to generate concrete eBPF witness programs for each precision gain (column 5), providing evidence that these improvements are observable in a real execution. These synthesized programs complement the hand-written examples that often accompany kernel patches, reinforcing the role of automated witness generation in kernel development and validation.

```
1  set r1            ; r1 unknown r1([S64_min, S64_max], [S32_min, S32_max])
2  r1 = r1 & 15      ; r1([0, 15], [0, 15])
3  r1 = r1 - 10      ; r1([-10, 5], [-10, 5])
4  r1 = r1 * -5      ; our bpf_mul: r1([-75, 50], [-75, 50])
5                    ; old bpf_mul: r1([S64_min, S64_max], [S32_min, S32_max])
6  exit
```

Listing 1.1. Witness eBPF program demonstrating improved precision in the multiplication abstract operator bpf_mul for signed interval domains (A_{s64}, A_{s32}). The old operator yields overly conservative intervals, whereas our operator computes exact bounds.

***Generating Witness of Precision for* bpf_mul *and* bpf_and.** Here, we present two witness programs generated by our synthesizer for our improved multiplication abstract operator (Sect. 3) and for the bitwise *and* abstract operator bpf_and [8]. These witnesses are real eBPF programs that exhibits the precision merits of these operators. We illustrate our multiplication operator's performance on signed values in Listing 1.1 using two domains, A_{s64} and A_{s32}. The program exemplifies how the operator handles multiplying two signed intervals $[-10, 15] \times [-5, -5]$. We observe that the old multiplication operator (line 5) yields the widest range possible for these domains while our operator yields the exact result expected for this multiplication $[-75, 50]$. This improvement in precision could practically mean the verifier would accept a program in which the $r1$ register might be later used to access memory. Importantly, in our patch to the Linux kernel, we included such an automatically generated witness embedded in its commit message. This patch is now upstreamed to kernel version v6.14 and beyond [7].

Our second witness example (Listing 1.2) illustrates precision improvement in the A_{s64} domain for the bpf_and operator. The patch itself aimed at improving the handling of negative values when performing the bitwise *and* operation, since it would result in verifier rejections detailed in [8]. Our synthesizer generates a program which performs bitwise *and* on two signed intervals where the old operator (line 5) results in $\top$ and the proposed version (line 4) returns a more precise interval $[-2^{40}, \approx 2^{40}]$.

```
1   set r1                ; set r1 to unknown r1([S64_min, S64_max])
2   set r2                ; set r2 to unknown r2([S64_min, S64_max])
3   r1 = r1 s>> 23        ; r1([-1099511627776, 1099511627775])
4   r2 = r2 s>> 32        ; r2([-2147483648, 2147483647])
5   r1 = r1 & r2          ; new bpf_and: r1([-1099511627776, 1099511627775])
6                         ; old bpf_and: r1([S64_min, S64_max])
7   exit
```

Listing 1.2. Witness eBPF program illustrating precision gap in abstract operator bpf_and for the signed interval domain (A_{s64}).

Evaluating the Reduction Operator (RQ3). To assess the precision benefits of the verifier's reduction operator (BPF_SYNC), we systematically compared a set of arithmetic and logical abstract operators with and without reduction, using Linux kernel version v6.10. The reduction operator, invoked at the tail end of every abstract operator execution, has been the focus of multiple precision-focused kernel patches [3,6,18]. While its soundness has been formally established [65], its precision impact had not been rigorously evaluated prior to this work.

Table 4 summarizes our findings and reveals several important insights. First, as shown in columns 2 and 3, all operators augmented with reduction are always at least as precise, and some may also be strictly more precise, than operators without reduction. Second, column 4 illustrates that the reduction operator can enhance precision across a wide range of domains, frequently yielding improvements in all five abstract domains. Third, our framework was able to successfully synthesize witness eBPF programs (column 5) for all operators and for most domains where precision gains were possible. However, we were not able to generate witnesses that expose improvements in the tnum domain for any of the bitwise/shift operations given the program length and time constraints used in this experiment. This reflects the inherent limitations of bounded enumeration; we cannot know if limited sequence length prevented reaching the input abstract

Table 4. Precision gains from applying the reduction operator (BPF_SYNC) to arithmetic eBPF instructions (Linux v6.10). Operators with reduction ($F_R^\#$) are consistently at least as precise as those without ($F_{\neg R}^\#$), and for some inputs strictly more so (cols. 2–3). Precision testing shows the reduction operator can improve precision in almost all abstract domains (col. 4). Our synthesizer is able to produce witness programs for most of these domains which require four or less instructions to expose precision gaps (cols. 5–6). This demonstrates both the broad utility of reduction and the effectiveness of our approach.

eBPF insn	$F_R^\# \preceq F_{\neg R}^\#$	$F_{\neg R}^\# \preceq F_R^\#$	Improved domains?	Synthesized witness for	Witness length?
BPF_RSH	✓	✗	All	$A_{u64}, A_{u32}, A_{s64}, A_{s32}$	≤ 4
BPF_ARSH	✓	✗	All	$A_{u64}, A_{u32}, A_{s64}, A_{s32}$	≤ 4
BPF_LSH	✓	✗	All	$A_{u64}, A_{u32}, A_{s64}, A_{s32}$	≤ 4
BPF_ADD	✓	✗	All	All	≤ 3
BPF_SUB	✓	✗	All	All	≤ 3
BPF_AND	✓	✗	All	A_{u64}, A_{s64}	≤ 4
BPF_OR	✓	✗	$A_{u64}, A_{u32}, A_{s64}, A_{s32}$	A_{u64}, A_{s64}	≤ 4
BPF_XOR	✓	✓	None	—	—

states necessary to expose precision differences or if such inputs are unreachable regardless of sequence length. Lastly, our results indicate that many of these witnesses required multi-instruction sequences to manifest observable differences (column 6), underscoring the importance of bounded program synthesis beyond single-instruction analysis. Taken together, our evaluation demonstrates that the reduction operator is an effective, general-purpose mechanism for improving the precision of value tracking in the eBPF verifier.

6 Related Work

Verifying Correctness of the eBPF Verifier. This paper is closest in approach to our prior work verifying the value tracking of the eBPF verifier [65,73]. These automatically verify the soundness of abstract operators by generating verification conditions directly from C code of the Linux eBPF verifier. When a proof of correctness is unattainable, our prototype, Agni [72], generates witness programs illustrating unsound behavior in the verifier. This paper is similar in its approach, but our main focus here is proving precision properties of abstract operator implementations rather than proving their correctness, with the goal of reducing verifier rejections of safe programs. As such, we adapt our differential synthesis to produce witness programs illustrating precision gaps between operators.

Synthesizing Abstract Operators. Manually crafting sound and precise abstract operators is non-trivial and error-prone. Research on developing automated approaches is ongoing [36,62,63,69]. Amurth [43] automatically synthesizes abstract operators for non-relational domains with a user provided DSL. Amurth explores the search space using a dual CEGIS [66] loop with positive (soundness) and negative (precision) counter-examples guaranteeing that when an abstract operator is synthesized, it is sound and the most precise possible in the given language. This approach is extended for reduced-product domains [44]. Our work complements these efforts, allowing precision comparison of operators generated automatically for non-relational domains. Our precision comparison framework along with automated approaches to generating abstract operators could provide a sound and precise foundation for abstract operators in the eBPF verifier.

Domain Refinement and Abstract Interpretation. Our work builds on foundational ideas in abstract interpretation [30,32,33], particularly the use of lattice-theoretic structures to reason about precision. We focus on non-relational domains such as intervals and bitwise abstractions [52,53], and define precision comparisons over abstract operators using their ordering in the lattice. Our witness generation approach led us to explore how the eBPF verifier combines information from multiple domains, which is non-standard but loosely follows the literature on reduced products domain refinements [33,53]. Improving cross-domain interaction remains an area of interest [21,27,29,70]. For a broader overview, we refer the reader to an existing survey on product operators [28].

7 Conclusion

The eBPF verifier's *precision* is vital for practical eBPF deployment: overly coarse abstract operators cause the kernel to reject programs that are, in fact, safe. In this work, we propose a systematic approach that leverages formal specifications and program synthesis to compare and validate the precision of competing abstract operator implementations. We introduce a formal precision specification rooted in abstract interpretation, allowing us to precisely define and verify precision relationships between competing operator implementations. When precision gaps are identified, our approach synthesizes concrete eBPF programs demonstrating these differences in real executions. We applied our framework to our improved bpf_mul operator and several other precision-related kernel patches, successfully generating witness programs for each, confirming their precision improvements. We propose this methodology as a principled way to ensure that future kernel patches targeting abstract operator precision are effective across all relevant inputs.

Acknowledgements. This paper is based upon work supported in part by the National Science Foundation under FMITF-Track I Grant No. 2019302 and FMITF-Track II Grant No. 2422076, the Facebook Systems and Networking Award, and the eBPF Foundation Award. We thank the anonymous reviewers for their insightful feedback. We also thank Eduard Zingerman and Alexei Starovoitov for their feedback on our patches.

References

1. bpf: fix a verifier failure with xor. https://lore.kernel.org/bpf/20200825064608.2017937-1-yhs@fb.com/
2. bpf: fix incorrect sign extension in check_alu_op(). https://github.com/torvalds/linux/commit/95a762e2c8c942780948091f8f2a4f32fce1ac6f
3. bpf: Fix reg_bound_offset 64->32 var_off subreg propagation. https://lore.kernel.org/linux-patches/20230508094431.898575322@linuxfoundation.org/
4. bpf, Harden and/or/xor value tracking in verifier. https://git.kernel.org/pub/scm/linux/kernel/git/bpf/bpf-next.git/commit/?id=1f586614f3ff
5. bpf selftests. https://git.kernel.org/pub/scm/linux/kernel/git/torvalds/linux.git/tree/tools/testing/selftests/bpf/
6. bpf: Verifer, adjust_scalar_min_max_vals to always call update_reg_bounds(). https://lkml.iu.edu/hypermail/linux/kernel/2208.1/01778.html
7. bpf, verifier: Improve precision of BPF_MUL. https://git.kernel.org/pub/scm/linux/kernel/git/bpf/bpf-next.git/commit/?id=9aa0ebde0014
8. bpf, verifier: improve signed ranges reasoning for BPF_AND. https://lore.kernel.org/bpf/20240719110059.797546-6-xukuohai@huaweicloud.com/
9. bpf, x32: Fix bug with ALU64 LSH, RSH, ARSH BPF_X shift by 0. https://github.com/torvalds/linux/commit/68a8357ec15bdce55266e9fba8b8b3b8143fa7d2
10. CVE-2017-16996 Mishandling of register truncation. https://nvd.nist.gov/vuln/detail/CVE-2017-16996
11. CVE-2017-17852 Mishandling of 32-bit ALU ops. https://nvd.nist.gov/vuln/detail/CVE-2017-17852
12. CVE-2017-17853 Mishandling of 32-bit ALU ops. https://nvd.nist.gov/vuln/detail/CVE-2017-17853
13. CVE-2017-17864 Mishandled comparison between pointer and unknown data types. https://nvd.nist.gov/vuln/detail/CVE-2017-17864
14. CVE-2018-18445 Mishandling of 32-bit RSH op. https://nvd.nist.gov/vuln/detail/CVE-2018-18445
15. CVE-2020-8835 Mishandling of bounds tracking for 32-bit JMPs. https://nvd.nist.gov/vuln/detail/CVE-2020-8835
16. CVE-2021-3490 The eBPF ALU32 bounds tracking for bitwise ops (AND, OR and XOR) in the Linux kernel did not properly update 32-bit bounds. CVE-2021-3490
17. Facebook's Katran load balancer: Kernel XDP program. https://github.com/facebookincubator/katran/blob/master/katran/lib/bpf/balancer_kern.c
18. Merge branch 'bpf-register-bounds-logic-and-testing-improvements'. https://git.kernel.org/pub/scm/linux/kernel/git/bpf/bpf-next.git/commit/?id=cd9c127069c040d6b022f1ff32fed4b52b9a4017
19. Netconf 2018 day 1. https://lwn.net/Articles/757201/
20. bpf, tnums: Provably sound, faster, and more precise algorithm for tnum_mul (2021). https://git.kernel.org/pub/scm/linux/kernel/git/bpf/bpf-next.git/commit/?id=05924717ac70. Accessed 19 Oct 2022

21. Amadini, R., et al.: Combining string abstract domains for JavaScript analysis: an evaluation. In: Legay, A., Margaria, T. (eds.) TACAS 2017. LNCS, vol. 10205, pp. 41–57. Springer, Heidelberg (2017). https://doi.org/10.1007/978-3-662-54577-5_3
22. Bhat, S., Shacham, H.: Formal verification of the linux kernel ebpf verifier range analysis (2022). https://sanjit-bhat.github.io/assets/pdf/ebpf-verifier-range-analysis22.pdf
23. Borkmann, D.: bpf: Fix scalar32_min_max_or bounds tracking (2020). https://github.com/torvalds/linux/commit/5b9fbeb75b6a98955f628e205ac26689bcb1383e
24. Borkmann, D.: bpf: Undo incorrect __reg_bound_offset32 handling (2020). https://git.kernel.org/pub/scm/linux/kernel/git/netdev/net-next.git/commit/?id=f2d67fec0b43edce8c416101cdc52e71145b5fef
25. Borkmann, D.: bpf: Fix alu32 const subreg bound tracking on bitwise operations (2021). https://git.kernel.org/pub/scm/linux/kernel/git/bpf/bpf.git/commit/?id=049c4e13714ecbca567b4d5f6d563f05d431c80e
26. Borkmann, D.: bpf: Fix signed_sub,add32_overflows type handling (2021). https://git.kernel.org/pub/scm/linux/kernel/git/torvalds/linux.git/commit/?id=bc895e8b2a64e502fbba72748d59618272052a8b
27. Cheng, X., Wang, J., Sui, Y.: Precise sparse abstract execution via cross-domain interaction. In: Proceedings of the IEEE/ACM 46th International Conference on Software Engineering. ICSE 2024. Association for Computing Machinery, New York (2024). https://doi.org/10.1145/3597503.3639220
28. Cortesi, A., Costantini, G., Ferrara, P.: A survey on product operators in abstract interpretation. Electron. Proc. Theor. Comput. Sci. **129**, 325–336 (2013). https://doi.org/10.4204/eptcs.129.19
29. Cousot, P., Cousot, R.: Higher-order abstract interpretation (and application to comportment analysis generalizing strictness, termination, projection and per analysis of functional languages). In: Proceedings of 1994 IEEE International Conference on Computer Languages (ICCL 1994), pp. 95–112 (1994). https://doi.org/10.1109/ICCL.1994.288389
30. Cousot, P.: Lecture 13 notes: Mit 16.399, abstract interpretation (2005). http://web.mit.edu/afs/athena.mit.edu/course/16/16.399/www/lecture_13-abstraction1/Cousot_MIT_2005_Course_13_4-1.pdf
31. Cousot, P., Cousot, R.: Static determination of dynamic properties of programs. In: Proceedings of the 2nd International Symposium on Programming, Paris, France, pp. 106–130. Dunod (1976)
32. Cousot, P., Cousot, R.: Abstract interpretation: a unified lattice model for static analysis of programs by construction or approximation of fixpoints. In: Proceedings of the 4th ACM SIGACT-SIGPLAN Symposium on Principles of Programming Languages, POPL 1977, pp. 238–252. Association for Computing Machinery, New York (1977). https://doi.org/10.1145/512950.512973
33. Cousot, P., Cousot, R.: Systematic design of program analysis frameworks. In: Proceedings of the 6th ACM SIGACT-SIGPLAN Symposium on Principles of Programming Languages, POPL 1979, pp. 269–282. Association for Computing Machinery, New York (1979). https://doi.org/10.1145/567752.567778
34. Cree, E.: bpf/verifier: fix bounds calculation on BPF_RSH (2017). https://git.kernel.org/pub/scm/linux/kernel/git/torvalds/linux.git/commit/?id=4374f256ce8182019353c0c639bb8d0695b4c941
35. Moura, L., Bjørner, N.: Z3: an efficient SMT solver. In: Ramakrishnan, C.R., Rehof, J. (eds.) TACAS 2008. LNCS, vol. 4963, pp. 337–340. Springer, Heidelberg (2008). https://doi.org/10.1007/978-3-540-78800-3_24

36. Elder, M., Lim, J., Sharma, T., Andersen, T., Reps, T.: Abstract domains of affine relations. ACM Trans. Program. Lang. Syst. **36**(4) (2014). https://doi.org/10.1145/2651361
37. Fabre, A.: L4drop: Xdp ddos mitigations. https://blog.cloudflare.com/l4drop-xdp-ebpf-based-ddos-mitigations/
38. Gershuni, E., et al.: Simple and precise static analysis of untrusted linux kernel extensions. In: Proceedings of the 40th ACM SIGPLAN Conference on Programming Language Design and Implementation, PLDI 2019, pp. 1069–1084. Association for Computing Machinery, New York (2019). https://doi.org/10.1145/3314221.3314590
39. Horn, J.: Arbitrary read+write via incorrect range tracking in ebpf. https://bugs.chromium.org/p/project-zero/issues/detail?id=1454
40. Horn, J.: bpf: fix 32-bit ALU op verification (2017). https://git.kernel.org/pub/scm/linux/kernel/git/torvalds/linux.git/commit/?id=468f6eafa6c44cb2c5d8aad35e12f06c240a812a
41. Horn, J.: bpf: 32-bit RSH verification must truncate input before the ALU op (2018). https://git.kernel.org/pub/scm/linux/kernel/git/torvalds/linux.git/commit/?id=b799207e1e1816b09e7a5920fbb2d5fcf6edd681
42. Hung, H.W., Amiri Sani, A.: BRF: fuzzing the eBPF runtime. Proc. ACM Softw. Eng. **1**(FSE) (2024). https://doi.org/10.1145/3643778
43. Kalita, P.K., Muduli, S.K., D'Antoni, L., Reps, T., Roy, S.: Synthesizing abstract transformers. Proc. ACM Program. Lang. **6**(OOPSLA2) (2022). https://doi.org/10.1145/3563334
44. Kalita, P.K., Reps, T., Roy, S.: Synthesizing abstract transformers for reduced-product domains. In: Giacobazzi, R., Gorla, A. (eds.) Static Analysis, pp. 147–172. Springer, Cham (2025). https://doi.org/10.1007/978-3-031-74776-2_6
45. Kline, E.: BPF instruction set architecture (ISA). https://www.kernel.org/doc/html/latest/bpf/standardization/instruction-set.html
46. Li, Y., Niu, W., Zhu, Y., Gong, J., Li, B., Zhang, X.: Fuzzing logical bugs in eBPF verifier with bound-violation indicator. In: ICC 2023 - IEEE International Conference on Communications, pp. 753–758 (2023). https://doi.org/10.1109/ICC45041.2023.10278676
47. Lian, Z., Li, Y., Chen, Z., Shan, S., Han, B., Su, Y.: eBPF-based working set size estimation in memory management. In: 2022 International Conference on Service Science (ICSS), pp. 188–195. IEEE (2022)
48. Linux eBPF maintainers: Bounds syncing for abstract registers (2023). https://github.com/torvalds/linux/blob/v6.0/kernel/bpf/verifier.c#L1565
49. Lu, D., Tang, B., Paper, M., Kogias, M.: Towards functional verification of eBPF programs. In: Proceedings of the ACM SIGCOMM 2024 Workshop on EBPF and Kernel Extensions, eBPF 2024, pp. 37–43. Association for Computing Machinery, New York (2024). https://doi.org/10.1145/3672197.3673435
50. Lucas Leong: ZDI-20-1440: An incorrect calculation bug in the linux kernel eBPF verifier. https://www.zerodayinitiative.com/blog/2021/1/18/zdi-20-1440-an-incorrect-calculation-bug-in-the-linux-kernel-ebpf-verifier
51. Manfred Paul: CVE-2020-8835: Linux kernel privilege escalation via improper eBPF program verification. https://www.zerodayinitiative.com/blog/2020/4/8/cve-2020-8835-linux-kernel-privilege-escalation-via-improper-ebpf-program-verification
52. Miné, A.: Abstract domains for bit-level machine integer and floating-point operations. In: WING'12 - 4th International Workshop on invariant Generation, p. 16. Manchester, United Kingdom (2012). https://hal.science/hal-00748094

53. Miné, A.: Tutorial on static inference of numeric invariants by abstract interpretation. Found. Trends® Program. Lang. **4**(3-4), 120–372 (2017). https://doi.org/10.1561/2500000034
54. Mohamed, M.H.N., Wang, X., Ravindran, B.: Understanding the security of linux eBPF subsystem. In: Proceedings of the 14th ACM SIGOPS Asia-Pacific Workshop on Systems, APSys 2023, pp. 87–92. Association for Computing Machinery, New York (2023). https://doi.org/10.1145/3609510.3609822
55. Monniaux, D.: Verification of device drivers and intelligent controllers: a case study. In: Proceedings of the 7th ACM & IEEE International Conference on Embedded Software, pp. 30–36 (2007). https://doi.org/10.1145/1289927.1289937
56. Moore, R.E.: Interval Analysis. Prentice-Hall (1966)
57. Nakryiko, A.: BPF register bounds logic and testing improvements (2023). https://git.kernel.org/pub/scm/linux/kernel/git/bpf/bpf-next.git/commit/?id=cd9c127069c0
58. Onderka, J., Ratschan, S.: Fast three-valued abstract bit-vector arithmetic. In: Finkbeiner, B., Wies, T. (eds.) VMCAI 2022. LNCS, vol. 13182, pp. 242–262. Springer, Cham (2022). https://doi.org/10.1007/978-3-030-94583-1_12
59. Palmiotti, V.: Kernel pwning with eBPF: a love story. https://www.graplsecurity.com/post/kernel-pwning-with-ebpf-a-love-story
60. Peng, C., Jiang, M., Wu, L., Zhou, Y.: Toss a fault to bpfchecker: revealing implementation flaws for eBPF runtimes with differential fuzzing. In: Proceedings of the 2024 on ACM SIGSAC Conference on Computer and Communications Security, CCS 2024, pp. 3928–3942. Association for Computing Machinery, New York (2024). https://doi.org/10.1145/3658644.3690237
61. Regehr, J., Duongsaa, U.: Deriving abstract transfer functions for analyzing embedded software. In: Proceedings of the 2006 ACM SIGPLAN/SIGBED Conference on Language, Compilers, and Tool Support for Embedded Systems, LCTES 2006, pp. 34–43. Association for Computing Machinery, New York (2006). https://doi.org/10.1145/1134650.1134657
62. Reps, T., Sagiv, M., Yorsh, G.: Symbolic implementation of the best transformer. In: Steffen, B., Levi, G. (eds.) VMCAI 2004. LNCS, vol. 2937, pp. 252–266. Springer, Heidelberg (2004). https://doi.org/10.1007/978-3-540-24622-0_21
63. Reps, T., Thakur, A.: Automating abstract interpretation. In: Jobstmann, B., Leino, K.R.M. (eds.) VMCAI 2016. LNCS, vol. 9583, pp. 3–40. Springer, Heidelberg (2016). https://doi.org/10.1007/978-3-662-49122-5_1
64. Rick Larabee: eBPF and Analysis of the get-rekt-linux-hardened.c Exploit for CVE-2017-16995. https://ricklarabee.blogspot.com/2018/07/ebpf-and-analysis-of-get-rekt-linux.html
65. Shachnai, M., Vishwanathan, H., Narayana, S., Nagarakatte, S.: Fixing latent unsound abstract operators in the eBPF verifier of the linux kernel. In: International Static Analysis Symposium, pp. 386–406. Springer (2024)
66. Solar-Lezama, A.: Program sketching. Int. J. Softw. Tools Technol. Transfer **15**(5), 475–495 (2013)
67. Sun, H., Su, Z.: Validating the eBPF verifier via state embedding. In: 18th USENIX Symposium on Operating Systems Design and Implementation (OSDI 2024), pp. 615–628. USENIX Association, Santa Clara, CA (2024). https://www.usenix.org/conference/osdi24/presentation/sun-hao
68. Sun, H., Xu, Y., Liu, J., Shen, Y., Guan, N., Jiang, Y.: Finding correctness bugs in eBPF verifier with structured and sanitized program. In: Proceedings of the

Nineteenth European Conference on Computer Systems, EuroSys 2024, pp. 689–703. Association for Computing Machinery, New York (2024). https://doi.org/10.1145/3627703.3629562
69. Thakur, A., Reps, T.: A method for symbolic computation of abstract operations. In: Madhusudan, P., Seshia, S.A. (eds.) CAV 2012. LNCS, vol. 7358, pp. 174–192. Springer, Heidelberg (2012). https://doi.org/10.1007/978-3-642-31424-7_17
70. Toubhans, A., Chang, B.-Y.E., Rival, X.: Reduced product combination of abstract domains for shapes. In: Giacobazzi, R., Berdine, J., Mastroeni, I. (eds.) VMCAI 2013. LNCS, vol. 7737, pp. 375–395. Springer, Heidelberg (2013). https://doi.org/10.1007/978-3-642-35873-9_23
71. Vishwanathan, H., Shachnai, M., Narayana, S., Nagarakatte, S.: Sound, precise, and fast abstract interpretation with tristate numbers. In: Proceedings of the 20th IEEE/ACM International Symposium on Code Generation and Optimization, CGO 2022, pp. 254–265. IEEE Press (2022). https://doi.org/10.1109/CGO53902.2022.9741267
72. Vishwanathan, H., Shachnai, M., Narayana, S., Nagarakatte, S.: Agni: Verifying the Verifier (eBPF Range Analysis Verification) (2023). https://github.com/bpfverif/ebpf-range-analysis-verification-cav23
73. Vishwanathan, H., Shachnai, M., Narayana, S., Nagarakatte, S.: Verifying the verifier: eBPF range analysis verification. In: Computer Aided Verification: 35th International Conference, CAV 2023, Paris, France, 17–22 July 2023, Proceedings, Part III, pp. 226–251. Springer, Heidelberg (2023). https://doi.org/10.1007/978-3-031-37709-9_12
74. Yang, J., Chen, L., Bai, J.: Redis automatic performance tuning based on eBPF. In: 2022 14th International Conference on Measuring Technology and Mechatronics Automation (ICMTMA), pp. 671–676. IEEE (2022)

Bounded-Exhaustive Subspace Diversification for SMT Solver Testing

Junda Zheng and Peisen Yao(✉)

The State Key Laboratory of Blockchain and Data Security, Zhejiang University,
Hangzhou, China
{zhengjd04,pyaoaa}@zju.edu.cn

Abstract. SMT solvers form critical infrastructure for many verification and program analysis systems. Recent fuzzing efforts since 2019 have significantly improved solver robustness, yet these approaches often fall short of systematically probing the diverse semantic subspaces within a formula's satisfiability domain. This paper introduces subspace diversification, which systematically partitions the solution space of seed formulas to guide solvers into exploring different behavioral regions. We instantiate the idea using three general, bounded, and efficient mutation strategies that confine the space with cubes, numerical domains, and quantifiers. An extensive evaluation on Z3 and CVC4 demonstrates the effectiveness of our implementation, Canary, which uncovered 108 confirmed bugs across multiple theories and bug types.

1 Introduction

Satisfiability Modulo Theories (SMT) solvers determine the satisfiability of formulas over first-order theories, such as integers, reals, bit-vectors, and strings. SMT solvers have been widely used in various techniques such as symbolic execution [1–3], program verification [4–6], program synthesis [7,8], program repair [9,10], refinement types [11,12], among others. SMT solvers have also been successfully deployed in the industry to address practical software engineering programs, such as finding zero-day software vulnerabilities [13], verifying the safety of radiotherapy machines [14], and enforcing the access control policies of Amazon Web Services [15,16].

Despite substantial advances, modern SMT solvers remain susceptible to bugs [17–20], such as soundness issues, invalid models, and runtime crashes. These faults compromise the reliability of tools that rely on SMT solvers, particularly in safety-critical software systems. Ensuring the correctness of these solvers is a persistent challenge, particularly in developing effective testing methodologies. In particular, it is challenging to generate test formulas that thoroughly exercise the solver's diverse components, such as preprocessing routines, general frameworks, and theory-specific engines.

Existing approaches to test formula generation generally fall into two categories: generative and mutational. Generative approaches create formulas from scratch—typically by randomly assembling syntactically valid expressions according to target theory grammars [18,21–23]—and can produce many variants. However, it is often hard to steer them toward testing specific solver features. In contrast, mutational approaches systematically transform existing formulas [17,19,20,24,25]. By starting from known "seed" formulas, these techniques generate small changes that preserve much of the original structure while exploring new solver behaviors.

Yet, even sophisticated mutation strategies tend to focus on localized edits—altering a constraint, flipping a logical operator, or adding redundant terms. Although such transformations can explore a range of syntactic variations, they often fail to expose deeper semantic differences in solver behavior. In particular, they lack mechanisms for deliberately probing distinct logical regions within a formula's satisfiability space. As a result, significant portions of the solver's decision-making paths may remain untested, leaving certain bugs hidden.

This paper presents a novel mutational testing approach for SMT solvers, termed *subspace diversification*. The key insight is that, for a given formula φ, many SMT solvers exhibit deterministic search behaviors that focus on narrow regions of the solution space, potentially overlooking significant unexplored areas. These underexamined sub-regions may conceal latent bugs that evade detection by conventional tests. Subspace diversification addresses this limitation by systematically partitioning the solution space of a formula φ using a set of constraints $M_1, \ldots, M_n$, where each M_i restricts φ to a distinct subspace of the solution space. By guiding the solver to explore these regions, our approach can potentially expose unexpected behaviors or faults.

We evaluate Canary on two widely used SMT solvers—Z3 and CVC4—and demonstrate its effectiveness by uncovering 108 confirmed bugs, many of which have since been fixed. These bugs span multiple theories and encompass critical issues, including soundness violations, invalid model generation, and crashes. Our evaluation also shows that Canary can help improve code coverage and bug detection efficiency of baseline fuzzers. Furthermore, our head-to-head comparison with state-of-the-art fuzzers (HistFuzz and Yinyang) demonstrates that Canary can discover bugs that are missed by existing techniques. When integrated with these baseline fuzzers, Canary improves bug detection across all categories, showing that subspace diversification is complementary to existing approaches and can uncover deeper semantic errors.

In summary, our contributions are as follows:

- We introduce subspace diversification, a novel mutation-based testing methodology for exploring under-tested regions of SMT solver behavior.
- We instantiate the methodology by proposing three mutation strategies focused on cubes, numerical domains, and quantifiers.

2 Overview

SMT-LIB2 Language. SMT extends the classical Boolean satisfiability (SAT) problem by incorporating reasoning over first-order theories, such as linear integer arithmetic, real numbers, and strings. The SMT-LIB2 format has become the de facto standard for expressing SMT constraints, offering a unified language for defining variables, asserting conditions, and invoking satisfiability checks. For instance, the following SMT-LIB2 code snippet defines two integer variables and asserts a constraint that both must satisfy:

```
1  (set-logic QF_LIA)
2  (declare-const x Int)
3  (declare-const y Int)
4  (assert (and (> x 1) (< y 3)))
5  (check-sat)
```

2.1 SMT Formula Generation

The development of rigorous test formulas is central to evaluating the correctness and performance of SMT solvers. These formulas aim to explore solver behavior under diverse and challenging conditions. Two prevailing methodologies exist in the literature: generative and mutational approaches.

Generative Approach. Generative methods produce entirely new formulas from scratch, often guided by the grammar and semantics of the target logic. Several notable strategies include:

- FuzzSMT [21] is the first, grammar-based blackbox fuzzing tool developed to validate SMT solvers.
- StringFzz [22] uses grammar-based generation to construct formulas tailored to specific theories systematically.
- BanditFuzz [24] uses reinforcement learning-based generation, which adapts its generation policy based on feedback from solver performance.
- Falcon [23] focuses on mutating solver configuration options using a feedback-driven mechanism to test solver behaviors.
- ET [26] is a grammar-based enumerator for systematically validating the correctness and performance of SMT solvers.

Mutational Approach. Mutational approaches modify existing seed formulas to generate new test inputs. This category is further divided based on the use of oracles that preserve or evaluate the satisfiability status.

Oracle-Guided Mutations: These techniques rely on known solver outputs or structural transformations that maintain satisfiability. For instance:

- Bugariu and Müller [18] presents formula transformations that preserve satisfiability and create increasingly complex formulas to test string solvers.
- Storm [19] generates satisfiable formulas that are structurally different from the original seeds.
- Yiyang [20] combines formulas with identical satisfiability outcomes to create new variants.

- Sparrow [25]: generates formulas using approximation strategies, enabling the construction of test oracles.
- Diver [27]: uses random mutations and assignment-based oracles to test SMT solvers, focusing on satisfiable formulas.

Oracle-Less Mutations: These methods operate without oracle feedback, often using syntactic heuristics or probabilistic models:

- OpFuzz [20] uses a type-aware operator mutation technique targeting first-order logic formulas.
- HistFuzz [28] leverages historical bug-triggering inputs. The method extracts skeletons (core structures) and atomic formulas from past bug reports, then uses association rule mining to guide the generation of new test formulas.

Limitations. Although these techniques can explore nuanced input variations, they often fall short in systematically directing solvers toward semantically distinct regions within a seed formula's satisfiability space. SMT solvers typically employ deterministic search strategies that concentrate on narrow solution regions, neglecting potentially significant unexplored areas. Mutation-based approaches may generate syntactically different formulas without challenging solvers to navigate fundamentally different search spaces. As a result, substantial portions of a solver's decision space may remain untested, allowing subtle bugs to persist undetected.

2.2 Subspace Diversification

To bridge this gap, we propose a new mutation strategy called *subspace diversification*. Rather than relying on random edits or broad syntactic changes, our approach systematically explores unexplored logical sub-regions within a base formula. The central idea is rooted in the observation that SMT solvers often follow deterministic paths during satisfiability checking. As a result, large portions of the formula's solution space may remain unvisited.

Subspace diversification aims to expose these latent execution paths by selectively constraining or activating specific subformulas. This targeted perturbation increases the likelihood of triggering divergent solver behaviors.

To illustrate the approach, consider the following seed formula, which we use for triggering a confirmed bug in CVC4:

```
1  (set-logic QF_NIA)
2  (declare-const a Int)
3  (declare-const b Int)
4  (declare-const c Int)
5  (declare-const d Bool)
6  (declare-const e Int)
7  (assert (or (= (* (+ 0 0 e 0 888) c b a) 0) d))
8  (check-sat)
```

This formula is satisfiable if either disjunct holds. After we replace "check-sat" with "(check-sat-assuming (d))", CVC4 can solve the formula instantly. However, if we replace "check-sat" with "(check-sat-assuming ((= (* (+ 0 0 e 0 888) c b a) 0)))", CVC4 experiences significant performance degradation. Both cases correspond to distinct branches of the disjunction, yet they elicit dramatically different solver behaviors.

The discrepancy was traced to a bug in the branching heuristic of CVC4. The developers acknowledged the issue and subsequently fixed it. This example showcases the importance of systematically probing alternative semantic paths within a formula, an objective directly addressed by our work.

3 Approach

This section presents our methodology for systematically uncovering bugs in SMT solvers by decomposing the original formula into logically distinct subspaces. We begin by formalizing the solution space partitioning problem (§ 3.1). We then describe three complementary strategies for generating sub-formulas that explore these subspaces (§ refsubsec:partitionspsstrategies). Finally, we describe how our method integrates with a differential testing workflow to identify and categorize solver inconsistencies (§ 3.3).

3.1 Solution Space Partition

Given an SMT formula φ, its solution space consists of all interpretations (or models) under which φ evaluates to true. We formalize this as follows:

Definition 1. *(Solution Space) The solution space $S(\varphi)$ of a formula φ comprises all interpretations under which φ evaluates to true:*

$$S(\varphi) = \{I \mid I \vdash \varphi\}$$

Example 1. Let $\varphi \equiv p \vee q$, where p and q are Boolean variables. The formula evaluates to true under the following interpretations:

$$S(p \vee q) = \{\{p \mapsto true,\ q \mapsto false\},$$
$$\{p \mapsto false,\ q \mapsto true\},$$
$$\{p \mapsto true,\ q \mapsto true\}\}$$

Modern SMT solvers typically follow deterministic search trajectories when exploring solution spaces.[1] While this determinism benefits reproducibility and robustness, it creates a critical limitation: during any single execution, large portions of the solution space may remain entirely unexplored.

---

[1] We can set the random seed and other parameters to diversify the runtime behavior to a certain degree.

To address this, we design a method to produce syntactic mutations of φ that apply targeted constraints, effectively dividing the solution space into multiple, non-overlapping sub-regions. Each resulting sub-formula explores a distinct portion of $S(\varphi)$, encouraging solvers to exercise different decision paths.

Problem Statement. Given a formula φ, our objective is to generate a collection of formulas $\varphi_1, \ldots, \varphi_n$ such that:

- Each φ_i restricts φ to a specific segment of its solution space.
- Each sub-formula φ_i preserves the syntactic and semantic properties necessary for meaningful SMT solver testing.

The key challenge is how to construct informative sub-formulas that prompt diverse solver behavior, without relying on exhaustive enumeration, which is infeasible for formulas with combinatorial or infinite solution spaces, common in theories involving integers, reals, arrays, or strings.

3.2 Partition Strategies

We introduce three strategies for constructing sub-formulas that partition the solution space of a given formula φ: (i) numerical domain constraints, (ii) Boolean cubes, and (iii) quantifier-based transformations. Each strategy is designed to satisfy the following criteria:

- *Diversification* Each strategy helps target distinct logical regions of the solution space.
- *Generality* The strategies should be broadly applicable.
- *Efficiency* The mutations should be fast to enable testing throughput.

Partition via Numerical Domains. First, for formulas over numeric theories, we partition the solution space by constraining variables to lie within specific abstract domains [29,30]. This strategy draws on techniques from abstract interpretation, using domains such as intervals, zones, and octagons to define semantically meaningful subregions.

Example 2. For an integer formula $\varphi(x, y)$, we can partition its solution space into $\varphi \wedge x > a$ and $\varphi \wedge x \leq a$, where a represents a randomly-generated constant.

For arithmetic-heavy theories, such as nonlinear arithmetic and floating-point logic, solver behavior is often sensitive to the magnitude of numeric values. Partitioning by value range may expose corner cases in arithmetic reasoning, overflow handling, or rounding behavior.

Besides, this approach generalizes naturally to multiple variables and more expressive domains. For instance, we can partition using relational constraints such as $x-y \leq c$ (zones) or $x+y \leq c$ and $x-y \leq c$ (octagons). These abstractions allow us to define subregions that are both expressive and tractable.

Partition via Cubes. Second, inspired by cube-and-conquer approaches in parallel SAT solving [31,32], we define Boolean cubes as conjunctions of literals (atoms or their negations) to form partitions.

Definition 2. *(Partition Cube)* *Given a formula φ and a set S of partition predicates, a k-dimensional partition cube C is defined as the conjunction $l_1 \wedge \cdots \wedge l_k$, where each l_i is either a predicate or the negation of a predicate $p \in S$.*

Example 3. Consider the formula $\varphi \equiv p \wedge (q \vee \neg s) \wedge (r \vee s)$, with atoms p, q, r, s. Possible cubes include:

- 1-dimensional: p, $\neg p$, r;
- 2-dimensional: $p \wedge q$, $p \wedge \neg s$;
- 3-dimensional: $p \wedge q \wedge r$, $p \wedge \neg q \wedge \neg s$.

By forcing the solver to commit to specific cubes, we can guide it toward decision paths that may otherwise remain unexplored. Cubes can be constructed over both propositional and theory-level atoms. For instance, in string logic, predicates may include $x =$ "alice" or $z =$ str.++(x, y). In array logic, predicates may include $a[i] = v$ or $select(a, i) = v$. Because cube construction operates over literals, it generalizes across theories without requiring theory-specific reasoning.

This strategy offers two key advantages. First, it provides bounded combinatorial complexity: for k predicates, there are at most 2^k cubes. This allows controlled exploration of the solution space by adjusting k. Second, it is syntactically lightweight: cube construction requires only syntactic analysis of φ, without invoking expensive semantic reasoning.

Partition via Quantifiers. Finally, quantifiers significantly enhance the expressive power of SMT formulas and are essential for modeling systems with variable scope or data abstraction. However, supporting quantifiers introduces significant complexity into SMT solving and is often a source of incompleteness or performance degradation, such as incomplete instantiation strategies that miss relevant ground terms and improper handling of quantifier alternation or variable shadowing.

To further diversify test instances, we apply transformations that inject quantifiers into seed formulas.

Example 4. Given the quantifier-free formula $\varphi(x, y) \equiv x + y < 1$, we may construct quantified variants as follows:

- Universal quantification: $\forall z.\varphi(x, z)$;
- Existential quantification: $\exists z.\varphi(z, y)$;
- Quantifier alternation: $\forall z.\exists w.\forall v.\varphi(z, w, v)$.

Notably, this strategy can also indirectly stress the quantifier-free reasoning engines, since quantifier-handling algorithms, such as MBQI (model-based quantifier instantiation) [33] and E-matching [34], typically employ quantifier-free decision procedures as fundamental subroutines.

Algorithm 1: Search Space Partition-Based Differential Testing

Input: $solver1, solver2$: SMT solvers under test
Input: Φ: a set of input seed formulas
Input: N: number of mutations per seed formula
Output: $bugs$: set of bug-triggering formulas

1 $bugs \leftarrow \emptyset$;
2 **foreach** $\varphi \in \Phi$ **do**
3   **if** φ *is unsat* **then**
4          $\varphi \leftarrow \neg \varphi$;   /* negation an unsatisfiable seed */
5   **for** $i = 1$ **to** N **do**
6          $s \leftarrow$ randomly select a mutation strategy;
7          $\psi \leftarrow$ apply the strategy to φ;
8          $r1 \leftarrow solver1.\text{solve}(\psi)$;
9          $r2 \leftarrow solver2.\text{solve}(\psi)$;
10   **if** $r1 = crash$ **or** $r2 = crash$ **or** $r1 \neq r2$ **then**
11             $bugs \leftarrow bugs \cup \{\psi\}$;
12 **return** $bugs$

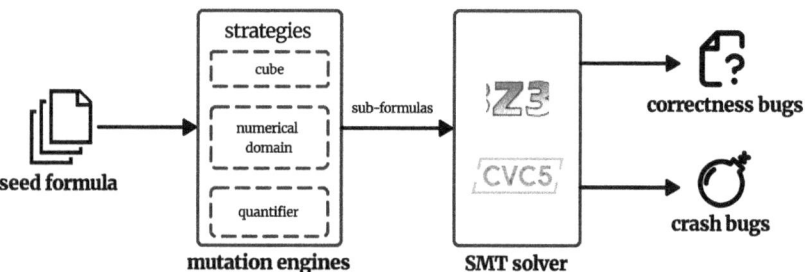

Fig. 1. Overall workflow of Canary.

3.3 Testing Workflows

Our testing framework utilizes a multi-strategy partitioning scheme, combined with differential testing, to identify discrepancies and crashes in SMT solvers. By generating logically distinct sub-formulas from an original formula φ, we drive solvers into varied execution paths.

Overall Workflow. Algorithm 1 presents the complete testing pipeline. The algorithm accepts two SMT solvers, a set of seed formulas, and a mutation count per seed. For each seed formula, it first checks satisfiability; if the formula is unsatisfiable, it is negated to ensure a satisfiable starting point. Given a satisfiable seed φ, the algorithm generates N test cases by applying randomly selected mutation strategies. Each mutation yields a variant formula ψ, which is evaluated by both solvers. A discrepancy—either a crash or a disagreement in satisfiability results—signals a potential bug (Fig. 1).

It is worth noting that while the quantifier partition strategy can be applied to unsatisfiable seeds, the current implementation focuses on satisfiable formulas by negating unsatisfiable seeds to align with the other mutation strategies.

Bug Categorization. For each subspace ψ, the workflow performs *differential testing*, comparing the results of multiple SMT solvers. This involves running ψ across all solvers and checking for:

- Correctness bugs: Cases where solvers disagree on the satisfiability of ψ (e.g., one returns SAT while another returns UNSAT).
- Crash bugs: Instances where a solver terminates unexpectedly due to internal errors or resource exhaustion.

Any sub-formula that triggers a crash or disagreement is added to the candidate bug set, denoted as bugs in Algorithm 1. To streamline debugging and facilitate triage, we apply automated formula minimization tools such as ddSMT. Crashing instances are grouped by failure trace (e.g., assertion location or memory errors), while correctness bugs are categorized and reported to developers by theory (e.g., linear arithmetic, strings).

While our approach is inspired by the idea of bounded-exhaustive testing, our implementation does not attempt to exhaustively enumerate all possible subspaces. Instead, we sample a representative subset of partitions under a given resource budget to strike a balance between coverage and efficiency.

4 Evaluation

This section presents a comprehensive assessment of Canary, aiming to answer the following research questions:

- **RQ1**: How effective is Canary in uncovering previously unknown bugs in state-of-the-art SMT solvers (§ 4.1)?
- **RQ2**: How does Canary impact code coverage, and can it enhance the effectiveness of existing SMT fuzzers (§ 4.2)?
- **RQ3**: Can Canary detect bugs effectively compared to existing fuzzers (§ 4.3)?

Tested Solvers. We have selected Z3 and CVC4, the two most popular SMT solvers, for the experimental evaluation because they are popular and widely used in academia and industry, support most of the SMT-LIB2 theories [35], and have been extensively tested by previous efforts [17, 19–24]. We primarily focus on the solvers' default modes. For CVC4, we enable options such as produce-models, incremental, and strings-exp to support all the seed formulas. We use the check-models option for CVC4 and model.validate=true for Z3 to detect invalid model bugs. Additionally, we test a new SMT core of Z3, which can be activated via the options tactic.default_tactic=smt sat.euf=true.

Baselines. We compare Canary against three state-of-the-art and mutational SMT fuzzing techniques, including HistFuzz [28] and Yinyang [20].

Environment. All experiments are conducted on a Linux workstation equipped with an 80-core Intel(R) Xeon(R) 2.2 GHz processor and 256 GB of RAM. We compile Z3 and CVC4 using GCC 5.4.0, with assertions and AddressSanitizer [36] enabled. We use Gcov [37] to measure the code coverage.

4.1 Analysis of the Discovered Bugs

This section summarizes the bugs identified during testing with Canary and categorizes them based on their nature and severity.

Number of the Bugs. Over a nine-month evaluation period from June 2021 to March 2022, Canary uncovered 123 unique bugs across Z3 and CVC4. Table 1 summarizes the status of these bugs. Out of the total, 108 were confirmed by solver developers, and 107 have already been addressed through patches. These outcomes demonstrate Canary's capacity to surface substantive issues in mature, production-grade solvers.

Types of the Bugs. Table 2 categorizes the confirmed bugs according to their type. Crash bugs form the majority (71 out of 108), followed by invalid model bugs (28) and soundness errors (9). Invalid model bugs indicate situations where the solver produces a model that does not satisfy the input formula, while soundness bugs involve incorrect satisfiability results. Notably, correctness issues (invalid models and soundness bugs) account for over 35% of the confirmed bugs, emphasizing Canary's strength in detecting deep semantic flaws.

Table 1. Summary of the bugs found by Canary.

Status	Z3	CVC4	Total
Reported	83	40	123
Confirmed	75	33	108
Fixed	75	32	107
Duplicate	1	5	6
Won't fix	7	2	9

Table 2. Bug types among the confirmed bugs.

Type	Z3	CVC4	Total
Soundness	6	3	9
Invalid model	21	7	28
Crash	48	23	71

Diversity of the Theories. Figure 2 depicts the distribution of theories among bug-triggering formulas. While AUFLIA, QF_BV, and AUFBV were the most frequent, a broad range of logics were represented, showcasing Canary's generality across multiple theory combinations. Notably, QF_BV—one of the most mature and widely adopted SMT theories—accounts for a substantial portion of the triggered bugs, underscoring the practical relevance of Canary's findings.

Impact on Solvers' Codebase. To assess the development effort required to resolve identified bugs, we analyzed the corresponding commits. Specifically, we examined the number of files and lines of code modified in each commit. As illustrated in Fig. 3, most fixes altered fewer than five files, suggesting localized

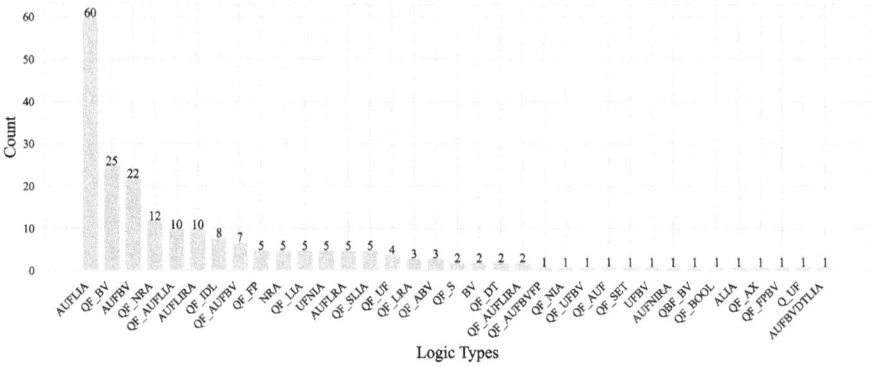

Fig. 2. The number of bug-triggering formulas from different theories.

issues, yet some required broader changes, highlighting how a single bug may uncover structural weaknesses. In total, 196 files and 5,669 lines of code were modified to fix bugs discovered by Canary.

In Fig. 4, we studied the most changed files in these commits fixing bugs found by Canary. In Z3, the most modified files concern the array theory solver and EUF solver, among others. In contrast, the most frequently fixed files in CVC4 are the theory model builder, the quantifiers rewriter, and the sequences rewriter. These results provide insight into the solver components most susceptible to errors uncovered by Canary.

Summary. Our evaluation demonstrates that Canary is highly effective in testing SMT solvers. Here are the key highlights:

- Canary identified 123 bugs, with 108 confirmed and 107 already addressed.
- Bugs span a diverse set of SMT-LIB2 theories, including strings, (non-)linear arithmetic, bit-vectors, uninterpreted functions, floating-point operations, and combinations thereof.
- Many confirmed bugs were triggered in the solvers' default configurations, demonstrating the tool's ability to expose real-world failures without relying on exotic options.

4.2 Code Coverage

In addition to bug discovery, we evaluated Canary's ability to increase code coverage in SMT solvers.

Experimental Design. We used the seed formulas from HistFuzz, which are sampled from the SMT-LIB2 library to represent a diverse range of theories and complexity levels. We generated 100 mutants for each seed using Canary's partition-based strategies. First, we ran the baseline fuzzers to collect their coverage results. Then, we layered Canary's partitioning techniques onto these fuzzers to measure the incremental improvement in coverage.

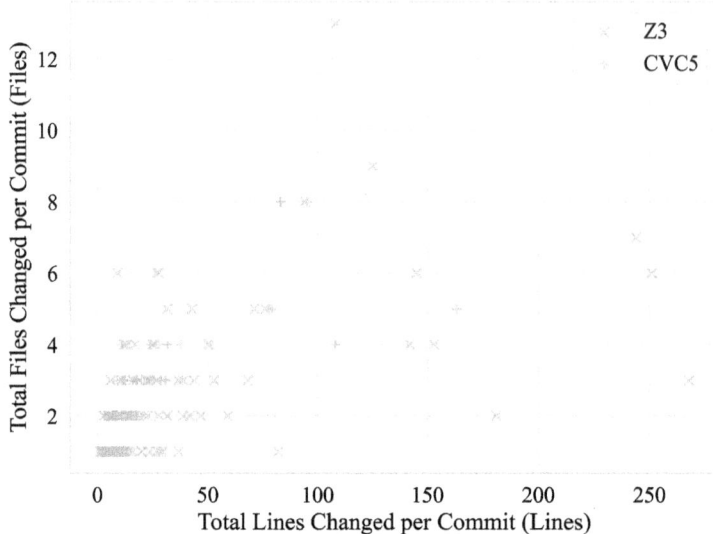

Fig. 3. Distribution of file changes and lines of code changes for Z3 and CVC4 bug-fixing commits.

To ensure fair and reproducible comparisons, we set the solver timeout to two seconds per formula—enough time to process most formulas without excessive resource consumption. We compiled both Z3 and CVC4 in debug mode without optimizations to enable accurate coverage measurement. We used `gcov` to record three key coverage metrics: line coverage (l), function coverage (f), and branch coverage (b). Each experiment was run three times, and we report the average results to account for any variability.

Integration with Other Fuzzers. To assess the compatibility and impact of Canary's core partitioning strategies when integrated with existing fuzzing frameworks, we combined Canary with two leading fuzzers, HistFuzz and Yinyang. Table 3 presents the resulting coverage metrics, illustrating the benefits of augmenting these state-of-the-art tools with our approach.

The results highlight that Canary's partitioning techniques serve as effective, modular enhancements to existing approaches. When integrated with other fuzzing strategies, our approach yields consistent improvements across all coverage metrics. For Z3, combining Canary with HistFuzz increased line coverage by 0.7% points, function coverage by 0.7% points, and branch coverage by 0.6% points. Similarly, the Yinyang integration showed improvements of 0.6, 0.5, and 0.6% points, respectively. For CVC4, both combinations demonstrated notable improvements, with HistFuzz+Canary achieving particularly strong results: 33.1% line coverage, 46.9% function coverage, and 26.9% branch coverage. The consistency of these improvements across both solvers indicates that Canary's partitioning strategy offers fundamental benefits that transcend specific solver implementations.

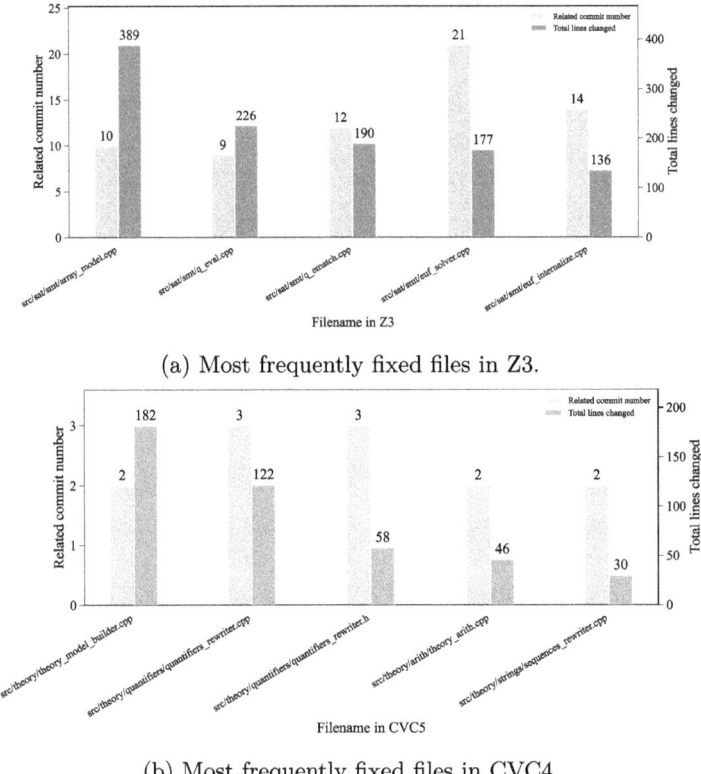

(a) Most frequently fixed files in Z3.

(b) Most frequently fixed files in CVC4.

Fig. 4. Number of commits and changed lines of Top 5 fixed files in Z3 and CVC4.

These results are particularly significant because they demonstrate that Canary can enhance even the most sophisticated existing fuzzers. The improvements stem from Canary's ability to generate semantically diverse yet valid formulas that exercise different solver components through targeted partitioning.

Ablation Study. We conducted an ablation study to understand the contribution of each component of Canary to the overall improvement in coverage. We created three variants by selectively removing one core component at a time:

- Canary-NoCube: Excludes cube-based partitioning;
- Canary-NoDomain: Excludes numerical domain constraints;
- Canary-NoQuant: Excludes quantifier manipulations.

Table 4 presents the coverage results for each variant across different baseline fuzzers. The patterns revealed by this ablation study are nuanced and informative. While removing any component generally reduced overall coverage, certain variants performed better in specific contexts, indicating that the optimal configuration may depend on both the target solver and the baseline fuzzer.

Table 3. Line coverage (l), function coverage (f), and branch coverage (b) results of using Canary to enhance existing fuzzers.

Tool	Z3 (l/f/b)	CVC4 (l/f/b)
Canary	24.4% / 27.0% / 20.6%	27.9% / 43.5% / 22.5%
HistFuzz	32.4% / 32.9% / 28.8%	32.1% / 46.2% / 25.9%
HistFuzz+Canary	33.1% / 33.6% / 29.4%	33.1% / 46.9% / 26.9%
Yinyang	27.0% / 28.8% / 24.0%	27.9% / 43.8% / 22.6%
Yinyang+Canary	27.6% / 29.3% / 24.6%	28.8% / 44.3% / 23.5%

Table 4. Line coverage (l), function coverage (f), and branch coverage (b) results for different variants of Canary.

Baseline	Canary variant	Z3 (l/f/b)	CVC4 (l/f/b)
HistFuzz	Canary-NoCube	33.1% / 33.6% / 29.6%	32.2% / 45.6% / 26.4%
	Canary-NoDomain	32.8% / 33.4% / 29.4%	32.4% / 45.9% / 26.5%
	Canary-NoQuant	33.3% / 33.8% / 29.8%	32.8% / 45.9% / 26.8%
Yinyang	Canary-NoCube	25.0% / 27.2% / 21.3%	28.5% / 43.7% / 23.3%
	Canary-NoDomain	27.9% / 29.5% / 24.6%	28.5% / 43.7% / 23.3%
	Canary-NoQuant	27.4% / 28.9% / 24.4%	28.0% / 43.5% / 22.6%

For instance, for HistFuzz, Canary-NoQuant unexpectedly achieved better coverage compared to Canary-NoCube. This suggests that cube-based partitioning may be more important than quantifier manipulations when starting from HistFuzz's mutation strategy. The most interesting variation appeared with Yinyang as the baseline. For Z3, Canary-NoQuant achieved notably higher coverage than Canary-NoCube, while for CVC4, the opposite was true—Canary-NoCube performed better than Canary-NoQuant.

These results have important implications for Canary's design and deployment. They suggest that: (1) No single component is universally dominant; the effectiveness depends on the context; (2) Different solvers benefit from different aspects of Canary's partitioning strategy; (3) There may be interaction effects between Canary's components and the baseline fuzzer's mutation strategy.

Summary. These results indicate that Canary can help improve code coverage across multiple dimensions—line, function, and branch—when used alone or in conjunction with existing fuzzers. While code coverage is a useful metric, it has its limitations. The relative coverage gains shown in our results may appear modest, as the baseline fuzzers are already effective at exploring many of the simpler execution paths in the solvers. However, the small percentage improvements still represent meaningful absolute increases in the number of lines, functions, and branches of code being tested. The coverage also provides a complementary set of stress-testing mechanisms that can uncover new and interesting solver behaviors.

Table 5. Comparison of bugs found by different tools within one week.

Tool	Z3			CVC4		
	Soundness	Invalid Model	Crash	Soundness	Invalid Model	Crash
HistFuzz	2	2	5	1	1	3
HistFuzz+Canary	4	2	6	3	1	4
Yinyang	4	0	3	2	1	1
Yinyang+Canary	4	1	5	3	1	3

4.3 Controlled Experiments for Bug Detection

To further evaluate the effectiveness of Canary, we conducted a head-to-head comparison with two state-of-the-art SMT solver fuzzing tools, including HistFuzz [28] and Yinyang [20].

Experimental Design. All tools were evaluated under identical experimental conditions: each was run for one week on the same hardware platform, using an identical set of seed formulas. During this period, we systematically recorded both the number and types of unique bugs uncovered in Z3-4.8.7 and CVC4-1.8. The results of this comparative study are presented in Table 5.

Quantitative Analysis. The integration of Canary with baseline fuzzers shows consistent improvements. For HistFuzz, the combination with Canary increased the total number of bugs found from 14 to 20, with notable gains in soundness bugs and crash bugs. Similarly, for Yinyang, the integration improved the total bug count from 11 to 17, with significant improvements in crash bugs and the discovery of invalid model bugs.

Qualitative Analysis. The results reveal several important patterns. First, Canary demonstrates particular strength in detecting soundness bugs—the most critical type of correctness issues. When combined with HistFuzz, it doubled the number of soundness bugs found, and when combined with Yinyang, it maintained the high detection rate. This suggests that subspace diversification is particularly effective at uncovering deep semantic errors that affect solver correctness. Second, the integration shows consistent improvements in crash detection. Both HistFuzz+Canary and Yinyang+Canary found more crash bugs than their baseline counterparts, indicating that our partitioning strategies can expose execution paths that lead to unexpected termination. Third, the discovery of invalid model bugs by Yinyang+Canary where the baseline Yinyang found none demonstrates that Canary's approach can uncover bugs that are missed by existing techniques.

Cross-Solver Analysis. The results also show interesting patterns across different SMT solvers. For Z3, the improvements are more pronounced, with HistFuzz+Canary finding 12 bugs compared to HistFuzz's 9, and Yinyang+Canary finding 10 bugs compared to Yinyang's 7. For CVC4, the improvements are more modest but still consistent, with both combinations showing better performance than their baselines. This cross-solver analysis suggests that Canary's effectiveness may be influenced by the specific characteristics of each solver's implementation. Z3's more complex architecture and broader theory support may provide more opportunities for subspace diversification to uncover bugs, while CVC4's more focused design may require more targeted partitioning strategies.

Complementarity Analysis. Notably, Canary is able to find bugs that are not detected by other state-of-the-art fuzzers, indicating that our approach can uncover unique issues missed by existing techniques. This confirms that subspace diversification is an effective strategy for uncovering deep and subtle semantic errors that are often overlooked by existing fuzzing techniques. The fact that different combinations (HistFuzz+Canary vs. Yinyang+Canary) find different sets of bugs suggests that Canary's partitioning strategies can adapt to and enhance different baseline approaches.

Summary. These results confirm that Canary is not only effective in finding a large number of bugs, but also excels at uncovering critical correctness issues in SMT solvers compared to state-of-the-art fuzzers under the same testing budget. We believe that combining complementary testing techniques within a unified system represents a promising direction. Such a system would leverage the strengths of individual methods while mitigating their weaknesses, yielding a more robust and comprehensive testing pipeline for SMT solvers.

4.4 Assorted Sample Bugs

In this section, we select and discuss six reported Z3 and CVC4 bugs. classifications and status.

Figure 5a shows a refutation soundness bug in Z3. The reason is that models are prematurely reported invalid when the EUF (Equality with Uninterpreted Functions) solver is active. The developers fixed the issue by deferring certain validation checks until after the EUF-specific model construction is completed.

Figure 5b shows a solution to a soundness bug in CVC4's quantifier instantiation engines. It is marked as "major", which is the highest severity in CVC4's bug tracking system. The bug is caused by allowing ineligible terms to appear in the instantiations.

Figure 5c shows a crash bug in CVC4 caused by an assertion that requires the model to always have a shared term for the real term in the conversion from real to floating-point value.

Figure 5d shows an invalid model bug in Z3's bit-vector solver. This bug is triggered by a corner case in the signed arithmetic solver, where the input has a bit-width of 1.

Figure 5e shows an invalid model bug in CVC4's ALIRA logic. This is because the sanity check for integer models in linear arithmetic was too strict when the linear solver had assigned a real value to an integer variable.

```
1 (declare-fun x () Real)
2 (assert (and (> 0.0 x) (= 0.0
      (/ 0.0 x))))
3 (check-sat-using (then
      add-bounds propagate-ineqs
      purify-arith uflra))
```

(a) A refutation soundness bug in Z3.

```
1 (declare-datatypes ((E 0))
      (((c (a Bool)))))
2 (assert (forall ((v E)) (and
      (a v))))
3 (check-sat)
```

(b) A solution soundness bug in CVC4.

```
1 (declare-const X (_
      FloatingPoint 8 24))
2 (declare-const R Real)
3 (assert (= X ((_ to_fp 8 24)
      RTZ (- R))))
4 (assert (= X ((_ to_fp 8 24)
      RTZ 0)))
5 (check-sat)
```

(c) A crash bug in CVC4.

```
1 (set-option :model_validate
      true)
2 (declare-fun bv_4-0 () (_
      BitVec 1))
3 (assert (not (bvsmul_noovfl
      bv_4-0 bv_4-0)))
4 (check-sat)
```

(d) An invalid model bug in Z3.

```
1 (set-logic ALIRA)
2 (declare-const x Real)
3 (declare-fun i () Int)
4 (declare-fun i1 () Int)
5 (push)
6 (assert (< 1 (- i)))
7 (check-sat)
8 (pop)
9 (push)
10 (assert (or (>= i1 (* 5 (- i)
      ))))
11 (check-sat)
12 (pop)
13 (assert (or (> i1 1) (= x (
      to_real i))))
14 (check-sat)
15 (assert (not (is_int x)))
16 (check-sat)
```

(e) An invalid model bug in CVC4

```
1 (set-option :smt.arith.
      eager_eq_axioms false)
2 (declare-fun z () Int)
3 (declare-fun y () Int)
4 (declare-fun x () Int)
5 (declare-fun named3 () Bool)
6 (declare-fun named5 () Bool)
7 (declare-fun named6 () Bool)
8 (declare-fun named7 () Bool)
9 (assert (and (= y (+ x 1)) (=
      1 (* z z))))
10 (assert (or named6 (not
      named3)))
11 (assert (or (not named5) (= y
      0)))
12 (assert (or named7 (= z y)))
13 (get-consequences (named5) (
      named3 named7))
```

(f) A crash bug in Z3.

Fig. 5. Sampled bugs detected by Canary.

Figure 5f shows a crash bug in Z3's eager generation of axioms. This is due to the unconditional eager generation of axioms for arithmetic disequalities. The developers fixed the issue by controlling the generation of this axiom.

4.5 Discussions

Limitations. While Canary has demonstrated effectiveness in uncovering bugs and improving solver coverage, several limitations merit discussion. First, the efficacy of partition-based mutation is theory-dependent; certain SMT fragments may not benefit uniformly from the same mutation strategies. Second, our evaluation assumes deterministic solver behavior. Solvers employing randomized heuristics may exhibit variability across runs, complicating reproducibility and analysis. Third, as solvers evolve and adapt to current mutation patterns, the marginal utility of existing strategies may diminish, necessitating continual refinement of mutation operators to maintain effectiveness.

Adaptivity and Mutation Strategy Evolution. To sustain long-term effectiveness, mutation strategies must evolve. One avenue is to monitor metrics such as coverage growth or behavioral divergence over time; a plateau in these metrics may signal the need for strategy revision. Canary's modular design facilitates the integration of adaptive mechanisms, such as online bandit algorithms that reallocate probability mass among operators based on empirical utility. Additionally, synthesizing new mutation operators—e.g., via SyGuS or learned models—offers a principled path to expanding the mutation space.

Program Analysis for Targeted Mutation. Incorporating program analysis—both static and dynamic—can potentially improve the relevance and effectiveness of mutations. Static analysis of seed formulas can uncover logical dependencies among variables or subformulas, enabling the generation of non-trivial subspace partitions, such as those that preclude trivially inconsistent cubes. Complementarily, dynamic analysis (e.g., runtime coverage profiling, logs of SMT solvers) can identify under-tested components of SMT solvers, guiding the mutation engine to generate inputs that stress these components, thereby improving bug exposure and coverage.

Applications Beyond Solver Testing. The partition-based mutation approach introduced in Canary has potential applications beyond SMT solver testing. Similar principles could be adapted to test other formal reasoning tools, such as theorem provers and program verifiers. Additionally, the generated diverse yet semantically connected formula sets could serve as benchmarks for evaluating solver performance or as training data for machine learning models to predict solver behavior [38]. The semantic partitioning approach might also inform strategies for distributed solving [31,32], where formula space is partitioned intelligently among parallel solver instances.

5 Related Work

SMT Solver Testing. FuzzSMT [21] introduced grammar-based fuzzing to evaluate SMT solvers, marking one of the earliest efforts in this domain. Subsequent tools such as StringFuzz [22] and Winterer et al. [20] contributed a type-aware mutation strategy to improve the generation of diverse SMT formulas. However, these methods primarily rely on differential testing—comparing the outputs of multiple solvers—to detect inconsistencies. To address this issue, more recent approaches have focused on generating formulas with known satisfiability outcomes. Bugariu et al. [18] proposed constructing increasingly complex string formulas through satisfiability-preserving transformations. Winterer et al. [17] introduced semantic fusion to obtain mutants of formulas whose satisfiability status remains unchanged. Existing mutation techniques either focus on localized syntactic changes or changes vastly different from the seed, but the seed formula's original search space may not be thoroughly tested. Subspace diversification explicitly partitions a formula's solution space into disjoint regions using additional constraints.

Bounded-Exhaustive Testing. The principle behind bounded-exhaustive testing (BET) [39–42] is to systematically explore all inputs up to a predefined size or complexity. The underlying assumption is that many software defects are exposed by relatively small inputs, making exhaustive testing over these inputs an effective strategy for bug discovery. There are two prominent approaches in this space: declarative and imperative enumeration. Declarative methods [39] leverage logical invariants to constrain the space of valid inputs, while imperative strategies [43] construct inputs procedurally based on specific structural specifications. While BET offers thorough coverage, it faces challenges related to scalability and efficiency. To mitigate these issues, several optimization techniques have been proposed, such as sparse test generation [44] and structural test merging [45]. Our work draws inspiration from BET by employing small, bounded syntactical modifications. However, a key distinction is that our mutations also aim to constrain the search space semantically, guiding the generation towards more meaningful variations beyond purely structural exploration.

6 Conclusion

We have presented bounded-exhaustive subspace diversification, a principled approach to testing SMT solvers that targets underexplored regions of the solution space. Our implementation, Canary, uncovered 108 previously unknown bugs in Z3 and CVC4. These bugs span a wide range of bug types, input logics, and solver configurations, demonstrating the generality and effectiveness of our approach.

Acknowledgements. We would like to thank the reviewers for their helpful feedback. This work is supported by the National Key R&D Program of China (2023YFB3106000), the National Natural Science Foundation of China (62302434, U2341212, 62302442), and ZJU-China Unicom Digital Security Joint Laboratory. Peisen Yao is the corresponding author.

References

1. Sen, K., Marinov, D., Agha, G.: Cute: a concolic unit testing engine for c. In: Proceedings of the 10th European Software Engineering Conference Held Jointly with 13th ACM SIGSOFT International Symposium on Foundations of Software Engineering, ESEC/FSE-13, pp. 263–272, New York, NY, USA, 2005. ACM. https://doi.org/10.1145/1081706.1081750
2. Cadar, C., Ganesh, V., Pawlowski, P.M., Dill, D.L., Engler, D.R.: Exe: automatically generating inputs of death, pp. 322–335 (2006) .https://doi.org/10.1145/1180405.1180445
3. Huang, H., Yao, P., Wu, R., Shi, Q., Zhang, C.: Pangolin: incremental hybrid fuzzing with polyhedral path abstraction. In: 2020 IEEE Symposium on Security and Privacy, SP 2020, San Francisco, CA, USA, May 18–21, 2020, pp. 1613–1627. IEEE (2020). https://doi.org/10.1109/SP40000.2020.00063
4. Alt, L., et al.: Hifrog: SMT-based function summarization for software verification. In: International Conference on Tools and Algorithms for the Construction and Analysis of Systems, pp. 207–213. Springer (2017)
5. Yao, P., Shi, Q., Huang, H., Zhang, C.: Program analysis via efficient symbolic abstraction. In: Proceedings of the ACM Program Language 5(OOPSLA) (2021)
6. Heizmann, M., Hoenicke, J., Podelski, A.: Software model checking for people who love automata. In: International Conference on Computer Aided Verification, pp. 36–52. Springer (2013)
7. Solar-Lezama, A., Bodik, R.: Program synthesis by sketching. Citeseer (2008)
8. Blazytko, T., Contag, M., Aschermann, C., Holz, T.: Syntia: synthesizing the semantics of obfuscated code. In: Kirda, E., Ristenpart, T., eds., In: 26th USENIX Security Symposium, USENIX Security 2017, Vancouver, BC, Canada, August 16-18, 2017, pp. 643–659. USENIX Association (2017)
9. Mechtaev, S., Yi, J., Roychoudhury, A.: Angelix: scalable multiline program patch synthesis via symbolic analysis. In: Proceedings of the 38th International Conference on Software Engineering, ICSE '16, pp. 691–701, New York, NY, USA (2016). ACM. https://doi.org/10.1145/2884781.2884807
10. Nguyen, H.D.T., Qi, D., Roychoudhury, A., Chandra, S.: Semfix: program repair via semantic analysis. In: Proceedings of the 2013 International Conference on Software Engineering, ICSE '13, pp. 772–781, Piscataway, NJ, USA (2013). IEEE Press
11. Vazou, N., Seidel, E.L., Jhala, R., Vytiniotis, D., Peyton-Jones, S.: Refinement types for haskell. In: Proceedings of the 19th ACM SIGPLAN International Conference on Functional Programming (ICFP), pp. 269–282. ACM (2014). https://doi.org/10.1145/2628136.2628161
12. Champion, A., Chiba, T., Kobayashi, N., Sato, R.: ICE-based refinement type discovery for higher-order functional programs. In: Beyer, D., Huisman, M. (eds.) TACAS 2018. LNCS, vol. 10805, pp. 365–384. Springer, Cham (2018). https://doi.org/10.1007/978-3-319-89960-2_20
13. Avgerinos, T., Rebert, A., Cha, S.K., Brumley, D.: Enhancing symbolic execution with veritesting. In: Proceedings of the 36th International Conference on Software Engineering, ICSE 2014, pp. 1083–1094, New York, NY, USA. (2014). ACM. https://doi.org/10.1145/2568225.2568293
14. Pernsteiner, S., et al.: Investigating safety of a radiotherapy machine using system models with pluggable checkers. In: Chaudhuri, S., Farzan, A. (eds.) CAV 2016. LNCS, vol. 9780, pp. 23–41. Springer, Cham (2016). https://doi.org/10.1007/978-3-319-41540-6_2

15. Cook, B.: Formal reasoning about the security of amazon web services. In: International Conference on Computer Aided Verification, pp. 38–47. Springer (2018)
16. Bouchet, M. et al.: Block public access: trust safety verification of access control policies. In: Devanbu, P., Cohen, M.B., Zimmermann, T., eds., ESEC/FSE '20: 28th ACM Joint European Software Engineering Conference and Symposium on the Foundations of Software Engineering, Virtual Event, USA, November 8-13, 2020, pp. 281–291. ACM (2020). https://doi.org/10.1145/3368089.3409728
17. Winterer, D., Zhang, C., Su, Z.: Validating SMT solvers via semantic fusion. In: Donaldson, A.F., Torlak, E., eds., In: Proceedings of the 41st ACM SIGPLAN International Conference on Programming Language Design and Implementation, PLDI 2020, London, UK, June 15-20, 2020, pp. 718–730. ACM, (2020). https://doi.org/10.1145/3385412.3385985
18. Bugariu, A., Müller, P.: Automatically testing string solvers. In: Rothermel, G., Bae, G.-H., eds., In: ICSE '20: 42nd International Conference on Software Engineering, Seoul, South Korea, 27 June - 19 July, 2020, pp. 1459–1470. ACM (2020). https://doi.org/10.1145/3377811.3380398
19. Numair Mansur, M., Christakis, M., Wüstholz, V., Zhang, F.: Detecting critical bugs in SMT solvers using blackbox mutational fuzzing. In: Proceedings of the 28th ACM Joint European Software Engineering Conference and Symposium on the Foundations of Software Engineering (ESEC/FSE), pp. 1–12, New York, NY, USA, 2020. ACM. https://doi.org/10.1145/3368089.3409736
20. Winterer, D., Zhang, C., Su, Z.: On the unusual effectiveness of type-aware operator mutations for testing SMT solvers. In: Proceedings of the ACM Programming Language, vol. 4,(OOPSLA):193:1–193:25 (2020). https://doi.org/10.1145/3428261
21. Brummayer, R., Biere, A.: Fuzzing and delta-debugging SMT solvers. In: Proceedings of the 7th International Workshop on Satisfiability Modulo Theories, SMT '09, page 1–5, New York, NY, USA, 2009. Association for Computing Machinery (2009). ISBN 9781605584843. https://doi.org/10.1145/1670412.1670413
22. Blotsky, D., Mora, F., Berzish, M., Zheng, Y., Kabir, I., Ganesh, V.: Stringfuzz: a fuzzer for string solvers. In: Chockler, H., Weissenbacher, G., eds., Computer Aided Verification - 30th International Conference, CAV 2018, Held as Part of the Federated Logic Conference, FloC 2018, Oxford, UK, July 14-17, 2018, Proceedings, Part II, vol. 10982 of LNCS, pp. 45–51. Springer (2018). https://doi.org/10.1007/978-3-319-96142-2_6. URL https://doi.org/10.1007/978-3-319-96142-2_6
23. Yao, P., Huang, H., Tang, W., Shi, Q., Wu, R., Zhang, C.: Fuzzing SMT solvers via two-dimensional input space exploration. In: ISSTA'21: 30th ACM SIGSOFT International Symposium on Software Testing and Analysis, Virtual Event, USA (2021). https://doi.org/10.1145/3460319.3464803
24. Scott, J., Mora, F., Ganesh, V.: Banditfuzz: a reinforcement-learning based performance fuzzer for SMT solvers. In: Christakis, M., Polikarpova, N., Sidhar Duggirala, P., Schrammel, P., eds., Software Verification - 12th International Conference, VSTTE 2020, and 13th International Workshop, NSV 2020, Los Angeles, CA, USA, July 20-21, (2020), Revised Selected Papers https://doi.org/10.1007/978-3-030-63618-0_5
25. Yao, P., Huang, H., Tang, W., Shi, Q., Wu, R., Zhang, C.: Skeletal approximation enumeration for smt solver testing. In: Proceedings of the 29th ACM Joint European Software Engineering Conference and Symposium on the Foundations of Software Engineering, ESEC/FSE 2021. Association for Computing Machinery, (2021).

26. Winterer, D., Su, Z.: Validating SMT solvers for correctness and performance via grammar-based enumeration. In: Proceedings of the ACM on Programming Languages, 8(OOPSLA2):355:1–355:24, (2024). https://doi.org/10.1145/3689795
27. Kim, J., So, S., Oh, H.: Diver: Oracle-guided SMT solver testing with unrestricted random mutations. In: Proceedings of the 45th International Conference on Software Engineering (ICSE 2023), pp. 2224–2236. IEEE (2023). https://doi.org/10.1109/ICSE48619.2023.00187
28. Sun, M., Yang, Y., Wen, M., Wang, Y., Zhou, Y., Jin, H.: Validating smt solvers via skeleton enumeration empowered by historical bug-triggering inputs. In: 2023 IEEE/ACM 45th International Conference on Software Engineering (ICSE), pp. 69–81. IEEE, 2023. ISBN 9798350323701. https://doi.org/10.1109/ICSE48619.2023.00020
29. Miné, A.: The octagon abstract domain. Higher-order and symbolic computation **19**(1), 31–100 (2006)
30. Fan, G., Chen, L., Yin, B., Zhang, W., Yao, P., Wang, J.: Program analysis combining generalized bit-level and word-level abstractions. In: Proceedings of the ACM SIGSOFT International Symposium on Software Testing and Analysis, ISSTA '25. ACM (2025)
31. Heule, M.J.H., Kullmann, O., Wieringa, S., Biere, A.: Cube and conquer: guiding CDCL SAT solvers by lookaheads. In: Eder, K., Lourenço, J., Shehory, O. (eds.) HVC 2011. LNCS, vol. 7261, pp. 50–65. Springer, Heidelberg (2012). https://doi.org/10.1007/978-3-642-34188-5_8
32. Tak, P., Heule, M.J.H., Biere, A.: Concurrent cube-and-conquer. In: Cimatti, A., Sebastiani, R. (eds.) SAT 2012. LNCS, vol. 7317, pp. 475–476. Springer, Heidelberg (2012). https://doi.org/10.1007/978-3-642-31612-8_42
33. Ge, Y., De Moura, L.: Complete instantiation for quantified formulas in satisfiability modulo theories. In: Computer Aided Verification, 21st International Conference, CAV, pp. 306–320 (2009)
34. Leino, K.R.M., Pit-Claudel, C.: Trigger selection strategies to stabilize program verifiers. In: Computer Aided Verification: 28th International Conference (CAV'16)
35. Barrett, C., Stump, A., Tinelli, C.: The satisfiability modulo theories library (smt-lib). www. SMT-LIB. org **15**, 18–52 (2010)
36. Serebryany, K., Bruening, D., Potapenko, A., Vyukov, D.: Addresssanitizer: a fast address sanity checker. In: Heiser, G., Hsieh, W.C., eds., In: 2012 USENIX Annual Technical Conference, Boston, MA, USA, June 13-15, 2012, pp. 309–318. USENIX Association (2012)
37. Team, G.: Gcov-using the gnu compiler collection (gcc). Online, disponıvel em.http://gccgnu.org/onlinedocs/gcc/Gcov.html-Ultimoacessoem, **26**(02), 2015 (2014)
38. Balunovic, M., Bielik, P., Vechev, M.: Learning to solve SMT formulas. In: Advances in Neural Information Processing Systems, pp. 10317–10328 (2018)
39. Marinov, D., Khurshid, S.: Testera: a novel framework for automated testing of java programs. In: Proceedings of the 16th IEEE International Conference on Automated Software Engineering (ASE), pp. 22–31. IEEE Computer Society (2001). https://doi.org/10.1109/ASE.2001.989792
40. Sullivan, K., Yang, J., Coppit, D., Khurshid, S., Jackson, D.: Software assurance by bounded exhaustive testing. In: Proceedings of the 2004 ACM SIGSOFT International Symposium on Software Testing and Analysis, pp. 133–142 (2004)
41. Zhang, Q., Sun, C., Su, Z.: Skeletal program enumeration for rigorous compiler testing. In: Proceedings of the 38th ACM SIGPLAN Conference on Programming Language Design and Implementation, pp. 347–361 (2017)

42. Usman, M., Wang, W., Khurshid, S.: Testmc: testing model counters using differential and metamorphic testing. In: 35th IEEE/ACM International Conference on Automated Software Engineering, ASE 2020, Melbourne, Australia, September 21-25, 2020, pp. 709–721. IEEE (2020). https://doi.org/10.1145/3324884.3416563
43. Boyapati, C., Khurshid, S., Marinov, D.: Korat: automated testing based on java predicates. In: Proceedings of the 2002 ACM SIGSOFT International Symposium on Software Testing and Analysis (ISSTA), pp. 123–133. ACM (2002). https://doi.org/10.1145/566172.566191
44. Kim, Y., Hong, S.: Deminer: test generation for high test coverage through mutant exploration. Softw. Test., Verif. Reliab. **31**(1–2), e1715 (2021). https://doi.org/10.1002/stvr.1715
45. Offutt, J., Liu, S., Abdurazik, A., Ammann, P.: Generating test data from state-based specifications. Softw. Test., Verif. Reliab. **13**(1), 25–53 (2003). https://doi.org/10.1002/stvr.264

Abstracting Concolic Execution for Soft Contract Verification

Bram Vandenbogaerde[1](✉), Quentin Stiévenart[2], and Coen De Roover[1]

[1] Vrije Universiteit Brussel, Ixelles, Belgium
{bram.vandenbogaerde,coen.de.roover}@vub.be
[2] Université du Québec à Montréal, Montreal, Canada
stievenart.quentin@uqam.ca

Abstract. Design-by-technique for *CESK* machines. Intended solely to introduce the concept of soft contract verification, these purpose-built analyses lack configurability. In this paper, we propose a novel static analysis for soft contract verification called *abstract concolic execution*. We systematically abstract a concolic execution, which is a form of dynamic symbolic execution, into abstract concolic execution, rendering the technique terminating and sound for any program input. To show that our analysis is more configurable than the state-of-the-art analysis supporting soft contract verification, we propose two variations of the analysis. Finally, we show that our approach is comparable to if not more precise than the state of the art at the cost of performance. We find that in 10 out of the 24 benchmark programs, our approach is more precise than the state-of-the-art approach, while being as precise in 9 of them and less precise in 5.

1 Introduction

Design-by-contract [14] is a programming methodology where program elements (e.g., classes or functions) are annotated with *contracts*. These contracts usually encoded invariants or pre- and post-conditions on the program element. In the case of a function, its pre-conditions are usually about the arguments of the function, while its post-conditions are about its return value and potential side effects. Expanding upon the work of Meyer et al. [14], Felleisen [5] et al. propose a contract language for *higher-order* programming languages. A well-known implementation of their language can be found in *Racket*, where contracts are embedded and implemented in the same language as the elements they annotate. Unfortunately, as these contracts are often highly dynamic (e.g., depend on the function input, or change over time), they require *run-time contract checks*, resulting in a large performance penalty when executing the program.

Multiple approaches, collectively known as *soft contract verifiers* [16,17,24], have been proposed to verify as many contracts as possible before running the program. The first incarnation of this approach by Nguyen et al. [17] relies on *higher-order symbolic execution*, a calculus of opaque or *symbolic* values refined with predicates originating from contracts in the code. Unfortunately, their approach is not suitable for more complex programs that exhibit *side effects*. Thus, in follow-up work [16], Nguyen et al. propose a soft contract verifier that also takes side effects into account. The approach is based on the systematic abstraction of a concrete *CESK* machine, adding machinery for tracking symbolic variables and symbolic path constraints along the way.

More specifically, Nguyen et al. [16] extend the *CESK* machine with a *store cache* and *path constraint*. The store cache tracks *locally-precise* information about the in-scope variables by mapping variables to *post-values* which are combinations of abstract and symbolic values. The resulting abstract machine implements a form of *static symbolic execution* but renders it finite by carefully constructing and updating its store caches. Unfortunately, this renders the resulting analysis less *configurable* and precludes the application of common optimizations such as global store widening. This is because the store cache must be at a specific location in the state space and is governed by rules tailored to the analysed programming language.

Instead, we propose systematic abstraction of a *concolic execution* of the program to determine the reachability of contract violations. Concolic execution is a form of *dynamic symbolic execution* in which the program is executed concretely while keeping a symbolic representation alongside each program value. To this end, the program is instrumented to track each branching point in its execution as well as the conditions leading to that branching point. When the execution has terminated, the satisfiability of the conditions of the non-taken branches is checked, and a *model* is generated representing a mapping of symbolic variables to values that satisfy the selected condition. The program is executed again with the newly-obtained values. This process is repeated until all possible branches have been explored or until a time budget is exceeded. Unfortunately, concolic execution is not suitable for fully automated program verification as it is not guaranteed to terminate. This potentially leads to false negatives as it might fail to discover contract violations in the program. Abstracting a concolic execution engine solves this limitation by computing an over-approximation of the program behaviour, eliminating false negatives at the cost of introducing false positives.

In short, the contributions of this paper are as follows:

- We are the first to explore the idea of *abstract concolic execution* as an abstract interpretation of concolic execution for soft contract verification. We do so by systematically abstracting a $CESK_\varphi$ machine, a new variation on a *CESK* machine augmented with failure continuations and path constraints. We claim that this systematic abstraction results in a more configurable analysis compared to the state-of-the-art soft contract verification approaches.

Furthermore, we demonstrate this claim by proposing two variations of the abstract machine.
- We formulate and prove a soundness and termination theorem for the resulting analysis, showing that the analysis terminates for any analysed program, and that its results are guaranteed to over-approximate the actual run-time behaviour of the program.
- Finally, we apply this novel analysis technique to the problem of *soft contract verification* [16,17,24]. Our analysis enables novel configurations of the resulting abstract machine, yielding different trade-offs between performance and precision.

In what follows we recall existing soft contract verification techniques and highlight their shortcomings. Next, we proceed by explaining why concrete concolic execution is not sufficient for the purposes of soft contract verification, and highlight challenges for its abstraction process. Next, we formalize a *concrete* version of a concolic execution engine using a variation on the $CESK$ machine called the $CESK_\varphi$ machine. Then, we systematically abstract this machine by applying the AAM method [13] to obtain a finite and sound static analysis. We show that the resulting analysis is more configurable than state-of-the-art soft contract verification approaches by formalizing two variations of the abstract machine. We conclude with an evaluation of our approach by applying it to benchmark programs found in other related soft contract verification work.

2 State of the Art in Soft Contract Verification

In this paper we consider functional design-by-contract languages, more specifically the contract model introduced by Findler et al. [9] as implemented in Racket. Listing 1 depicts the `square` function and its contract. The contract stipulates that if the arguments of the function are numbers, the function's return value will be a positive number. Analysing the function's implementation carefully, one can deduce that this is indeed the case since squaring a number always results in a positive number.

Listing 1 A `square` function annotated with a contract stipulating that if the input is a number, the output will be a positive number.

```
def square(x: number?): positive? =
    return x*x
```

Contracts are not only used in user-defined functions, but also for primitive functions provided by the host programming language. The multiplication operator, for instance, requires that its arguments are numbers. Failing to provide numbers as arguments results in a contract violation at run time. In the example depicted in Listing 1, however, such a contract violation is not possible because the contract on the argument of the function already requires that the argument is a number. Thus, the program would fail if the `square` function was not called with a number before reaching the multiplication operator. This results in more helpful error messages, as errors are reported at the earliest location where expectations are not met. The example also shows that the multiplication operator can never be called with an invalid argument, as the execution of the program halts before the execution of the body of `square`. Note that all paths to the multiplication operator have a `number?` constraint, highlighting the need for *path-sensitive* reasoning when verifying contract validity.

In general, contracts in functional programs can encode arbitrary predicates on the arguments and return value of a function. The contract system proposed by Findler et al. even allows for contracts on the return value of the function to be specified in terms of the arguments of the function, resulting in a *dependent contract*. This highlights the need for reasoning about arbitrary constraints on unknown (user) input.

Combining these needs naturally leads to *static symbolic execution* which represents unknown (user) input and subsequent operations on this input symbolically, and in tandem keeps track of a *path constraint* encoding the symbolic conditions necessary for a particular program state to be reached. These path constraints are updated whenever execution reaches a *branching point* (e.g., an *if statement*). Upon a branching point, a symbolic condition is added to the path constraint. Unfortunately, static symbolic execution is known to not always terminate such as when programs have an unbounded number of `input` statements, or whose `input` statements are under-constrained. Static symbolic execution is therefore unsuitable for verification purposes.

Nguyen et al. [16] instead propose *symbolic verification* which ensures a sound and terminating process for checking the reachability of contract violations. To this end, they abstract a *CESK* machine and extend the abstracted machine with a path constraint and a *store cache*. This store cache keeps track of symbolic information about the variables in scope. To ensure termination, Nguyen et al. only consider looping through recursion (i.e., through function calls) and carefully adapt the store cache to ensure termination. In the case of function calls, function arguments are replaced with symbolic variables corresponding to the names of the parameters of function. This ensures that a symbolic expression tree remains finite, but also discards potentially essential information from the caller of the function.

Summarising the discussion, we identify the following shortcomings of existing soft contract verification approaches:

- **Unnecessary precision loss** Simply discarding symbolic information from the caller of the function and replacing it with a symbolic variable for each parameter results in unnecessary precision loss. The caller of the function no longer controls which symbolic variables it passes to the callee. There is no longer a connection of the path constraint from the caller of the function with that of the callee.

– **Ad-hoc store cache management** Store caches represent *locally precise* information about the variables in scope of the current program state. Their contents and update rules are determined by analysis developers based on factors such as precision and termination. In the case of the state-of-the-art soft contract verification work, store caches are invalidated at function call boundaries, and whenever mutation of variables occurs. This ad-hoc management of the store cache makes common systematic optimizations such as global store widening more difficult to implement and formalize.

We address these shortcomings by proposing *abstract concolic execution*, a novel abstraction interpretation of concolic execution. In this setting, the abstract machine is no longer extended with a store-cache that collects locally precise information. Instead, we guarantee termination by properly abstracting symbolic variables and symbolic expressions. In the remainder of this paper we assume (as demonstrated in Sect. 7), without loss of generality, that all contract checks can be translated to first-class `assert` statements.

3 From Concrete to Abstract Concolic Execution

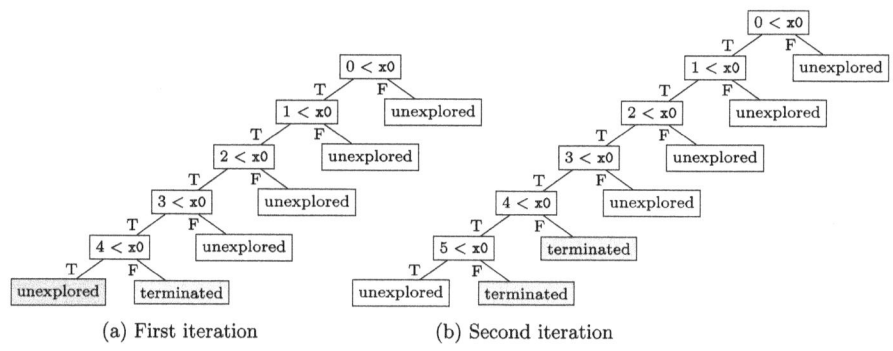

Fig. 1. Execution tree after two concolic execution of the `square` program

In the listing below, we present a program that computes the square of a number through repeated additions of x coming from user input. A concolic execution engine executes this program by first generating a *concolic value*, consisting of a program value and symbolic variable, that substitutes the missing user input. In the remainder of this paper, symbolic variables are typeset with a monospace letter (usually x) followed by a unique number (e.g., x0 for the first symbolic variable being generated). Next, the concolic execution engine executes the `square` function which contains a branching point, i.e., to stop the loop if i >= x and to continue whenever i < x. This is represented in a *symbolic execution tree* as a node created for each branching point, labelled with the conditions leading to the next branching point in the program. The edges of the tree are labelled with truth values for the conditions (T for true, F for false). Assuming that the initial input, named x0, has been arbitrarily chosen to be 4, the symbolic execution tree grows to contain 5 branching points, one for each iteration of the loop. This execution is depicted in Fig. 1a. The first execution eventually reaches the node highlighted in green, and then terminates.

```
def square(x) =
    y = 0
    i = 0
    while i < x do
        y = y+x
        i++
    return y

print(square(input()))
```

Next, the concolic execution engine selects an unexplored node in its execution tree (highlighted in red in Fig. 1a), collects all constraints alongside the path leading up to that unexplored node and subsequently generates inputs (i.e., a model) satisfying these constraints. These inputs result into a new value for x used in the next execution of the program. In this case, the value 5 is chosen as the input for x in the next concolic execution (Fig. 1b). Normally, this process is repeated until all nodes in the execution tree have been explored. Unfortunately, in this case the execution tree continues to grow indefinitely because different values for x0 can continue to be computed and the exploration never finishes. Thus, in this example, the execution can only terminate after a set timeout has been reached rendering the program exploration incomplete. To summarize, this example illustrates a number of problems with dynamic symbolic execution:

- **Exploration of redundant states:** A concolic execution engine might explore nodes that are *behaviourally equivalent* to another node in the execution tree but differ in its path condition. In the example program, increasing the number of iterations of the loop does not yield any new interesting behaviour, yet their concolic execution states are considered different.
- **Non-termination:** The concolic execution approach is not guaranteed to terminate. This problem is illustrated in the example above as the execution tree keeps growing with increasing values for x. This results in an *unsound* analysis from a static analysis point of view, as it does not consider *all possible paths* in the program. This is problematic for verification purposes as the program cannot be verified without considering all of its paths.

Abstract interpretation [4] could offer a solution to these problems by defining an abstraction for each component of the concolic execution engine. Abstract interpretation solves the first problem by abstracting concolic execution states, rendering identical those that do not differ in the property of interest. The second problem is solved by abstracting reoccurring subtrees into a graph shared between all parts of the tree in which the subtree occurs.

In this paper, we investigate whether this approach can be applied for abstracting concolic execution. This problem is challenging because a number of concolic execution aspects that need to be abstracted:

– **Symbolic representations:** A symbolic execution engine uses *symbolic representations* of program values in order to constrain them through the program's path condition. These symbolic representations are not necessarily finite (e.g., a loop containing an assignment $x = x + 1$, resulting in repeated suffixes of $+1$ in the symbolic expression). To guarantee termination without complex widening operators, an abstract interpretation of a concolic execution engine needs to abstract these symbolic representation so that a finite number of them is present at all times.
– **Symbolic variables:** In a concrete run of a concolic execution engine, the same input statement may be executed multiple times (e.g., in a loop), resulting in distinct concrete values and symbolic variables for each execution. Unfortunately, this is often a source of non-termination in a concolic execution engine. An abstract interpretation needs to abstract multiple concrete executions into a single abstract execution having a single abstract value with a corresponding abstract symbolic variable.
– **Path constraints:** Since the path constraint consists of first-order logic assertions over a number of symbolic expressions, the interpretation of the truth values of its abstract counterpart needs to account for abstract symbolic expressions too. Moreover, as infinite path constraints often give rise to non-terminating concolic execution engines, they need to be rendered finite for the resulting analysis to terminate without complex widening.
– **Model:** After each concrete symbolic execution run, a *model* is computed which maps symbolic variables to concrete values so that the next iteration follows the intended path to an unexplored node of the execution tree. Since abstract symbolic variables could correspond to multiple input statements, an abstract version of this model needs to map the statement's abstract symbolic variable to an abstract value that subsumes all possible invocations of the same input statement.

In this paper, we propose an abstraction of the $CESK_\varphi$ machine, a new variation of the CESK machine [8], by applying the *abstracting abstract machines* (or AAM) recipe [13]. We investigate whether this process results in an efficient and precise static analysis for the analysed program. And if so, what machine configurations work best in terms of precision and performance.

4   Concrete Concolic Execution

In this section we present a concrete version of a concolic execution engine. This concrete version largely follows the standard concolic execution semantics [20]. However, it does not explicitly model the execution as an execution tree. Instead, it relies on failure continuations to model backtracking and program re-execution. We do so in order to make the abstraction of the resulting machine easier. We formalize the concolic execution engine for a language λ_s. The semantics is defined as a small-step relation over a $CESK\varphi$ machine, extending the standard $CESK$ machine [8] with constraints and failure continuations.

4.1 Syntax

Figure 2 depicts the syntax of our language. The language is an *A-normal form* version of the λ-calculus, extended with support for if expressions, let expressions and input statements.

$$e ::= \text{let } x = e \text{ in } e \mid \text{if } ae\ e\ e \mid ae\ ae \mid \text{input}$$
$$ae \in Atomic ::= n \mid b \mid x \mid \lambda x.e \qquad x \in Identifier \qquad n \in \mathbb{N} \qquad b \in \mathbb{B} ::= \text{true} \mid \text{false}$$

Fig. 2. Syntax of λ_s

4.2 Semantics

Figure 3 depicts the state space of λ_s's semantics. Concolic values are represented by the *Value* sort. Such concolic values consist of a program value and symbolic expression of the *SymbolicValue* sort. This symbolic expression can be empty (denoted by $\emptyset$) to indicate that the corresponding program value does not have a suitable symbolic representation, such as closures. Addresses are represented by their allocation site and combined with a calling context consisting of a call-site history. The allocation site for a variable x is denoted as $\ell(x)$, assuming that an injective labelling function ℓ is defined for any program expression e. This choice for the address representation automatically yields a valid *address allocation* strategy where the new address is derived from the calling context and the label of the expression at the allocation-site. Addresses generated according to this

$\varsigma \in \Sigma ::= \langle c, \sigma, \kappa, \psi, \text{ctx}, M, \phi, V \rangle \qquad c \in Control ::= \text{ev}(e, \rho) \mid \text{ap}(v)$

$\sigma \in Store = Address \mapsto Value \qquad \kappa \in Continuation ::= \text{let}(x, e, \rho) :: \kappa \mid \emptyset$

$\psi \in FailContinuation ::= \text{branch}(\phi) :: \psi \mid \emptyset \qquad M \in Model ::= SymVar \mapsto ProgramVal$

$\rho \in Environment = Identifier \mapsto Address \qquad \alpha \in Address = Label \times Context$

$\text{ctx} \in Context = \overline{Label} \qquad v_p \in ProgramVal ::= n \mid b \mid (\lambda x.e, \rho)$

$s \in SymbolicVal ::= b \mid \emptyset \mid x \mid op(s, \ldots, s) \qquad \text{xi} \in SymVar = Address$

$v \in Value = ProgramVal \times SymbolicVal \qquad \phi, \varphi_1, \varphi_2 \in Formula ::= \varphi_1 \wedge \varphi_2 \mid s \mid \neg s$

$b \in \mathbb{B} ::= \text{true} \mid \text{false} \qquad Label \text{ is a program location}$

Fig. 3. State space of λ_s. A sequence is denoted by an overline, for instance, the set of sequences of elements $a \in A$ is denoted as $\overline{A}$.

allocation strategy are *unique* since each allocation site can repeat only when the program contains a loop. However, since the λ_s language does not contain any looping constructs, looping can only occur through function calls, meaning that our calling context provides a sufficient distinction from addresses of previous loop iterations. Symbolic variables are treated identically to addresses but are generated by another meta-function called fresh.

The state space is derived from the possible program states which consist of the following components: a control (c), a store (σ), a continuation stack (κ), a failure continuation stack (ψ), a model (M), an unbounded calling context (ctx), a path condition (ϕ), and the set of visited branches. The control component is either an *ev*aluation state, or a continuation *ap*plication state. The former includes an environment ρ in which an expression e is to be evaluated. The latter includes the value that should be sent to the continuation on top of the continuation stack. The model consists of a mapping from addresses to program values. A lookup in this mapping is denoted as $M(x)$ where x denotes the address. If the mapping is undefined for some x a random value is returned instead.

Next, as depicted in below, we define an atomic evaluation function $[\![\cdot]\!]$ and a small-step relation $\rightsquigarrow$ (Fig. 4). The atomic evaluation function is defined as expected. Literal numbers and boolean literals map to their respective concolic value, and λ expressions evaluate to closure values which do not have a symbolic counterpart. Variable references are evaluated to their respective concolic values by looking up their address and values from the environment and store.

$$[\![b]\!](\rho, \sigma) = (b, b) \qquad [\![n]\!](\rho, \sigma) = (n, n)$$
$$[\![\lambda x.e]\!](\rho, \sigma) = ((\lambda x.e, \rho), \emptyset) \qquad [\![x]\!](\rho, \sigma) = \sigma(\rho(x))$$

The evaluation of function applications proceeds as usual. Rules [ST-LET1] and [ST-LET2] depict the semantics for introducing new lexical scopes. [ST-LET1] first evaluates the binding expression e_1 to a value by transitioning to an ev control state, and pushing a let continuation on the continuation stack. This continuation is applied in rule [ST-LET2] by binding the value of the evaluated expression to the variable x. Conditional expressions require more attention as they introduce additional constraints in the path condition. This is depicted by rule [ST-IFTRUE] and [ST-IFFALSE] which first evaluate the condition to a concolic value, check whether the concolic value is true or false, and evaluate the consequent and alternative branch accordingly. While doing so, the failure continuation stack is extended with a branch failure continuation, tracking which branch has not been taken. Metafunction in accepts four arguments: a path constraints, a visited set and two failure continuations. The metafunction returns the third argument whenever the path constraint is not in the visited set and returns the fourth argument otherwise. This ensures that the same branch is not repeatedly executed in subsequent concolic execution runs by checking whether the alternative path constraint is part of the visited set. Finally, rule [INPUT] reduces an input expression to either a new random value or to a value from the model M if one is defined in its mapping.

$\langle \mathsf{ev}(ae, \rho), \sigma, \kappa, \psi, \mathsf{ctx}, M, \varphi, V \rangle \rightsquigarrow \langle \mathsf{ap}(\llbracket ae \rrbracket(\rho, \sigma), \sigma, \kappa, \psi, \mathsf{ctx}, M, \varphi, V \rangle$ ST-ATOMIC

$$\frac{\llbracket ae \rrbracket(\rho, \sigma) = (true, s) \quad \varphi_t = \varphi \wedge s}{\varphi_f = \varphi \wedge \neg s \quad \psi' = \mathsf{in}(\varphi_f, V, \mathsf{branch}(\varphi_f) :: \psi, \psi)} \text{ST-IFTRUE}$$
$$\langle \mathsf{ev}(\mathsf{if}\ ae\ e_1\ e_2, \rho), \sigma, \kappa, \psi, \mathsf{ctx}, M, \varphi, V \rangle$$
$$\rightsquigarrow \langle \mathsf{ev}(e_1, \rho), \sigma, \kappa, \psi', \mathsf{ctx}, M, \varphi_t, \{\varphi_f\} \cup V \rangle$$

$$\frac{\llbracket ae \rrbracket(\rho, \sigma) = (false, s) \quad \varphi_t = \varphi \wedge s}{\varphi_f = \varphi \wedge \neg s \quad \psi' = \mathsf{in}(\varphi_t, V, \mathsf{branch}(\varphi_t) :: \psi, \psi)} \text{ST-IFFALSE}$$
$$\langle \mathsf{ev}(\mathsf{if}\ ae\ e_1\ e_2, \rho), \sigma, \kappa, \psi, \mathsf{ctx}, M, \varphi, V \rangle$$
$$\rightsquigarrow \langle \mathsf{ev}(e_2, \rho), \sigma, \kappa, \psi', \mathsf{ctx}, M, \varphi_f, \{\varphi_t\} \cup V \rangle$$

$$\frac{\langle \mathsf{ev}(\mathsf{let}\ x{=}e_1\ \mathsf{in}\ e_2, \rho), \sigma, \kappa, \psi, \mathsf{ctx}, M, \varphi, V \rangle}{\rightsquigarrow \langle \mathsf{ev}(e_1, \rho), \sigma, \mathsf{let}(x, e_2, \rho) :: \kappa, \psi, \mathsf{ctx}, M, \varphi, V \rangle} \text{ST-LET1}$$

$$\frac{\alpha = \mathsf{alloc}(\ell(x), \mathsf{ctx})}{\langle \mathsf{ap}(v), \sigma, \mathsf{let}(x, e_2, \rho) :: \kappa, \psi, \mathsf{ctx}, M, \varphi, V \rangle} \text{ST-LET2}$$
$$\rightsquigarrow \langle \mathsf{ev}(e_2, \rho[x \mapsto \alpha]), \sigma[\alpha \mapsto v], \kappa, \psi, \mathsf{ctx}, M, \varphi, V \rangle$$

$$\frac{\llbracket ae_1 \rrbracket \rho, \sigma = (\lambda x.e, \rho') \quad \llbracket ae_2 \rrbracket(\rho, \sigma) = v \quad \alpha = \mathsf{alloc}(\ell(x), \mathsf{ctx})}{\langle \mathsf{ev}(ae_1\ ae_2, \rho), \sigma, \kappa, \psi, \mathsf{ctx}, M, \varphi, V \rangle} \text{ST-APP}$$
$$\rightsquigarrow \langle \mathsf{ev}(e, \rho'[x \mapsto \alpha]), \sigma[\alpha \mapsto v], \kappa, \psi, \ell(ae_1\ ae_2) :: \mathsf{ctx}, M, \varphi, V \rangle$$

$$\frac{(v, \overline{v'}) = M(\mathbf{x}) \quad \mathbf{x} = \mathsf{fresh}(\ell(\mathsf{input}), \mathsf{ctx})}{\langle \mathsf{ev}(\mathsf{input}, \rho), \sigma, \kappa, \psi, \mathsf{ctx}, M, \varphi, V \rangle} \text{INPUT}$$
$$\rightsquigarrow \langle \mathsf{ap}((v, \mathbf{x})), \sigma, \kappa, \psi, \mathsf{ctx}, M, \varphi, V \rangle$$

$$\frac{M' = \mathsf{model}(\varphi)}{\langle \mathsf{ap}(v), \sigma, \emptyset, \mathsf{branch}(\varphi) :: \psi, \mathsf{ctx}, M, \varphi', V \rangle \rightsquigarrow \langle \mathsf{ev}(e_0, \rho_0), \sigma_0, \emptyset, \psi, \emptyset, M', \emptyset, V \rangle} \text{ST-BACKTRACK}$$

Fig. 4. Small-step semantics of the concolic execution for λ_s

Rule [ST-BACKTRACK] enables backtracking to program states that were not executed in the previous concolic execution. It does so by applying the failure continuation whenever the program terminates, and by restarting the program execution with an empty calling context and a model M' generated by meta-function model giving an assignment of symbolic variables to program values that satisfies the path constraint stored in the failure continuation. This corresponds to a depth-first search (*DFS*) of the concolic execution tree.

The complete concolic execution is defined as the least-fixed point of the small-step evaluation relation, as depicted by *Eval* and *Run*. Variables ρ_0 and σ_0 denote the initial environment and store respectively.

$$Eval(\Sigma) = \Sigma \cup \bigcup_{\substack{\varsigma \in \Sigma \\ \varsigma \rightsquigarrow \varsigma'}} \{\varsigma'\} \qquad Run(e_0) = \mathit{lfp}\ Eval\ \{\langle \mathsf{ev}(e_0, \rho_0), \sigma_0, \emptyset, \emptyset, \emptyset, \emptyset, \emptyset, \emptyset \rangle\}$$

5 Abstracting Concolic Execution

In this section we develop a sound over-approximation of the concolic execution semantics from the previous section. We do so by following the *AAM* [13] approach which proposes to abstract a concrete machine and its operational semantics in a component-wise manner. This results in a sound over-approximation of the concrete machine's semantics. While doing so, we establish a Galois connection between the concrete operational semantics and the abstract ones which we use for formulating and proving soundness of the resulting static analysis.

5.1 Preliminaries

We first present some standard notions of abstract interpretation required for the remainder of this section.

Definition 5.1.1. *A join-semilattice, denoted $\langle A, \leq, \sqcup \rangle$ is a partially ordered set $\langle A, \leq \rangle$ with a least-upper bound $\sqcup$ defined for every two elements in the set.*

Definition 5.1.2. *A **Galois connection** between two partially ordered sets A and B is a pair of functions α and γ, denoted as $\langle A, \leq_A \rangle \xrightarrow[\alpha]{\gamma} \langle B, \leq_B \rangle$, such that:*

$$\forall a \in A : a \leq_A \gamma(\alpha(a))$$

Definition 5.1.3. *An abstract function $\hat{f}$ is said to be sound with respect to its concrete counterpart f iff:*

$$\forall a \in \hat{A} : \alpha_{\hat{B}}(f(a)) \leq_{\hat{B}} \hat{f}(\alpha_{\hat{A}}(a))$$

where α_x is the abstraction function corresponding to the partially ordered set x.

In what follows, we will overload the notation by using the same α and γ functions for different value types whenever no ambiguities can arise. In ambiguous contexts, a subscript will be used to differentiate the intended function from other potential candidates.

5.2 Standard Component-Wise Abstractions

Before abstracting the components of our abstract machine, we apply a transformation that store-allocates continuations instead of keeping them in a stack. The details of this transformation are available in the online appendix[1]. We continue the abstraction process on this version of the concrete machine.

Figure 5 depicts an abstraction of the concolic machine. The control component of the abstract machine is adapted so that each continuation is applied to an *abstract value* instead of a concrete one. The machine's stores are also

---
[1] https://doi.org/10.5281/zenodo.16568308.

abstracted, so that they form mappings from abstract addresses to abstract values or to sets of abstract continuations. The abstraction of a continuation is defined as a straightforward point-wise abstraction of its components. More specifically, the program continuation for implementing let is adapted to include abstract environments and abstract addresses instead of concrete ones. Furthermore, the failure continuation is adapted to include an abstraction of the path constraint. Both continuations are adapted so that they refer to an abstract continuation address as their next continuation. Abstractions for these addresses are omitted from this paper, as any sound abstraction will do (e.g., one that limits the number of calling contexts).

Finally, the model component (M) and the path constraint component (φ) are abstracted to obtain a fully abstracted concolic machine. To do so, we render symbolic formulae, symbolic expressions, and symbolic variables abstract, as discussed in the following sections.

$$\widehat{\varsigma} \in \widehat{\Sigma} ::= \langle \widehat{c}, \widehat{\sigma}, \widehat{a_\kappa}, \widehat{\kappa}, \widehat{a_\psi}, \widehat{\psi}, \widehat{M}, \widehat{\mathsf{ctx}}, \widehat{\varphi}, \widehat{V} \rangle \qquad \widehat{c} \in \widehat{Control} ::= \mathsf{ev}(e, \widehat{\rho}) \mid \mathsf{ap}(\widehat{v})$$

$\widehat{a_\kappa} \in \widehat{KAdr} ::= \ldots \mid \mathsf{Hlt} \quad \widehat{a_\psi} \in \widehat{FAdr} ::= \ldots \mid \mathsf{Hlt}$ $\widehat{\mathsf{ctx}}$ is a finite abstraction of the context
$\widehat{\varphi} \in \widehat{Formula} \quad \widehat{M} \in \widehat{Model}$ $\widehat{\kappa} \in \widehat{KontSto} ::= \widehat{KAdr} \to \mathcal{P}(Continuation)$
$\widehat{\psi} \in \widehat{FailSto} ::= \widehat{FAdr} \to \mathcal{P}(FailureContinuation) \quad \widehat{v} \in \widehat{Value} = ProgramValue \times \widehat{SymbolicValue}$
$\widehat{\rho} \in \widehat{Environment} = Identifier \to \widehat{Value} \qquad \widehat{V} \in \widehat{Visited}$

Fig. 5. Abstraction of the state space as a component-wise abstraction of the concrete state space

5.3 Abstracting Symbolic Representations

As concrete symbolic variables have the same representation as concrete addresses, any suitable address abstraction can also be used for their abstraction. However, since the abstraction of symbolic variables is central to our approach we define their representation explicitly below.

Definition 5.3.1. *Abstract symbolic variables are constructed from a program label and a finite abstraction of a calling context.*

$$\widehat{\mathsf{x}} \in \widehat{SymbolicVariable} = Label \times \widehat{Context}$$

The power set of these abstract symbolic variables trivially forms a join-semilattice with the subset relation as its partial order, and the union as its least upper bound. Having defined this lattice, we define a Galois connection between the concrete and abstract representations of symbolic variables.

Definition 5.3.2. $\mathcal{P}(SymbolicVariable)$ *and* $\mathcal{P}(\widehat{SymbolicVariable})$ *form a Galois connection* $\langle \mathcal{P}(SymbolicVariable), \subseteq \rangle \xleftrightarrow[\alpha_x]{\gamma_x} \langle \mathcal{P}(\widehat{SymbolicVariable}), \subseteq \rangle$, *where* α *and* γ *are defined as follows:*

$$\alpha_x(SV) = \bigcup_{(\ell, \mathsf{ctx}) \in SV} \{(\ell, \alpha(\mathsf{ctx}))\} \qquad \gamma_x(\widehat{SV}) = \bigcup_{(\ell, \widehat{\mathsf{ctx}}) \in \widehat{SV}} \{(\ell, \mathsf{ctx}) \mid \widehat{\mathsf{ctx}} \subseteq \mathsf{ctx}\}$$

It is important to note that a single abstract symbolic variable could correspond to multiple concrete symbolic variables. This is because the abstraction of the context makes a possibly infinite concrete context finite, resulting in a potentially infinite number of corresponding concrete symbolic variables. The same does not hold for the reverse case: abstractions of concrete symbolic variables only result in a single abstract symbolic variable as witnessed by the usage of singleton sets in the definition of the abstraction function.

Next, we define a lattice of symbolic expressions ($\widehat{e} \in \widehat{SymbolicValue}$). This lattice is defined as a flat lattice that consists of $\mathsf{sym}(e)$ as its elements, and fresh as its top element with the usual partial-ordering and least-upper bound.

Having defined the partial ordering relation, and having established that this representation forms a join-semilattice, we define a Galois connection between the power set of concrete symbolic expressions $\mathcal{P}(SymbolicValue)$ and the abstract symbolic expressions $\widehat{SymbolicValue}$ defined earlier.

Definition 5.3.3. *The sets $\mathcal{P}(SymbolicValue)$ and $\widehat{SymbolicValue}$ form a Galois connection $\langle \mathcal{P}(SymbolicValue), \subseteq \rangle \xrightleftharpoons[\alpha]{\gamma} \langle \widehat{SymbolicValue}, \leq \rangle$ where α and γ are defined as follows:*

$\alpha(S) = \bigsqcup_{e \in S} \alpha_e(e)$

$\alpha_e(n) = \mathsf{sym}(n), n \in \mathbb{N}$
$\alpha_e(b) = \mathsf{sym}(b), b \in \mathbb{B}$
$\alpha_e(x) = \mathsf{sym}(\alpha_x(x))$

$\alpha_e(op(e_1, \ldots e_n)) = op(\alpha(e_1), \ldots, \alpha(e_n))$

$\gamma(\bot) = \{\}$

$\gamma(\mathsf{sym}(n)) = \{n\}, n \in \mathbb{N}$
$\gamma(\mathsf{sym}(b)) = \{b\}, b \in \mathbb{B}$
$\gamma(\mathsf{sym}(x)) = \gamma(x)$
$\gamma(\mathsf{fresh}) = SymbolicValue$
$\gamma(\mathsf{sym}(op(\widehat{e}_1, \ldots, \widehat{e}_n))) = \{op(e_1, \ldots, e_n) \mid e_i \in \gamma(\widehat{e}_i)\}$

Intuitively, the partial ordering is guided by the concrete symbolic expressions corresponding to an abstract symbolic expression. For instance, an abstract expression e corresponds to the singleton set of concrete expression e, whereas fresh corresponds to all possible symbolic expressions. The choice for representing this abstract value using a fresh symbolic variable is not a coincidence. For example, a symbolic variable y0 would subsume a symbolic expression x0 > 0 as the former evaluates to any value while the latter evaluates to a boolean value after computing the inequality with zero.

Other, more precise abstractions can also be defined for symbolic expressions. However, for simplicity of our presentation, we chose to represent abstract symbolic expressions as a flat lattice consisting of a bottom element, a concrete symbolic expression, and a fresh symbolic variable.

5.4 Path Constraints Abstractions

In the previous section, we defined abstractions for symbolic expressions. These abstractions are used for abstracting the store and its concolic values as well as the symbolic expressions in the path constraint. In this section, we discuss how abstract symbolic expressions are integrated with a symbolic path constraint in order to obtain an abstract path constraint.

Definition 5.4.1. *An abstract path constraint is formed by an abstract formula* $\widehat{Formula}$ *which is defined as follows:*

$$\widehat{\varphi_1}, \widehat{\varphi_2} \in \widehat{Formula} ::= \widehat{\varphi_1} \wedge \widehat{\varphi_2} \mid \neg \widehat{e} \mid \widehat{e} \mid \emptyset$$

Thus, abstract formulae share the same structure as their concrete counterpart but use abstract symbolic expressions as their constraints. A natural partial order on both concrete and abstract formulae can be defined using the logical implication ($\Rightarrow$). Consequently, the least-upper bound can be defined as the least generalization such that if $\varphi_1 \sqcup \varphi_2 = \varphi_3$ then $\varphi_1 \Rightarrow \varphi_3$ and $\varphi_2 \Rightarrow \varphi_3$.

Definition 5.4.2. *Concrete formulae from Formula form a Galois connection with abstract formulae $\widehat{Formula}$ denoted by* $\langle Formula, \Rightarrow \rangle \xleftrightarrow[\alpha]{\gamma} \langle \widehat{Formula}, \Rightarrow \rangle$, *where α and γ are defined as follows:*

$$\alpha(\varphi_1 \wedge \varphi_2) = \alpha(\varphi_1) \wedge \alpha(\varphi_2) \qquad \gamma(\widehat{\varphi_1} \wedge \widehat{\varphi_2}) = \bigsqcup_{\substack{\varphi_1 \in \widehat{\varphi_1} \\ \varphi_2 \in \widehat{\varphi_2}}} \varphi_1 \wedge \varphi_2$$

$$\alpha(\neg e) = \neg \alpha(e) \qquad \gamma(\neg \widehat{e}) = \bigsqcup \{\neg e \mid e \in \gamma_e(\widehat{e})\}$$
$$\alpha(e) = \alpha_s(e) \qquad \gamma(\widehat{e}) = \bigsqcup \{e \mid e \in \gamma_e(\widehat{e})\}$$

5.5 Satisfiability Checking and Abstract Counting

Since an abstract formula corresponds to one or more concrete formulae, *satisfiability checking* of these formulae also need to be adapted. To this end, we define a *translation* function that translates abstract formulae into *SMT* formulae that can be used in any SMT solver.

Imprecise Translations The definition of an *SMT* formula is depicted below. The structure of an *SMTFormula* largely corresponds to the structure of concrete and abstract formulae, except that symbolic variables are generated from the set of natural numbers ($\mathbb{N}$) instead of program locations and their context.

$$\varphi'_1, \varphi'_2 \in SMTFormula ::= \varphi'_1 \wedge \varphi'_2 \mid \mathrm{x}' \mid \varphi'_1 \mid \neg \varphi'_1 \qquad \mathrm{x}' \in SMTVariable ::= \mathrm{x} n, n \in \mathbb{N}$$

Below we define the translation function from abstract symbolic formulae to *SMT* formulae. We assume an infinite pool of natural numbers shared between all invocations of translate. A selection from this pool is denoted by $n \in \mathbb{N}$.

translate $:\widehat{Formula} \to SMTFormula$ 　　translate$(\widehat{\varphi_1} \wedge \widehat{\varphi_2}) = $ translate$(\widehat{\varphi_1}) \wedge $ translate$(\widehat{\varphi_2})$
translate(sym($\neg e$)) = $\neg$translate(e) 　　translate(sym(n)) = $n, n \in \mathbb{N}$
translate(sym(b)) = $b, b \in \mathbb{B}$ 　　translate(sym(x)) = $\mathrm{x}n, n \in \mathbb{N}$
translate($\bot$) = $\emptyset$ 　　translate(fresh) = $\mathrm{x}n, n \in \mathbb{N}$

Note that the translation of abstract symbolic variables to SMT variables requires a unique SMT variable for every occurrence of an abstract symbolic variable, even if these abstract symbolic variables are identical. This is because abstract symbolic variables originate from input statements, and are allocated by combining the location of the input statement in the source program with an abstraction of the current calling context of the program execution. Thus, if such input statements repeat in the same execution, multiple concrete input statements could result in the same abstract symbolic variable, while getting a unique symbolic variable in the concrete execution. Therefore, each symbolic variable needs to be translated to a unique SMT variable.

Precise Translations with Abstract Counting The above translation is suboptimal as every occurrence of an abstract symbolic variable is translated to a distinct *SMT* variable. The code example depicted below illustrates in which situations this suboptimal translation is warranted.

```
y = 0
while True:
    y = x
    x = input()
    if x > y: error
```

In this example, the error is reachable as the user input from the previous loop iteration could be smaller than the current one. To detect is error, a concrete concolic execution engine generates an infinite number of symbolic variables for the input statement on line 4. To render the abstract execution finite, the abstracted version of the concolic execution engine associates a *single* abstract variable with that input statement, yielding the following path constraint at the error statement after two iterations of the `while` loop (where x0 is an abstract symbolic variable associated with the input statement on line 4).

$$x0 > x0 \wedge x0 > x0$$

In this case, the abstract symbolic variable x0 cannot refer to the same concrete symbolic variable as the path constraint would become unsatisfiable. Therefore, the imprecise translation is warranted when abstract symbolic variables refer to multiple concrete symbolic variables.

However, abstract symbolic variables can usually occur more than once in a symbolic path constraint, as illustrated by the code listing depicted below. An abstract concolic execution of this program yields to following path constraint at the error statement: $x0 > 5 \wedge x0 < 4$, which is clearly unsatisfiable. However, since all occurrences of abstract symbolic variables are replaced by fresh ones, the formula becomes satisfiable again, resulting in the imprecise conclusion that the error statement is reachable.

```
x = input()
if x < 4:
    if x > 5: error
```

This problem arises from the absence of information regarding the *cardinality* of a symbolic variable. To render the translation more precise, we propose to conservatively approximate this cardinality by counting the number of concrete symbolic variables corresponding to an abstract symbolic variable. This approach is commonly referred to as *abstract counting* [15], and has been used for soundly implementing *strong updates*. We apply this same concept for determining whether a symbolic variable corresponds to zero, one or more concrete symbolic variables.

Definition 5.5.1. *An abstract count is defined as follows:*

$$c \in AbstractCount ::= 0 \mid 1 \mid \infty$$

The elements of *AbstractCount* form a join-semilattice, where the partial order is defined as $0 \leq 1 \leq \infty$ and the least-upper bound as $0 \sqcup x = x$ (idem for the symmetric case), $1 \sqcup 1 = 1$ and $x \sqcup \infty = \infty$ (idem for the symmetric case). Having defined a lattice structure, we can define an abstract operation called inc which increases the abstract count by one.

$$\mathsf{inc}(0) = 1 \quad \mathsf{inc}(1) = \infty \quad \mathsf{inc}(\infty) = \infty$$

To determine the abstract count for each symbolic variable, we introduce an abstract count *mapping* C which maps symbolic variables to their abstract count. The mapping is initially set to zero for every abstract symbolic variable. The definition of this mapping is depicted below:

$$C \in AbstractCountMap = \widehat{SymbolicVariable} \rightarrow AbstractCount$$

Mapping C is used for rendering the translation function more precise. In the definition below, we assume that a mapping $\mathcal{N} : \widehat{SymbolicVariable} \rightarrow SMTVariable$ exists and is updated accordingly when SMT variables are generated from abstract symbolic variables. We denote a successful lookup from this mapping using $\mathcal{N}(\mathsf{x})$. The definition below only depicts the translation of symbolic variables, as the translation of other types of formulae remains identical, except for passing the abstract count mapping alongside the formula that is being translated.

$$\mathsf{translate}(\mathsf{x}, C) = \begin{cases} \mathcal{N}(\mathsf{x}) & \text{if } C(\mathsf{x}) = 1 \\ \mathsf{x}n, n \in \mathbb{N} & \text{otherwise} \end{cases}$$

The translation function handles the satisfiability checking in one direction: the direction from the analysis to the SMT solver. A concolic execution engine, however, requires bidirectional communication by constructing a model satisfying the path constraint and feeding it back to the next concolic execution.

To this end, we define an inverse function getModel (depicted below), to compute an abstract model from the SMT model. We also define a mapping from *SMT* variables to their original abstract symbolic variables so that an abstract model can be computed from the *SMT* model.

$$SMTModel = SMTVariable \rightarrow ProgramValue \quad \mathcal{N}^{-1} :: SMTVariable \rightarrow \widehat{SymbolicVariable}$$
$$\mathsf{getModel} :: SMTModel \times \mathcal{N}^{-1} \rightarrow \widehat{Model} \quad \mathsf{getModel}(M, N) = \bigsqcup_{x \in M} [N(x) \mapsto M(x)]$$

As every abstract symbolic variable can have multiple corresponding SMT variables, all corresponding SMT variables are joined into a single abstract symbolic variable, resulting in an over-approximation of the concrete model.

5.6 Abstracting the Visited Set

The visited set is an important component in the concrete semantics as it ensures that the concrete concolic execution engine does not perpetually alternate between same branches of the program. This visited set needs to be abstracted too, as it would otherwise lead the abstract interpreter to conclude that the concolic execution never finishes, resulting in a $\bot$ value.

Definition 5.6.1. *An abstracted visited is formed by a* has*-visited and a* may*-visited set. The former corresponds to the branches that have been visited, while the latter corresponds to the branches that may have been taken.*

$$\hat{V} \in \widehat{Visited} ::= \mathcal{P}(Formula) \times \mathcal{P}(Formula)$$

Definition 5.6.2. *The least upper bound $\sqcup$ and partial ordering $\leq$ for $\widehat{Visited}$ is defined as follows.*

$$(h_1, m_1) \leq (h_2, m_2) \triangleq h_1 \supseteq h_2 \wedge m_1 \subseteq m_2 \quad (h_1, m_1) \sqcup (h_2, m_2) \triangleq (h_1 \cap h_2, m_1 \Delta m_2)$$

where $m_1 \Delta m_2$ is the symmetric union of m_1 and m_2.

When computing the least upper bound of two states of the concolic machine, paths visited in both states end up in the has-set while the others are kept in the may-set. This leads us to the following definition of the abstract in operation.

Definition 5.6.3. *The abstract* in *operation is defined as follows.*

$$\mathsf{in}(e, (h, m), a_\psi 1, a_\psi 2) = \begin{cases} \{a_\psi 1, a_\psi 2\} & \text{if } e \in m \\ \{a_\psi 1\} & \text{if } e \notin h \wedge e \notin m \\ \{a_\psi 2\} & \text{if } e \in h \wedge e \notin m \end{cases}$$

We also define an abstract operation to add elements to the visited set.

Definition 5.6.4. *The operation* add *is defined as follows:*

$$\mathsf{add}(e, (h, m)) = (\{e\} \cup h, m)$$

5.7 Abstract Stepping Relation

Having defined an abstraction of the standard *CESK* machine components, an abstraction of symbolic expressions and their formulae and a translation to SMT formulae, we can put everything together and define an abstract version of the small-stepping relation $\widehat{\leadsto}$ on the concolic machine (depicted in Fig. 6).

Atomic evaluation remains largely unchanged except that literals are now injected in the abstract domain (through their abstraction functions α) for program and symbolic values. All rules are adapted to take the abstract count mapping C into account. This mapping propagates mostly unchanged through the stepping relation except for the [INPUT] and [ST-BACKTRACK] rules. The [INPUT] rule "allocates" a fresh abstract symbolic variable based on the source location of the matching input statement and the current abstract program context. The abstract count mapping is then updated to take this allocation into account by applying the inc meta-function to the current abstract count for that abstract symbolic variable. [ST-BACKTRACK'] *resets* the abstract count mapping as the program execution is restarted.

The remaining rules also need to take the abstractions of the continuation stores into account. Rules [ST-IFTRUE'] and [ST-IFFALSE'] perform *weak updates* on both the continuation and the value store. This weak update is performed by joining the new value at a specified address with its old value. While our semantics does not preclude *strong updates*, incorporating them would require additional changes to the abstract count mapping. Finally, rule [ST-BACKTRACK'] is updated to first translate the abstract path condition to one suitable for the model function and then translating its results back into an abstract model using the getModel function. The new model M' is joined with the old model M so that the number of possible abstract models remain finite. Next, we formulate and prove soundness of our abstract concolic semantics and prove that the resulting analysis terminates on any program input.

Theorem 5.7.1. $\widehat{\leadsto}$ *is a sound over-approximation of* $\leadsto$. *That is, for every* $\varsigma \leadsto \varsigma'$ *there exists an approximation* $\hat{\varsigma} \widehat{\leadsto} \hat{\varsigma}'$ *given that* $\alpha(\varsigma) \sqsubseteq \hat{\varsigma}$ *such that* $\alpha(\varsigma') \sqsubseteq \hat{\varsigma}'$.

Proof. Assuming that there exists a concrete transition, $\varsigma \leadsto \varsigma'$, we show by case analysis on the applied rules that there is an abstract transition $\hat{\varsigma} \widehat{\leadsto} \hat{\varsigma}'$ so that the proposition $\alpha(\varsigma') \sqsubseteq \hat{\varsigma}'$ holds for any given $\alpha(\varsigma) \sqsubseteq \hat{\varsigma}$. A full version of the proof is available in the online appendix.[2]   □

Theorem 5.7.2. *Termination.* $\widehat{Eval}$ *always terminates.*

Proof. Proof by analysis of the cardinality of each state-space component. A full version of the proof is available in the online appendix.   □

---

[2] https://doi.org/10.5281/zenodo.16568308.

$$\frac{(v, \overline{v'}) = \mathsf{lookupModel}(M, \mathbf{x}, \overline{v}) \qquad \mathbf{x} = \mathsf{fresh}(\ell(\mathsf{input}), \mathsf{ctx})}{\langle \mathsf{ev}(\mathsf{input}, \rho), \sigma, a_\kappa, \kappa, a_\psi, \psi, \overline{v}, \mathsf{ctx}, M, C, \varphi, \widehat{V} \rangle} \quad \text{INPUT}$$
$$\widehat{\leadsto} \langle \mathsf{ap}((v, \mathbf{x})), \sigma, a_\kappa, \kappa, a_\psi, \psi, \overline{v'}, \mathsf{ctx}, M, \boxed{C[\mathbf{x} \mapsto \mathsf{inc}(C(\mathbf{x}))]}, \varphi, \widehat{V} \rangle$$

$$\frac{\begin{array}{c}[\![ae]\!](\rho,\sigma) \ni (\mathit{true}, s) \qquad \varphi_t = \varphi \wedge s \qquad \varphi_f = \varphi \wedge \neg s \\ a'_\psi \in \mathsf{in}(\varphi_f, \widehat{V}, \mathsf{alloc}(\ell(ae)), a_\psi) \qquad \psi' = \psi'[a'_\psi \mapsto \boxed{\psi(a'_\psi)} \sqcup \{\,\mathsf{branch}(\varphi_f) :: a_\psi\,\}\,] \\ \langle \mathsf{ev}(\mathsf{if}\ ae\ e_1\ e_2, \rho), a_\kappa, \sigma, \kappa, a_\psi, \psi, \overline{v}, \mathsf{ctx}, M, \boxed{C}, \varphi, \widehat{V} \rangle \\ \widehat{\leadsto} \langle \mathsf{ev}(e_1, \rho), \sigma, a_\kappa, \kappa, a'_\psi, \psi', \overline{v}, \mathsf{ctx}, M, \boxed{C}, \varphi_t, \boxed{\mathsf{add}(\varphi_f, \widehat{V})} \rangle \end{array}} \quad \text{ST-IfTrue'}$$

$$\frac{\begin{array}{c}[\![ae]\!](\rho,\sigma) \ni (\mathit{false}, s) \qquad \varphi_t = \varphi \wedge s \qquad \varphi_f = \varphi \wedge \neg s \\ a'_\psi = \mathsf{in}(\varphi_t, \widehat{V}, \mathsf{alloc}(\ell(ae)), a_\psi) \qquad \psi' = \psi'[a'_\psi \mapsto \boxed{\psi(a_\psi)} \sqcup \{\mathsf{branch}(\varphi_t) :: a_\psi\}] \\ \langle \mathsf{ev}(\mathsf{if}\ ae\ e_1\ e_2, \rho), \sigma, a_\kappa, \kappa, a_\psi, \psi, \overline{v}, \mathsf{ctx}, M, \boxed{C}, \varphi, \widehat{V} \rangle \\ \widehat{\leadsto} \langle \mathsf{ev}(e_2, \rho), \sigma, a_\kappa, \kappa, a'_\psi, \psi', \overline{v}, \mathsf{ctx}, M, \boxed{C}, \varphi_f, \boxed{\mathsf{add}(\varphi_t, \widehat{V})} \rangle \end{array}} \quad \text{ST-IfFalse'}$$

$$\text{ST-Backtrack'}$$
$$\frac{M' = \mathsf{getModel}(\mathsf{model}(\mathsf{translate}(\varphi))) \qquad \mathsf{branch}(\varphi, \overline{x'}) :: a'_\psi \in \psi(a_\psi)}{\langle \mathsf{ap}(v), \sigma, \mathsf{Hlt}, \kappa, a_\psi, \psi, \overline{v}, \mathsf{ctx}, M, \boxed{C}, \varphi', \widehat{V} \rangle \widehat{\leadsto} \langle \mathsf{ev}(e_0, \rho_0), \sigma_0, \mathsf{Hlt}, \emptyset, a'_\psi, \psi, \overline{v'}, \emptyset, \boxed{M \sqcup M'}, \emptyset, \emptyset, \widehat{V} \rangle}$$

Fig. 6. Abstract stepping relation $\widehat{\leadsto}$, highlighted in grey are the parts changed in comparison to the concrete stepping relation. Rules for atomic evaluation, [St-Let1] and [St-Let2] are omitted for brevity but are available in the online appendix.

6 Variations on the Analysis

In contrast to the state of the art in soft contract verification, the systematic abstraction of a concolic execution machine enables a number of variations on the resulting abstract machine. These variations either render the analysis results more precise, or improve the analysis' performance. To demonstrate the possible variations, we take a similar approach as in Glaze et al. [11] and vary the machine by global widening and per-state widening.

6.1 Global Widening

One variation of the machine is to widen its components so that they become *shared* between all program states. More specifically, all machine components can be widened except for the control component, the addresses for the top of the failure and regular continuation stack, and the program and iteration context. One could also widen *path constraint* so that it becomes shared between all program states, which leads to a whole-program invariant. However, since the path constraints across a whole program can differ substantially, the most generic path constraint usually is the empty one. The *model*, on the other hand, can be widened to a global version since its symbolic variables are indexed by the path constraint for which the model was computed. Widening the model to be shared with all program states therefore does not impact its values since its values would be joined anyway. Finally, widening the abstract counts leads to imprecise information for the count of each symbolic variable. Every abstract count will be widened to ∞ causing each symbolic variable in the path condition to be translated into a unique SMT variable.

The widened state space Σ', consisting of a set of small step states, and the shared components, is depicted below. The abstracted evaluation function $\widehat{Eval}$ is adapted to operate on these widened states by iterating over each of its small-step states, lifting them to a non-widened small-step state, applying the evaluation relation and joining its results together. Note that this transformation does not impact the formal semantics.

$$\varsigma \in \Sigma ::= \langle c, a_\kappa, a_\psi, \text{ctx}, \varphi \rangle$$
$$\Sigma' = \mathcal{P}(\Sigma) \times (Store \times ContSto \times FailSto \times Model)$$
$$\text{lift}(\langle c, a_\kappa, a_\psi, \text{ctx}, \varphi \rangle, (\sigma, \kappa, \psi, M)) = \langle c, \sigma, a_\kappa, \kappa, a_\psi, \psi, M, \text{ctx}, \varphi \rangle$$
$$\widehat{Eval}(\Sigma, S) = \Sigma \sqcup \bigsqcup_{\substack{\varsigma \in \Sigma \\ \text{lift}(\varsigma, S) \rightsquigarrow \varsigma' \\ \text{lift}(\varsigma'', S') = \varsigma'}} (\{\varsigma''\}, S')$$

Conclusion This transformation shows that our abstract machine can be easily adapted to globally widen its components. Although this global widening drastically decreases the time complexity of resulting analysis, we argue against widening the symbolic execution components of the machine, as they will decrease the precision of its results.

6.2 Per-state Widening

A more practical form of widening is *per-state widening*. This form of widening entails that some analysis components are passed onto the next analysis states instead of making them part of the next analysis state itself. The widened state space Σ', depicted below, consists of pairs of which the second element is a mapping between abstract states $\varsigma \in \Sigma$ and their widened components. The abstract evaluation function $\widehat{Eval}$ is adapted accordingly.

$$\varsigma \in \Sigma = \langle c, a_\kappa, a_\psi, \text{ctx}, PC \rangle \qquad \Sigma' = \mathcal{P}(\Sigma) \times S$$
$$S = \Sigma \rightarrow (Store \times ContSto \times FailSto \times Model)$$
$$\text{lift}_1(\langle c, a_\kappa, a_\psi, \text{ctx}, \varphi \rangle, (\sigma, \kappa, \psi, M)) = \langle c, \sigma, a_\kappa, \kappa, a_\psi, \psi, M, \text{ctx}, \varphi \rangle$$
$$\text{lift}_2(\varsigma, S) = \text{lift}_1(\varsigma, S(\varsigma))$$
$$\widehat{Eval}(\Sigma, S) = \Sigma' \cup \bigsqcup_{\substack{\varsigma \in \Sigma \\ \text{lift}_2(\varsigma, S) \rightsquigarrow \varsigma' \\ \text{lift}_1(\varsigma'', S') = \varsigma'}} (\{\varsigma''\}, S[\varsigma'' \mapsto S'])$$

This reduces the number of states drastically, as each modification to the shared components no longer leads to a different program state.

Having defined the widened transfer function, we can assess its impact on the precision of the analysis result. Widening per state usually results in widening of components in the presence of *loops*. This means that components such as the path constraint get widened to loop iterations resulting in a *loop invariant*. The abstract count mapping gets similarly widened to each loop iteration, resulting in a ∞ count for symbolic variables that get produced in a loop. Again, the results of the model are not affected by these changes as they are already uniquely identified by their symbolic variable combined with the path constraint for which the model was computed.

> **Conclusion:** Again, our abstract machine can be easily adapted to support per-state widening. This widening approach is preferable over globally widening the symbolic components, as per-state widening naturally leads to widening at loop-heads, which is preferable is most cases.

7 Evaluation

We evaluate our approach by instantiating it for the problem of *soft contract verification* [16,17,24]. In this evaluation, we instantiate our abstract concolic execution engine for soft contract verification. To this end, contract specifications are compiled into low-level *assertions* that can be checked by the machinery of our approach. We compare our approach to traditional soft contract verification on a dataset provided by the state of the art. This dataset consists of a number of Racket programs annotated with contract specifications. All programs in this dataset are considered to be *safe* (e.g., do not contain any contract violations) by the original authors [16], and we also manually verified that this was indeed the case. We use this ground truth to compare our approach to traditional soft contract verification by measuring the number of unverified contracts.

Listing 2 The rules central to the translation from CFCP to ordinary λ-calculus.

$$\text{mon}^{j,k} \ (\text{flat } v_1) \ v_2 \rightarrow \text{if } (v_1 \ v_2) \ v_2 \ (\text{blame } j)$$
$$\text{mon}^{j,k} \ (\kappa_1 \rightarrow \kappa_2) \ (\lambda x.e) \rightarrow (\lambda x.\text{mon}^{j,k} \ \kappa_2 \ (e[x \mapsto \text{mon}^{k,j} \ \kappa_1 \ x]))$$

7.1 Instantiating Soft Contract Verification

Findler et al. [14] propose a contract system for specifying the expected behaviour of higher-order functions. In the listing shown below, we again depict a contract for the `square` function, stating that its input should be a number while guaranteeing that its output will be positive:

```
def square(x: number?): positive? = return x*x
```

In the language proposed by Findler et al., called CPCF, this code example would be translated into the following term:

$$\text{letrec } square = \text{mon}^{j,k} \ (number? \rightarrow positive?) \ (\lambda x.(x * x))$$

The contract-annotated function is transformed to a λ-expression containing the original parameters of the function and its body. Furthermore, the contract is translated to a *contract monitor*, mon, which attaches the contract to the function so that when the function is applied the *number?* contract is checked on the input value and the *positive?* contract is checked on the output value.

The translation of these contract systems into the language used in our approach is straightforward and partially given by Dimoulas et al. [5,6]. Listing 2 depicts the rules for translating CFCP terms to ordinary λ-calculus terms. These rules can then be applied recursively to obtain a contract-free program that can be analysed using our approach.

The full translation is a bit more involved, as it also translates Racket-specific constructs such as contract-out and contracts on structs, but their translations are omitted here for brevity.[3]

7.2 Implementation

We implemented our approach in Monarch [25], a framework for static analysis through abstract interpretation written in Haskell. This implementation is **publicly available as a replication package at** https://doi.org/10.5281/zenodo.16410896. The implementation follows the formalization for the most part, but extends the analysed language with support for strings, heap-allocated pairs, and vectors. Moreover, the analysed language also supports functions accepting multiple arguments. It uses a constant propagation domain as the abstract domain for program values, and power-set lattices for abstracting pointers and closures. Z3 is used an SMT solver.

7.3 Experimental Setup

To measure the performance and accuracy of our approach, we run our analysis on a collection of benchmark programs from existing soft contract verification work [24], and we compare the number of false positives detected by our approach to the number of false positives detected by related work. The ground truth is constructed by looking at benchmark programs that contain no contract violations, making every detected contract violation a false positive.

We first translate the benchmark programs to *ANF*, compile each contract down to λ_s in the manner described above, and insert function calls to each contracted function. A summary of the resulting set of programs is depicted in Table 1. The translated programs are larger than the original programs because they are translated into an *ANF* form, include a prelude of primitive functions

---
[3] The full translation is included in our replication package.

Table 1. An overview of the set of benchmark programs. Depicted are the number of lines of code (according to `sloc`) in the original and translated program.

Name	Original	Processed	Name	Original	Processed
games-snake	134	4525	mochi-zip	13	2684
games-tetris	250	6690	sergey-blur	12	2570
games-zombie	230	5110	sergey-eta	8	2543
mochi-fold-div	11	2657	sergey-kcfa2	10	2563
mochi-hors	12	2613	sergey-kcfa3	15	2573
mochi-hrec	8	2648	sergey-loop2	18	2593
mochi-l-zipunzip	15	2712	sergey-mj09	12	2560
mochi-map-foldr	9	2707	sergey-sat	28	2675
mochi-mappend	10	2689	softy-append	6	2595
mochi-mem	11	2695	softy-cpstak	21	2637
mochi-mult	7	2645	softy-last-pair	5	2573
mochi-neg	10	2610	softy-last	13	2626
mochi-nth0	11	2608	softy-length-acc	8	2589
mochi-r-file	25	2719	softy-length	6	2583
mochi-r-lock	8	2609	softy-member	6	2579
mochi-reverse	9	2620	softy-recursive-div2	8	2598
mochi-sum	7	2581	softy-subst	9	2617
			softy-tak	9	2616

annotated with contracts and some built-in contracts, and have the contract specifications compiled down into base-level assertions. To measure the precision of the analysis, the analysis is executed and the number of unique contract violations is counted.

The evaluation features two configurations of the analysis: a version, called "local" with no widening mirroring our formalization closely, and a version with per-state widening called "flow". Both configurations are instantiated with k-CFA context sensitivity for function calls, and with path constraints as its branching sensitivity. In the evaluation, we compare multiple values for k bounded to 5 call-sites, and measure whether it has an impact on the analysis precision.

For comparing the precision and performance of our approach with the state of the art, we replicate the results from Vandenbogaerde et al. [24] by running their replication package on the aforementioned benchmarks and measuring their running time and precision. For measuring the performance, we repeated the analysis of each benchmark program *20 times* with a timeout of 15 min and report its summary statistics. The benchmarks are executed on a *AMD EPYC 9384X* machine having 12 GiB of available memory. No limitations on garbage collection have been imposed.

7.4 Results

Precision Results Table 2 depicts the precision results of our benchmark programs. Benchmark programs for which all configurations result in either a timeout, or an error (in case of missing features in the analysed programming language), are omitted from the table. The omitted benchmarks comprise 11 out of the 35 benchmarks from the benchmark set. The state of the art did not time out on the omitted benchmarks. The table is split into three parts. The first part depicts the number of false positives found in the state-of-the-art approach [24], the second and third part depict the "flow" and "local" configurations (cf. above). These configurations are further subdivided into different values for k, which a tunable parameter changing how many function calls should be retained in the calling context. Higher values of k typically result in a higher precision at the cost of performance. However, as we noticed in the benchmarks such as *sergey_eta*, a higher precision could also lead to improved performance as abstract values grow smaller due to the increased precision of the analysis.

Table 2. Precision results for each benchmark program. Cells containing a ∞ indicate a timeout for that combination of benchmark and configuration.

Name	[24]	Flow 0 1 2 3 4 5	Local 0 1 2 3 4 5	Name	[24]	Flow 0 1 2 3 4 5	Local 0 1 2 3 4 5
mochi_fold-div	5	4 1 1 1 1 1	$\infty\infty\infty\infty\infty\infty$	mochi_sum	4	0 0 0 0 0 0	0 0 0 0 0 0
mochi_hors	2	3 3 3 3 3 3	$\infty\infty\infty\infty\infty\infty$	sergey_eta	0	0 0 0 0 0 0	0 0 0 0 0 0
mochi_hrec	5	6 $\infty\infty\infty\infty\infty$	$\infty\infty\infty\infty\infty\infty$	sergey_kcfa2	0	0 0 0 0 0 0	0 0 0 0 0 0
mochi_l-zipunzip	7	2 2 $\infty\infty\infty$ 2	$\infty\infty\infty\infty\infty\infty$	sergey_kcfa3	0	0 0 0 0 0 0	0 0 0 0 0 0
mochi_map-foldr	1	1 $\infty\infty\infty\infty\infty$	$\infty\infty\infty\infty\infty\infty$	sergey_mj09	0	0 0 0 0 0 ∞	0 0 0 0 0
mochi_mappend	4	1 $\infty\infty\infty\infty\infty$	$\infty\infty\infty\infty\infty\infty$	sergey_sat	0	0 0 $\infty\infty\infty\infty\infty$	$\infty\infty\infty\infty\infty$
mochi_mem	20	3 $\infty\infty\infty\infty\infty$	$\infty\infty\infty\infty\infty\infty$	softy_append	3	1 $\infty\infty\infty\infty\infty$	$\infty\infty\infty\infty\infty\infty$
mochi_mult	5	4 $\infty\infty\infty\infty\infty$	$\infty\infty\infty\infty\infty\infty$	softy_cpstak	3	3 3 $\infty\infty\infty\infty$	$\infty\infty\infty\infty\infty\infty$
mochi_neg	4	4 4 4 4 4	$\infty\infty\infty\infty\infty\infty$	softy_last	0	1 $\infty\infty\infty\infty\infty$	$\infty\infty\infty\infty\infty\infty$
mochi_nth0	3	4 3 3 3 3 3	$\infty\infty\infty\infty\infty\infty$	softy_length	6	2 $\infty\infty\infty\infty\infty$	$\infty\infty\infty\infty\infty\infty$
mochi_r-file	1	0 0 0 0 0	$\infty\infty\infty\infty\infty\infty$	softy_length-acc	6	2 $\infty\infty\infty\infty\infty$	$\infty\infty\infty\infty\infty\infty$
mochi_r-lock	2	4 4 4 4 4	$\infty\infty\infty\infty\infty\infty$	softy_tak	0	3 3 3 $\infty\infty\infty\infty$	$\infty\infty\infty\infty\infty\infty$

The results show that the "local" configuration of the analysis is barely useable with only 5 out of the 24 benchmarks terminating before the timeout is reached. This outcome is expected, as the "local" configuration results in an exponential number of states, as has been observed in prior work on AAM [11].

The results for the "flow" configuration are more interesting, as they are more likely to terminate before the timeout is reached. We found that in 10 out of the 24 benchmark programs our approach reports fewer false positives than the state-of-the-art approach. In 9 out of the 24 benchmark programs, the number of reported false positives is the same as the state-of-the-art approach, while for 5 benchmark programs, our approach reports more false positives.

> **Conclusion:** The results show that our approach is able to achieve a higher or equal level of precision in the majority of tested benchmark programs, at the cost of being slower than existing approaches and failing to analyse 10 out of the 34 benchmark programs within a time budget of 15 minutes.

Table 3. Performance results for each benchmark program. Each cell contains the mean running time or ∞ indicating a timeout for that combination of benchmark program and configuration. For each combination, the coefficient of variation never exceeds 21.9%, however in 75% of the combinations never exceed 1.3%.

Name	State-of-the-art	Flow						Local					
		0	1	2	3	4	5	0	1	2	3	4	5
mochi_fold-div	0.059 s	9.10 s	2.32 s	2.34 s	2.35 s	2.37 s	2.38 s	∞	∞	∞	∞	∞	∞
mochi_hors	0.063 s	39.65 s	99.83 s	289.14 s	168.42 s	492.21 s	791.92 s	∞	∞	∞	∞	∞	∞
mochi_hrec	0.055 s	834.24 s	∞	∞	∞	∞	∞	∞	∞	∞	∞	∞	∞
mochi_l-zipunzip	0.074 s	146.97 s	1566.51 s	∞	∞	∞	525.16 s	∞	∞	∞	∞	∞	∞
mochi_map-foldr	0.061 s	1104.61 s	∞	∞	∞	∞	∞	∞	∞	∞	∞	∞	∞
mochi_mappend	0.055 s	773.74 s	∞	∞	∞	∞	∞	∞	∞	∞	∞	∞	∞
mochi_mem	1.239 s	498.28 s	∞	∞	∞	∞	∞	∞	∞	∞	∞	∞	∞
mochi_mult	0.058 s	347.69 s	∞	∞	∞	∞	∞	∞	∞	∞	∞	∞	∞
mochi_neg	0.043 s	132.16 s	405.17 s	774.56 s	1135.49 s	1251.37 s	1503.50 s	∞	∞	∞	∞	∞	∞
mochi_nth0	0.033 s	56.58 s	78.22 s	81.52 s	83.02 s	83.73 s	86.27 s	∞	∞	∞	∞	∞	∞
mochi_r-file	0.062 s	14.53 s	62.26 s	397.81 s	672.42 s	1588.63 s	∞	∞	∞	∞	∞	∞	∞
mochi_r-lock	0.076 s	30.29 s	64.99 s	90.67 s	103.44 s	119.79 s	154.05 s	∞	∞	∞	∞	∞	∞
mochi_sum	0.047 s	0.19 s	0.18 s	0.17 s	0.18 s	0.18 s	0.18 s	0.15 s	0.16 s	0.16 s	0.16 s	0.16 s	0.16 s
sergey_eta	0.002 s	0.44 s	0.27 s	0.19 s	0.19 s	0.19 s	0.19 s	1.52 s	0.33 s	0.19 s	0.19 s	0.19 s	0.19 s
sergey_kcfa2	0.045 s	1.13 s	1.69 s	1.98 s	1.57 s	1.45 s	1.25 s	8.52 s	111.47 s	36.05 s	7.71 s	7.83 s	4.18 s
sergey_kcfa3	0.035 s	1.43 s	2.64 s	2.02 s	1.98 s	2.34 s	2.52 s	12.33 s	624.24 s	107.40 s	251.81 s	105.78 s	45.88 s
sergey_mj09	0.020 s	1.69 s	3.43 s	0.20 s	0.20 s	0.20 s	0.20 s	121.53 s	∞	0.21 s	0.21 s	0.22 s	0.22 s
sergey_sat	0.039 s	170.62 s	979.98 s	∞	∞	∞	∞	∞	∞	∞	∞	∞	∞
softy_append	0.039 s	887.45 s	∞	∞	∞	∞	∞	∞	∞	∞	∞	∞	∞
softy_cpstak	0.084 s	151.59 s	1291.34 s	∞	∞	∞	∞	∞	∞	∞	∞	∞	∞
softy_last	0.040 s	1241.82 s	∞	∞	∞	∞	∞	∞	∞	∞	∞	∞	∞
softy_length	0.059 s	708.55 s	∞	∞	∞	∞	∞	∞	∞	∞	∞	∞	∞
softy_length-acc	0.082 s	764.85 s	∞	∞	∞	∞	∞	∞	∞	∞	∞	∞	∞
softy_tak	0.059 s	92.14 s	1225.51 s	1673.31 s	∞	∞	∞	∞	∞	∞	∞	∞	∞

Table 3 depicts the running times for each combination of benchmark programs and configurations. The results show that our approaches is able to analyse each program in a few minutes. More interestingly, different values of k seem to increase and sometimes decrease the running times of the analysis. In the case of sergey_kcfa the resulting difference is quite pronounced since the benchmark program is designed to decrease running times with higher values of k. Others, such as mochi_neg only increase their running times with higher values of k. We conclude that impact of k is highly dependent on the benchmark program. Again, we observe that the "local" configuration is outperformed by the "flow" configuration. The results show that the "flow" configuration outperforms the "local" configuration by several orders of magnitude.

Comparing our approach with the state-of-the-art approach for soft contract verification, we observe that our approach is several orders of magnitude slower, but still takes only a couple of minutes to complete. This is because the state-of-the-art approach uses a bespoke *compositional analysis* design for their analysis. Since their approach is compositional, functions can be analysed in isolation regardless of on which paths calls to those functions occur. This substantially reduces the size of the state space, but reduces the precision of the analysis since function calls are no longer analysed in a path sensitive manner. Moreover, while doing so the state-of-art approach chooses an ad-hoc configuration for its abstract machine, and does not consider abstractions for its path constraint, symbolic variables and expressions. Instead, when detecting loops, the state-of-art approach simply discards the path constraint instead of widening it to the least general constraint. A similar phenomenon occurs for its symbolic expressions which are simply discarded instead of widened.

However, one of the strengths of our approach is that it is amenable to a myriad of optimizations proposed in the *AAM* literature, ranging from store deltas [11], to modularization [18], parallelization [22], and abstract garbage collection [7,10]. In Sect. 6 we already demonstrated *global store widening*, a common optimization in *AAM* literature. This shows that these common optimizations can be easily adapted to our context.

Timed-Out Benchmarks. Compared to the terminated benchmarks, the timed-out ones are typically larger and contain more complex contracts. For instance, the *games* benchmarks contain contracts on more complex nested data structures for representing elements of the game. Since our analysis is *path-sensitive*, these constraints often result in an exponentially larger state space. Again, other performance-enhancing techniques from the AAM literature might be used to reduce this state space further.

> **Conclusion:** The results demonstrate that most benchmark programs can be analysed within a few minutes. They also highlight the importance of incorporating widening techniques, as the "local" approach alone proves to be insufficient. Compared to the state-of-the-art, our approach achieves higher precision, though at the expense of performance. Our approach is the first to systematically abstract concolic execution, and explore its different configurations. Thus, it remains amenable to a myriad of *AAM* optimizations that have been successful in the past for rendering other *AAM*-based analysis techniques scalable.

8 Related Work

State Merging. Sen et al. [21] propose a state merging technique for reducing the path explosion problem in dynamic symbolic execution. They do so by merging multiple *DSE* states together into a *value summary* therefore reducing the number of states to be explored. Moreover, these summaries allow redundant execution paths to be pruned reducing the state space even more. However, these summaries still contain concrete path constraints and concrete values, thereby only solving the problem of redundant state exploration, but not of termination.

Other state merging techniques, also in the context concolic execution, have been proposed [26] with the same termination problem.

Subsumption Checking. Anand et al. [1,2] propose symbolic execution with subsumption checking. Their approach differs from our approach in two ways. First, their approach targets static symbolic execution, while our approach targets a variant of dynamic symbolic execution called *concolic execution*. Using dynamic symbolic execution instead of static symbolic execution allows our approach to replace symbolic values with a symbolic representation of the computed (abstract) program value, instead of reasoning over program values in a purely symbolic way. Therefore, our approach is more precise since it computes an *abstract model* that contains concrete values (depending on the abstract domain used) whenever possible. The second difference is that their analysis results in an under-approximation of the program behaviour, while our analysis is designed to return an over-approximation of the program behaviour at the cost of running into false positives. However, their proposed shape abstractions could be used to improve the abstract domain of *symbolic expressions* in our approach in order to make them more precise.

Combining Symbolic Execution and Abstract Interpretation. The idea of combining symbolic execution with abstract interpretation is not new. For instance, Permenev et al. [19] propose combining static symbolic execution with predicate abstractions [12] through *delayed predicate abstractions*. In their approach, static symbolic execution is used to execute the majority of the program, but then switches over to predicate abstractions to verify the property of interest. The reasoning is that their properties of interest require deep exploration of the static symbolic execution tree, and that using delayed predicate abstraction decreases the required exploration to prove or disprove a property. We follow a similar approach, but use an abstracted version of the state space *right away*. However, depending on the configuration of the abstract machine, we could achieve similar results. For instance, the machine could be configured to reason in a precise way about the possible program states and up to point that the delayed predicate abstraction should occur. To this end, the context component can be modified to include precise calling contexts, and to remove those whenever delayed abstraction is needed.

Sound Symbolic Execution. Tiraboschi et al. [23] propose *(relational) sound symbolic execution*. Their approach achieves termination by applying a form of *bounded symbolic execution* after which the symbolic execution context is overapproximated to also render the analysis sound. These bounds are implemented through *counters* that are part of the symbolic execution state. Our approach in contrast depends on *arbitrary contexts* to differentiate different abstract concolic states from each-other, which are only joined (i.e., over-approximated) when they are no longer distinguishable. Moreover, our approach is derived from a systematic abstraction of the $CESK_\varphi$ machine using the AAM methodology, which opens it up to a myriad of common optimizations (cf. Section 6), and precision-enhancing techniques (e.g., variants of context sensitivity).

Soft Contract Verification. Nguyen et al. [17] propose *soft contract verification* which is a technique to static analyse software contracts in higher-order programming languages. This work has since been extended to include stateful programs [16], and has been rendered compositional [24]. Our work offers a more generalized way of expressing this soft contract verification. Nguyen et al. propose a machine where the path constraint and symbolic store (i.e., a mapping from addresses to concolic values) is always included in the program state (i.e., corresponding to our "local" configuration), and is never widened to a more abstract value. Instead, their approach solves this problem in ad-hoc manner by simply removing all symbolic expressions and path constraints whenever the program execution reaches a loop. Our approach, in contrast, does not require this loop detection and widens the affected machines components naturally. Finally, the work by Nguyen et al. use a form of static symbolic execution, whereas we use *concolic execution*. The main difference is that their work does not require multiple concolic executions of the same machine, and does not require the computation and therefore abstraction of a model. The lack of a model potentially introduces more imprecision in the analysis results and leads to a higher number of false positives.

Relational Analysis. In a relational analysis, program states are explored in a path-sensitive manner by indexing the program state with predicates on a set of program variables. To render the analysis finite, this set of program variables needs to be finite, and so do their predicates. In traditional relational analyses this set of variables is determined before running the analysis. Other techniques have been proposed to iteratively refine [3] this set of variables until the desired level of precision is reached, or until the precision no longer improves by adding additional variables. Our approach instead derives symbolic variables from the program location of input statements, and counts them to determine the number of corresponding concrete symbolic variables.

9 Future Work

In this paper we presented the first systematic abstraction of concolic execution for soft contract verification. In contrast to the state of the art, this systematic abstraction results in a more configurable abstract machine, leading to multiple avenues for future work. As demonstrated by the results, our approach is somewhat slower than the existing state-of-the-art approach for soft contract verification, Therefore, a natural avenue for future work is to further apply several *AAM* optimizations [11,18] to render our analysis scalable to larger programs. Finally, another avenue of future work is refining the abstract representation of symbolic expressions. Our representation is currently limited to three levels, a bottom value, a symbolic expression or a fresh value. Other representations could be used to make the analysis more precise, such as those found in [1].

10 Conclusion

We have introduced *abstract concolic execution* as a systematically-derived static analysis supporting soft contract verification. The static analysis is sound and is guaranteed to terminate. The downside is that false positives may be returned, so the analysis is incomplete. We demonstrated, however, that the benefits of concolic execution are retained. For instance, our approach enables analysis developers to replace symbolic representations with abstract values whenever the solver is not sufficiently powerful to solve some of the introduced constraints, or whenever modelling certain programming language features (e.g., closures) becomes a burden on the performance of the solver. To render concolic execution abstract, we introduced a novel extension to the *CESK* machine, $CESK_\varphi$, which models both the instrumented version of the program and the concolic iteration loop itself. Inspired by the *AAM* recipe, we then abstracted this semantics by abstracting the components of the machine, and its small-stepping relation. We have shown that the resulting machine predicts all behaviour found by the concrete machine (i.e., is sound), and that it terminates for any program input. When applying abstract concolic execution to soft contract verification, we found that it outperforms the state-of-the-art approaches in terms of precision while being somewhat slower. We have also demonstrated that our approach is more *configurable* than existing approaches by relying on real abstractions of path constraints, symbolic expressions, and symbolic variables, eliminating the need for a store caches and ad-hoc rules for updating them.

Acknowledgements. This work is partially funded by Research Foundation Flanders (FWO) (grant number 1187122N).

References

1. Anand, S., Păsăreanu, C.S., Visser, W.: Symbolic execution with abstract subsumption checking. In: Valmari, A. (ed.) SPIN 2006. LNCS, vol. 3925, pp. 163–181. Springer, Heidelberg (2006). https://doi.org/10.1007/11691617_10
2. Anand, S., Pasareanu, C.S., Visser, W.: Symbolic execution with abstraction. Int. J. Softw. Tools Technol. Transf. **11**(1), 53–67 (2009). https://doi.org/10.1007/S10009-008-0090-1
3. Ball, T., Rajamani, S.K.: The SLAM project: debugging system software via static analysis. In: Proceedings of the 29th ACM SIGPLAN-SIGACT Symposium on Principles of Programming Languages, pp. 1–3 (2002)
4. Cousot, P., Cousot, R.: Abstract interpretation: a unified lattice model for static analysis of programs by construction or approximation of fixpoints. In: Proceedings of the 4th ACM SIGACT-SIGPLAN Symposium on Principles of Programming Languages, pp. 238–252 (1977)
5. Dimoulas, C., Findler, R.B., Flanagan, C., Felleisen, M.: Correct blame for contracts: no more scapegoating. In: Proceedings of the 38th ACM SIGPLAN-SIGACT Symposium on P rinciples of Programming Languages, POPL, 26–28 January 2011, pp. 215–226. ACM (2011)

6. Dimoulas, C., Tobin-Hochstadt, S., Felleisen, M.: Complete monitors for behavioral contracts. In: Proceedings of the 21ste European Symposium on Programming Languages and Systems, ESOP 2012, Held as Part of the European Joint Conferences on Theory and Practice of Software, ETAPS 2012. LNCS, vol. 7211, pp. 214–233. Springer (2012)
7. Van Es, N., Stiévenart, Q., De Roover, C.: Garbage-free abstract interpretation through abstract reference counting. In: 33rd European Conference on Object-Oriented Programming, ECOOP. LIPIcs, 15–19 July 2019, vol. 134, pp. 10:1–10:33. Schloss Dagstuhl - Leibniz-Zentrum für Informatik (2019). https://doi.org/10.4230/LIPICS.ECOOP.2019.10
8. Felleisen, M., Friedman, D.P.: A calculus for assignments in higher-order languages. In: Conference Record of the Fourteenth Annual ACM Symposium on Principles of Programming Languages, 21–23 January 1987, pp. 314–325. ACM Press (1987). https://doi.org/10.1145/41625.41654
9. Findler, R.B., Felleisen, M.: Contracts for higher-order functions. In: Proceedings of the Seventh ACM SIGPLAN International Conference on Functional Programming, pp. 48–59 (2002)
10. Germane, K., McCarthy, J.: Newly-single and loving it: improving higher-order must-alias analysis with heap fragments. Proc. ACM Program. Lang. **5**(ICFP), 1–28 (2021). https://doi.org/10.1145/3473601
11. Glaze, D., Labich, N., Might, M., Van Horn, D.: Optimizing abstract abstract machines. SIGPLAN Not. **48**(9), 443–454 (2013). https://doi.org/10.1145/2544174.2500604
12. Graf, S., Saïdi, H.: Construction of abstract state graphs with PVS. In: Proceedings of the 9th International Conference on Computer Aided Verification (CAV). LNCS, 22–25 June 1997, vol. 1254, pp. 72–83. Springer (1997). https://doi.org/10.1007/3-540-63166-6_10
13. Van Horn, D., Might, M.: Abstracting abstract machines. In: Proceedings of the 15th ACM SIGPLAN International Conference on Functional Programming, ICFP 2010, 27–29 September 2010, pp. 51–62. ACM (2010). https://doi.org/10.1145/1863543.1863553
14. Meyer, B.: Design by contract: the Eiffel method. In: 26th International Conference on Technology of Object-Oriented Languages and Systems (Tools), p. 446. IEEE Computer Society (1998)
15. Might, M., Shivers, O.: Improving flow analyses via GammaCFA: abstract garbage collection and counting. In: Proceedings of the 11th ACM SIGPLAN International Conference on Functional Programming, ICFP, 16–21 September 2006, pp. 13–25. ACM (2006). https://doi.org/10.1145/1159803.1159807
16. Nguyen, P.C., Gilray, T., Tobin-Hochstadt, S., Van Horn, D.: Soft contract verification for higher-order stateful programs. Proc. ACM Program. Lang. **2**(POPL), 51:1–51:30 (2018). https://doi.org/10.1145/3158139
17. Nguyen, P.C., Tobin-Hochstadt, S., Van Horn, D.: Soft contract verification. In: Proceedings of the 19th ACM SIGPLAN International Conference on Functional programming, 1–3 September 2014, pp. 139–152 (2014). https://doi.org/10.1145/2628136.2628156
18. Nicolay, J., Stiévenart, Q., De Meuter, W., De Roover, C.: Effect-driven flow analysis. In: Proceedings of the 20th International Conference on Verification, Model Checking, and Abstract Interpretation, VMCAI. LNCS, 13–15 January 2019, vol. 11388, pp. 247–274. Springer (2019). https://doi.org/10.1007/978-3-030-11245-5_12

19. Permenev, A., Dimitrov, D.K., Tsankov, P., Drachsler-Cohen, D., Vechev, M.T.: VerX: safety verification of smart contracts. In: 2020 IEEE Symposium on Security and Privacy, SP, 18–21 May 2020, pp. 1661–1677. IEEE (2020). https://doi.org/10.1109/SP40000.2020.00024
20. Sen, K., Marinov, D., Agha, G.: CUTE: a concolic unit testing engine for C. In: Proceedings of the 10th European Software Engineering Conference held jointly with 13th ACM SIGSOFT International Symposium on Foundations of Software Engineering, 5–9 September 2005, pp. 263–272 (2005). https://doi.org/10.1145/1081706.1081750
21. Sen, K., Necula, G.C., Gong, L., Choi, W.: MultiSE: multi-path symbolic execution using value summaries. In: Proceedings of the 2015 10th Joint Meeting on Foundations of Software Engineering, ESEC/FSE 2015, 30 August–4 September 2015, pp. 842–853. ACM (2015)
22. Stiévenart, Q., Van Es, N., Van der Plas, J., De Roover, C.: A parallel worklist algorithm and its exploration heuristics for static modular analyses. J. Syst. Softw. **181**, 111042 (2021). https://doi.org/10.1016/J.JSS.2021.111042
23. Tiraboschi, I., Rezk, T., Rival, X.: Sound symbolic execution via abstract interpretation and its application to security. In: Proceedings of the 24th International Conference on Verification, Model Checking, and Abstract Interpretation, VMCAI 2023. LNCS, vol. 13881, pp. 267–295. Springer (2023). https://doi.org/10.1007/978-3-031-24950-1_13
24. Vandenbogaerde, B., Stiévenart, Q., De Roover, C.: Summary-based compositional analysis for soft contract verification. In: Proceedings of the 22nd IEEE International Working Conference on Source Code Analysis and Manipulation, SCAM 2021, pp. 186–196 (2021). https://doi.org/10.1109/SCAM55253.2022.00028
25. Vandenbogaerde, B., Verbelen, S., Van Es, N., De Roover, C.: Monarch: a modular framework for abstract definitional interpreters in Haskell. In: Proceedings of the 32nd International Symposium on Static Analysis, SAS. LNCS, 12–18 October 2025. Springer (2025)
26. Vandercammen, M., De Roover, C.: State merging for concolic testing of event-driven applications. Sci. Comput. Program. **242**, 103264 (2025). https://doi.org/10.1016/J.SCICO.2025.103264

Enhancing Neural Network Robustness via Synthesis of Repair Programs

Tom Yuviler(✉)[iD] and Dana Drachsler-Cohen[iD]

Technion, Haifa, Israel
tom.yuviler@campus.technion.ac.il, ddana@ee.technion.ac.il

Abstract. Adversarial examples undermine the reliability of neural networks. To defend against attacks, multiple approaches have been proposed. However, many of them introduce high training overhead or high inference overhead, some significantly decrease the network's accuracy or insufficiently increase the network's robustness, and others do not scale to deep networks. To mitigate all these shortcomings, we propose a new form of defense: optimal program synthesis of short *repair programs*, integrated into a trained network. A repair program modifies a few neurons by using a few other neurons. The challenge is to identify the most successful combination of neurons to enhance the network's robustness while maintaining high accuracy. We introduce DefEnSyn, a stochastic synthesizer of repair programs. To cope with the exponential number of neuron combinations, DefEnSyn learns the effective combinations by synthesizing repair programs of increasing length. We evaluate DefEnSyn on classifiers for ImageNet and CIFAR-10 and show it enhances the robustness of networks to L_∞-, L_2-, and L_0- black-box adversarial example attacks and to backdoor attacks. DefEnSyn's repair programs enhance the networks' robustness on average by $+40\%$ and up to $+71\%$. DefEnSyn decreases the network's accuracy by only $\approx -1\%$. We demonstrate that DefEnSyn outperforms existing state-of-the-art defenses based on adversarial training, randomization, and repair, in both robustness and accuracy.

Keywords: Neural Network Robustness · Program Synthesis

1 Introduction

Despite the immense success of neural networks, their reliability is still an open challenge due to their vulnerability to various kinds of attacks. One of the widely studied attacks is the adversarial example attack, where an adversary computes a small perturbation that causes the network to predict the wrong output [4,11,26,36,50,71,73,84]. When the attacked network is an image classifier, the attacker typically aims at generating an imperceptible perturbation. Formally, the attacker computes a perturbation whose magnitude is smaller than a predefined small threshold, where the magnitude is measured with respect to a given *p*-norm, such as L_∞ [26,50], L_2 [4,11], L_1 [12,17], or L_0 [16,71]. These

Table 1. Adversarial defenses: advantages and disadvantages (yes ✓, partly ✓, no ×).

	High clean accuracy	High robust accuracy	Scalability for large networks	Low training overhead	Low inference overhead
Adv. training	✓	✓	✓	×	✓
Randomization	✓	✓	✓	✓	✓
Repair	✓	✓	✓	✓	✓
DefEnSyn (ours)	✓	✓	✓	✓	✓

adversarial examples raise concerns about deploying AI in safety-critical applications, leading to new regulations by the European Union [22] and guidelines for secure AI system development by the NSA [54].

To mitigate adversarial attacks, many *adversarial defenses* have been proposed. An adversarial defense aims to make a network more robust to adversarial attacks without significantly decreasing the network's accuracy. This is commonly obtained by modifying the network's computations or the input to the network during training or inference. Existing adversarial defenses are thus required to carefully balance all these conflicting goals: high accuracy on unperturbed inputs (called *clean accuracy*), high accuracy on adversarially perturbed inputs (called *robust accuracy*), low training overhead, low inference overhead, and scaling to large networks. This has led to three kinds of defenses: adversarial training, randomization, and post-training repair (repair for short). Adversarial training alters the training to consider adversarial examples [1,36,50,64,66,79]. Often, these defenses obtain high clean accuracy and high robust accuracy (with respect to the given attack types). However, they introduce significant overhead in computational resources and training time (e.g., several days). This overhead becomes significant when newly discovered attacks necessitate repeated retraining of the network to enhance its robustness. Randomization adds stochastic noise to the input [9,10,15,39,53,62,82] or to the network's computations [37,45]. While randomization defenses have a lighter training overhead than adversarial training, they tend to decrease the network's clean accuracy and still introduce some time overhead during both training and inference. Repair techniques introduce post-training modifications to the neural network, like parameter adjustments [49,67,72,74,77] or architectural modifications [23,38,70]. Most repair techniques do not aim to defend against adversarial examples but rather repair benign misclassifications [23,49,67,70,74] or enforce specifications, e.g., linear constraints over the network's output [38]. However, repair has also been proposed for adversarial defense [77]. Its main disadvantage is that it often relies on expensive analysis, which does not scale to large networks. There are two exceptions [70,74], but they focus on provable repair, which becomes infeasible when the number of inputs required to be defended is more than a few hundred. Table 1 summarizes the advantages and disadvantages of the defense types.

We propose a novel form of defense: optimal program synthesis [8,13,51] of *short repair programs*, integrated into a trained network, that enhance robustness with a minimal decrease in the clean accuracy. Program synthesis relies on

Enhancing Neural Network Robustness via Synthesis of Repair Programs   223

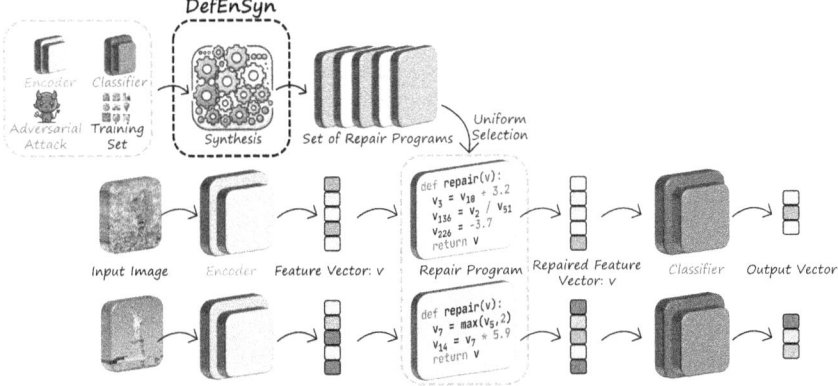

Fig. 1. Illustration of `DefEnSyn`, an adversarial defense via optimal program synthesis.

training, enabling us to look for a repair that maximizes both the robust and clean accuracies. It is also commonly restricted to a short solution, enabling us to lower the training and inference overhead. To scale to deep networks, a *repair program* is integrated into a trained network between the network's *encoder* and *classifier* (illustrated by Fig. 1). The encoder consists of the first layers, transforming an input into a lower-dimensional feature vector, and the classifier consists of the other layers, mapping the feature vector to a probability vector over the classes. Defending a network by modifying the network's extracted features has been shown to be successful [41,83]. Our repair programs modify the values of a *few* neurons using a *few* other neurons. This idea builds on the observation that certain parts of neural networks act as *program modules* and can be recomposed to achieve a task *without retraining* [55,58]. Our defense has several advantages: (1) it is applicable to any network architecture and does not make any assumptions about its layer types, (2) it is computed *after* the network has been trained, and (3) during synthesis, evaluating candidate programs requires only the classifier part, keeping the synthesis overhead relatively low, even for deep networks. Our focus is *optimal* program synthesis since the goal of adversarial defense is to *maximize* the clean and robust accuracies on a given training set. This is different from provable repair [70,74], which looks for a repair with perfect accuracy on the training set and fails if there is none. Naturally, for large training sets (more than a few hundred), provable repair fails more often.

Computing a repair program that maximizes the clean and robust accuracies is highly challenging. First, it requires identifying the best neurons to include in the repair program (on the left-hand side and the right-hand side of its instructions) out of an exponential number of possibilities. The challenge is that neurons are not standard program variables but rather functions over the network's inputs, and some of them are correlated. Second, there is no monotonicity between the effectiveness of a program and programs that extend it. Thus, greedy synthesis, iteratively generating the next best instruction, is unsuitable.

Third, stochastic synthesis that samples full programs (e.g., [21,60]) requires an infeasible number of samples to converge. To illustrate, if there are 100 neurons and the repair program can have up to ten instructions, only checking a single program for each possibility of repaired neurons requires 10^{13} samples. Even if evaluating a single sample takes one millisecond, this basic sampling requires over 300 years. To the best of our knowledge, choosing a small set of variables out of a large set of correlated variables is a new challenge in program synthesis.

We introduce DefEnSyn, a synthesizer that computes a set of repair programs. It relies on two ideas. First, to cope with the exponential number of possibilities, it learns the effectiveness of each neuron *separately* (not as part of sets). Second, although there is no monotonicity between programs and their extensions, it uses short programs, whose search space is smaller, as guidance towards the effective neurons in longer programs. Technically, it learns two distributions over the neurons, for the left-hand side of the instructions (the *repaired* neurons), and for the right-hand side (the *repairing* neurons). To this end, it iterates over program lengths from 1 to k. For each, it samples full programs based on the distributions learned by previous iterations. It updates these distributions by the average accuracies of candidate programs. This sampling method helps it to identify the more suitable neurons for repair when sampling programs of length k. Thus, it converges to effective repair programs with relatively few samples ($k \cdot 10^6$). Like randomization defenses, DefEnSyn leverages stochastic noise: it computes a *set* of programs and, at inference, one program from the set is randomly selected. Unlike randomization defenses, this form of stochastic noise has negligible overhead, and it leads to a minor decrease in clean accuracy.

We evaluate DefEnSyn on ImageNet classifiers: ConvNeXt [48], DeiT [76], ViT [20], and ResNet-18 [28], consisting of up to 22 million parameters. We consider the more realistic black-box setting, where the attacker has no access to the defended network and can only query it. DefEnSyn enhances the robustness of networks against state-of-the-art L_∞ adversarial attacks by +71%, against L_2 attacks by +15%, and against L_0 attacks by +44%. This increase in robust accuracy exceeds the increase of state-of-the-art adversarial training and randomization defenses. DefEnSyn also outperforms repair defenses: it increases the robust accuracy of a CIFAR-10 classifier against a backdoor attack [27,46,61] by +27%, compared to +4% obtained by an existing repair [77]. In all experiments, DefEnSyn slightly decreases the clean accuracy by about −1%, outperforming existing defenses. It computes repair programs within a few hours, unlike adversarial training, which requires several days. Integrating repair programs into the network poses a negligible overhead during inference: less than $3 \cdot 10^{-5}$ seconds.

In summary, our main contributions are:

- A post-training defense that integrates short repair programs into a network.
- A synthesizer of repair programs that identifies the best neurons for them.
- Extensive evaluation showing that our defense outperforms existing adversarial training, randomization, and repair defenses.

2 Problem Definition

In this section, we define the problem of adversarial defense.

Neural Network Classifiers. We focus on classifiers for images. An image is a $d_1 \times d_2$ matrix, consisting of RGB pixels in $[0,1]^3$. A classifier maps an image to a score vector over the classes $[c] = \{1, \ldots, c\}$, i.e., $N : [0,1]^{d_1 \times d_2 \times 3} \to \mathbb{R}^c$. The classification of image x is the class with the highest score, $c' = \operatorname{argmax}(N(x))$. We focus on classifiers implemented by neural networks. Neural networks process data through a series of interconnected layers. Generally, a layer consists of multiple neurons, where a neuron performs some computation (e.g., a weighted sum of its inputs, followed by a non-linear activation function). The exact connections between neurons and the definition of the weights are determined by the network architecture. For example, in a fully connected network [44,75], neurons between two adjacent layers are fully interconnected, and each connection has a unique weight. Other architectures, shown to be highly effective for image processing tasks, are Convolutional Neural Networks (CNNs) [28,35,48,65] and Vision Transformers (ViTs) [20,47,76]. Since the definition of these architectures is not required for understanding our paper, we omit their definition. The effectiveness of a classifier is commonly defined by the *clean accuracy*. This is the percentage of inputs, in a given data set $\mathcal{D}$, that are correctly classified by N:

$$Acc_C(N, \mathcal{D}) = 100 \cdot \frac{\sum_{(x_i, c_i) \in \mathcal{D}} \mathbb{1}\{\operatorname{argmax}(N(x_i)) = c_i\}}{|\mathcal{D}|} \quad (1)$$

Attacks. An adversarial example attack introduces a small perturbation to a correctly classified input image with the goal of misleading the classifier. Typically, the magnitude of the perturbation is constrained with respect to a chosen norm, such as L_∞, L_2, L_1, or L_0. Formally, given a perturbation bound ϵ and a p-norm, an adversarial attack is a function $\mathcal{A}$ mapping a classifier N, a correctly classified input x and its class c_x to a perturbed image $\mathcal{A}(N, x, c_x) = x' \in [0,1]^{d_1 \times d_2 \times 3}$ such that $\|x - x'\|_p \leq \epsilon$. The attack succeeds if N classifies x' not as c_x (i.e., $\operatorname{argmax}(N(x')) \neq c_x$). This attack is called an *untargeted attack*. Our work can also be extended to targeted attacks, where the goal is that N classifies x' as a target class $c_t \neq c_x$. We note that constraining the attack's perturbation by a single norm is the most widely used attack model; however, there are attack models constraining the perturbation by several norms [18,31,32]. We focus on black-box attacks, where the attacker has no access to the network's internals and can only query the network to obtain the outputs of given inputs (specifically, *score-based attacks*). This setting is more realistic [4,40,56,87], in particular for machine-learning-as-a-service (MLaaS) deployments, where users can only submit queries to the network and observe its outputs (e.g., the scores). Similar to prior work [14,30,40,52], we assume an attacker that adapts its attack by querying the network multiple times. To evaluate the resilience of a classifier against an adversarial attack, it is common to measure the *robust accuracy* [1,15,30,66,80,81]. The robust accuracy is the percentage of inputs, in a given data set $\mathcal{D}$, that are correctly classified by N when adversarially perturbed:

$$Acc_R(N, \mathcal{D}) = 100 \cdot \frac{\sum_{(x_i, c_i) \in \mathcal{D}} \mathbb{1}\{argmax(N(\mathcal{A}(N, x_i, c_i))) = c_i\}}{|\mathcal{D}|} \quad (2)$$

Adversarial Defense. An adversarial defense is an algorithm whose goal is to increase the robust accuracy of a classifier while maximizing the clean accuracy. Ideally, the goal would be to obtain perfect clean and robust accuracies on any input and for any attack. However, this goal is infeasible for many reasons. For example, some attacks are unknown and some inputs are on the decision boundaries. Instead, the vast majority of adversarial defenses [1,10,15,39,66,77] are given an adversarial attack $\mathcal{A}$ as well as training and test sets $\mathcal{D}_{Tr}, \mathcal{D}_{Ts}$ for evaluating the defended network. Note that $\mathcal{A}$ can be any adversarial attack and can even combine multiple attacks. In this setting, the defense computes a defended network given $2 \cdot |\mathcal{D}_{Tr}|$ requirements (two for each input: classifying the input correctly and classifying its perturbed version by $\mathcal{A}$ correctly) and evaluates the result by measuring the clean and robust accuracies on $\mathcal{D}_{Ts}$. Since these requirements are often conflicting, and since the space of defenses is highly complex, it is common to look for a defense that maximizes the number of satisfied requirements. Formally, an adversarial defense is defined as follows.

Definition 1 (A Defense). *Given a classifier* $N : [0, 1]^{d_1 \times d_2 \times 3} \to \mathbb{R}^c$, *a data set of image-class pairs* $\mathcal{D}_{Tr} \subseteq [0, 1]^{d_1 \times d_2 \times 3} \times [c]$, *and an adversarial attack* $\mathcal{A}$, *a defense computes a defended network* N' *maximizing the robust and clean accuracies* $Acc_R(N', \mathcal{D}_{Tr}) + \lambda \cdot Acc_C(N', \mathcal{D}_{Tr})$, *where* λ *is a balancing factor.*

3 Adversarial Defense by Repair Programs

In this section, we describe our defense by a set of *repair programs*.

Our Defense. Our defense assumes a network that can be viewed as a composition of an encoder and a classifier, i.e., $N = C \circ E$. Intuitively, E extracts the input's features and passes a feature vector to C to compute the classification. We denote the number of extracted features by m. Formally, $E : \mathbb{R}^{d_1 \times d_2 \times 3} \to \mathbb{R}^m$ and $C : \mathbb{R}^m \to \mathbb{R}^c$. Most popular network architectures can be viewed as a composition of an encoder and a classifier, including fully connected networks, CNNs, and ViTs. Our defense adds a repair program P between the encoder E and classifier C, that is, the defended network is $N' = C \circ P \circ E$. Repair programs are short, and each of their instructions modifies a single entry of the feature vector. Integrating a program into the network is similar to adding a layer to the network, but the program supports more complex computations (e.g., piecewise polynomial functions). Integrating a repairing layer has been proposed [38]; however, only for enforcing linear constraints over the output vector, which cannot express the requirements of clean and robust accuracy. Other defenses that repair a single layer modify an *existing* layer [25,41,77]. While both our approach and existing repairs are post-training, our approach is a new form of defense: unlike

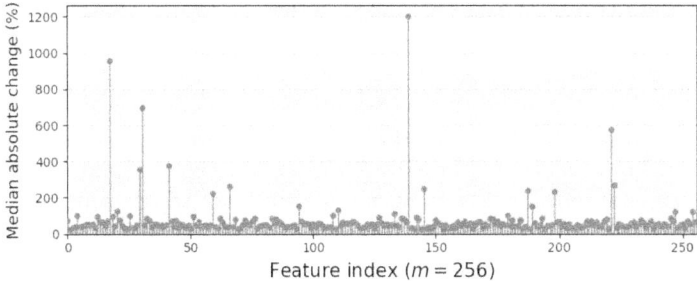

Fig. 2. The median absolute change (%) of every feature of a CIFAR-10 Wide-ResNet classifier following the L_0 `Pixle` attack. Most features are slightly changed.

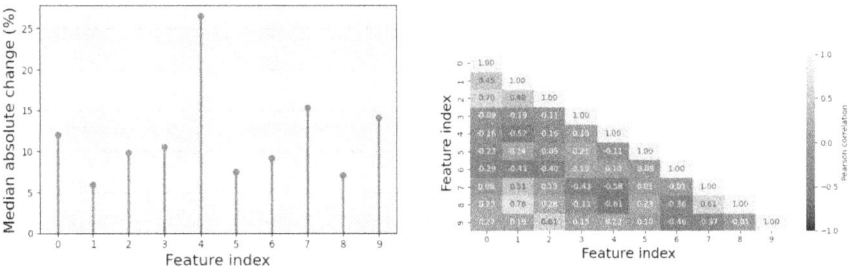

Fig. 3. Left: The median absolute change (%) of the first ten features of a CIFAR-10 Wide-ResNet classifier following the L_∞ `Square` attack. Right: The pairwise Pearson-correlation matrix of these features (computed on clean inputs).

existing repairs, it does not modify the network parameters or manipulate the network's output. Instead, it *synthesizes a program*, over a (restricted) programming language, which is added *between the network's layers*. This difference is similar to the difference between program repair and program synthesis.

Advantages. There are several advantages to repairing the input of the network's classifier part. First, its input dimension tends to be smaller than the input dimensions of previous layers, which reduces the search space of the repair. Second, adversarial attacks tend to change a small subset of these latent features (as demonstrated in Fig. 2); thus, identifying and modifying them can mitigate the attack. Third, due to redundancy, features tend to have strong linear correlations with some of the other features [5,6]. This suggests that we can increase the network's robustness without significantly changing its computation by replacing the output of vulnerable features with a linear combination of robust features that have strong correlation with them. To illustrate, we consider a CIFAR-10 [34] classifier and compute the maximal change of its features as a result of the `Square` attack [4]. Figure 3 (left) shows this change for the first ten features (in total there are $m = 256$ features), where feature 4 is one of the top-10 features exhibiting the maximal absolute change. Figure 3 (right) shows the correlation between the first ten features. Features 4 and 8 have a strong negative linear correlation (whereas feature 4 has a lower correlation with the other features). This suggests that replacing the 4th feature (heavily affected by the adversarial attack) with the 8th feature (less affected by the attack) multiplied by a negative constant could mitigate the attack's impact without significantly changing the classifier's computation. Fourth, the synthesis of repair programs does not involve repeatedly running inputs through the full network, but only through the repair program and the classifier part. This reduces the synthesis overhead. Lastly, short repair programs introduce low inference overhead.

Randomization. Our defense benefits from randomization without its costs (time overhead and clean accuracy decrease). The motivation for adding randomization is that it challenges attackers in crafting their adversarial examples: despite the black-box access to the network, a fixed defense is known to be more vulnerable, especially if the attacker can pose an unlimited number of queries [29,82]. Thus, our defense generates a *set* of repair programs and at inference, upon every input, randomly selects a program, adds it between the encoder and classifier, and propagates the input through this defended network. This form of stochastic noise enhances the network's robustness with very low overhead, since it only picks one of K programs. Moreover, due to the synthesis, the generated set of repair programs introduces a minor decrease in clean accuracy.

Program Space. Our program search space is inspired by fully connected layers. A repair program repairs features (i.e., entries of the feature vector) using arithmetic expressions of (usually other) features. The expressions include standard arithmetic operations (e.g., addition, multiplication), generalizing the weighted sum computed by fully connected layers, and piecewise linear functions (minimum and maximum), generalizing the popular, piecewise linear ReLU activation function [2]. Figure 4 presents the grammar of our repair programs. A repair program P is a sequence of assignment instructions. An assignment A assigns a data element or an operation over two data elements to an entry $\mathbf{v}_i$ of the feature vector ($i \in [m]$). A data element d is a real number r or a feature $\mathbf{v}_i$. An operation Op is an arithmetic operation (addition, subtraction, multiplication, or division) or a comparative function (the minimum or maximum of two data elements). The semantics of repair programs is as expected, except that if a division by zero occurs when running a program, the effect of the respective instruction is removed (i.e., the program runs as if this instruction does not exist).

Example. The program: $\boxed{\mathbf{v}_3 = \mathbf{v}_{100} + 3.267;\ \mathbf{v}_{136} = \mathbf{v}_2\ /\ \mathbf{v}_{51};\ \mathbf{v}_{121} = -3.761}$ has been synthesized for the CIFAR-10 [34] Wide-ResNet-34-10 [85] classifier against the L_2 Square attack [4]. It repairs the 3rd, 136th, and 121st entries of the feature vector. The 3rd feature is the sum of the 100th feature and a constant. The 136th feature is the division of the 2nd and 51st features. The 121st feature is set to a constant. All other features are unchanged. Figure 1 shows two more examples.

$$\begin{array}{rrcl}
(Program) & P & ::= & A \mid P_1; P_2 \\
(Assignment) & A & ::= & \mathbf{v}_i = d \mid \mathbf{v}_i = Op\,(d_1, d_2) \\
(Operation) & Op & ::= & add \mid sub \mid mul \mid div \mid max \mid min \\
(Data\ Element) & d & ::= & \mathbf{v}_i \mid r \\
(Variable) & \mathbf{v}_i & \in & \{\mathbf{v}_1, \mathbf{v}_2, \ldots, \mathbf{v}_m\} \\
(Constant) & r & \in & \mathbb{R}
\end{array}$$

Fig. 4. The domain-specific language of our repair programs.

4 DefEnSyn: A Program Synthesizer of Repair Programs

In this section, we present DefEnSyn (**Def**ending by **En**umerative Stochastic **Syn**thesis), our synthesizer for computing a set of repair programs as an adversarial defense. We begin by discussing the challenge and our idea. We then explain how DefEnSyn computes a set of programs. Lastly, we show its algorithm.

Challenge. The goal of DefEnSyn is to compute effective repair programs. Given a network $N = C \circ E$ and a training set $\mathcal{D}_{Tr}$, the effectiveness of a program P is the weighted sum of the clean and robust accuracies of the defended network: $score(P) = Acc_R(C \circ P \circ E, \mathcal{D}_{Tr}) + \lambda \cdot Acc_C(C \circ P \circ E, \mathcal{D}_{Tr})$. The higher the score, the more effective the program. Since our program space consists of a small number of operators and since searching for constants in arithmetic expressions over *given* variables is amenable to efficient search procedures (discrete or numerical optimization), we view the main challenge in our program space as selecting the best features to use as variables. The challenge is intensified in our setting for several reasons. First, the features are not standard input variables but rather functions over the network's inputs and some are correlated (Fig. 3), which complicates the task of identifying the most suitable features (unlike standard variables which are commonly independent). Further, there is a large set of features (several hundred), which makes this task even more complex. Third, there is no monotonicity between a program's score and the scores of programs that subsume it, which would provide a partial order on the program space and could enable pruning. To the best of our knowledge, identifying an effective small subset of input variables out of a large set of variables, which some are correlated, without a partial order over the programs is a new challenge in program synthesis. To illustrate our problem's complexity, assume a limited program space consisting only of feature assignments $\boxed{\mathbf{v}_{i_1} = \mathbf{v}_{j_1}; \ldots; \mathbf{v}_{i_k} = \mathbf{v}_{j_k}}$. Assume that the feature vector dimension is $m = 100$ (in our experiments, $m \in [256, 512]$), and that it takes one millisecond to compute a program's score. It would take about 300 days to enumerate all programs of length three (DefEnSyn looks for programs up to length ten). One may consider, as an alternative, stochastic synthesis which learns a distribution over (full) programs to converge to an effective one (e.g., [21,60]). However, even if we check a single program for every possible left-hand side (i.e., without even searching for effective right-hand side expressions), we would need 10^{13} samples for program length ten, which is infeasible.

Key Idea. Our key idea is to employ stochastic search to learn the best set of features (as opposed to stochastic synthesis, which learns programs). To cope with the exponential number of possibilities, we learn for each feature *separately* how effective it is as a repaired feature and as a repairing feature. That is, we learn two distributions, each over all m features. We consider the dependencies between the features by (1) defining the effectiveness of a feature to be the average scores of repair programs that include it, and (2) considering programs of increasing lengths, from 1 to k. The ascending program lengths enable us to approximate the effectiveness of a set of features in smaller search spaces. For the sake of explanation, ignore the constants in our language, and assume there are $m = 100$ features and that $k = 10$. In programs of length one, the program space is relatively small: $m \cdot (m + 6 \cdot m^2) = 6{,}010{,}000$ (i.e., the number of possibilities for the left-hand side multiplied by the number of possibilities for the right-hand side, consisting of a single variable or one of our six operators with two operands). Even if we consider constants, 10^6 samples provide good coverage of the programs of length one. Although these programs do not capture dependency between features, we can use the sampled programs' scores to identify effective features for the repair. In programs of length two, the search space is larger: $\approx 6{,}010{,}000^2$ – sampling 10^6 programs covers only $10^{-6}\%$ of the program space. However, if our sampling is biased towards features that are more promising for programs of length one, the search explores programs containing them more frequently. Since there is no monotonicity, some of these promising features may be included in programs with higher scores, while others in programs with lower scores. Accordingly, the learned distributions are updated. Generally, for length i, we sample full programs of length i where the variables are chosen by the learned distributions of the previous program lengths and update the distributions based on these programs' scores. While there is no monotonicity, if a feature is effective for multiple program lengths, it may hint that this feature is effective in longer programs. Thus, when we sample programs of length k, we have a good approximation of the better features for the repair. Consequently, even if we sample a very low number of programs (10^6 is less than $10^{-62}\%$ of the programs of length 10), we can identify effective programs.

Computing a Set of Programs. Recall that our defense leverages randomization to enhance robustness and thus DefEnSyn generates a set of repair programs. If the synthesized programs are very similar, the randomization would have little effect. Thus, naively returning the K highest-scored programs would be less effective. Instead, DefEnSyn forces diversity in the set of programs by requiring that each program has a different set of repaired features. Our diversity definition ignores the right-hand side expressions, including the repairing features, since it may lead to programs with identical repaired features, which will be easier for the attacker to exploit. To compute this set of programs, DefEnSyn maintains a dictionary whose keys are sets of repaired features, and the entry for a key is the highest-scored program for this set of repaired features and its score. At the end, DefEnSyn returns the K highest-scored repair programs in this dictionary.

Algorithm 1: DefEnSyn (E, C, $\mathcal{D}_{Tr}$, $\mathcal{A}$)

Input : Encoder E, classifier C, training set $\mathcal{D}_{Tr}$, adversarial attack $\mathcal{A}$.
Output: A set of repair programs $\mathcal{P}$.

1 features $= [E(x_i) \mid (x_i, c_i) \in \mathcal{D}_{Tr}]$
2 adv_features $= [E(\mathcal{A}(C \circ E, x_i, c_i)) \mid (x_i, c_i) \in \mathcal{D}_{Tr}]$
3 class $= [c_i \mid (x_i, c_i) \in \mathcal{D}_{Tr}]$
4 progs $= \{\}$ // The dictionary for the repair programs
5 $\overline{S}_L = \overline{0}; \overline{S}_R = \overline{0}$ // The average scores of LHS/RHS variables
6 $S_L = \overline{0}; S_R = \overline{0}$ // The sum of scores of LHS/RHS variables
7 $Z_L = \overline{0}; Z_R = \overline{0}$ // The number of occurrences of LHS/RHS variables
8 $Dist_{LHS} = \text{softmax}(\overline{S}_L); Dist_{RHS} = \text{softmax}(\overline{S}_R)$ // The distributions
9 prev $= 0$ // The sum of the top-K scores
10 **for** prog_length $= 1$ **to** MAX_NUM_ASSIGNMENTS **do**
11   **for** $i = 1$ **to** MAX_ITER_PER_LENGTH **do**
12         $P = []$ // Init a new program
13   **for** length $= 1$ **to** prog_length **do**
14   P.append(generate_random_assignment($Dist_{LHS}, Dist_{RHS}$))
15   score $= 0$ // Init the program's score
16   **for** $j = 1$ **to** $|\mathcal{D}_{Tr}|$ **do**
17   **if** $argmax(C \circ P(\text{adv\_features}[j])) == \text{class}[j]$ **then** score$+= 1$
18   **if** $argmax(C \circ P(\text{features}[j])) == \text{class}[j]$ **then** score $+= \lambda$
19   lhs_v, rhs_v $=$ extract_vars(P)
20   **for** $i = 1$ **to** m **do**
21   **if** $\mathbf{v}_i \in \text{lhs\_v}$ **then** $S_L[i] += \text{score}; Z_L[i] += 1$
22   **if** $\mathbf{v}_i \in \text{rhs\_v}$ **then** $S_R[i] += \text{score}; Z_R[i] += 1$
23             $\overline{S}_L[i] = S_L[i]/Z_L[i]; \overline{S}_R[i] = S_R[i]/Z_R[i]$
24   **if** lhs_v not in progs.keys() or progs[lhs_v].score $<$ score **then**
25   progs[lhs_v] $= (P, \text{score})$
26     $Dist_{LHS} = \text{softmax}(\overline{S}_L); Dist_{RHS} = \text{softmax}(\overline{S}_R)$
27   curr $= \Sigma_{\text{score} \in \text{topK(progs)}} \text{score}$
28   **if** prog_length > 1 and curr/prev $<$ IMPROVE **then break**
29   prev $=$ curr
30 **return** top-K programs in progs

Synthesis. Algorithm 1 shows the algorithm of DefEnSyn. Its inputs are a network, given by an encoder E and a classifier C, a training set of images and their classes $\mathcal{D}_{Tr}$, and an adversarial attack $\mathcal{A}$. It returns a set of repair programs $\mathcal{P}$ with different sets of repaired features. DefEnSyn begins by computing the feature vectors of the inputs, computing the feature vectors of the adversarial examples, and storing the true classes (Line 1–Line 3). It then initializes the dictionary progs mapping a set of repaired features to their best program and score (Line 4). Then, it initializes the vectors $\overline{S}_L$ and $\overline{S}_R$, which store the average scores of each feature on the left-hand and right-hand sides (Line 5). Next, it initializes vectors that enable the computation of these average scores:

two vectors for storing the sum of scores S_L and S_R and two vectors for storing the number of feature occurrences Z_L and Z_R (Line 6–Line 7). Afterwards, it initializes the probability distributions to uniform distributions by invoking the softmax operation over the score vectors (Line 8). Next, it initializes the variable prev that stores the sum of the scores of the top-K programs, which will be used in an early stopping condition (Line 9). Then, DefEnSyn begins synthesizing programs of increasing length from one to MAX_NUM_ASSIGNMENTS (Line 10). For every program length, DefEnSyn synthesizes MAX_ITER_PER_LENGTH programs (Line 11). A program P is synthesized by sampling its instructions using Algorithm 2, given the probability distributions (Line 12–Line 14). Then, it computes the program's score $Acc_R(N', \mathcal{D}_{Tr}) + \lambda \cdot Acc_C(N', \mathcal{D}_{Tr})$, where $N' = C \circ P \circ E$ (Line 15–Line 18). Note that to compute the score of a given input, DefEnSyn passes its stored feature vector through the program P and then through the classifier C. That is, every input passes through the encoder E only twice (Line 1–Line 2), rather than for *every* candidate repair program. This significantly reduces the synthesis time, since the encoder consists of most of the layers and thus involves many computations. Then, to update the score vectors and progs, DefEnSyn extracts from P the features on the left-hand side and on the right-hand side (Line 19). Accordingly, it updates the average vectors (Line 20–Line 23) and updates progs if P's set of repaired features is new or if its score is better (Line 24–Line 25). After synthesizing all programs for a given length, DefEnSyn updates the probability distributions using the softmax operation (Line 26). Then, it checks whether it can stop early by checking the improvement of this iteration (Line 27–Line 29). This is checked by computing the ratio of the sum of the scores of the current top-K programs and this sum in the previous iteration. If the ratio is below a threshold IMPROVE, DefEnSyn terminates. Otherwise, it updates prev and continues to another iteration. At the end, DefEnSyn returns the top-K programs in progs, to obtain a diverse set of repair programs. We note that, in practice, synthesizing effective repair programs can be achieved with a small training set $\mathcal{D}_{Tr}$ (several hundred suffice). In case the network's original training set is unavailable, it is possible to synthesize a training set, as suggested by [42, 56, 86].

Sampling Instructions. Algorithm 2 generates a random instruction. Its inputs are the probability distributions for selecting the features for the left-hand side and the right-hand side. It first samples the candidates for operands: the feature to repair, the two repairing features, and a real-valued constant (within a predetermined interval $[l, u]$). It then determines the first and second operands (d1 and d2) by uniformly sampling from the two repairing features and the constant. Next, it uniformly samples an operator. Lastly, it uniformly samples the right-hand side over the constant, the first repairing feature, and the arithmetic computation. This form of sampling expresses our preference for simple assignments over arithmetic operations, since they provide simpler repairs.

Algorithm 2: generate_random_assignment($Dist_{LHS}, Dist_{RHS}$)

input : $Dist_{LHS}, Dist_{RHS} \in [0,1]^m$, probability distributions over the features for the left-hand side and the right-hand side.
output: An assignment instruction.

1   lhs_v $\sim Dist_{LHS}(\{\mathbf{v}_1, \ldots, \mathbf{v}_m\})$
2   rhs_v1 $\sim Dist_{RHS}(\{\mathbf{v}_1, \ldots, \mathbf{v}_m\})$
3   rhs_v2 $\sim Dist_{RHS}(\{\mathbf{v}_1, \ldots, \mathbf{v}_m\})$
4   const $\sim$ Uniform($[l, u]$)
5   d1 $\sim$ Uniform($\{$const, rhs_v1, rhs_v2$\}$)
6   d2 $\sim$ Uniform($\{$const, rhs_v1, rhs_v2$\}$)
7   op $\sim$ Uniform($\{$+, -, /, •, max, min$\}$)
8   rhs $\sim$ Uniform($\{$const, rhs_v1, op(d1,d2)$\}$)
9   **return** lhs_v = rhs

A Running Example. Figure 5 shows a running example of DefEnSyn. Its inputs are a network split into an encoder E and a classifier C, a training set of three images, and an attack $\mathcal{A}$. DefEnSyn begins by iterating over the training set and computing for each image its perturbed image using $\mathcal{A}$. It then passes the image and the perturbed image through E and stores the feature vectors in features and adv_features (Fig. 5(a)). In this example, there are three features ($\mathbf{v} \in \mathbb{R}^3$). Then, DefEnSyn enumerates programs by incrementally increasing the programs' lengths, from one to MAX_NUM_ASSIGNMENTS = 10. For each length, it generates MAX_ITER_PER_LENGTH = 10^6 programs. For program length 1, the left-hand side $Dist_{LHS}$ and the right-hand side $Dist_{RHS}$ distributions are uniform: $(1/3, 1/3, 1/3)$. After generating 10^6 programs of length 1, $Dist_{LHS}$ and $Dist_{RHS}$ are updated based on their scores (Fig. 5(b), top left). It then continues to program length 2 and generates 10^6 programs. Figure 5(b) shows the last iteration of prog_length = 2 (i.e., $i = 10^6$). In this iteration, the sampled program is $\boxed{\text{P: } \mathbf{v}_1 = \mathbf{v}_3 + 3.5; \mathbf{v}_2 = -1.7}$. It is constructed by calling Algorithm 2 twice with $Dist_{LHS}$ and $Dist_{RHS}$. DefEnSyn computes P's score by passing each feature vector and each adversarial feature vector through P and then C. For each, it checks whether the predicted class is correct. If so, the score increases by $\lambda = 1$ for a feature vector and by 1 for an adversarial feature vector. In this example, the score is 4. Then, for each LHS feature, $\mathbf{v}_1$ and $\mathbf{v}_2$, it adds 1 to its entry in Z_L and adds the score to its entry in S_L. Similarly, it updates the entry of the RHS feature $\mathbf{v}_3$ in Z_R and S_R. Then, DefEnSyn checks the dictionary progs at the entry of the repaired feature set $\{\mathbf{v}_1, \mathbf{v}_2\}$. In this example, 4 is a better score and thus progs is updated (Fig. 5(b), right). After this iteration, which completes the sampling for length 2, it updates $Dist_{LHS}$ and $Dist_{RHS}$ given S_L, S_R, Z_R, and Z_L. For instance, the probability of selecting $\mathbf{v}_1$ for the left-hand side rises from 0.1 to 0.2, whereas that of $\mathbf{v}_2$ drops from 0.7 to 0.6 (Fig. 5(c), left). DefEnSyn next checks whether the program length 2 yields a sufficient improvement in the cumulative score of the top-K programs. In this example, it does, and so it proceeds to length 3. Figure 5(c) shows its first itera-

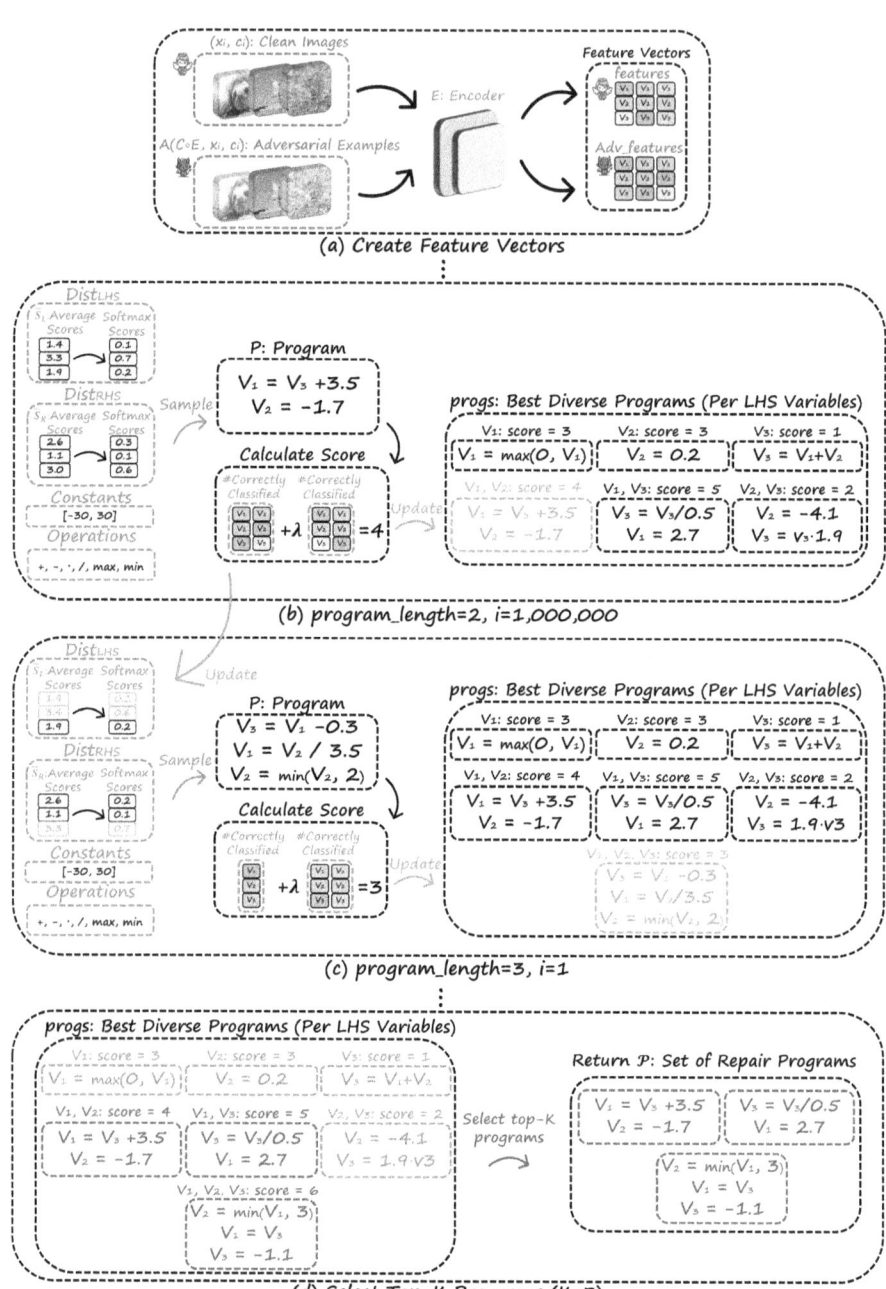

Fig. 5. Illustration of DefEnSyn.

tion, where $P: \mathbf{v}_3 = \mathbf{v}_1 - 0.3; \mathbf{v}_1 = \mathbf{v}_2/3.5; \mathbf{v}_2 = min(\mathbf{v}_2, 2)$ and its score is 3. It updates S_L, S_R, Z_R, Z_L and then updates progs, since P is the first program with left-hand side $\{\mathbf{v}_1, \mathbf{v}_2, \mathbf{v}_3\}$ (Fig. 5(c), right). When DefEnSyn completes, it returns the top-K (in the example, $K = 3$) programs with the highest scores in progs, each repairing a different set of features (Fig. 5(d)).

Limitations. DefEnSyn has two main limitations. First, it is an empirical defense and does not guarantee soundness or completeness, i.e., the synthesized programs may not always ensure robustness, and DefEnSyn may miss programs that could ensure robustness. Second, to keep the synthesis overhead tractable, it does not analyze dependencies among features or relations between the repair programs.

5 Evaluation

In this section, we evaluate DefEnSyn and show: (1) it improves the robustness of networks against state-of-the-art black-box L_∞, L_2, and L_0 adversarial attacks, outperforming state-of-the-art adversarial training and randomization defenses, (2) it only slightly reduces the clean accuracy of the defended networks, with a maximum decrease of -2%, (3) it can synthesize effective repair programs within a few hours, unlike existing adversarial training posing a training overhead of 1-2 days, (4) the inference overhead stemming from incorporating its repair programs into a network is negligible, (5) it effectively counters backdoor attacks, outperforming an existing repair [77], and (6) its synthesis components are important for achieving both high clean accuracy and high robust accuracy.

Implementation and Setup. We implemented DefEnSyn[1] in Python using PyTorch. Our implementation supports GPU parallelization. Experiments ran on an Ubuntu 20.04.2 OS on a dual AMD EPYC 7742 server with 1TB RAM and eight NVIDIA A100 GPUs. Unless otherwise stated, the hyper-parameters are $|\mathcal{D}_{Tr}| = 750$, MAX_NUM_ASSIGNMENTS $= 10$, MAX_ITER_PER_LENGTH $= 10^6$, IMPROVE $= 1.01$, $\lambda = 1$, $K = 30$, and $[l, u] = [-30, 30]$ (Algorithm 2). We evaluate DefEnSyn on two image data sets, CIFAR-10 [34] and ImageNet [19], consisting of $d \times d \times 3$ colored images, where $d = 32$ for CIFAR-10 and $d = 224$ for ImageNet. An image is classified as one of 10 classes for CIFAR-10 and as one of 1,000 classes for ImageNet. We consider different networks, where for each, we consider as the encoder all layers but the last one and as the classifier the last layer. The feature vector dimension m is between 256 and 512. We measure the clean and robust accuracies over inputs in the test sets of CIFAR-10 or ImageNet, which are disjoint from the training sets DefEnSyn uses.

5.1 Defense Against L_∞, L_2, and L_0 Adversarial Example Attacks

We next evaluate DefEnSyn's effectiveness for black-box adversarial example attacks. We compare DefEnSyn with several state-of-the-art defenses to assess

---
[1] https://github.com/TomYuviler/DefEnSyn.

its effectiveness. The selected baselines represent diverse approaches in adversarial defense. The first baseline is the adversarial training proposed by [66], denoted as `AdvTrain`, which is the current state-of-the-art defense against L_∞ adversarial attacks. The second baseline is the diffusion-based randomization defense introduced by [10], denoted as `DiffRandom`. This approach utilizes a pre-trained denoising diffusion model to modify the inference phase without additional training or synthesis and stands as the state-of-the-art randomization-based defense against L_2 adversarial attacks. The third baseline is the randomized smoothing technique developed by [15], which incorporates Gaussian noise during both training and inference phases to defend against L_2 adversarial attacks, denoted as `GausRandom`. The fourth baseline is the randomization-based defense customized for L_0 attacks, proposed by [39], which performs a randomized ablation of image pixels. This defense is the state-of-the-art defense against L_0 attacks and is denoted as `AblaRandom`. For all baselines, we use the authors' code with their default hyper-parameters. In this experiment, we focus on large networks for which no scalable repair defense currently exists against adversarial attacks.

Evaluated Networks. We consider four network classifiers for ImageNet. The first network, denoted as `ConvNeXt`, is Isotropic ConvNeXt-S [48], one of the state-of-the-art models for ImageNet classification using convolutional neural networks, with 22 million parameters. The second network, denoted as `DeiT`, is Data-Efficient Image Transformer [76], which is a Vision Transformer model [20] with an efficient training process and 22 million parameters. The third network, denoted as `ViT`, is a Vision Transformer model [20], with 6 million parameters. The fourth network, denoted as `ResNet18`, is ResNet-18 [28], which is a convolutional neural network with 12 million parameters. The weights for `ConvNeXt` were obtained from the original ConvNeXt repository[2]. The weights of the other networks were obtained from `timm` [78], an open-source collection of classifiers.

Adversarial Example Attacks. We evaluate `DefEnSyn` against the `Square` attack [4], which is the state-of-the-art black-box adversarial example attack (based on a recent benchmark [87]), for the L_∞ and L_2 norms. The perturbation limits are $\epsilon = 4/255$ for the L_∞ norm and $\epsilon = 0.5$ for the L_2 norm. For the L_0 norm, we evaluate `DefEnSyn` against two state-of-the-art black-box attacks: the `Pixle` attack [57] and the `Sparse-RS` attack [16]. For the `Square` and the `Pixle` attacks, we use the implementation in Torchattacks [33], and for the `Sparse-RS` attack, we use the authors' code. For all attacks, we use the default hyper-parameters.

Results. We run the attacks on the defended networks over 10,000 randomly selected images from ImageNet's test set. Table 2 reports the clean accuracy, robust accuracy, training/synthesis overhead, and inference time. The results show that `DefEnSyn`'s repair programs significantly increase the models' robust accuracy against the L_∞ `Square` attack by +70.6%, with a minor decrease in

---
[2] https://github.com/facebookresearch/ConvNeXt.

Table 2. DefEnSyn vs. state-of-the-art adversarial training and randomization defenses.

Classifier (# Params.)	Attack	Defense	Clean acc. (%)	Robust acc. (%)	Training/synthesis overhead (H)	Inference time (S)
ConvNeXt (22M)	Square (L_∞)	No defense	79.72	7.69	-	2.9×10^{-5}
		AdvTrain	66.11	51.97	49.4	2.9×10^{-5}
		DefEnSyn	79.52	77.38	1.0	2.9×10^{-5}
DeiT (22M)	Square (L_∞)	No defense	79.21	4.99	-	3.1×10^{-5}
		AdvTrain	67.23	54.36	45.2	3.1×10^{-5}
		DefEnSyn	78.77	76.44	0.9	3.2×10^{-5}
ResNet18 (12M)	Square (L_2)	No defense	71.36	55.97	-	2.9×10^{-5}
		GausRandom	50.08	49.61	31.8	0.17
		DefEnSyn	71.15	70.96	2.2	2.9×10^{-5}
ViT (6M)	Square (L_2)	No defense	69.33	54.21	-	2.9×10^{-5}
		DiffRandom	62.86	62.86	0	59.75
		DefEnSyn	69.28	69.21	1.5	3.1×10^{-5}
ResNet18 (12M)	Pixle (L_0)	No defense	71.04	10.71	-	2.9×10^{-5}
		AblaRandom	35.13	32.53	26.3	6.89
		DefEnSyn	69.98	40.75	1.5	3.2×10^{-5}
ResNet18 (12M)	Sparse-RS (L_0)	No defense	71.79	6.56	-	2.9×10^{-5}
		AblaRandom	35.73	34.47	26.3	6.89
		DefEnSyn	70.46	65.0	2.1	3.1×10^{-5}

clean accuracy of less than -1%. In contrast, AdvTrain, the state-of-the-art adversarial training, increases the models' robust accuracy by $+46.9\%$ against the L_∞ Square attack, with a decrease in clean accuracy of -12.4%. For the L_2 Square attack, DefEnSyn increases the robust accuracy by $+15.0\%$, with a minor decrease in clean accuracy of -1%. In contrast, the state-of-the-art randomization-based defenses, GausRandom and DiffRandom, on average increase the robust accuracy by $+1.2\%$, with a significant decrease in clean accuracy of -14%. For the L_0 attacks, DefEnSyn increases the robust accuracy by $+44.2\%$, with a minor decrease in the clean accuracy of -1%. In contrast, AblaRandom, the state-of-the-art defense for L_0 attacks, enhances the robust accuracy by $+24.9\%$ and significantly decreases the clean accuracy by -36%. Additionally, on average, DefEnSyn's synthesis overhead is 1.5 hours, while the average training overhead of AdvTrain is 47.3 hours, of GausRandom is 31.8 hours, and of AblaRandom is 26.3 hours. The DiffRandom defense does not require any training, but it assumes access to a pre-trained denoiser, unlike DefEnSyn and the other baselines. The average inference time per image of DefEnSyn and AdvTrain is similar to that of the original (undefended) network: approximately 3×10^{-5} seconds. In contrast, the inference time of the randomization-based techniques is significantly higher and can reach up to one minute in the worst case.

Table 3. DefEnSyn vs. NNRepair on a CIFAR-10 classifier against a backdoor attack.

Classifier (# Params.)	Attack	Defense	Clean acc. (%)	Robust acc. (%)
ConvCIFAR(0.9M)	Backdoor	No defense	72.26	15.89
		NNRepair-I	72.28	16.70
		NNRepair-L	71.65	19.66
		DefEnSyn-30	70.29	34.18
		DefEnSyn-1	70.69	43.06

5.2 Defense Against Backdoor Attacks

Next, we compare DefEnSyn to a repair defense against a backdoor attack [27,46,61]. Backdoor attacks embed malicious behaviors into a classifier during its training phase by introducing a small proportion of poisoned data into the training set, each containing a specific pattern ("trigger"), such as a small white square. The model, once trained with this poisoned data set, behaves normally on standard inputs but produces a specific incorrect output when the trigger is present in the input. We note that, unlike the majority of adversarial example attacks, the perturbation is constant and is not influenced by the original input image.

Setting. We compare to NNRepair [77], which utilizes a constraint solver to make minor adjustments to the weights of specific network layers to mitigate the backdoor attack's effects. We consider two variants of NNRepair: NNRepair-I, which modifies an intermediate layer, and NNRepair-L, which modifies the last layer. We evaluate DefEnSyn and NNRepair on the convolutional classifier for CIFAR-10, ConvCIFAR, evaluated by NNRepair[3]. This network has 890,000 parameters and achieves a test accuracy of 72.26% on clean inputs. However, its accuracy drops significantly to 15.89% for inputs with the trigger of a 3×3 white square positioned at the bottom-right corner of the image. The defense's objective is to enhance the classification accuracy for inputs with the trigger without decreasing the clean accuracy. Since the attack is independent of the input image, introducing randomness into the network as a defense mechanism is unnecessary. Thus, in this experiment, we consider a variant of DefEnSyn that defends using the repair program with the highest score seen during the synthesis process, instead of defending using a set $\mathcal{P}$ of K=30 repair programs. We denote DefEnSyn's defense by DefEnSyn-30 and its variant by DefEnSyn-1.

Results. We run a backdoor attack on all 10,000 images from CIFAR-10's test set. The attack adds the trigger: a 3×3 white square placed at the bottom-right corner. Table 3 shows the results. While both approaches reduce the network's clean accuracy by at most -2%, DefEnSyn significantly enhances the robust accuracy: by $+18.29\%$ when K=30 and by $+27.17\%$ when K=1. In contrast, NNRepair enhances the robust accuracy of the network by at most $+3.77\%$.

---
[3] https://github.com/nnrepair.

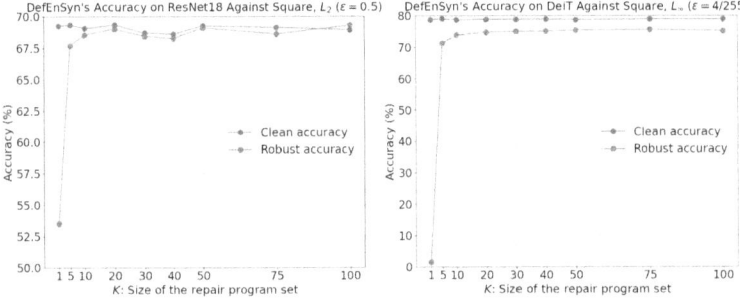

Fig. 6. The impact of different values of K (top-K) on the robust and clean accuracies.

5.3 Ablation Study

Lastly, we provide an ablation study showing the importance of: (1) defending by a *set* of repair programs, (2) synthesizing programs and sampling variables from learned distributions (showing that merely hiding the chosen repair program from the attacker is not enough), and (3) allowing multiple instructions in the repair programs (justifying our large program space). In addition, we analyze the impact that key hyper-parameters have on the performance of DefEnSyn.

Set of Programs. We evaluate the importance of defending using a set of repair programs by running DefEnSyn with different values of K (i.e., the size of the repair program set $\mathcal{P}$). We focus on two ImageNet classifiers, ResNet18 and DeiT, and the Square attack, which runs over 10,000 random images from ImageNet's test set. We defend the first model against the L_2 Square attack and the second model against the L_∞ Square attack. Figure 6 shows the results. It shows that with $K = 1$ (a single repair program), the robust accuracy does not increase. This is expected since the attacker can query the network multiple times (in a black-box fashion) to adapt its attack to the defense. As K increases, the robust accuracy increases and it stabilizes around $K \geq 20$. Results also show that the value of K has a low impact on the clean accuracy.

Synthesis and Learned Distributions. Next, we compare DefEnSyn to two variants: Random and Uniform-DefEnSyn. Random generates a random program upon each input during inference (i.e., it randomly selects a program length (1–10) and generates instructions using Algorithm 2 with uniform probability distributions). Uniform-DefEnSyn runs the synthesis (Algorithm 1) but does not update the variable distributions, i.e., $Dist_{LHS}$ and $Dist_{RHS}$ remain uniform distributions. We compare the three algorithms on ResNet18 for the L_∞ Square attack, with a perturbation limit of $\epsilon = 4/255$, and 10,000 random images from ImageNet's test set. Table 4 presents the results. The results show that Random improves the robust accuracy by $+21\%$, but decreases the clean accuracy significantly by -44.8%. Uniform-DefEnSyn increases the robust accuracy by $+54.6\%$, but

Table 4. Effectiveness of DefEnSyn's synthesis and learned distributions.

Defense	Clean accuracy (%)	Robust accuracy (%)
No defense	71.88	5.21
Random	27.09	26.21
Uniform-DefEnSyn	69.90	59.79
DefEnSyn	70.83	65.00

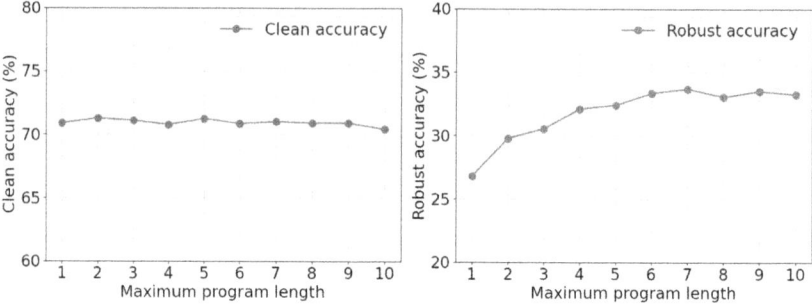

Fig. 7. Clean accuracy (left) and robust accuracy (right) for different program lengths.

decreases the clean accuracy by -2%. DefEnSyn increases the robust accuracy by $+59.8\%$ and decreases the clean accuracy by only -1%. This shows the importance of our synthesis and learned distributions.

Multiple Instructions. Next, we show the importance of DefEnSyn's ability to synthesize repair programs with multiple instructions. We focus on the CIFAR-10 classifier and the backdoor attack (Sect. 5.2), evaluated over all 10,000 images from CIFAR-10's test set. We run DefEnSyn and report the clean and robust accuracies of the top-K (for $K = 30$) repair programs after each iteration of prog_length. Figure 7 shows the results. The results indicate that the synthesis of multiple instructions allows DefEnSyn to increase the robust accuracy.

Training Set Size. We next evaluate the impact of the size of the training set $\mathcal{D}_{Tr}$ by running DefEnSyn with training sets of different sizes. We focus on the widely known Wide-ResNet-28-4 CIFAR-10 classifier [85], with 6 million parameters, and the L_∞ Square attack, with a perturbation limit of $\epsilon = 8/255$. We evaluate DefEnSyn's defense over all 10,000 images from the CIFAR-10 test set. Figure 8 shows the clean and robust accuracies as a function of the training set size. It shows that even a very small training set of 10 images enhances the robust accuracy by almost $+20\%$, with a decrease of -3% in the clean accuracy. With 50 images, the robust accuracy increases by an additional $+2\%$, and the decrease in clean accuracy drops to -1%. The robust and clean accuracies slightly improve with larger training sets and stabilize when the training set size is 250.

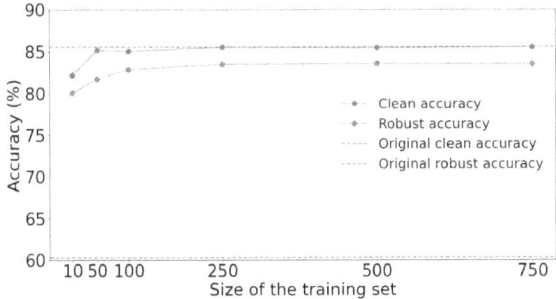

Fig. 8. The impact of the training set size $|\mathcal{D}_{Tr}|$ on the robust and clean accuracies.

Table 5. The impact of the constant interval $[l, u]$ on the robust and clean accuracies.

$[l, u]$	Clean accuracy (%)	Robust accuracy (%)
$[-5, 5]$	85.22	83.55
$[-15, 15]$	85.39	83.57
$[-30, 30]$	85.53	83.55
No defense	85.59	60.30

Constant Interval. We next analyze the impact of the size of the interval $[l, u]$, which defines the range of the constants in the synthesized repair programs (Algorithm 2). We run DefEnSyn with different intervals $[l, u]$ where $[l, u] \in \{[-5, 5], [-15, 15], [-30, 30]\}$. We focus on the Wide-ResNet-28-4 CIFAR-10 classifier and the L_∞ Square attack with a perturbation limit of $\epsilon = 8/255$. We evaluate DefEnSyn's defense over all 10,000 images from the CIFAR-10 test set. Table 5 shows the clean and robust accuracies. The results show that the clean and robust accuracies are very similar, suggesting that further increasing the interval is unnecessary.

Balancing Factor. Lastly, we analyze the impact of the balancing factor λ, which weights the importance of the clean accuracy relative to the robust accuracy in the program's score function. We run DefEnSyn with different values of λ on the Wide-ResNet-28-4 CIFAR-10 classifier and the L_∞ Square attack with a perturbation limit of $\epsilon = 8/255$. We evaluate DefEnSyn's defense over all 10,000 images from the CIFAR-10 test set. Table 6 shows the clean and robust accuracies. The results show the expected trade-off: higher values of λ lead to better clean accuracy at the expense of robust accuracy, while lower values improve robustness but cause a decrease in clean accuracy.

6 Related Work

In this section, we discuss the closest related work.

Table 6. The impact of the balancing factor λ on the robust and clean accuracies.

λ	Clean accuracy (%)	Robust accuracy (%)
0	84.09	83.59
0.5	85.39	83.57
1	85.53	83.55
5	85.58	81.99
100	85.59	77.19
No defense	85.59	60.30

Neural Network Repair. Several repair techniques have been proposed for neural networks. NNRepair enhances robustness by modifying the weights in a single layer using constraint solvers [77]. MODE performs model state differential analysis to pinpoint network parameters responsible for undesired behaviors, followed by network retraining with selected inputs [49]. REGLO applies a verification-guided algorithm to detect and rectify violations of the global robustness property by adjusting the weights in the network's last layer [24]. CARE repairs multiple layers via causality-based fault localization, targeting weight adjustments in neurons linked to undesired behavior [72]. Several works identify the minimal weight modifications necessary to modify the network's behavior [25,59,69]. Arachne repairs weights via Differential Evolution [67]. APRNN provides a provable repair [74], looking for a repair that is correct for all inputs within a convex bounded polytope. Several works repair via architectural modifications, such as integrating a compact patch network [23], adding a self-correcting layer [38], and decoupling the network into separate activation and value networks [70].

Randomization Defenses. Like DefEnSyn, several defenses incorporate randomness into the classification process. One defense modifies the classification by randomly selecting multiple samples and then predicting the class based on a majority vote among these samples [9]. Others rely on randomized smoothing, wherein Gaussian noise layers are added to the model, which is then trained with these layers [15,37,45]. During inference, multiple copies of the original input are generated, and the prediction relies on the average of the predictions. Another approach modifies only the inference procedure [10,62]. Given a (pre-trained) classifier, they create Gaussian noise-corrupted copies of the input image, denoise them, and then base the classification on the majority vote across all denoised images. Others use a diffusion model to introduce random noise into an adversarial example and then employ a reverse denoising process to purify the image before classification [53]. A different approach defends against L_0 adversarial example attacks using randomized ablation of pixels [39].

Program Synthesis. Like DefEnSyn, several works guide a synthesizer by learning. Probe introduces just-in-time learning, which guides the search by leveraging partial solutions (programs) and probabilistic models [7]. Counterexample

Guided Inductive Synthesis (CEGIS) prunes the search space using counterexamples [68]. Divide-and-conquer independently enumerates smaller expressions that are suitable for specific subsets of inputs [3]. Large language models (LLMs) have been shown to be effective in directing the synthesizer through an iterative feedback loop between the LLM and the synthesizer [43]. Some works employ Bayesian methods to adjust the sampling distributions for programs [21,60], while others rely on Markov Chain Monte Carlo to synthesize programs [63].

7 Conclusion

We present DefEnSyn, a synthesizer of repair programs for enhancing the robustness of neural network classifiers. A repair program repairs a few neurons using other neurons. DefEnSyn performs a stochastic search to identify effective neurons for the repair. To scale, it samples programs of increasing lengths. DefEnSyn synthesizes a set of diverse repair programs so that, at inference, a program can be randomly selected for the repair. We evaluate DefEnSyn on large networks for ImageNet and CIFAR-10 against black-box adversarial example attacks. The evaluation shows that DefEnSyn's repair programs enhance the networks' robust accuracy on average by $+71\%$ against L_∞ attacks, by $+15\%$ against L_2 attacks, by $+44\%$ against L_0 attacks, and by $+27\%$ against backdoor attacks. DefEnSyn decreases the clean accuracy by approximately -1%. These accuracies exceed those of state-of-the-art customized defenses relying on adversarial training, randomization, or repair. DefEnSyn's synthesis overhead is a few hours, and its inference overhead is negligible.

References

1. Addepalli, S., Jain, S., Sriramanan, G., Babu, R.V.: Scaling adversarial training to large perturbation bounds. In: ECCV (2022). https://doi.org/10.1007/978-3-031-20065-6_18
2. Agarap, A.F.: Deep learning using rectified linear units (relu). CoRR abs/1803.08375 (2018). http://arxiv.org/abs/1803.08375
3. Alur, R., Radhakrishna, A., Udupa, A.: Scaling enumerative program synthesis via divide and conquer. In: TACAS (2017). https://doi.org/10.1007/978-3-662-54577-5_18
4. Andriushchenko, M., Croce, F., Flammarion, N., Hein, M.: Square attack: a query-efficient black-box adversarial attack via random search. In: ECCV (2020). https://doi.org/10.1007/978-3-030-58592-1_29
5. Ayinde, B.O., Inanc, T., Zurada, J.M.: On correlation of features extracted by deep neural networks. In: IJCNN (2019). https://doi.org/10.1109/IJCNN.2019.8852296
6. Ayinde, B.O., Inanc, T., Zurada, J.M.: Redundant feature pruning for accelerated inference in deep neural networks. Neural Netw. **118** (2019). https://doi.org/10.1016/j.neunet.2019.04.021
7. Barke, S., Peleg, H., Polikarpova, N.: Just-in-time learning for bottom-up enumerative synthesis. In: OOPSLA (2020). https://doi.org/10.1145/3428295
8. Bornholt, J., Torlak, E., Grossman, D., Ceze, L.: Optimizing synthesis with metasketches. In: POPL (2016). https://doi.org/10.1145/2837614.2837666

9. Cao, X., Gong, N.Z.: Mitigating evasion attacks to deep neural networks via region-based classification. In: ACSAC (2017). https://doi.org/10.1145/3134600.3134606
10. Carlini, N., Tramèr, F., Dvijotham, K.D., Rice, L., Sun, M., Kolter, J.Z.: (certified!!) adversarial robustness for free! In: ICLR (2023). https://openreview.net/pdf?id=JLg5aHHv7j
11. Carlini, N., Wagner, D.A.: Towards evaluating the robustness of neural networks. In: IEEE Symposium on Security and Privacy, SP (2017). https://doi.org/10.1109/SP.2017.49
12. Chen, P., Sharma, Y., Zhang, H., Yi, J., Hsieh, C.: EAD: elastic-net attacks to deep neural networks via adversarial examples. In: AAAI (2018). https://www.aaai.org/ocs/index.php/AAAI/AAAI18/paper/view/16893
13. Chen, Q., Lamoreaux, A., Wang, X., Durrett, G., Bastani, O., Dillig, I.: Web question answering with neurosymbolic program synthesis. In: PLDI (2021). https://doi.org/10.1145/3453483.3454047
14. Chen, S., Carlini, N., Wagner, D.A.: Stateful detection of black-box adversarial attacks. CoRR abs/1907.05587 (2019). http://arxiv.org/abs/1907.05587
15. Cohen, J., Rosenfeld, E., Kolter, J.Z.: Certified adversarial robustness via randomized smoothing. In: ICML (2019). http://proceedings.mlr.press/v97/cohen19c.html
16. Croce, F., Andriushchenko, M., Singh, N.D., Flammarion, N., Hein, M.: Sparse-RS: a versatile framework for query-efficient sparse black-box adversarial attacks. In: AAAI (2022). https://doi.org/10.1609/aaai.v36i6.20595
17. Croce, F., Hein, M.: Mind the box: l_1-APGD for sparse adversarial attacks on image classifiers. In: ICML (2021). http://proceedings.mlr.press/v139/croce21a.html
18. Croce, F., Hein, M.: Adversarial robustness against multiple and single l_p-threat models via quick fine-tuning of robust classifiers. In: ICML (2022). https://proceedings.mlr.press/v162/croce22b.html
19. Deng, J., Dong, W., Socher, R., Li, L.J., Li, K., Fei-Fei, L.: Imagenet: a large-scale hierarchical image database. In: CVPR (2009). https://doi.org/10.1109/CVPR.2009.5206848
20. Dosovitskiy, A., et al.: An image is worth 16x16 words: transformers for image recognition at scale. In: ICLR (2021). https://openreview.net/forum?id=YicbFdNTTy
21. Ellis, K., Solar-Lezama, A., Tenenbaum, J.: Sampling for Bayesian program learning. In: NIPS (2016). https://proceedings.neurips.cc/paper/2016/hash/afd4836712c5e77550897e25711e1d96-Abstract.html
22. Fiscutean, A.: How the EU AI act regulates artificial intelligence: what it means for cybersecurity (2023). https://www.csoonline.com/article/1258597
23. Fu, F., Li, W.: Sound and complete neural network repair with minimality and locality guarantees. In: ICLR (2022). https://openreview.net/forum?id=xS8AMYiEav3
24. Fu, F., et al.: REGLO: provable neural network repair for global robustness properties. In: NeurIPS Workshop (2022). https://openreview.net/forum?id=FRTXdodwsoA
25. Goldberger, B., Katz, G., Adi, Y., Keshet, J.: Minimal modifications of deep neural networks using verification. In: LPAR (2020). https://doi.org/10.29007/699q
26. Goodfellow, I.J., Shlens, J., Szegedy, C.: Explaining and harnessing adversarial examples. In: ICLR (2015). http://arxiv.org/abs/1412.6572
27. Gu, T., Dolan-Gavitt, B., Garg, S.: Badnets: identifying vulnerabilities in the machine learning model supply chain. CoRR abs/1708.06733 (2017). http://arxiv.org/abs/1708.06733

28. He, K., Zhang, X., Ren, S., Sun, J.: Deep residual learning for image recognition. In: CVPR (2016). https://doi.org/10.1109/CVPR.2016.90
29. He, Z., Rakin, A.S., Fan, D.: Parametric noise injection: trainable randomness to improve deep neural network robustness against adversarial attack. In: CVPR (2019). http://openaccess.thecvf.com/content_CVPR_2019/html/He_Parametric_Noise_Injection_Trainable_Randomness_to_Improve_Deep_Neural_Network_CVPR_2019_paper.html
30. Hung-Quang, N., Lao, Y., Pham, T., Wong, K., Doan, K.D.: Understanding the robustness of randomized feature defense against query-based adversarial attacks. In ICLR (2024). https://openreview.net/forum?id=vZ6r9GMT1n
31. Jiang, E., Singh, G.: RAMP: boosting adversarial robustness against multiple l_p perturbations for universal robustness. In: NeurIPS (2024). http://papers.nips.cc/paper_files/paper/2024/hash/4d5ce4a7ebf588834db127965cdb5ccb-Abstract-Conference.html
32. Jiang, E., Singh, G.: Towards universal certified robustness with multi-norm training. CoRR abs/2410.03000 (2024). https://doi.org/10.48550/arXiv.2410.03000
33. Kim, H.: Torchattacks: a pytorch repository for adversarial attacks. arXiv preprint arXiv:2010.01950 (2020). https://github.com/Harry24k/adversarial-attacks-pytorch
34. Krizhevsky, A.: Learning multiple layers of features from tiny images (2009). https://www.cs.toronto.edu/~kriz/learning-features-2009-TR.pdf
35. Krizhevsky, A., Sutskever, I., Hinton, G.E.: Imagenet classification with deep convolutional neural networks. In: NeurIPS (2012). https://proceedings.neurips.cc/paper/2012/hash/c399862d3b9d6b76c8436e924a68c45b-Abstract.html
36. Kurakin, A., Goodfellow, I.J., Bengio, S.: Adversarial examples in the physical world. In: ICLR (2017). https://openreview.net/forum?id=HJGU3Rodl
37. Lécuyer, M., Atlidakis, V., Geambasu, R., Hsu, D., Jana, S.: Certified robustness to adversarial examples with differential privacy. In: IEEE Symposium on Security and Privacy (SP) (2019). https://doi.org/10.1109/SP.2019.00044
38. Leino, K., Fromherz, A., Mangal, R., Fredrikson, M., Parno, B., Pasareanu, C.S.: Self-correcting neural networks for safe classification. In: CAV Workshops (2022). https://doi.org/10.1007/978-3-031-21222-2_7
39. Levine, A., Feizi, S.: Robustness certificates for sparse adversarial attacks by randomized ablation. In: AAAI (2020). https://ojs.aaai.org/index.php/AAAI/article/view/5888
40. Li, H., Shan, S., Wenger, E., Zhang, J., Zheng, H., Zhao, B.Y.: Blacklight: scalable defense for neural networks against query-based black-box attacks. In: USENIX (2022). https://www.usenix.org/conference/usenixsecurity22/presentation/li-huiying
41. Li, J., Guo, Y., Lao, S., Wu, Y., Bai, L., Wei, Y.: Towards a high robust neural network via feature matching. Int. J. Multim. Inf. Retr. (2021). https://doi.org/10.1007/s13735-021-00219-0
42. Li, Q., Guo, Y., Chen, H.: Practical no-box adversarial attacks against DNNs. In: NeurIPS (2020). https://proceedings.neurips.cc/paper/2020/hash/96e07156db854ca7b00b5df21716b0c6-Abstract.html
43. Li, Y., Parsert, J., Polgreen, E.: Guiding enumerative program synthesis with large language models. CoRR abs/2403.03997 (2024). http://arxiv.org/abs/2403.03997
44. Lin, Z., Memisevic, R., Konda, K.R.: How far can we go without convolution: improving fully-connected networks. CoRR abs/1511.02580 (2015). http://arxiv.org/abs/1511.02580

45. Liu, X., Cheng, M., Zhang, H., Hsieh, C.: Towards robust neural networks via random self-ensemble. In: ECCV (2018). https://doi.org/10.1007/978-3-030-01234-2_23
46. Liu, Y., et al.: Trojaning attack on neural networks. In: NDSS (2018). https://www.ndss-symposium.org/wp-content/uploads/2018/02/ndss2018_03A-5_Liu_paper.pdf
47. Liu, Z., et al.: Swin transformer: hierarchical vision transformer using shifted windows. In: ICCV (2021). https://doi.org/10.1109/ICCV48922.2021.00986
48. Liu, Z., Mao, H., Wu, C., Feichtenhofer, C., Darrell, T., Xie, S.: A convnet for the 2020s. In: CVPR (2022). https://doi.org/10.1109/CVPR52688.2022.01167
49. Ma, S., Liu, Y., Lee, W., Zhang, X., Grama, A.: MODE: automated neural network model debugging via state differential analysis and input selection. In: ESEC/SIGSOFT (2018). https://doi.org/10.1145/3236024.3236082
50. Madry, A., Makelov, A., Schmidt, L., Tsipras, D., Vladu, A.: Towards deep learning models resistant to adversarial attacks. In: ICLR (2018). https://openreview.net/forum?id=rJzIBfZAb
51. Mell, S., Zdancewic, S., Bastani, O.: Optimal program synthesis via abstract interpretation. In: POPL (2024). https://doi.org/10.1145/3632858
52. Nayak, G.K., Khatri, I., Rawal, R., Chakraborty, A.: Data-free defense of black box models against adversarial attacks. In: CVPR Workshops (2024). https://doi.org/10.1109/CVPRW63382.2024.00030
53. Nie, W., Guo, B., Huang, Y., Xiao, C., Vahdat, A., Anandkumar, A.: Diffusion models for adversarial purification. In: ICML (2022). https://proceedings.mlr.press/v162/nie22a.html
54. NSA Media Relations: Guidance for securing AI issued by NSA, NCSC-UK, CISA, and partners (2023). https://www.nsa.gov/Press-Room/Press-Releases-Statements/Press-Release-View/Article/3598020/guidance-for-securing-ai-issued-by-nsa-ncsc-uk-cisa-and-partners/. Accessed 18 Mar 2024
55. Pan, R., Rajan, H.: On decomposing a deep neural network into modules. In: Devanbu, P., Cohen, M.B., Zimmermann, T. (eds.) ESEC/FSE, pp. 889–900. ACM (2020)
56. Papernot, N., McDaniel, P.D., Goodfellow, I.J., Jha, S., Celik, Z.B., Swami, A.: Practical black-box attacks against machine learning. In: AsiaCCS (2017). https://doi.org/10.1145/3052973.3053009
57. Pomponi, J., Scardapane, S., Uncini, A.: Pixle: a fast and effective black-box attack based on rearranging pixels. In: IJCNN (2022). https://doi.org/10.1109/IJCNN55064.2022.9892966
58. Qi, B., Sun, H., Gao, X., Zhang, H.: Patching weak convolutional neural network models through modularization and composition. In: ASE (2022). https://doi.org/10.1145/3551349.3561153
59. Refaeli, I., Katz, G.: Minimal multi-layer modifications of deep neural networks. In: CAV Workshops (2022). https://doi.org/10.1007/978-3-031-21222-2
60. Saad, F.A., Cusumano-Towner, M.F., Schaechtle, U., Rinard, M.C., Mansinghka, V.K.: Bayesian synthesis of probabilistic programs for automatic data modeling. In: POPL (2019). https://doi.org/10.1145/3290350
61. Saha, A., Subramanya, A., Pirsiavash, H.: Hidden trigger backdoor attacks. In: AAAI (2020). https://doi.org/10.1609/aaai.v34i07.6871
62. Salman, H., Sun, M., Yang, G., Kapoor, A., Kolter, J.Z.: Denoised smoothing: a provable defense for pretrained classifiers. In: NeurIPS (2020). https://proceedings.neurips.cc/paper/2020/hash/f9fd2624beefbc7808e4e405d73f57ab-Abstract.html

63. Schkufza, E., Sharma, R., Aiken, A.: Stochastic program optimization. Commun. ACM (2016). https://doi.org/10.1145/2863701
64. Shafahi, A., et al.: Adversarial training for free! In: NeurIPS (2019). https://proceedings.neurips.cc/paper/2019/hash/7503cfacd12053d309b6bed5c89de212-Abstract.html
65. Simonyan, K., Zisserman, A.: Very deep convolutional networks for large-scale image recognition. In: ICLR (2015). http://arxiv.org/abs/1409.1556
66. Singh, N.D., Croce, F., Hein, M.: Revisiting adversarial training for imagenet: architectures, training and generalization across threat models. In: NeurIPS (2023). http://papers.nips.cc/paper_files/paper/2023/hash/2d3b007613940def7a5ec9d6d635937b-Abstract-Conference.html
67. Sohn, J., Kang, S., Yoo, S.: Arachne: search-based repair of deep neural networks. ACM Trans. Softw. Eng. Methodol. (2023). https://doi.org/10.1145/3563210
68. Solar-Lezama, A.: Program synthesis by sketching. University of California, Berkeley (2008)
69. Sotoudeh, M., Thakur, A.V.: Correcting deep neural networks with small, generalizing patches. In: NeurIPS Workshop (2019). https://thakur.cs.ucdavis.edu/assets/pubs/SRDM2019.pdf
70. Sotoudeh, M., Thakur, A.V.: Provable repair of deep neural networks. In: PLDI (2021). https://doi.org/10.1145/3453483.3454064
71. Su, J., Vargas, D.V., Sakurai, K.: One pixel attack for fooling deep neural networks. CoRR abs/1710.08864 (2017). http://arxiv.org/abs/1710.08864
72. Sun, B., Sun, J., Pham, L.H., Shi, T.: Causality-based neural network repair. In: ICSE (2022). https://doi.org/10.1145/3510003.3510080
73. Szegedy, C., Zaremba, W., Sutskever, I., Bruna, J., Erhan, D., Goodfellow, I.J., Fergus, R.: Intriguing properties of neural networks. In: ICLR (2014). http://arxiv.org/abs/1312.6199
74. Tao, Z., Nawas, S., Mitchell, J., Thakur, A.V.: Architecture-preserving provable repair of deep neural networks. In: PLDI (2023). https://doi.org/10.1145/3591238
75. Tolstikhin, I.O., et al.: MLP-mixer: an all-MLP architecture for vision. In: NeurIPS (2021). https://proceedings.neurips.cc/paper/2021/hash/cba0a4ee5ccd02fda0fe3f9a3e7b89fe-Abstract.html
76. Touvron, H., Cord, M., Douze, M., Massa, F., Sablayrolles, A., Jégou, H.: Training data-efficient image transformers & distillation through attention. In: ICML (2021). http://proceedings.mlr.press/v139/touvron21a.html
77. Usman, M., Gopinath, D., Sun, Y., Noller, Y., Pasareanu, C.S.: Nnrepair: constraint-based repair of neural network classifiers. In: CAV (2021). https://doi.org/10.1007/978-3-030-81685-8_1
78. Wightman, R.: Pytorch image models (2019). https://doi.org/10.5281/zenodo.4414861. https://github.com/rwightman/pytorch-image-models
79. Wong, E., Rice, L., Kolter, J.Z.: Fast is better than free: revisiting adversarial training. In: ICLR (2020). https://openreview.net/forum?id=BJx040EFvH
80. Wu, Y., Liu, F., Simon-Gabriel, C., Chrysos, G., Cevher, V.: Robust NAS under adversarial training: benchmark, theory, and beyond. In: ICLR (2024). https://openreview.net/forum?id=cdUpf6t6LZ
81. Xiao, C., Zhong, P., Zheng, C.: Enhancing adversarial defense by k-winners-take-all. In: ICLR (2020). https://openreview.net/forum?id=Skgvy64tvr
82. Xie, C., Wang, J., Zhang, Z., Ren, Z., Yuille, A.L.: Mitigating adversarial effects through randomization. In: ICLR (2018). https://openreview.net/forum?id=Sk9yuql0Z

83. Xie, C., Wu, Y., van der Maaten, L., Yuille, A.L., He, K.: Feature denoising for improving adversarial robustness. In: CVPR (2019). http://openaccess.thecvf.com/content_CVPR_2019/html/Xie_Feature_Denoising_for_Improving_Adversarial_Robustness_CVPR_2019_paper.html
84. Yuan, X., He, P., Zhu, Q., Li, X.: Adversarial examples: attacks and defenses for deep learning. IEEE Trans. Neural Netw. Learn. Syst. (2019). https://doi.org/10.1109/TNNLS.2018.2886017
85. Zagoruyko, S., Komodakis, N.: Wide residual networks. In: BMVC (2016). https://bmva-archive.org.uk/bmvc/2016/papers/paper087/index.html
86. Zhang, Q., Zhang, C., Li, C., Song, J., Gao, L., Shen, H.T.: Practical no-box adversarial attacks with training-free hybrid image transformation. CoRR abs/2203.04607 (2022). https://doi.org/10.48550/arXiv.2203.04607
87. Zheng, M., Yan, X., Zhu, Z., Chen, H., Wu, B.: Blackboxbench: a comprehensive benchmark of black-box adversarial attacks. CoRR abs/2312.16979 (2023). https://doi.org/10.48550/arXiv.2312.16979

Relating Distances and Abstractions
An Abstract Interpretation Perspective

Marco Campion[1]($^{\boxtimes}$), Isabella Mastroeni[2], and Caterina Urban[1]

[1] Inria and ENS, PSL, Paris, France
{marco.campion,caterina.urban}@inria.fr
[2] Department of Computer Science, University of Verona, Verona, Italy
isabella.mastroeni@univr.it

Abstract. We establish a formal relation between quantitative and semantic approximations—formalized by pre-metrics and upper closure operators (ucos), respectively—by means of Galois connections. This connection reveals that it is far from trivial for a pre-metric to uniquely identify a uco, highlighting the structural constraints and, more generally, the distinct identity inherent to semantic approximations.

Building on this foundation, we introduce a general composition of semantic and quantitative approximations. This allows us to define a new confidentiality property, called Partial Abstract Non-Interference, that measures bounded variations in program behavior over abstract properties of data. We then relate this property to Partial Completeness in abstract interpretation, revealing a deeper connection between static analysis precision and security guarantees.

Keywords: Distances · Abstractions · Abstract Interpretation · Partial Abstract Non-Interference · Partial Completeness

1 Introduction

Understanding the behavior of programs is a fundamental challenge in computer science. Due to inherent undecidability, some degree of approximation is unavoidable, both in how we observe program behavior and in how we formalize the properties we aim to analyze. Broadly speaking, we can distinguish between two main paradigms of approximation: semantic and quantitative. *Semantic* approximations capture qualitative properties of data and computations, often abstracting over irrelevant details to retain logical or behavioral correctness. *Quantitative* approximations, on the other hand, measure similarity or closeness between elements using metrics or more relaxed forms of distances.

These two perspectives can be pursued *independently*, or *combined* for a unified approach to approximation. Semantic approximations are at the heart of abstract interpretation [14,16], a foundational framework for soundly approximating program behavior through *abstractions*. They are also intrinsic to properties such as Abstract Non-Interference [24], a relaxation of classic

Non-Interference [27] that captures variations in the semantic properties that may influence program computations. In contrast, quantitative approximations underpin distance-based properties, useful when reasoning about approximations in a meaningful distance space. Notable examples include Approximate Non-Interference [18], which permits some exactly quantified leakage of information, as well as Program Continuity and Robustness [9–11], which ensure that arbitrarily small changes to inputs only cause arbitrarily small changes to program outputs, and Differential Privacy [20], which formalizes privacy loss as a bounded statistical difference in output distributions. In some cases, semantic and quantitative perspectives are *combined* to define a more general approximation approach. For instance, Partial Completeness in abstract interpretation [5] leverages pre-metrics compatible with the underlying domain structure to quantify precision loss in program analysis [8]. Similarly, Abstract Robustness [25], characterizes the robustness of deep neural networks against adversarial attacks by combining a distance over inputs with an abstraction of the outputs.

In general, semantic and quantitative approaches offer distinct perspectives on the problem of approximation, each relying on different formal frameworks to capture its nuances. In this work, we aim to explore whether and how these two methodologies relate:

Are they fundamentally distinct tools for approximations, or can one be systematically derived from the other?

Can we formalize a way to combine their respective advantages into a unifying approximation framework?

Our Contribution. We explore a formal correspondence between semantic approximations, modeled here as *upper closure operators* (ucos), and quantitative approximations, modeled here as *pre-metrics*. We show how semantic approximations can be derived from distance functions (and vice versa), through a process of abstractions using Galois connections. On the one hand, this connection confirms that ucos can be viewed as particular instances of pre-metrics— specifically, those that assign a distance of zero to elements sharing the same abstraction. On the other hand, however, it is far from trivial for a pre-metric to uniquely identify a uco, highlighting the structural constraints and, more generally, the distinct identity inherent to semantic approximations.

Building on this foundation, we formalize a *composition* operator of pre-metrics that first selects the domain of comparison and then measures distances within this selected domain, thereby enabling a form of layered abstraction. Such a composition, when involving a distance characterizing a semantic abstraction and a distance characterizing a quantitative abstraction, defines a new form of approximation, called *general approximation*, combining semantic and quantitative approaches while keeping the two types of approximations distinct.

This approach allows us to define a new confidentiality property, called *Partial Abstract Non-Interference*, that generalizes both Abstract Non-Interference and Approximate Non-Interference in a unifying view by combining both semantic and quantitative approximations. Partial Abstract Non-Interference allows bounded variations in the abstract program behavior over inputs sharing a similar abstract property. We then relate this property to Partial Completeness in abstract interpretation, revealing a deeper connection between bounded (im)precision in abstract interpretation and security guarantees.

Structure of the Paper. In Sect. 2 we formalize semantic approximations via upper closure operators, and quantitative approximations by pre-metrics, recalling their respective definitions from the literature. Section 3 establishes a formal relation between the two forms of approximations. This consists in an abstraction process—formalized by a series of Galois connections—from the domain of pre-metrics to the domain of ucos by passing through equivalence relations. Section 4 formally defines a possible way to combine pre-metrics, characterizing quantitative approximations, with distances characterizing semantic abstractions. This will form a general approximation framework which will be used in Sect. 6 to define a new confidentiality property based on the notion of Abstract Non-Interference, called Partial Abstract Non-Interference that quantifies semantic variations in the output domain. This newly defined property is then compared with the Partial Completeness property to establish a relation between them. A background on the Partial Completeness notion in abstract interpretation, and the Abstract Non-Interference property, is provided in Sect. 5.

2 Abstractions and Distances

In many domains, approximations are a fundamental tool for simplifying reasoning while retaining essential properties. Broadly speaking, we can distinguish between *semantic* (or *qualitative*) approximations, and *quantitative* approximations. Here we formalize semantic approximations via *upper closure operators* and quantitative approximations by means of *pre-metrics*.

2.1 Semantic Approximations via Upper Closure Operators

Qualitative or semantic approximations preserve certain *semantic properties* of the approximated data. Semantic approximations are at the hearth of *abstract interpretation* [14,16], which offers a general methodology for approximating computations by evaluating functions (e.g., program semantics) over an abstract domain A instead of the concrete domain C. This approach is especially valuable when exact analysis is computationally infeasible or undecidable, trading precision for decidability. In this setting, A is referred to as an *abstraction* of C whenever there is a *Galois Connection* (GC), or a *Galois Insertion* (GI), between the two domains. More formally, given a partially ordered set (poset, for short) $\langle C, \leq_C \rangle$, called the concrete domain, and a poset $\langle A, \leq_A \rangle$, called the abstract domain, a GC is denoted by $\langle C, \leq_C \rangle \xleftrightarrow[\alpha]{\gamma} \langle A, \leq_A \rangle$ where $\alpha \colon C \to A$ is the (monotone) abstraction function, sometimes referred to as the lower adjoint, and $\gamma\colon \mathtt{A} \to \mathtt{C}$ is the (monotone) concretization function, also referred to as the upper adjoint, both satisfying the following condition $\forall a \in \mathtt{A}$ and $\forall c \in \mathtt{C}$:

$$\alpha(c) \leq_{\mathtt{A}} a \Leftrightarrow c \leq_{\mathtt{C}} \gamma(a)$$

A GC is a GI, denoted by $\langle \mathtt{C}, \leq_{\mathtt{C}} \rangle \xrightarrow[\alpha]{\gamma} \langle \mathtt{A}, \leq_{\mathtt{A}} \rangle$, when $\alpha \circ \gamma = \iota$, namely when their composition is the identity function ($\iota \stackrel{\text{def}}{=} \lambda x.\, x$). An essential property of a GC is that an upper/lower adjoint of a GC uniquely determines the other: $\alpha(c)$ is the least element a with $c \leq_{\mathtt{C}} \gamma(a)$, and $\gamma(a)$ is the largest element c with $\alpha(c) \leq_{\mathtt{A}} a$. In particular, when both $\langle \mathtt{C}, \leq_{\mathtt{C}} \rangle$ and $\langle \mathtt{A}, \leq_{\mathtt{A}} \rangle$ are complete lattices, respectively $\langle \mathtt{C}, \leq_{\mathtt{C}}, \vee_{\mathtt{C}}, \wedge_{\mathtt{C}}, \top_{\mathtt{C}}, \bot_{\mathtt{C}} \rangle$ and $\langle \mathtt{A}, \leq_{\mathtt{A}}, \vee_{\mathtt{A}}, \wedge_{\mathtt{A}}, \top_{\mathtt{A}}, \bot_{\mathtt{A}} \rangle$, then $\alpha(c) = \wedge_{\mathtt{A}} \{a \in \mathtt{A} \mid c \leq_{\mathtt{C}} \gamma(a)\}$ and $\gamma(a) = \vee_{\mathtt{C}} \{c \in \mathtt{C} \mid \alpha(c) \leq_{\mathtt{A}} a\}$. It turns out that α is a complete join-morphism (sometimes also referred to as an additive function), namely for all $S \subseteq \mathtt{C}$: $\alpha(\vee_{\mathtt{C}} S) = \vee_{\mathtt{A}} \{\alpha(c) \mid c \in S\}$, dually γ is a complete meet-morphism (co-additive function), namely for all $S \in \mathtt{A}$: $\gamma(\wedge_{\mathtt{A}} S) = \wedge_{\mathtt{A}} \{\gamma(a) \mid a \in S\}$.

Galois connections/insertions can be equivalently formulated in terms of upper closure operators [16] (ucos or closures, for short).

Definition 1 (Upper Closure Operator). *An upper closure operator on a poset $\langle \mathtt{C}, \leq_{\mathtt{C}} \rangle$ is a function $\rho\colon \mathtt{C} \to \mathtt{C}$ with the following properties $\forall c, c' \in \mathtt{C}$:*

(i) $c \leq_{\mathtt{C}} c' \Rightarrow \rho(c) \leq_{\mathtt{C}} \rho(c')$; *(monotonicity)*
(ii) $c \leq_{\mathtt{C}} \rho(c)$; *(extensivity)*
(iii) $\rho(\rho(c)) = \rho(c)$. *(idempotence)*

Ucos are uniquely determined by the set of their fixpoints: $\rho(C) = \{c \in \mathtt{C} \mid \rho(c) = c\}$. For instance, the composition $\gamma \circ \alpha$ is a uco of $\mathtt{C}$. In the following, the set of all upper closure operators on a poset $\mathtt{C}$ is denoted by $Uco(\mathtt{C})$.

Example 1 (Sign and Parity Abstractions). The closure $\mathsf{Sign} \in Uco(\wp(\mathbb{Z}))$ abstracts a set of integers by discarding all information except the sign of its values. It corresponds to the identity function when applied to the empty set or in case the set contains the value zero only. The closure is defined by the set of fixpoints:

$$\mathsf{Sign}(\wp(\mathbb{Z})) \stackrel{\text{def}}{=} \{\varnothing, \{0\}, \{z \in \mathbb{Z} \mid z \leq 0\}, \{z \in \mathbb{Z} \mid z \geq 0\}, \mathbb{Z}\}$$

Similarly, we can define the parity abstraction closure $\mathsf{Par} \in Uco(\wp(\mathbb{Z}))$ as:

$$\mathsf{Par} \stackrel{\text{def}}{=} \{\varnothing, Even \stackrel{\text{def}}{=} \{n \in \mathbb{Z} \mid n \bmod 2 = 0\}, Odd \stackrel{\text{def}}{=} \{n \in \mathbb{Z} \mid n \bmod 2 = 1\}, \mathbb{Z}\} \quad \triangleleft$$

Whenever $\mathtt{C}$ is a complete lattice, then also $Uco(\mathtt{C})$, ordered point-wise, is a complete lattice denoted by $\langle Uco(\mathtt{C}), \sqsubseteq, \sqcup, \sqcap, \lambda x.x, \lambda x.\top \rangle$. Here, for every $\rho, \eta \in Uco(\mathtt{C})$, $\{\rho_i\}_{i \in I} \subseteq Uco(\mathtt{C})$ where I is an index set of ucos, and $x \in \mathtt{C}$: $\rho \sqsubseteq \eta$ iff $\forall c \in \mathtt{C}.\, \rho(c) \leq_{\mathtt{C}} \eta(c)$ iff $\eta(\mathtt{C}) \subseteq \rho(\mathtt{C})$; $(\sqcap_{i \in I} \rho_i)(c) = \wedge_{i \in I} \rho_i(c)$; and $(\sqcup_{i \in I} \rho_i)(c) = c \Leftrightarrow \forall i \in I.\, \rho_i(c) = c$. Then, $Uco(\mathtt{C})$ is the so-called *lattice of abstractions* of

C [16], i.e., the complete lattice of all possible abstractions (up to isomorphic representation of their objects) of the concrete domain C.

Henceforth, we formally model semantic approximation through ucos:

Definition 2 (Semantic Approximation). *Given a poset $\langle C, \leq_C \rangle$ and the abstraction $\rho \in Uco(C)$, an element $x \in C$ is semantically approximated by $\rho(x)$, and the set $\{y \in C \mid \rho(y) = \rho(x)\}$ represents all elements in C sharing the same semantic approximation as x.*

Example 2. Let $\mathsf{Int}\colon \wp(\mathbb{Z}) \to \wp(\mathbb{Z})$ map a set of integers $S \in \wp(\mathbb{Z})$ to the smallest interval $[l, u] \stackrel{\text{def}}{=} \{i \in \mathbb{Z} \mid l \leq i \leq u\}$ that contains it, namely such that $S \subseteq [l, u]$, where $l \in \mathbb{Z} \cup \{-\infty\}$, $u \in \mathbb{Z} \cup \{+\infty\}$ and $l \leq u$. This is the well known interval abstraction $\mathsf{Int} \in Uco(\wp(\mathbb{Z}))$ [13]. So, for instance, the set of integers $\{0, 1, 4\}$ can be semantically approximated by the interval $[0, 4]$ through Int. Moreover, the set $\{\{0,4\}, \{0,1,4\}, \{0,2,4\}, \{0,3,4\}, \{0,1,2,4\}, \{0,1,3,4\}, \{0,1,2,3,4\}\}$ contains all sets of integers S such that $\mathsf{Int}(S) = [0, 4]$. ◁

2.2 Quantitative Approximations via Pre-metrics

Quantitative approximations preserve *closeness* of the approximated data, typically measured through a distance function in a suitable topological space. Here, we model distance functions using (pre-)metrics.

Let $\mathbb{R}^\infty$ be the set of real numbers extended with the infinite symbol ∞, such that for all $r \in \mathbb{R}$, $r < \infty$. Let $\mathbb{R}_{\geq n}$ be the restriction of $\mathbb{R}$ to values greater or equal than $n \in \mathbb{N}$. For instance, $\mathbb{R}^\infty_{\geq 0} \stackrel{\text{def}}{=} \{r \in \mathbb{R} \mid r \geq 0\} \cup \{\infty\}$.

Definition 3 (Metric). *Given a non-empty set L, a metric is a binary function $\delta : L \times L \to \mathbb{R}^\infty$ with the following properties $\forall x, y, z \in L$:*

(1) $\delta(x, y) \geq 0$;	*(non-negativity)*
(2) $x = y \Leftrightarrow \delta(x, y) = 0$;	*(iff-identity)*
(3) $\delta(x, y) = \delta(y, x)$;	*(symmetry)*
(4) $\delta(x, y) \leq \delta(x, z) + \delta(z, y)$.	*(triangle-inequality)*

The pair $\langle L, \delta \rangle$ is called a metric space.

A classic metric example is the Euclidean distance measuring the distance between two real values as the absolute value of their difference.

Due to their axioms, metrics are among the strongest types of distances. However, depending on what we want to measure and on which domain, a distance function may not satisfy all axioms of a metric, but only, e.g., *(non-negativity)* and *(if-identity)*, thereby being a pre-metric instead (cf. Figure 1). As we will see in Sect. 6, understanding the type of distance function we are manipulating is essential for proving some implications between properties of programs (such as between Partial Completeness and Partial Abstract Non-Interference in Sect. 6).

In particular, a metric that does not satisfy symmetry is called a *quasi-metric*, while a metric that does not satisfy the $\Leftarrow$ implication of *(iff-identity)* is called a

	pre-	quasisemi-	semi-	quasi-	pseudo-	metric
(non-negativity)	✓	✓	✓	✓	✓	✓
(if-identity)	✓	✓	✓	✓	✓	✓
(iff-identity)	✗	✓	✓	✓	✗	✓
(symmetry)	✗	✗	✓	✗	✓	✓
(triangle-inequality)	✗	✗	✗	✓	✓	✓

Fig. 1. Metrics and their relaxed forms.

pseudo-metric. Semi-metrics satisfy all the axioms except for the triangle inequality. The function δ is called a *pre-metric* [8,17] if it only satisfies (*non-negativity*) and the $\Rightarrow$ implication of the (*iff-identity*), i.e., the (*if-identity*) axiom. All the other metric axioms are not required, making the definition of pre-metric one of the weakest possible distance function. By composing the words pseudo-, quasi- and semi- we obtain different distance flavors by simply keeping the axioms that are satisfied by all the combined words. For instance, a quasisemi-metric is a pre-metric that additionally satisfies the (*iff-identity*). Figure 1 summarizes the above distance notions and their properties. We will occasionally use the subscript δ_L in cases where the set L may not be immediately clear from the context. From this point forward, whenever we say that a function δ is a distance, we assume that it satisfies, at least, the axioms of a pre-metric.

Example 3 (Size Distance). Consider the powerset $\wp(L)$ of a set L. We write $Count(S)$ for the number of elements in the set $S \in \wp(L)$. We define the distance $\delta_{siz} : \wp(L) \times \wp(L) \to \mathbb{R}^\infty$ between two sets $S_1, S_2 \in \wp(L)$ as the absolute value of the difference in their size, i.e., $\delta_{siz}(S_1, S_2) \stackrel{\text{def}}{=} |Count(S_2) - Count(S_1)|$. Note that δ_{siz} is not a metric, but a pseudo-metric since it does not satisfy the (*iff-identity*) axiom: two sets may have the same size yet being different.

In program analysis, δ_{siz} could be used to count, for instance, the number of spurious elements added by an abstract sound computation with respect to the abstraction of a concrete computation. For instance, if $[0, 0]$ is the (interval abstraction of the) strongest numerical invariant of a program variable x at certain program point, while $[0, 10]$ is the abstract invariant generated by an abstract interpretation over Int, then $\delta_{siz}^{\text{Int}}([0,0], [0,10]) = 10$ indicates that the abstract interpretation added 10 spurious values with respect to the (interval abstraction of the) concrete execution. A similar example can be considered when counting the false positives generated by a static analysis while checking an abstract specification (e.g., whether $x \in [0, 0]$). ◁

Example 4 (Volume Distance). Let us consider the ordered domain of convex octagons (Oct, $\leq_{\text{Oct}}$) [39]. We define the distance

$$\delta_{\mathit{Vol}}(o_1, o_2) \stackrel{\text{def}}{=} Av(\mathit{Vol}(o_1) - \mathit{Vol}(o_2))$$

calculating the absolute value of the difference between the volume of two convex octagons $o_1, o_2 \in$ Oct. The volume function Vol: Oct $\to \mathbb{R}_{\geq 0}^\infty$ could be a monotone (namely, if $\gamma(o_1) \subseteq \gamma(o_2)$ then $Vol(o_1) \leq Vol(o_2)$) overapproximation of the exact volume computation. δ_{Vol} satisfies all the axioms of a metric except for (*iff-identity*) since two octagons may have they same volume yet not representing the same octagon. Thus, δ_{Vol} qualifies as a pseudo-metric. In program analysis, δ_{Vol} could be used to quantify the difference between the (numerical) invariants of program variables generated by the abstraction of a concrete computation with respect to an abstract computation. ◁

For additional examples of pre-metrics and their applications in domains used within the context of program analysis, we refer to [8].

We formally define quantitative approximations via pre-metrics as follows:

Definition 4 (Quantitative Approximation). *Given a pre-metric space $\langle C, \delta \rangle$ and a fixed constant $\varepsilon \in \mathbb{R}^{\infty}_{\geq 0}$, an element $x \in C$ is quantitatively approximated by any element in the set $\{y \in C \mid \delta(x, y) \leq \varepsilon\}$.*

Example 5. Continuing Example 2, we may approximate sets of integer numbers by the size distance δ_{siz} defined in Example 3. For instance, $\{0, 1, 4\}$ can be quantitatively approximated by any set of integers whose maximum distance from it is at most $\varepsilon = 1$. Examples of such approximations include sets $\{0, 1\}$ and $\{5, 6, 8, 10\}$. ◁

Here, the admitted noise concerns elements that are topologically close to the original one but that may share no semantic property.

3 From Pre-Metrics to Upper Closure Operators

Semantic and quantitative approaches offer distinct perspectives on the problem of approximation, relying on different formal frameworks to capture its nuances. This naturally raises the question: are these two perspectives entirely orthogonal, or is there a deeper *relation* between them? Understanding this connection is the main goal of this section. Specifically, in the following, we establish a formal relation between quantitative and semantic approximations—formalized by pre-metrics and ucos, respectively—by means of Galois connections.

Let us start by assuming to work with a complete lattice $\langle C, \leq_C, \vee_C, \wedge_C, \top_C, \bot_C \rangle$. Pre-metrics provide a quantitative measure of the difference between elements in C. Such distances cannot be derived from the order structure alone, they must be explicitly defined. As a result, the only viable approach to relate pre-metrics and ucos is to derive the latter as abstractions of the former. The abstraction process moves from pre-metrics to ucos by passing through *equivalence relations*:

$$\text{Pre-Metrics} \longrightarrow \text{Equivalence Relations} \longrightarrow \text{Uco}$$

More in detail, we first identify a subset of pre-metrics (called 0-*pseudo-metrics*) on which we can obtain equivalence relations as an abstraction. The underlying intuition is that we can represent a semantic approximation $\rho \in Uco(\mathsf{C})$ by means of a pre-metric δ that assigns distance 0 to elements $x, y \in \mathsf{C}$ with the same abstraction $\rho(x) = \rho(y)$, and assigns distance ∞ otherwise. Elements assigned with a distance of zero are the equivalence classes of the equivalence relation induced by the 0-pseudo-metrics. On the other hand, ucos satisfy structural properties—monotonicity, extensivity, idempotence—that are not automatically satisfied by pre-metrics, 0-pseudo-metrics, or equivalence relations. These properties have to be enforced through suitable constraints imposed by the abstractions. We derive ucos in two further steps: forcing *extensivity* first, and *monotonicity* and *idempotence* afterward, leveraging [15].

3.1 The Domain M(C) of Pre-Metrics

The first step in formalizing the abstraction process from pre-metrics to ucos is to define the underlying domain on which the construction operates. In the following, we introduce the domain of pre-metrics. In the next subsections, we progressively derive the domain of ucos as an abstraction.

Let $\mathsf{M}(\mathsf{C})$ be the set of all pre-metrics $\delta : \mathsf{C} \times \mathsf{C} \longrightarrow \mathbb{R}^\infty$ defined on C, i.e., $\mathsf{M}(\mathsf{C}) \stackrel{def}{=} \{\delta \mid \delta \text{ is a pre-metric on } \mathsf{C}\}$. We equip $\mathsf{M}(\mathsf{C})$ with a partial order $\sqsubseteq_m$ that compares pre-metrics based on the cardinality of sets of pairs of elements with a distance of zero. Formally, for $\delta_1, \delta_2 \in \mathsf{M}(\mathsf{C})$, we define:

$$\delta_1 \sqsubseteq_m \delta_2 \stackrel{def}{\Leftrightarrow} \forall x, y \in \mathsf{C} . \, \delta_2(x,y) = 0 \vee (\delta_1(x,y) \neq 0 \wedge \delta_1(x,y) \leq \delta_2(x,y))$$

Intuitively, moving upward in the ordering corresponds to enlarging the sets of pairs of elements that are assigned a distance of zero: pairs of elements that are distinguished (assigned a non-zero distance) by a more concrete pre-metric δ_1 may become indistinguishable (assigned a zero distance) by a more abstract pre-metric δ_2. The distance between elements that remain distinguishable in δ_2 may stretch, possibly to ∞, reflecting the underlying intuition mentioned above.

Example 6. Suppose $\mathsf{C} = \wp(\{1,2,3,4\})^1$. Let δ and δ' be pre-metrics on C such that $\delta(1,3) = \delta(13,12) = \delta(2,12) = \delta(34,234) = 0$, $\delta(12,14) = 2$, $\delta(12,34) = 2$ while all the other elements are at distance ∞, and $\delta' = \delta$ except for $\delta'(1,23) = 0$ ($\delta(1,23) = \infty$) and $\delta'(12,34) = 3 > 2 = \delta(12,34)$, graphically:

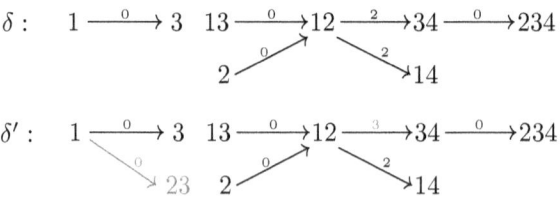

---

[1] For the sake of readability, in the following, we represent sets of numbers by the sequences of their elements without separators, e.g., $\{1,2\}$ is represented by 12.

(The distances not depicted above are ∞. The differences are colored in red.) We clearly have $\delta \sqsubseteq_m \delta'$. ◁

Let $N \subseteq \mathbb{N}$ and $x, y \in \texttt{C}$. We define the join and meet operators, $\bigsqcup_m$ and $\bigsqcap_m$, over sets of pre-metrics $\{\delta_i(x,y) \in \texttt{M}(\texttt{C}) \mid i \in N\}$ as follows:

$$\bigsqcup_m \{\delta_i\}_{i \in N} \stackrel{\text{def}}{=} \lambda(x,y). \begin{cases} \max\{\delta_i(x,y) \mid i \in N\} & \forall i \in N \colon \delta_i(x,y) \neq 0 \\ 0 & \text{otherwise} \end{cases}$$

$$\bigsqcap_m \{\delta_i\}_{i \in N} \stackrel{\text{def}}{=} \lambda(x,y). \begin{cases} m & m = \min\{\delta_i(x,y) \mid i \in N\} \neq \bot \\ \text{undefined} & \text{otherwise} \end{cases}$$

where the max and min operators:

$$\max\{\delta_i(x,y) \mid i \in N\} \stackrel{\text{def}}{=} \begin{cases} d & \exists m \in N \colon \forall i \in N \colon \infty \neq d = \delta_m(x,y) \geq \delta_i(x,y) \\ \infty & \text{otherwise} \end{cases}$$

$$\min\{\delta_i(x,y) \mid i \in N\} \stackrel{\text{def}}{=} \begin{cases} 0 & \forall i \in N \colon \delta_i(x,y) = 0 \\ d & \exists m \in N \colon \forall i \in N \colon 0 < d = \delta_m(x,y) \leq \delta_i(x,y)) \\ \bot & \text{otherwise} \end{cases}$$

find the distances within the given set of pre-metrics that are largest (but different from ∞) and smallest (possibly equal to ∞), respectively. It is clear that the bottom element of $\texttt{M}(\texttt{C})$ does not exist in general. It is $\delta_\bot$ such that $\forall x, y \in \texttt{C} \colon \delta_\bot(x,y) \stackrel{\text{def}}{=} 1$, if pre-metrics are restricted to assign discrete distances over natural numbers. The top element of $\texttt{M}(\texttt{C})$ is $\delta_\top$ such that $\forall x, y \in \texttt{C} \colon \delta_\top(x,y) \stackrel{\text{def}}{=} 0$.

Proposition 1. $\langle \texttt{M}(\texttt{C}), \sqsubseteq_m, \bigsqcup_m, \bigsqcap_m, \delta_\top \rangle$ *is a join-complete semi-lattice.*

3.2 The Domain $\texttt{M}_0(\texttt{C})$ of 0-Pseudo-Metrics

$$\texttt{M}(\texttt{C}) \xleftarrow{\rho_0} \texttt{M}_0(\texttt{C})$$

We observe that not all pre-metrics in $\texttt{M}(\texttt{C})$ are meaningful representations of semantic approximations. For instance, the pre-metric in Example 6 is not a meaningful semantic approximation because it is neither symmetric nor transitive between elements at distance zero, e.g., δ identifies a semantic equivalence between 1 and 3 ($\delta(1,3) = 0$) but not between 3 and 1 ($\delta(3,1) = \infty$).

The domain $\texttt{M}_0(\texttt{C})$. We define a restriction of pre-metrics—called 0-pseudo-metrics—satisfying symmetry and transitivity between elements that are assigned a distance of zero.

Definition 5. (0-Pseudo-Metrics). *A 0-pseudo-metric* $\delta \colon \texttt{C} \times \texttt{C} \to \mathbb{R}^\infty$ *is a pre-metric that additionally satisfies the following conditions, for all $x, y, z \in \texttt{C}$:*

1. $\delta(x,y) = 0 \Rightarrow \delta(y,x) = 0;$ \hfill *(0-distance symmetry)*

2. $(\delta(x,y) = 0 \land \delta(y,z) = 0) \Rightarrow \delta(x,z) = 0$ (0-distance transitivity)

Let $M_0(C)$ be the set of all 0-pseudo-metrics defined on C. It is clear that, by definition, $M_0(C) \subset M(C)$, hence $\langle M_0(C), \sqsubseteq_m \rangle$, i.e., the domain of 0-pseudo-metrics, is still a poset preserving the same characteristics as $M(C)$.

Proposition 2. $\langle M_0(C), \sqsubseteq_m, \sqcup_m, \sqcap_m, \delta_\top \rangle$ *is a join-complete semi-lattice.*

Abstracting pre-metrics into 0-pseudo-metrics. We show here that 0-pseudo metrics can be obtained from pre-metrics by forcing both symmetry and transitivity between elements assigned with a distance of zero.

Let $S \colon M(C) \to M(C)$ be the operator forcing symmetry only between the elements with distance zero:

$$S(\delta) \stackrel{\text{def}}{=} \lambda(x,y). \begin{cases} 0 & \delta(y,x) = 0 \\ \delta(x,y) & \text{otherwise} \end{cases}$$

Clearly, if a pre-metric δ is already symmetric, then $S(\delta) = \delta$.

Similarly, we define the operator $T \colon M(C) \to M(C)$ forcing transitivity, again only between elements with distance zero:

$$T(\delta) \stackrel{\text{def}}{=} \mathit{lfp}_\delta^{\sqsubseteq_m} \mathfrak{t}$$

$$\mathfrak{t}(\delta) \stackrel{\text{def}}{=} \lambda(x,y). \begin{cases} 0 & \exists z \in C \colon \delta(x,z) = 0 \land \delta(z,y) = 0 \\ \delta(x,y) & \text{otherwise} \end{cases}$$

Note that, if a pre-metric δ satisfies the triangle inequality, then $T(\delta) = \delta$.

Let $\rho_0 \stackrel{\text{def}}{=} T \circ S$. By construction, given a pre-metric $\delta \in M(C)$, we have that $\rho_0(\delta) \in M_0(C)$ is a 0-pseudo-metric. More generally, ρ_0 is a uco on $M(C)$ and $M_0(C)$ is the set of its fixpoints $\rho_0(M(C))$.

Theorem 1. $\rho_0 \in Uco(M(C))$ *and* $M_0(C) = \rho_0(M(C))$.

Example 7. Suppose $C = \wp(\{1,2,3,4\})$ and consider δ of Example 6. Let $\delta_s \stackrel{\text{def}}{=} S(\delta)$, such that $\delta_s = \delta$ except for $\delta_s(3,1) = \delta_s(12,13) = \delta_s(12,2) = \delta_s(234, 34) = 0$.

$\delta_s: \quad 1 \xleftrightarrow{0} 3 \quad 13 \xleftrightarrow{0} 12 \xrightarrow{2} 34 \xleftrightarrow{0} 234$
$\qquad\qquad\qquad\qquad\quad 2 \nwarrow^0 \qquad \searrow^2 14$

Note that δ_s is not transitive, e.g., $\delta_s(2,12) = 0 = \delta_s(12,13)$, but $\delta_s(2,13) = \delta(2,13) = \infty$. Let us consider now $\delta_t = T(\delta_s)$ (which preserves symmetry).

$\delta_t: \quad 1 \xleftrightarrow{0} 3 \quad 13 \xleftrightarrow{0} 12 \xrightarrow{2} 34 \xleftrightarrow{0} 234$
$\qquad\qquad\qquad\qquad\; \updownarrow^0 \nwarrow^0 \qquad \searrow^2 14$
$\qquad\qquad\qquad\qquad\quad 2$

After one iteration of $\mathfrak{t}$ we reach the fix-point and $\delta_t(2,13) = \delta_t(13,2) = 0$. Note that the triangle inequality does not hold among elements with a distance greater than zero, e.g., $\delta_t(2,14) = \infty$ while $\delta_t(2,12) = 0$ and $\delta_t(12,14) = 2$. ◁

3.3 From $M_0(C)$ to Equivalence Relations: The Domain $M_\top(C)$

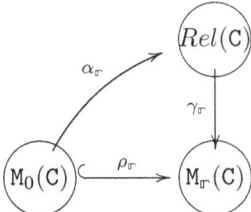

At this point we can observe that 0-pseudo-metrics naturally induce an equivalence relation between elements with a distance of zero. In this section, we thus abstract 0-pseudo-metrics into the equivalence relations induced by them.

Let $Rel(C)$ be the set of equivalence relations on C. In the following, given an element $x \in C$ and an equivalence relation $R \in Rel(C)$, $[x]_R$ denotes the equivalence class of x induced by R, i.e., $[x]_R \stackrel{def}{=} \{y \in C \mid y\,R\,x\}$. We define a partial order $\preccurlyeq$ on $Rel(C)$ such that, for any $R, S \in Rel(C)$, $R \preccurlyeq S$ if and only if $\forall x \in C : [x]_R \subseteq [x]_S$. We have the following Galois insertion

$$\langle M_0(C), \sqsubseteq_m \rangle \xrightarrow[\alpha_\top]{\gamma_\top} \!\!\!\!\!\!\!\!\twoheadrightarrow \langle Rel(C), \preccurlyeq \rangle$$

where the abstraction function $\alpha_\top : M_0(C) \to Rel(C)$ is

$$\alpha_\top(\delta) \stackrel{def}{=} \{(x,y) \in C \times C \mid \delta(x,y) = 0\}$$

and the concretization function $\gamma_\top : Rel(C) \to M_0(C)$ is

$$\gamma_\top(R) \stackrel{def}{=} \lambda(x,y).\begin{cases} 0 & x\,R\,y \\ \infty & \text{otherwise} \end{cases}$$

Thus, the domain $\langle Rel(C), \preccurlyeq \rangle$ is an abstraction of $\langle M_0(C), \sqsubseteq_m \rangle$. Let $\rho_\top \stackrel{def}{=} \gamma_\top \circ \alpha_\top$, we have that $\rho_\top$ is a uco on $M_0(C)$.

Theorem 2. $\rho_\top \in Uco(M_0(C))$.

Note that $\rho_\top$ is not an isomorphism since a 0-pseudo-metric δ may also assign non-zero distances between elements. However, through the abstraction, these distances are stretched to ∞ in $\rho_\top(\delta)$. More generally, $\rho_\top$ abstracts 0-pseudo-metrics into pseudo-metrics, ignoring all non-zero distances between elements.

Let $M_\top(C) \stackrel{def}{=} \rho_\top(M_0(C)) = \rho_\top \circ \rho_0(M(C))$ and let $\delta_\infty \in M_\top(C)$ be defined as:

$$\delta_\infty \stackrel{def}{=} \lambda(x,y).\begin{cases} 0 & x = y \\ \infty & \text{otherwise} \end{cases}$$

Proposition 3. $\langle M_\top(C), \sqsubseteq_m, \sqcup_m, \sqcap_m, \delta_\top, \delta_\infty \rangle$ is a complete lattice.

Note that $\delta_\top = \gamma_\pi(\top)$, where $\top \in Rel(C)$ is such that $\forall x, y \in C \colon x\top y$, and $\delta_\infty = \gamma_\pi(\mathrm{id})$, where $\mathrm{id} \in Rel(C)$ is such that $x\,\mathrm{id}\,y \stackrel{\text{def}}{\Leftrightarrow} x = y$. Thus, $M_\pi(C) \subset M_0(C) \subset M(C)$ is the complete sub-lattice of $M(C)$ *uniquely identifying equivalence relations*.

Example 8. Let us consider δ_t of Example 7. Its abstraction $\delta_r \stackrel{\text{def}}{=} \rho_\pi(\delta_t)$ is such that $\delta_r = \delta_t$ except for $\delta_r(12, 14) = \delta_r(12, 34) = \infty$.

$\delta_r:\quad 1 \xleftrightarrow{0} 3 \quad 13 \xleftrightarrow{0} 12 \quad 34 \xleftrightarrow{0} 234 \quad \equiv \quad \boxed{1\ \ 3}\ \ \boxed{2\ \ 12\ \ 13}\ \ \boxed{34\ \ 234}$
$\phantom{\delta_r:\quad 1 \xleftrightarrow{0} 3 \quad}{\downarrow}{\ \ }{\nearrow}^{0}$
$\phantom{\delta_r:\quad 1 \xleftrightarrow{0} 3 \quad\ \ }2 \swarrow$

In the depiction above on the right, we show an equivalent representation of δ_r where different elements inside the same box are assigned with a distance of zero, while all other distances between elements in different boxes or between the other, not depicted, elements of C are ∞. ◁

3.4 From Equivalence Relations to Upper Closure Operators

$$Rel(C) \xrightarrow{\alpha_e} Ext(C) \xhookrightarrow{\rho_{\mathit{fun}}} Uco(C)$$
$$\underset{\gamma_e}{\longleftarrow}$$

The next step in the abstraction process is to move from equivalence relations towards (extensive) functions and afterward to upper closure operators.

Let $Fun(C)$ be the set of total functions on C ordered point-wise, i.e., $f \dot{\leq}_C g \stackrel{\text{def}}{\Leftrightarrow} \forall x \in C\,.\,f(x) \leq_C g(x)$.

Proposition 4. $\langle Fun(C), \dot{\leq}_C, \dot{\vee}_C, \dot{\wedge}_C, \lambda x.\top_C, \lambda x.\bot_C \rangle$ *is a complete lattice.*

Given an equivalence relation $R \in Rel(C)$ we can construct a total function $f\colon C \to C$ that maps each element in C to a representative element of its equivalence class under R. Various choices are possible for this representative element, but since our ultimate goal is to characterize ucos, which in particular are extensive functions, we define f such that each equivalence class is mapped to its least upper bound, thus ensuring that f is extensive.

Formally, let $Ext(C) \stackrel{\text{def}}{=} \{f : C \to C \mid \forall x \in C\,.\,x \leq_C f(x)\} \subset Fun(C)$ be the set of all extensive functions on C. Clearly $Ext(C)$ forms a complete sub-lattice of $Fun(C)$. Note that $\lambda x.\bot_C$ is the smallest function with respect to the point-wise order in $Fun(C)$ but, not being extensive, it cannot be the smallest function in $Ext(C)$, where the bottom element is the identity function ι.

Proposition 5. $\langle Ext(C), \dot{\leq}_C, \dot{\vee}_C, \dot{\wedge}_C, \lambda x.\top_C, \iota \rangle$ *is a complete lattice.*

We define the following function $\alpha_e \colon Rel(C) \to Ext(C)$ as

$$\alpha_e(R) \stackrel{\text{def}}{=} \lambda x \in C\,.\,\bigvee([x]_R)$$

Note that α_e is not surjective since an extensive function could lead the elements to be greater than the least upper bound.

Example 9. Suppose $\mathsf{C} = \wp(\{1,2,3,4\})$ and consider δ_r of Example 8. Let R the corresponding equivalence relation depicted in Example 8. Its abstraction $f \stackrel{\text{def}}{=} \alpha_e(\mathsf{R})$ is the identity function except for $f(1) = f(3) = 13$, $f(2) = f(12) = f(13) = 123 = f(123)$, $f(34) = f(234) = 234$. Hence, f collapses the image of 123 with the one of 2, 12, and 13, since, for instance, $f(12) = \bigvee([12]_\mathsf{R}) = \bigvee\{2,12,13\} = 123$. ◁

From the domain of extensive function $Ext(\mathsf{C})$, we can use the construction in [15] to further enforce monotonicity and idempotence thus characterizing the complete sub-lattice of ucos on C, i.e., $\langle Uco(\mathsf{C}), \dot\leq_\mathsf{C}, \dot\vee_\mathsf{C}, \dot\wedge_\mathsf{C}, \lambda x. \top_\mathsf{C}, \iota \rangle$, where the point-wise order $\dot\leq_\mathsf{C}$ reflects the relative precision between ucos.

Let $Mon(\mathsf{C}) \stackrel{\text{def}}{=} \{f \in Ext(\mathsf{C}) \mid \forall x,y \in \mathsf{C} . \, x \leq_\mathsf{C} y \Rightarrow f(x) \leq_\mathsf{C} f(y)\}$ be the set of monotone extensive functions. To enforce monotonicity, we leverage the operator $\mathsf{M} : Ext(\mathsf{C}) \to Mon(\mathsf{C})$ [15] defined as

$$\mathsf{M}(f) \stackrel{\text{def}}{=} \lambda x. \bigvee \{f(y) \mid y \leq_\mathsf{C} x\}$$

which, given an extensive function $f \in Ext(\mathsf{C})$, yields the least monotone extensive function greater than f. This means that $\mathsf{M} \in Uco(Ext(\mathsf{C}))$, identifying the sub-lattice of monotone and extensive functions [15].

To enforce idempotence, we leverage $\mathsf{I} : Mon(\mathsf{C}) \to Uco(\mathsf{C})$ [15] defined as

$$\mathsf{I}(f) \stackrel{\text{def}}{=} lfp_f^{\dot\leq_\mathsf{C}} (\lambda g. g \circ g)$$

which, given a monotone and extensive function $f \in Mon(\mathsf{C})$, yields the smallest idempotent function greater than f. Thus, $\mathsf{I} \in Uco(Mon(\mathsf{C}))$ and, by defining $\rho_{\mathsf{Im}} \stackrel{\text{def}}{=} \mathsf{I} \circ \mathsf{M} \in Uco(Ext(\mathsf{C}))$, we have $Uco(\mathsf{C}) = \rho_{\mathsf{Im}}(Ext(\mathsf{C}))$.

We now define the following Galois insertion

$$\langle Rel(\mathsf{C}), \preccurlyeq \rangle \xleftrightarrow[\alpha_\mathsf{f}]{\gamma_\mathsf{f}} \langle Uco(\mathsf{C}), \dot\leq_\mathsf{C} \rangle$$

where the abstraction $\alpha_\mathsf{f} : Rel(\mathsf{C}) \to Uco(\mathsf{C})$ is

$$\alpha_\mathsf{f}(\mathsf{R}) \stackrel{\text{def}}{=} \rho_{\mathsf{Im}} \circ \alpha_e(\mathsf{R})$$

and the concretization $\gamma_\mathsf{f} : Uco(\mathsf{C}) \to Rel(\mathsf{C})$ is

$$\gamma_\mathsf{f}(\rho) \stackrel{\text{def}}{=} \{(x,y) \in \mathsf{C} \times \mathsf{C} \mid \rho(x) = \rho(y)\}$$

We have that $\rho_\mathsf{f} \stackrel{\text{def}}{=} \gamma_\mathsf{f} \circ \alpha_\mathsf{f}$ defines a uco on $Rel(\mathsf{C})$.

Theorem 3. $\rho_\mathsf{f} \in Uco(Rel(\mathsf{C}))$.

Example 10. Consider $\mathsf{C} = \wp(\{1,2,3,4\})$ and f of Example 9. Then $f_m \stackrel{\text{def}}{=} \mathsf{M}(f)$ is such that $f_m = f$ except for $f_m(14) = 134$, $f_m(23) = 123$, and $f_m(24) = f_m(124) = f_m(134) = f_m(1234) = 1234 = f_m(34) = f_m(234)$ (since $f_m(3)$ adds 1 and 3, while $f_m(34)$ adds 2 and 4). Finally, $\rho = \mathsf{I}(f_m)$ is such that $\rho = f_m$ except for $\rho(1) = \rho(3) = 123$ (since $f_m(1) = f_m(3) = 13$ and $f_m(13) = 123 = f_m(123)$) and $\rho(14) = 1234$ (since $f_m(14) = 134$ and $f_m(134) = 1234 = f_m(1234)$). The corresponding equivalence relation $R_\rho \stackrel{\text{def}}{=} \gamma_{\mathfrak{f}}(\rho)$ is

$$R_\rho : \boxed{1 \quad 2 \quad 3 \quad 12 \quad 13 \quad 23 \quad 123} \boxed{14 \quad 24 \quad 34 \quad 124 \quad 134 \quad 234 \quad 1234}$$

representing a uco over $C = \wp(\{1, 2, 3, 4\})$ with fix points $\{\emptyset, 4, 123, 1234\}$. ◁

3.5 Upper Closure Operators as Pre-Metrics: The Domain $M_u(C)$

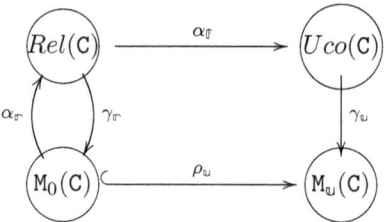

The last step consists of identifying the pre-metrics that can be uniquely associated with a uco. We define the following Galois insertion

$$\langle M_0(C), \sqsubseteq_m \rangle \xleftrightarrow[\alpha_u]{\gamma_u} \langle Uco(C), \dot{\leq}_c \rangle$$

where the abstraction $\alpha_u : M_0(C) \to Uco(C)$ is

$$\alpha_u \stackrel{\text{def}}{=} \alpha_{\mathfrak{f}} \circ \alpha_{\mathfrak{r}}$$

and the concretization $\gamma_u : Uco(C) \to M_0(C)$ is

$$\gamma_u(\rho) \stackrel{\text{def}}{=} \gamma_{\mathfrak{r}} \circ \gamma_{\mathfrak{f}} = \lambda(x, y). \begin{cases} 0 & \rho(x) = \rho(y) \\ \infty & \text{otherwise} \end{cases}$$

We have that $\rho_u \stackrel{\text{def}}{=} \gamma_u \circ \alpha_u$ defines a uco on $M_0(C)$ forcing all the properties described in the previous sections on the collections of elements with 0-distance and forgetting (setting to ∞) all the other distances.

Theorem 4. $\rho_u \in Uco(M_0(C))$.

Let $M_u(C) \stackrel{\text{def}}{=} \rho_u(M_0(C)) = \rho_u \circ \rho_0(M(C))$.

Proposition 6. $\langle M_u(C), \sqsubseteq_m, \sqcup_m, \sqcap_m, \delta_\top, \delta_\infty \rangle$ is a complete lattice.

We finally have the following increasing chain between pre-metric domains:

$$M_u(C) \subset M_{\mathfrak{r}}(C) \subset M_0(C) \subset M(C)$$

In particular, $M_u(C)$ is the sub-lattice of pre-metrics *uniquely identifying* ucos on the complete lattice C.

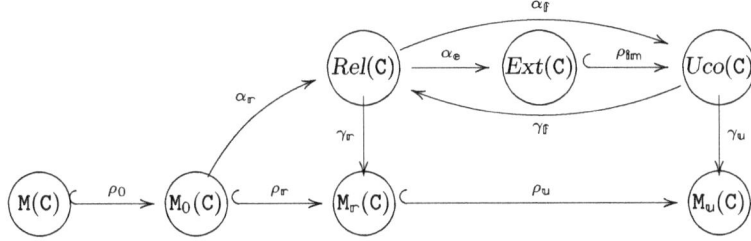

Fig. 2. From pre-metrics to ucos, and back.

Figure 2 illustrates the full abstraction process from pre-metrics to ucos developed in this section. It shows that ucos can, in general, be viewed as specific instances of pre-metrics (via γ_u). However, ucos are far from trivial: deriving one from a pre-metric requires that the distance satisfy specific and often stringent conditions. As a result, ucos obtained through abstraction ($\alpha_f \alpha_r \rho_u$) retain a distinct identity, reflecting structural properties of the underlying domain C.

4 Combining Distances (and Abstractions)

In this section, building on our view of ucos as abstractions of pre-metrics, we study a way to compose pre-metrics—akin to how compositions of ucos can be defined. Specifically, we define a combination of pre-metrics that enables a *layered abstraction*: a first pre-metric determines how to aggregate elements (at distance zero)—to select the domain of comparison—and a second pre-metric measures distances within this selected domain between the identified aggregations.

Let us consider $\delta_1, \delta_2 \in \text{M}(C)$, and let $f[\delta_1]$ be a *selector map* $f[\delta_1] : C \to C$ associating with each element $z \in C$ a unique element $f_z \in C$ at distance of zero from z with respect to δ_1, i.e., such that if $f_z \stackrel{\text{def}}{=} f[\delta_1](z)$ then $\delta_1(f_z, z) = 0$. Then, we can *combine* δ_1 and δ_2, leveraging $f[\delta_1]$, as follows:

$$\delta_1 \triangleright_f \delta_2 \stackrel{\text{def}}{=} \lambda(x,y). \begin{cases} 0 & \delta_1(x,y) = 0 \\ \delta_2(f[\delta_1](x), f[\delta_1](y)) & \text{otherwise} \end{cases}$$

Proposition 7. *Let $\delta_1, \delta_2 \in \text{M}(C)$. Then also $\delta_1 \triangleright_f \delta_2 \in \text{M}(C)$.*

Example 11. Let Σ be a chosen alphabet (finite set of characters) and let Σ^* be the Kleene closure of Σ, i.e., the set of all strings of finite length over Σ. We consider the poset $\langle \wp(\Sigma^*), \subseteq \rangle$. Let us define $\delta_\Sigma : \wp(\Sigma^*) \times \wp(\Sigma^*) \to \mathbb{N}^\infty$ to compute the absolute difference between the number of string lengths between two sets of strings $W_1, W_2 \in \wp(\Sigma^*)$. Formally:

$$\delta_\Sigma(W_1, W_2) \stackrel{\text{def}}{=} \delta_{siz}(\{\text{length}(w_1) \mid w_1 \in W_1\}, \{\text{length}(w_2) \mid w_2 \in W_2\})$$

where δ_{siz} is the size distance of Example 3 and length(w) is the number of characters composing the (finite) string w.

The composition $\delta_{siz} \triangleright_f \delta_\Sigma$, with $f[\delta_{siz}] = \iota$, computes the distance between the cardinality of string lengths only when the string sets have different cardinality. For instance, given $W_1 = \{a\}$ and $W_2 = \{bb\}$, then $\delta_{siz}(W_1, W_2) = 0$ and therefore $\delta_{siz} \triangleright_f \delta_\Sigma(W_1, W_2) = 0$. Instead, given W_1 and $W_3 = \{a, bb, cc\}$, we have $\delta_{siz} \triangleright_f \delta_\Sigma(W_1, W_2) = 2$ and thus $\delta_{siz} \triangleright_f \delta_\Sigma(W_1, W_3) = \delta_\Sigma(W_1, W_3) = 1$.

Vice versa, $\delta_\Sigma \triangleright_f \delta_{siz}$, with $f[\delta_\Sigma] = \iota$, computes the distance between the cardinality of the string sets only when the sets of their strings lengths have different lengths. For instance, $\delta_\Sigma(W_1, W_2) = 0$ and thus $\delta_\Sigma \triangleright_f \delta_{siz}(W_1, W_2) = 0$, while $\delta_\Sigma(W_1, W_3) = 1$ and therefore $\delta_\Sigma \triangleright_f \delta_{siz}(W_1, W_3) = \delta_{siz}(W_1, W_3) = 2$. ◁

At this point, we can use the operation $\triangleright_f$ for *combining* a distance $\delta_\rho \in M_u(C)$ characterizing a semantic abstraction $\rho \in Uco(C)$ (cf. Sect. 3.5), and another distance $\delta_C \in M(C)$ that we want to use for measuring the distances between abstract elements, i.e. elements in $\rho(C)$. As for selector function $f[\delta_\rho]$, we can exploit precisely the structure of the elements assigned with a distance of zero in δ_ρ. Namely, we can take the least upper bound of the elements at distance zero, which by construction is at distance zero (cf. Sect. 3.4). Formally, let us define $\delta_C^\rho \stackrel{def}{=} \delta_\rho \triangleright_f \delta_C$ with $f[\delta_\rho] \stackrel{def}{=} \lambda x. \bigvee \{w \mid \delta_\rho(x, w) = 0\}$. Note that the definition of $f[\delta_\rho]$ satisfies the condition to be a selector function since, by construction of $\delta_\rho \in M_u(C)$, we have that: $\forall x \in C$. $\delta_\rho(f[\delta_\rho](x), x) = 0$. The combination distance $\delta_\rho \triangleright_f \delta_C$ is the conjunction of a semantic approximation ρ (cf. Definition 2) and a quantitative approximation δ_C (cf. Definition 4):

Proposition 8. *Let $\delta_\rho \in M_u(C)$ characterize $\rho \in Uco(C)$ and let $\delta_C \in M(C)$. Let $f[\delta_\rho] = \lambda x. \bigvee \{w \mid \delta_\rho(x, w) = 0\}$ on C, then*

$$\forall x, y \in C . (\delta_\rho \triangleright_f \delta_C)(x, y) = \delta_C(\rho(x), \rho(y))$$

We formally define this general notion of approximation below.

Definition 6. (General Approximation). *Let $\langle C, \leq_C \rangle$ be a poset and $\langle C, \delta_C \rangle$ be a pre-metric space, and let $\rho \in Uco(C)$. We define the general approximation as follows for any $x, y \in C$:*

$$\delta_C^\rho(x, y) \stackrel{def}{=} \delta_C(\rho(x), \rho(y))$$

An element $x \in C$ is semantically approximated with ρ and quantitatively approximated by δ_C, up to $\varepsilon \in \mathbb{R}_{\geq 0}^\infty$, by any element in the set $\{y \in C \mid \delta_C^\rho(x, y) \leq \varepsilon\}$.

That is, $\delta_C^\rho(x, y)$ calculates the distance between the semantic approximations of x and y with ρ. Clearly, when considering the identity function $\iota \in Uco(C)$ as abstraction, it holds that $\delta_\iota \triangleright_f \delta_C = \delta_C^\iota(x, y) = \delta_C(x, y)$ for any $x, y \in C$.

Example 12. Continuing Example 2 and Example 5, the set $\{0,1,4\}$ can be semantically and quantitatively approximated by $\delta_{\mathsf{Int}} \triangleright_f \delta_{siz} = \delta_{siz}^{\mathsf{Int}}$ and $\varepsilon = 1$ in any set in

$$\{S \in \wp(\mathbb{Z}) \mid \delta_{siz}^{\mathsf{Int}}(\{0,1,4\}, S) \leq 1\} = \{S \in \wp(\mathbb{Z}) \mid \mathsf{Int}(S) = [-1,4] \vee \mathsf{Int}(S) = [0,5]\} \quad \triangleleft$$

In the following sections, we build on this general approximation framework a new confidentiality property—based on the notion of Abstract Non-Interference—that quantifies semantic variations in the output domain. This leads to a novel property we call *Partial Abstract Non-Interference*. We prove that it has a strong relation with Partial Completeness [5,7,8], a property modeling imprecision of an abstraction in the context of abstract interpretation, but it provides a novel *perspective* on precision, as it happens for the (not partial) corresponding notions.

5 (Partial) Completeness and Abstract Non-interference

We briefly recall the notions of Completeness and Partial Completeness in abstract interpretation, as well as Abstract Non-Interference (ANI).

Completeness. Given a monotone function $f \colon \mathsf{C} \to \mathsf{D}$ over posets $\langle \mathsf{C}, \leq_\mathsf{C} \rangle$ and $\langle \mathsf{D}, \leq_\mathsf{D} \rangle$, the abstractions $\eta \in Uco(\mathsf{C})$ and $\rho \in Uco(\mathsf{D})$ can be used to approximate computations, thus defining an abstract version $f^\natural \colon \eta(\mathsf{C}) \to \rho(\mathsf{D})$ of f. An abstract function $f^\natural$ is *sound* when $\rho \circ f \leq_\mathsf{D} f^\natural \circ \eta$ [14]. A sound by construction approximation is $f^\alpha \stackrel{\mathrm{def}}{=} \rho \circ f \circ \eta$, called the *best correct approximation* (bca) [14] of f. Any $f^\natural$ soundly approximating f is, in fact, equal or less precise than the bca, formally: $\rho \circ f \leq_\mathsf{D} f^\alpha \leq_\mathsf{D} f^\natural \circ \eta$ [14].

A sound abstract computation $f^\natural \colon \eta(\mathsf{C}) \to \rho(\mathsf{D})$ performs a *precise* approximation of a (concrete) monotone function $f \colon \mathsf{C} \to \mathsf{D}$ whenever $\rho \circ f = f^\natural \circ \eta$. It has been proved that for a precise abstract approximation to exist, the bca f^α must also be precise [13,26]. In particular, if $f^\natural$ is a precise abstract approximation of f then $f^\natural = f^\alpha$. *Completeness* [13,26] in abstract interpretation is a desirable property that ensures the existence of a precise abstract approximation of a (concrete) monotone function f. Formally[2]:

Definition 7 (Completeness *[13,26]*). *Let $\langle \mathsf{C}, \leq_\mathsf{C} \rangle$ and $\langle \mathsf{D}, \leq_\mathsf{D} \rangle$ be posets, and let $\eta \in Uco(\mathsf{C})$ and $\rho \in Uco(\mathsf{D})$ be the input and output abstractions, respectively. A monotone function $f \colon \mathsf{C} \to \mathsf{D}$ satisfies* Completeness *w.r.t. $\langle \eta, \rho \rangle$ when the following condition holds: $\forall x \in \mathsf{C} \,.\, \rho \circ f(x) = \rho \circ f \circ \eta(x)$.*

In other words, proving the Completeness of f w.r.t. the input and output abstractions $\langle \eta, \rho \rangle$ means proving the bca $\rho \circ f \circ \eta$ is precise.

Partial Completeness. In practice, Completeness is rarely satisfied. For this reason, Campion et al. [5,7,8] introduced a weaker notion of completeness, called *Partial Completeness*, by the use of pre-metrics *compatible* with the ordering of the underlying poset.

---
[2] This definition of Completeness is also called Backward-Completeness [26].

Definition 8 (Order-Compatible Distance [8]). *Let $\langle L, \leq_L \rangle$ be a poset. A distance $\delta : L \times L \to \mathbb{R}^\infty$ is said to be compatible with the ordering $\leq_L$ or, in short, $\leq_L$-compatible, if and only if it also satisfies the following property $\forall x, y, z \in L$:*

$$x \leq_L y \leq_L z \Rightarrow \delta(x,y) \leq \delta(x,z) \wedge \delta(y,z) \leq \delta(x,z). \text{ (chains-order)}$$

A poset $\langle L, \leq_L \rangle$ equipped with a $\leq_L$-compatible distance δ is called a distance compatible space and is denoted by the triple $\langle L, \leq_L, \delta \rangle$.

The purpose of the *(chains-order)* axiom is to give a meaning to distances between comparable elements. Notably, let $f_1^\natural$ and $f_2^\natural$ be sound abstract approximations of a concrete monotone function $f \colon \mathsf{C} \to \mathsf{D}$, i.e., $\rho \circ f \leq_D f_1^\natural \circ \eta$ and $\rho \circ f \leq_D f_2^\natural \circ \eta$. If $f_1^\natural$ is more precise than $f_2^\natural$, i.e., $f_1^\natural \leq_D f_2^\natural$, we expect a decrease in the imprecision (distance) with respect to the concrete computation when using $f_1^\natural$ rather than $f_2^\natural$, i.e., $\forall x \in \mathsf{D} \colon \delta(\rho \circ f(x), f_1^\natural \circ \eta(x)) \leq \delta(\rho \circ f(x), f_2^\natural \circ \eta(x))$.

Example 13 The poset $\langle \wp(L), \subseteq \rangle$ and the size distance δ_{siz} from Example 3 form a pseudo-metric compatible space. ◁

For additional examples of order-compatible pre-metrics and their applications in domains used within the context of program analysis, we refer to [8]. Definition 8 is general enough to be instantiated with other definitions of distances used in the literature of abstract interpretation (see, e.g., [5,19,30,31,41]).

We can now recall the definition of ε-Partial Completeness, adapted here in the context of ucos and by leveraging Definition 6 for rewriting the condition.

Definition 9 (ε-Partial Completeness [5,8]). *Let $\langle \mathsf{C}, \leq_\mathsf{C} \rangle$ be a poset and $\langle \mathsf{D}, \leq_\mathsf{D}, \delta_\mathsf{D} \rangle$ be a pre-metric compatible space, let $\eta \in Uco(\mathsf{C})$ and $\rho \in Uco(\mathsf{D})$ be the input and output abstractions, respectively. Let $\varepsilon \in \mathbb{R}^\infty_{\geq 0}$. A monotone function $f : \mathsf{C} \to \mathsf{D}$ satisfies ε-Partial Completeness w.r.t. $\langle \eta, \delta_\mathsf{D}^\rho \rangle$ if and only if the following condition holds: $\forall x \in \mathsf{C}$. $\delta_\mathsf{D}^\rho(f(x), f \circ \eta(x)) \leq \varepsilon$.*

The equality requirement of Definition 7 is relaxed by admitting a bounded imprecision, i.e. a bounded distance, between $\rho \circ f(x)$ and the bca $\rho \circ f \circ \eta(x)$ for all $x \in C$, which must not exceed ε. The imprecision to be measured and bounded is encoded in the pre-metric $\leq_\mathsf{D}$-compatible δ_D defined on the output domain D.

Example 14 We consider the pre-metric compatible space $\langle \wp(\mathbb{Z}), \subseteq, \delta_{siz} \rangle$ where δ_{siz} is the size distance defined in Example 3, the complete lattice $\langle \wp(\mathbb{Z}), \subseteq , \cup, \cap, \mathbb{Z}, \varnothing \rangle$, and the standard denotational collecting semantics over it $[\![Q]\!] \colon \wp(\mathbb{Z}) \to \wp(\mathbb{Z})$ of the following program $Q \in \mathsf{Prog}$:

while $x > 1$ **do** $x := x - 2$

Let us set $\rho = \eta = \mathsf{Int}$. Then $[\![Q]\!]$ does not satisfy Completeness for $\langle \mathsf{Int}, \mathsf{Int} \rangle$ because for the input $\{2, 4\}$ we get:

$$\mathsf{Int}([\![Q]\!]\{2,4\}) = [0,0] \subset [0,1] = \mathsf{Int}([\![Q]\!]\{2,3,4\}) = \mathsf{Int}([\![Q]\!]\mathsf{Int}(\{2,4\}))$$

However, if we allow an imprecision quantified by $\varepsilon = 1$, which for δ_{siz} corresponds to accepting one spurious element between the two results, we get:

$$\delta_{siz}^{\mathsf{Int}}(\llbracket \mathsf{Q} \rrbracket \{2,4\}, \llbracket \mathsf{Q} \rrbracket \mathsf{Int}(\{2,4\})) = \delta_{siz}([0,0],[0,1]) \leq 1$$

In particular, it is easy to note that $\delta_{siz}^{\mathsf{Int}}(\llbracket \mathsf{Q} \rrbracket S, \llbracket \mathsf{Q} \rrbracket \mathsf{Int}(S)) \leq 1$, for all input sets $S \in \wp(\mathbb{Z})$, which implies that $\llbracket \mathsf{Q} \rrbracket$ satisfies 1-Partial Completeness w.r.t. $\langle \mathsf{Int}, \delta_{siz}^{\mathsf{Int}} \rangle$. ◁

It is worth noting that, if a function f is proved to satisfy Completeness for abstractions $\langle \eta, \rho \rangle$, then f is also 0-Partial Complete for $\langle \eta, \delta_{\mathsf{D}}^{\rho} \rangle$ with respect to any pre-metric order-compatible δ (thanks to the (*if-identity*) axiom). However, the converse does not hold if the (*iff-identity*) axiom is not satisfied by δ, e.g., when δ is a pseudo-metric.

Abstract Non-Interference. Non-Interference [27] is a confidentiality policy that safeguards sensitive input information from affecting observable computation results. This concept has been relaxed to encompass variations in properties that might influence computations [21,22,24,32,33]. Additionally, the distinction between secret/relevant and public/observable data can be interpreted as an abstraction of data. In particular, Non-Interference has been extended and refined through abstract interpretation, yielding a confidentiality policy called Abstract Non-Interference [24]. Following [35], we will focus on the flavor of Abstract Non-Interference considering an input data property to protect, when assuming an abstract observation of computations (this notion is called narrow in [24]).

Definition 10 (Abstract Non-Interference [24]). *Let $\langle \mathsf{C}, \leq_{\mathsf{C}} \rangle$ and $\langle \mathsf{D}, \leq_{\mathsf{D}} \rangle$ be posets, and let $\eta \in Uco(\mathsf{C})$ and $\rho \in Uco(\mathsf{D})$ be abstractions. A function $f \colon \mathsf{C} \to \mathsf{D}$ satisfies* Abstract Non-Interference *(ANI for short) w.r.t. $\langle \eta, \rho \rangle$ when:*

$$\forall x, y \in \mathsf{C} \,.\, \eta(x) = \eta(y) \;\Rightarrow\; \rho \circ f(x) = \rho \circ f(y)$$

Example 15 Consider the complete lattice $\langle \wp(\mathbb{Z}), \subseteq, \cup, \cap, \mathbb{Z}, \varnothing \rangle$, the standard collecting semantics $\llbracket \mathsf{P} \rrbracket \colon \wp(\mathbb{Z}) \to \wp(\mathbb{Z})$, and the following program P:

if $(x \bmod 2 = 0 \wedge x \neq 0)$ **then** $x := (x/2)^2$ **else** $x := -x^2 + (1 - |x|)$

where MOD is the modulo operation. Let $\mathsf{Par} \in Uco(\wp(\mathbb{Z}))$ be the parity abstraction over input values, and $\mathsf{Sign} \in Uco(\wp(\mathbb{Z}))$ the sign abstraction over output values (cf. Example 1). In this program, for any even value, we return a positive number; for 0, we return 1 (hence a positive value), while for odd numbers, we return a negative value. Formally, for all $N, M \in \wp(\mathbb{Z})$, if $\mathsf{Par}(N) = \mathsf{Par}(M)$ then we have $\mathsf{Sign}(\llbracket P \rrbracket N) = \mathsf{Sign}(\llbracket P \rrbracket M)$, thus $\llbracket \mathsf{P} \rrbracket$ satisfies ANI w.r.t. $\langle \mathsf{Par}, \mathsf{Sign} \rangle$. It should be clear that, if we consider as input abstractions any convex abstract domain other than Par (mixing in the same abstract value even and odd values) such as Sign or Int, then ANI w.r.t. Sign as output abstraction (e.g., $\langle \mathsf{Sign}, \mathsf{Sign} \rangle$ or $\langle \mathsf{Int}, \mathsf{Sign} \rangle$) does not hold anymore. ◁

Although Abstract Non-Interference and Completeness may initially appear to be distinct notions, they have been proved to be equivalent in [35]. This equivalence enables the reuse of verification mechanisms for ANI to verify Completeness. Conversely, domain transformers that induce Completeness (e.g., [3,26]) can also be repurposed to enforce ANI.

6 A *General Approximated* Confidentiality Property

Non-Interference [27] has been widely adopted to model various security properties, particularly confidentiality, which concerns the control of information flow within a computer system. Despite its widespread use in academic research, Non-Interference is rarely achievable in real-world systems for two main reasons: first, it is a very strong property that requires complete indistinguishability of data; second, practical systems often need to reveal some information to function—for example, a password checker necessarily leaks some information about the input when indicating whether access is granted. As a result, several weakened variants of Non-Interference have been proposed. Broadly, these relaxations fall into two categories, which correspond to the two types of approximation discussed in Sect. 4: *semantic* approximation and *quantitative* approximation.

Abstract Non-Interference (cf. Definition 10) adopts a semantic approach, replacing indistinguishability between *data* with indistinguishability between *properties of data*. This constitutes a semantic approximation, as it requires the abstraction of the program semantics to be indistinguishable whenever the inputs are indistinguishable with respect to a given abstract property. In language-based security, it means that if the observable output remains within the group of all acceptable outputs (modeled as an abstraction), the system is deemed secure.

Approximate Non-Interference [18] follows a quantitative approach, where *indistinguishability* between data is replaced by *similarity*. Originally introduced in the context of probabilistic process algebras, this notion requires that the observable behaviors of two agents differ by no more than a threshold ε, rather than being strictly identical as in standard Non-Interference [27].

Our idea is to *combine* the two approximation strategies (cf. Sect. 4)—semantic and quantitative—while keeping the two types of approximation explicitly distinct. This leads to a new notion called *Partial Abstract Non-Interference*, where *indistinguishability* between *data* is replaced by *similarity* between *properties of data*. In security, Partial ANI would offer a more refined modeling capability. Instead of requiring outputs to be indistinguishable under a coarse abstraction, it allow outputs to vary, as long as the variation remains within a specified quantitative bound. This enables a more nuanced treatment of security policies, especially when small, bounded differences in outputs are tolerable.

6.1 Partial Abstract Non-Interference

Partial Abstract Non-Interference is a novel relaxation of Non-Interference that combines both semantic and quantitative approximations. Specifically, it observes properties of data (as in ANI) rather than raw data, while allowing for a bounded distance between these observed properties.

Definition 11 (ε-Partial Abstract Non-Interference). *Let $\langle C, \preceq_C \rangle$ be the input domain and $\langle D, \preceq_D \rangle$ be the output one (posets), respectively. Let $\langle C, \delta_C \rangle$ and $\langle D, \delta_D \rangle$ be pre-metric spaces. Let $\eta \in Uco(C)$, $\rho \in Uco(D)$ be the abstractions of the input and output domains, respectively, and $\varepsilon \in \mathbb{R}_{\geq 0}^{\infty}$. A function $f: C \to D$ satisfies ε-Partial Abstract Non-Interference (ε-Partial ANI for short) w.r.t. $\langle \delta_C^\eta, \delta_D^\rho \rangle$ when the following implication holds:*

$$\forall x, y \in C \, . \, \delta_C^\eta(x,y) = 0 \implies \delta_D^\rho(f(x), f(y)) \leq \varepsilon$$

Starting from inputs whose property distance is zero according to δ_C^η, i.e., $\delta_C^\eta(x,y) = 0$, Partial ANI allows the function to produce different outputs, potentially with different properties under δ_D^ρ, as long as the variation remains bounded, specifically not exceeding a given threshold ε, i.e. $\delta_D^\rho(f(x), f(y)) \leq \varepsilon$. It is important to note that the condition $\delta_C^\eta(x,y) = 0$ does not imply $\eta(x) = \eta(y)$ (as required for ANI, cf. Definition 10) since δ_C is a pre-metric and may therefore violate the *(iff-identity)* axiom. As a result, on the left-hand side of the implication, Partial ANI allows inputs to be mapped by η to different abstract properties, while still being indistinguishable with respect to δ_C.

Example 16 Consider the program R: **if** $x > 0$ **then** $x := x - 1$ **else** $x := x + 1$. and the standard collecting denotational semantics $[\![R]\!]: \wp(\mathbb{Z}) \to \wp(\mathbb{Z})$. Let us consider the counting distance δ_{siz}, defined in Example 3 and the abstract domain of intervals $\mathsf{Int} \in Uco(\wp(\mathbb{Z}))$. In this program, if we start from an interval composed by positive values only (e.g. $[1,8]$), then $[\![R]\!]$ decreases all the values by one (i.e., $[0,7]$). Something similar happens when all the elements in the interval are negative, e.g., $[-5,-2]$ returning $[-4,-1]$. The only case in which the dimension of an input interval changes is when the lower bound is non-positive (and thus increased by one) and the upper bound is positive (and thus decreased by one), e.g., $[-2,5]$ becomes $[-1,4]$. This means that starting from two sets $S_1, S_2 \in \wp(\mathbb{Z})$ whose interval abstraction has the same number of values (i.e., $\delta_{siz}^{\mathsf{Int}}(S_1, S_2) \leq 0$), e.g. $\delta_{siz}^{\mathsf{Int}}(\{-9,-2\},\{1,3,5,8\}) = 0$, we obtain as output two respective intervals with the same number of elements, e.g. $\delta_{siz}^{\mathsf{Int}}(\{-8,-1\},\{0,2,4,7\}) = \delta_{siz}([-8,-1],[0,7]) = 0$, or, in the worst case, with a difference of two, i.e., $\delta_{siz}^{\mathsf{Int}}([\![R]\!]S_1, [\![R]\!]S_2) \leq 2$. For instance, $\delta_{siz}^{\mathsf{Int}}(\{-5,0,2\},\{1,8\}) = 0$ in input, and $\delta_{siz}^{\mathsf{Int}}(\{-4,1\},\{0,7\}) = 2$ in output. Hence, we can say that the collecting semantics of the program R satisfies 2-Partial ANI w.r.t. $\langle \delta_{siz}^{\mathsf{Int}}, \delta_{siz}^{\mathsf{Int}} \rangle$.

Conversely, consider this time the program R* where * is the Kleene closure of regular commands [40] whose semantics is defined as follows: $\forall S \in \wp(\mathbb{Z})$. $[\![R^*]\!]S \stackrel{\text{def}}{=} \bigcup \{ [\![R]\!]^n S \mid n \in \mathbb{N} \}$ and where $[\![R]\!]^n$ is the composition of program R n times. Then Partial ANI does not hold for any ε (except for the trivial case $\varepsilon = \infty$). In particular, for any input whose interval abstraction has bounds of opposite sign, e.g., $[-2,4]$, the result is precisely the same interval since the collecting semantics keeps the greater collection; if the lower bound is not negative, e.g., $[2,6]$, then it is pushed to 0 in the output, i.e., $[0,6]$; while if the upper bound is not positive, e.g., $[-4,-2]$, then this is pushed to 1, i.e., $[-4,1]$. This means that for instance $\delta_{siz}([2,6],[21,25]) \leq 0$ but $\delta_{siz}^{\mathsf{Int}}([\![R^*]\!][2,6],[\![R^*]\!][21,25]) = \delta_{siz}([0,6],[0,25]) = 19$, and this difference may increase without limit. ◁

By fixing the bound on the difference between output properties to $\varepsilon = 0$, Partial ANI reduces to the following slight generalization of ANI:

$$\forall x,y \in \mathsf{C} \,.\, \delta_\mathsf{C}^\eta(x,y) = 0 \Rightarrow \delta_\mathsf{D}^\rho(f(x),f(y)) \leq 0$$

This notion collapses to ANI (cf. Definition 10) when both δ_C and δ_D satisfy the (*iff-identity*) axiom, namely when both are quasisemi-metrics.

On the other hand, if we move into the field of process algebra, if we consider $\eta = \top$ (i.e., we do not have constraints on the input processes), δ_C is any quasisemi-metric, and we consider as ρ the observation of the processes, then Partial ANI (cf. Definition 11) collapses to Approximate Non-interference [18].

6.2 On the Relation with Partial Completeness

In the last decade, it has been proved that there is a strong relation between the property of Completeness in abstract interpretation and Abstract Non-Interference [35]. Specifically, we know that requiring Completeness of a function w.r.t. an input and output abstractions, is equivalent to requiring that function inputs sharing the same property are mapped to outputs that also share the same property (i.e., ANI).

In this section, we study the relation between Partial Completeness (cf. Definition 9) and Partial ANI (cf. Definition 11). When generalizing ANI to Partial ANI by combining semantic and quantitative approximations, the equivalence between Completeness and ANI (proved in [35]) becomes an implication between ε-Partial ANI and ε-Partial Completeness. Vice versa, when we are considering a quasisemi-metric space and a pseudo-metric space for the input and output domains, respectively, there is an implication between ε-Partial Completeness and 2ε-Partial ANI. These statements are proved in the following two theorems:

Theorem 5 (ε-Partial ANI $\Rightarrow$ ε-Partial Completeness). *Let $\langle \mathsf{C}, \preceq_\mathsf{C} \rangle$ be a poset equipped with a pre-metric (not necessarily order-compatible) δ_C, and $\langle \mathsf{D}, \preceq_\mathsf{D}, \delta_\mathsf{D} \rangle$ be a pre-metric compatible space. Let $\eta \in Uco(\mathsf{C})$, $\rho \in Uco(\mathsf{D})$ be abstractions and $\varepsilon \in \mathbb{R}_{\geq 0}^\infty$. If a monotone function $f \colon \mathsf{C} \to \mathsf{D}$ satisfies ε-Partial ANI w.r.t. $\langle \delta_\mathsf{C}^\eta, \delta_\mathsf{D}^\rho \rangle$ then f satisfies ε-Partial Completeness w.r.t. $\langle \eta, \delta_\mathsf{D}^\rho \rangle$, namely:*

$$[\forall x,y \in \mathsf{C}. \delta_\mathsf{C}^\eta(x,y) \leq 0 \Rightarrow \delta_\mathsf{D}^\rho(f(y),f(x)) \leq \varepsilon] \Rightarrow [\forall x \in \mathsf{C}. \delta_\mathsf{D}^\rho(f(x),f \circ \eta(x)) \leq \varepsilon]$$

Example 17 Consider again the pre-metric compatible space $\langle \wp(\mathbb{Z}), \subseteq, \delta_{siz} \rangle$ and the abstraction $\mathsf{Int} \in Uco(\wp(\mathbb{Z}))$. From Example 16, we know that $[\![R]\!]$ satisfies 2-Partial ANI w.r.t. $\langle \delta_{siz}^{\mathsf{Int}}, \delta_{siz}^{\mathsf{Int}} \rangle$, i.e., $\delta_{siz}^{\mathsf{Int}}(X,Y) \leq 0 \Rightarrow \delta_{siz}^{\mathsf{Int}}([\![R]\!]X,[\![R]\!]Y) \leq 2$ for any $X, Y \in \wp(\mathbb{Z})$. Thus, by Theorem 5, it satisfies 2-Partial Completeness w.r.t. $\langle \mathsf{Int}, \delta_{siz}^{\mathsf{Int}} \rangle$, i.e., $\delta_{siz}^{\mathsf{Int}}([\![R]\!]X,[\![R]\!]\mathsf{Int}(X)) \leq 2$ for any $X \in \wp(\mathbb{Z})$. In fact, the bound 2 for Partial Completeness is not tight as $[\![R]\!]$ also satisfies 1-Partial Completeness w.r.t. $\langle \mathsf{Int}, \delta_{siz}^{\mathsf{Int}}\rangle$. Indeed, given $X = \{-1,1\}$, we have $\delta_{siz}^{\mathsf{Int}}([\![R]\!]\{-1,1\}, [\![R]\!]\mathsf{Int}(\{-1,1\})) = \delta_{siz}([0,0],[0,1])) \leq 1$, while for any $Y \in \wp(\mathbb{Z}) \setminus \{-1,1\}$ we have $\delta_{siz}^{\mathsf{Int}}([\![R]\!]Y, [\![R]\!]\mathsf{Int}(Y)) \leq 0$. ◁

Theorem 6 (ε-Partial Completeness $\Rightarrow 2\varepsilon$-Partial ANI). *Let $\langle \mathsf{C}, \preceq_\mathsf{C}\rangle$ be a poset equipped with a quasisemi-metric (not necessarily order-compatible) δ_C, and $\langle \mathsf{D}, \preceq_\mathsf{D}, \delta_\mathsf{D}\rangle$ be a pseudo-metric compatible space. Let $\eta \in Uco(\mathsf{C})$, $\rho \in Uco(\mathsf{D})$ be the input and output abstractions, respectively, and $\varepsilon \in \mathbb{R}_{\geq 0}^\infty$. If a monotone function $f\colon \mathsf{C} \to \mathsf{D}$ satisfies ε-Partial Completeness w.r.t. $\langle \eta, \delta_\mathsf{D}^\rho\rangle$ then f satisfies 2ε-Partial ANI w.r.t. $\langle \delta_\mathsf{C}^\eta, \delta_\mathsf{D}^\rho\rangle$, namely:*

$$[\forall x \in \mathsf{C}. \delta_\mathsf{D}^\rho(f(x), f\circ\eta(x)) \leq \varepsilon] \Rightarrow [\forall x,y \in \mathsf{C}. \delta_\mathsf{C}^\eta(x,y) \leq 0 \Rightarrow \delta_\mathsf{D}^\rho(f(y), f(x)) \leq 2\varepsilon]$$

Theorem 5 shows that having a proof of ε-Partial ANI of f w.r.t. $\langle \delta_\mathsf{C}^\eta, \delta_\mathsf{D}^\rho\rangle$, implies that f is partial complete w.r.t. $\langle \eta, \delta_\mathsf{D}^\rho\rangle$ with the same bound of imprecision ε. In other words, if f maps distinct inputs but having a zero distance according to δ_C, to corresponding outputs that differ by an ε amount according to δ_D (i.e., f satisfies ε-Partial ANI), then there exists a sound abstract approximation of f over $\langle \eta, \rho\rangle$, namely $\rho\circ f\circ\eta$, capable of producing a results with an imprecision, measured by δ_D, not greater than the bound ε.

On the other hand, the use of δ_C^η and δ_D^ρ in the definitions of Partial ANI (cf. Definition 11) and Partial Completeness (cf. Definition 9) amplifies the bound on the output error by a constant factor in Theorem 6. This is because Partial ANI bounds the distance between $\rho\circ f(x)$ and $\rho\circ f(y)$, for all $x,y \in \mathsf{C}$ that have distance smaller or equal than zero through the abstraction η, but Partial Completeness only guarantees a bound on the distance between $\rho\circ f(x)$ and $\rho\circ f(y)$, for all $x \in C$ with $y = \eta(x)$. We thus bound the output error for Partial ANI by adding up the distance between $\rho\circ f(x)$ and $\rho\circ f\circ\eta(x) = \rho\circ f\circ\eta(y)$, and between $\rho\circ f\circ\eta(x) = \rho\circ f\circ\eta(y)$ and $\rho\circ f(y)$.

Note also that Theorem 6 imposes stronger requirements than Theorem 5 on δ_C and δ_D. Its applicability is more limited and strongly depends on which imprecision we are interested to measure, i.e. the type of distances used over the input and output domains, as shown by the following example.

Example 18 Consider again the pre-metric compatible space $\langle \wp(\mathbb{Z}), \subseteq, \delta_{siz}\rangle$ and the abstraction $\mathsf{Int} \in Uco(\wp(\mathbb{Z}))$. The collecting semantics $[\![R]\!]$ from Example 16 satisfies 1-Partial Completeness w.r.t. $\langle \mathsf{Int}, \delta_{siz}^{\mathsf{Int}}\rangle$ (cf. Example 17). However, we cannot apply Theorem 6 to derive that $[\![R]\!]$ also satisfies 2-Partial ANI w.r.t. $\langle \delta_{siz}^{\mathsf{Int}}, \delta_{siz}^{\mathsf{Int}}\rangle$ because δ_{siz} is not a quasisemi-metric (it does not satisfy the (*iff-identity*) axiom). ◁

The relation between 0-Partial ANI and Completeness (cf. Definition 7) is a straightforward corollary of Theorem 5 and Theorem 6.

Corollary 1 0-Partial ANI $\Leftrightarrow$ Completeness). *Let $\langle \mathsf{C}, \preceq_\mathsf{C}\rangle$ be a poset that is equipped with a (not necessarily order-compatible) pre-metric δ_C, and let $\langle \mathsf{D}, \preceq_\mathsf{D}$*

, $\delta_D\rangle$ be a quasisemi-metric order-compatible space. Let $\eta \in Uco(C)$, $\rho \in Uco(D)$ be abstractions, and $\varepsilon \in \mathbb{R}_{\geq 0}^\infty$. A monotone function $f: C \to D$ satisfies 0-Partial ANI w.r.t. $\langle \delta_C^\eta, \delta_D^\rho \rangle$ if and only if f satisfies Completeness w.r.t. $\langle \eta, \rho \rangle$, namely:

$$[\forall x, y \in C.\; \delta_C^\eta(x,y) \leq 0 \Rightarrow \delta_D^\rho(f(y), f(x)) \leq 0] \Leftrightarrow [\forall x \in C.\; \rho f(x) = \rho \circ f \circ \eta(x)]$$

7 Related Work

The approach we propose, transitioning from pre-metrics to ucos, involves proving a non-trivial abstraction relation between equivalence relations and ucos. This is not the first work in this direction; indeed, in the literature [29], it has been shown that equivalence relations on a domain C correspond to ucos on $\wp(C)$ (and more generally, the most concrete uco associated with an equivalence relation R, has R as its kernel). In the present work, we needed to associate any equivalence relation on C with a uco defined directly on C, rather than on $\wp(C)$. This shift in the domain where the uco is formalized introduces a significant difference and makes the correspondence notably less straightforward. Indeed, defining a uco on $\wp(C)$ can be done straightforwardly by mapping each $x \in C$ to its equivalence class (a subset of C) as shown in [29]. In contrast, our approach requires defining a uco directly on C, which means selecting a representative element within C for each equivalence class. This selection is nontrivial, as there is no canonical or optimal choice that naturally leads to a well-defined uco.

Another strongly related work is [15], where the authors define the function transformers making any total function in $Fun(C)$ a uco. In particular, they define the monotonicity transformer M and an extensivity transformer, let us call it E, on generic total functions $Fun(C)$, showing also that $M \circ E = E \circ M$. In our work, we start from $Rel(C)$ (instead of $Fun(C)$), and we observed that it was possible to move from $Rel(C)$ to $Ext(C)$ directly, avoiding so far the application of E and applying M to extensive functions, thanks to the commutativity between the two transformers [15]. Finally, I is applied precisely to monotone and extensive functions, as it happens in [15], inhering so far all the results.

When considering the general approximation based on the combination of pre-metrics and abstractions, we can identify related ideas in other existing works. Partial Completeness (discussed in Sect. 5 and 6.2) is such an example. More recently, a similar idea has been explored in the context of Deep Neural Networks (a multi-layered machine learning model) robustness, where resistance to adversarial attacks is modeled by combining a distance over inputs with an abstraction of the outputs [25].

We also have a correspondence between ANI and Input Data (Non-) Usage [42] when f is deterministic, i.e., Input Data (Non-) Usage is an instance of ANI [36].

Although Partial ANI is a novel notion, Theorem 6 (and Corollary 1) ensures that verification mechanisms developed for Partial Completeness can be reused to verify Partial ANI. For example, in [5], the authors introduced a proof system for deriving triples of the form $[Pre]P[Post, \varepsilon]$, meaning that the distance $\delta_D^\rho(\llbracket P \rrbracket(Pre), Post) \leq \varepsilon$ holds. In light of Theorem 6, a proof of $[Pre]P[\llbracket P \rrbracket \rho(Pre), \varepsilon]$, that is, $\llbracket P \rrbracket$ satisfies ε-Partial Completeness w.r.t. $\langle \iota, \delta_D^\rho \rangle$, implies that $\llbracket P \rrbracket$ also satisfies 2ε-Partial ANI with respect to $\langle \delta_C^\iota, \delta_D^\rho \rangle$, assuming δ_C^ι is a quasi-metric. A similar reasoning applies to the proof system proposed in [23] to derive Completeness, which, under the premises of Corollary 1, also yield a proof of 0-Partial ANI. Moreover, existing (and potentially future) domain transformer techniques developed to enforce Completeness (e.g., [2,26]) and Partial Completeness can similarly be adapted to enforce Partial ANI.

8 Conclusion

We established a formal relation between quantitative approximations, formalized by pre-metrics, and semantic approximations, captured by upper closure operators, through a chain of Galois connections. This result shows that, under certain structural conditions on a pre-metric, a corresponding semantic abstraction can be derived via Galois connections. Conversely, abstractions defined via ucos can be interpreted as specific instances of pre-metrics, highlighting a bidirectional connection between the two frameworks. We then formalized a composition of pre-metrics that first selects the domain of comparison and then measures distances within this selected domain, thereby enabling a form of layered abstraction. Such a composition, when involving a distance characterizing a semantic abstraction and a distance characterizing a quantitative abstraction, defines a new form of approximation, called general approximation, combining semantic and quantitative approaches while keeping the two types of approximations distinct. This general approximation captures the idea of allowing an approximate observation of data through abstraction, while also tolerating a certain error in the observation, quantified by a distance between abstractions. We believe that this is a promising approach to approximation, already used in some way in the literature, as we have seen in Sect. 7. In particular, we exploit this approach for defining a new partial form of ANI, where we accept an error in the observed output properties. We showed that this notion is strongly connected to the well-established property of Partial Completeness in abstract interpretation, mirroring the relation between the standard versions of ANI and Completeness.

As future work, we plan to formalize a deductive system specialized for proving Partial ANI of programs. Other deductive systems for the verification of Completeness [23] (and its local version [3]), Partial Completeness [5] and ANI [35] have already been formalized in the literature. As already discussed in Sect. 6, a verification mechanism for Partial ANI could build upon the framework developed for Partial Completeness and ANI [21], particularly in light of Theorem 6. This connection is promising, even though the approach in [5] focuses on a local variant of the property. Moreover, this future direction could inspire the development of an abstract interpretation-based static analyzer for verifying the Partial ANI property of programs. The challenge here lies in the fact that Partial ANI is a hyperproperty [12], and thus the standard abstract interpretation-based overapproximations of sets of traces cannot be directly applied.

The proposed Partial ANI notion is a *global* property, in the sense that it is universally quantified over all inputs. As a future work, we plan to formalize its *local* version, namely requiring Partial ANI over a strict subset of the input domain, and study its relation with other local properties in the context of abstract interpretation [1,3,6,34]. Dropping the universal quantification may invalidate the correlation already established between the global counterparts.

We formalized abstractions as ucos, which have been proven to be equivalent to Galois insertions [16]. In the future, we would like to consider weaker abstraction notions able to formalize properties that do not necessarily admit a best abstraction, such as the domain of convex polyhedra [28] or formal languages [4]. In this direction, the notion of weak closures defined in [35] could be considered.

Finally, in the literature there are numerous quantitative program properties under various formalisms (e.g. Quantitative Data Usage [37,38], Approximated Non-Interference [18], etc.) and other could be obtained by applying the general approximation mechanism of Sect. 4 (e.g. a quantitative general version of program monotonicity [6] or program continuity [9,11]). It could be interesting to build a taxonomy of quantitative program properties, in which the quantification mechanisms are expressed within a unified formalism, such as the combination of pre-metrics and abstractions presented in Sect. 4, and to study the assumptions under which one property implies another.

Acknowledgements. This work was partially supported by the project SERICS (PE00000014) under the MUR National Recovery and Resilience Plan funded by the European Union - NextGenerationEU; by PRIN2022PNRR "RAP-ARA" (PE6) - codice MUR: P2022HXNSC; by the SAIF project, funded by the "France 2030" government investment plan managed by the French National Research Agency, under the reference ANR-23-PEIA-0006.

References

1. Bruni, R., Giacobazzi, R., Gori, R., Ranzato, F.: A logic for locally complete abstract interpretations. In: 36th Annual ACM/IEEE Symposium on Logic in Computer Science, LICS 2021, pp. 1–13. IEEE (2021). https://doi.org/10.1109/LICS52264.2021.9470608
2. Bruni, R., Giacobazzi, R., Gori, R., Ranzato, F.: Abstract interpretation repair. In: Jhala, R., Dillig, I. (eds.) PLDI '22: 43rd ACM SIGPLAN International Conference on Programming Language Design and Implementation. pp. 426–441. ACM (2022). https://doi.org/10.1145/3519939.3523453
3. Bruni, R., Giacobazzi, R., Gori, R., Ranzato, F.: A correctness and incorrectness program logic. J. ACM **70**(2), 15:1–15:45 (2023). https://doi.org/10.1145/3582267
4. Campion, M., Dalla Preda, M., Giacobazzi, R.: Abstract interpretation of indexed grammars. In: Chang, B.E. (ed.) 26th Static Analysis Symposium (SAS 2019). Lecture Notes in Computer Science, vol. 11822, pp. 121–139. Springer (2019). https://doi.org/10.1007/978-3-030-32304-2_7
5. Campion, M., Dalla Preda, M., Giacobazzi, R.: Partial (in)completeness in abstract interpretation: limiting the imprecision in program analysis. Proc. ACM Program. Lang. **6**(POPL), 1–31 (2022). https://doi.org/10.1145/3498721

6. Campion, M., Dalla Preda, M., Giacobazzi, R., Urban, C.: Monotonicity and the precision of program analysis. Proc. ACM Program. Lang. **8**(POPL), 1629–1662 (2024). https://doi.org/10.1145/3632897
7. Campion, M., Preda, M.D., Giacobazzi, R.: On the properties of partial completeness in abstract interpretation. In: Lago, U.D., Gorla, D. (eds.) Proceedings of the 23rd Italian Conference on Theoretical Computer Science, ICTCS 2022, Rome, Italy, September 7-9, 2022. CEUR Workshop Proceedings, vol. 3284, pp. 79–85. CEUR-WS.org (2022). https://ceur-ws.org/Vol-3284/8665.pdf
8. Campion, M., Urban, C., Preda, M.D., Giacobazzi, R.: A formal framework to measure the incompleteness of abstract interpretations. In: Hermenegildo, M.V., Morales, J.F. (eds.) Static Analysis - 30th International Symposium, SAS 2023. Lecture Notes in Computer Science, vol. 14284, pp. 114–138. Springer (2023). https://doi.org/10.1007/978-3-031-44245-2_7
9. Chaudhuri, S., Gulwani, S., Lublinerman, R.: Continuity analysis of programs. In: Proceedings of the 37th Annual ACM SIGPLAN-SIGACT Symposium on Principles of Programming Languages, pp. 57–70. POPL '10, Association for Computing Machinery (2010). https://doi.org/10.1145/1706299.1706308
10. Chaudhuri, S., Gulwani, S., Lublinerman, R.: Continuity and robustness of programs **55**(8), 107–115 (2012). https://doi.org/10.1145/2240236.2240262
11. Chaudhuri, S., Gulwani, S., Lublinerman, R., NavidPour, S.: Proving programs robust. In: Gyimóthy, T., Zeller, A. (eds.) SIGSOFT/FSE'11 19th ACM SIGSOFT Symposium on the Foundations of Software Engineering (FSE-19), pp. 102–112. ACM (2011). https://doi.org/10.1145/2025113.2025131
12. Clarkson, M.R., Schneider, F.B.: Hyperproperties. J. Comput. Secur. **18**(6), 1157–1210 (2010). https://doi.org/10.3233/JCS-2009-0393
13. Cousot, P.: Principles of Abstract Interpretation. The MIT Press, Cambridge, Mass (2021)
14. Cousot, P., Cousot, R.: Abstract interpretation: a unified lattice model for static analysis of programs by construction or approximation of fixpoints. In: Graham, R.M., Harrison, M.A., Sethi, R. (eds.) Conference Record of the Fourth ACM Symposium on Principles of Programming Languages, Los Angeles, California, USA, January 1977, pp. 238–252. ACM (1977). https://doi.org/10.1145/512950.512973
15. Cousot, P., Cousot, R.: A constructive characterization of the lattices of all retractions, preclosure, quasi-closure and closure operators on a complete lattice. Portugaliae Mathematica **38**(1-2), 185–198 (1979). http://eudml.org/doc/115380
16. Cousot, P., Cousot, R.: Systematic design of program analysis frameworks. In: Aho, A.V., Zilles, S.N., Rosen, B.K. (eds.) Conference Record of the Sixth Annual ACM Symposium on Principles of Programming Languages, pp. 269–282. ACM Press (1979). https://doi.org/10.1145/567752.567778
17. Geometry of Cuts and Metrics. AC, vol. 15. Springer, Heidelberg (1997). https://doi.org/10.1007/978-3-642-04295-9
18. Di Pierro, A., Hankin, C., Wiklicky, H.: Approximate non-interference. J. Comput. Secur. **12**(1), 37–82 (2004). https://doi.org/10.3233/JCS-2004-12103
19. Di Pierro, A., Wiklicky, H.: Measuring the precision of abstract interpretations. In: Lau, K. (ed.) 10th Logic Based Program Synthesis and Transformation (LOPSTR'00). LNCS, vol. 2042, pp. 147–164. Springer (2000)
20. Dwork, C., McSherry, F., Nissim, K., Smith, A.D.: Calibrating noise to sensitivity in private data analysis. In: Halevi, S., Rabin, T. (eds.) Theory of Cryptography, Third Theory of Cryptography Conference, TCC 2006. LNCS, vol. 3876, pp. 265–284. Springer (2006). https://doi.org/10.1007/11681878_14

21. Giacobazzi, R., Mastroeni, I.: Proving abstract non-interference. In: Marcinkowski, J., Tarlecki, A. (eds.) CSL 2004. LNCS, vol. 3210, pp. 280–294. Springer, Heidelberg (2004). https://doi.org/10.1007/978-3-540-30124-0_23
22. Giacobazzi, R., Mastroeni, I.: Adjoining classified and unclassified information by abstract interpretation. J. Comput. Secur. **18**(5), 751–797 (2010)
23. Giacobazzi, R., Logozzo, F., Ranzato, F.: Analyzing program analyses. In: Rajamani, S.K., Walker, D. (eds.) Proceedings of the 42nd Annual ACM SIGPLAN-SIGACT Symposium on Principles of Programming Languages, POPL 2015, pp. 261–273. ACM (2015). https://doi.org/10.1145/2676726.2676987
24. Giacobazzi, R., Mastroeni, I.: Abstract non-interference: a unifying framework for weakening information-flow. ACM Trans. Priv. Secur. **21**(2), 9:1–9:31 (2018). https://doi.org/10.1145/3175660
25. Giacobazzi, R., Mastroeni, I., Perantoni, E.: Adversities in abstract interpretation - accommodating robustness by abstract interpretation. ACM Trans. Program. Lang. Syst. **46**(2), 5 (2024). https://doi.org/10.1145/3649309
26. Giacobazzi, R., Ranzato, F., Scozzari, F.: Making abstract interpretations complete. J. ACM **47**(2), 361–416 (2000). https://doi.org/10.1145/333979.333989
27. Goguen, J.A., Meseguer, J.: Security policies and security models. In: 1982 IEEE Symposium on Security and Privacy, Oakland, CA, USA, April 26-28, 1982, pp. 11–20. IEEE Computer Society (1982). https://doi.org/10.1109/SP.1982.10014
28. Grünbaum, B., Klee, V., Perles, M.A., Shephard, G.C.: Convex polytopes, vol. 16. Springer (1967)
29. Hunt, S., Mastroeni, I.: The PER model of abstract non-interference. In: Hankin, C., Siveroni, I. (eds.) Static Analysis, 12th International Symposium, SAS 2005, London, UK, September 7-9, 2005, Proceedings. Lecture Notes in Computer Science, vol. 3672, pp. 171–185. Springer (2005). https://doi.org/10.1007/11547662_13
30. Liew, D., Cogumbreiro, T., Lange, J.: Sound and partially-complete static analysis of data-races in GPU programs. Proc. ACM Program. Lang. **8**(OOPSLA2), 2434–2461 (2024). https://doi.org/10.1145/3689797
31. Logozzo, F.: Towards a quantitative estimation of abstract interpretations. In: Workshop on Quantitative Analysis of Software. Microsoft (2009). https://www.microsoft.com/en-us/research/publication/towards-a-quantitative-estimation-of-abstract-interpretations/
32. Mastroeni, I.: On the role of abstract non-interference in language-based security. In: Yi, K. (ed.) 3rd Asian Symp. on Programming Languages and Systems (APLAS '05). Lecture Notes in Computer Science, vol. 3780, pp. 418–433. Springer
33. Mastroeni, I.: Abstract interpretation-based approaches to security - a survey on abstract non-interference and its challenging applications. Electron. Proc. Theoretical Comput. Sci. **129**, 41–65 (2013). https://doi.org/10.4204/eptcs.129.4
34. Mastroeni, I.: Abstract local completeness - a local form of abstract non-interference. In: Krishna, S., Sankaranarayanan, S., Trivedi, A. (eds.) 26th Verification, Model Checking, and Abstract Interpretation (VMCAI 2025). Lecture Notes in Computer Science, vol. 15530, pp. 3–25. Springer (2025). https://doi.org/10.1007/978-3-031-82703-7_1
35. Mastroeni, I., Pasqua, M.: Domain precision in galois connection-less abstract interpretation. In: Hermenegildo, M.V., Morales, J.F. (eds.) Static Analysis - 30th International Symposium, SAS 2023, Cascais, Portugal, October 22-24, 2023, Proceedings. Lecture Notes in Computer Science, vol. 14284, pp. 434–459. Springer (2023). https://doi.org/10.1007/978-3-031-44245-2_19

36. Mazzucato, D.: Static analysis by abstract interpretation of quantitative program properties. (Analyse Statique par Interprétation Abstraite de Propriétés Quantitatives de Programmes). Ph.D. thesis, École Normale Supérieure, Paris, France (2024). https://tel.archives-ouvertes.fr/tel-04886659
37. Mazzucato, D., Campion, M., Urban, C.: Quantitative input usage static analysis. In: Benz, N., Gopinath, D., Shi, N. (eds.) NASA Formal Methods - 16th International Symposium, NFM 2024, Moffett Field, CA, USA, June 4-6, 2024, Proceedings. Lecture Notes in Computer Science, vol. 14627, pp. 79–98. Springer (2024). https://doi.org/10.1007/978-3-031-60698-4_5
38. Mazzucato, D., Campion, M., Urban, C.: Quantitative static timing analysis. In: Giacobazzi, R., Gorla, A. (eds.) Static Analysis - 31st International Symposium, SAS 2024, Pasadena, CA, USA, October 20-22, 2024, Proceedings. Lecture Notes in Computer Science, vol. 14995, pp. 268–299. Springer (2024). https://doi.org/10.1007/978-3-031-74776-2_11
39. Miné, A.: The octagon abstract domain. In: Burd, E., Aiken, P., Koschke, R. (eds.) Proc. of the 8th Working Conf. on Reverse Engineering, WCRE'01. p. 310. IEEE Computer Society (2001). https://doi.org/10.1109/WCRE.2001.957836
40. O'Hearn, P.W.: Incorrectness logic. Proc. ACM Program. Lang. **4**(POPL), 10:1–10:32 (2020). https://doi.org/10.1145/3371078
41. Sotin, P.: Quantifying the precision of numerical abstract domains. Research Report (2010). https://inria.hal.science/inria-00457324
42. Urban, C., Müller, P.: An abstract interpretation framework for input data usage. In: Ahmed, A. (ed.) 27th European Symposium on Programming, ESOP 2018. Lecture Notes in Computer Science, vol. 10801, pp. 683–710. Springer (2018). https://doi.org/10.1007/978-3-319-89884-1_24

DUCTAPE: Optimizing Dynamically Typed Programs Using Ahead-of-Time Compilation and Data-Flow Analysis

Adi Harif(✉) and Shachar Itzhaky

Technion—Israel Institute of Technology, Haifa, Israel
adi.harift@gmail.com

Abstract. The software landscape is showing consistent, accelerated growth in the volume of code developed using dynamic languages. These languages are characterized by dynamic typing and more lax preemptive checks, which allow rapid application development and shorter development cycles. The vast majority of these languages are interpreted; that is, programs are executed by an interpreter in a managed runtime environment. Such interpreters incur significant performance hits, and, to counter that, modern runtime environments usually employ some sort of optimization. The most common one is Just-in-Time compilation (JIT), which translates source code on-demand into native code that can run much faster. Some notable JIT engines (such as V8 for JavaScript) exhibit impressive speedups. Still, in most realistic scenarios, they cannot surpass the performance of hand-crafted native code written in a low-level language like C.

There are inherent reasons for why *Ahead-of-Time* compilation (AOT) is rarely practiced with dynamic languages. Since variables are dynamically typed, this will require most of the type-checking to be done at runtime still, thus limiting the range of optimization that can be performed ahead of time, consequently limiting the benefit of AOT compilation. We propose an approach that utilizes static analysis for the purpose of *sound* type inference, which can then be leveraged for code generation requiring a minimal amount of runtime type checks. Unlike previous work in this area, our approach eliminates the need for the JIT at runtime. Indeed, for programs that avoid using inherently dynamic features (such as `eval` or reflection) we can eliminate the need for a managed runtime altogether.

Our preliminary results show that programs compiled ahead-of-time using our approach achieve substantial speedups compared to execution in a purely interpreted environment. These speedups are greater than previous efforts in that area. In some cases, our results even come close to execution times using an interpreter with a JIT compiler. This lets us believe that, with further improvements, this methodology can be utilized to surpass JIT speedups.

Keywords: Static Analysis · Optimizing Compilation · Dynamic Types · Type Inference · Abstract Interpretation

1 Introduction

Recent surveys show that JavaScript is the language of choice of ~60% of software developers [27–29]. Dynamic programming languages, overall, are exploding in popularity [12]. The term "dynamic programming language" typically refers to an ecosystem in which execution is based on an interpreter, which in turns admits a range of decisions that can be made at runtime. In particular, most of these languages feature *dynamic typing*, meaning that identifiers are not necessarily bound to specific types; variables can be assigned values, and the values can have types, all of which are determined and checked for correctness at runtime. Not surprisingly, using interpreted, dynamic runtime environments has a huge impact on performance [18]. These overheads stem from several factors, some of which are: F1 **erratic control**, F2 **runtime checks**, and F3 **memory layout**. In more detail: F1 The interpreter is essentially a loop with a giant `switch` statement, branching to implement a different functionality for different kinds of instructions. This is disastrous to some fundamental optimizations present in modern compute architectures, such as prefetching and caching [23]. F2 Dynamic typing requires the interpreter to perform frequent type checks at runtime to determine the appropriate operations and detect potential errors. F3 The memory layout of program data is affected by the dynamic nature of the language. Data structures have to be tagged with metadata, and oftentimes, data elements have to be accessed by literal name, typically a string. This makes the memory footprint larger, and also severely damages spatial locality for the program using them—both leading to reduced cache utilization and significant slowdown in programs that are more memory-bound.

In order to provide a viable solution for execution of dynamic code without prohibitive overheads, most interpreted runtimes use some form of Just-in-Time compilation (JIT). JIT compilers, such as TurboFan [4] (part of the V8 JavaScript runtime), reduce interpretation overhead by compiling, on the fly, portions of the code that are found to be "busy", i.e. are executed frequently, thus constituting performance bottlenecks. In those parts of the code, they are able to completely eliminate F1. To some extent, they also counter F2, by obviating most of the type checks within the compiled code fragment; some checks are still needed, especially at the boundary between uncompiled and compiled code. Some of these checks may be quite cheap, such as checking that the argument value fits in a 31-bit integer (commonly referred to as "small integer"). Certain checks—such as whether an entire array consists of only 31-bit integer values—can be prohibitively expensive for large arrays. As a result, JIT engines often avoid emitting code that would require these checks, thereby foregoing opportunities to represent arrays using better, compact memory layouts, even when such layouts would be applicable and beneficial.

For example, the function `arrmax` in Fig. 1 reads values from an input array and computes the maximum value. Each array element needs to be checked that it is indeed a number, before the comparison (>) can take place. Even if the function is always called with arrays containing integer values, and the two functions are JIT-compiled for this type, this runtime check *per element* cannot be avoided.

```
function arrmax(a) {
    let m = 0;
    for (let i = 0;
         i < a.length; i++)
        m = max(m, a[i]);
    return m;
}
```

```
function max(a, b) {
    let m;
    if (a > b) m = a;
    else m = b;
    return m;
}
```

Fig. 1. An example program; computes the maximal value stored in an array.

As for F3, JIT cannot do much,[1] since it has to remain faithful to the interpreted runtime in which it is embedded, and as such, cannot change the memory layout of stored data—unless said data is copied on entry to the compiled code and back on exit, which, again, may be too expensive for large structures. It appears that in the case of large data structures, esp. those containing collections such as arrays and maps, JIT falls short; but these are precisely the situations in which compilation to native code would be most beneficial.

Some more advanced optimizations, such as whole-program optimizations, link-time optimizations, superoptimization, etc., are not available to JIT engines, due to the incremental nature in which it operates and to avoid delays during runtime. On top of that, JIT itself has some non-negligible memory footprint, and cannot be deployed on very low-memory devices, such as IoT. The combination of all of these arguments above gives rise to insofar untapped opportunities for further performance gains offered by Ahead-of-Time (AOT) compilation.

In principle, compilation of dynamic languages to native code ahead-of-time can be done in much the same way that it is done for static languages: each operator in the source language has its predefined semantics, for which the corresponding low-level IR can be emitted by traversing the abstract syntax tree, passing intermediate results through temporary variables in the traditional way. This eliminates the interpreter loop F1, and does result in some speedup [23], but does nothing to alleviate F2 and F3. The emitted code remains dependent on the original language runtime, including its memory model and built-in primitives. In fact, in sense of runtime type-checks, this solution is *inferior* to JIT, as the JIT compiler makes use of type information available at runtime while emitting the code, information that is not available to the AOT compiler backend.

Our insight, based on the discussion above, is that a-priori type inference for data elements in a dynamic language is beneficial for ahead-of-time compilation, and can produce higher speedups than the speedups manifested by the naïve

---

[1] There are *some* (limited) optimizations that a JIT can do to improve memory representation, such as storing object properties in arrays instead of hash maps when they can infer consistent offsets for them. [13].

code generation of LuaAOT [23]. To obtain these, some type information needs to be inferred, in order to both reduce the volume of runtime type checks (F2) and accommodate a more efficient data layout (F3). The more precise that information, the better the code that is eventually generated. We propose DUCTAPE, a TypeScript ahead-of-type compiler, at the core of which is a static analysis that uses a specialized type domain to reason about all the possible types that can occur at any program location. From these types, DUCTAPE derives the appropriate data representation and emits code for corresponding operations, such as integer addition, string concatenation, array element access, and so forth. This code is then passed through the LLVM compiler toolchain, to take advantage of more traditional, tried-and-true compile-time optimizations, which indeed were engineered with statically-typed code in mind. Compiling the source program using DUCTAPE results in a standalone binary, which no longer requires the presence of a managed runtime environment. The absence of the interpreter does pose some limitations of the language features DUCTAPE supports, as further described in Subsect. 2.4.

Our Contributions. This paper offers the following contributions:

- We define a type domain suitable for representing types in the form of a lattice. Notably, the domain includes collection types and union types.
- We describe a static analysis over the type domain, which infers sound overapproximations for types of values occurring in untyped programs. This includes a clever combination of a type domain with pointer analysis, which we argue is crucial for soundness.
- We implement a proof-of-concept compiler prototype that incorporates this analysis. Our tool takes a TypeScript program as input, and outputs a corresponding C++ program, which can then be compiled using Clang.
- We perform an empirical evaluation, comparing the performance of programs compiled with DUCTAPE to execution using an interpreter, with and without JIT compilation. Our evaluation shows that DUCTAPE greatly improves the performance of these programs compared to JIT-less, interpreted execution. In some cases, the performance of the pre-compiled program is close to the performance achieved by the V8 JIT engine.

2 Overall Description

Here we will describe the general structure of DUCTAPE, a framework for analysis and ahead-of-time compilation of TypeScript programs into binary executables. DUCTAPE utilizes a specialized intermediate representation (IR) called DUCTIR, as well as Clang and LLVM toolchains to do so.

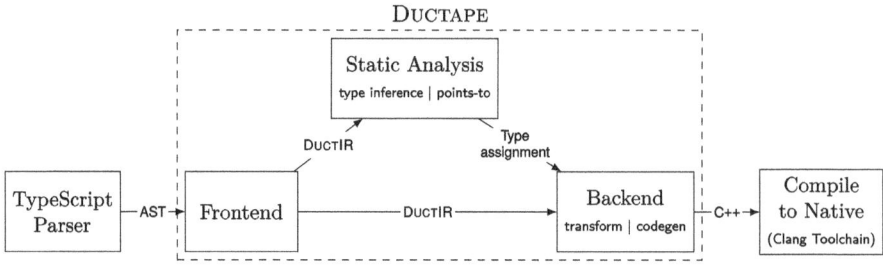

Fig. 2. DUCTAPE Architecture

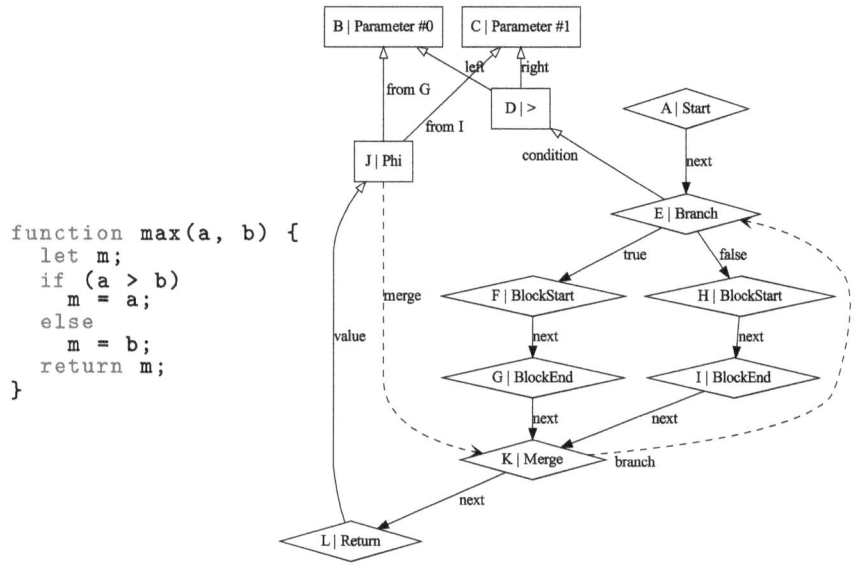

Fig. 3. DUCTIR – a small example (part of the program in Fig. 1).

The general structure of DUCTAPE, as depicted in Fig. 2, is as follows:

| Frontend | Utilizes the TypeScript Compiler (TSC) infrastructure to parse the input program and transform it into DUCTIR.

| Static Analysis | Reasons about the input program via analyzing its DUCTIR, inferring types of the program's values in a way that is sound, via a conservative overapproximation.

| Backend | Translates the DUCTIR into a low-level C++ representation according to the inferred types and metadata. This low-level code is then compiled to native machine code using Clang.

2.1 Frontend

The frontend accepts as input an AST of the TypeScript program, as produced by the TypeScript compiler. The output is the given program, represented in the form of a graph. We call this intermediate representation DUCTIR.

Program Dependency Graph. DUCTIR is a graph-based intermediate representation designed to facilitate flexible, composable static analysis of software. It has the structure of a Program Dependency Graph (PDG) in Static Single Assignment (SSA) form. A PDG [9] is a representation that carries both the program's control flow and its data dependencies. Vertices correspond to program elements: statements and expressions; edges represent control and data connections. Our flavor is similar to the one used by GraalVM [8], but somewhat simplified and relaxed. DUCTAPE uses DUCTIR both for the static analysis phase, and for code generation in the backend.

As an introductory example, Fig. 3 shows the DUCTIR of the function max from Fig. 1. Diamond-shaped vertices form the control-flow of the program. Rectangular vertices represent input values (parameters) and intermediate values. It should be noted that local variable names are not included in the graph; and that, following the style of SSA, multiple assignments to the same variable in divergent branches are merged using a Phi operator (see vertex J). More details on particular features of DUCTIR are explained in Sect. 3.

2.2 Static Analysis

A central challenge in compiling dynamically typed code to binary is determining how to represent program values. In dynamically typed languages, it is common for variables to assume different types over the course of execution, e.g. starting as undefined and later being assigned a number or an array. One theoretical approach would be to represent all variables and parameters with a uniform dynamic type that resolves to the actual runtime type, as is common in some interpreter and runtime engine designs. However, since DUCTAPE aims to optimize programs ahead of time, we chose to represent values with a single static type wherever possible, enabling more aggressive preemptive optimizations. Importantly, because the type systems of dynamic languages including TypeScript's are not sound [5], we could not rely solely on declared or inferred types from the source program for our low-level representations, as doing so could lead to undefined behavior. To address this, DUCTAPE performs a sound type inference on the input program, leveraging the program,s DUCTIR to ensure safe typing for subsequent compilation stages.

The static analysis performed by DUCTAPE assigns a type to each value in the program, specifically to each data vertex in the program's DUCTIR. These types are drawn from an abstract type domain designed to represent the most common types used in TypeScript. The type domain includes atomic types such as Integer, Number (floating-point), Undefined, String, and others. It also supports Union types, which model values that may assume different types during execution, as well as Array types for variable-size, homogeneous arrays. A specification of

max(3, 1.5);

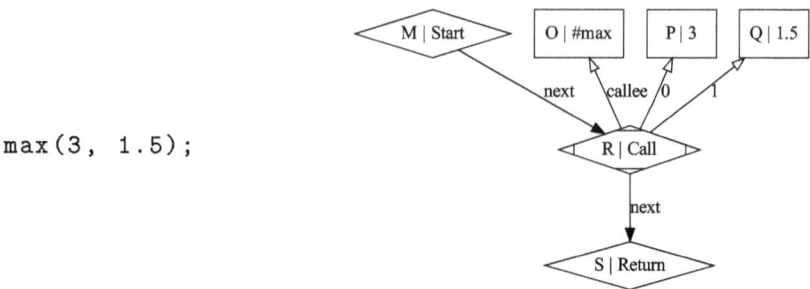

Fig. 4. DUCTIR – function call

the type domain can be found in Subsect. 4.1. Additionally, we define a partial ordering over the types, forming a lattice structure that is used during the type inference process.

For every data vertex in the graph, DUCTAPE infers its associated type based on the types of its data dependencies, and according to a set of typing rules that soundly encode the (runtime) semantics of TypeScript. This process iteratively applies the rules until a fixpoint is reached, which yields the least solution to the constraints imposed by the type system.

Consider the code snippet and corresponding DUCTIR shown in Fig. 3. Suppose we know that the parameters a and b are of types Integer and Number (floating-point), respectively. These variables correspond to parameter vertices in the graph; therefore, the type Integer is attached to vertex B, representing parameter a, and the type Number is attached to vertex C, representing b. Now, observe vertex D, which represents a "greater-than" binary operation. In TypeScript, the result of a comparison operation is always a Boolean value; accordingly, the inference rule assigns the type Boolean to such vertices.

As another example, consider vertex J, which is a Phi vertex. Since Phi vertices can take on the value of any of their operands, the type inferred for them is the *least upper bound* of the operand types. That is, the most specific type capable of representing all operand types. In our case, because the operands are of types Integer and Number, the type attached to vertex J is inferred as Integer⊔Number = Number, which can safely represent both integer and floating-point values.

It is important to note that local type inference alone is typically insufficient to infer types for all values in a program. Inter-procedural analysis is essential for sound translation in our setting, as we cannot rely on the type annotations present in the input program. Another limitation of local inference arises when reasoning about object operations, as Load and Store vertices referring to the same object may be located far apart in the program's DUCTIR, or in different functions. Considering the immediate neighbors of the operation will not give enough information to maintain the types. To overcome these obstacles and enhance the completeness of our analysis, DUCTAPE incorporates some basic pointer analyses. These analyses track which objects in the program may hold references to other objects, and identify which vertices may serve as aliases of other ones, such as arguments passed to a function call and the corresponding function Parameter vertices.

Consider a case in which the input program contains a call to the previously discussed max function, with arguments 3 and 1.5. The corresponding DUCTIR for this call is shown in Fig. 4. Our pointer analysis includes a rule specifically designed for function calls, which establishes connections between the parameter vertices of the called function and the data vertices representing the arguments at the call site. In this example, the call vertex R invokes the max function, as indicated by its callee outbound edge. Based on this, the analysis infers that the parameter vertices B and C in the DUCTIR of max may alias the argument vertices P and Q, respectively. This inference allows us to propagate type information from the arguments to the parameters: the types assigned to the parameter vertices must generalize over all argument types observed at call sites. Specifically, the types of B and C are computed as the least upper bound of the types of the corresponding arguments across all call sites. (The set of all call sites is over-approximated using pointer analysis.)

This pointer analysis is also crucial in order to maintain soundness of the type analysis, not merely to enhance its completeness. Consider the following code snippet:

```
const outer = [[1, 2]];
const inner = outer[0];
inner[0] = "thx";
```

This snippet allocates a two-dimentional array containing only integers, loads its first array element and then assigns a new values to one of its elements. Notably, using the rules demonstrated so far, DUCTAPE can infer the type of outer array is Array⟨Array⟨Integer⟩⟩. It is also inferred that its element, called inner, is of type Array⟨Integer⟩. However, the assignment inner[0] ="thx" forces the inferred type upwards, to Array⟨Union⟨Integer, String⟩⟩. As a result, the type of outer cannot remain Array⟨Array⟨Integer⟩⟩—as that would be unsound. Any changes to the type of inner must also be reflected in the type of any containing arrays. The analysis must track therefore "element-of" relationships between arrays and objects, to preserve consistent and sound typing. We track these relations using our pointer analysis, as described in Subsect. 4.3.

2.3 Backend

We have implemented a backend for DUCTAPE that uses the results of the static analysis to compile a binary executable out of the program's DUCTIR. The backend outputs C++ code, which incorporates the semantics of given DUCTIR objects, and is later compiled into a binary executable using the Clang toolchain. We chose C++ as our target language, rather than lower level IRs such as LLVM IR, to utilize higher-level language features, such as RAII for simpler memory management.

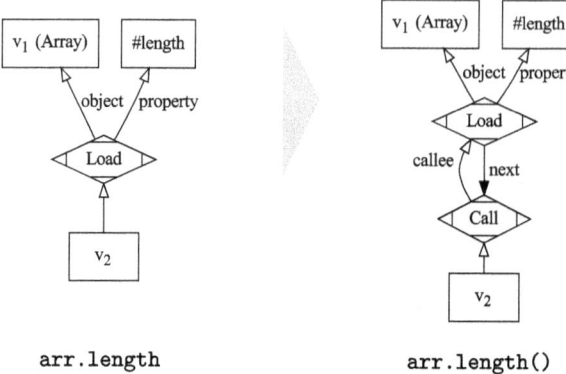

arr.length   arr.length()

Fig. 5. DuctIR Transformation

Before translating it to the target language, DUCTAPE's backend applies a few transformations to the given DUCTIR. This is done primarily to compensate for the source language and DUCTIR features which are not supported by the target language. One such feature is object property accessors (setters and getters), which are supported in TypeScript but not in C++ and are represented in DUCTIR as an object load operation rather than a method call. For example, TypeScript arrays have a length getter. In C++, we implemented a class, DynamicArray (thin wrapper over std::vector), to be used in the target code. The backend transforms arr.length into arr.length() by modifying the IR prior to code emission, as shown in Fig. 5.

After all necessary transformations have been applied, DUCTAPE translates the modified DUCTIR into low-level C++ code. During this process, DUCTAPE traverses the graph, assigning each data vertex to a local variable with an appropriate type based on the results of the type analysis. Each vertex is then translated into a C++ statement encapsulating its semantics, depending on the vertex kind. Conditional branches and merges of divergent control flows are converted into goto statements at this stage. We chose C++ as the target language because it allows convenient representation of complex data structures such as tagged unions and dynamic arrays, while also providing fine-grained control over the program's control flow through goto statements.

2.4 Limitations

DUCTAPE is a prototype, proof-of-concept implementation, and does not support all of the syntactic constructs and features of TypeScript. Major features that are currently not supported are class types and modules. This prototype is therefore applicable to a small subset of existing programs. The frontend checks the program and rejects any that contain unsupported features, so, at the very least, this limitation does not lead to unsoundness.

Naturally, due to the fact that DUCTAPE eliminates the use of a managed runtime, it is unable to support inherently dynamic language features that require one. The two main features DUCTAPE does not support for this reason are `eval` and reflection. Any use of the `eval` function or reflection (e.g. accessing the `__proto__` field of an object) will cause DUCTAPE to reject the source program. We see this as a minor limitation of the tool, as using these features is usually considered bad practice in modern TypeScript.

Another language feature currently unsupported by DUCTAPE is closures. Variables captured from an outer scope are inherently stateful and may outlive the execution of the capturing function, therefore treating them as regular, function-scoped variables can lead to unsound translations. A possible approach to handling closures is to represent them as objects, with accesses to captured variables transformed into explicit Load and Store operations. This is beyond the scope of this paper.

One source of unsoundness currently exhibited by DUCTAPE comes from the semantics of arrays in TypeScript. Arrays offer a very lax behavior with respect to index bounds: accessing the array at an out-of-bounds index results in the built-in value `undefined`. In contrast, DUCTAPE treats out-of-bounds access as undefined behavior. Indeed, one can expect well-behaved programs to respect array bounds; and our experiments comprise solely of ones that do. In principle, this property can be checked automatically by additional analysis of the numeric index domain; this is, however, orthogonal to the problem of types and AOT compilation, and approaches towards this aspect of static analysis, well, abound (e.g. [6,11,25]). We have therefore opted to separate this concern and not address it in this current work.

3 Intermediate Representation (DUCTIR)

A DUCTIR graph models the top level-scope of a module. Each function defined in the module is represented by a subgraph, containing its entire control flow and all declared and allocated values. Nested functions, including anonymous function definitions, are also represented as embedded subgraphs within the parent function's graph.

Structure. Vertices in DUCTIR fall into two categories: **Control** and **Data**.

- ⋄ **Control Vertices** model the control flow of a program and include vertex kinds such as Start, Return, Branch and Merge. These vertices form the backbone of the control-flow structure and determine the order of execution.
- □ **Data Vertices** represent program values and expressions and model the program's data flow. Common data vertex kinds include Binary Op, Unary Op, Literal, Parameter, and Phi. These vertices are primarily concerned with the representation of computation results and their propagation.

Some vertices belong to both categories, such as Allocation, Load and Call vertices. These vertices represent stateful program instruction that produce data in a flow-sensitive manner, and therefore should be anchored in the control-flow structure of the program. They also yield values, and participate in the data-flow within the program.

Edges in DUCTIR are directed and labeled, with three primary types used to encode different program semantics:

- **Control Edges** define the execution order between control vertices. They represent constructs such as sequential execution, branching, and merging of control flows.
- **Data Edges** indicate the flow of data between vertices. These capture data dependencies between different expressions in the program.
- **Association Edges** are used to connect auxiliary information or metadata between vertices, typically representing structural or semantic relationships that do not fall strictly under control or data dependencies.

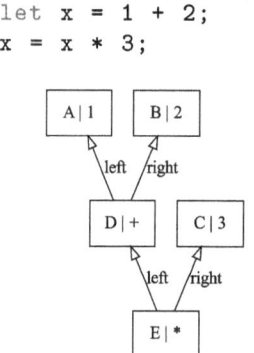

Fig. 6. DUCTIR– simple data flow in expressions.

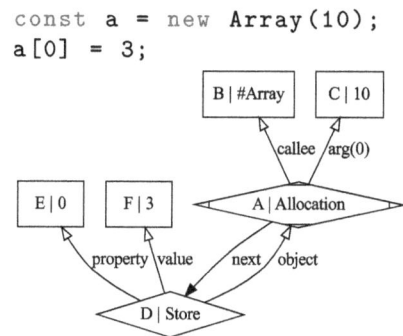

Fig. 7. DUCTIR– array allocation and store.

For example, consider code snippet and its corresponding DUCTIR in Fig. 6. The binary operators "+" and "*" are represented by the vertices D and E, respectively. Data edges connect each operator to its operands, which are the literals ("1", "2", "3") or previous applications. Note that the name of the local variable, x, is absent from the graph. This is generally true for local variables: they can be assigned multiple times, and each assignment manifests as a separate vertex, representing the assigned value, in the style of SSA. The first assignment to x is represented by D, and the second by E. Note that the first assignment (D) is used as the left operand of the second assignment (E), and is directly connected by a data edge. The actual name "x" is therefore not needed.

Local Variables and Memory. Multiple assignments to a local variables on separate control paths are handled with a Phi operator, as is demonstrated in Fig. 3. A Phi vertex is always associated with a Merge control vertex, via an association edge; and has outgoing data edges corresponding to that Merge's predecessors. This way, Phi vertices are used to merge assignments from different execution paths, such as those introduced by conditional statements and loops. (This is isomorphic to similar elements in other SSA-based IRs, such as LLVM's phi instruction.)

Memory access is governed by Allocation, Store, and Load vertices. These kinds are all control vertices; Allocation and Load are also data vertices, since they yield values. An example for creating an array and setting one of its elements is shown in Fig. 7.

Modularity. Each function subgraph has a single Start vertex, which is the entry point of the function and at least one return vertex. Each function corresponds to a single Symbol vertex that acts as a reference to the function. In Typescript, function are first-class citizen values, therefore these symbol vertices can be treated just like any other data vertex.

Construction of DUCTIR. To generate a DUCTIR representation of the program, the frontend traverses the AST in a bottom-up fashion as it translate each AST node into several DUCTIR vertices and edges. The translation is mostly straightforward, although some care is needed to make it right.

TypeScript's semantics is not SSA, and one of the frontend's primary tasks is to perform name resolution for local variables, keeping track of data vertices representing the current value of each variable at every program point, and translating uses to appropriate data edges. When creating a Merge vertex, the frontend merges the information from incoming branches, creating Phi vertices as necessary.

As for global variables, keeping track of their current value at compile time is not possible, as these values should survive between function calls and across different functions. Instead, we represent all global variables as fields of a single, global object, and translate their accesses to Loads and Stores. This preserves the lifetime and stateful semantics of global variables.

4 DUCTAPE's Static Analysis, Formally

To generate efficient low-level code from dynamically-typed programs, DUCTAPE depends on comprehensive static analysis. This section introduces the key analyses implemented in the system, with an emphasis on type inference and pointer analysis. As TypeScript does not provide sound static type guarantees, we define a custom type domain designed to support sound reasoning about types. These analyses operate over DUCTAPE's intermediate representation, DUCTIR, and are critical for ensuring soundness in the translation process. We formalize the structure of the type domain, outline the inference rules used in both the type and pointer analyses, and describe how the two analysis work together.

$L \triangleq \langle T \cup \{\top, \bot\} / \leftrightarrow, \sqsubseteq \rangle$

$T ::= B \mid \mathsf{Tuple}\langle(T, ...)\rangle \mid \mathsf{Array}\langle T \rangle \mid \mathsf{Union}\langle\{T, ...\}\rangle \mid \mathsf{Function}\langle RT, \mathsf{Tuple}\langle(T, ...)\rangle\rangle$
$B ::= \mathsf{Undefined} \mid \mathsf{Boolean} \mid \mathsf{Integer} \mid \mathsf{Number} \mid \mathsf{String}$
$RT ::= T \mid \mathsf{Void} \mid \mathsf{Union}\langle\{\mathsf{Void}, T, ...\}\rangle$

$$\frac{}{\mathsf{Integer} \sqsubseteq \mathsf{Number}} \,(1) \qquad \frac{K \in S}{K \sqsubseteq \mathsf{Union}\langle S \rangle} \,(2) \qquad \frac{S_1 \subseteq S_2}{\mathsf{Union}\langle S_1 \rangle \sqsubseteq \mathsf{Union}\langle S_2 \rangle} \,(3)$$

$$\frac{K_1 \sqsubseteq K_2}{\mathsf{Array}\langle K_1 \rangle \sqsubseteq \mathsf{Array}\langle K_2 \rangle} \,(4) \qquad \frac{R_1 \sqsubseteq R_2 \wedge P_1 \sqsubseteq P_2}{\mathsf{Function}\langle R_1, P_1 \rangle \sqsubseteq \mathsf{Function}\langle R_2, P_2 \rangle} \,(5)$$

$$\frac{}{\mathsf{Union}\langle\{\mathsf{Array}\langle I_1 \rangle, \mathsf{Array}\langle I_2 \rangle, I_3, ...\}\rangle \sqsubseteq \mathsf{Union}\langle\{\mathsf{Array}\langle\mathsf{Union}\langle\{I_1, I_2\}\rangle\rangle, I_3, ...\}\rangle} \,(6)$$

$$\frac{\forall i : K_i \sqsubseteq K_i'}{\mathsf{Tuple}\langle(K_1, \ldots, K_n)\rangle \sqsubseteq \mathsf{Tuple}\langle(K_1', \ldots, K_n')\rangle} \,(7)$$

Fig. 8. Type domain lattice.

4.1 Type Domain

Figure 8 presents the type domain used in our analysis. This domain encompasses a set of atomic types such as Integer, Number, String, and Undefined, along with composite types including Union, Array, Tuple and Function. The design of this domain is derived from TypeScript's type system, as it serves to model the semantics of the input programs of DUCTAPE; but also from the intended low-level target language. Our domain makes an explicit distinction between integers and floating-point numbers, captured as Integer and Number respectively, a refinement that enables optimizations opportunities downstream. The type domain forms a lattice, L, structured by a partial ordering relation $\sqsubseteq$, also described in Fig. 8, which enables us the use of monotone dataflow analysis techniques. To support TypeScript's object semantics, our type domain also includes object types, Object$\langle T \rangle$—representing an associative array with String-typed keys. It is elided from the definitions in Fig. 8 to keep the presentation concise, and because its ordering rules are analogous to those of Array$\langle T \rangle$.

Note that our definition of L admits some syntactically different types which are semantically equivalent; *i.e.*, there exist multiple representations for a single type. For example, Number and Union$\langle$Integer, Number$\rangle$: in essence, Number subsumes Integer, hence this type covers the exact same set of runtime values as just Number. From rules (1) and (2) we can derive that Number $\sqsubseteq$ Union$\langle$Integer, Number$\rangle$. It is *not* possible to introduce the converse, Union$\langle$Integer, Number$\rangle \sqsubseteq$ Number, since $\sqsubseteq$ must be antisymmetric.

These multiple representations are caused by the rather permissive definition of the Union$\langle\rangle$ type, and are undesirable, as they lead to imprecisions in

$$\dot{L} \triangleq L / \leftrightarrow \qquad \tau_1 \leftrightarrow \tau_2 \iff \exists \tau.\; \tau_1 \rightarrowtail^* \tau \land \tau_2 \rightarrowtail^* \tau$$

$$\mathsf{Union}\langle \varnothing \rangle \rightarrowtail \bot \qquad (a)$$
$$\mathsf{Union}\langle \{T\} \rangle \rightarrowtail T \qquad (b)$$
$$\mathsf{Union}\langle \{\mathsf{Union}\langle S \rangle, T_1, ... T_n\} \rangle \rightarrowtail \mathsf{Union}\langle S \cup \{T_1, ... T_n\} \rangle \qquad (c)$$
$$\mathsf{Union}\langle \{K_1, K_2, ...\} \rangle \rightarrowtail \mathsf{Union}\langle \{K_2, ...\} \rangle \quad \text{if } K_1 \sqsubseteq K_2 \qquad (d)$$

Fig. 9. Type domain — equivalence relation.

the analysis later on. Rather than try to work out a stricter, but more convoluted, definition for $\mathsf{Union}\langle\rangle$, we address this issue by introducing an equivalence relation, $\leftrightarrow$, on top of the existing domain. The relation is defined by a set of rewrite rules (Fig. 9), which yield, for every type term, a *normal form*. Types are deemed equivalent if they have the same normal form.

In the small example mentioned above, applying normalization rules (d) and (b) leads to a common normal form:

$$\mathsf{Union}\langle \mathsf{Integer}, \mathsf{Number} \rangle \xrightarrow[(d)]{} \mathsf{Union}\langle \mathsf{Number} \rangle \xrightarrow[(b)]{} \mathsf{Number}$$

Let us take as another example the type $\mathsf{Union}\langle \mathsf{Array}\langle \mathsf{Number} \rangle, \mathsf{Array}\langle \mathsf{String} \rangle \rangle$. By rule (6), we infer that

$$\mathsf{Union}\langle \mathsf{Array}\langle \mathsf{Number}\rangle, \mathsf{Array}\langle \mathsf{String}\rangle \rangle \sqsubseteq \mathsf{Union}\langle \mathsf{Array}\langle \mathsf{Union}\langle \mathsf{Number}, \mathsf{String}\rangle\rangle\rangle$$

Clearly, the outer $\mathsf{Union}\langle\rangle$ of the right-hand side is redundant, as it is a union of a single type. Applying rewrite rule (b) simplifies it to $\mathsf{Array}\langle \mathsf{Union}\langle \mathsf{Number}, \mathsf{String}\rangle\rangle$, hence $\mathsf{Union}\langle \mathsf{Array}\langle \mathsf{Number}\rangle, \mathsf{Array}\langle \mathsf{String}\rangle\rangle \sqsubseteq \mathsf{Array}\langle \mathsf{Union}\langle \mathsf{Number}, \mathsf{String}\rangle\rangle$. In similar fashion, for every set of types $\{K_i\}$, we can generally infer:

$$\mathsf{Union}\langle \mathsf{Array}\langle K_1\rangle, \mathsf{Array}\langle K_2\rangle, ...\rangle \sqsubseteq \mathsf{Array}\langle \mathsf{Union}\langle K_1, K_2, ...\rangle\rangle$$

We then refine our previous definition of the lattice L by taking the quotient of L over $\leftrightarrow$. The partial order naturally extends to equivalence classes. In the sequel, whenever a type term occurs in the context of the analysis domain, the semantics is that of the equivalence class in which it resides.

4.2 Type Analysis

Based on the type domain lattice (Fig. 8) and the graph-based IR DUCTIR, we define a data-flow analysis that infers sound types associated with vertices of the graph. Our analysis is flow-insensitive, and, following the methodology of data-flow analysis, consists of constructing data-flow equations and computing the least solution through least-fixed-point calculation. Every data vertex v in the program graph is assigned a distinct type variable, denoted $|v|$, which is then used in constraints that encode program semantics. The constraints are written in the form of (conditional) inequalities, using the order relation $\sqsubseteq$. The nature

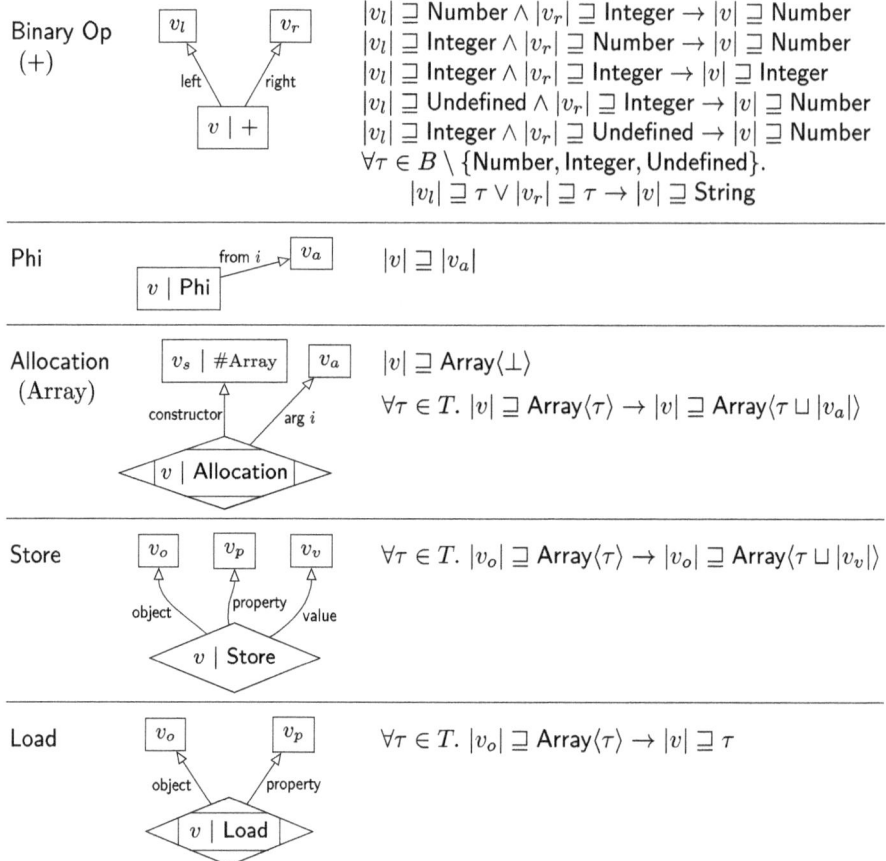

Fig. 10. Pattern rules for type-inference data-flow equations

of the constraint depends on the type of the vertex (or vertices) involved. We use simple pattern matching on the PDG to identify the constraint appropriate for each location.

Figure 10 shows a selection of the rules used to generate constraints for type analysis. There is a variety of operators in JavaScript, each with its own semantics and typing rules. We show the rule for binary '+', which is representative and also not quite trivial, due to JavaScript's predefined implicit coercions: when both operands are numeric, the result is numeric; When one is numeric and the other Undefined, the result is NaN (which is a special floating-point value); and in all other cases, both operands are coerced to String and concatenated.

The rules for array allocation, storing an element in an array, and loading an element from an array, encode the flow of type information through collections. At the allocation site, an array is empty, which is expressed by the type $\mathsf{Array}\langle\bot\rangle$. Storing an element lifts the type of the array by asserting the least upper bound of any element type τ and the type of the value being stored ($\tau \sqcup |v_v|$).

These usages demonstrate how the type lattice comes into play: in the case of arithmetic expressions, the least solution will pick the Integer if only $|v| \sqsubseteq$ Integer is present, otherwise it will pick Number. The constraint seamlessly addresses union types via the rule $K \in S \rightarrow K \sqsubseteq \text{Union}\langle S \rangle$ (rule (2) in Fig. 8). In the case of array stores, the least solution will be Array$\langle \tau \rangle$ where τ is the least upper bound of the types of all values that may be stored into the array, such that i.e. if both Integer and Number values are stored into some array v, the result would be $|v| = $ Array$\langle$Number$\rangle$; and in case String is stored as well, $|v| = $ Array$\langle$Union$\langle$Number, String$\rangle\rangle$.

All the rules take the form of Horn clauses, making them suitable for encoding and solving using SOUFFLÉ. This encoding is described in Sect. 5.

4.3 Pointer Analysis

The type analysis described so far works well for cases where the types of values remain stable throughout execution. This is typically true for immutable types, but not for mutable types like arrays and objects. As demonstrated in 2.2, an array initially allocated with type Array$\langle$Integer$\rangle$ may later "evolve" into Array$\langle$Union$\langle$Integer, String$\rangle\rangle$ if a string is stored into it. While our type inference includes rules to update an array's type in response to store operations, applying these rules soundly requires identifying all arrays that may be affected by a given store. This becomes non-trivial, since arrays are passed by reference, and the store vertex in the DUCTIR may not directly refer to the original allocation site.

To address these concerns, DUCTAPE incorporates pointer analysis alongside the type analysis. We use a standard, flow-insensitive, context-insensitive data-flow analysis with allocation-site heap abstraction. This flavor combines algorithmic simplicity with a natural affinity to type checking (which is also, mostly, flow-insensitive and context-insensitive, for the purpose of modularity) [1,2].

While this analysis is quite standard, we do highlight a few points specific to its application to DUCTIR and its combination with the points-to analysis. Our analysis has two facets:

Refers-To. In the reference points-to domain, we define an aliasing vertex as a vertex kind that may, at runtime, hold a reference to a value produced by another vertex. In DUCTIR, this includes vertex kinds such as Phi, Load, Call, and Parameter. We write RefersTo(v_1,v_2) to denote that the aliasing vertex v_1 may refer to another data vertex v_2.

Object-Member. Object-member points-to analysis, on the other hand, applies specifically to object *allocation sites*, addressed via their respective Allocation vertices in DUCTIR. We write ObjectMember(v_1,v_2) to express that the allocation vertex v_1 may represent objects that contain values produced by v_2 as elements. They may be array elements or values referenced by object fields.

It is important to note that DUCTAPE conservatively over-approximates both relations to ensure soundness. Since this information feeds into the type analysis,

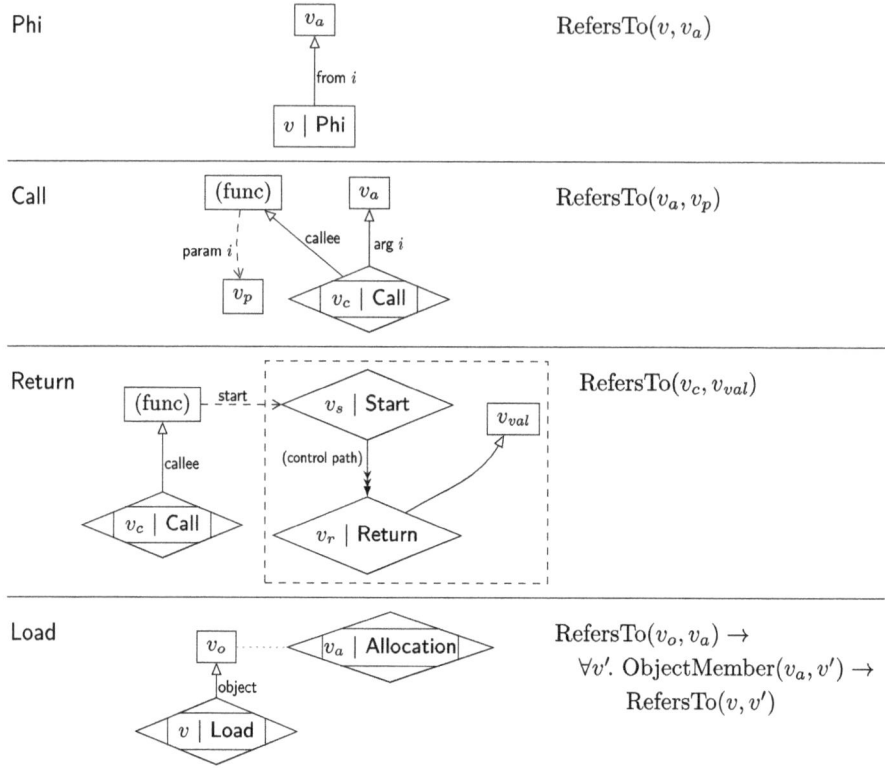

Fig. 11. Inference rules – Refers-to

any imprecision must err on the side of safety. We use a rather coarse analysis based on allocation-site heap abstraction as it is conceptually simple. Our working hypothesis is that the level of precision obtained by such analyses is adequate for the rather modest requirements of type inference.

In Fig. 11, we present a selection of inference rules used in the refers-to analysis. Unlike the type inference ones, these are standard Datalog rules, i.e. can be expressed with vanilla Datalog. The rules for RefersTo and ObjectMember are mutually dependent.

The first rule follows directly the semantics of Phi vertices. Since a Phi vertex may take the value of any of its operands, depending on the control-flow path taken, it can serve as a secondary reference to each of those operand vertices.

The second and third rules incorporate the semantics of function calls, covering both parameter passing and return value handling. In DuctIR, as in TypeScript, non-primitive values are passed by reference rather than by copy or move. Primitive values, on the other hand, are immutable, and since DuctIR uses SSA form, referencing a primitive is semantically equivalent to copying it in TypeScript. As a result, a parameter vertex in a function may refer to the corresponding data vertex passed at a call site, and a call vertex itself may be

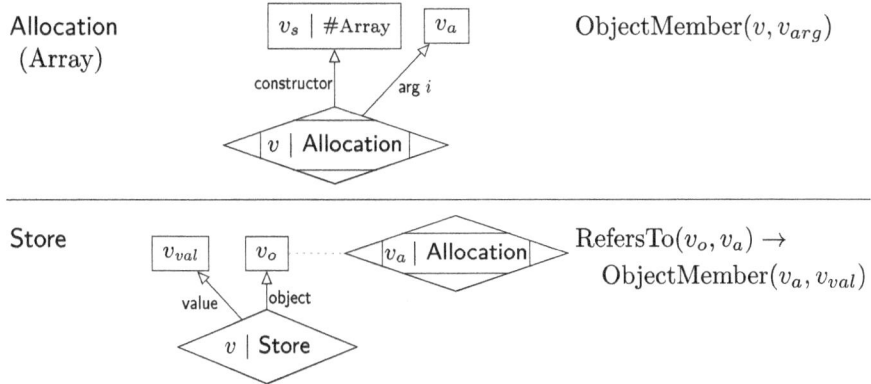

Fig. 12. Inference rules – Object-Member Points-to

a reference for any value returned by the function via a Return vertex. These inference rules also rely on auxiliary association edges in the graph, labeled "start" and "param i", which are constructed during DUCTIR graph generation by DUCTAPE's frontend.

The final rule in Fig. 11 addresses value loading from objects or arrays and depends on the object-member points-to relation. Because the analysis is field-insensitive, we conservatively infer that any Load vertex may refer to any value previously stored in the associated object, regardless of the specific field or index.

In Fig. 12, we present the rules for inferring the object-member relations. Each of these rules capture one of the two ways a value can become a member of an array or an object: (1) during allocation as part of the constructor and (2) when storing it to a field of the object.

To incorporate the points-to and object-member relations into our type inference process, we derive two additional inference rules that enhance the precision of the analysis.

(1) $\text{RefersTo}(v_1, v_2) \rightarrow |v_1| \sqsupseteq |v_2|$
(2) $|v_1| \sqsupseteq \text{Array}\langle \bot \rangle \wedge \text{ObjectMember}(v_1, v_2) \rightarrow |v_1| \sqsupseteq \text{Array}\langle |v_2| \rangle$

The first rule ensures that a data vertex is used as an alias for another vertex, has a type at least as general as that of the vertex being referred. The second rule keeps track of array elements and adjusts the type of the array to faithfully describe all of its elements. (An analogous rule is provided for $\text{Object}\langle\rangle$ types.)

Example. To illustrate how pointer information is used to extend type inference, we show the typing constraints involved in the analysis of the simple code snippet that was presented in 2.2. Figure 13 shows the relevant parts of the code's PDG (control edges omitted for readability), and the typing constraints for it. From these typing constraints alone, the least solution for A would be $\text{Array}\langle \text{Array}\langle \text{Integer}\rangle\rangle$ (shown in blue in the figure). As mentioned before, this

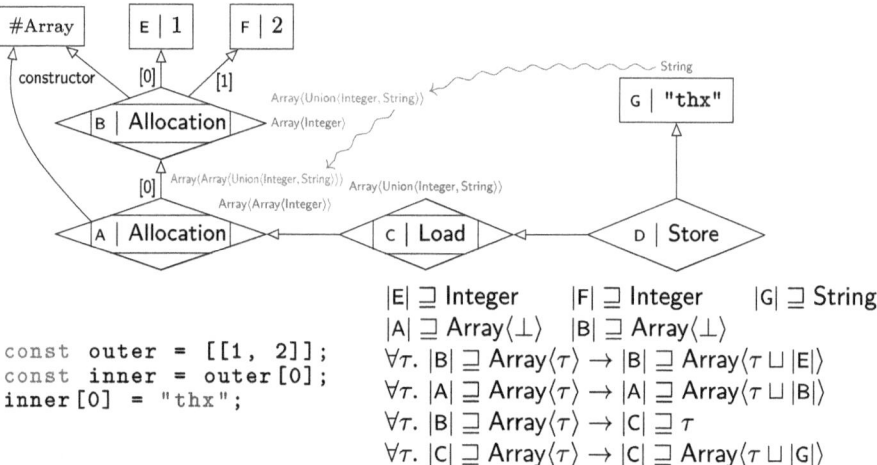

```
const outer = [[1, 2]];
const inner = outer[0];
inner[0] = "thx";
```

Fig. 13. Example of types inferred, combining information from the type domain and the pointer domain. (Color figure online)

would be unsound; the Store operation causes the array allocated at B to contain a String element. To this end, we turn to the results of the pointer analysis. From the Allocation rule, we can infer ObjectMember(A, B). From the latter and Load, we get RefersTo(C, B), and from that and Store, ObjectMember(B, G).

At this point, the second rule above enforces a constraint on the type of B, that it must be general enough to describe all of its (possible) members. With this constraint, the least solution will have $|B| = \text{Array}\langle\text{Union}\langle\text{Integer}, \text{String}\rangle\rangle$, as expected. Moreover, combined with the Allocation rule for A, it will also be that $|A| = \text{Array}\langle\text{Array}\langle\text{Union}\langle\text{Integer}, \text{String}\rangle\rangle\rangle$ (as shown in red).

5 Implementation

DUCTAPE is implemented mostly in TypeScript, and integrates several components as described in Fig. 2. It also uses SOUFFLÉ [17], a Datalog engine designed for large scale static analysis, to implement it's type inference and pointer analysis. In this section, we describe the key stages and tools used in implementing the static analysis component of DUCTAPE, focusing on how DUCTIR is encoded and processed using the SOUFFLÉ Datalog engine.

The first step in performing static analysis is converting DUCTAPE's intermediate representation, DUCTIR, into a relational format suitable for processing by SOUFFLÉ. This involves encoding the graph structure as a set of Datalog relations and exporting them as CSV files. The two core components of DUCTIR, its vertices and edges, are each represented by a dedicated relation. The **vertex** relation records the unique ID of each vertex along with its kind and label. The **edge** relation captures the graph edges, with each entry specifying a source ID, a destination ID, the edge kind, and an associated label. These relations are then used for implementing DUCTAPE's static analysis inference rules.

SOUFFLÉ rules are declarative logic statements that derive new facts from existing relations. Each rule has a head, which specifies the new fact it adds to the program, and a body, which lists the conditions that must be satisfied for the head to hold. These rules operate over input relations, producing new derived information based on pattern matching and variable binding. For example, given a vertex(id, kind, label) relation and an edge(src, dst, kind, label) relation, we can write rules to calculate a relation containing all pairs of vertices that are reachable from one to another:

```
reachable(v, u) :- edge(v, u, _, _).
reachable(v, u) :- reachable(v, w), edge(w, u, _, _).
```

The first rule seeds the relation with all pairs of directly connected vertices, based on the edge relation alone. The second rule propagates reachability transitively. SOUFFLÉ evaluates these rules iteratively, deriving new facts until a fixed point is reached, meaning no further inferences can be made. This fixpoint computation allows us to express complex static analyses as a collection of declarative rules and logical constraints over the input relations.

In order to implement our type inference rules, we first needed to encode the type lattice into SOUFFLÉ. Luckily, SOUFFLÉ enables us to define lattices by specifying a domain, a least-upper-bound function ($\sqcup$) and a greatest-lower-bound function ($\sqcap$).

The type domain is defined in SOUFFLÉ by an ADT (algebraic data type) that enumerates all possible type constructors used in our analysis. These contain atomic types, such as Integer, Number, String, Boolean and more. It also includes parameterized types such as Array$\langle T \rangle$. These values of the ADT, can then be used as fields in relation entries.

We then define the LUB and GLB functions as SOUFFLÉ functors, implemented in C++. These definition are derived from the partial ordering of the type domain and let us use values of the domain's ADT as part of our inference rules implementation.

Consider the following rule:

```
inferred_type(v, $Integer()) :-
    vertex(v, "BinaryOperation", "+"),
    edge(v, left, _, "left"),
    edge(v, right, _, "right"),
    inferred_type(left, $Integer()),
    inferred_type(right, $Integer()).
```

This rule corresponds to one of the inference rules for the + operator in Fig. 10. When executing the rule, SOUFFLÉ first matches the variables v, left, and right to vertex identifiers that satisfy the specified constraints over the vertex and edge relations. It then looks up the types currently associated with left and right in the inferred_type relation, if available. Using the GLB functor, SOUFFLÉ checks whether these types are compatible with the expected operand types by ensuring that they are below or equal to the required types in the lattice. If this constraint is satisfied for both operands, the rule fires, and a new type is inferred for v, in this case Integer.

If v already has a type recorded in the `inferred_type` relation, SOUFFLÉ updates it using the LUB of the existing type and the newly inferred one. This guarantees that types in the `inferred_type` relation are monotonically increasing within the lattice.

After the analysis completes, DUCTAPE imports the results produced by SOUFFLÉ and attaches the inferred information back to its internal DUCTIR representation. As a result, each data vertex in the graph is now annotated with its soundly inferred type. With this enriched IR, DUCTAPE can generate appropriate C++ code by translating each vertex into one or more C++ statements, tailored to the vertex's inferred type. Once the entire IR has been translated, DUCTAPE uses the Clang toolchain to compile the generated C++ code into a binary executable. Additionally, DUCTAPE links a dedicated library that provides implementations for several complex types used in the output program, such as `DynamicArray` (used to represent TypeScript arrays) and `Union`.

6 Evaluation

6.1 Experimental Setup

In this part, we evaluate the effectiveness of DUCTAPE on 6 benchmarks. The primary metric used in this evaluation is execution time, measuring the entire execution of the test program compiled with DUCTAPE, from start to finish. (Compilation time is *not* counted towards execution time.) For comparison, we also compiled these benchmarks using Microsoft's TypeScript Compiler (TSC) and then executed them using NodeJS, as this is a common workflow for executing TypeScript programs. We compared the performance of the benchmarks compiled with DUCTAPE to running them using NodeJS in two modes—with and without JIT optimizations enabled.

The benchmark suite we used also contained alternative implementations, written in other programming languages. We took the execution time of C implementations as references to compare them with DUCTAPE's compiled binary performance. We refer to these alternative implementations as "Handcrafted Native" in our results.

All executions and measurements were conducted on a desktop computer with an Intel i5-13400F processor and 32GB of RAM, running Fedora Linux 39, and using Clang 17.0.6 with the highest optimization level (`-O3`). Each benchmark in each workflow was executed 10 times, sequentially; Fig. 14 shows the average of all 10 executions in seconds.

6.2 Benchmark Suite

We chose to evaluate DUCTAPE's performance using the Ostrich benchmark suite [15]. Ostrich is aimed at measuring performance of different languages and contains 12 benchmarks, each associated with a different class of numerical algorithms and computationally intensive workloads. These classes, also known as dwarfs, include workloads such as graph traversals, linear algebra algorithms, dynamic programming problems, and more. We chose using Ostrich to evaluate Ductape because we expected these kinds of workload could benefit from ahead-of-time compilation and be more heavily impacted by code optimizations. Ostrich benchmarks are implemented in several languages, including JavaScript and C. We ported these JavaScript implementations into TypeScript in order to use them as input for DUCTAPE, and used these ports throughout the evaluation. We also used the C implementations as references in our results. Note that we evaluated DUCTAPE using a subset of 6 benchmarks from Ostrich and not all available benchmarks from the suite. In our evaluation we have ignored benchmarks that contain usage of language features that DUCTAPE does not yet support, such as classes. We also did not include benchmarks for which DUCTAPE's analysis could not infer all required information for the tool to fully compile the source code.

6.3 Results

Our results, shown in Fig. 14, report execution times in seconds for each benchmark. In most benchmarks, DUCTAPE demonstrates substantial performance improvements over the JIT-less NodeJS baseline, with an order of magnitude speedups in cases such as "crc" and "lud". On average, DUCTAPE achieves a 5.2x improvement (calculated by geometric average), with a peak speedup of 16.8x observed in the "lud" benchmark. Furthermore, in some cases, programs optimized by DUCTAPE have execution times comparable to JIT optimized code and even handcrafted implementation in statically typed languages, making DUCTAPE a viable alternative to JIT optimizers for executing TypeScript programs.

One exception, the "bfs" benchmark, exhibits worse performance in DUCTAPE than in the baseline interpreter. This highlights a shortcoming of DUCTAPE with its current representation of objects: they are represented by a map (red-black tree) from string keys to values, where all values have the same type, since the type analysis is field-insensitive. This design ensures correctness and generality, but, unsurprisingly, introduces significant overhead for field accesses, which are frequent. The "bfs" benchmark creates objects (representing nodes and edges of a graph) through *object literals*, such as dest": d, "weight": w"dest": d, "weight": w. This is a common idiom in TypeScript (which has a structural type system), where the fields are allocated as keys and remain unchanged throughout execution A more careful, field-sensitive analysis would admit a compact representation in these common situations, eliminating this performance gap.

Overall, these results highlight that DUCTAPE's static analysis and ahead-of-time compilation pipeline can yield considerable speedups for many compute-intensive workloads, while still leaving room for future improvements.

We also analyzed the compilation pipeline of DUCTAPE to understand the time distribution across its major stages. As shown in Fig. 15, the frontend and

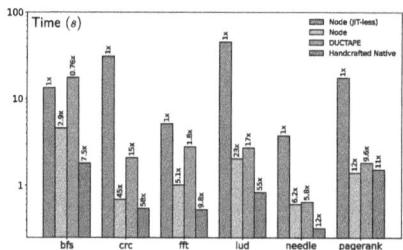
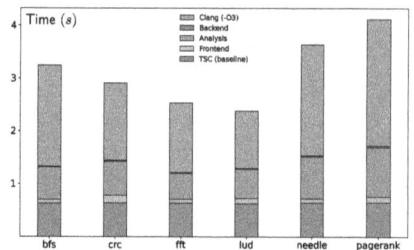

Fig. 14. Execution time comparison (Time axis is log-scale, data labels show speedup compared to the baseline).

Fig. 15. AOT compilation breakdown by phases. (Blocks above 'TSC' represent DUCTAPE's compilation time overhead.)

backend phases of DUCTAPE are marginal compared to the total compilation time. A more significant portion is taken up by the static analysis stage and the execution of the TypeScript compiler (TSC). The most time-consuming phase, accounting for roughly 50% of the overall compilation time, is the final stage, where the Clang toolchain compiles and optimizes the generated C++ code.

7 Related Work

Approaches to AOT Compilation. Ahead-of-time (AOT) compilation traditionally refers to performing a compilation step prior to and independently of a program's execution. In practice, AOT compilation can take many different forms, particularly when applied to languages that are typically interpreted. One notable class of approaches revolves around specializing the interpreter with respect to the program being compiled. This technique, a form of partial evaluation commonly known as the first-order Futamura projection [10], can span a spectrum of strategies. On the simpler end, it may involve bundling an interpreter with the program to produce a standalone executable. On the more advanced end, it can lead to the derivation of an optimizing compiler from the semantics or implementation of the interpreter [16,31].

Zhuykov and Sharygin [32] present a distinct interpretation of ahead-of-time (AOT) compilation in the context of dynamically typed languages. Rather than replacing or fully decoupling from just-in-time (JIT) compilation, their approach integrates an AOT phase that offloads certain early-stage compilation tasks prior to runtime. This interpretation of AOT focuses less on optimizing the code by transforming it ahead of execution and more on reducing the burden on the JIT compiler by preparing intermediate representations in advance. In contrast, DUCTAPE adopts a more traditional, optimization-centric view of AOT compilation, where static analysis and code transformations play a central role in improving runtime performance without relying on a JIT engine. Another interesting approach to AOT compilation, which is somewhat between the previous two is demonstrated in HERMES by Meta [20]. HERMES offloads several tasks usually performed at the start of runtime, such as parsing the input program into bytecode, into an AOT stage as well. In addition to that, HERMES also attempts at optimizing said bytecode in advance, in order to reduce the burden on the runtime environment. We note that HERMES does *not* produce native code, and the resulting code runs in the interpreter.

Optimization by AOT Compilation. Another attempt at optimizing dynamically typed programs is demonstrated in LUAAOT by Musso Gualandi and Ierusalimschy [23], a lightweight ahead-of-time compiler for Lua designed with a minimalist philosophy. LUAAOT compiles Lua programs by embedding the input program's bytecode in the Lua interpreter, and as a result eliminates the overhead cause by the instruction dispatch in the interpreter loop. In contrast to DUCTAPE, which leverages extensive static analysis to guide its optimizations, LUAAOT performs no static analysis whatsoever. Another key difference between the two systems lies in their runtime dependencies, as LUAAOT relies on the Lua interpreter to be present during execution, while DUCTAPE produces fully self-contained binaries with no external runtime dependencies. Although LUAAOT achieves speedups of up to 2.5x over the baseline Lua interpreter, DUCTAPE demonstrates significantly larger gains, up to 16x in some cases. We attribute this performance advantage primarily to DUCTAPE's use of static analysis to enable more efficient memory representations and control flow decisions.

Abstract Interpretation and Types. Abstract interpretation, a theoretical framework introduced by Cousot and Cousot [7], is a well-established foundation for static program analysis. Several efforts have applied this framework for type inference [14,19,26], often focusing on statically typed functional languages such as ML. These languages typically enforce immutability and disallow implicit union types, that is, values whose types can vary at runtime depending on the execution path. In contrast, DUCTAPE addresses two key challenges that arise in reasoning about gradually typed imperative languages like TypeScript: (1) accurately representing union types and (2) soundly reasoning about mutable data structures such as arrays and objects. These capabilities are central innovations of DUCTAPE's analysis and its abstract type domain. It is also worth noting that, unlike traditional abstract domains which are often finite or bounded to ensure termination, the type domain used in DUCTAPE is infinite. While, theoretically, this may cause the analysis, to diverge, it only occurs in corner cases which we have not encountered in any of our surveyed benchmarks.

Soundness of Gradual Typing. One notable advantage of DUCTAPE, beyond improving runtime performance, is its ability to enforce type safety. In gradually typed languages, ensuring type correctness typically requires inserting runtime checks at the boundaries between dynamically and statically typed code, which may introduce substantial overhead to program execution [3,30]. In the case of TypeScript, whose type system is unsound by design [5], even the statically typed portions of code can harbor type inconsistencies, meaning type checks should, in principle, be applied universally. However, because runtime type checks can be costly, most execution environments opt to skip them altogether, sacrificing safety for speed. Recent advancements in static reasoning about gradually typed programs have made sound gradual typing more feasible and practical [21,22,24]. Nonetheless, these approaches often introduce non-negligible runtime overhead compared to unsound but faster execution strategies. By contrast, DUCTAPE shifts this burden to compile time, using static analysis to eliminate the need for runtime checks while preserving type correctness.

8 Conclusion

In this work, we presented DUCTAPE, an ahead-of-time (AOT) compiler for TypeScript that leverages static analysis to generate efficient native code. DUCTAPE introduces a custom intermediate representation, DUCTIR, designed to bridge the gap between a dynamically typed source language and statically typed low-level code, as well as support advance static analysis of input programs. Our approach is centered around a novel type inference system, augmented with a lightweight pointer analysis, both of which are implemented declaratively using the SOUFFLÉ Datalog engine.

Through these analyses, DUCTAPE is able to infer types for data values, track aliasing relationships, and propagate type updates soundly across mutable structures like arrays and objects. This information enables DUCTAPE to generate statically typed C++ code that is then compiled into standalone binaries. Our results show that this method yields significant performance improvements—achieving up to 16× speedup compared to a JIT-less baseline interpreter. While DUCTAPE does not yet surpass the performance of state of the art JIT compilers or alternative hand crafted implementations in static languages, it shows promising potential for optimizing dynamic languages through static techniques.

References

1. Andersen, L.O.: Program analysis and specialization for the C programming language (1994)
2. Avots, D., Dalton, M., Livshits, V.B., Lam, M.S.: Improving software security with a C pointer analysis. In: Proceedings of the 27th International Conference on Software Engineering, ICSE 2005, pp. 332–341, Association for Computing Machinery, New York (2005). ISBN 1581139632. https://doi.org/10.1145/1062455.1062520
3. Bauman, S., Bolz-Tereick, C.F., Siek, J., Tobin-Hochstadt, S.: Sound gradual typing: only mostly dead. Proc. ACM Program. Lang. 1(OOPSLA) (2017). https://doi.org/10.1145/3133878
4. Titzer, B.L.: Digging into the TurboFan JIT (2015). https://v8.dev/blog/turbofan-jit
5. Bierman, G., Abadi, M., Torgersen, M.: Understanding TypeScript. In: Jones, R. (ed.) ECOOP 2014. LNCS, vol. 8586, pp. 257–281. Springer, Heidelberg (2014). https://doi.org/10.1007/978-3-662-44202-9_11
6. Chen, L., Miné, A., Wang, J., Cousot, P.: An abstract domain to discover interval linear equalities. In: Barthe, G., Hermenegildo, M. (eds.) VMCAI 2010. LNCS, vol. 5944, pp. 112–128. Springer, Heidelberg (2010). https://doi.org/10.1007/978-3-642-11319-2_11

7. Cousot, P., Cousot, R.: Abstract interpretation: a unified lattice model for static analysis of programs by construction or approximation of fixpoints. In: Conference Record of the Fourth Annual ACM SIGPLAN-SIGACT Symposium on Principles of Programming Languages, pp. 238–252, ACM Press, New York (1977)
8. Duboscq, G., Stadler, L., Würthinger, T., Simon, D., Wimmer, C., Mössenböck, H.: Graal IR: an extensible declarative intermediate representation. In: Proceedings of the Asia-Pacific Programming Languages and Compilers Workshop, pp. 1–9 (2013)
9. Ferrante, J., Ottenstein, K.J., Warren, J.D.: The program dependence graph and its use in optimization. ACM Trans. Program. Lang. Syst. **9**(3), 319–349 (1987). ISSN 0164-092. https://doi.org/10.1145/24039.24041
10. Futamura, Y.: Partial evaluation of computation process—an approach to a compiler-compiler. Higher Order Symbol. Comput. **12**(4), 381–391 (1999). ISSN 1388-369. https://doi.org/10.1023/A:1010095604496
11. Gershuni, E., et al.: Simple and precise static analysis of untrusted linux kernel extensions. In: McKinley, K.S., Fisher, K. (eds.) Proceedings of the 40th ACM SIGPLAN Conference on Programming Language Design and Implementation, PLDI 2019, Phoenix, AZ, USA, June 22–26, 2019, pp. 1069–1084, ACM (2019). https://doi.org/10.1145/3314221.3314590
12. GitHub: Octoverse 2024 (2024). https://github.blog/news-insights/octoverse/octoverse-2024/#the-most-popular-programming-languages
13. Gong, L., Pradel, M., Sen, K.: JITProf: pinpointing JIT-unfriendly javascript code. In: Proceedings of the 2015 10th Joint Meeting on Foundations of Software Engineering, pp. 357–368, ESEC/FSE 2015, Association for Computing Machinery, New York (2015). ISBN 9781450336758. https://doi.org/10.1145/2786805.2786831
14. Gori, R., Levi, G.: An experiment in type inference and verification by abstract interpretation. In: Cortesi, A. (ed.) Verification, Model Checking, and Abstract Interpretation, pp. 225–239, Springer Berlin Heidelberg, Berlin, Heidelberg (2002). ISBN 978-3-540-47813-3
15. Herrera, D., Chen, H., Lavoie, E., Hendren, L.: Numerical computing on the web: benchmarking for the future. SIGPLAN Not. **53**(8), 88–100 (2020). ISSN 0362-134. https://doi.org/10.1145/3393673.3276968
16. Jones, N.D.: Transformation by interpreter specialisation. Sci. Comput. Program. **52**(1–3), 307–339 (2004). ISSN 0167-6423. https://doi.org/10.1016/j.scico.2004.03.010
17. Jordan, H., Scholz, B., Subotić, P.: Soufflé: On synthesis of program analyzers. In: Chaudhuri, S., Farzan, A. (eds.) Computer Aided Verification, pp. 422–430, Springer International Publishing, Cham (2016). ISBN 978-3-319-41540-6
18. Lion, D., Chiu, A., Stumm, M., Yuan, D.: Investigating managed language runtime performance: Why JavaScript and python are 8x and 29x slower than c++, yet java and go can be faster? In: 2022 USENIX Annual Technical Conference (USENIX ATC 22), pp. 835–852, USENIX Association, Carlsbad, CA (2022). ISBN 978-1-939133-29-40. https://www.usenix.org/conference/atc22/presentation/lion
19. Lu, L.: Type analysis of logic programs in the presence of type definitions. In: Proceedings of the 1995 ACM SIGPLAN Symposium on Partial Evaluation and Semantics-Based Program Manipulation, PEPM 1995, pp. 241–252, Association for Computing Machinery, New York (1995). ISBN 0897917200. https://doi.org/10.1145/215465.215597
20. Meta: Hermes: An open source JavaScript engine optimized for mobile apps, starting with React Native (2019). https://engineering.fb.com/2019/07/12/android/hermes/

21. Moy, C., Nguyen, P.C., Tobin-Hochstadt, S., Van Horn, D.: Corpse reviver: sound and efficient gradual typing via contract verification. Proc. ACM Program. Lang. **5**(POPL) (2021). https://doi.org/10.1145/3434334
22. Muehlboeck, F., Tate, R.: Sound gradual typing is nominally alive and well. Proc. ACM Program. Lang. **1**(OOPSLA) (2017). https://doi.org/10.1145/3133880
23. Musso Gualandi, H., Ierusalimschy, R.: A surprisingly simple Lua compiler. In: Proceedings of the 25th Brazilian Symposium on Programming Languages, SBLP 2021, pp. 1–8, Association for Computing Machinery, New York (2021). ISBN 978145039062. https://doi.org/10.1145/3475061.3475077
24. Rastogi, A., Swamy, N., Fournet, C., Bierman, G., Vekris, P.: Safe & efficient gradual typing for TypeScript. SIGPLAN Not. **50**(1), 167–180 (2015). ISSN 0362-134. https://doi.org/10.1145/2775051.2676971
25. Rugina, R., Rinard, M.: Symbolic bounds analysis of pointers, array indices, and accessed memory regions. In: Proceedings of the ACM SIGPLAN 2000 Conference on Programming Language Design and Implementation, PLDI 2000, pp. 182–195, Association for Computing Machinery, New York, NY, USA (2000). ISBN 158113199https://doi.org/10.1145/349299.349325
26. Simon, A.: Deriving a complete type inference for Hindley-Milner and vector sizes using expansion. In: Proceedings of the ACM SIGPLAN 2013 Workshop on Partial Evaluation and Program Manipulation, PEPM 2013, pp. 13–22, Association for Computing Machinery, New York (2013). ISBN 978145031842. https://doi.org/10.1145/2426890.2426895
27. Stack Overflow: Stack Overflow Developer Survey (2022). https://survey.stackoverflow.co/2022/#technology
28. Stack Overflow: Stack Overflow Developer Survey (2023). https://survey.stackoverflow.co/2023/#technology
29. Stack Overflow: Stack Overflow Developer Survey (2024). https://survey.stackoverflow.co/2024/technology
30. Takikawa, A., Feltey, D., Greenman, B., New, M.S., Vitek, J., Felleisen, M.: Is sound gradual typing dead? SIGPLAN Not. **51**(1), 456–468 (2016). ISSN 0362-134. https://doi.org/10.1145/2914770.2837630
31. Wimmer, C., Würthinger, T.: Truffle: a self-optimizing runtime system. In: Proceedings of the 3rd Annual Conference on Systems, Programming, and Applications: Software for Humanity, SPLASH 2012, pp. 13–14, Association for Computing Machinery, New York (2012). ISBN 9781450315630. https://doi.org/10.1145/2384716.2384723
32. Zhuykov, R., Sharygin, E.: Ahead-of-time compilation of JavaScript programs. Program. Comput. Softw. **43**(1), 51–59 (2017). https://doi.org/10.1134/S036176881701008X

Automated Catamorphism Synthesis for Solving Constrained Horn Clauses over Algebraic Data Types

Hiroyuki Katsura[1]($\boxtimes$), Naoki Kobayashi[1], Ken Sakayori[1], and Ryosuke Sato[2]

[1] The University of Tokyo, Tokyo, Japan
{h.katsura,koba,sakayori}@is.s.u-tokyo.ac.jp
[2] Tokyo University of Agriculture and Technology, Tokyo, Japan
rsato@acm.org

Abstract. We propose a novel approach to satisfiability checking of Constrained Horn Clauses (CHCs) over Algebraic Data Types (ADTs). CHC-based automated verification has gained considerable attention in recent years, leading to the development of various CHC solvers. However, existing solvers for CHCs over ADTs are not fully satisfactory, due to their limited ability to find and express models involving inductively defined functions/predicates (e.g., those about the sum of list elements). To address this limitation, we consider *catamorphisms* (generalized fold functions), and present a framework for automatically discovering appropriate catamorphisms on demand and using them to express a model of given CHCs. We have implemented a new CHC solver called Catalia based on the proposed method. Our experimental results for the CHC-COMP 2024 benchmark show that Catalia outperforms state-of-the-art solvers in solving satisfiable CHCs over ADTs. Catalia was also used as a core part of the tool called ChocoCatalia, which won the ADT-LIA category of CHC-COMP 2025.

Keywords: Constrained Horn Clauses · Algebraic Data Types · Catamorphisms · Automated Verification

1 Introduction

Fully automated verification of programs through satisfiability checking of constrained Horn clauses (CHCs) has attracted considerable attention in recent years, as it offers a uniform and language-agnostic framework for verifying diverse program properties [1,12,16,25]. For example, consider the following functional program.

```
let rec plus m n = if n=0 then m else (plus m (n-1))+1
let main m n = if n>=0 then assert(plus m n >= m)
```

The lack of assertion failures in the above program can be reduced to the satisfiability of the following CHCs, i.e., the problem of whether there exists a predicate *Plus* that satisfies them:

$$\forall m.\ Plus(m, 0, m).$$
$$\forall m, n, r.\ Plus(m, n, r+1) \Leftarrow Plus(m, n-1, r).$$
$$\forall m, n, r.\ \mathbf{ff} \Leftarrow Plus(m, n, r) \wedge n \geq 0 \wedge r < m.$$

Here, **ff** represents false. The predicate *Plus* may be considered an invariant among arguments m, n and the corresponding return value r; indeed, $Plus(m, n, r) \equiv m + n = r$ satisfies the above CHCs. State-of-the-art CHC solvers [4,5,13,14,22] can quickly solve problems like the above, finding an appropriate invariant ($Plus(m, n, r) \equiv m + n = r$ or $Plus(m, n, r) \equiv r \geq m$ in this case), enabling fully automated program verification.

Despite various efforts, however, the current CHC solvers are not very good at dealing with data structures. For example, consider the following variant of the example above, where natural numbers are represented as data structures.

$$\forall m.\ PlusNat(m, Z, m).$$
$$\forall m, n, r.\ PlusNat(m, S(n), S(r)) \Leftarrow PlusNat(m, n, r).$$
$$\forall n.\ Lt(Z, S(n)). \qquad \forall m, n.\ Lt(S(m), S(n)) \Leftarrow Lt(m, n).$$
$$\forall m, n, r.\ \mathbf{ff} \Leftarrow PlusNat(m, n, r) \wedge Lt(r, m).$$

Z3 Spacer [22], a state-of-the-art CHC solver, fails to prove the satisfiability of the CHCs above. A problem is that while a model for *Plus* can be expressed by a simple linear arithmetic formula ($m + n = r$), an inductively defined predicate is required to express a model for *PlusNat*, and it is, in general, hard to automatically find such an inductively defined predicate and check that it is indeed a model (i.e., satisfies all the clauses).

To address the issue above, we propose a method for abstracting CHCs by using a *catamorphism* [26] from data structures to (tuples of) integers, on which existing CHC solvers perform well in practice. For the example above, we can abstract Z and S respectively to 0 and $\lambda x.x + 1$[1], and obtain the following "abstract" CHCs over integers, whose satisfiability implies that of the original CHCs.

$$\forall m.\ \overline{PlusNat}(m, 0, m).$$
$$\forall m, n, r.\ \overline{PlusNat}(m, n+1, r+1) \Leftarrow \overline{PlusNat}(m, n, r).$$
$$\forall n.\ \overline{Lt}(0, n+1). \qquad \forall m, n.\ \overline{Lt}(m+1, n+1) \Leftarrow \overline{Lt}(m, n).$$
$$\forall m, n, r.\ \mathbf{ff} \Leftarrow \overline{PlusNat}(m, n, r) \wedge \overline{Lt}(r, m).$$

Universal quantifiers are now over integers, and for the sake of simplicity, we have omitted some conditions on the variables; see later sections. State-of-the-art

---

[1] Actually, we do not lose any information using this *abstraction*, as the induced catamorphism is injective. In general, however a catamorphism may not be injective, hence introducing abstraction.

solvers can instantly deduce its satisfiability, which also implies the satisfiability of the original CHCs.

The remaining question is how to automatically find appropriate catamorphisms. In the above example, the required catamorphism is just the "size" function incorporated by default in some CHC solvers like Eldarica [14], but as we will see later, the size function is not always sufficient. To this end, we propose a method for automatically finding appropriate catamorphisms in a counterexample-guided manner. We have implemented the proposed method and developed a new CHC solver called CATALIA. According to our experiments using the benchmark set of the ADT category of CHC-COMP 2024, CATALIA significantly outperformed state-of-the-art CHC solvers for SAT instances.

Our contributions are summarized as follows.

- Formalization of abstraction of CHCs using catamorphisms.
- Counterexample-guided automatic synthesis of appropriate catamorphisms.
- Implementation of the proposed method and experimental evaluation.

The idea of using catamorphisms for verification of programs with ADTs itself is not new [9,15,28,30,34]. Thus, our main contributions lie in the formalization and implementation of the procedure for automatically discovering catamorphisms in the context of CHC solving.

The rest of this paper is organized as follows. Section 2 reviews CHCs over ADTs and catamorphisms for ADTs. Section 3 gives an overview of our framework. Section 4 formalizes our catamorphism-based abstraction, and Sect. 5 introduces our template-based catamorphism synthesis procedure. Section 6 reports the experimental results. Section 7 discusses related work, and Sect. 8 concludes the paper.

2 Preliminaries

2.1 Constrained Horn Clauses Modulo Algebraic Data Types and Integer Arithmetic

We consider a standard first-order logic and a theory of algebraic data types and integer arithmetic, which is written as $T_{\text{ADT}+\mathbb{Z}}$. We also denote the theory of integer arithmetic by $T_{\mathbb{Z}}$. For simplicity, we consider formulas that involve only integers and a single algebraic data type (ADT) $(\delta, \{C_1, \ldots, C_k\})$ where δ is a sort and C_i is a function symbol called a *constructor*.[2] Each constructor C_i is assumed to be a function of $m_i + n_i$ arguments with its sort specified as

$$(\overbrace{\mathit{int} \times \cdots \times \mathit{int}}^{m_i} \times \overbrace{\delta \times \cdots \times \delta}^{n_i}) \to \delta.$$

---

[2] Extending our proposed method to support multiple ADTs is straightforward. As detailed in Sect. 6, our implementation is already capable of handling multiple ADTs within a single instance. In a standard theory of algebraic data types, projections and testers are used as the standard connectives for algebraic data types in addition to constructors. We omit them for simplicity, since they can be easily removed by standard preprocessing techniques (c.f. Sect. 4.5 of [23]).

Note that $m_i + n_i$ can be 0. We often simply write δ to mention the ADT.

Example 1. An algebraic data type for natural numbers *nat* in the introduction is defined as $(nat, \{Z, S\})$ where Z is a constant of sort *nat* and S has the sort $nat \to nat$. An algebraic data type for integer lists, written as *ilist*, is defined as $(ilist, \{nil, cons\})$ where *nil* is a constant of sort *ilist* and *cons* has the sort $int \times ilist \to ilist$. A list $[1; 2]$ is written as $cons(1, cons(2, nil))$. □

The sets of *terms* and *constraint formulas* are defined by:

$$(terms) \quad t ::= x \mid n \mid C_i(\widetilde{t_i}) \mid t_1 \text{ op } t_2$$
$$(constraint\ formulas) \quad \theta ::= \mathbf{tt} \mid \mathbf{ff} \mid \theta_1 \wedge \theta_2 \mid \theta_1 \vee \theta_2 \mid t_1 \bowtie t_2 \mid \exists x^\xi.\,\theta \mid \forall x^\xi.\,\theta.$$

Here, x, n, and ξ are metavariables for variables, integers, and sorts respectively, $\bowtie$ ranges over binary predicates in $\{=_{int}, \neq_{int}, >, \leq, =_\delta\}$ and **op** ranges over binary arithmetic operations $\{+, -, \times\}$. We also write $\widetilde{t_i}$ for a sequence of terms $t_1, \ldots, t_k$. The predicate $=_\delta$ takes two terms of sort δ, while others take two terms of sort *int*. For technical convenience, we omit the disequality $\neq_\delta$ for ADT; it can be encoded using CHCs. (c.f. Section 4.4 of [23]). We also use $(t_1, \ldots, t_k) =_{int^k} (t'_1, \ldots, t'_k)$ as a syntax sugar for the conjunction of equalities $t_1 =_{int} t'_1 \wedge \cdots \wedge t_k =_{int} t'_k$.

We write $\mathrm{FV}(t)$ and $\mathrm{FV}(\theta)$ for the set of free variables, and $\forall\theta$ and $\exists\theta$ for the universal and existential closures of θ, respectively. We also write $\mathcal{H}_\delta$ for the set of ground terms (i.e., with no free variables) of sort δ. We call non-ground terms *open terms*, and terms without constructors *arithmetic terms*. A constraint formula θ is *quantifier-free* if no quantifier occurs in θ. We consider only well-sorted terms and formulas, where well-sortedness is defined in the standard manner. Substitutions such as $[t/x]t'$ and $[t/x]\theta$ are defined as usual. The semantics of terms and formulas are also given in the standard way.

A *constrained Horn clause* (CHC) (over algebraic data types and integer arithmetic) is a formula of the form

$$\forall \widetilde{x^{int}}, \widetilde{y^\delta}.\ H \Leftarrow \theta \wedge P_1(\widetilde{t_1}) \wedge \cdots \wedge P_k(\widetilde{t_k}).$$

Here, $P_i(\widetilde{t_i})$ is a predicate application, θ is a quantifier-free constraint formula, and H is either **ff** or a predicate application $P(\widetilde{t_{k+1}})$. For simplicity, universal quantifiers are often omitted. We call a finite set of CHCs *a system of CHCs*. We use $\mathbb{C}$ and $\mathbb{S}$ as the metavariables for CHCs and systems of CHCs, respectively. A system of CHCs is (or simply, CHCs are) said to be *satisfiable* if there is an interpretation of predicate variables that makes all the clauses valid.

Example 2. Recall the CHCs over the ADT *nat* in Sect. 1, consisting of the predicates *PlusNat* and *Lt*. The CHCs are satisfiable under the model:

$$PlusNat(x, y, z) \stackrel{\Delta}{=} size(x) + size(y) = size(z) \quad Lt(x, y) \stackrel{\Delta}{=} size(x) < size(y),$$

where the function *size* from *nat* to integers is defined by $size(S^n(Z)) = n$. □

2.2 Catamorphisms

We introduce *catamorphisms* for δ, which are generalized fold functions that map instances of $\mathcal{H}_\delta$ to N-tuples of integers. Here, N is called the *approximation degree*. A catamorphism $\mathcal{C}$ (for δ) is defined as a map constructed as follows:

$$\mathcal{C}(x) \triangleq \text{match } x \text{ with}$$
$$\text{case } C_1(\widetilde{y_1}, z_1, \ldots, z_{n_1}) \Rightarrow \mathcal{F}_1(\widetilde{y_1}, \mathcal{C}(z_1), \ldots, \mathcal{C}(z_{n_1}))$$
$$\vdots$$
$$\text{case } C_k(\widetilde{y_k}, z_1, \ldots, z_{n_k}) \Rightarrow \mathcal{F}_k(\widetilde{y_k}, \mathcal{C}(z_1), \ldots, \mathcal{C}(z_{n_k})).$$

Here, $\mathcal{F}_i$ is called a *structure map* for C_i. Recall that the constructor C_i takes m_i arguments of sort *int* and n_i arguments of sort δ. The structure map $\mathcal{F}_i$ takes m_i integers and n_i N-tuples of integers, and returns an N-tuple of integers. We also write $\mathcal{C}^{\mathcal{F}_1, \ldots, \mathcal{F}_k}$ for $\mathcal{C}$ when clarifying the structure maps. Furthermore, if a catamorphism has free variables $a_1, \ldots, a_l$ in the definition, we write $\overline{\mathcal{C}}^{\mathcal{F}_1, \ldots, \mathcal{F}_k}_{\{a_1, \ldots, a_l\}}$.

Example 3. A catamorphism for *ilist* is of the form

$$\mathcal{C}^{\mathcal{F}_{nil}, \mathcal{F}_{cons}}(x) \triangleq \text{match } x \text{ with}$$
$$\text{case } nil \Rightarrow \mathcal{F}_{nil}$$
$$\text{case } cons(x, l) \Rightarrow \mathcal{F}_{cons}(x, \mathcal{C}^{\mathcal{F}_{nil}, \mathcal{F}_{cons}}(l))$$

where $\mathcal{F}_{nil}$ and $\mathcal{F}_{cons}$ are structure maps for the two constructors *nil* and *cons*, respectively. For $\mathcal{F}_{nil} = 0$ and $\mathcal{F}_{cons}(x, l) = 1 + l$, $\mathcal{C}^{\mathcal{F}_{nil}, \mathcal{F}_{cons}}$ is the list length function, and for $\mathcal{F}_{nil} = 0$ and $\mathcal{F}_{cons}(x, l) = x + l$, $\mathcal{C}^{\mathcal{F}_{nil}, \mathcal{F}_{cons}}$ is the function for computing the sum of list elements. The catamorphism defined by the structure maps $\mathcal{F}_{nil} = (0, 0)$ and $\mathcal{F}_{cons}(x, (l_1, l_2)) = (1 + l_1, x + l_2)$ has the approximation degree 2; it maps an integer list to a pair consisting of the list length and the sum of elements.

Similarly, we define a catamorphism $\mathcal{C}_{size}$ for *nat* as $\mathcal{C}^{\mathcal{F}_Z, \mathcal{F}_S}$ where $\mathcal{F}_Z = 0$ and $\mathcal{F}_S(x) = 1 + x$. This corresponds to *size* used in Example 2. □

3 Overview

This section gives an overview of the proposed procedure, called CATALIA, which follows a framework of template-based synthesis and counterexample-guided abstraction refinement (CEGAR) [6], as illustrated in Fig. 1.

Given a system $\mathbb{S}$ of CHCs over algebraic data types and integer arithmetic, we first abstract them to a system $\mathbb{S}'$ of CHCs over integer arithmetic. When $\mathbb{S}'$ is unsatisfiable, CATALIA generates a constraint formula θ (called a counterexample), which witnesses the possible unsatisfiability of $\mathbb{S}$, based on a resolution proof for unsatisfiability of $\mathbb{S}'$. If θ is satisfiable, $\mathbb{S}$ is indeed unsatisfiable; otherwise, we refine the catamorphism $\mathcal{C}$ using θ in the refinement phase.

Below, we briefly explain the abstraction, counterexample generation, and synthesis phases of CATALIA. We will provide more details for the abstraction and synthesis phases in Sects. 4 and 5, respectively.

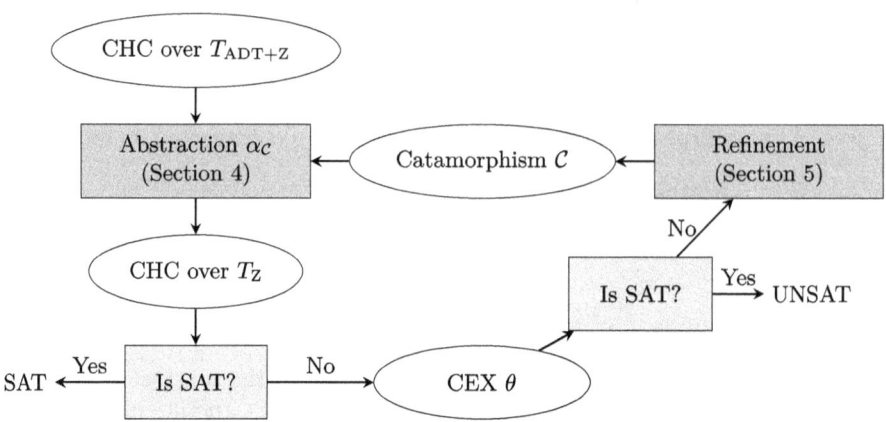

Fig. 1. Overview of CATALIA

3.1 Abstraction

Recall the following system of CHCs given in Sect. 1.

(i) $PlusNat(m, Z, m)$.
(ii) $PlusNat(m, S(n), S(r)) \Leftarrow PlusNat(m, n, r)$.
(iii) $< (Z, S(n))$.   (iv) $< (S(m), S(n)) \Leftarrow < (m, n)$.
(v) $\mathrm{ff} \Leftarrow PlusNat(m, n, r) \land < (r, m)$.

Using the catamorphism $\mathcal{C}^{\mathcal{F}_Z, \mathcal{F}_S}$ where $\mathcal{F}_Z = 0$ and $\mathcal{F}_S(x) = 1+x$, we obtain the following abstracted version of CHCs.

$\overline{PlusNat}(m, 0, m) \Leftarrow \overline{P_\delta}(m)$.
$\overline{PlusNat}(m, n+1, r+1) \Leftarrow \overline{P_\delta}(m) \land \overline{P_\delta}(n) \land \overline{P_\delta}(r) \land \overline{PlusNat}(m, n, r)$.
$\overline{Lt}(0, n+1) \Leftarrow \overline{P_\delta}(n)$. $\overline{Lt}(m+1, n+1) \Leftarrow \overline{P_\delta}(m) \land \overline{P_\delta}(n) \land \overline{Lt}(m, n)$.
$\mathrm{ff} \Leftarrow \overline{P_\delta}(m) \land \overline{P_\delta}(n) \land \overline{P_\delta}(r) \land \overline{PlusNat}(m, n, r) \land \overline{Lt}(r, m)$.
$\overline{P_\delta}(0)$. $\overline{P_\delta}(n+1) \Leftarrow \overline{P_\delta}(n)$.

Here, we have replaced each variable or term of sort *nat* with one of sort *int* by applying the catamorphism. We have also added $\overline{P_\delta}(x)$ for each universally quantified variable x (whose sort is *nat* in the original CHCs and *int* after the abstraction); this is for the purpose of restricting the range of the variable to the image of the catamorphism. (In other words, a formula $\forall x^{nat}.\varphi(x)$ is abstracted to $\forall x^{int}.\overline{P_\delta}(x) \Rightarrow \varphi'(x)$ where $\varphi'(x)$ is an abstract version of $\varphi(x)$.) The definition of $\overline{P_\delta}$, called the *C-admissibility predicate*, is obtained automatically from the following predicate that should be satisfied by every variable of sort *nat*, which was implicit in the original CHCs.

$$P_\delta(Z). \qquad P_\delta(S(x)) \Leftarrow P_\delta(x).$$

Note that, without the predicate P, the abstraction would be too coarse. For example, consider a CHC $\forall x^{nat}.\ \mathrm{ff} \Leftarrow S(x) = Z$, which is valid (as $S(x) = Z$ never holds). Without the P predicate, however, it would be abstracted to $\forall x^{int}.\ \mathrm{ff} \Leftarrow x + 1 = 0$, which is invalid.

The abstracted CHCs above are satisfiable with the following model:

$$\overline{PlusNat}(m,n,r) \triangleq m+n=r \qquad \overline{Lt}(x,y) \triangleq x<y \qquad \overline{P_\delta}(n) \triangleq n \geq 0.$$

We can therefore conclude that the original CHCs are also satisfiable, with the following model:

$$PlusNat(m,n,r) \triangleq \mathcal{C}(m) + \mathcal{C}(n) = \mathcal{C}(r) \qquad Lt(x,y) \triangleq \mathcal{C}(x) < \mathcal{C}(y).$$

A remaining issue is how to abstract the primitive equality predicate $=_{nat}$. We can simply replace it with $=_{int}$; this is a sound abstraction, since $x =_{nat} y$ implies $\mathcal{C}(x) =_{int} \mathcal{C}(y)$. In contrast, $x \neq_{nat} y$ does NOT imply $\mathcal{C}(x) \neq_{int} \mathcal{C}(y)$; that is why we exclude out $\neq_\delta$ from the set of primitive predicates (recall Sect. 2), and encode the inequality by using CHCs.

3.2 Counterexample Generation

Now, we consider the case where the abstracted CHCs are unsatisfiable. If the catamorphism $\mathcal{C}^{0,\lambda x.0}$ (which maps all the natural numbers to 0) were used instead of $\mathcal{C}^{0,\lambda x.x+1}$, the original CHCs would be abstracted to the following CHCs over T_Z, which are unsatisfiable.

(i') $\overline{PlusNat}(m,0,m) \Leftarrow \overline{P_\delta}(m)$.
(ii') $\overline{PlusNat}(m,0,0) \Leftarrow \overline{P_\delta}(m) \wedge \overline{P_\delta}(n) \wedge \overline{P_\delta}(r) \wedge \overline{PlusNat}(m,n,r)$.
(iii') $\overline{\mathrm{\lessdot}}(0,0) \Leftarrow \overline{P_\delta}(n)$.   (iv') $\overline{\mathrm{\lessdot}}(0,0) \Leftarrow \overline{P_\delta}(m) \wedge \overline{P_\delta}(n) \wedge \overline{\mathrm{\lessdot}}(m,n)$.
(v') $\mathrm{ff} \Leftarrow \overline{P_\delta}(m) \wedge \overline{P_\delta}(n) \wedge \overline{P_\delta}(r) \wedge \overline{PlusNat}(m,n,r) \wedge \overline{\mathrm{\lessdot}}(r,m)$.
(vi') $\overline{P_\delta}(0)$.   (vii') $\overline{P_\delta}(0) \Leftarrow \overline{P_\delta}(m)$.

Notice that the abstracted CHCs $(i') - (v')$ correspond to the original CHCs $(i) - (v)$.

Suppose the following (SLD-)resolution proof was generated by a CHC solver as a witness of unsatisfiability.

$$\cfrac{\cfrac{\cfrac{\mathrm{ff} \Leftarrow \overline{P_\delta}(m) \wedge \overline{P_\delta}(n) \wedge \overline{P_\delta}(r) \wedge \overline{PlusNat}(m,n,r) \wedge \overline{Lt}(r,m)}{\mathrm{ff} \Leftarrow \overline{P_\delta}(m) \wedge \overline{P_\delta}(n) \wedge \overline{P_\delta}(r) \wedge n=0 \wedge m=r \wedge \overline{P_\delta}(m) \wedge \overline{Lt}(r,m)}\ (i')}{\mathrm{ff} \Leftarrow \overline{P_\delta}(m) \wedge \overline{P_\delta}(n) \wedge \overline{P_\delta}(r) \wedge n=0 \wedge m=r \wedge \overline{P_\delta}(m) \wedge m=r=0 \wedge \overline{P_\delta}(n')}\ (iii')}{\mathrm{ff} \Leftarrow m=n=r=n'=0}\ (vi')$$

The derivation starts with the goal clause, and in the last step, the resolution on multiple occurrences of $\overline{P_\delta}$ has been performed in one step. We have indicated which CHC has been used in each resolution step. Note that the last clause is invalid, which indicates that the abstracted CHCs are unsatisfiable.

From the resolution proof for the abstract CHCs above, we construct the following candidate of a resolution proof for the unsatisfiability of the original CHCs, by applying the corresponding clause of the original CHCs (i.e., the clauses (i) and (iii) instead of (i') and (iii') respectively) except for the clauses on the $\mathcal{C}$-admissibility predicate.

$$\frac{\dfrac{\text{ff} \Leftarrow PlusNat(m,n,r) \wedge Lt(r,m)}{\text{ff} \Leftarrow m = r \wedge n = Z \wedge Lt(r,m)} \ (i)}{\text{ff} \Leftarrow m = r \wedge n = Z \wedge r = Z \wedge m = S(n')} \ (iii)$$

The right-hand side of the last clause can be simplified to: $\theta \triangleq Z = S(n')$. We call θ a *counterexample* (against the satisfiability of the original CHCs); it serves as a possible witness of the unsatisfiability of the original CHCs, in the sense that if θ were satisfiable, we could conclude that the original CHCs were unsatisfiable. In this case, however, θ is unsatisfiable; the abstract CHCs yielded a spurious resolution proof for the original CHCs.

3.3 Synthesis

For the example in the previous subsection (where $\theta \equiv Z = S(n')$), we need to find a catamorphism $\mathcal{C}' = \mathcal{C}^{\mathcal{F}_Z, \mathcal{F}_S}$ such that

$$\exists n^{nat}. \mathcal{F}_Z = \mathcal{F}_S(\mathcal{C}'(n))$$

is invalid. By preparing a template $\mathcal{F}_Z = a$ and $\mathcal{F}_S(\overline{n}) = b \times \overline{n} + c$ for $\mathcal{F}_Z$ and $\mathcal{F}_S$, the problem above is reduced to the satisfiability problem:

$$\exists a, b, c. \forall n^{nat}. a \neq b \times \mathcal{C}^{\mathcal{F}_Z, \mathcal{F}_S}(n) + c.$$

Solving the above satisfiability problem is costly, since it is an $\exists\forall$-formula and also involves the recursive function $\mathcal{C}^{\mathcal{F}_Z, \mathcal{F}_S}$. We thus provide a procedure for solving this $\exists\forall$-formula based on counterexample-guided inductive synthesis (CEGIS), which we will explain in detail in Sect. 5. This procedure may return $a = 0$ and $b = c = 1$ as a witness and synthesize a new catamorphism $\mathcal{C}^{0, \lambda x. x+1}$. We then go back to the abstraction step of the CEGAR cycle, and in this case, succeed in proving the satisfiability of the original CHCs, as explained in Sect. 3.1.

4 Abstraction

This section explains more details about the abstraction step.

In this section, we use the following more tricky example as a running example. To the best of our knowledge, most of the previous approaches [14,15,22,23] struggle with the example, while our approach can easily solve it.

Example 4. We consider the following CHCs:

$$G(nil, 0, 0). \qquad G(cons(x, l), x + n, m) \Leftarrow G(l, m, n).$$
$$Gen(nil, 0). \qquad Gen(cons(x, cons(x - 1, l)), n) \Leftarrow Gen(l, n - 1).$$
$$\text{ff} \Leftarrow m - n \neq x \land x \geq 0 \land Gen(l, x) \land G(l, m, n).$$

Here, G and Gen are predicate symbols of sorts $ilist \times int \times int \to bool$, and $ilist \times int \to bool$ respectively. Intuitively, $G(l, m, n)$ means that the sums of elements of l at even and odd indices are m and n respectively (where an index starts from 0). The predicate $Gen(l, n)$ holds if l is a list of the form $[m_0; m'_0; \cdots; m_{n-1}; m'_{n-1}]$ where $m_i = m'_i + 1$ for each $i = 0, \ldots, n - 1$. The last clause asserts that if $Gen(l, x)$ holds, then the difference between the sums of elements at even and odd indices is x. The above system of CHCs is satisfiable, where the models of G and Gen are as informally explained above.

Let $\mathcal{C}_{eo}$ be $\mathcal{C}^{\mathcal{F}_{nil}, \mathcal{F}_{cons}}$ where $\mathcal{F}_{nil} = 0$ and $\mathcal{F}_{cons}(x, l) = x - l$. This catamorphism is sufficient for proving the satisfiability of the CHCs above. □

Suppose the approximation degree is N, and we have a catamorphism $\mathcal{C}^{\mathcal{F}_1, \ldots, \mathcal{F}_k}$, which is a map from $\mathcal{H}_\delta$ to $\mathbb{Z}^N$. We define an abstraction of CHCs $\alpha_\mathcal{C}$ induced by $\mathcal{C}$.

Before applying the abstraction, we add the atom $P_\delta(x)$, where P_δ is a unary predicate that takes a value of sort δ, to the body of each clause, for each variable x of sort δ. Intuitively, $P_\delta(x)$ means that x ranges over the set of terms of sort δ. We add the following clause for each constructor C_i of sort $(\overbrace{int \times \cdots \times int}^{m_i} \times \overbrace{\delta \times \cdots \times \delta}^{n_i}) \to \delta$.

$$P_\delta(C_i(x_1, \ldots, x_{m_i}, y_1, \ldots, y_{n_i})) \Leftarrow P_\delta(y_1) \land \cdots \land P_\delta(y_{n_i}).$$

It ensures that the least model of P_δ indeed has the meaning described above. Obviously, the CHCs augmented with P_δ is equi-satisfiable with the original CHCs. Nonetheless, P_δ is added because the abstraction of P_δ yields the "$\mathcal{C}$-admissibility predicate" mentioned in Sect. 3. The abstraction of $P_\delta(x)$ ensures the integer variables obtained by abstracting x to range over the image of the catamorphism.

Example 5. For the example in Example 4, the augmented CHCs are:

(i) $G(nil, 0, 0)$. (ii) $G(cons(x, l), x + n, m) \Leftarrow P_{ilist}(l) \land G(l, m, n)$.
(iii) $Gen(nil, 0)$.
(iv) $Gen(cons(x, cons(x - 1, l)), n) \Leftarrow P_{ilist}(l) \land Gen(l, n - 1)$.
(v) $\text{ff} \Leftarrow m - n \neq x \land x \geq 0 \land P_{ilist}(l) \land Gen(l, x) \land G(l, m, n)$.
(vi) $P_{ilist}(nil)$. (vii) $P_{ilist}(cons(x, l)) \Leftarrow P_{ilist}(l)$.

The augmented CHCs are abstracted as follows. Let $\mathbb{C}$ be a clause $\forall \widetilde{x^{int}}, \widetilde{y^{\delta}}.\ H \Longleftarrow \theta \wedge P_1(\widetilde{t_1}) \wedge \cdots \wedge P_n(\widetilde{t_n})$, and Ξ be a variable abstraction environment, which is a finite map from variables to N-tuples of variables, such that $\Xi(y_i) = (y_1^i, \ldots, y_N^i)$ for each $y_i \in \{\widetilde{y^{\delta}}\} = \{y^1, \ldots, y^l\}$. We define $\alpha_{\mathbb{C}}(\mathbb{C})$ as

$$\forall \widetilde{x}, \widetilde{y_j^i}.\ \alpha_{\mathcal{C},\Xi}(H) \Longleftarrow \alpha_{\mathcal{C},\Xi}(\theta) \wedge \alpha_{\mathcal{C},\Xi}(P_1(\widetilde{t_1})) \wedge \cdots \wedge \alpha_{\mathcal{C},\Xi}(P_n(\widetilde{t_n})).$$

Here, $\widetilde{y_j^i}$ denotes $y_1^1, \ldots, y_N^1, \ldots, y_1^l, \ldots, y_N^l$, and the abstraction $\alpha_{\mathcal{C},\Xi}$ for atoms, constraint formulas, and terms is defined by:

$$\alpha_{\mathcal{C},\Xi}(P(\widetilde{t})) = \overline{P}(\alpha_{\mathcal{C},\Xi}(\widetilde{t})) \qquad \alpha_{\mathcal{C},\Xi}(\mathbf{tt}) = \mathbf{tt} \qquad \alpha_{\mathcal{C},\Xi}(\mathbf{ff}) = \mathbf{ff}$$
$$\alpha_{\mathcal{C},\Xi}(t_1 =_{\delta} t_2) = \alpha_{\mathcal{C},\Xi}(t_1) =_{int^N} \alpha_{\mathcal{C},\Xi}(t_2)$$
$$\alpha_{\mathcal{C},\Xi}(\mathbf{p}(\mathbf{a}_1, \ldots, \mathbf{a}_l)) = \mathbf{p}(\mathbf{a}_1, \ldots, \mathbf{a}_l) \qquad \text{(if $\mathbf{p}$ is a built-in predicate on integers)}$$
$$\alpha_{\mathcal{C},\Xi}(\varphi_1 \wedge \varphi_2) = \alpha_{\mathcal{C},\Xi}(\varphi_1) \wedge \alpha_{\mathcal{C},\Xi}(\varphi_2) \qquad \alpha_{\mathcal{C},\Xi}(\varphi_1 \vee \varphi_2) = \alpha_{\mathcal{C},\Xi}(\varphi_1) \vee \alpha_{\mathcal{C},\Xi}(\varphi_2)$$
$$\alpha_{\mathcal{C},\Xi}(x) = \begin{cases} \Xi(x) & \text{if } x \in \text{dom}(\Xi) \\ x & \text{otherwise} \end{cases} \qquad \alpha_{\mathcal{C},\Xi}(\mathbf{a}) = \mathbf{a} \ \text{(if $\mathbf{a}$ is an integer term)}$$
$$\alpha_{\mathcal{C},\Xi}(C_i(\mathbf{a}_1, \ldots, \mathbf{a}_{m_i}, t_1, \ldots, t_{n_i})) = \mathcal{F}_i(\mathbf{a}_1, \ldots, \mathbf{a}_{m_i}, \alpha_{\mathcal{C},\Xi}(t_1), \ldots, \alpha_{\mathcal{C},\Xi}(t_{n_i})).$$

As defined above, we just recursively replace each constructor C_i with the corresponding structure map $\mathcal{F}_i$, and the equality $=_\delta$ on ADT with the equality $=_{int^N}$ on integer tuples.

Example 6. Recall the augmented CHCs in Example 5 and the catamorphism $\mathcal{C}_{eo}$ given in Example 4. We obtain the following abstracted CHCs.

$$\overline{G}(0,0,0). \qquad \overline{G}(x-l, x+n, m) \Leftarrow \overline{P}_{ilist}(l) \wedge \overline{G}(l, m, n).$$
$$\overline{Gen}(0,0). \qquad \overline{Gen}(x - ((x-1) - l), n) \Leftarrow \overline{P}_{ilist}(l) \wedge \overline{Gen}(l, n-1).$$
$$\mathbf{ff} \Leftarrow m - n \neq x \wedge x \geq 0 \wedge \overline{P}_{ilist}(l) \wedge \overline{Gen}(l, x) \wedge \overline{G}(l, m, n).$$
$$\overline{P}_{ilist}(0). \qquad \overline{P}_{ilist}(x - l) \Leftarrow \overline{P}_{ilist}(l).$$

They have the following model.

$$\overline{G}(l, y, z) \stackrel{\triangle}{=} l = y - z \qquad \overline{Gen}(l, y) \stackrel{\triangle}{=} l = y \qquad \overline{P}_{ilist}(l) \stackrel{\triangle}{=} \mathbf{tt}.$$

We have $\overline{P}_{ilist}(l) \stackrel{\triangle}{=} \mathbf{tt}$ because the image of $\mathcal{C}_{eo}$ is $\mathbb{Z}$, but we note that this is not the case in general.[3]

By the soundness theorem given below, we can conclude that the original CHCs given in Example 4 are satisfiable. Indeed, the following is the model for the original CHCs.

$$G(l, y, z) \stackrel{\triangle}{=} \mathcal{C}_{eo}(l) = y - z \quad \text{and} \quad Gen(l, y) \stackrel{\triangle}{=} \mathcal{C}_{eo}(l) = y.$$

---

[3] For example, a model for the predicate $\overline{P}_\delta$ in Sect. 3.1 is given by $\overline{P}_\delta(x) \stackrel{\triangle}{=} x \geq 0$.

We now discuss the soundness of abstraction. The following lemma follows immediately from the above construction.

Lemma 1. *For any system $\mathbb{S}$ of CHCs, $\alpha_\mathcal{C}(\mathbb{S})$ is a system of CHCs defined over integer arithmetic.*

The following theorem states the soundness, and also describes how a model of the original CHCs can be constructed from that of the abstract CHCs.

Theorem 1 (Soundness). *Let $\mathbb{S}$ be a system of CHC over T_{ADT+Z}. If $\alpha_\mathcal{C}(\mathbb{S})$ is satisfiable, then so is $\mathbb{S}$. Furthermore, from a model $\mathcal{M}_1$ of $\alpha_\mathcal{C}(\mathbb{S})$, we can construct a model $\mathcal{M}_2$ for $\mathbb{S}$. The interpretation of a predicate $P\colon \delta^m \times \mathit{int}^n$ in $\mathcal{M}_2$ is given as a function $P^{\mathcal{M}_2}(x_1,\ldots,x_m,\widetilde{y}) = \overline{P}^{\mathcal{M}_1}(\mathcal{C}(x_1),\ldots,\mathcal{C}(x_m),\widetilde{y})$, where $\overline{P}^{\mathcal{M}_1}$ is the interpretation of $\overline{P}$ in $\mathcal{M}_1$.*

A proof is given in the longer version of this paper [19]. Here we provide an informal argument. Notice that, for any predicate $P\colon \delta^m \times \mathit{int}^n$, ground terms $t_1,\ldots,t_m$ and integers $\widetilde{k}$, $P(t_1,\ldots,t_m,\widetilde{k})$ holds under $\mathcal{M}_2$ (i.e., $P^{\mathcal{M}_2}(t_1,\ldots,t_m,\widetilde{k})$ holds) if and only if $\alpha_\mathcal{C}(P(t_1,\ldots,t_m,\widetilde{k})) = \overline{P}(\mathcal{C}(t_1),\ldots,\mathcal{C}(t_m),\widetilde{k})$ holds under $\mathcal{M}_1$ (i.e., $\overline{P}^{\mathcal{M}_1}(\mathcal{C}(t_1),\ldots,\mathcal{C}(t_m),\widetilde{k})$ holds). For any ground constraint formula θ, $\neg\alpha_\mathcal{C}(\theta)$ implies $\neg\theta$. Thus, for any ground clause $H \Leftarrow \theta \wedge P_1(\widetilde{t_1}) \wedge \cdots \wedge P_k(\widetilde{t_k})$, if $\mathcal{M}_1$ is a model of $\alpha_\mathcal{C}(H) \Leftarrow \alpha_\mathcal{C}(\theta) \wedge \alpha_\mathcal{C}(P_1(\widetilde{t_1})) \wedge \cdots \wedge \alpha_\mathcal{C}(P_k(\widetilde{t_k}))$, then $\mathcal{M}_2$ is a model of $H \Leftarrow \theta \wedge P_1(\widetilde{t_1}) \wedge \cdots \wedge P_k(\widetilde{t_k})$.

Recall the model of the original CHCs in Example 6. The interpretation $G^{\mathcal{M}_2}(l,x,y) \triangleq (\mathcal{C}_{eo}(l) = x - y)$ for G has been obtained from $\overline{G}^{\mathcal{M}_1}(l,x,y) \triangleq (l = x - y)$, by just replacing l with $\mathcal{C}_{eo}(l)$ based on the theorem above.

5 Template-Based and Counterexample-Guided Catamorphism Synthesis

We adopt a *template-based approach* to catamorphism synthesis; we prepare a set of predefined template catamorphisms and derive constraints for $\mathcal{C}$ to satisfy. As detailed later, such constraints involve universal quantifiers over ADTs and recursively defined functions, which are difficult for SMT solvers to handle. To address this problem, we employ a *counterexample-guided approach with testing*.

5.1 Template-Based Catamorphism Synthesis

We define a *template catamorphism* as a catamorphism parameterized by integers. Here, each constructor C_i has an associated *template structure map* represented by a tuple of open terms $(t_i^{(1)}[\widetilde{x},\widetilde{a}],\ldots,t_i^{(N)}[\widetilde{x},\widetilde{a}])$ of sort $\mathit{int} \times \cdots \times \mathit{int}$ where $\widetilde{x}$ are arguments of the catamorphism and $\widetilde{a}$ are integer parameters.

Let $\mathcal{T}$ be a template catamorphism, and $\mathcal{M}$ be an assignment of the parameters $\widetilde{a}$ to integers. A catamorphism $\mathcal{M}(\mathcal{T})$, a catamorphism obtained by substituting each parameter a_i with $\mathcal{M}(a_i)$ in $\mathcal{T}$, is said to be an *instantiation* of the template catamorphism $\mathcal{T}$.

We often use *linear* template catamorphisms, which are template catamorphisms whose associated template structure maps are affine functions. We denote a linear template catamorphism of degree 1 by $\mathcal{L}$.

Example 7. For *ilist*, $\mathcal{L}$ is given by the template structure maps:

$$\mathcal{F}_{nil} = d, \quad \mathcal{F}_{cons}(x, l) = a \times l + b \times x + c$$

with parameters a, b, c, d. □

Remark 1. In practice, we design our templates based on a trade-off between the expressive power of the abstraction and the cost of catamorphism synthesis. As explained in Sect. 6, our implementation uses restricted linear template catamorphisms $\mathcal{L}_{[a,b]}$ to efficiently explore the search space, where the range of each parameter of $\mathcal{L}$ is limited to $[a, b]$. For example, a restricted linear template catamorphism for *ilist*, denoted by $\mathcal{L}_{[-1,1]}$, is given by:

$$\mathcal{F}_{nil} = d, \quad \mathcal{F}_{cons}(x, l) = a \times l + b \times x + c \quad \text{where } a, b, c, d \in [-1, 1].$$

We gradually increase the expressiveness of the templates by increasing the parameter ranges and the approximation degree, until they suffice to prove the satisfiability of the given CHCs. In our implementation, we prepare the following sequence of template catamorphisms:

$$\mathcal{L}_{[-1,1]}, (\mathcal{L}_{[-1,1]}, \mathcal{L}_{[-1,1]}), (\mathcal{L}_{[-1,1]}, \mathcal{L}_{[-1,1]}, \mathcal{L}_{[-1,1]}), (\mathcal{L}_{[-2,2]}, \mathcal{L}_{[-2,2]}, \mathcal{L}_{[-2,2]}),$$
$$(\mathcal{L}_{[-4,4]}, \mathcal{L}_{[-4,4]}, \mathcal{L}_{[-4,4]}), \ldots.$$

Here, we assume each $\mathcal{L}_{[a,b]}$ has its own unique set of parameters, and an N-tuple of template catamorphisms $(T_1, \ldots, T_k)$ represents a template catamorphism of N-approximation degree, defined by $\lambda \tilde{x}. (T_1(\tilde{x}), \ldots, T_k(\tilde{x}))$.

We could also consider templates containing disjunctive properties, but inferring such templates would be more costly; it is left for future work.

Note that the templates are prepared and fixed in advance, and are independent of specific CHCs or data structures. The parameters required for each constructor are determined by its sort, and can be derived automatically. □

We introduce a constraint generation map $\langle \cdot \rangle_T$, which is used later to find appropriate instantiations of template catamorphisms. It is defined by:

$$\langle \forall x. \theta \rangle_T = \forall x. \langle \theta \rangle_T \quad \langle t_1 =_\delta t_2 \rangle_T = (T(t_1) =_{int^N} T(t_2)) \quad \langle \mathbf{p}(\tilde{a}) \rangle_T = \mathbf{p}(\tilde{a})$$
$$\langle \theta_1 \star \theta_2 \rangle_T = \langle \theta_1 \rangle_T \star \langle \theta_2 \rangle_T \text{ for } \star \in \{\wedge, \vee\} \quad \langle \neg \theta \rangle_T = \neg \langle \theta \rangle_T.$$

Here, we assume that T is a symbol of a recursively defined function of sort $\delta \to int^N$ that encodes the template catamorphism. Note that in Sect. 5 we use an extended form of constraint formulas (used only for our catamorphism synthesis) that allows the negation operator $\neg$ for convenience.

Procedure 1. Counterexample-Guided Catamorphism Synthesis

1: **Input:** CHCs over $\mathcal{T}_{\text{ADT}+\mathbb{Z}}$ $\mathbb{S}$
2: **Output:** satisfiable / unsatisfiable / unknown
3: $(C, S) \leftarrow (\mathcal{C}_0, \emptyset)$
4: **for** $\mathcal{T}$ in $\mathfrak{T}$ **do**
5: $\quad \Theta \leftarrow \text{tt}$
6: $\quad$ **loop**
7: $\quad\quad \mathbb{S}' \leftarrow \alpha_C(\mathbb{S})$
8: $\quad\quad r \leftarrow \text{check\_sat\_chc}(\mathbb{S}')$
9: $\quad\quad$ **if** $r = \text{satisfiable}$ **then return** satisfiable
10: $\quad\quad \theta \leftarrow \text{get\_cex}(r, \mathbb{S})$
11: $\quad\quad$ **if** $\text{check\_sat\_smt}(\theta)$ **then return** unsatisfiable
12: $\quad\quad S \leftarrow S \cup \{\forall \neg \theta\}$
13: $\quad\quad (C, \Theta) \leftarrow \text{synthesis}(\bigwedge S, C, \Theta, \mathcal{T})$
14: $\quad\quad$ **if** (C, Θ) is None **then break**
15: $\quad$ **end loop**
16: **end for**
17: **return** unknown

Example 8. Let θ be the (extended) constraint formula $\neg(cons(0, cons(0, l)) =_\delta nil)$, and $\mathcal{T}$ be the linear template catamorphism $\overline{C}_{\{a,b,c,d\}}^{\mathcal{F}_{nil},\mathcal{F}_{cons}}$ in Example 7. By applying $\langle \cdot \rangle_{\mathcal{T}}$ to θ, we obtain $\neg(\mathcal{T}(cons(0, cons(0, l))) =_{int} \mathcal{T}(nil))$, which can be simplified to

$$a \times (a \times \mathcal{T}(l) + c) + c \neq_{int} d$$

by using the defining axioms of $\mathcal{T}$. □

5.2 Counterexample-Guided Catamorphism Synthesis

We now discuss the CEGAR procedure of CATALIA in more detail, shown in Procedure 1.

The procedure maintains two internal states: the current catamorphism C and a set S of the negations of counterexample formulas. We call elements of S *proof obligations*; they are valid formulas over ADTs, whose validity should be preserved by the catamorphism-based abstraction. Initially, we set C to the default catamorphism $\mathcal{C}_0$ and S to the empty set. The choice of $\mathcal{C}_0$ is arbitrary.

We iterate over a sequence of template catamorphisms $\mathfrak{T}$, which is prepared in advance as described in Remark 1. For now, let us ignore Θ and focus on the inner loop (line 6–15). The first part of the inner loop (line 7–11) is the same as described in Sect. 3. When a candidate counterexample θ for $\mathbb{S}$ is spurious, we add $\forall \neg \theta$ to the set S and proceed to the synthesis phase (line 12–13). When the synthesis phase fails to find a new catamorphism, we break the loop and try another template catamorphism (line 14).

A notable difference from the standard CEGAR approach is to relax the goal of the synthesis procedure: to tackle the challenges described below, we allow it

Procedure 2. Procedure synthesis

1: **Input:** θ, $\mathcal{C}$, Θ, and $\mathcal{T}$
2: **Output:** $\mathcal{C}'$ and Θ'
3: $\theta' \leftarrow$ a quantifier-free formula such that $\theta \equiv \forall \tilde{x}.\,\theta'$
4: timeout $\leftarrow \infty$
5: loop
6:    $[\tilde{x} \mapsto \tilde{v}] \leftarrow$ check_sat_with_TO($\neg\langle\theta'\rangle_\mathcal{C}$, timeout)   ▷ Testing
7:    if $[\tilde{x} \mapsto \tilde{v}]$ is None or timeout then return $(\mathcal{C}, \Theta)$
8:    timeout $\leftarrow$ defaultTimeout
9:    $\Theta \leftarrow \Theta \wedge \theta''$ where $\theta'' \equiv [\tilde{v}/\tilde{x}]\langle\theta'\rangle_\mathcal{T}$ ▷ $\mathcal{T}$ does not occur in θ''
10:    $\mathcal{M} \leftarrow$ check_sat(Θ)   ▷ SAT modulo NIA
11:    if $\mathcal{M}$ is None then return None
12:    $\mathcal{C} \leftarrow \mathcal{M}(\mathcal{T})$
13: end loop

to return a catamorphism $\mathcal{C}$ that does not necessarily preserve the validity of the proof obligation $\bigwedge S$. As a result, the same spurious counterexample θ might be encountered multiple times at line 10. To prevent it, we store a constraint formula Θ, which accumulates information from the synthesis exploration. This formula represents necessary conditions for the template parameters, enabling the synthesis process to resume from its previous state when needed, as detailed below.

Challenges in Catamorphism Synthesis. Synthesizing a catamorphism from the proof obligation $\bigwedge S$ faces two main challenges:

1. The proof obligation involves universal quantifiers over ADTs and recursive definitions, which SMT solvers struggle to handle.
2. Even after synthesizing a catamorphism $\mathcal{C}$, checking whether $\mathcal{C}$ preserves the validity of $\bigwedge S$ remains costly as it still involves recursively defined functions and ADTs.

To address these challenges, we adopt an approach proposed by Reynolds et al. [31], a variant of counterexample-guided inductive synthesis (CEGIS), combined with a lightweight testing approach.

Procedure synthesis. Procedure 2 shows the synthesis procedure. This procedure takes a proof obligation θ, a current catamorphism $\mathcal{C}$, a constraint formula Θ, and a template catamorphism $\mathcal{T}$ as inputs. Here, θ and $\mathcal{C}$ satisfy $\not\models \langle\theta\rangle_\mathcal{C}$ but $\models \theta$. The goal of the procedure is to find a new catamorphism $\mathcal{C}'$ that is *likely* to satisfy $\models \langle\theta\rangle_{\mathcal{C}'}$.

As in ordinary CEGIS, the procedure consists of two phases: (a) verification (line 6) and (b) synthesis (line 10). The former checks whether the current candidate of $\mathcal{C}$ satisfies $\forall \tilde{x}.\,\theta'$ by checking whether $\neg\langle\theta'\rangle_\mathcal{C}$ is satisfiable. If so, we obtain ground terms $\tilde{v}$ such that $[\tilde{v}/\tilde{x}]\langle\theta'\rangle_\mathcal{C}$ is invalid, and update Θ to (a formula equivalent to) $\Theta \wedge [\tilde{v}/\tilde{x}]\langle \theta' \rangle_\mathcal{T}$. This enables us to synthesize a new catamorphism in a counterexample-guided manner on line 10.

A difference from the standard CEGIS is that we give up checking the satisfiability of $\neg\langle \theta' \rangle_\mathcal{C}$ upon a time-out on line 6. This is because an SMT prover is not good at proving the unsatisfiability of $\neg\langle \theta' \rangle_\mathcal{C}$. If the satisfiability check times out, then we optimistically assume that $\langle \theta' \rangle_\mathcal{C}$ is valid, and returns the current catamorphism $\mathcal{C}$ as a candidate solution. In that case, it remains unknown whether $\langle \theta \rangle_\mathcal{C}$ is indeed valid; thus, the same counterexample as the previous might be encountered in Procedure 1 again.

To ensure the progress even with this relaxation, we accumulate the necessary conditions Θ for the template parameters of $\mathcal{T}$ inside the synthesis loop (line 9) and return Θ to Procedure 1. This allows Procedure 2 to resume from the previous state whenever Procedure 1 encounters the same counterexample again. For the progress, we must additionally require that the given catamorphism is refined at least once during each synthesis call. To this end, we initialize the timeout to ∞ (line 4) and later reset it to a default finite value (line 8). This is justified by the fact that $\langle \theta \rangle_\mathcal{C}$ for the given catamorphism $\mathcal{C}$ is already known to be invalid by Procedure 1; therefore, an SMT solver should be able to find a model for $\neg\langle \theta' \rangle_\mathcal{C}$ on line 6.

Example 9. Let $\mathcal{C}$ be $\mathcal{C}^{\mathcal{F}_{nil,0}, \mathcal{F}_{cons,0}}$ where $\mathcal{F}_{nil,0} = 0$ and $\mathcal{F}_{cons,0}(x,l) = 0$, θ be $\forall l^\delta$. θ' where $\theta' \triangleq \neg(cons(0, cons(0,l)) =_\delta nil)$, Θ be tt, and $\mathcal{T}$ be the linear template catamorphism in Example 7 for *ilist*. We execute Procedure 2 with these inputs: $\theta, \mathcal{C}, \Theta, \mathcal{T}$. We first check whether $\neg\langle \theta' \rangle_\mathcal{C} \equiv \mathcal{C}(cons(0, cons(0,l))) =_{int} \mathcal{C}(nil)$ is satisfiable, and find a model $[l \mapsto nil]$. As all arguments of sort δ in the catamorphism applications within $[nil/l]\langle \theta' \rangle_\mathcal{T}$ are ground terms, $[nil/l]\langle \theta' \rangle_\mathcal{T}$ can be simplified to: $a \times (a \times d + c) + c \neq d$. We then update Θ to $a \times (a \times d + c) + c \neq d$. Suppose an SMT solver yields the following model for Θ: $\mathcal{M} \equiv \{a \mapsto 0, b \mapsto 0, c \mapsto 1, d \mapsto 0\}$. Based on this model, we have a new catamorphism $\mathcal{C}_1$ defined by $\mathcal{C}^{\mathcal{F}_{nil,1}, \mathcal{F}_{cons,1}}$ where $\mathcal{F}_{nil} = 0$ and $\mathcal{F}_{cons}(x,l) = 1$. Now the backend SMT solver either proves that $\models \langle \theta \rangle_{\mathcal{C}_1}$ holds or times out. Therefore, we return $\mathcal{C}_1$ and Θ as the result of Procedure 2. □

5.3 Discussions

We discuss properties of the overall procedure of CATALIA in this subsection. We have already shown the soundness of the procedure in Sect. 4 (Theorem 1). Other important questions are:

1. Relative completeness: Let $\mathbb{S}$ be a system of CHCs, and suppose that $\alpha_\mathcal{C}(\mathbb{S})$ is satisfiable for some $\alpha_\mathcal{C}$ (where $\mathcal{C}$ belongs to the class of catamorphisms expressed by a given set of templates). Assuming that the backend CHC solver over integers and SMT solver were sound and complete, does CATALIA eventually prove that $\mathbb{S}$ is satisfiable?
2. Refutational completeness: Let $\mathbb{S}$ be a system of CHCs, and suppose that $\mathbb{S}$ is unsatisfiable. Assuming that the backend CHC solver over integers and

SMT solver were sound and complete, does CATALIA eventually prove that $\mathbb{S}$ is unsatisfiable?

We need to make some modifications and further assumptions to guarantee that relative completeness and refutational completeness hold.

We can ensure relative completeness by ensuring that the values of template parameters are chosen from a *finite* set, and the set and the approximation degree N are gradually increased (as explained in Remark 1) when there is no solution for the constraints in the current template, so that the whole class of catamorphisms being considered is eventually covered. Note that given a template catamorphism, the same catamorphism is not encountered again since the necessary conditions are accumulated in Θ in Procedure 2. Thus, if $\alpha_\mathcal{C}(\mathbb{S})$ is satisfiable for some $\alpha_\mathcal{C}$ and such $\alpha_\mathcal{C}$ is an instance of the current template catamorphism, it will eventually be found.

Refutational completeness holds if the underlying solver for CHC (over integers) generates resolution proofs in a *fair* manner, in the sense that, given an infinite sequence of unsatisfiable CHCs $\mathbb{S}_1, \mathbb{S}_2, \ldots$ if every $\mathbb{S}_i$ has a resolution proof of the same "shape" (except for constraint formulas), then that resolution proof is eventually produced. That is because if $\mathbb{S}$ is unsatisfiable, then its augmented version also has a resolution proof, and all of its abstractions $\alpha_{\mathcal{C}_1}(\mathbb{S}), \alpha_{\mathcal{C}_2}(\mathbb{S}), \ldots$ have the resolution proof of the same shape. Thus, by the assumption of fairness, that resolution proof is eventually generated.

The assumption on the fairness above may be too strong in practice; in fact, we do not think an existing CHC solver satisfies that property. A more reasonable requirement would be to ensure that a CHC solver generates a resolution proof of the smallest size. Then, it suffices to ensure that a resolution proof of the same shape is never re-encountered, e.g., by removing a prior bound on the approximation degree N and removing the timeout on line 9 of Procedure 2.

6 Implementation and Evaluation

We have implemented CATALIA, a solver for the satisfiability checking problem of CHCs over ADT and LIA. In this section, we describe the implementation details and evaluate CATALIA on the benchmark set from CHC-COMP 2024 [10]. As stated in the abstract, CATALIA was used as a core part of the tool called ChocoCatalia, which won the ADT-LIA category of CHC-COMP 2025 (which is the only category ChocoCatalia participated in). ChocoCatalia relies on another independent, complementary technique to be reported elsewhere, but CATALIA alone would have won the competition, judging from the evaluation result reported below for the CHC-COMP 2024 benchmark.

Table 1. Number of Solved Instances

Instance	CATALIA	RInGen	Spacer	Eldarica
# SAT	67	54	48	50
# UNSAT	80	46	86	87
# ALL	147	100	134	137
# UNIQUE (SAT)	18	14	3	1
# UNIQUE (UNSAT)	2	3	4	1

6.1 Implementation

The solver consists of the following four components:

(i) **Preprocessing:** To handle testers and selectors that are not directly supported by our framework, we have implemented preprocessing steps described in Sect. 4 of [23].
(ii) **Abstraction:** This is an implementation of the procedure described in Sect. 4. We utilized a portfolio of Spacer [22], Eldarica [14], and HoICE [5] as the backend solver for satisfiability checking problems of CHCs over integer arithmetic.
(iii) **Counterexample Generation:** We extract a (hyper-)resolution proof generated by Z3/Spacer [22,27], when a system of abstracted CHCs over integer arithmetic is unsatisfiable. We parse the result, and obtain a counterexample θ as described in Sect. 3.2.
(iv) **Refinement:** Our implementation of the synthesis procedure from Sect. 5 employs multiple linear templates (see Remark 1). The testing component (line 6–8 in Procedure 2) is executed by running Z3 with a timeout of one second.

While the formalization in the previous sections was for CHCs over a single ADT δ, the implementation can handle general CHCs over ADTs, including those with mutually recursive definitions.

6.2 Evaluation

We evaluated CATALIA on the ADT-LIA division of *CHC-COMP 2024* [10], which consists of 300 benchmark instances of satisfiable and unsatisfiable CHCs over algebraic data types and linear integer arithmetic. The benchmark set is publicly available [11]. For comparison, we selected three state-of-the-art CHC solvers that support the theory of ADTs and LIA: Spacer [22], RInGen [23], and Eldarica [14]. All the experiments were conducted on a machine with Intel Xeon Gold 6242 CPU and 64GB of RAM. We set the timeout to 300 s. Further details of the evaluation are publicly available [18].

The results, summarized in Table 1 and Fig. 2, show that CATALIA performs particularly well on satisfiable instances. It solved 67 satisfiable instances, the

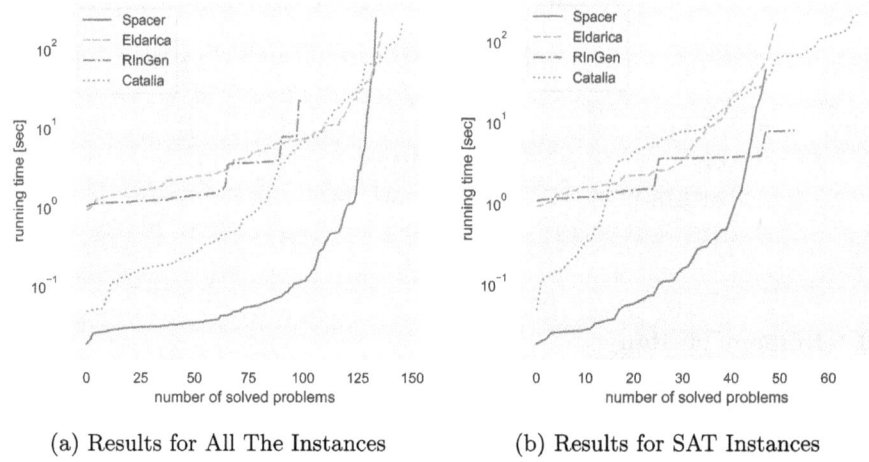

(a) Results for All The Instances (b) Results for SAT Instances

Fig. 2. Cactus plots. The horizontal axis shows the number of solved instances, and the vertical axis shows the time required to solve them.

most among all solvers. Additionally, it uniquely solved 18 satisfiable instances that no other solver could solve successfully within 300 s. Our approach primarily targets satisfiable CHCs, and the results confirm its effectiveness in this category. Catamorphisms that CATALIA successfully found include the list length, the sum of an integer list, the evenness of the list length, and their combinations. In terms of uniquely satisfiable instances, CATALIA and RInGen are complementary because they handle different classes of invariants. For example, CATALIA can handle the list length, whereas RInGen cannot. Conversely, RInGen can handle invariants involving the last element of a list, which CATALIA cannot. The latter is due to CATALIA's restriction of template catamorphisms to linear ones (cf. Remark 1). We expect that, by extending templates with conditional expressions, CATALIA will subsume RInGen's capability; we leave this extension for future work. For unsatisfiable instances, CATALIA performed slightly worse than Spacer and Eldarica. We also leave this issue for future work; random testing techniques [17] may help address it.

Figure 2 provides a detailed efficiency comparison across solvers. Spacer demonstrates the fastest solving times overall, efficiently handling numerous instances. However, its advantage lies primarily in speed rather than the number of solved satisfiable instances; in fact, it uniquely solves only a few problems. In contrast, CATALIA, while slower in terms of solving time than Spacer, successfully solves more satisfiable instances, aligning with its design goal of handling more complex invariants.

7 Related Work

We discuss related work on SMT solvers and CHC solvers that support ADTs.

7.1 SMT Solvers

The theory of ADT has been incorporated into the SMT-LIB Standard [3], the de facto standard language specification for SMT solvers, and leading SMT solvers such as Z3 [27], CVC5 [2] and Princess [33] already support this theory. Since Oppen's work [29], various decision procedures [24,30,32,34–36,38] have been proposed to handle ADTs.

Among these, several approaches [30,32,34,35] address satisfiability modulo ADT and recursively defined functions (RDFs). The approaches by Reynolds and Kuncak [32] and Yang et al. [36] tackled automated inductive reasoning on ADTs and RDFs by an efficient enumeration of lemmas. Suter et al. [34,35] introduced an abstraction method based on catamorphisms, which is similar to our approach. They also proposed decision procedures based on the abstraction, which were later refined by Pham et al. [30]. Our abstraction, however, differs in that it is tailored for CHCs (e.g., by introducing $\mathcal{C}$-admissibility predicates). In particular, our approach is capable of automatically synthesizing catamorphisms, leveraging the result of CHC solving.

7.2 CHC Solvers

Various approaches have been proposed to solve CHCs over ADTs in order to capture more complex properties of ADTs [5,7,9,14,15,21,23,37]. Eldarica [14] utilizes size constraints that represent the size of a given term to capture properties such as the list length. Size functions, which are also utilized in the decision procedures by Zhang et al. [38], can be seen as a special case of the catamorphisms introduced in this paper. De Angelis et al. [7] proposed fold/unfold transformation with techniques such as difference predicates [8] and catamorphic abstractions [9] to efficiently transform CHCs over ADTs to those without ADTs. However, their solver is not capable of yielding a model even when it successfully proves the satisfiability, and it requires users to manually supply catamorphisms. Kostyukov et al. [23] reduced satisfiability checking of CHCs to finite model finding of first-order logic, by approximating constructors with uninterpreted functions. A notable limitation of this approach is its inability to combine the theory of ADT with other theories such as linear integer arithmetic (LIA) and arrays. Krishnan et al. [15] have proposed a Spacer-like procedure for CHC over ADT and RDFs that preserves the refutational completeness of the original Spacer algorithm. While their approach requires users to provide catamorphisms, ours automatically synthesizes them. Some approaches [5,37] transform predicates in CHCs to RDFs, thereby reducing the problem to checking the satisfiability of formulas over ADTs and RDFs. However, as discussed above, solving such a formula in SMT solvers can be challenging. Furthermore, syntactically transforming predicates to functions is difficult especially when the CHCs are generated from compiler intermediate representations (e.g., LLVM), where the functional structure is often lost. Kobayashi and Wu [21] employed a machine learning technique to synthesize inductive invariants over lists. They train a recurrent neural network using an ICE learning framework and extract a fold (catamorphism) function using the technique proposed by Kobayashi et al. [20]. Although their approach can, in theory, synthesize general recursive functions, its scalability remains a significant challenge.

8 Conclusion

We have proposed a method to solve the satisfiability checking problem of constrained Horn clauses over algebraic data types and integer arithmetic. To find models defined inductively on the structure of algebraic data types, we employed catamorphisms to express inductive properties, and formalized a framework for automatically discovering appropriate catamorphisms on demand. We also implemented a CHC solver CATALIA based on the proposed method, and evaluated CATALIA against the benchmark sets taken from CHC-COMP 2024 ADT-LIA division. According to the evaluation results, CATALIA outperformed the previous methods in solving SAT instances, indicating that CATALIA is superior at discovering invariants that the previous solvers failed to find.

In future work, we plan to introduce more expressive catamorphism templates than linear ones. As this may incur a cost in efficiency, an important direction is to develop strategies for selectively applying different templates in the refinement phase of CATALIA.

Acknowledgments. We would like to thank anonymous reviewers for useful comments. This work was supported by JSPS KAKENHI Grant Numbers JP23KJ0546 and JP20H05703.

References

1. Alt, L., Blicha, M., Hyvärinen, A.E.J., Sharygina, N.: SolCMC: solidity compiler's model checker. In: Shoham, S., Vizel, Y. (eds.) Computer Aided Verification - 34th International Conference, CAV 2022, Haifa, Israel, August 7–10, 2022, Proceedings, Part I. Lecture Notes in Computer Science, vol. 13371, pp. 325–338. Springer (2022). https://doi.org/10.1007/978-3-031-13185-1_16
2. Barbosa, H., et al.: cvc5: A versatile and industrial-strength SMT solver. In: Fisman, D., Rosu, G. (eds.) Tools and Algorithms for the Construction and Analysis of Systems - 28th International Conference, TACAS 2022, Held as Part of the European Joint Conferences on Theory and Practice of Software, ETAPS 2022, Munich, Germany, April 2–7, 2022, Proceedings, Part I. Lecture Notes in Computer Science, vol. 13243, pp. 415–442. Springer (2022). https://doi.org/10.1007/978-3-030-99524-9_24
3. Barrett, C., Fontaine, P., Tinelli, C.: The SMT-LIB Standard: version 2.6. Technical Report. Department of Computer Science, The University of Iowa (2017). Available at. www.SMT-LIB.org
4. Blicha, M., Fedyukovich, G., Hyvärinen, A.E.J., Sharygina, N.: Transition power abstractions for deep counterexample detection. Presented at the (2022). https://doi.org/10.1007/978-3-030-99524-9_29

5. Champion, A., Chiba, T., Kobayashi, N., Sato, R.: ICE-based refinement type discovery for higher-order functional programs. J. Autom. Reason. **64**(7), 1393–1418 (2020). https://doi.org/10.1007/S10817-020-09571-Y
6. Clarke, E.M., Grumberg, O., Jha, S., Lu, Y., Veith, H.: Counterexample-guided abstraction refinement for symbolic model checking. J. ACM **50**(5), 752–794 (2003). https://doi.org/10.1145/876638.876643
7. Angelis, E., Fioravanti, F., Pettorossi, A., Proietti, M.: Solving horn clauses on inductive data types without induction. Theory Pract. Log. Program. **18**(3–4), 452–469 (2018). https://doi.org/10.1017/S1471068418000157
8. De Angelis, E., Fioravanti, F., Pettorossi, A., Proietti, M.: Removing algebraic data types from constrained horn clauses using difference predicates. In: Peltier, N., Sofronie-Stokkermans, V. (eds.) IJCAR 2020. LNCS (LNAI), vol. 12166, pp. 83–102. Springer, Cham (2020). https://doi.org/10.1007/978-3-030-51074-9_6
9. De Angelis, E., Fioravanti, F., Pettorossi, A., Proietti, M.: Catamorphic abstractions for constrained Horn clause satisfiability. Theory Pract. Log. Program. **25**(1), 64–91 (2025). https://doi.org/10.1017/S147106842400019X
10. Ernest, G., Morales, J.F.: CHC COMP 2024 Report (2024). https://chc-comp.github.io/2024/
11. Ernest, G., Morales, J.F.: CHC COMP benchmarks (2024). https://github.com/chc-comp/chc-comp24-benchmarks/tree/main/ADT-LIA
12. Gurfinkel, A., Kahsai, T., Komuravelli, A., Navas, J.A.: The SeaHorn verification framework. In: Kroening, D., Pasareanu, C.S. (eds.) Computer Aided Verification - 27th International Conference, CAV 2015, San Francisco, CA, USA, July 18–24, 2015, Proceedings, Part I. Lecture Notes in Computer Science, vol. 9206, pp. 343–361. Springer (2015). https://doi.org/10.1007/978-3-319-21690-4_20
13. Hoder, K., Bjørner, N.: Generalized property directed reachability. In: Cimatti, A., Sebastiani, R. (eds.) SAT 2012. LNCS, vol. 7317, pp. 157–171. Springer, Heidelberg (2012). https://doi.org/10.1007/978-3-642-31612-8_13
14. Hojjat, H., Rümmer, P.: The ELDARICA Horn solver. In: Proceedings of FMCAD 2018, pp. 1–7. IEEE (2018). https://doi.org/10.23919/FMCAD.2018.8603013
15. K., H.G.V., Shoham, S., Gurfinkel, A.: Solving constrained Horn clauses modulo algebraic data types and recursive functions. Proceedings ACM Program. Language **6**(POPL), 1–29 (2022). https://doi.org/10.1145/3498722
16. Kahsai, T., Rümmer, P., Sanchez, H., Schäf, M.: Jayhorn: A framework for verifying Java programs. In: Chaudhuri, S., Farzan, A. (eds.) Computer Aided Verification - 28th International Conference, CAV 2016, Toronto, ON, Canada, July 17–23, 2016, Proceedings, Part I. Lecture Notes in Computer Science, vol. 9779, pp. 352–358. Springer (2016). https://doi.org/10.1007/978-3-319-41528-4_19
17. Katsura, H., Kobayashi, N., Sakayori, K., Sato, R.: Mode-based reduction from validity checking of fixpoint logic formulas to test-friendly reachability problem. In: Kiselyov, O. (ed.) Programming Languages and Systems - 22nd Asian Symposium, APLAS 2024, Kyoto, Japan, October 22–24, 2024, Proceedings. Lecture Notes in Computer Science, vol. 15194, pp. 325–345. Springer (2024). https://doi.org/10.1007/978-981-97-8943-6_16
18. Katsura, H., Kobayashi, N., Sakayori, K., Sato, R.: Artifact: automated catamorphism synthesis for solving constrained horn clauses over algebraic data types (2025). https://doi.org/10.5281/zenodo.16220747
19. Katsura, H., Kobayashi, N., Sakayori, K., Sato, R.: Automated catamorphism synthesis for solving constrained horn clauses over algebraic data types (2025). https://arxiv.org/abs/2507.20726

20. Kobayashi, N., Sekiyama, T., Sato, I., Unno, H.: Toward neural-network-guided program synthesis and verification. In: Dragoi, C., Mukherjee, S., Namjoshi, K.S. (eds.) Static Analysis - 28th International Symposium, SAS 2021, Chicago, IL, USA, October 17–19, 2021, Proceedings. Lecture Notes in Computer Science, vol. 12913, pp. 236–260. Springer (2021). https://doi.org/10.1007/978-3-030-88806-0_12
21. Kobayashi, N., Wu, M.: Neural network-guided synthesis of recursive list functions. In: Sankaranarayanan, S., Sharygina, N. (eds.) Tools and Algorithms for the Construction and Analysis of Systems - 29th International Conference, TACAS 2023, Held as Part of the European Joint Conferences on Theory and Practice of Software, ETAPS 2022, Paris, France, April 22–27, 2023, Proceedings, Part I. Lecture Notes in Computer Science, vol. 13993, pp. 227–245. Springer (2023). https://doi.org/10.1007/978-3-031-30823-9_12
22. Komuravelli, A., Gurfinkel, A., Chaki, S.: SMT-based model checking for recursive programs. Formal Methods Syst. Design **48**(3), 175–205 (2016). https://doi.org/10.1007/s10703-016-0249-4
23. Kostyukov, Y., Mordvinov, D., Fedyukovich, G.: Beyond the elementary representations of program invariants over algebraic data types. In: Freund, S.N., Yahav, E. (eds.) PLDI '21: 42nd ACM SIGPLAN International Conference on Programming Language Design and Implementation, Virtual Event, Canada, June 20–25, 2021, pp. 451–465. ACM (2021). https://doi.org/10.1145/3453483.3454055
24. Leino, K.R.M.: Automating induction with an SMT solver. In: Kuncak, V., Rybalchenko, A. (eds.) VMCAI 2012. LNCS, vol. 7148, pp. 315–331. Springer, Heidelberg (2012). https://doi.org/10.1007/978-3-642-27940-9_21
25. Matsushita, Y., Tsukada, T., Kobayashi, N.: RustHorn: CHC-based verification for rust programs. In: Müller, P. (ed.) Programming Languages and Systems - 29th European Symposium on Programming, ESOP 2020, Held as Part of the European Joint Conferences on Theory and Practice of Software, ETAPS 2020, Dublin, Ireland, April 25–30, 2020, Proceedings. Lecture Notes in Computer Science, vol. 12075, pp. 484–514. Springer (2020). https://doi.org/10.1007/978-3-030-44914-8_18
26. Meijer, E., Fokkinga, M.M., Paterson, R.: Functional programming with bananas, lenses, envelopes and barbed wire. In: Hughes, J. (ed.) Functional Programming Languages and Computer Architecture, 5th ACM Conference, Cambridge, MA, USA, August 26–30, 1991, Proceedings. Lecture Notes in Computer Science, vol. 523, pp. 124–144. Springer (1991). https://doi.org/10.1007/3540543961_7
27. de Moura, L.M., Bjørner, N.S.: Z3: an efficient SMT solver. In: Ramakrishnan, C.R., Rehof, J. (eds.) Tools and Algorithms for the Construction and Analysis of Systems, 14th International Conference, TACAS 2008, Held as Part of the Joint European Conferences on Theory and Practice of Software, ETAPS 2008, Budapest, Hungary, March 29-April 6, 2008. Proceedings. Lecture Notes in Computer Science, vol. 4963, pp. 337–340. Springer (2008). https://doi.org/10.1007/978-3-540-78800-3_24
28. Mukai, R., Kobayashi, N., Sato, R.: Parameterized recursive refinement types for automated program verification. In: Singh, G., Urban, C. (eds.) Static Analysis - 29th International Symposium, SAS 2022, Auckland, New Zealand, December 5–7, 2022, Proceedings. Lecture Notes in Computer Science, vol. 13790, pp. 397–421. Springer (2022). https://doi.org/10.1007/978-3-031-22308-2_18
29. Oppen, D.C.: Reasoning about recursively defined data structures. J. ACM **27**(3), 403–411 (1980). https://doi.org/10.1145/322203.322204

30. Pham, T., Gacek, A., Whalen, M.W.: Reasoning about algebraic data types with abstractions. J. Autom. Reason. **57**(4), 281–318 (2016). https://doi.org/10.1007/S10817-016-9368-2
31. Reynolds, A., Deters, M., Kuncak, V., Tinelli, C., Barrett, C.: Counterexample-guided quantifier instantiation for synthesis in SMT. In: Kroening, D., Păsăreanu, C.S. (eds.) CAV 2015. LNCS, vol. 9207, pp. 198–216. Springer, Cham (2015). https://doi.org/10.1007/978-3-319-21668-3_12
32. Reynolds, A., Kuncak, V.: Induction for SMT solvers. In: D'Souza, D., Lal, A., Larsen, K.G. (eds.) VMCAI 2015. LNCS, vol. 8931, pp. 80–98. Springer, Heidelberg (2015). https://doi.org/10.1007/978-3-662-46081-8_5
33. Rümmer, P.: A constraint sequent calculus for first-order logic with linear integer arithmetic. In: Cervesato, I., Veith, H., Voronkov, A. (eds.) LPAR 2008. LNCS (LNAI), vol. 5330, pp. 274–289. Springer, Heidelberg (2008). https://doi.org/10.1007/978-3-540-89439-1_20
34. Suter, P., Dotta, M., Kuncak, V.: Decision procedures for algebraic data types with abstractions. In: Hermenegildo, M.V., Palsberg, J. (eds.) Proceedings of the 37th ACM SIGPLAN-SIGACT Symposium on Principles of Programming Languages, POPL 2010, Madrid, Spain, January 17–23, 2010, pp. 199–210. ACM (2010). https://doi.org/10.1145/1706299.1706325
35. Suter, P., Köksal, A.S., Kuncak, V.: Satisfiability modulo recursive programs. In: Yahav, E. (ed.) Static Analysis - 18th International Symposium, SAS 2011, Venice, Italy, September 14–16, 2011. Proceedings. Lecture Notes in Computer Science, vol. 6887, pp. 298–315. Springer (2011). https://doi.org/10.1007/978-3-642-23702-7_23
36. Yang, W., Fedyukovich, G., Gupta, A.: Lemma synthesis for automating induction over algebraic data types. In: Principles and Practice of Constraint Programming: 25th International Conference, CP 2019, Stamford, CT, USA, September 30-October 4, 2019, Proceedings 25, pp. 600–617. Springer (2019)
37. Zavalía, L., Chernigovskaia, L., Fedyukovich, G.: Solving constrained Horn clauses over algebraic data types. In: Dragoi, C., Emmi, M., Wang, J. (eds.) Verification, Model Checking, and Abstract Interpretation - 24th International Conference, VMCAI 2023, Boston, MA, USA, January 16–17, 2023, Proceedings. Lecture Notes in Computer Science, vol. 13881, pp. 341–365. Springer (2023). https://doi.org/10.1007/978-3-031-24950-1_16
38. Zhang, T., Sipma, H.B., Manna, Z.: Decision procedures for term algebras with integer constraints. Inf. Comput. **204**(10), 1526–1574 (2006). https://doi.org/10.1016/J.IC.2006.03.004

Formal Analysis of Networked PLC Controllers Interacting with Physical Environments

Jaeseo Lee and Kyungmin Bae(✉)

Pohang University of Science and Technology, Pohang, South Korea
kmbae@postech.ac.kr

Abstract. Programmable logic controllers (PLCs) are widely used in industrial systems to control physical plants. Ensuring their correctness is important due to their safety-critical nature. However, existing formal analysis techniques focus on individual PLC programs in isolation, often neglecting interactions with physical plants and networked communication between different controllers. This limitation poses significant challenges in analyzing real-world industrial systems, where continuous dynamics and distributed coordination play a central role. This paper presents a unified formal framework that integrates discrete PLC semantics, networked communication, and continuous physical behaviors. To mitigate state explosion in model checking, we apply partial order reduction to reduce the number of explored states while preserving correctness. Our framework enables precise analysis of PLC-based cyber-physical systems.

Keywords: Programmable logic controller · Structured Text · Formal semantics · Continuous dynamics · Partial order reduction

1 Introduction

Industrial automation systems rely on programmable logic controllers (PLCs) to execute control tasks across various domains, including robotic assembly lines, power distribution systems, and autonomous production machinery. The IEC 61131-3 standard [18] defines a set of domain-specific languages that support PLC programming. A PLC program typically controls a physical plant with continuous behaviors. Ensuring the correctness of PLC programs is crucial, as they are often deployed in safety-critical industrial environments.

The need for rigorous verification of PLC programs has attracted significant research interest from both academia and industry. As a result, various formal techniques and tools have been developed for analyzing PLC programs, such as [7,

8,11,19], spanning various PLC programming languages. Among these languages, Structured Text (ST)—a high-level imperative programming language—is the most expressive and widely adopted for formal analysis [12].

However, existing work on formal analysis of PLC programs mostly focuses on a single program in isolation, neglecting interactions with physical environments and networked communication between multiple PLCs. Some approaches attempt to integrate physical dynamics and communication, but they often rely on abstract PLC models that omit key programming constructs such as function blocks. As a result, they fail to capture the full expressiveness of PLC languages, which is crucial for accurately modeling real-world industrial automation systems.

The goal of this paper is to develop formal analysis techniques for general PLC applications by integrating three important aspects: the semantics of PLC programming languages, networked communication between PLC controllers (with explicit consideration of network delays), and the behavior of physical plants with continuous dynamics. Rather than addressing these aspects separately, we aim to develop a unified formal framework that supports faithful reasoning about system-level properties involving all three aspects.

Achieving this goal is challenging. Traditionally, each aspect of PLC systems has been modeled and analyzed using a different formalism, without an integrated approach for the full PLC-controlled system:

- **PLC programs**: Translated into the input language of another model checker [7,11], or given formal semantics of the language directly [17,26,39];
- **Communications**: Modeled using communication models such as process calculi [20] and colored Petri nets [15]; and
- **Physical Environments**: Typically using hybrid automata [16,29], where PLC program behaviors are encoded as guarded transition systems.

Combining these approaches is nontrivial due to high verification complexity from complex PLC programs, interleavings from asynchronous communication, and continuous behaviors. For example, hybrid automata can model physical environments and communications, but only under the unrealistic assumption that PLC programs—with features of general-purpose imperative languages—are simplified to finite state machines. Even with such assumptions, the resulting models often become infeasible for formal analysis (see Sect. 8).

This paper proposes a novel integration—tailored to the PLC domain—of three well-established methods: (i) object-oriented modeling of PLC programs, communication, and physical dynamics within a unified rewriting logic framework; (ii) symbolic reachability analysis using Maude combined with SMT solving [40]; and (iii) partial order reduction to mitigate state-space explosion from concurrency. While each technique has been studied individually, the novelty of our approach lies in their nontrivial integration into a single coherent framework.

We provide an *object-oriented rewriting-based specification*, where each PLC controller, interacting with a physical plant and communicating with other controllers, is encapsulated as an object, based on rewriting logic [28]. The attributes of a PLC object include timers, physical parameters, and a "processor" containing the entire configuration of a PLC ST program. The behavior of these objects is specified using an existing rewriting-based semantics for PLC ST [17,39], supporting a full subset of the language with minimal modification.

A communication model for PLCs with continuous behaviors can be effectively captured using *distributed real-time object-based systems* [32]. This approach provides a structured way to represent interactions between PLC controllers and their physical environment. As is common in distributed systems, communication between objects is modeled as asynchronous message passing. A key advantage is that it enables a direct and faithful representation of PLC communication mechanisms as specified in industrial standards.

To enable efficient verification, we apply partial order reduction (POR) [34] to mitigate the state explosion caused by redundant interleavings. Consider two PLC objects, each running a simple PLC program. Due to interleaving, the number of possible execution sequences grows exponentially. However, only statements that send and receive messages can produce different outcomes. By integrating POR with symbolic rewriting-based model checking, we significantly reduce the number of explored states while preserving correctness.

This integration is nontrivial because PLC systems exhibit unique features that are rarely addressed together by typical POR techniques. PLC programs use encapsulated function blocks with internal state, execute in periodic scan cycles with strict real-time constraints, and operate in distributed settings where each object interacts with physical plants. We address these challenges by exploiting the modularity of rewriting-based specifications, which facilitates the characterization of independent rewrite rules specialized for PLC communication models.

Our approach is implemented in Maude [10], a tool for modeling and analyzing rewriting logic specifications. We evaluate it on a set of benchmark models, including *new PLC ST benchmarks* we developed to explicitly incorporate PLC semantics, networked communication, and continuous dynamics—an integration not addressed in prior benchmarks. We compare our approach with a hybrid-automata-based tool, SpaceEx [14], showing that our method, combined with POR, outperforms SpaceEx by an order of magnitude.

The key contribution of our paper is to enable *unified formal analysis for PLCs* by tailoring the framework to the PLC domain, leveraging core concepts from the PLC standard, such as sensing and actuation, scan cycles, and communication. While each underlying method has been explored previously, their integration in the PLC context has not been developed. We believe this work is the first to jointly address PLC scan-cycle semantics, function block behavior, and networked physical interactions within a single formal analysis tool.

This paper is organized as follows. Section 2 provides background on rewriting logic, PLC ST, and POR. Section 3 introduces a motivating example. Section 4 presents the object-oriented semantics of PLCs with physical environments. Section 5 formalizes PLC communication. Section 6 presents our POR method specialized for PLCs. Section 7 explains symbolic analysis using rewriting modulo SMT. Section 8 reports the experimental results. Section 9 discusses related work. Finally, Sect. 10 presents some concluding remarks.

2 Preliminaries

2.1 Rewriting Logic and Maude

Rewrite Theories. A *rewrite theory* [28] is a formal specification of concurrent systems. States are specified as elements of algebraic data types, and transitions are specified using rewrite rules. A rewrite theory is a tuple $\mathcal{R} = (\Sigma, E, R)$, where: (i) (Σ, E) is an equational theory with Σ an algebraic signature (declaring sorts, subsorts, and function symbols) and E a set of equations; and (ii) R is a set of rewrite rules of the form $l : q \longrightarrow r$ **if** ψ, where l is a label, q and r are terms, and ψ is a conjunction of equations and rewrites. A *rewrite* $t \longrightarrow_{\mathcal{R}}^{*} t'$ holds if t' is reachable from t using the rewrite rules in $\mathcal{R}$.

To specify real-time systems, real-time rewrite theories [31] use *tick* rewrite rules of the form $l : \{t\} \longrightarrow \{t'\}$ **in time** τ **if** ψ, where the entire state is represented as $\{t\}$. This rule specifies that the transition from state t to t' takes time τ. Because the whole state has the form $\{t\}$, time elapses uniformly across the entire system when a tick rule is applied. Other (non-tick) rewrite rules are considered instantaneous, taking zero time.

Rewriting Modulo SMT. A *constrained term* is a pair $\phi(x_1, \ldots, x_n) \parallel t(x_1, \ldots, x_n)$ of a constraint ϕ and a term t over SMT variables $x_1, \ldots, x_n$ [4,35]. A constrained term $\phi \parallel t$ symbolically represents the set of all instances of t satisfying ϕ, denoted by $[\![\phi \parallel t]\!]$. A *symbolic rewrite* $\phi_t \parallel t \leadsto_{\mathcal{R}}^{*} \phi_u \parallel u$ on constrained terms symbolically represents the set of all "concrete" rewrites $t' \longrightarrow_{\mathcal{R}}^{*} u'$ such that $t' \in [\![\phi_t \parallel t]\!]$ and $u' \in [\![\phi_u \parallel u]\!]$. For any concrete rewrite $t' \longrightarrow_{\mathcal{R}}^{*} u'$ with $t' \in [\![\phi_t \parallel t]\!]$, there exists a symbolic rewrite $\phi_t \parallel t \leadsto_{\mathcal{R}}^{*} \phi_u \parallel u$ with $u' \in [\![\phi_u \parallel u]\!]$.

Symbolic rewrites can be "implemented" using ordinary rewrite rules on constrained terms [35]. For example, a rule $l : q \longrightarrow r$ **if** ψ is transformed into a constrained-term rule $l : \mathtt{PHI} \parallel q \longrightarrow (\mathtt{PHI}\ \text{and}\ \psi) \parallel r$ **if** $\mathtt{smtCheck}(\mathtt{PHI}\ \text{and}\ \psi)$ where $\mathtt{PHI}$ is a Boolean variable and $\mathtt{smtCheck}$ is a function that checks the satisfiability of a given SMT formula.

Maude. Maude [10] is a language and tool for specifying and analyzing rewrite theories. In Maude, rules are declared with the syntax `rl [l]: q => r`, and, for conditional rules, `crl [l]: q => r if` ψ. Similarly, equations are declared with the syntax `eq u = v`, and `ceq u = v if` ψ. Operators are declared with the syntax `op f : `$s_1 \ldots s_n$` -> s`, where $s_1, \ldots, s_n$ denote the argument sorts and s denotes the result sort. An operator declared with the `ctor` attribute is a *constructor* that defines the data elements of a sort.

A class declaration `class C | `$att_1 : s_1, \ldots, att_n : s_n$ declares a class C with attributes att_1 to att_n of sorts s_1 to s_n. An instance of a class C is represented as a term `< `O` : C | `$att_1 : v_1, \ldots, att_n : v_n$` >` of sort `Object`, where O is the object's identifier, and v_i is the value of each attribute att_i. A message is a term of sort `Msg`. A global system state is a term of sort `Configuration` that has the structure of a multiset composed of objects and messages, where multiset union is denoted by juxtaposition (empty syntax).

Maude supports a wide range of formal analysis commands. In particular, the command `search [n,m]: t =>* t'` such that Ψ searches for n states that are reachable from a ground term t within m steps, match the pattern t', and satisfy the condition Ψ, where n and m are optional.

In addition to explicit-state analysis methods, Maude provides SMT solving and symbolic reachability analysis for constrained terms. Maude-SE [40] extends Maude with extra functionality for rewriting modulo SMT, including witness generation and the `smtCheck` function that invokes the underlying SMT solver to check the satisfiability of SMT formulas.

2.2 Partial Order Reduction

A *transition system* $\mathcal{S}$ is defined as a tuple (S, s_0, T, AP, L) [5,34], where: S is the set of states, $s_0 \in S$ is the initial state, T represents the set of transitions such that each transition $\alpha \in T$ is a partial function $\alpha : S \to S$, AP is a collection of atomic propositions, and $L : S \to 2^{AP}$ is a labeling function that associates states with sets of atomic propositions.

A transition $\alpha \in T$ is considered *enabled* in a state $s \in S$ if $\alpha(s)$ is defined. The set of all transitions enabled in state s is denoted by $enabled(s)$. We often use the notation $s \xrightarrow{\alpha} s'$ to indicate that $\alpha(s) = s'$ for states $s, s' \in S$. Given a rewrite system, a transition system is naturally defined by a mapping from terms to states and rewrites to transitions.

Consider a transition system $\mathcal{S} = (S, s_0, T, AP, L)$. A transition $\alpha \in T$ is defined as *invisible* if $s \xrightarrow{\alpha} s'$ implies that $L(s) = L(s')$. An *independence relation* $I \subseteq T \times T$ is a symmetric and anti-reflexive relation, such that for any pair of transitions $(\alpha, \beta) \in I$ and a state $s \in S$, where $\alpha, \beta \in enabled(s)$, the following conditions hold: (i) $\alpha \in enabled(\beta(s))$ and $\beta \in enabled(\alpha(s))$, and (ii) $\alpha(\beta(s)) = \beta(\alpha(s))$. The complement of I, denoted by $D = (T \times T) \setminus I$, is referred to as a dependency relation.

We use partial order reduction via ample sets [34]. An *ample set* for a state $s \in S$ is a subset of the enabled transitions, represented as $ample(s) \subseteq enabled(s)$. A state $s \in S$ is considered *fully expanded* when $ample(s) = enabled(s)$. During state space exploration, only the transitions in $ample(s)$ are examined rather than all transitions in $enabled(s)$. This process produces a reduced transition system $\hat{\mathcal{S}}$, which maintains behavioral equivalence with the original system when ample sets are chosen correctly.

The following conditions ensure behavioral equivalence between the original transition system $\mathcal{S}$ and its reduced version $\hat{\mathcal{S}}$ [34]:[1] (i) $ample(s) \neq \emptyset$ if and only if $enabled(s) \neq \emptyset$; (ii) any transition that depends on a transition in $ample(s)$ cannot occur until a transition in $ample(s)$ occurs first;[2] (iii) if s is not fully expanded, then all transitions in $ample(s)$ must be invisible; and (iv) every cycle in the reduced state space $\hat{\mathcal{S}}$ includes at least one fully expanded state.

---

[1] More precisely, $\mathcal{S}$ and $\hat{\mathcal{S}}$ are stuttering bisimilar [5].
[2] For $s \xrightarrow{\beta_1} \cdots \xrightarrow{\beta_n} s_n \xrightarrow{\alpha} t$ with α depends on $ample(s)$, $\beta_i \in ample(s)$ for some $i \leq n$.

2.3 K Framework

K [36] is a rewrite-based semantic framework for defining the semantics of programming languages, grounded in rewriting logic [28]. It has been extensively used to formalize a wide range of languages, including C [13], Java [6], and JavaScript [33], Several tools can be used to execute and analyze languages using the K framework, including the K tool [21] and Maude [9,38].

In K, program states are represented as multisets of nested cells, called *configurations*. Each cell within a configuration represents a component of a program state, such as variable environments or memory stores. Transitions between configurations are specified as rewrite rules, written in a notation that concisely specifies only the relevant parts of these cells.

A computation in K is represented as a $\curvearrowright$-separated sequence of computational tasks. E.g., $t_1 \curvearrowright \ldots \curvearrowright t_n$ represents a computation where t_i is followed by t_{i+1} for $1 \leq i < n$. A task can be decomposed into a sequence of simpler tasks, and the result of a task is forwarded to the subsequent tasks. For instance, $(5 + x) * 2$ is decomposed into $x \curvearrowright 5 + \square \curvearrowright \square * 2$, where $\square$ is a placeholder. If x evaluates to a value v, then $v \curvearrowright 5 + \square \curvearrowright \square * 2$ becomes $5 + v \curvearrowright \square * 2$.

The following shows a typical K rule for variable lookup, labeled lookup. It involves three cells: k holds a computation; env, a map from variables to locations; and $store$, a map from locations to values:

$$\text{lookup:} \quad \frac{\langle x \curvearrowright \ldots \rangle_k \ \langle \ldots x \mapsto l \ldots \rangle_{env} \ \langle \ldots l \mapsto v \ldots \rangle_{store}}{v}$$

This rule specifies that if the first task in k is x, then x is replaced by value v in its location l. K rules can be translated into ordinary rewrite rules [36].

2.4 PLC ST

Structured text (ST) is a textual programming language defined in the IEC 61131-3 international standard [18]. ST supports typical features of imperative programming languages, including variable assignments, conditionals, loops, and functions. ST also has unique constructs such as function blocks, which are callable objects with state variables. In PLC, functions, function blocks, and programs are called *program organization units* (POUs).

Programs are declared using the syntax PROGRAM *Name* ... END_PROGRAM, and each program is composed of variable declarations and a code body. Variables are declared with the syntax VAR *SectionType* ... END_VAR, where *SectionType* may be GLOBAL, INPUT, or OUTPUT; if omitted, the variables are considered local. Global variable sections are defined outside of the program. The code body starts after the variable declaration sections.

PLC behavior consists of repeated *scan cycles*—a continuous loop where the controller reads inputs, executes programs, and updates outputs. In each scan cycle, the PLC first reads the status of all input devices (e.g., sensors and switches) and stores them in memory. It then executes control programs based on these inputs and updates output devices (e.g., motors, lights) accordingly.

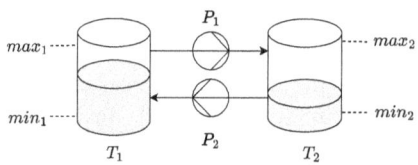
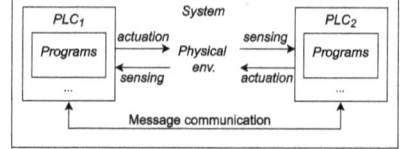

Fig. 1. Control system with PLCs

Fig. 2. System representation

The K semantics of PLC ST has been defined in prior work [17,26,39]. K configurations in this semantics include the k, env, and $store$ cells mentioned above, along with other cells for PLC-specific features such as POUs. Thanks to the modularity of K, the rules for typical imperative constructs are (almost) identical to those used for other imperative languages (e.g., see [37]).

3 Motivating Example: A Chemical Plant

Our motivating example, shown in Fig. 1, is a chemical plant adapted from [29]. The plant consists of two tanks, T_1 and T_2, where water is transferred between them by using pumps P_1 and P_2 based on user input. Pump P_1 moves water from T_1 to T_2, and P_2 moves water from T_2 to T_1, while maintaining the water levels of both tanks within specified intervals. The plant is controlled by two PLCs: PLC_i controls pump P_i for $i = 1, 2$.

While each PLC runs its own program, external behavior governs how water levels change. When P_1 is on, the water level in T_1 decreases and that of T_2 increases by the same amount. Conversely, when P_2 is on, the water level in T_2 decreases while T_1's increases by the same amount.

PLCs operate cyclically through input, execution, and output stages. In the input stage (sensing), sensor values are copied into input variables. In the output stage (actuation), output variables update physical components. In between, the PLC programs execute based on the sensed inputs to determine output values. During the execution stage, PLC programs run internally, while externally, physical *flow* occurs (i.e., continuous changes in physical attributes), typically modeled by ordinary differential equations or continuous functions.

PLC communication is managed using standard function blocks specified in [18], such as CONNECT, USEND, and URCV. The CONNECT function block establishes or disconnects a communication link between two PLCs based on a Boolean trigger. Once the connection is established, USEND can asynchronously send data, and URCV can asynchronously receive it. Figure 2 illustrates the interplay between PLC program execution, continuous dynamics, and inter-PLC communication.

Our goal is to develop a model that natively captures the full system behavior. For example, the property "*The water level in T_1 is always between 20 and 80*" depends on the combined effects of program logic, the physical environment, and inter-PLC communication. Defining semantics that cover these diverse system aspects is challenging due to the complex interplay among them.

4 Behavior of PLCs with Physical Environment

This section explains how we define the semantics, which includes PLCs' interaction with the environment. A PLC system is a set of PLC objects, which exhibit both programmatic and physical behavior. A PLC object is composed of the PLC's program state, a timer for scan cycles, a mapping of physical states, and a flow function that models the evolution of physical quantities over time.

The environment interacts with the programs by sensing and actuation at the beginning of every scan cycle. Sensing and actuation are overwriting values from physical state to program memory back and forth. We define the *timeEffect* that defines the time evolution of the system, which updates the environmental state according to the flow function. We define the `tick` rule, which uses the `timeEffect` function to evolve the whole system temporally, and the `start` rule, which starts new scan cycles. Especially, the `tick` rule captures time progression as discrete transitions, making it suitable for POR discussed in Sect. 6.

4.1 Object-Oriented Representation

The following illustrates the class definitions of PLC, which encapsulates the programmatic aspect of PLCs and the external interactions.

```
class PLC | proc: KConfig, timer: Time, state: State, flow: Flow .
```

The programmatic part of the PLC is captured in `proc` attribute, which stores the program configuration in K [26,37] and describes the state of internal PLC programs. The `timer` attribute tracks the remaining time in the current scan cycle. The `state` is a mapping of actuating/sensing attribute names to their corresponding values, and the `flow` defines the system's physical dynamics. The flow function can be defined as a polynomial equation of arbitrary degree.

Suppose a system where the current water level `wl` is 10 and the pump switch `ps` is zero. `wl` decreases by 1 per time unit when `ps` is 1 and remains unchanged when `ps` is 0. The following represents the object with the `timer` of value 10.

```
< T1 : PLC | proc : app', timer : 10, state : (wl |-> 10, ps |-> 0),
             flow : wl(t) = wl - ps * t >
```

4.2 Semantics of PLC Machines with Physical Attributes

The following show two key rewrite rules that specify the real-time behavior of PLCs. The `start` rule initiates new scan cycles for due objects. The `tick` rule (nondeterministically) advances time (by duration T). These rules are defined using three auxiliary functions `start`, `timeEffect`, and `mte`.

```
crl [start] : {Conf} => {start(Conf)}  if Conf =/= start(Conf) .
crl [tick]  : {Conf} => {timeEffect(Conf,T)} in time T  if T <= mte(Conf) .
```

A new scan cycle may start when two conditions hold: (1) the PLC's `timer` attribute has reached zero, and (2) all programs have completed execution. There are two equations for `start` operation. The first initiates a new scan cycle for such PLC objects, while the other ensures that objects not due for a new cycle remain unchanged.

The `start` function resets the timer and loads the program definitions to begin the next cycle. The specific process of loading and executing programs is assumed to be governed by the semantics of the internal PLC programming language, similar to those in [25,26]. On top of that, `start` also contains sensing and actuating behavior. The `actuate` and the `sense` are functions for actuation and sensing described in Sect. 3. The `callP` is a K label that loads the programs.

```
var KC : KConfig .      var FLOW : Flow .           var ENV : Map{Id,Loc} .
vars T TIMER : Time .   var STORE : Map{Loc,Val} .  var STATE : Map{Id,Val} .

eq start(< O : PLC | timer : 0, state : STATE,
                     proc : k(.) cycleTime(T) env(ENV) store(STORE) KC >)
 = < O : PLC | timer : T, state : actuate(ENV, STORE, STATE)
               proc : k(callP) cycleTime(T) env(ENV)
               store(sense(ENV, STORE, STATE)) KC > .
eq start(< O : PLC | timer : T >) = < O : PLC | > [owise] .
```

To model the passage of time, the system defines the *time effect function*. The following equation describes the *time effect* of duration T for a single PLC object, provided that T does not exceed the object's current `timer` value TIMER. The function x monus y is defined as max(x - y, 0), ensuring that time never progresses past zero. A PLC also must reflect the physical behavior by updating the `state` attribute according to the `flow` attribute. The `eval` function in the `state` attribute evaluates the result of the physical flow of a given duration.

```
eq timeEffect(< O : PLC | timer: TIMER, flow: FLOW, state: STATE >, T)
 = < O : PLC | timer: TIMER monus T, state: eval(FLOW, STATE, T) > .
```

The `mte` (*maximal time elapse*) function determines the maximum duration the system can advance before another transition (such as a new scan cycle) must occur. For a single PLC object, the `mte` value is simply the `timer` value, ensuring that time does not surpass the scan cycle boundary.

```
eq mte(< O : PLC | timer : TIMER >) = TIMER .
```

4.3 Example

We revisit the motivating example introduced in Sect. 3, but without communication. The whole system, including two PLCs and their physical environment, must be handled at once, but we only explain in the view of one PLC machine for the sake of simplicity. The program in Fig. 3 is loaded in the PLC machine.

```
PROGRAM T1                                  IF input THEN ps := 1;
VAR_INPUT wl : REAL; END_VAR                ELSE ps := 0;
VAR_OUTPUT ps : INT; END_VAR                END_IF;
VAR input : BOOL;   ...      END_VAR       END_PROGRAM
```

Fig. 3. ST program for a chemical plant

input is a Boolean value that is directly linked to a user input. Depending on the user input, ps is 1 or 0.

Figure 4 shows an execution sequence starting from the initial state s_1. There is one sensor attribute wl and one actuation attribute ps. The app is a K configuration including the code, store, and environment. The flow attribute flow : wl(t) = wl - ps * t is omitted, since it stays the same.

Applying the tick rule of duration 10 will result in s_2. Since ps has value 0 in state attribute, the flow function returns the current wl, which is 10. Note that the timer value is reduced to 0. Assume that the user input 1 is given. We have s_3 after this scan cycle, where app' represents the final program state after execution, with ps in proc is 1.

The start rule applies and produces s_4, as it performs actuation, sensing, program reloading, and resetting the PLC's timer to the cycle time. Since wl remains unchanged, sensing has no effect. However, actuation updates ps in state from 0 to 1. The app" is the result of reloading the programs in app'. After 6 time units elapses, since ps in state has value 1, the water level becomes 4 according to the flow function.

```
s1 < T1 : PLC | proc : app  , timer : 10, state : wl |-> 10, ps |-> 0, ... >
s2 < T1 : PLC | proc : app  , timer :  0, state : wl |-> 10, ps |-> 0, ... >
s3 < T1 : PLC | proc : app' , timer :  0, state : wl |-> 10, ps |-> 0, ... >
s4 < T1 : PLC | proc : app'', timer : 10, state : wl |-> 10, ps |-> 1, ... >
s5 < T1 : PLC | proc : app'', timer :  4, state : wl |->  4, ps |-> 1, ... >
```

Fig. 4. Example of an execution sequence

5 Semantics of Communication

In this section, we describe our formal semantics of communication that conforms to IEC 61131 [18] standard. We focus on the connection establishment and the asynchronous send/receive functionality.

We define the behavior of communication function blocks in ST in the form of user-defined function blocks. These function blocks are stateful and operate across multiple steps, so it is inappropriate to model them as single transitions. Specifically, a single run of a function block call involves conditional branching, flag settings, and operations such as connection establishment and data transmission. To enable POR, we carefully identify atomic operations and encode communicating behavior using function blocks constructed from these operations.

We formulate the *Conn* class representing a connection, which collects sent messages so that the receivers can retrieve them. A *Conn* object may exist for every pair of PLCs in the system. It stores the messages in their transmission and the network delay constraint.

The handling of connection establishment, message transmission, and message reception necessitates the introduction of new semantic components. To address this, we define atomic operations within the proc attribute to structure these operations: connectRequest for initiating connection establishment, disconnect for severing a connection, isConnected for checking connection establishment, sendData for transmitting data, and rcvData for receiving data.

5.1 Encoding of Communication Function Blocks

Figure 5 is the function block definition of CONNECT. The function block has two inputs: ENC, a Boolean that triggers the connection process, and PARTNER, a string identifying the target device. It produces four outputs: VALID, indicating a successful connection; ERROR, set to TRUE if a failure occurs; STATUS, an integer representing the connection state (0 for success, 1 for failure); and ID, storing the connected partner's identifier. The connection process starts when ENC is TRUE, initiating a request to PARTNER. If the connection is valid and ENC switches to FALSE, a disconnection follows. The block continuously checks the connection status using isConnected(PARTNER), updating the outputs accordingly: if connected, VALID is TRUE, ERROR is FALSE, STATUS is 0, and ID is updated; otherwise, VALID is FALSE, ERROR is TRUE, and STATUS is 1. For other function block definitions, please refer to our longer version of this paper [24].

```
FUNCTION_BLOCK CONNECT
VAR_INPUT
ENC : BOOL; PARTNER : STRING;
END_VAR
VAR_OUTPUT
VALID : BOOL := FALSE;
ERROR : BOOL := FALSE;
STATUS : DINT := 0;
ID : STRING;
END_VAR
  IF ENC = TRUE THEN
    connectRequest(PARTNER);
  END_IF ;
```

```
IF VALID AND NOT ENC THEN
   disconnect(PARTNER);
END_IF;
IF isConnected(PARTNER) THEN
   VALID := TRUE;   ERROR := FALSE;
   STATUS := 0;
   ID := PARTNER;
ELSE
   VALID := FALSE;
   ERROR := TRUE;
   STATUS := 1;
END_IF;
END_FUNCTION_BLOCK
```

Fig. 5. Function block encoding of CONNECT

5.2 Semantics of Communication Between PLCs

All communication behaviors are captured by functions that modify or refer to Conn objects. The following is the class definition of Conn, the constructor for its identifiers, and the constructor of messages.

```
class Conn | validity: Bool, buffer: Set{Msg}, delay: Pair{Time,Time} .

op conn : Oid Oid -> Oid [ctor comm] .
op m : Oid Oid Id Id Any Time Time -> Msg [ctor] .
```

The validity attribute denotes if the connection is successfully established. The buffer stores the sent message along with the information about the source and destination function block instances. The delay contains the minimum and maximum message delays specified by the delay annotation (to be explained shortly). The identifier of the *Conn* between PLCs O and O' is conn(O, O'). To avoid redundant definitions for the same pair of PLCs (e.g., conn(O, O') and conn(O', O)), the constructor is defined commutative using the comm axiom.

A message is composed of the sender's ID, the receiver's ID, the identifiers of the sending and receiving function block instances, the transmitted data, and two message delay timers. Each message is assigned delay timers upon creation according to the delay annotation. The timeEffect function decreases the delay timers of all messages by the elapsed time. A message becomes receivable when its minimum delay timer reaches zero, and must be accepted once its maximum delay timer expires. The decreaseTimer function iterates through messages in the buffer, reducing the delay timers by the specified amount.

```
vars C O O' : Oid .       var BUFFER : Set{Msg} .    var K : K .        vars L U : Time .
var DATA : Val .          var B : Bool .             vars T T2 : Time .
vars MIN MAX MIN' MAX' : Time .                      vars SFBID RFBID : Id .

eq timeEffect(< C : Conn | buffer : BUFFER >, T) =
                < C : Conn | buffer : decreaseTimer(BUFFER, T) > .

eq decreaseTimer(empty, T) = empty .
eq decreaseTimer((m(O, O', SFBID, RFBID, DATA, MIN, MAX) BUFFER), T)
 = m(O, O', SFBID, RFBID, DATA, MIN monus T, MAX monus T)
     decreaseTimer(BUFFER) .
```

The maximal time elapse of Conn object is the minimum value of all the messages' maximum delay.

```
op minMaxDelay : Set{Msg} ~> Time .

eq mte(< C : Conn | buffer : BUFFER >) = minMaxDelay(BUFFER) .

eq minMaxDelay(empty) = infinity .
eq minMaxDelay((m(O, O', SFBID, RFBID, DATA, MIN, MAX), BUFFER))
 = min(MAX, minMaxDelay(BUFFER)) .
```

The following describes the atomic operations for communication, including connectRequest, isConnected, sendData, and rcvData. The connectRequest function takes a PLC id and opens a connection. The conSucc and the conFail rules respectively define the success or failure of the requested connection.

```
rl [conSucc] :
   < O : PLC | proc : k(connectRequest(O') ~> K) KC >
   < conn(O, O') : Conn | validity : false >
=> < O : PLC | proc : k(K) KC > < conn(O, O') : Conn | validity : true > .

rl [conFail] :
   < O : PLC | proc : k(connectRequest(O') ~> K) KC >
   < conn(O, O') : Conn | validity : false >
=> < O : PLC | proc : k(K) KC > < conn(O, O') : Conn | > .
```

The isConnected function checks if the desired connection is successfully established. It takes a PLC name and returns either TRUE or FALSE depending on the presence of the established connection to that PLC.

```
rl [conCheck]: < O : PLC | proc : k(isConnected(O') ~> K) KC >
               < conn(O, O') : Conn | validity : B >
            => < O : PLC | proc : k(if B then TRUE else FALSE fi ~> K) KC >
               < conn(O, O') : Conn | > .
```

The sendData function sends data when given the sender's and receiver's PLC identifiers and the function block instance identifiers of USEND and URCV. The message delay setting is in the delay attribute. The sendData and sendDataFail rules respectively succeed and fail to dispatch the data.

```
rl [sendData] :
< O : PLC | proc: k(sendData(O', SFBID, RFBID, DATA) ~> K) KC >
< conn(O, O') : Conn | validity : true, buffer : BUFFER, delay :(MIN, MAX) >
=> < O : PLC | proc : k(TRUE ~> K) KC >
< conn(O, O') : Conn |
  buffer : insert(BUFFER, m(O, O', SFBID, RFBID, DATA, MIN, MAX)) > .

rl [sendDataFail] :
< O : PLC | proc : k(sendData(O', SFBID, RFBID, DATA) ~> K) KC >
< conn(O, O') : Conn | validity : false, buffer : BUFFER >
=> < O : PLC | proc : k(FALSE ~> K) KC > < conn(O, O') : Conn | > .
```

The rcvData function accepts the data if available in the corresponding buffer of the connection. The series of rules in the following describes the success (rcvData), the failure due to lost connection (rcvFail), or accepting no message (rcvNo). The rcvError label indicates the failure of receiving message. The checkMsg function checks if there is a transmitted message in the buffer.

```
crl [rcvData] : < O : PLC | proc : k(rcvData(O', SFBID, RFBID) ~> K) KC >
< conn(O, O') : Conn |
validity : true, buffer : (BUFFER m(O', O, SFBID, RFBID, DATA, MIN, MAX)) >
=> < O : PLC | proc : k(DATA ~> K) KC >
   < conn(O, O') : Conn | buffer : BUFFER > if MIN == 0 .

rl [rcvFail] : < O : PLC | proc : k(rcvData(O', SFBID, RFBID) ~> K) KC >
< conn(O, O') : Conn | validity : false, buffer : BUFFER >
=> < O : PLC | proc : k(rcvError ~> K) KC > < conn(O, O') : Conn | > .

crl [rcvNo] : < O : PLC | proc : k(rcvData(O', SFBID, RFBID) ~> K) KC >
   < conn(O, O') : Conn | validity : true, buffer : BUFFER >
=> < O : PLC | proc : k(rcvError ~> K) KC >
   < conn(O, O') : Conn | > if not checkMsg(BUFFER, O', SFBID, RFBID) .
```

We introduce a time assertion annotation to specify that a statement must execute after a certain time has elapsed since the start of the scan cycle. Although our formal semantics is designed to accommodate arbitrary execution times of statements within a scan cycle, this can lead to overly conservative or unrealistic behavior during analysis. The time assertion annotation takes //assertTime(min, max) form. The following restricts the invocation of rcv to take place from 50 to 80 ms since the beginning of the cycle, where con is a connection object and send' is a USEND instance in the other end of the con.

```
//assertTime(50, 80)        rcv(TRUE, con, send');
```

The range of message delays can also be configured. The delay annotation is represented as //delay(P1, P2, m, M), where P1 and P2 are object ids, m is a minimum message delay, and M is a maximum message delay. The following annotation makes the data arrive in 10 to 20 ms after the message creation.

```
//delay(P1, P2, 10, 20)     send(TRUE, con, rcv', data);
```

The following shows the constructor definitions and rules for time annotations. The assertTime rule checks that the elapsed time from the beginning of the current cycle T2 - T is in the assertion range [L,U]. The rule delay rule replaces the original content of delay attribute with the given values.

```
sort Annotation .           subsort Annotation < K .
op //assertTime : Time Time -> Annotation [ctor] .
op //delay : Oid Oid Time Time -> Annotation [ctor] .

crl [assertTime] :
< O : PLC | timer : T,
            proc : k(//assertTime(L, U) ~> K) cycleTime(T2) KC, ATTRS > =>
< O : PLC | timer : T,
      proc : k(K) cycleTime(T2) KC, ATTRS > if L <= T2 - T and U >= T2 - T .

rl [delay] : < O : PLC | proc : k(//delay(O, O', MAX, MIN) ~> K), ATTRS >
   < conn(O, O') : Conn | delay : (MAX', MIN') >
=> < O : PLC | proc : k(K), ATTRS >
   < conn(O, O') : Conn | delay : (MAX, MIN) > .
```

5.3 Example

```
PROGRAM T1
VAR_INPUT    wl : REAL;    END_VAR
VAR_OUTPUT   ps : INT;     END_VAR
VAR
  input  : INT;    comm     : CONNECT;
  send   : USEND;  rcv      : URCV;
  sig_in : INT;    sig_out  : INT;  ...
END_VAR
  comm(TRUE , "T2");
  IF NOT comm.VALID THEN RETURN;
  END_IF;
  sig_out := input;
  send(TRUE, "T2", "rcv", sig_out);
  rcv(TRUE, "T2", "send");
  sig_in := rcv.DATA;
  ps := sig_out - sig_in;
END_PROGRAM
```

```
PROGRAM T2
VAR_INPUT    wl : REAL;    END_VAR
VAR_OUTPUT   ps : INT;     END_VAR
VAR
  input  : INT;    comm     : CONNECT;
  send   : USEND;  rcv      : URCV;
  sig_in : INT;    sig_out  : INT;  ...
END_VAR
  comm(TRUE , "T1");
  IF NOT comm.VALID THEN RETURN;
  END_IF;
  sig_out := input;
  send(TRUE, "T1", "rcv", sig_out);
  rcv(TRUE, "T1", "send");
  sig_in := rcv.DATA;
  ps := sig_out - sig_in;
END_PROGRAM
```

Fig. 6. ST programs for a chemical plant

Consider the example in Sect. 4.3, but this time with communication. Figure 6 shows the programs installed in T_1 and T_2. The process begins with an attempt to establish a connection using the comm(TRUE,"T2") function, where "T2" represents T_2. After initiating communication, the program verifies the connection establishment by checking comm.VALID. If the connection is invalid, the program terminates early using the RETURN statement. Otherwise, the program assigns the value of input to signal_out, preparing the data for transmission. The send(TRUE, "T2", "rcv", signal_out) function sends signal_out to T_2's receiving function block instance rcv. The program then executes rcv(TRUE, "T2", "send"), which retrieves data from T_2 that was sent by a function block instance send. The received data in rcv.DATA is assigned to signal_in. Finally, the difference between signal_out (the sent data) and signal_in (the received data) is computed and stored in pump_switch. This ensures that when both tanks receive positive input (+1) from users, they do not activate their pumps simultaneously, preventing meaningless water exchange.

Figure 7 shows an execution sequence with communication between T_1 and T_2. In the initial state s_1, connectRequest(T2) is ready to execute. The message delay time is given as 5 to 10 ms. After the conSucc rule applies, the connection's validity is true, and we have s_2 after some program transitions. The signal is given as 1 by the user. The sendData rule applies and inserts the message to the buffer in the connection object, as shown in s_3. After 5 milliseconds, during T_2's invocation of the function block instance rcv, rcvData is ready, as shown in s_4. In s_5, the data is transferred from the connection object to T_2 by rcvData.

```
        ┌──────────────────────────────────────────────────────────────────────────────┐
    s₁  │ < T1 : PLC | proc : k(connectRequest(T2) ~> ...) ..., timer : 10, ... >       │
        │ < T2 : PLC | proc : k(...) ...,                        timer : 10, ... >     │
        │ < conn(T1, T2) : Conn | validity: false, delay : (5, 10), buffer : empty >   │
        ├──────────────────────────────────────────────────────────────────────────────┤
    s₂  │ < T1 : PLC | proc : k(sendData(T2, "send", "rcv", 1) ~> ...) ..., timer : 10, ... > │
        │ < T2 : PLC | proc : k(...) ...,                        timer : 10, ... >     │
        │ < conn(T1, T2) : Conn | validity : true, delay : (5, 10), buffer : empty >   │
        ├──────────────────────────────────────────────────────────────────────────────┤
    s₃  │ < T1 : PLC | proc : k(...) ..., timer : 10, ... >                            │
        │ < T2 : PLC | proc : k(...) ..., timer : 10, ... >                            │
        │ < conn(T1,T2) : Conn | validity : true, delay: (5, 10),                       │
        │                       buffer : (T1, T2, "send", "rcv", 1, 5, 10) >           │
        ├──────────────────────────────────────────────────────────────────────────────┤
    s₄  │ < T1 : PLC | proc : k(...),                             timer : 5, ... >    │
        │ < T2 : PLC | proc : k(rcvData(T1, "send", "rcv") ~> ...), timer : 5, ... >   │
        │ < conn(T1 , T2) : Conn | validity : true, delay : (5, 10),                    │
        │                       buffer : (T1, T2, "send", "rcv", 1, 0, 5) >            │
        ├──────────────────────────────────────────────────────────────────────────────┤
    s₅  │ < T1 : PLC | proc : k(...) ...,       timer : 5, ... >                       │
        │ < T2 : PLC | proc : k(1 ~> ...) ..., timer : 5, ... >                        │
        │ < conn(T1 , T2) : Conn | validity : true, buffer : empty, delay : (5, 10) > │
        └──────────────────────────────────────────────────────────────────────────────┘
```

Fig. 7. Example of an execution sequence with communication

6 Partial Order Reduction

Despite the conciseness of our semantics, state explosion remains an issue due to redundant state exploration. Consider the state transition diagram in Fig. 8. In the top-left state, two PLCs are ready to execute their own *main* function, and the system clock is 0. The system can take one of the three choices: to execute PLC_1's program, to execute PLC_2's program, and to elapse time by 3 unit. Similarly, each of the resulting three states has two choices, and finally, they converge to one state in the bottom-left.

However, we do not need to explore all of these states since they do not change the properties of interest, which only regard the physical environment such as the location of PLC machine parts. For example, suppose PLC_1 moves one unit per time unit along the x-axis, starting from $(0,0)$, while PLC_2 travels in parallel with PLC_1 from $(0, 10)$. Regardless of the execution path taken, the system transitions from the state where PLC_1 is at $(0,0)$ and PLC_2 is at $(0,10)$ to the state where PLC_1 reaches $(3,0)$ and PLC_2 reaches $(3,10)$. Thus, instead of exploring 8 states, we can only explore one path consisting of 4 states.

Partial order reduction (POR) is a model checking optimization technique that reduces the number of explored states by identifying independent transitions that can occur in different orders without affecting the final system behavior. By selectively exploring only a subset of execution sequences, POR mitigates state explosion while preserving the correctness of verification results. We apply the ample-set based POR technique. By using our ample set approach, the state explosion only takes the left-most path in Fig. 8.

A transition is specified by a rule label and substitution. When $s \xrightarrow{\alpha} s'$ in our semantics, s' is the outcome of applying l with σ to s for some rule label l and a substitution σ. We denote this transition as $l(\sigma)$. When a rule label alone can determine a single enabled transition, we omit the substitution. Similarly, we only need a part of the substitution as long as it singles out the possible transition. For example, rcvData(0 ← P1) is a transition of rcvData where P1 is the recipient. For simplicity, rule label(O ← P) is abbreviated as rule label(P) for some object P. A timed transition of duration τ is represented as tick(τ).

We exploit the fact that physical behaviors for a scan cycle are determined by the actuation, which is dependent on the outcome of the previous cycle. We assume that actuation does not happen mid-cycle, which is a common practice in various PLC implementations. Thus, all the in-program transitions are independent of the external environment's time evolution tick and the starting of the new scan cycle start, except for the communication functions. In addition, programs in different PLCs do not affect each other except for communication, because their transitions take place in strictly separate objects. Since there are independent groups of transitions, POR is suitable for reducing the state space.

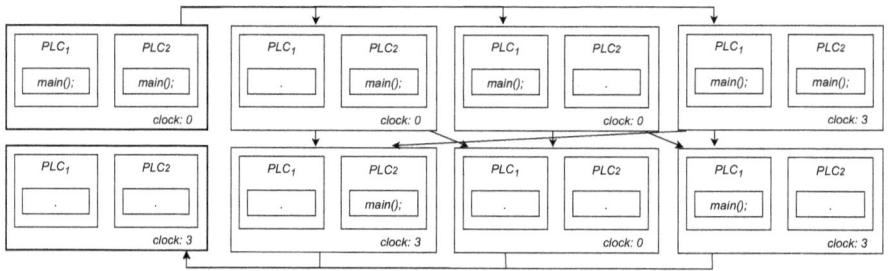

Fig. 8. State transition diagram without POR

Another major source of the state explosion is communication. Communication transitions can interleave with other transitions, such as assignments, start, and tick. However, communication happens independently of other types of transitions. Thus, we can allow the interleaving only among communication transitions.

We also define internal transitions for individual PLCs, which do not involve any inter-PLC interaction. Since these transitions and communication transitions are independent, we only need to consider the interleaving among the same groups. Definition 1 are formal definitions of those groups of transitions.

Definition 1 (Transition sets). *(1) Given a PLC object P, its internal transition set $P_{internal}$ contains transitions that modify proc of P. (2) The communication transitions set comm = {sendData(P), rcvData(P), rcvFail(P), rcvNo(P), isConnected(P), connectRequest(P) | for all PLC object P}.*

Our ample set definition is as follows. The basic idea is that start is in the ample set when enabled. If not, the ample set contains transitions of the object with the lowest index with at least one enabled transition. The function $\iota : id \to \mathbb{N}$ is a one-to-one mapping from PLC identifiers to distinct indices.

Definition 2 (Ample set). *For a system S and a state s, ample is defined as follows: (1) ample(s) = {start}, if start $\in$ enabled(s). (2) ample(s) =*

($P_{internal} \cap enabled(s)$), if start $\notin enabled(s)$ and $\iota(P)$ is the minimal number such that $P_{internal} \cap enabled(s)$ is not empty. (3) $ample(s) = comm \cap enabled(s)$ if start $\notin enabled(s)$ and $comm \cap enabled(s) \neq \emptyset$ and $P_{internal} = \emptyset$ for all P. (4) $ample(s) = enabled(s)$ otherwise.

Ultimately, we need to prove that the above definition of ample satisfies the four ample set conditions explained in Sect. 2. To achieve this goal, we first prove the independence between groups of transitions.

Lemma 1. *The followings hold: (1) For any state s where* start $\in enabled(s)$, *then* start *is independent of all transitions in* $enabled(s)$. *(2) For any state s,* tick *is independent of all transitions in* $enabled(s)$. *(3) For any two objects P_1 and P_2, for any a_1 and a_2 such that $a_1 \in transition_{P_1}$, $a_2 \in transition_{P_2}$, a_1 and a_2 are independent. (4) Let P be the object with the minimum numbering function in the system. Then, for any $a \in P_{internal}$ and $c \in comm$ are independent.*

Proof. (1) If start rule modifies a PLC object P, then any of P-specific transition are not enabled by definition of start. (2) tick rule updates the time and continuous attribute of PLC objects. The continuous attribute's behavior is only affected by the previous cycle of those PLC objects, so they are independent of transitions regarding PLC objects in the current cycle. (3) When a_1 and a_2 are non-communication transitions, let $P_1 \xrightarrow{a_1} P'_1$ and $P_2 \xrightarrow{a_2} P'_2$. Then, $P_1\ P_2\ Conf \xrightarrow{a_1} P'_1\ P_2\ Conf \xrightarrow{a_2} P'_1\ P'_2\ Conf$ and $P_1\ P_2\ Conf \xrightarrow{a_2} P_1\ P'_2\ Conf \xrightarrow{a_1} P'_1\ P'_2\ Conf$. (4) If c is not a communication transition related to P, the lemma holds trivially. In the remaining case, the statement is vacuously true since transitions in $P_{internal}$ and communication transitions involving P cannot be enabled simultaneously by construction of our semantics, where no two instructions are enabled at the same time. □

Using the Lemma 1, we have Theorem 1 stating that the ample set definition in Definition 2 satisfies all the conditions required to be met when taking the ample set approach.

Theorem 1. *The ample set defined in Definition 2 satisfies the four conditions of partial order reduction.*

Proof. (1) Immediately follows from Definition 2. There is no case where $enabled(s)$ is an empty set, since tick is always enabled. (2) When $ample(s) = \{$start$\}$, then by (1) of Lemma 1, there is no dependent transition enabled. When $ample(s) = (P_{internal} \cap enabled(s))$ for some PLC P, by Lemma 1, all transitions that are dependent on any transition in $ample(s)$ are transitions in $P_{internal}$. When $ample(s) = (comm \cap enabled(s))$ or $ample(s) =$ tick, there is no dependent transition with transitions in $ample(s)$ by Definition 2 and (2) of Lemma 1. (3) The property of interest is about continuous attributes, which are only affected by tick rule. Thus, all rules except tick rule are invisible. For any s, s is not fully expanded iff tick $\in enabled(s)$, since tick is always enabled. Thus, when not fully expanded, transitions in $ample(s)$ are all invisible for any

s. (4) By construction of our semantics, the cycle in the transition system can occur only with an infinite loop. Since while is only in the ample set when fully expanded, the cycle in a transition system contains at least one fully expanded state. □

7 Formal Analysis Using Rewriting Modulo SMT

7.1 Symbolic Semantics

Two key elements can be represented using SMT terms: the values stored in the proc attribute (internal) and the values mapped in state (external). The internal SMT constraints govern conditional statements and minimum message delay constraints, and the external SMT constraints reason the conformance of properties of the physical environment.

Generally, the external constraints are heavier to solve because they handle the flow functions, whereas the internal constraints are confined to Boolean or linear constraints. In the semantics introduced so far, tick evolves time for both inside and outside the PLC programs. This introduces inefficiency of SMT solving, because not both types of constraints have to be checked every time tick applies.

We can introduce two separate clocks—one for the environment and another for the programs to address this problem. As discussed in the first part of Sect. 6, the physical behavior within a scan cycle is dictated by the results of the previous cycle, meaning that external behavior for the current cycle is already established at its onset. Consequently, the physical environment can progress continuously until the end of the current cycle. The internal clock must advance independently of the environmental clock to account for message delays. With this clock separation method, we can achieve higher efficiency while preserving the same result on analyses regarding the endpoints of scan cycles.

To accomplish this, an additional timer is required to track the progression of time in the physical environment. The PLC class has new attributes envTimer and constraints. The envTimer attribute contains the external time that can elapse without a change in physical dynamics, and constraints collects the internal constraints for the enclosing PLC's programs.

```
class PLC | state: Map{Id, Val}, flow: Flow,
            envTimer: Time, timer: Time, constraints: BooleanExpr .
```

Figure 9 presents two state transition diagrams. The left diagram illustrates the transitions without clock separation, while the right diagram depicts the transitions with clock separation. The system consists of PLC_1, PLC_2, and PLC_3 with scan cycle duration 10, and PLC_1 sends data to PLC_2 and PLC_3 (PLC_2 and PLC_3 are omitted in the figure for brevity). The system must take at least two transitions to distinguish whether two sent messages can be received. It is important to note that SMT solving costs regarding the environment is much higher than solving internal constraints. On the left, where the clock is not separated, we must solve the internal and external constraints for all the

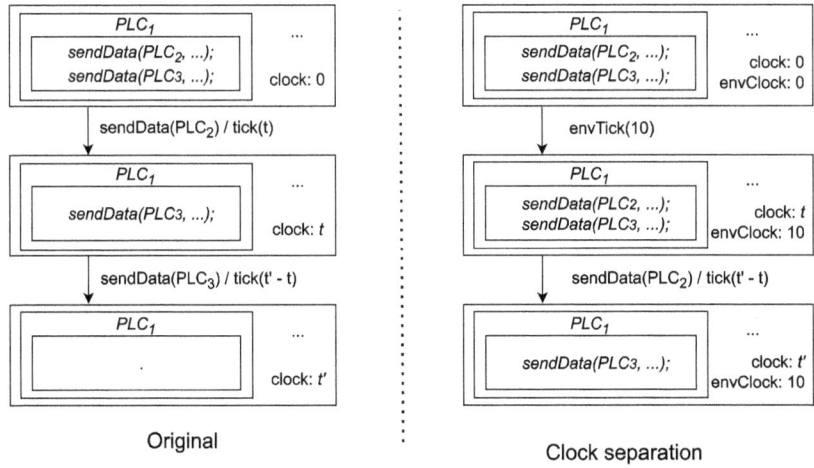

Fig. 9. State transition before and after applying clock separation

tick rules. However, on the right side, the environmental clock can immediately jump to 10, solving the SMT constraints for the physical environment just once, and internal time jumps (tick) only regard the message delay constraint.

The definition of tick, timeEffect, and mte for symbolic execution are shown below. They are now only for internal time elapses. The freshVarGen function generates a fresh SMT variable to denote the duration of newly elapsed time. mte returns Boolean expression that the newly elapsed time is less than the maximal time elapse. The addConst function adds the constraints to all PLC objects.

```
var PLC : Object .      var S : Stmt .  var CONF : Configuration .
vars CONST BE : BooleanExpr .           vars V1 V2 : Val .
vars R1 R2 : Map{Id,Val} .              vars ATTRS1 ATTRS2 : AttributeSet .

rl [tick] : { CONF } => { addConst(timeEffect(CONF, T), mte(CONF)) }
if T := freshVarGen(CONF) .

eq mte(PLC CONF, T) = mte(PLC, T) AND mte(CONF, T) .
eq mte(< O : PLC | timer : TIMER >, T) = T <= TIMER .
eq mte(CONF, T) = true [owise] .

eq addConst(PLC CONF, COSNT) = addConst(PLC,CONST) addConst(CONF,CONST) .
eq addConst(CONF, CONST) = CONF [owise] .
eq addConst(< O : PLC | constraints : CONST >, CONST') =
            < O : PLC | constraints : CONST and CONST' > .
```

The constraints attribute also collects the constraints from executing conditional statements. smtCheck checks if the given SMT formula is satisfiable (supported in Maude).

```
crl < O : PLC | proc : k(if BE then S else S' ~> ...) ...,
             constraints : CONST >
 => < O : PLC | proc : k(S ~> ...) ...,
             constraints : CONST and BE > if smtCheck(CONST and BE) .
crl < O : PLC | proc : k(if BE then S else S' ~> ...) ...,
             constraints : CONST >
 => < O : PLC | proc : k(S' ~> ...) ..., constraints : CONST and not BE >
 if smtCheck(CONST and not BE) .
```

The start rule now checks that the current timer value C *can be* zero, accounting for the accumulated constraints CONST.

```
crl start(< O : PLC | proc : k(.K) cycleTime(T) env(ENV) store(STORE) KC,
                    timer : TIMER, state : STATE, constraints(CONST) >)
 => < O : PLC |  proc : k(callP) cycleTime(T) env(ENV)
                      store(sense(ENV, STORE, STATE)) KC, timer : T,
                 state : actuate(ENV, STORE, STATE) >
 if smtCheck(TIMER == 0 and CONST) .
```

Similarly, rcvData is modified to check whether the message can be accepted.

```
crl [rcvData] : < O : PLC | proc : k(rcvData(O', SFBID, RFBID) ~> K) KC >
 < conn(O, O') : Conn | validity : true,
                  buffer: (BUFFER m(O', O, SFBID, RFBID, DATA, L, U)) >
 => < O : PLC | proc : k(DATA ~> K) KC >
    < conn(O, O') : Conn | validity : true, buffer : BUFFER >
 if smtCheck(L == 0 and U >= 0) .
```

The physical part of the tick rule introduced in Sect. 4 is separated to the envTick rule, where minEnv returns the smallest time duration to reach any end of the PLCs' scan cycles.

```
crl [envTick] : {CONF} => {envTimeEffect(CONF, minEnv(CONF))}
 if minEnv(CONF) > 0 .

eq minEnv(< O : PLC | envTimer : TIMER, flow : FLOW, state : STATE > CONF)
 = min(TIMER, minEnv(CONF)) .

eq minEnv(none) = infinity .
```

Accordingly, envTimeEffect is defined. It updates envTimer instead of timer.

```
eq envTimeEffect(
 < O : PLC | envTimer : TIMER, flow : FLOW, state: STATE >, T) =
 < O : PLC | envTimer : monus(TIMER, T), state : eval(FLOW, STATE, T) > .
```

7.2 Formal Analysis

We aim to run a reachability analysis on the chemical plant with two tanks explained in Sect. 3. Consider the following initial state. The clock attribute is newly introduced to represent the total elapsed system time, allowing for the specification of the analysis scope in terms of system time.

```
op init : Configuration .

eq init =
< "plc1" : PLC | proc : app1, timer : 0, envTimer : 0, clock : 0,
                state : wl |-> 20, ps |-> 0, flow : wl(t) = wl - ps * t >
< "plc2" : PLC | proc : app2, timer : 0, envTimer : 0, clock : 0,
                state : wl |-> 20, ps |-> 0, flow : wl(t) = wl - ps * t >
< conn("plc1", "plc2") : Conn | validity : false, buffer : empty > .
```

We want to check if the water level always stays between 2 and 35 within the time bound 20 ms. The time bound is enforced by adding an equation that converts the whole system into an operator that cannot be rewritten again.

```
op boundReached : GlobalSystem [ctor] .
ceq { < O : PLC | ATTRS, clock : T > Conf } = boundReached if T > 20 .
```

The following search command searches for a reachable state that goes outside the specified range of water level. The result suggests that both tanks in the system maintain the specified water levels up to 20 time units.

```
Maude> search [1] init =>*
{< "plc1" : PLC | state : (wl |-> V1, R1), ATTRS1 >
 < "plc2" : PLC | state : (wl |-> V2, R2), ATTRS2 > CONF }
such that smtCheck(V1 < 2 or V1 > 35 or V2 < 2 or V2 > 35) .
No solution.
```

Now, we want to check that the two tanks have exactly the same water levels from the state with unbalanced water levels. Consider the following initial state.

```
eq init =
< "plc1" : PLC | proc : app1, timer : 0, envTimer : 0, clock : 0,
                state : wl |-> 5,  ps |-> 0, flow : wl(t) = wl - ps * t >
< "plc2" : PLC | proc : app2, timer : 0, envTimer : 0, clock : 0,
                state : wl |-> 45, ps |-> 0, flow : wl(t) = wl - ps * t >
< conn("plc1", "plc2") : Conn | validity : false, buffer : empty > .
```

The following search command looks for the reachable state where the two water levels are the same. This search command finds a reachable state and presents it to the user. ATTRS1 and ATTRS2 are omitted for brevity.

```
Maude> search [1] init =>*
{< "plc1" : PLC | state : (w1 |-> V1, R1), ATTRS1 >
 < "plc2" : PLC | state : (w1 |-> V2, R2), ATTRS2 >}
such that smtCheck(V1 === V2) .

Solution 1 (state 828) states: 829   rewrites: 160521 in 2220ms cpu
(2220ms real) (72306 rewrites/second)
ATTRS1 -->  ...      V1 --> 25     ATTRS2 -->  ...     V2 --> 25  CONF -->
< conn("plc1", "plc2") : Conn | validity : true, buffer : empty >
```

8 Experimental Evaluation

To assess the effectiveness of our approach, we implemented our semantics and state space reduction techniques in Maude [9], a high-performance rewriting engine. Nondeterministic time evolution is handled using symbolic execution methods, such as those described in [26]. We developed a total of eight benchmark models using both our semantics and the SpaceEx model. In our framework, modeling requires minimal effort, as the PLC ST code itself serves as the model; only the physical environment and Conn settings need to be configured. In contrast, the SpaceEx model requires manually constructing all models from scratch. All Maude and SpaceEx benchmark models are publicly available at https://github.com/postechsv/plc-release/releases/tag/sasfinal.

The first research question examines whether our approach is more efficient than the previous hybrid automata-based approach using SpaceEx. To evaluate this, we compare the time required for full-state exploration in Maude and SpaceEx. The second research question regards the effectiveness of our state space reduction technique. We compare the space and time spent in full-state exploration before and after applying the state space reduction techniques. All experiments were conducted on Intel Xeon 2.8 GHz with 256 GB memory. Timeout is set to 10 min in all settings. For more information about our benchmark models and full tables, please refer to our longer version of this paper [24].

Benchmark Models. Previous benchmark sets for PLC programs are often limited in scope, focusing on isolated control logic without modeling communication or physical dynamics. Many benchmarks consist of single-task programs. As a result, they fail to capture essential aspects of PLC systems, such as concurrent execution, communication, and interaction with continuous physical processes.

We obtain models with physical dynamics, programming logic, and inter-PLC communication by adapting hybrid automata benchmarks. They often include both discrete control logic and continuous physical dynamics by themselves, and it is possible to encode simplified message-passing logic.

Besides models for hybrid automata, we construct the secure water treatment (SWaT) model, which is a standard industrial control system model. They have communication, physical environment, and programming logic altogether. Our work is the first to construct comprehensive SWaT models, which closely model a real-world example, that can be utilized in formal analysis to our knowledge.

We have eight benchmark models, including a chemical plant with two pumps [29], railed vehicles, and networked thermostats [3], each implemented with and without explicit communication. On top of that, we have two models for two parts of SWaT process [2]. In the models without explicit communication, multiple PLCs are consolidated into a single PLC that runs multiple programs and encapsulates all physical behaviors. The models with explicit communication maintain multiple PLC objects that exchange data. The *chemical plant* models are already covered in Sect. 3, Sect. 5.3, and Sect. 7.2.

Time Comparison with Hybrid Automata-Based Approach. We compare the full-state exploration time of our rewrite-based approach, which incorporates state space reduction techniques, with that of the SpaceEx tool. To enable a meaningful comparison, we manually constructed SpaceEx models that approximate the behavior of our approach in a simplified manner: mode transitions encode blocked code segments rather than one-step rewrites. On top of that, the complex behavior of communication function blocks such as connection checking and flag settings are completely abstracted out.

While our framework currently supports polynomial dynamics of arbitrary degree, for this experiment, we restrict the dynamics to linear functions to align with the capabilities of the SpaceEx tool under the PHAVer scenario.

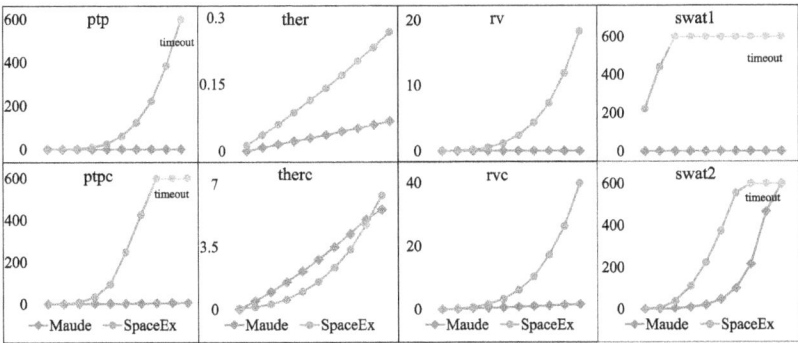

Fig. 10. Time comparison between our approach and SpaceEx (Color figure online)

Figure 10 presents 8 graphs that compare analysis times between our approach (Maude) and SpaceEx. The model names 'ptp', 'ther', and 'rv' correspond to a chemical plant, a thermostat, and a railed vehicle without communication. When 'c' is appended to the model name, it indicates that the model includes explicit communication. 'swat1' and 'swat2' correspond to the first and second halves of the SWaT process. For each graph, the x-axis is the increasing time bounds from 1 cycle to 10 cycles. The y-axis shows the time taken for the full state exploration in seconds. The timed-out data are shown as 600 s and highlighted yellow.

The execution time comparison between our approach (blue diamonds) and the SpaceEx tool (gray dots) shows significant differences in efficiency, particularly as the system complexity increases. For models without explicit communication, the execution time for our approach remains relatively low even as the time bound increases. In contrast, the SpaceEx execution time grows exponentially, particularly for ptp-* models. This trend is evident across all models, demonstrating how our method effectively controls state space growth.

For models with explicit communication, a natural increase in execution time is observed due to the additional complexity of message passing. However, our approach still performs significantly better than SpaceEx. 'ptpc' shows the greatest time gap between our approach and SpaceEx. The thermostat model (therc-*) exhibits a similar pattern. Although SpaceEx outperform our approach in some model bound settings, our approach eventually outperforms SpaceEx again with larger bounds. This result suggests that our rewrite-based approach is more promising for large-scale industrial control systems than SpaceEx.[3]

Effectiveness of State Space Reduction. To demonstrate the effectiveness of our state space reduction techniques, we compare the full-state space exploration time before and after their application. Similar to Fig. 10, Fig. 11 shows 8 graphs that compare the original and reduced semantics analysis time.

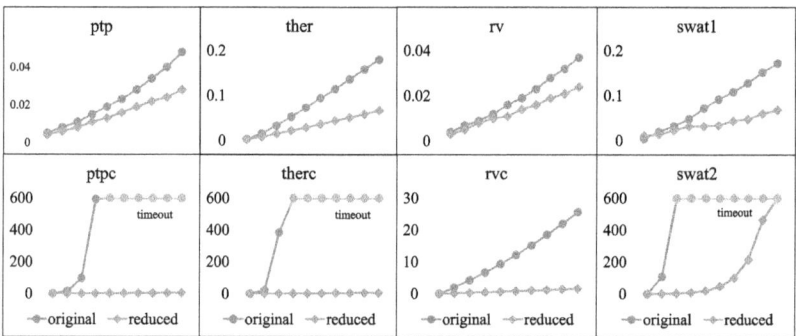

Fig. 11. Time comparison before and after state space reduction (Color figure online)

The results in Fig. 11 highlight the impact of state space reduction. Across all benchmark models, applying state space reduction reduces execution time, with drastic improvements observed in models with explicit communication.

For models without communication, execution time is mildly lowered, visually expressed that blue dots (original) are above the gray diamonds (reduced). For

---

[3] In [29], their approach for the chemical plant with two pumps without communication takes 69.0 s to complete the analysis on their machine.

models with explicit communication, the benefits of state space reduction are more pronounced. The gray diamonds are tightly aligned with the x-axis.

Across all communication-based models, the original approach results in rapid state space growth, leading to timeouts in larger instances, whereas the reduced version remains computationally feasible. The blue bars that reach 600 in 'ptpc', 'therc' and 'swat2' are timed out data before state space reduction.

These results demonstrate that state space reduction is crucial for handling complex PLC-based systems with communication, where nondeterminism plays a significant role in increasing verification complexity.

9 Related Work

Various methods have been developed for the formal analysis of PLC programs written in different languages, including Structured Text [7,11,17,39], Sequential Function Chart [16,19], and Instruction List [8]. However, most of these approaches focus only on analyzing single PLC programs in isolation, without considering interactions with physical environments or communication between multiple PLC controllers. In contrast, our work explicitly models both physical environment interactions and PLC communication.

The papers [16,29] address the verification of PLC-controlled systems while incorporating physical dynamics. These approaches employ a hybrid automata-based framework and introduce a tool capable of reasoning about both control programs and their surrounding physical environments. In particular, [29] utilizes a CEGAR approach, where the abstract model assumes arbitrary dynamics, and refinement progressively adds concrete dynamics. However, these works do not consider communication between different PLC controllers.

The work in [25] defines a formal semantics for PLC ST with preemptive multitasking using the K framework and introduces state space reduction techniques. However, it does not consider interactions with the physical environment or communication between PLC controllers. In contrast, our work focuses on multiple single-task PLC controllers that communicate with each other and interact with physical environments. While the paper [25] applies partial order reduction in the context of multitasking, we use it to address state explosion caused by communication. These differences suggest that our approach and the technique in [25] are complementary.

Only a few studies focus on the semantics of communicating PLCs, including [15,20]. The paper [20] defines a process calculus for runtime enforcement, enhancing security against malware, and [15] models of PLC-based networked control systems using colored Petri nets. A key similarity between their approaches and ours is the formal semantics for PLCs with communication. However, both are based on highly abstracted formalisms, lacking concrete semantics for any specific PLC programming language. In contrast, our work explicitly considers both physical interactions and PLC communications in PLC ST.

Rewriting logic has been extensively applied to specifying and analyzing distributed object systems, real-time and cyber-physical systems, and programming language semantics [27]. In particular, rewriting modulo SMT [35] has gained increasing attention as a symbolic analysis method. Applications of rewriting modulo SMT include security protocols [1], soft agents [30], and cyber-physical systems [22,23]. Within this research direction, our paper presents the first attempt to combine partial order reduction with symbolic reachability analysis.

10 Concluding Remarks

In this work, we have presented a formal semantics for industrial control systems modeled using programmable logic controllers (PLCs). Our framework integrates PLC program execution, interactions with the physical environment, and networked communication, enabling a unified analysis of system behavior. By incorporating rewriting logic, we have provided a modular and expressive formalization that faithfully represents real-world industrial automation scenarios.

To address the state explosion problem inherent in formal verification, we have introduced a state space reduction technique based on partial order reduction and significantly improved the analysis efficiency. Our approach is implemented in Maude and evaluated using benchmark models, demonstrating its scalability and effectiveness. Compared to SpaceEx, our method requires less modeling effort while offering a more precise and scalable verification framework.

Future work includes extending our semantics to support more complex multitasking and real-time scheduling features, as well as further optimizing state space reduction techniques. Additionally, we aim to integrate our approach with existing PLC verification tools to provide a more comprehensive and practical formal analysis framework for industrial control systems.

Acknowledgement. This work was supported in part by the National Research Foundation of Korea (NRF) grant (No. RS-2021-NR060080) and the Institute of Information & Communications Technology Planning & Evaluation (IITP) grant (No. RS-2024-00439856), both funded by the Korea government (MSIT).

References

1. Aires Urquiza, A., et al.: Resource-bounded intruders in denial of service attacks. In: CSF 2019, pp. 382–396. IEEE (2019)
2. Antonioli, D., Tippenhauer, N.O.: MiniCPS: a toolkit for security research on CPS networks. In: CPS-SPC, pp. 91–100. ACM (2015)
3. Bae, K., Ölveczky, P.C., Kong, S., Gao, S., Clarke, E.M.: SMT-based analysis of virtually synchronous distributed hybrid systems. In: HSCC. ACM (2016)
4. Bae, K., Rocha, C.: Symbolic state space reduction with guarded terms for rewriting modulo SMT. Sci. Comput. Program. **178**, 20–42 (2019)
5. Baier, C., Katoen, J.P.: Principles of Model Checking. MIT Press (2008)
6. Bogdanas, D., Roşu, G.: K-Java: A complete semantics of Java. In: POPL, pp. 445–456. ACM (2015)

7. Bohlender, D., Hamm, D., Kowalewski, S.: Cycle-bounded model checking of PLC software via dynamic large-block encoding. In: SAC, pp. 1891–1898. ACM (2018)
8. Canet, G., Couffin, S., Lesage, J.J., Petit, A., Schnoebelen, P.: Towards the automatic verification of PLC programs written in Instruction List. In: SMC, vol. 4, pp. 2449–2454. IEEE (2000)
9. Clavel, M., et al.: Maude manual (version 3.5.1) (2025)
10. Clavel, M., et al.: All About Maude – A High-Performance Logical Framework. LNCS, vol. 4350. Springer, Heidelberg (2007)
11. Darvas, D., Blanco Vinuela, E., Fernández Adiego, B.: PLCverif: a tool to verify PLC programs based on model checking techniques. In: Accelerator and Large Experimental Physics Control Systems (2015)
12. Darvas, D., Majzik, I., Viñuela, E.B.: PLC program translation for verification purposes. Period. Polytech. Elec. Eng. and Comput. Sci. **61**(2), 151–165 (2017)
13. Ellison, C., Rosu, G.: An executable formal semantics of C with applications. In: POPL, vol. 47, pp. 533–544. ACM (2012)
14. Frehse, G., et al.: SpaceEx: scalable verification of hybrid systems. In: Gopalakrishnan, G., Qadeer, S. (eds.) CAV 2011. LNCS, vol. 6806, pp. 379–395. Springer, Heidelberg (2011). https://doi.org/10.1007/978-3-642-22110-1_30
15. Ghanaim, A., Frey, G.: Modeling and control of closed-loop networked PLC-systems. In: ACC, pp. 502–508. IEEE (2011)
16. Hassapis, G., Kotini, I., Doulgeri, Z.: Validation of a SFC software specification by using hybrid automata. IFAC Proc. Vol. **31**(15), 107–112 (1998)
17. Huang, Y., Bu, X., Zhu, G., Ye, X., Zhu, X., Shi, J.: KST: executable formal semantics of IEC 61131-3 structured text for verification. IEEE Access **7** (2019)
18. International Electrotechnical Commission: Programmable controllers - part 3: Programming languages. IEC 61131-3 (1993)
19. Lampérière-Couffin, S., Lesage, J.J.: Formal verification of the sequential part of PLC programs. In: Discrete Event Systems: Analysis and Control. SECS, vol. 569, pp. 247–254. Springer (2000)
20. Lanotte, R., Merro, M., Munteanu, A., et al.: A process calculus approach to correctness enforcement of PLCs. In: CEUR Workshop Proceedings, vol. 2756 (2020)
21. Lazar, D., et al.: Executing formal semantics with the K tool. In: FM. LNCS, vol. 7436, pp. 267–271. Springer, Heidelberg (2012)
22. Lee, J., Bae, K., Ölveczky, P.C., Kim, S., Kang, M.: Modeling and formal analysis of virtually synchronous cyber-physical systems in AADL. Int. J. Softw. Tools Technol. Transf. **24**, 1–38 (2022)
23. Lee, J., Kim, S., Bae, K., Ölveczky, P.C.: HYBRID SYNCHAADL: modeling and formal analysis of virtually synchronous CPSs in AADL. In: Silva, A., Leino, K.R.M. (eds.) CAV 2021. LNCS, vol. 12759, pp. 491–504. Springer, Cham (2021). https://doi.org/10.1007/978-3-030-81685-8_23
24. Lee, J., Bae, K.: Formal analysis of networked PLC controllers interacting with physical environments (2025). https://arxiv.org/abs/2507.15596
25. Lee, J., Bae, K.: Formal semantics and analysis of multitask PLC ST programs with preemption. In: Formal Methods. LNCS, vol. 14933, pp. 425–442. Springer, Cham (2025)
26. Lee, J., Kim, S., Bae, K.: Bounded model checking of PLC ST programs using rewriting modulo SMT. In: FTSCS, pp. 56–67. ACM (2022)
27. Meseguer, J.: Twenty years of rewriting logic. J. Logic Algebraic Program. **81**(7–8), 721–781 (2012)
28. Meseguer, J.: Conditional rewriting logic as a unified model of concurrency. Theoret. Comput. Sci. **96**(1), 73–155 (1992)

29. Nellen, J., Driessen, K., Neuhäußer, M.R., Ábrahám, E., Wolters, B.: Two CEGAR-based approaches for the safety verification of PLC-controlled plants. Inf. Syst. Front. **18**(5), 927–952 (2016)
30. Nigam, V., Talcott, C.: Automating safety proofs about cyber-physical systems using rewriting modulo SMT. In: WRLA. LNCS, vol. 13252. Springer, Cham (2022)
31. Ölveczky, P.C., Meseguer, J.: Abstraction and completeness for real-time maude. Electron. Notes Theor. Comput. Sci. **176**(4), 5–27 (2007)
32. Ölveczky, P.C., Meseguer, J.: Semantics and pragmatics of real-time maude. Higher-Order Symb. Comput. **20**, 161–196 (2007)
33. Park, D., Ştefănescu, A., Roşu, G.: KJS: a complete formal semantics of JavaScript. In: PLDI, pp. 346–356. ACM (2015)
34. Peled, D.: Partial-order reduction. In: Clarke, E.M., Henzinger, T.A., Veith, H., Bloem, R. (eds.) Handbook of Model Checking, pp. 173–190. Springer, Cham (2018)
35. Rocha, C., Meseguer, J., Muñoz, C.: Rewriting modulo SMT and open system analysis. J. Logical Algebraic Methods Program. **86**(1), 269–297 (2017)
36. Rosu, G., Şerbănuţă, T.F.: An overview of the K semantic framework. J. Log. Algebr. Methods Program. **79**(6), 397–434 (2010)
37. Roşu, G., Şerbănuţă, T.F.: K overview and simple case study. Electron. Notes Theor. Comput. Sci. **304**, 3–56 (2014)
38. Şerbănuţă, T.F., Roşu, G.: K-Maude: a rewriting based tool for semantics of programming languages. In: Ölveczky, P.C. (ed.) WRLA 2010. LNCS, vol. 6381, pp. 104–122. Springer, Heidelberg (2010). https://doi.org/10.1007/978-3-642-16310-4_8
39. Wang, K., Wang, J., Poskitt, C.M., Chen, X., Sun, J., Cheng, P.: K-ST: a formal executable semantics of the structured text language for PLCs. IEEE Trans. Software Eng. **49**(10), 4796–4813 (2023)
40. Yu, G., Bae, K.: A flexible framework for integrating Maude and SMT solvers using Python. In: WRLA. LNCS, vol. 14953, pp. 179–192. Springer, Cham (2024)

Monarch: A Modular Framework for Abstract Definitional Interpreters in Haskell

Bram Vandenbogaerde[ID], Sarah Verbelen[✉][ID], Noah Van Es[ID], and Coen De Roover[ID]

Vrije Universiteit Brussel, Brussels, Belgium
{bram.vandenbogaerde,sarah.verbelen,noah.van.es,coen.de.roover}@vub.be

Abstract. Abstract definitional interpreters are an approach to developing abstract interpretation-based static analyses in which language semantics are expressed through monadic recursive interpreters. These interpreters are then instantiated with an abstract value domain and executed in a suitable monadic context that carries abstract program state. Unfortunately, correctly implementing these definitional interpreters remains a difficult task. Moreover, instantiating analyses requires configuring many components. In this tool paper, we present the design of a framework called MONARCH that provides reusable components to programmers for implementing abstract definitional interpreters. Our design consists of the following components: abstract domains, a framework for expressing program semantics, and analysis instantiation techniques. Finally, we present an implementation in Haskell and give example instantiations in Scheme and Python to show how these components are used.

Keywords: Abstract Definitional Interpreters · Abstract Intepretation · Static Analysis

1 Introduction

Static analyses aim to decide behavioral program properties without actually running the program. Their use is widespread in compilers, integrated development environments, software verification, and so on. Abstract interpretation is a principled approach to static analysis design where program properties are computed through an abstraction of concrete program semantics. For example, whereas a concrete program semantics calculates the value of `fac(5)` to be `120`, an abstract interpreter might only compute its sign (i.e., +). Abstract definitional interpreters [5] (ADI) offer a recipe for constructing such abstract program semantics by deriving them from a recursive evaluation function parametrized by a computational context (i.e., a monad) and an abstract value domain (e.g., the sign). This computational context and abstract value domain are then instantiated to obtain a functioning abstract interpretation based static analysis.

Unfortunately, developing such abstract definitional interpreters remains a non-trivial task. For this reason, we present our design of MONARCH, a framework for constructing static analyses based on the abstract definitional interpreter approach. We highlight how we use advanced programming language concepts to create reusable building blocks that can be used by analysis developers.

To summarise, we make the following contributions in this tool paper:

- We present a modular design of a framework for static analysis using abstract interpretation called MONARCH. Our design consists of foundational building blocks and combinators for abstract domains, a monadic framework to specify program semantics, and techniques based on monad transformers to enable flexible and layered instantiations of program analyses. Our design focuses on modularity and composability.
- We present two case studies to show how several practical challenges are addressed, such as non-determinism and control flow (i.e., escaping control flow using `MonadEscape`), reusing semantics using effect polymorphism, and providing an efficient way to represent abstract values (i.e., sparse labeled products introduced in Sect. 4.1).

2 Motivation

In this section, we first introduce the key components of abstract definitional interpreters through the implementation of a toy language derived from the λ-calculus. Moreover, we will discuss the difficulties in implementing such abstract definitional interpreters. The toy language is depicted in Listing 1 and consists of lambda expressions, applications, numbers, `if` expressions, assignments, sequencing, and exceptions. The language lacks booleans for simplicity. Instead, the number 0 represents falsehood and any other number represents truthiness.

Abstract definitional interpreters derive their semantics starting from a concrete recursive interpreter. The listing below depicts an interpreter that consists of an evaluation function `eval` and a closure application function called `apply`. The evaluation function is executed in a monadic context `m` which supports effects for tracking the store and the environment, and for catching and throwing exceptions. The effects to track the environment and the store are generated through the `MonadEnvironment` and the `MonadStore` type class, respectively. These type classes contain operations to get the current store and environment,

```
data Exp = Lam String Exp    | Num Int | Var String | App Exp Exp
         | If Exp Exp Exp    | Set String Exp       | Seq Exp Exp
         | Throw Exp         | Catch String Exp Exp

type Env = Map String Val
data Val = Clo Exp Env | NumV Int
```

Listing 1: A toy language based on the λ-calculus. It supports lambda abstraction, application, if, assignments, sequencing, exceptions, variables, and number literals.

as well as to change them. The effects to catch and throw exceptions are generated through the `catchError` and `throwError` operations respectively, specified in the `MonadError` type class.

```
eval :: (MonadEnvironment m, MonadStore m, MonadError m)
        => Exp -> m Val
eval (Lam x e)     = bind getEnv (\env -> unit (Clo (Lam x e) env))
eval (Num n)       = unit (NumV n)
eval (Var x)       = lookupEnv x >>= lookupSto
eval (App e1 e2)   = do
  { v1 <- eval e1 ; v2 <- eval e2 ; apply v1 v2 }
eval (If e1 e2 e3) = ifM (eval e1) (eval e2) (eval e3)
eval (Set x e)     = do
  { v <- eval e ; a <- lookupEnv x ; setSto a v }
eval (Seq e1 e2) = eval e1 >> eval e2
eval (Throw e) = eval e >>= throwError
eval (Catch x e1 e2) =
    eval e1 `catchError` (\v -> do env <- getEnv
                                   let clo = (Clo (Lam x e2) env)
                                   apply clo v)

apply :: (MonadEnvironment m, MonadStore m, MonadError m)
         => Val -> Val -> m Val
apply (Clo (Lam x e) lenv) v2 = do
  a <- alloc x
  updateSto a v2
  withEnv (extendEnv a lenv) (eval e)
```

From this concrete interpreter, an abstract definitional interpreter can be derived [5, 25]. To this end, the concrete interpreter needs to undergo a number of transformations. First, the concrete values (represented by `Val`) of the language need to be abstracted. As an example, closures are abstracted to sets of abstract closures and numbers to their sign. The goal of this abstraction is to render the state space finite such that the evaluation terminates for any program input.

Next, several operations within the semantics need to be adapted according to the change in the value domain. For example, the `apply` function uses pattern matching to determine which closure needs to be applied to value v2. When using sets as an abstraction, this pattern matching needs to be replaced by a traversal over all elements of the set in such a way that each closure can be applied to v2 separately and their results can be joined together.

The evaluation of `if` expressions is another example. As numbers are abstracted to their sign, it is possible that the condition is simultaneously true and false. To overapproximate the program behavior in this case, operations such as `ifM` need to be adapted so that the consequent and alternative of the `if` expression are both executed and the results of both branches are joined afterwards. To support these changes, the evaluation function can be executed in a different monadic context that supports non-deterministic computations. An example of such monadic context is the `MonadPlus` type class. This type class specifies an `mplus` function, which executes two computations non-deterministically, and an `mzero` function, which represents the empty computation.

Overapproximating exception handling is challenging, as the exception handler (i.e., `Catch`) must account for both execution paths in which an exception is thrown and those in which no exception occurs. In this example, we make use of the `MonadEscape` type class to accomplish this. This type class is explained in more detail in Sect. 4.2.

The final step is to render the number of calls to `eval` finite. To ensure termination, the number of inputs need to be finite and the outputs should converge to a stable value. This is usually accomplished by caching the results of `eval` for any given input, and returning the cached result if `eval` is executed another time with input that has been evaluated before.

```
eval :: ( MonadPlus m , MonadEscape m ,
          MonadEnvironment m, MonadStore m)
         => Exp -> m AVal
eval (Lam x e)      = bind getEnv (\env ->
     unit ( Set.singleton  (Clo (Lam x e) env)))
eval (Num n)        = unit (NumV ( sign n))
eval (Var x)        = lookupEnv x >>= lookup
eval (App e1 e2)    = do
   { v1 <- eval e1 ; v2 <- eval e2 ; apply v1 v2 }
eval (If e1 e2 e3)  = mplus  (eval e2) (eval e3)
eval (Set x e)      = do
    { v <- eval e ; a <- lookupEnv x ; update a v }
eval (Seq e1 e2) = eval e1 >> eval e2
eval (Throw e) = eval e >>= throw
eval (Catch x e1 e2) =
    eval e1 `catch` (\v -> do
                            env <- getEnv
                            let clo = (Clo (Lam x e2) env)
```

```
                       apply (Set.singleton clo) v)

apply :: (MonadPlus m, MonadEscape m,
          MonadEnvironment m, MonadStore m)
              => AVal -> AVal -> m AVal
apply clos v2 =
    foldr mplus mzero (Set.map
       (\case (Clo (Lam x e) lenv) -> do
               a <- alloc x
               updateSto a v2
               withEnv (extendEnv a lenv) (eval e)
              (NumV _) -> mzero)
       clos)
```

The code listing shown above depicts the changes necessary for rendering our concrete interpreter abstract. Highlighted in orange are changes made to render the value domain abstract and finite, highlighted in blue are changes concerning the semantics. This example illustrates the intersection of various analysis concerns, as well as the need for suitable abstractions for implementing these analysis concerns. In the rest of this paper, we propose a set of abstractions formulated as type classes to address these concerns.

3 Background

In this section we review the concepts underpinning the design of abstract definitional interpreters. We start by recalling the concept of a *monad* which enables expressing computational effects in a definitional interpreter. Next, we illustrate how functions that are polymorphic in their computational effects can be expressed, and show how they are used to configure an abstract definitional interpreter for a specific analysis.

3.1 Monads

Monads are a key ingredient of our conceptual framework. Monads enable separating computational effects from the actual results of a computation [18,19]. They are characterised by two functions (depicted below): a unit and a bind. The unit function embeds an effect-free computation a into an effectful computation m a, while the bind function extracts the value from an effectful computation and applies an effectful function to it, essentially providing the ability for two computations to be executed in *sequence*.

```
class Monad m where
    unit :: a -> m a
    bind :: m a -> (a -> m b) -> m b
```

In Haskell, to avoid having to nest bind expressions, the so-called do-notation can be used. The code listing below demonstrates its usage and its bind.

```
example = do                    example =
   a <- m1                         bind m1 (\a ->
   b <- m2                         bind m2 (\b ->
   return (a + b)                  return (a+b))
```

A classic example of monadic computations is computations that carry *state*. Such computations can be characterised by the interface described in MonadState.

```
class (Monad m) => MonadState s m | m -> s where
   put :: s -> m ()
   get :: m s
```

The MonadState type class states that for some monad m and state s, the interface can be used if functions put and get are implemented. A suitable candidate for m in this case is a function forall a . s -> (a, s) for some fixed s. We will refer to such functions with the type State s. The implementation of these instances for the Monad and MonadState type classes are shown below.

```
type State s = forall a . s -> (a, s)
instance Monad (State s) where
   unit v   = \s -> (v, s)
   bind m f = \s -> let (a, s') = (m s) in (f a) s'
instance MonadState s (State s) where
   put s = \_ -> ((), s)
   get   = \s -> (s, s)
```

3.2 Effect Polymorphism

The previous section introduced the MonadState type class. One might wonder why such a type class is needed, as computations carrying state can be readily expressed using State s. Encoding MonadState as a type class enables *effect polymorphism*. Consider, for example, a function inc (depicted below) that implements incrementing an integer statefully. The function is not concerned with the internal representation of this state in the monadic structure. Thus, its type reflects that it can be executed in any monadic context m, given that this context implements the MonadState type class and provides functions put and get.

```
inc :: MonadState Int m => m ()
inc = bind get (\n -> put (n+1))
```

In Sect. 4.2, we discuss how this effect polymorphism enables reusable semantics for different analysis instantiations.

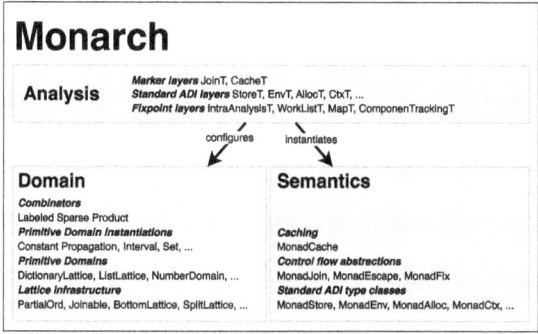

Fig. 1. Architecture of MONARCH.

4 Architecture

Figure 1 depicts the architecture of MONARCH. The framework consists of three major parts. The DOMAIN part depicted in the bottom left provides building blocks for abstract domains. It is detailed in Sect. 4.1. Section 4.2 presents the SEMANTICS part depicted in the bottom right, which provides monadic interfaces for specifying abstract semantics. In Sect. 4.3, the final part ANALYSIS (depicted at the top) is discussed. This part provides building blocks for instantiating an abstract semantics into a *static program analysis*. It does so by providing *monad transformers* that implement the monadic interfaces of the semantics.

4.1 Domain

In this section we first introduce the primitive building blocks for creating representations of abstracted primitive values. Next, we propose *combinators* to combine these primitive building blocks into representations of abstractions of more complex values. Finally, we discuss efficiency and performance implications of such representations and we propose a memory-efficient and type-safe one.

Primitive Building Blocks: Lattices. MONARCH follows a similar design as [3], using lattices. Lattices are a mathematical structure formed using partially ordered sets for which each finite subset has a supremum and an infimum. Mathematically, it is sufficient to define the elements of the set and its partial ordering relation. However, in practice, it is often more efficient to formulate the operations for computing the supremum and infimum explicitly. These operations are called the *join* and *meet* of a lattice respectively. For the purposes of this paper, we discuss *join* only. Thus we arrive at a structure with two operations and two elements: a partial order, a join, a top element, and a bottom element.

```
class PartialOrder v where
    leq    :: v -> v -> v
```

```
class (PartialOrder v) => BottomLattice v where
   bottom :: v
class (PartialOrder v) => TopLattice v where
   top    :: v
class (PartialOrder v) => Joinable v where
   join   :: v -> v -> v
```

All abstract domains are an instance of a *join semi-lattice* which is described in MONARCH by four type classes: `PartialOrder`, `Joinable`, `BottomLattice` and `TopLattice` (depicted above). Splitting the operations of a join semi-lattice in this way provides more flexibility for creating instances of these type classes when a type does not implement all of them. For example, the top element of a *powerset lattice* of closures cannot be defined without access to the analyzed program, and thus lacks an implementation for `TopLattice`.

Primitive Building Blocks: Domain. Lattices form *domains* by extending them with domain-specific operations. For example, lattices for representing *numbers* can form a *number domain* by implementing abstract versions of operations such as +, *, etc. These operations are combined into type classes.

A minimal domain needs an operation for converting concrete values to values belonging to that domain and an operation to check whether a concrete value is covered by an abstract value. We combine these operations into a `Domain` type class (depicted below), which serves as the superclass for more specific domains.

```
class (PartialOrder v) => Domain v c where
   alpha :: c -> v
   gamma :: c -> v -> Bool
   gamma c v = leq (alpha c) v
```

The `alpha` function converts concrete values c to abstract values v, while the `gamma` function checks whether a concrete value is covered by the abstract value. These functions borrow their names from *Galois connections*, which are often used to describe abstract semantics in abstract interpreters.

Combinators: Products. We conclude this section by discussing how to combine multiple domains. Program analyses typically require combinations of domains to reason about program behavior. These combinations are usually composed of multiple primitive domains and can be expressed as their product. The main problem of product values is their memory consumption when implemented naively. A naive implementation could represent this product as a structure with a field for each possible value. Some of these fields would then be set to $\bot$ to indicate their absence in the abstract value. However, this means that most product values will contain only a few distinct values (as most values are absent and thus $\bot$), resulting into inefficient memory utilisation.

We demonstrate this using empirical evidence gathered by running static analyses on a total of 129 Scheme benchmark programs, grouped into six benchmark suites. Table 1 shows the origin of these benchmark suites, as well as their number of lines of code excluding comments and blank lines.

Table 1. LoC for programs in each benchmark.

benchmark	count	mean	min	50%	max
ad	20	105.55	23	52	604
gabriel	11	109.00	19	46	570
gambit	25	154.68	1	33	632
scp1	57	42.60	4	26	318
toplas98	3	317.67	188	188	577
wcr2019	13	119.46	1	51	437

We show the inefficiency by measuring the number of distinct values within a product on a number of Scheme programs. The benchmark analysis is based on the modular analysis of Nicolay et al. [20,24] and computes an abstraction of the program's memory. The analysis is configured as follows:

- **Domain:** we configured the analysis to compute its analysis results in a *constant propagation domain* (i.e., for computing the set of constant variables), except for pointers and closures which are stored as sets of abstract addresses and pairs of expressions with their environment, respectively.
- **Context sensitivity:** we configured the analysis to be context insensitive meaning that calls are only differentiated based on the closure being called and not, for example, based on the call-site.

These parameters affect the precision of the resulting analysis. We chose these parameters since, in practice, they offer a good trade-off between precision and performance. However, we argue that our results present a best-case estimation of the real memory usage when using a naive implementation of a product.

Table 2. Percentage of values of a certain size, computed for 119 benchmark programs.

	1	2	3	4	5	6	7	8
min	32.04	0.00	0.00	0.00	0.00	0.00	0.00	0.00
25%	86.10	1.72	0.00	0.00	0.00	0.00	0.00	0.00
50%	92.63	5.58	0.88	0.00	0.00	0.00	0.00	0.00
75%	98.05	9.34	2.04	0.21	0.00	0.00	0.00	0.00
max	100.00	65.25	20.64	25.46	12.04	1.58	56.57	22.33

Table 2 depicts the results of our study. We instrumented the analysis to keep track of the number of constituents for each product value being created. The Scheme domain implemented in the analysis consists of *18 constituents*. However, in our benchmarks, only 8 distinct constituents were inhabited. The table shows the minimum, maximum, and median values for the number of values in each category.

Our results demonstrate that in most cases, abstract product values contain only one constituent. In more precise analyses with more precise domains and choice for sensitivity, the proportion of values with only one constituent is likely to increase. This is because a value with more constituents is less precise than values with fewer constituents. A more precise domain gives rise to more precise analysis results therefore increasing the likehood of fewer constituents in the product. Note that we measure the number of values created during an analysis in order to show the potential impact on memory consumption. Our results do not show the precision of the final analysis result.

Based on the results of our empirical study, we recommend implementing product values as sparse labeled products. To this end, MONARCH provides a SparseLabeledProduct data structure that is internally implemented as a heterogeneous map. Its function is to express the product's constituents at a type-level, while providing an efficient run-time memory representation. An excerpt of the sparse labeled product for representing Scheme values is depicted below.

```
data SchemeType = IntType | BoolType | PaiType |
                  CloType | PrimType | ...
type Values     = '[  IntType  ::-> CP Integer,
                      BoolType ::-> CP Bool,
                      PaiType  ::-> Set Addr,
                      CloType  ::-> Set (Exp, Env),
                      PrimType ::-> Set String, ...]

type SchemeVal  = LabeledSparseProduct Values
```

The constituents of the sparse labeled product are expressed as a type-level list of key-value pairs (denoted by `key ::-> value`). At run time `key` types are demoted to data values so that they can be used as keys in a map datastructure. This enables the efficient memory representation of the labeled product, since absent constituents do not need to be stored in the map datastructure. Moreover, expressing the product as a type-level list enables reasoning about its constituents through typeclass constraints.

This representation renders the combination of various abstract domains trivial. Moreover, it provides both type-safety and a memory-efficient run-time representation that only stores the present subdomains.

4.2 Semantics

In MONARCH, programming language semantics are expressed as recursive definitional interpreters. These interpreters are rendered compatible with the abstract interpretation framework through a library of monadic type classes that allow expressing programming language semantics. Most of our monadic type classes are standard for abstract definitional interpreters [1,5,13]. MONARCH provides type classes for interacting with abstract environments (MonadEnvironment), abstract stores (MonadStore) and abstract memory allocation (MonadAlloc).

In addition to these standard type classes, MONARCH defines interfaces for expressing conditional control flow and escaping control flow, as well as for expressing and automatically deriving fixpoint combinators.

Environments. Most languages provide variables for keeping track of arbitrary state or for naming complex program terms. These variables also need to be modeled by the abstract interpreter. To do so, a mapping from variables to their memory locations (address) needs to be provided. This can also be seen in the toy example fron Sect. 2. This mapping can be summarized through three functions: lookupEnv, withEnv and getEnv, shown below.

```
class (Monad m) => MonadEnvironment adr m where
   lookupEnv :: String -> m adr
   withEnv   :: [(String, adr)] -> m a -> m a
   getEnv    :: m [(String, adr)]
```

The lookupEnv function returns a computation that results in the address of the given variable name. The withEnv function runs the given computation m a (e.g., a call to eval) in the environment described by the list of mappings in the first argument. Finally, the getEnv function captures the current environment, which is needed for implementing language features such as closures.

Stores. A store provides a mapping from addresses to values and models the program's memory. In a concrete semantics, functions lookupSto and updateSto (depicted below) suffice to express the interactions with the store. However, abstract interpretation necessitates an additional function which we call extendSto.

```
class (Monad m) => MonadStore adr v m where
   lookupSto :: adr -> m v
   extendSto :: adr -> v -> m ()
   updateSto :: adr -> v -> m ()
```

The difference between updateSto and extendSto is that updateSto changes the value of an *existing* address, while extendSto adds a new address to the store and associates a value with it. This distinction is required for enabling support for *strong updates* since they need to differentiate between an existing binding being updated or a new binding being introduced in the store. Note that depending on the analysis, both extendSto and updateSto could join the new value with the previously stored value. They merely signal the intention of the semantics to introduce a new address (i.e., extendSto) or to update an existing one (i.e., updateSto).

Nondeterminism. In contrast to a single execution path in a concrete interpretation of the program, an abstract interpretation might explore multiple execution paths. This is because the interpreter has to reason with approximate values. For instance, evaluating the condition of an if expression can yield true, false or both meaning that both of its branches have to be approximated.

To this end, MONARCH exposes the MonadJoin type class, which executes two monadic computations and combines their results together. Its definition, depicted below, consists of two functions: mjoin and mbottom. This type class is similar to MonadPlus where mjoin corresponds to mplus and mbottom corresponds to mzero. In contrast to MonadPlus, however, MonadJoin adds lattice constraints on the output of its computations m a. This is because implementations of MonadJoin can either choose to combine all results into a set, akin to the non-determinism monad, or to join results of two computations together using join. Therefore, a Joinable constraint is required for mjoin.

```
class (Monad m) => MonadJoin m where
    mjoin   :: Joinable a      => m a -> m a -> m a
    mbottom :: BottomLattice a => m a
```

This MonadJoin interface can be used to implement over-approximating conditional control flow. Below, we present the cond function for expressing this conditional control flow. It uses the MonadJoin interface to combine computations of the consequent and alternative branches of if expressions. It uses the mbottom function to represent *empty computations*. This is the case when the condition for one of the branches becomes infeasible.

```
cond :: (BoolDomain b, MonadJoin m, Joinable v, BottomLattice v)
     => m b -> m v -> m v -> m v
cond cnd csq alt = mjoin t f
    where t = cnd >>= (\b -> if isTrue b then csq else mbottom)
          f = cnd >>= (\b -> if isFalse b then alt else mbottom)
```

As an example, we implement semantics for evaluating if expressions. This implementation is straightforward because if expressions almost directly translate to cond actions. The semantics essentially states that the condition (cnd) is evaluated first, and based on its result the consequent (csq), alternative (alt), or both are evaluated. This implementation is nearly identical to a concrete semantics, but our framework enables the use of cond for expressing non-deterministic if expressions (when the condition could be both true or false).

```
eval (If cnd csq alt) = cond (eval cnd) (eval csq) (eval alt)
```

Escaping Control Flow. We define *escaping control flow* as control flow that interrupts normal sequential program execution. Examples of escaping control flow are not only exceptions or program errors, but also more complex language features such as *early function returns*, *loop breaking*, and so on.

MONARCH abstracts from these language features through a single monadic type class called *MonadEscape* which is depicted in the code listing below.

```
class MonadEscape m where
   type Esc m :: Type
   throw  :: JoinLattice a => Esc m -> m a
   catch  :: JoinLattice a => m a -> (Esc m -> m a) -> m a
```

`MonadEscape` resembles the `MonadError` type class from the well-known mtl library[1] Both type classes contain methods for signalling an escaping or error condition through `escape` and `throwError` respectively. Moreover, both feature a method for catching potential errors that occur in a given computation through `catch` (`catchError` resp.). They differ, however, in their constraints. Whereas `MonadError` does not constrain the output of its monadic computations, `MonadEscape` constrains the output to a `JoinLattice` which is an alias for a combination of `Joinable`, `PartialOrder` and `BottomLattice`. This is because an implementation of `catch` needs to potentially account for both an escaping program path and a normal program path by joining the results of its handler with the results from the normal program path.

Error `Esc m` is typically set to an abstract representation of potential program errors. For example, to represent errors of type `Error` abstractly, a `Set Error` can be used. In general, developers can use a `Domain` constraint to provide this mapping from a concrete error to its abstract representation:

```
type EscapeConstraints m = (Domain (Esc m) Error, MonadEscape m)
```

Fixpoint Infrastructure. The key idea of abstract definitional interpreters is that they express abstract program semantics through a recursive evaluation function. Unfortunately, naively applying this evaluation function might lead to undesired non-termination issues. Instead, abstract definitional interpreter frameworks typically require some additional bookkeeping. For instance, to make sure that the analysis terminates, an in-out caching [5] mechanism can be employed through open recursion. This in-out caching mechanism keeps track of earlier inputs to the evaluation function and their outputs, and returns the associated output when applied more than once to the same input.

We support these mechanisms through two type classes. The first, `MonadFix`, provides a fixpoint function that transforms Kleisli arrows [16] (monadic computations that still require an input) into cached Kleisli arrows.

```
type Kleisli m b c = b -> m c   -- Kleisli arrow
class MonadFix b c m where
   fix :: (Kleisli m b c -> Kleisli m b c) -> Kleisli m b c
```

---

[1] From: https://hackage.haskell.org/package/mtl.

The first argument of `fix` corresponds to a version of an evaluation function using open recursion. This can be seen by replacing `b` with `Exp` and `c` with `v`. This results in the following function signature:

```
eval :: (Exp -> m v) -> Exp -> m v
eval recur e = _
-- or equivalently with Kleisli arrows
eval :: Kleisli Exp v -> Kleisli Exp v
```

Then, when a cached version of `eval` is required, the `recur` function can be used. This enables polymorphism over the caching and fixpoint mechanism.

The second type class to support in-out caching mechanisms is `MonadCache`. The methods in this type class compute the complete inputs and outputs to the evaluation function. These inputs and outputs also include values encapsulated by the monad in addition to the value specified by the return type of the evaluation function. The `MonadCache` type class, along with its associated methods and types, is depicted in the code listing below.

```
class MonadCache m where
    type Key m k :: Type
    type Val m v :: Type
    type Base m   :: Type -> Type
    key :: k -> m (Key m k)
    val :: Val m v -> m v
    run :: (k -> m v) -> Key m k -> Base m (Val m v)
```

Associated type families `Key` and `Val` compute the *type* of input and output respectively. Note that `Key` is also indexed by a type `k` which represents the input to the evaluation function —or in general to the Kleisli arrow— being cached. `Val` is indexed similarly by the output type of the cached Kleisli arrow. Functions `key` and `val` allow the current input to be extracted and the given output to be restored respectively. The `run` function takes the cached Kleisli arrow and *runs* it by supplying it with the expected input. `Base` computes the type of the first layer in a monadic stack that does not require caching, which can be the identity monad or some other monad. This enables expressing effects that are global to the fixpoint iteration, such as a global store [9].

To illustrate this, we depict an instance of `MonadCache` for the `StateT` monad transformer below. For its `Key` it adds the input state `s` to input `k`, and does so similarly for its output state for `Val`. The implementation of `key` and `val` are straightforward since they simply extract the input state and restore the output state respectively. MONARCH provides instances of `MonadCache` for all major `mtl` monad transformers in a similar manner.

```
instance MonadCache m => MonadCache (StateT s m) where
    type Key (StateT s m) k = Key m (k, s)
    type Val (StateT s m) v = Val m (v, s)
    type Base (StateT s m)  = Base m
```

```
key k   = StateT $ \s -> (,s) <$> key (k, s)
val     = StateT . const . val
run f   = run (\(k,s) -> runStateT (f k) s)
```

4.3 Analysis

A semantics can be instantiated into an analysis by instantiating all type parameters used in the evaluation function. These type parameters correspond to different static analysis concerns. In MONARCH, these type parameters correspond to abstract domains and monad transformer stacks.

We discuss several areas of interest. The first is the instantiation of the domain. Next, we discuss *effect layering*, which enables combining effects into a single monad that supports all expected effects. Third, we explore some instantiations of monad transformers. Finally, we discuss integrating fixpoint algorithms.

Domain Instantiation. In addition to descriptions of abstract domains through a set of interfaces represented as type classes, MONARCH also provides a number of type class instances for these domains. For example, the `CP a` type provides a constant propagation lattice for any type `a`, while `CP Integer` implements a number domain. Similarly, MONARCH provides instances for other frequently used domains such as strings, lists, dictionaries, booleans, and so on. Moreover, MONARCH enables composing these instantiations into powerful domains using domain combinators such as the sparse labeled product described in Sect. 4.1.

Effect Layering. Monads do not compose [10], meaning that their operations (i.e., `unit` and `bind`) cannot be readably expressed as the composition of their individual operations. Instead, *monad transformers* [17] have been proposed, which are best described as monads with "a hole". Consider the *state monad transformer*, depicted in the code listing below, as an example.

```
newtype StateT s m a = StateT (s -> m (a, s))
```

The monad is parametrized by the type of state `s`, its result type `a`, but also by a monad `m`. It essentially allows for additional effects to be added around the resulting value and the output state. The idea is that computational effects can be composed using a set of smaller monads that are stacked on top of each-other by `lifting` operations from monads lower in the stack. Typically, monad transformers are presented as a library of transformers and their type classes. For example, `StateT` implements the type class `MonadState`. The idea is that all other transformers also implement this type class, and delegate state operations down to a state monad lower in the stack. Therefore, the entire stack now implements the required type class and becomes a suitable instantiation.

The example shown below declares the type of a stack that introduces effects for tracking an environment and store. This stack can subsequently be used for running semantics that require environment and store effects.

```
type EvalM =
  StoreT Address Value (EnvT String Address Identity)
```

The main problem with monad transformers is that for each new type class and transformer combination a corresponding instance needs to be implemented, which leads to poor scalability. This is because not all operations can be expressed simply as a lifting of lower operations.

Therefore, monad transformers do not seem a suitable candidate for instantiating our semantics. Instead, inspired by the Haskell layers library[2], we propose a class called MonadLayer. This type class consists of two functions: upperM and lowerM. The former fulfils the role of lift. The latter is somewhat more complex, and fulfils the role of "lowering" a monadic computation into the stack.

```
class MonadLayer l where
  upperM :: Monad m => m a -> l m a
  lowerM :: (forall b . m b -> m b) -> l m a -> l m a
```

lowerM is a function that accepts two arguments. The first is another function that executes a monadic action on the lower layer. The second argument is a monadic computation l m a where l is a monad transformer, m is the monad one level below the transformer, and a is the result from the monadic computation.

It is important to note that type variable b is universally quantified inside the function in the first argument. This is because implementations of lowerM need to "push" information about their effects into the lower layer so that they are not lost in composition. For example, to remove a layer from StateT it needs to be executed with some initial state s. The output of this execution is a *pair* that consists of a value a and a new state s. Therefore, to execute an action on the lower layer, this pair needs to be part of the monadic computation. To illustrate, we provide the instance of MonadLayer for StateT below.

```
instance MonadLayer (StateT s) where
  upperM = lift
  lowerM f (StateT run) = StateT (f . run)
```

Below, we demonstrate how a MonadLayer can be used to delegate monadic actions to a lower monad. The code listing depicts an instance of MonadEnvironment for any monad layer l. The lookup and getEnv function can be implemented using upperM, while withEnv needs to be implemented using lowerM. Essentially, to delegate withEnv computations, the second argument of withEnv needs to be *lowered* into the layer below, so that the lower withEnv can be executed.

```
instance (MonadLayer l, MonadEnvironment m)
      => MonadEnvironment (l m) where
  getEnv         = upperM getEnv
  lookup var     = upperM (lookup var)
  withEnv bds ma = lowerM (withEnv bds) ma
```

---

[2] From: https://hackage.haskell.org/package/layers.

Effect Locality. Monad transformers and layers do not necessarily commute. The combination of a `Maybe` with a `State` monad for instance yields very different results depending on the order in which they are combined. For instance, composing `Maybe` after `State` results in a computation that can fail but retains its state up to the failure, while reversing this order results in a computation that can fail but loses its final state. This becomes more apparent when unfolding the type signature of the different composition orderings:

```
newtype MaybeT m a = MaybeT (m (Maybe a))
MaybeT (StateT Identity) a = s -> (Maybe a, s)
StateT (MaybeT Identity) a = s -> Maybe (a, s)
```

Thus, the depth of the monad transformer stack provides a *locality* dimension. The lower a monad is in the stack, the more global its effects become. In the earlier example, `MaybeT` is located lower in the stack, thus its failures are more global than the state so that the state is discarded when failure occurs.

Monad Transformers. For instantiating the monadic computation, the analysis developer is expected to construct a stack of monad transformers that provide implementations for each type class constraint of the evaluation function. To this end, MONARCH provides a library of monad transformers that have instances for these type classes. For example, to satisfy the `MonadStore` constraint, the framework provides a `StoreT` transformer that supports weak updates.

Interestingly, some monadic type classes have multiple implementations. One example is non-determinism, for which we describe two transformers that satisfy the `MonadJoin` constraint: `JoinT` and `NonDetT`. Recall that after one or more paths have been explored, their results need to be merged. The `JoinT` monad layer enables this by *joining* the results together so that only one path remains with a joined value (as is typically done when using traditional dataflow analyses). Alternatively, `NonDetT` can be used to accumulate each result into a list so that the semantics continues with the result of each path separately (as is typically done when using the AAM approach [25]).

```
newtype JoinT m a = JoinT (m a) deriving (Monad)
instance MonadJoin (JoinT m) where
    mzero = return bottom
    mjoin (JoinT ma) (JoinT mb) = join <$> ma <*> mb
runJoinT :: JoinT m a -> m a
runJoinT (JoinT m) = m
```

Essentially, `mjoin` runs both paths sequentially and then joins their results together. `NonDetT` works similarly but uses a list monad to capture all results.

```
newtype NondetT m a = NondetT (ListT m a) deriving (Monad)
```

The operations of `MonadJoin` can be trivially implemented as the empty list for `mzero` and as list concatination for `mjoin`.

Constructing Cached Fixpoint Computations. Finally, we briefly discuss instantiating an analysis with a fixpoint algorithm. To this end, we consider a simple evaluation function with the following constraints:

```
type EvalM v m = (MonadFix m Exp v, MonadJoin m, MonadStore m)
eval :: EvalM v m => Exp -> m v
```

The `Key` type (from `MonadCache`) gives rise to a *component*. A component typically represents a part of a program that is to be analyzed until its end and whose analysis does recurse infinitely. More concretely, it is the input to the `evaluation` function. Thus, most analyses can be structured as an *intra-component* analysis (i.e., `eval`) and an *inter-component* analysis. The inter-component analysis drives the intra-component analysis until it reaches a fixpoint.

The code listing below illustrates how to express this in our framework. We first define the monadic stack for the intra-analysis and separate out the remaining type class constraints. Then, we run the *inter-component* analysis. While doing so, we satisfy the remaining type class constraints by adding the appropriate monad transformer to the transformer stack.

```
type IntraT m  = MonadStack '[ JoinT, CacheT ] m
type Cmp       = Key (IntraT Identity) Exp
type Res       = Val (IntraT Identity) Val
type InterM    = (MonadStore m, MapM Cmp Res)
intra :: InterM m => Cmp -> m ()
intra e = runFixT @(IntraT (AnalysisT Cmp m) (eval e)
          & runAnalysisT e
-- computing a fixpoint over the intra analysis
inter = lfp intra
-- adding global effects and running the analysis
analyze :: Exp -> (Map Adr Val, Map Cmp Res)
analyze e = inter e & runStoreT emptyStore
            & runWithMapping @Cmp @Res & runIdentity
```

The result of this analysis is an abstraction of the heap (through `MonadStore` and `runStoreT`) and a mapping from each component in the program to its evaluated value (i.e., `Res`). MONARCH allows developers to instantiate the analysis with different fixpoint strategies. Some fixpoint strategies require additional bookkeeping that needs to be added to the set of global effects at the bottom of the monad transformer stack. Such bookkeeping can be added to the `runAnalysisT` monad transformer but is omitted for brevity. This design also allows reordering monad transformers to obtain different semantics [5], similar to Sect. 4.3. For example, moving `StoreT` to the intra-component analysis results in an analysis with *local stores* rather than a *global store* analysis [25].

Interestingly, this design also allows for effects that are neither global nor local, but sit somewhere in between. For instance, a *flow-sensitive* store is typically implemented by widening the store at the component level, keeping track of the store at the start (in-store) and at the end (out-store) of the analysis for that component. When components are function calls, on each function call the "in-store" is joined with the contents of the store at the call-site of the function. Then, the function body gets analyzed, after which the "out-store" is changed to the contents of the store at the end of the function body. This "out-store" is finally used to continue evaluation after calling the analysed function at each call-site.

This design can be implemented by moving the `StoreT` layer between the caching transformer and join transformers. The change causes the store to be no longer cached, as it is below the caching layer. Keeping the store above the join transformer ensures that stores are joined rather than threaded along multiple nondeterminstic program paths. Additional manual plumbing is required to update the store contents as described above. This is depicted below.

```
1   type IntraT = MonadStack '[ CacheT, StoreT, JoinT ]
2   intra :: forall obj m . AnalysisM m obj => Cmp -> m ()
3   intra e = runIntraAnalysisT e m
4     where m = do s <- fromJust <$> get (StoreIn e)
5                  r <- cache e (runCallT (uncurry callFix) . eval)
6                       & runStoreT s
7                       & runJoinT
8                  put (StoreOut e) s'
9                  return r
10            callFix :: Exp -> IntraT m Res
11            callFix bdy = do e' <- key bdy
12                             spawn e'
13                             changed <- joinWith (StoreIn e')
14                                 =<< currentStore
15                             if changed then mbottom
16                             else do rv <- cached e'
17                                     rs <- get (StoreOut e')
18                                     v <- maybe mbottom return rv
19                                     s <- maybe mbottom return rs
20                                     putStore s
21                                     return v
```

In this version, the transformers in the stack are rearranged to place the store transformer in between the caching and the joining layer. As mentioned before, this causes the store to be omitted from the keys and values of the cache, therefore becoming part of the global analysis state instead of the components themselves. The open recursion of the evaluation function through `runCallT` ensures that function calls are treated differently in order to change the contents of the store. The function calling semantics is depicted in the `callFix` function which takes the body of the function, checks whether the function has already been analyzed, and if so reads its result from the cache. Then, the function's "in-store" is updated to include the contents of the current store (i.e., the one at the call-site of the function). Then, after the function has been analyzed, the store at the call-site is updated through `putStore` (line 19).

Since the join and store transformers are no longer part of the cache, the `cache` (line 5) and `runIntraAnalysisT` (line 3) functions will no longer automatically run these layers. Hence, `runJoinT` and `runStoreT` need to be manually called after the cached layers have been executed through `cache`.

5 Instantiating the Framework

To illustrate the framework's use in practice, we discuss two case studies in which we instantiate two different types of analyses for two programming languages. The first analysis is for the Scheme language. The second analysis is for a subset of the Python language. Both analyses compute an abstraction of the program's memory, as well as its read, write and call effects. The languages differ significantly in their syntax, semantics, and types of run-time values. Table 3 summarizes the similarities and differences of the corresponding analysis implementations and connects them to the architecture of our framework (cf. Figure 1). For each implementation, we present the abstract domain, relevant semantics, and show how the analysis is instantiated using layers of monad transformers. **The source code for our case studies is available in the artifact**.

Table 3. Overview of ADI configuration per language

	Python	Scheme
Domain		
Primitive	Integer, Real, String	Integer, Real, Symbol
Combinator	sparse product in primitive fields, Dictionary, Tuple	coproduct abstracted as sparse product, Vector, Pair
Semantics		
Store	environment frames, objects	vector, pairs, strings, variables
Escape	return, break, errors	errors
Join	yes	yes

5.1 Domain

We use the labelled sparse product lattice proposed in Sect. 4.1 to represent Scheme's abstract domain. An excerpt of its implementation is depicted below. Labels and values are separated by a `::->` . Its definition is parametrized by a configuration m (represented by a type-level association list) which configures the domain with specific subdomains for each type of value.

```
type Values m = '[ IntKey  ::-> Assoc IntConf m,
                   BoolKey ::-> Assoc BoolConf m,
                   PaiKey  ::-> Set (Assoc PaiConf m),
                   CloKey  ::-> Set (Assoc ExpConf m, Assoc EnvConf m),
                   PrimKey ::-> Set String, ...]
type SchemeValue m = LabeledSparseProduct (Values m)
```

For instance, abstract closures are allocated at CloKey and are represented as sets of pairs consisting of an expression and an environment. Another example is the abstraction of Scheme numbers, which are allocated at the IntKey and map to a primitive integer sub-domain as configured by the IntConf key. The entire implementation of this Scheme domain is done in roughly 500 lines of code.

The implementation of the Python analysis takes a different approach. In Python all values are modelled as objects that have their own methods and associated class. Thus, a sparse product representation is no longer suitable to represent those values. Instead, we use an abstraction of dictionary values (similar to [7]) which stores method identifiers and field names as keys, and their abstracted value as values. An instantiation of this domain is depicted below. Again, parameter m is a *configuration* which configures the Python domain with specific primitive subdomains for each type of value.

```
data PyObj m = PyObj
  { dct :: CPDictionary String (Assoc ValueConf m),
    prm :: LabeledSparseProduct (PyPrm m) }
```

Our LabeledSparseProduct appears again here, to implement so-called *primitive fields*. These primitive fields are used to represent primitive values such as *integers* or *lists* which cannot be represented as an object and class, but can still be extended from in a class hierarchy. Thus we represent them as fields in every object that might be set if the object represents a primitive value such as integers. The definition of PyPrm is similar to Values and is left out for brevity. The implementation of the domain for Python objects is done in approximately 250 lines of code in total.

> **Conclusion.** Real-world abstract domains often consist of many subdomains. We provide modular, reusable primitive building blocks to represent these different subdomains and combinators to combine them. This saves analysis developers from performing the tedious and error-prone tasks of implementing abstract domains themselves.

5.2 Semantics

Depicted below are the type class constraints on the evaluation function for implementing the Python semantics (PyM, left) and the Scheme semantics (SchemeM, right) respectively. Both sets of constraints are similar: they both have a type class that describes their abstract domain (PyObj for Python and SchemeValue for Scheme), they both need MonadJoin and MonadEscape, and they need a representation of environment and store. Furthermore, we also use a monad called AllocM which enables the allocation of memory addresses.

```
type PyM m obj = (                type SchemeM m v = (
    PyObj' obj, MonadJoin m,          SchemeValue v, MonadJoin m,
    MonadEscape m,                    MonadEscape m,
    MonadEnvironment m ObjAdr PyEnv,  MonadEnvironment m (Adr v) (Env v),
    MonadStore m ObjAdr obj,          MonadStore m (PAdr v) (PaiDom v),
                                      MonadStore m (Adr v)  (VarDom v),
                                      MonadStore m (VAdr v) (VecDom v),
                                      MonadStore m (SAdr v) (StrDom v),
    AllocM m PyLoc ObjAdr,            AllocM m Ide (Adr v),
    AllocM m FrmLoc ObjAdr,           AllocM m Exp (PAdr v),
                                      AllocM m Exp (VAdr v),
    )                                 AllocM m Exp (SAdr v))
```

The language semantics differ more. We focus on the representation of primitive operations (e.g., arithmetic operations) since they show the interaction of language semantics with the abstract domains.

In the interpreter for Scheme, primitives are implemented as ordinary Haskell functions that accept a list of argument values as input. The interpreter applies an operation from the abstract domain and returns the result. In the abstract domain, primitives are then represented as sets of strings which are used as keys to find the associated Haskell function in a table of primitives. Below, we depict a number of simple arithmetic functions from the Scheme analysis. The full implementation of all Scheme primitives is approximately 150 lines of code.

```
fix2 :: String
     -> (forall m . PrimM m v => v -> v -> m v) -> Prim v
fix2 nam f = Prim nam (\_ [v1, v2] -> f v1 v2)
allPrimitives = [ fix2 "*" times, fix2 "+" plus,
                  fix2 "-" minus, ...]
```

Note that function fix2 which constructs primitives from ordinary Haskell functions allows the primitive to be executed in a monadic context m. This monadic context is necessary for primitives that need access to the store (i.e., MonadStore) or that might result in a failure (i.e., MonadEscape).

Primitives are implemented differently in the Python analysis. Instead of looking them up from a table by their name, primitives are represented as *methods* that operate on primitive fields (cf. Section 5.1). The latter is illustrated below by the implementation of prim2 which is the equivalent of fix2. The full implementation of all Python primitives is approximately 200 lines of code.

```
prim2 f loc [a1, a2] = do
   { o1 <- pyDeref' a1 ;
     o2 <- pyDeref' a2 ;
     r  <- f o1 o2    ;
     pyAlloc loc r }
```

This example illustrates that before applying a primitive operation represented as an ordinary Haskell function f, abstractions of Python objects first have to be dereferenced and looked up in the abstract memory. The final line shows that the result is an object and has to be allocated and stored in memory.

Finally, we show how the usage of MonadEscape differs between the Python and Scheme analyses. One major difference between Python and Scheme is the existence of *escaping control flow*. In Scheme, ignoring call/cc, the only way to return from a function is by evaluating its last expression. In contrast, Python supports a number of control flow statements that enable an early return from code blocks. For instance, break stops a loop iteration early.

These cases are supported by our MonadEscape infrastructure. Shown below is the evaluation of a return statement. The Python semantics support return statements that include expressions which evaluate to the *return value* of the enclosing function. If no expression is given, the enclosing function returns None.

```
execRet :: PyM pyM obj => Maybe PyExp -> pyM ()
execRet (Just exp) = eval exp >>= (escape . Return)
execRet Nothing    = escape (Return None)
```

This Return escape value needs to be intercepted at the top level of the evaluation so that it can be returned. This is shown below, highlighting the usefulness of our framework and its cond, escape, catch, etc. constructs.

```
evalBdy (FuncBdy _ bdy) = catchRet (exec bdy $> constant None)

catchRet :: PyM m obj => m PyVal -> m PyVal
catchRet = (`catch` \esc -> cond (return $ isReturn esc)
                                 (getReturn esc) (throw esc))
```

Another example of how our analysis framework facilitates implementing complex language features is depicted below. It shows the implementation of attribute lookup for Python objects. First, it checks whether the object contains the attribute, and looks it up in the fields of its class otherwise. Our framework enables expressing abstract semantics close to the concrete, as can be seen in hasAttr, getAttr, etc. These return abstract values which lead to approximation in the semantics, but the way they are expressed is close to a concrete semantics.

```
lookupAttr loc attr =
  pyDeref $ \adr obj ->
            cond (return $ hasAttr attr obj)
                 (return $ getAttr attr obj)
                 -- if not found locally => look in the class
                 (do cls <- atAttr "__class__" obj
                     lookupAttrInClass loc attr adr cls)
```

> **Conclusion.** Our type classes form a *framework* for defining abstract language semantics. Our case studies have shown that the framework is applicable to two very different semantics which demonstrates its power and expressiveness.

5.3 Analysis

Below we present the analysis instantiations for Scheme and Python. Both are implemented as a pair of functions `intra` and `analyze`. The former defines the set of layers which are cached by the caching mechanism and whose input and output will be used by the fixpoint iterator. The latter defines all the layers *outside* of the cache. This boundary is set by the `runBaseT` layer at the bottom of the stack defined in `intra`. Both instantiations place the store monad transformer below the cache layer. This is because the analyses use a *global store* which requires the store to remain outside of the cached state.

```
-- Scheme
intra :: (SchemeDomain v, AnalysisM m v) => Exp -> m v
intra e = eval e & runAlloc (PaiAdr @ctx)
                & runAlloc (VecAdr @ctx)
                & runAlloc (StrAdr @ctx)
                & runAlloc (EnvAdr @ctx)
                & runCtx ctx & runJoinT & runBaseT
analyze e = lfp (intra e)
          & runStoreT initialSto
          & runWithStore @(Map StrAdr (StrDom v))
          & runWithStore @(Map VecAdr (VecDom v))
          & runWithStore @(Map PaiAdr (PaiDom v))
          & runIdentity
-- Python
intra :: AnalysisM m obj => PyBdy -> m ()
intra bdy = evalBdy bdy & runMayEscape
                       & runEnvT initialEnv
                       & runAlloc (const . allocPtr)
                       & runAlloc (const . allocFrm)
                       & runCtxT () & runJoinT & runBaseT
analyze prg = lfp (intra prg)
            & runWithStore @(Map ObjAdr obj) @ObjAdr
            & runIdentity
```

The instantiations for Python and Scheme follow the same structure: both use the same fixpoint iterator function called `lfp`, need an environment and context, and use the `JoinT` layer for merging results from different paths in the analyzed program. Both instantiations are implemented in approximately 150 lines of code each. The major difference between the Scheme and Python analyses is in their use of *stores*. To run a Python analysis only a single store is required while a Scheme analysis requires four. This is because the Scheme analysis uses four memory segments: variable segment, vector segment, string segment and pair segment (in contrast, in Python everything is an object, and hence only an object segment is required). We chose this design because our memory allocation strategy never allocates values from different segments on the same address. Physically segmenting the stores allows enforcing this design at the type level. This usage also highlights how the `MonadStore` interface provides the correct `lookup` function by traversing the monad transformer stack, and uses the store that is applicable for the type of address used.

> **Conclusion.** We instantiated an analysis for Python and for Scheme subsets. These instantiations are similar, demonstrating that our monad transformer stack facilitates expressing effects for different semantics.

6 Related Work

In this section, we present other static analysis tools based on (definitional) abstract interpreters and discuss how our framework differs.

Monadic Abstract Interpreters. Sergey et al. [23] propose monadic abstractions for abstracting a CESK machine. To this end, they start from the AAM approach and derive monadic components. Although their work is the first to introduce monads in the context of abstracting abstract machines, it does not deal with the definitional aspect of the interpreter, nor does it integrate monad transformer stacks for composing different aspects of the analysis together.

Definitional Interpreters through Arrow Combinators. Keidel et al. [15] propose a library of *arrow combinators* [8] for expressing sound and composable abstract program semantics. Similar to their work, we also present a collection of type classes to describe the semantics of the analyzed language. However, we encode the expected abstractions as *monads* instead of *arrows*. We argue that arrow transformers are quite new and less supported by the Haskell ecosystem. Moreover, their abstraction of `ArrowPlus` (`MonadJoin` in our implementation) lacks a `Joinable` and `BottomLattice` constraint. This makes the implementation of this type class as a join of the values across program branches more difficult, as a layer within the monad transformer stack cannot assume the lattice structure of the values captured within the monadic computations.

In a follow-up work, Keidel et al. [14] propose fixpoint combinators for expressing the fixpoint algorithms for abstract definitional interpreters. Our work follows similar strategies but is specifically tailored to monadic abstract interpreters, rather than arrow transformers. The `MonadCache` type class essentially implements a caching mechanism specifically for Kleisli arrows. However, next to caching, the `MonadCache` type class also serves a more practical purpose: it allows to run a (part of) a monad transformer stack.

Abstract Definitional Interpreters Without Monads. Brandl et al. [1] propose a Scala framework for implementing abstract definitional interpreters. In contrast to our work, their framework proposes to eliminate the monad transformer stack by representing computational effects through an *imperative* effect stack. This reduces compilation times as the compiler no longer needs to aggressively inline each monadic operation across the transformer stack, but requires careful implementations of effect handlers to store and restore global state when appropriate. For instance, combining a store effect handler with a non-determinism handler requires that the store handler restores its state imperatively after the first branch is evaluated and before the execution moves on to the next branch. Monad transformers do not have an imperative state and do not require separate restore logic.

Other Abstract Interpretation Frameworks. MAF [24] is a framework for implementing modular analyses for higher-order programming languages. This work focuses on the *ModX* [20] approach to modular analyses and does not present abstractions for expressing abstract program semantics. Moreover, support for combining abstract domains is limited.

The MOPSA analyser [11] is a modular OCaml platform used to build sound semantic static analysers based on abstract interpretation. In contrast to our work, MOPSA does not follow the abstract definitional interpreter design.

LiSA [6] is a library for building analyses based on abstract interpretation. LiSA uses a control flow graph representation, allowing analysis implementers to reuse the library's existing analyses by only writing a parser and control flow graph builder for the language they want to analyse. In MONARCH this can be achieved by implementing an evaluation function for the language of interest. Other static analysis tools such as Soot [12], Phasar [22], ... also rely on control flow graphs but are tailored to specific programming languages such Java or LLVM IR. Although MONARCH currently focusses on Scheme and Python, it is designed in a language-agnostic manner.

CIAOPP [2] is an abstract interpretation-based preprocessor and analyser for Ciao Prolog programs. Similar to our work, the tool provides an interface to instantiate client analyses and the ability to configure the analysis in several ways. However, the tool is specialised to the Ciao Prolog programming language, while MONARCH provides many language-agnostic building blocks to allow analysis developers to create new analyses for other languages (as demonstrated by our case studies in Sect. 5).

Staged Abstract Interpreters. [26] Shows how an abstract interpreter can be specialised to a program to optimise it. Although this paper does not present any novel ideas specifically for abstract definitional interpreters, their optimisation steps could be of interest to integrate into the MONARCH framework.

Overall, our work follows a long tradition in abstract interpretation [4] and (abstract) definitional interpreters [14,21,23]. MONARCH combines this tradition into a single framework and proposes abstractions in the form of `MonadJoin`, `MonadEscape` and `MonadCache`. Moreover, our framework provides a strong foundation for building abstract domains through its rich set of primitive domains and its powerful domain combinators, such as sparse labeled products.

7 Conclusion

We have presented our framework called MONARCH for implementing abstract definitional interpreters in Haskell. Our design consists of three parts: abstract domains, abstract program semantics, and analysis instantiation. We have presented the key features of each part and how they integrate with one another. For its domain component, we found that a rich library of primitive domains and combinations thereof are the most suitable for representing abstract domains. We also found that type-level data structures are paramount for implementing complex abstract domains succinctly and efficiently by providing abstractions that reason about all subdomains automatically. For defining programming language semantics, we found that, similar to other abstract definitional interpreters, implementing language semantics is best performed in a polymorphic context expressed using a set of monadic type class constraints. Moreover, although nearly identical to their standard `mtl` counterparts, monadic type classes for abstract definitional interpreters require additional type class constraints relating to lattices and strong updates. We have also shown that caching infrastructure can be expressed in a generic manner through a `MonadCache` type class constraint without the need for less common representations of computations such as arrows. Finally, we discussed two different instantiations of analyses for Scheme and Python and showed how our design facilitated implementing these analyses.

Acknowledgments. This work was partially supported by an Innoviris grant for the ECOPIPE project (Joint R&D 2022, grant number 2022-PS-JRDIC-8), by the Research Foundation Flanders (FWO) (grant number 1187122N), and by the Cybersecurity Research Program Flanders.

Disclosure of Interests. The authors have no competing interests to declare that are relevant to the content of this article.

References

1. Brandl, K., Erdweg, S., Keidel, S., Hansen, N.: Modular abstract definitional interpreters for webassembly. In: 37th European Conference on Object-Oriented Programming, pp. 5:1–5:28 (2023). https://doi.org/10.4230/LIPICS.ECOOP.2023.5
2. Bueno, F., Hermenegildo, M., López, P., Morales, J.F., Puebla, G.: The ciaopp program processor (1996)

3. Cousot, P., Cousot, R.: Abstract interpretation: a unified lattice model for static analysis of programs by construction or approximation of fixpoints. In: Conference Proceedings of the 4th ACM Symposium on Principles of Programming Languages, pp. 238–252 (1977)
4. Cousot, P., Cousot, R.: Abstract interpretation: past, present and future. In: Proceedings of the Joint Meeting of the 23rd Annual Conference on Computer Science Logic and the 29th Annual ACM/IEEE Symposium on Logic in Computer Science, pp. 2:1–2:10 (2014)
5. Darais, D., Labich, N., Nguyen, P.C., Van Horn, D.: Abstracting definitional interpreters (functional pearl). Proc. ACM Program. Lang. **1**(ICFP), 1–25 (2017)
6. Ferrara, P., Negrini, L., Arceri, V., Cortesi, A.: Static analysis for dummies: experiencing lisa. In: Proceedings of the 10th ACM SIGPLAN International Workshop on the State of the Art in Program Analysis, p. 1–6 (2021). https://doi.org/10.1145/3460946.3464316
7. Fulara, J.: Generic abstraction of dictionaries and arrays. In: Proceedings of the 4th International Workshop on Numerical and Symbolic Abstract Domains. Electronic Notes in Theoretical Computer Science, vol. 287, pp. 53–64 (2012). https://doi.org/10.1016/J.ENTCS.2012.09.006
8. Hughes, J.: Generalising monads to arrows. Sci. Comput. Program. **37**(1–3), 67–111 (2000). https://doi.org/10.1016/S0167-6423(99)00023-4
9. Johnson, J.I., Labich, N., Might, M., Van Horn, D.: Optimizing abstract abstract machines. In: Proceedings of the 15th ACM SIGPLAN International Conference on Functional Programming, pp. 443–454 (2013)
10. Jones, M.P., Duponcheel, L.: Composing monads. Technical report, Technical Report YALEU/DCS/RR-1004, Department of Computer Science. Yale (1993)
11. Journault, M., Miné, A., Monat, R., Ouadjaout, A.: Combinations of reusable abstract domains for a multilingual static analyzer. In: Verified Software. Theories, Tools, and Experiments, pp. 1–18 (2020)
12. Karakaya, K., et al.: Sootup: a redesign of the soot static analysis framework. In: International Conference on Tools and Algorithms for the Construction and Analysis of Systems, pp. 229–247. Springer, Heidelberg (2024). https://doi.org/10.1007/978-3-031-57246-3_13
13. Keidel, S., Erdweg, S.: Sound and reusable components for abstract interpretation. Proc. ACM Program. Lang. **3**(OOPSLA), 176:1–176:28 (2019). https://doi.org/10.1145/3360602
14. Keidel, S., Erdweg, S., Hombücher, T.: Combinator-based fixpoint algorithms for big-step abstract interpreters. Proc. ACM Program. Lang. **7**(ICFP), 955–981 (2023). https://doi.org/10.1145/3607863
15. Keidel, S., Poulsen, C.B., Erdweg, S.: Compositional soundness proofs of abstract interpreters. Proc. ACM Program. Lang. **2**(ICFP), 72:1–72:26 (2018). https://doi.org/10.1145/3236767
16. Kleisli, H.: Every standard construction is induced by a pair of adjoint functors. Proc. Am. Math. Soc. **16**(3), 544–546 (1965)
17. Liang, S., Hudak, P., Jones, M.: Monad transformers and modular interpreters. In: Proceedings of the 22nd ACM SIGPLAN-SIGACT Symposium on Principles of Programming Languages, pp. 333–343 (1995). https://doi.org/10.1145/199448.199528
18. Moggi, E.: An abstract view of programming languages. University of Edinburgh. Department of Computer Science. Laboratory for Foundations of Computer Science (1990)

19. Moggi, E.: Notions of computation and monads. Inf. Comput. **93**(1), 55–92 (1991). https://doi.org/10.1016/0890-5401(91)90052-4
20. Nicolay, J., Stiévenart, Q., Meuter, W., Roover, C.: Effect-driven flow analysis. In: Enea, C., Piskac, R. (eds.) VMCAI 2019. LNCS, vol. 11388, pp. 247–274. Springer, Cham (2019). https://doi.org/10.1007/978-3-030-11245-5_12
21. Reynolds, J.C.: Definitional interpreters for higher-order programming languages. In: Proceedings of the ACM Annual Conference, vol. 2, pp. 717–740 (1972). https://doi.org/10.1145/800194.805852
22. Schubert, P.D., Hermann, B., Bodden, E.: Phasar: an inter-procedural static analysis framework for c/c++. In: International Conference on Tools and Algorithms for the Construction and Analysis of Systems, pp. 393–410. Springer, Heidelberg (2019)
23. Sergey, I., et al.: Monadic abstract interpreters. In: Proceedings of the 34th ACM SIGPLAN Conference on Programming Language Design and Implementation, pp. 399–410 (2013). https://doi.org/10.1145/2491956.2491979
24. Van Es, N., Van der Plas, J., Stiévenart, Q., De Roover, C.: MAF: a framework for modular static analysis of higher-order languages. In: Proceedings of the 20th IEEE International Working Conference on Source Code Analysis and Manipulation, pp. 37–42 (2020)
25. Van Horn, D., Might, M.: Abstracting abstract machines. In: Proceedings of the 15th ACM SIGPLAN International Conference on Functional Programming, pp. 51–62 (2010)
26. Wei, G., Chen, Y., Rompf, T.: Staged abstract interpreters: fast and modular whole-program analysis via meta-programming. Proc. ACM Program. Lang. **3**, 1–32 (10 2019). https://doi.org/10.1145/3360552

Delta Store Semantics: Abstract Garbage Collection for Abstract Definitional Interpreters

Noah Van Es(✉), Bram Vandenbogaerde, and Coen De Roover

Vrije Universiteit Brussel, Ixelles, Belgium
{noah.van.es,bram.vandenbogaerde,coen.de.roover}@vub.be

Abstract. Both the precision and performance of abstract interpreters can be improved greatly through the integration of abstract garbage collection (GC). Unfortunately, for abstract interpreters that do not explicitly model the stack (e.g., abstract definitional interpreters), this integration has proven cumbersome. Existing approaches either fail to exploit the full precision and performance benefits of abstract GC and pushdown control flow, and/or require complicated modifications to the abstract interpreter. In addition, the lack of global store widening, which is incompatible with abstract GC, often remains an obstacle for scalability.

In this work, we present delta store semantics (DSS), offering a novel yet simple approach to integrate abstract GC into big-step abstract definitional interpreters. DSS makes a simple change to the standard big-step language semantics, returning a delta store (representing changes to the original store) instead of an updated store, enabling the integration of a single evaluation rule to interleave GC into its semantics. Importantly, we show that DSS not only preserves the advantages of big-step abstract interpreters and abstract GC, but in fact can exploit greater precision benefits (due to more aggressive GC). We formulate this claim as a theorem, for which we provide both a mechanised proof in Rocq, as well as empirical evidence. Finally, we propose a new form of store widening for DSS, which tackles the scalability issues of abstract interpreters employing abstract GC without store widening. The result is similar to the traditional notion of flow sensitivity in data-flow analyses.

Keywords: Abstract Interpretation · Abstract Garbage Collection

1 Introduction

Abstract garbage collection is the application of garbage collection (GC) to an abstract interpreter. Similar to concrete GC, it reclaims memory locations that are no longer reachable. Its purpose, however, is entirely different: for a concrete interpreter, GC simply frees up memory resources, whereas in an abstract interpreter, its main purpose is to improve precision and scalability [21,22].

Abstract GC has frequently been integrated into abstract interpreters that employ *small-step* operational semantics, such as those obtained by following the *Abstracting Abstract Machines* (AAM) approach to abstract interpretation [21,30]. In contrast, for abstract interpreters that employ *big-step* definitional interpreters [28], this integration is inherently more challenging. The reason for this challenge is that for such *abstract definitional interpreters* [2], there is no explicit (abstraction of the) continuation. A direct application of GC requires access to the continuation to ensure that all addresses that are reachable therefrom are not accidentally reclaimed, as they might still be needed later on. That is, addresses reachable from the continuation are traditionally part of the GC root set.

Yet, at the same time, the lack of an explicit continuation on its own brings about key benefits to the precision and scalability of the abstract interpreter. These benefits are widely recognized under the umbrella of *pushdown control flow* models [3,11]. It should come as no surprise that various attempts [2,4,8] have been made to combine the benefits of such models with the benefits of abstract GC, aiming to realize "the best of both worlds". Unfortunately, these attempts often fall short of that promise, sacrificing some benefits of both abstract GC and pushdown control flow to enable their co-existence. Another issue is that these existing approaches overcomplicate the underlying machinery of the abstract interpreter, requiring significant engineering efforts and rendering formal reasoning about the interpreter's abstract semantics more challenging.

1.1 Motivation: The Best of Both Worlds

Both abstract GC and the pushdown control flow of abstract definitional interpreters offer significant precision and performance improvements.

Specifically, for abstract GC, we identify the following advantages:

Avoiding Garbage-Induced Imprecision. In order to ensure termination, an abstract interpreter needs to use a finite number of addresses. As such, multiple allocations may need to reuse the same address. All values allocated at the same address are *joined* together, causing a loss in precision. Abstract GC can prevent some of those precision-detrimental joins: by freeing up addresses that are unreachable, it prevents future allocations at those addresses from having to join the newly allocated value with the old "garbage values". When using abstract counting [16,21], which counts the number of concrete bindings for each abstract address, abstract GC can also prevent counting dead bindings.

Without abstract GC, these sources of imprecision in the heap are propagated, bringing garbage "back to life" and disturbing not only the data but also the control flow of the interpreter due to *spurious paths* [21]. Existing work has therefore shown that abstract GC can lead to order-of-magnitude improvements in precision (and performance, as the exploration of spurious paths is avoided).

Garbage Irrelevance. Another advantage of abstract GC relates not directly to the interpreter's precision, but to the scalability of the underlying fixpoint algorithm. Specifically, by removing garbage from the heap, the states explored by the abstract interpreter become smaller (i.e., the abstract interpreter only needs to explore the subset of the state space where all garbage is removed). This causes the interpreter to more frequently end up in the same states, allowing the reuse of previously computed analysis results for such states. In contrast, without abstract GC, the interpreter often has to analyze multiple states that are equivalent, but not equal, as they differ only in unreachable (garbage) bindings.

We refer to the examples given in [4,21,29] to illustrate the impact of these benefits. Only an interpreter that is entirely *garbage-free* [21,29] (i.e., eliminates all garbage immediately) enjoys the full benefit of both these advantages.

Similarly, we enumerate the advantages that are inherent to the pushdown control flow of abstract definitional interpreters.

Perfect Stack Precision. The big-step semantics of abstract definitional interpreters no longer model the continuation (i.e., "the stack"), and instead rely on the underlying continuation of the host language (or formalism) for recursive evaluation rules. Since the continuation is no longer modelled in the semantics, an abstraction of these semantics no longer requires an abstraction (i.e., approximation) of the continuation either. Such an abstraction of the continuation would otherwise cause imprecision in control flow, incorrectly matching callers and returns. In contrast, the pushdown control flow of abstract definitional interpreters entirely avoids this precision loss, resulting in "perfect stack precision" [2].

Context Irrelevance. Germane et al. [8] point out that big-step semantics, such as those of abstract definitional interpreters, also enjoy the benefit of context irrelevance. Analogous to garbage irrelevance, context irrelevance ensures that states are not differentiated based on their continuation component (i.e., their "context"). Therefore, when the same evaluation state is encountered in multiple contexts, the analysis results for that state can be reused in every context, improving scalability. The rationale is that just as garbage is not relevant to the evaluation of a current state, in many languages the continuation component also does not contribute to the result of an evaluation. Of course, the latter assumption does not hold when, for instance, first-class continuations are used.[1]

We refer to the examples in [3,4] to illustrate the impact of these benefits.

---

[1] However, it can be argued that a CPS transformation of the program under analysis can be used to support such language features.

In this work, we show that the combination of abstract GC and the pushdown control flow of abstract definitional interpreters can not only keep the advantages of both techniques, but can in fact do even better than "the best of both worlds". That is, we identify an additional benefit that can be exploited by abstract GC when applied to abstract definitional interpreters:

Stackless Abstract GC. As exemplified by the work of Germane et al. [8], abstract GC for big-step abstract interpreters can (temporarily) reclaim addresses that are still reachable from the (implicit) continuation. That is, such "stackless abstract GC" does not take references from the continuation into account, resulting in a smaller GC root set, and therefore also a more aggressive form of abstract GC (and therefore in turn amplifying its aforementioned advantages). We can illustrate this using the following Scheme program as an example:

```
(define (f n) (if (even? n)
                  (/ n 2)
                  (let ((r (f (+ n 1)))) (+ r n))))
(f 5)
```

For a context-insensitive abstract interpreter without abstract GC, the recursive call to f would allocate the argument (+ n 1) at the same address for the parameter n as the original argument 5, therefore joining both values at this address and losing precision. However, when abstract GC is applied to a small-step abstract interpreter with explicit continuations (e.g., à la AAM), this precision loss would also not be avoided. The reason is that n is still reachable by the continuation when the recursive call to f happens, and therefore its corresponding address can not be reclaimed. In contrast, when stackless abstract GC is applied to a big-step abstract interpreter, references from the stack do not contribute to the GC root set (i.e., only addresses reachable from the current environment are preserved). As such, n is not kept in scope, and its address can be reclaimed before it is reallocated for the recursive call to f, avoiding this precision loss.

1.2 Approach: Delta Store Semantics

In this work, we present delta store semantics (DSS), a new formalism to integrate abstract GC into abstract definitional interpreters, exploiting all the aforementioned advantages. DSS closely resembles the original big-step abstract semantics, making only a simple change by returning a *delta store* (containing all changes to the original store) instead of directly returning an updated store. This modification opens up two interesting opportunities:

- It enables a simple and efficient integration of abstract GC into the big-step abstract semantics (similar in spirit to the *effect logs* of Germane et al. [8, 9]). That is, when abstract GC is enabled, the delta store that is computed represents changes w.r.t. a minimal, garbage-collected store. Subsequently, we

can *replay* those changes on a non-garbage-collected store, where the bindings that are necessary for the continuation are still present.
- A delta store is a more efficient, minimal representation for the result of an evaluation compared to the full updated store. Just like regular stores, delta stores are joinable. We propose a novel form of store widening for DSS, which still allows for strong updates and (limited) abstract GC. Such store widening involves joining the results of evaluations at the same program point, which is more efficient using delta stores (as we only have to join the changed bindings instead of the entire stores).

These two opportunities form the outline for the core of this paper. Section 3 presents the big-step abstract semantics with delta stores; Sect. 4 and Sect. 5 show how abstract GC and flow-sensitive store widening can be integrated into this semantics, respectively. We evaluate the impact of both in Sect. 6.

Contributions. The contributions of this work are as follows:

- We present delta store semantics (DSS), a novel formulation of big-step abstract semantics where evaluation steps return *minimal* and *composable* delta stores (representing changes to a store) instead of full updated stores. Our formalism resembles the heap fragment semantics of Germane et al. [8,9], but is arguably simpler and closer to the original big-step semantics.
- We show how abstract GC can be integrated into DSS, exploiting the full potential of combining abstract GC with pushdown control flow (i.e., realizing all benefits listed in Sect. 1.1). As such, this integration achieves better precision than classical abstract GC for small-step abstract interpreters. We formulate this claim as a theorem, and provide a mechanised proof in Rocq.
- We show how a new form of store widening can be integrated into DSS, further exploiting the minimal and compositional nature of delta stores. This form of store widening closely resembles the traditional notion of flow sensitivity, and still allows for strong updates and (a limited form of) abstract GC.
- We provide an implementation of DSS (including the integrations of abstract GC and flow-sensitive store widening) in the MAF framework to abstract interpretation. Using this implementation, we conduct an empirical evaluation to measure the impact of abstract GC (specifically, the impact of the theorem formally shown in Rocq) and flow-sensitive store widening for DSS.

2 Background

We present the formal specification of a minimal higher-order language λ_{ANF} with support for mutable variables (to model strong updates). Below, we define the syntax of λ_{ANF}, based on the λ-calculus in A-Normal Form [5] (ANF).

$$
\begin{aligned}
e \in \mathsf{Exp} &::= ae \mid f(ae) & f, ae \in \mathsf{Atom} &::= x \mid lam \\
&\mid \mathbf{let}\ x = e_1\ \mathbf{in}\ e_2 & lam \in \mathsf{Lam} &::= \lambda x.e \\
&\mid \mathbf{set}\ x := ae\ \mathbf{then}\ e & x &\in \mathsf{Var}\ \text{(a set of identifiers)}
\end{aligned}
$$

ANF is a syntactic form restricting operators and operands to atomic expressions ae which can be evaluated immediately without impacting program state. This simplification can be automated, is purely cosmetic, and without loss of generality.

We define both the abstract small-step and big-step semantics for λ_{ANF}, and discuss the integration of abstract counting and abstract GC.

2.1 Small-Step Abstract Semantics of λ_{ANF}

We present the small-step abstract semantics of λ_{ANF} (the "operational semantics") using the AAM technique [30] to abstract interpretation.

State Space. The state space Σ of the abstract interpreter is given below.[2][3]

$$
\begin{aligned}
\varsigma \in \Sigma &::= \langle c, \sigma, \sigma_k, a_k \rangle & \sigma_k &\in \mathsf{KStore} = \mathsf{KAddr} \to \mathsf{Kont} \\
c \in \mathsf{Control} &::= \mathbf{ev}(e, \rho) \mid \mathbf{ap}(v) & \kappa &\in \mathsf{Kont} = \mathcal{P}(\mathsf{Frame}) \\
\rho \in \mathsf{Env} &= \mathsf{Var} \rightharpoonup \mathsf{Addr} & frm \in \mathsf{Frame} &::= \mathbf{letk}(x, e, \rho, a_k) \\
\sigma \in \mathsf{Store} &= \mathsf{Addr} \to \mathsf{Val} & l &\in \mathsf{Loc} = \mathsf{Addr} \cup \mathsf{KAddr} \\
v \in \mathsf{Val} &= \mathcal{P}(\mathsf{Clo}) & a &\in \mathsf{Addr}\ \text{(a finite set)} \\
clo \in \mathsf{Clo} &= \mathsf{Lam} \times \mathsf{Env} & a_k &\in \mathsf{KAddr}\ \text{(a finite set)}
\end{aligned}
$$

A state ς consists of a control component (either an expression e under evaluation paired with an environment ρ, or a resulting value v), a store σ (to model "the heap"), a continuation store σ_k (to model "the stack"), and the current continuation address a_k (pointing to "the top of the stack"). While the sets Addr and KAddr are infinite in a concrete interpreter (e.g., by picking $\mathsf{Addr} = \mathsf{KAddr} = \mathbb{N}$), for an abstract interpreter both sets should be finite. One can easily show that this restriction ensures that the state space Σ also remains finite.

As the abstract interpreter can only use a finite number of addresses, it may need to reuse the same address for multiple allocations. Closures and continuation frames that end up at the same address need to be *joined* together to obtain

---

[2] Note that it is often customary to put $\widehat{hats}$ on abstracted components, in order to distinguish them from their concrete counterparts. We only present the abstract semantics, and therefore omit these hats to improve readability.

[3] For a state ς, we implicitly use subscripted notations so that $\varsigma = \langle c_\varsigma, \sigma_\varsigma, \sigma_{k_\varsigma}, a_{k_\varsigma} \rangle$. For (partial) maps, $[]$ denotes the empty map, $[a \mapsto b]$ denotes a map m with a single binding (i.e., $dom(m) = \{a\}$ and $m(a) = b$), and the notation $m[a \mapsto b]$ extends the map m so that $m[a \mapsto b](a) = b$ and $m[a \mapsto b](x) = m(x)$ for $x \neq a$.

a sound, but finite approximation. Therefore, values and continuations are represented as *sets* of closures and continuation frames, respectively. We define the *join operator* ($\sqcup$), the *subsumption relation* ($\sqsubseteq$) and the *global lower bound* ($\bot$) for Val (and analogously for Kont): $v_1 \sqcup v_2 = v_1 \cup v_2, v_1 \sqsubseteq v_2 \iff v_1 \subseteq v_2$ and $\bot = \emptyset$. We trivially extend the definitions of ($\bot$), ($\sqcup$) and ($\sqsubseteq$) to functions and pairs. For example, $(a_1, b_1) \sqcup (a_2, b_2) = (a_1 \sqcup a_2, b_1 \sqcup b_2)$ and $(f_1 \sqcup f_2)(a) = f_1(a) \sqcup f_2(a)$, while ($\bot$) is defined so that $\bot \sqcup v = v \sqcup \bot = v$ and ($\sqsubseteq$) so that $a \sqsubseteq b \iff a \sqcup b = b$.

Evaluation Rules. Atomic expressions can be evaluated in a single step, without making any modifications to the store. To evaluate such atomic expressions, we introduce an auxiliary function $\mathcal{A} : \text{Atom} \times \text{Env} \times \text{Store} \to \text{Val}$.

$$\mathcal{A}(x, \rho, \sigma) = \text{lookup}(\sigma, \rho(x)) \qquad \mathcal{A}(lam, \rho, \sigma) = \{\langle lam, \rho\rangle\}$$

where currently, lookup is simply defined as $\text{lookup}(\sigma, a) = \sigma(a)$.

Below, we define the small-step transition relation $(\to) \subseteq \Sigma \times \Sigma$ for λ_{ANF}. Note that $(\to)$ is not deterministic due to its over-approximating behaviour.

$$\frac{v = \mathcal{A}(ae, \rho, \sigma)}{\langle\text{ev}(ae, \rho), \sigma, \sigma_k, a_k\rangle \to \langle\text{ap}(v), \sigma, \sigma_k, a_k\rangle} \quad (\textsc{St-Atom})$$

$$\frac{\langle\lambda x.e, \rho'\rangle \in \mathcal{A}(f, \rho, \sigma) \quad v = \mathcal{A}(ae, \rho, \sigma) \quad a = \text{alloc}(x)}{\langle\text{ev}(f(ae), \rho), \sigma, \sigma_k, a_k\rangle \to \langle\text{ev}(e, \rho'[x \mapsto a]), \text{extend}(\sigma, a, v), \sigma_k, a_k\rangle} \quad (\textsc{St-App})$$

$$\frac{a'_k = \text{alloc}_k(e_1) \quad \kappa = \{\text{letk}(x, e_2, \rho, a_k)\}}{\langle\text{ev}(\text{let } x = e_1 \text{ in } e_2, \rho), \sigma, \sigma_k, a_k\rangle \to \langle\text{ev}(e_1, \rho), \sigma, \text{extend}_k(\sigma_k, a'_k, \kappa), a'_k\rangle} \quad (\textsc{St-Let1})$$

$$\frac{\text{letk}(x, e, \rho, a'_k) \in \sigma_k(a_k) \quad a = \text{alloc}(x)}{\langle\text{ap}(v), \sigma, \sigma_k, a_k\rangle \to \langle\text{ev}(e, \rho[x \mapsto a]), \text{extend}(\sigma, a, v), \sigma_k, a'_k\rangle} \quad (\textsc{St-Let2})$$

$$\frac{v = \mathcal{A}(ae, \rho, \sigma) \quad a = \rho(x) \quad \sigma' = \text{update}(\sigma, a, v)}{\langle\text{ev}(\text{set } x := ae \text{ then } e, \rho), \sigma, \sigma_k, a_k\rangle \to \langle\text{ev}(e, \rho), \sigma', \sigma_k, a_k\rangle} \quad (\textsc{St-Set})$$

We leave the choice of sets Addr and KAddr, as well as the allocation functions alloc and alloc_k open as configuration parameters of the abstract interpreter (resulting in a particular *allocation policy*). Any allocation policy yields a sound and decidable analysis [30] (as long as the sets chosen for Addr and KAddr are finite). However, the choice is not arbitrary, as the allocation policy decides how often (determined by the size of Addr and KAddr) and when (determined by alloc and alloc_k) addresses need to be reused. This choice therefore affects the precision and *polyvariance* [10] of the abstract interpreter.[4]

---

[4] For the sake of simplicity, our abstract interpreter does not include a timestamp component (as in [30]), which could be used to express more complex allocation policies such as k-CFA with $k > 1$.

Currently, we define functions extend (analogously, extend$_k$) and update as:

$$\text{extend}(\sigma, a, v) = \text{update}(\sigma, a, v) = \sigma[a \mapsto \sigma(a) \sqcup v]$$

Abstract Counting. We can further improve the precision of the abstract interpreter using abstract counting [1,19]. With abstract counting, one keeps track for every allocated address a in σ whether it has been allocated (concretely) only once or possibly multiple times. Doing so can avoid joining the old and new value in the ST-SET rule in certain cases. Formally, we define

$$n \in \text{Count} := 0 \mid 1 \mid \infty$$

$$n_1 \sqcup n_2 = \begin{cases} n_2 & \text{if } n_1 \sqsubseteq n_2 \\ n_1 & \text{otherwise} \end{cases} \qquad \text{inc}(n) = \begin{cases} 1 & \text{if } n = 0 \\ \infty & \text{otherwise} \end{cases}$$

and the (reflexive and transitive) subsumption relation ($\sqsubseteq$) as $0 \sqsubseteq 1 \sqsubseteq \infty$. We then modify the definition of Store to keep track of abstract counts[5]:

$$\sigma \in \text{Store} = \text{Addr} \rightarrow (\text{Val} \times \text{Count})$$

Extending the store with a newly-allocated address (using extend) increases the abstract count at that location. Updating the address at an existing address (using update) does not increase the abstract count. If the existing abstract count for that address is ∞, we are not able to replace the value at that location (because that address may represent multiple allocations, and we are only updating one of them); in this case, the new value is still joined together with an old value (called a *weak update*). However, if the abstract count at this location is 1, then we know that we can safely replace the old value with the new one (called a *strong update*), thereby increasing the precision of the ST-SET rule. If $\langle v_a, c_a \rangle = \sigma(a)$, then:

$$\text{lookup}(\sigma, a) = v_a \qquad \text{extend}(\sigma, a, v) = \sigma[a \mapsto \langle v_a \sqcup v,\ \text{inc}(c_a)\ \rangle]$$

$$\text{update}(\sigma, a, v) = \begin{cases} \sigma[a \mapsto \langle v, 1 \rangle] & \text{if } c_a = 1 \\ \sigma[a \mapsto \langle v_a \sqcup v, c_a \rangle] & \text{otherwise} \end{cases}$$

Abstract Garbage Collection. We now add garbage collection to further improve precision. We use notation and definitions similar to those used by Might and Shivers [21]. First, we define a family of auxiliary functions $\mathcal{T}_X : X \rightarrow \mathcal{P}(\text{Loc})$ that return all addresses that are referenced directly by some element of type X.

---

[5] Important changes with respect to previous definitions are highlighted in *gray*.

$$\mathcal{T}_\Sigma(\langle c, \sigma, \sigma_k, a_k \rangle) = \mathcal{T}_{\mathsf{Control}}(c) \cup \{a_k\} \qquad \mathcal{T}_{\mathsf{Clo}}(\langle \lambda x.e, \rho \rangle) = \mathcal{T}_{\mathsf{Env}}(\rho)$$
$$\mathcal{T}_{\mathsf{Control}}(\mathsf{ev}(e, \rho)) = \mathcal{T}_{\mathsf{Env}}(\rho) \qquad \mathcal{T}_{\mathsf{Env}}(\rho) = \mathsf{range}(\rho)$$
$$\mathcal{T}_{\mathsf{Control}}(\mathsf{ap}(v)) = \mathcal{T}_{\mathsf{Val}}(v) \qquad \mathcal{T}_{\mathsf{Frame}}(\mathsf{letk}(x, e, \rho, a_k)) = \mathcal{T}_{\mathsf{Env}}(\rho) \cup \{a_k\}$$
$$\mathcal{T}_{\mathsf{Val}}(v) = \bigcup_{clo \in v} \mathcal{T}_{\mathsf{Clo}}(clo) \qquad \mathcal{T}_{\mathsf{Kont}}(\kappa) = \bigcup_{frm \in \kappa} \mathcal{T}_{\mathsf{Frame}}(frm)$$

Next, we introduce the adjacency relation between addresses ($\leadsto_\varsigma$) $\subseteq$ Loc $\times$ Loc, where intuitively $l \leadsto_\varsigma l'$ means that there is a reference from l to l'. We define ($\leadsto_\varsigma$) = ($\leadsto_\sigma$) $\cup$ ($\leadsto_{\sigma_{k_\varsigma}}$), using the following auxiliary adjacency relations:

$$a \leadsto_\sigma l \iff l \in \mathcal{T}_{\mathsf{Val}}(\mathsf{lookup}(\sigma, a)) \qquad a_k \leadsto_{\sigma_k} l \iff l \in \mathcal{T}_{\mathsf{Kont}}(\sigma_k(a_k))$$

The auxiliary function $\mathcal{R}_{(\leadsto)} : \mathcal{P}(\mathsf{Loc}) \to \mathcal{P}(\mathsf{Loc})$ computes all addresses transitively reachable from a given root set using a transition relation ($\leadsto$):

$$\mathcal{R}_{(\leadsto)}(\mathit{roots}) = \mathit{lfp}(f) \quad \mathbf{where} \quad f(S) = \mathit{roots} \cup \{l' \in \mathsf{Loc} \mid \exists l \in S : l \leadsto l'\}$$

The function $\mathcal{R} : \Sigma \to \mathcal{P}(\mathsf{Loc})$ computes all reachable addresses of a state:

$$\mathcal{R}(\varsigma) = \mathcal{R}_{(\leadsto_\varsigma)}(\mathcal{T}_\Sigma(\varsigma)).$$

Using these definitions, we can define garbage collection for a state ς as a function $\Gamma : \Sigma \to \Sigma$ that restricts the stores of ς to its reachable addresses $\mathcal{R}(\varsigma)$.

$$\Gamma(\varsigma) = \langle c_\varsigma, \sigma_\varsigma |_{\mathcal{R}(\varsigma)}, \sigma_{k_\varsigma} |_{\mathcal{R}(\varsigma)}, a_k \rangle$$

where $\sigma|_R(a) = \sigma(a)$ if $a \in R$ and $\langle \bot, 0 \rangle$ otherwise (analogously for $\sigma_k|_R$).

To incorporate garbage collection into our evaluation rules, we define a new transition relation ($\to_\Gamma$) as a composition of the garbage collection function Γ and the existing transition relation ($\to$), i.e. ($\to_\Gamma$) = $\Gamma \circ (\to)$. As such, ($\to_\Gamma$) applies GC after every step. This ensures that no garbage can be created by ($\to_\Gamma$), rendering the abstract interpreter *garbage-free* [29,30].

Note that abstract GC synergises with abstract counting: abstract counts for collected addresses are reset to 0, increasing opportunities for future strong updates. Conversely, by applying strong updates, more garbage can be collected, as addresses reachable from the overwritten value no longer contribute to $\mathcal{R}(\varsigma)$.

Program Semantics. The collecting semantics of a program can now be defined using the function $\mathcal{S} : \mathsf{Exp} \to \mathcal{P}(\Sigma)$, which computes all the states reachable by the abstract interpreter, starting from the initial state of the program:[6]

$$\mathcal{S}(e) = \{\varsigma \in \Sigma \mid \langle \mathsf{ev}(e, []), \bot_\sigma, \bot_{\sigma_k}, a_{\mathsf{halt}} \rangle \xrightarrow{*}_\Gamma \varsigma\}$$

where $\bot_\sigma(a) = \langle \bot, 0 \rangle$, $\bot_{\sigma_k}(a) = \bot$ and a_{halt} is a special address in KAddr. As Σ is finite, for any program e it is guaranteed that $\mathcal{S}(e)$ is finite and therefore computable. We can reason over the behaviour of e by reasoning over $\mathcal{S}(e)$,

---

[6] We write ($\xrightarrow{*}_\Gamma$) for the reflexive, transitive closure of ($\to_\Gamma$).

yielding a sound and decidable program analysis. Note that the definition of $\mathcal{S}$ reveals the benefit of garbage irrelevance: as $(\rightarrow_\Gamma)$ is garbage-free, $\mathcal{S}$ only needs to explore the subset of Σ where $\varsigma = \Gamma(\varsigma)$.

We also define a function eval : $\mathsf{Exp} \rightarrow \mathcal{P}(\mathsf{Val} \times \mathsf{Store})$, returning a set of all possible return values (along with their corresponding store) for a program:

$$\mathsf{eval}(e) = \{(v, \sigma) \mid \langle \mathbf{ap}(v), \sigma, \sigma_k, a_{\mathsf{halt}} \rangle \in \mathcal{S}(e)\}$$

2.2 Big-Step Abstract Semantics of λ_{ANF}

We present the big-step abstract semantics of λ_{ANF} (the "definitional semantics") following the approach of Darais et al. [2] to abstract interpretation.

Evaluation Rules. For an abstract definitional interpreter, the semantics are formulated as recursive evaluation rules using a big-step relation $(\Downarrow) \subseteq \mathsf{Config} \times \mathsf{Result}$. We define input configurations to evaluate (Config) and the result of the evaluation for that configuration (Result) as follows:

$$\mathit{conf} \in \mathsf{Config} = \mathsf{Exp} \times \mathsf{Env} \times \mathsf{Store} \qquad \mathit{res} \in \mathsf{Result} = \mathsf{Val} \times \mathsf{Store}$$

That is, a configuration $\langle e, \rho, \sigma \rangle$ contains an expression e to evaluate using the environment ρ and store σ. In contrast to states in Σ, configurations crucially do not carry a continuation component, which is key to achieve context irrelevance (as configurations with the same expression, environment and store, but used in different evaluation contexts are still considered equal) and avoids a loss in stack precision (since there is no need to approximate this component). The result of an evaluation $\langle v, \sigma' \rangle$ holds the resulting value v along with the updated store σ'.

The big-step transition relation $(\Downarrow)$ is defined below. Note again that—just as with the small-step transition relation $(\rightarrow)$—there is nondeterminism due to the over-approximating behaviour of the abstract interpreter.

$$\frac{v = \mathcal{A}(ae, \rho, \sigma)}{\langle ae, \rho, \sigma \rangle \Downarrow \langle v, \sigma \rangle} \quad (\text{E-ATOM})$$

$$\frac{\langle \lambda x.e, \rho' \rangle \in \mathcal{A}(f, \rho, \sigma) \quad a_x = \mathsf{alloc}(x) \quad v_x = \mathcal{A}(ae, \rho, \sigma)}{\langle e, \rho'[x \mapsto a_x], \mathsf{extend}(\sigma, a_x, v_x) \rangle \Downarrow \langle v, \sigma' \rangle} \quad (\text{E-APP})$$

$$\frac{\langle e_1, \rho, \sigma \rangle \Downarrow \langle v_x, \sigma' \rangle \quad a_x = \mathsf{alloc}(x)}{\langle e_2, \rho[x \mapsto a_x], \mathsf{extend}(\sigma', a_x, v_x) \rangle \Downarrow \langle v, \sigma'' \rangle} \quad (\text{E-LET})$$

$$\frac{a_x = \rho(x) \quad v_x = \mathcal{A}(ae, \rho, \sigma)}{\langle e, \rho, \mathsf{update}(\sigma, a_x, v_x) \rangle \Downarrow \langle v, \sigma' \rangle} \quad (\text{E-SET})$$

Note that strong updates are already supported in these semantics, since we are reusing the abstract-counting definitions of extend and update.

Abstract Garbage Collection. For the small-step abstract interpreter of Sect. 2.1, we computed the GC root set for the current state ς using the addresses directly reachable from the control component ($\mathcal{T}_{\mathsf{Control}}(c_\varsigma)$) and the current root of the continuation component (a_{k_ς}). For the abstract definitional interpreter presented here, we do not have access to the latter, as the continuation component is not explicitly reified. Nevertheless, addresses reachable from the continuation can not just be ignored: if they are not included in the GC root set, addresses that are used later on may accidentally be collected. The updated store σ' of an evaluation step $\langle e, \rho, \sigma \rangle \Downarrow \langle v, \sigma' \rangle$ is then no longer safe to continue evaluation with. For instance, in the E-LET rule, it is crucial that the updated store σ' (returned after evaluating e_1) still contains all addresses reachable from ρ, so that it can safely be used to evaluate e_2.

In order to address this, Darais et al. [2] show how abstract GC can still be integrated into an abstract definitional interpreter by explicitly passing along all addresses reachable from the (implicit) continuation (i.e., all addresses that need to be preserved, as they may be used after the current evaluation step). Concretely, this requires passing along a set of addresses ψ in each configuration:

$$conf \in \mathsf{Config} = \mathsf{Exp} \times \mathsf{Env} \times \mathsf{Store} \times \mathcal{P}(\mathsf{Addr})$$

Incorporating GC into the evaluation rules then requires two modifications:

- Each recursive evaluation step passes along the set of stack addresses ψ that need to be preserved, along with additional addresses that are still needed to continue with the remaining evaluation steps in that rule. The latter corresponds to the addresses that would previously be directly reachable from the Frame (i.e., using $\mathcal{T}_{\mathsf{Frame}}$) allocated in the corresponding rule of the small-step semantics. Due to our simplification to ANF, the only rule with multiple recursive evaluation steps is the E-LET rule; addresses still required for the second evaluation step (in this case, $\mathcal{T}_{\mathsf{Env}}(\rho)$) are therefore added to ψ for the first evaluation step. As the second evaluation step is also the final one (i.e., e_2 is evaluated in *tail* position, so it does not grow the (implicit) continuation), no additional addresses need to be preserved.
- We add a new rule to collect garbage: for a configuration $\langle e, \rho, \sigma, \psi \rangle$, it uses $\psi \cup \mathcal{T}_{\mathsf{Env}}(\rho)$ as the GC root set, using the garbage-collected store to evaluate e, and subsequently also cleans up the updated store σ' of the result $\langle v, \sigma' \rangle$ using the GC root set $\psi \cup \mathcal{T}_{\mathsf{Val}}(v)$.[7] To interleave this rule with the existing evaluation rules, we introduce a new relation ($\Downarrow_\Gamma$) with such a GC rule:

---

[7] Note that we are able to collect more garbage here compared to the original work of Darais et al. [2], as we GC not only the result store, but also the configuration store.

$$\frac{\sigma_{\mathsf{gc}} = \sigma|_{\mathcal{R}_{(\leadsto_\sigma)}(\psi \cup \mathcal{T}_{\mathsf{Env}}(\rho))} \quad \langle e, \rho, \sigma_{\mathsf{gc}}, \psi \rangle \Downarrow \langle v, \sigma' \rangle}{\langle e, \rho, \sigma, \psi \rangle \Downarrow_\Gamma \langle v, \sigma'_{\mathsf{gc}} \rangle} \quad \text{(E-GC)}$$

$$\sigma'_{\mathsf{gc}} = \sigma'|_{\mathcal{R}_{(\leadsto_{\sigma'})}(\psi \cup \mathcal{T}_{\mathsf{Val}}(v))}$$

Subsequently, we modify the other evaluation rules to use ($\Downarrow_\Gamma$) instead of ($\Downarrow$) for recursive evaluation steps. This effectively results in the big-step equivalent of the "GC at every step" policy used in ($\rightarrow_\Gamma$).

The updated evaluation rules are shown below:

$$\frac{v = \mathcal{A}(ae, \rho, \sigma)}{\langle ae, \rho, \sigma, \psi \rangle \Downarrow \langle v, \sigma \rangle} \quad \text{(E-ATOM)}$$

$$\frac{\langle \lambda x.e, \rho' \rangle \in \mathcal{A}(f, \rho, \sigma) \quad a_x = \mathsf{alloc}(x) \quad v_x = \mathcal{A}(ae, \rho, \sigma)}{\langle e, \rho'[x \mapsto a_x], \mathsf{extend}(\sigma, a_x, v_x), \psi \rangle \Downarrow_\Gamma \langle v, \sigma' \rangle} \quad \text{(E-APP)}$$
$$\langle f(ae), \rho, \sigma, \psi \rangle \Downarrow \langle v, \sigma' \rangle$$

$$\frac{\langle e_1, \rho, \sigma, \psi \cup \mathcal{T}_{\mathsf{Env}}(\rho) \rangle \Downarrow_\Gamma \langle v_x, \sigma' \rangle \quad a_x = \mathsf{alloc}(x)}{\langle e_2, \rho[x \mapsto a_x], \mathsf{extend}(\sigma', a_x, v_x), \psi \rangle \Downarrow_\Gamma \langle v, \sigma'' \rangle} \quad \text{(E-LET)}$$
$$\langle \mathsf{let}\ x = e_1\ \mathsf{in}\ e_2, \rho, \sigma, \psi \rangle \Downarrow \langle v, \sigma'' \rangle$$

$$\frac{a_x = \rho(x) \quad v_x = \mathcal{A}(ae, \rho, \sigma)}{\langle e, \rho, \mathsf{update}(\sigma, a_x, v_x), \psi \rangle \Downarrow_\Gamma \langle v, \sigma' \rangle} \quad \text{(E-SET)}$$
$$\langle \mathsf{set}\ x := ae\ \mathsf{then}\ e, \rho, \sigma, \psi \rangle \Downarrow \langle v, \sigma' \rangle$$

While this approach can safely collect garbage to improve precision, it still loses out on the full advantages of both abstract GC and pushdown control flow.

First, the abstract interpreter no longer enjoys context irrelevance. While the continuation itself is not directly part of a configuration, the addresses reachable from the continuation are. Configurations that only differ in the context in which they are used (i.e., they have different continuations), and that would otherwise be equal, may therefore be analysed multiple times by the analysis (i.e., when the set of reachable addresses ψ is also different, leading to multiple configurations).

Second, the abstract interpreter can not take advantage of the pushdown control flow to collect more garbage. That is, it can not reclaim any bindings reachable from the continuation (as these are kept alive by ψ), even though these are not actually used for the current evaluation step. An optimal approach would be able to more aggressively collect garbage using a smaller root set (i.e., without ψ), only adding back the bindings reachable by ψ *after* the evaluation step to construct the updated store to continue evaluation with.

Program Semantics. As with the small-step semantics, we can define a function eval : Exp $\to$ $\mathcal{P}$(Val $\times$ Store) that returns all possible return values (and stores):

$$\mathsf{eval}(e) = \{(v,\sigma) \mid \langle e, [], \bot_\sigma \rangle \Downarrow_\Gamma \langle v, \sigma \rangle\}$$

We refer to the work of Darais et al. [2] for a cache-based fixpoint algorithm to compute the (finite) big-step relation ($\Downarrow_\Gamma$). The same paper also shows how the evaluation rules can be instrumented to compute the collecting semantics.

3 Delta Store Semantics

We now present the core foundation of delta store semantics (DSS). DSS closely resembles the standard big-step semantics presented in Sect. 2.2. The main difference is that evaluation now returns a *delta store* (representing changes to the original store) instead of the entire updated store.

We first introduce delta stores in Sect. 3.1, along with a set of operations on delta stores defining how they are *joined* and *composed*. We also show how a delta store can be applied to the original store, in order to reconstruct the updated store. In Sect. 3.2, we then modify the abstract big-step semantics for λ_{ANF}, resulting in an equivalent semantics formulated using delta stores.

3.1 Delta Stores

A delta store captures bindings that were changed with respect to a given store σ. Put differently, it is the subset of the updated store containing all bindings that σ has potentially[8] been extended or updated with.

Formally, we define delta stores similarly to regular stores:

$$\delta \in \mathsf{Delta} = \mathsf{Addr} \rightharpoonup (\mathsf{Val} \times \mathsf{Count})$$

The difference is that a delta store is represented as a *partial* function, since it only maps addresses that have been modified w.r.t. the original store.

In what follows, we show how delta stores can be applied, composed, and joined.

Application. A delta store δ, representing changes over an original store σ, can be applied to σ in order to construct the updated store in which these changes are directly integrated. Since both stores and delta stores are represented as functions, we can use the mathematical *override* operator ($\triangleright$) for this purpose:

$$(f_1 \triangleright f_2)(a) = \begin{cases} f_1(a) & \text{if } a \in dom(f_1) \\ f_2(a) & \text{if } a \notin dom(f_1) \land a \in dom(f_2) \end{cases}$$

---

[8] A delta store may also contain updated bindings that happen to have the same value as in the original store σ, although this makes its usage slightly less efficient.

That is, we can write $\delta \triangleright \sigma$ to apply the changes of delta store δ to the original store σ. Note that the result of this operation is a Store, as $dom(\sigma) = \mathsf{Addr}$, so that $\delta \triangleright \sigma$ is always a total function $\mathsf{Addr} \to (\mathsf{Val} \times \mathsf{Count}) = \mathsf{Store}$. A lookup in this store will first look for the address in the delta store δ, and for unchanged bindings (i.e., that are not in δ) fall back to the original store σ.

Composition. We also require an operator to combine multiple delta stores that represent a sequence of changes (e.g., resulting from the evaluation of multiple expressions in a sequence). That is, given a delta store δ_1 (representing changes over a store σ) followed by a delta store δ_2 (representing changes over $\delta_1 \triangleright \sigma$), we want to be able to combine these changes into a single delta store.

To this end, we can use the same override operator ($\triangleright$) as an operator for composition. A series of changes represented in order by delta stores $\delta_1, \delta_2, ..., \delta_n$ can then be composed into a single delta store $\delta_n \triangleright ... \triangleright \delta_2 \triangleright \delta_1$, which (when applied to a store σ) will integrate all changes of these delta stores in that same order. Note that, when applied to two delta stores δ_1 and δ_2, the result of the composition is again a delta store (i.e., a partial function) with $dom(\delta_2 \triangleright \delta_1) = dom(\delta_1) \cup dom(\delta_2)$.

Join. Delta stores are joinable, but only when they represent changes over the same store σ, so that the resulting delta store also represents changes over σ. Therefore, we define a join operator ($\sqcup_\sigma$) parameterized over some store σ:

$$(\delta_1 \sqcup_\sigma \delta_2)(a) = \begin{cases} \delta_1(a) \sqcup \delta_2(a) & \text{if } a \in dom(\delta_1) \wedge a \in dom(\delta_2) \\ \delta_1(a) \sqcup \sigma(a) & \text{if } a \in dom(\delta_1) \wedge a \notin dom(\delta_2) \\ \sigma(a) \sqcup \delta_2(a) & \text{if } a \notin dom(\delta_1) \wedge a \in dom(\delta_2) \end{cases}$$

Note that $dom(\delta_1 \sqcup_\sigma \delta_2) = dom(\delta_1) \cup dom(\delta_2)$. When joining delta stores, it is important to consider what happens when an address is in one delta store, but not the other. In this case, we join the binding of the delta store with the binding of the original store σ, since the lack of a binding in the other delta store implies no change w.r.t. the original store (hence, the original binding is preserved).

The join operator ($\sqcup_\sigma$) is useful to handle non-determinism in the abstract semantics, as the results of multiple program paths (which each include a delta store) following a non-deterministic choice can be joined together into a single result. We will make use of this operator later in Sect. 5 when we integrate flow-sensitive store widening into the abstract semantics using delta stores.

3.2 Big-Step Abstract Semantics with Delta Stores for λ_{ANF}

We now formulate the big-step abstract semantics for λ_{ANF} using delta stores. The main difference to the big-step semantics presented in Sect. 2.2 is that all modifications to the store are now expressed as delta stores. We first adapt the auxiliary functions that modify the store, extend and update, to return a delta store (with a single change) instead of an updated store. If $\langle v_a, c_a \rangle = \sigma(a)$, then:

$$\text{extend}(\sigma, a, v) = [a \mapsto \langle v_a \sqcup v, \text{inc}(c_a) \rangle]$$

$$\text{update}(\sigma, a, v) = \begin{cases} [a \mapsto \langle v, 1 \rangle] & \text{if } c_a = 1 \\ [a \mapsto \langle v_a \sqcup v, c_a \rangle] & \text{otherwise} \end{cases}$$

Note that these definitions have remained mostly unchanged. The only difference is that the change is now expressed as a "portable" delta store, as opposed to being directly integrated into the store that is extended or updated.

Next, we introduce a new big-step evaluation relation ($\Downarrow^\Delta$), which returns a delta store instead of an updated store as part of the result. That is, we define:

$$res \in \text{Result} = \text{Val} \times \text{Delta}$$

The updated evaluation rules for ($\Downarrow^\Delta$) are given below:

$$\frac{v = \mathcal{A}(ae, \rho, \sigma)}{\langle ae, \rho, \sigma \rangle \Downarrow^\Delta \langle v, [] \rangle} \quad \text{(E-ATOM)}$$

$$\frac{\langle \lambda x.e, \rho' \rangle \in \mathcal{A}(f, \rho, \sigma) \quad a_x = \text{alloc}(x) \quad v_x = \mathcal{A}(ae, \rho, \sigma)}{\delta_x = \text{extend}(\sigma, a_x, v_x) \quad \langle e, \rho'[x \mapsto a_x], \delta_x \triangleright \sigma \rangle \Downarrow^\Delta \langle v, \delta \rangle}{\langle f(ae), \rho, \sigma \rangle \Downarrow^\Delta \langle v, \delta \triangleright \delta_x \rangle} \quad \text{(E-APP)}$$

$$\frac{\langle e_1, \rho, \sigma \rangle \Downarrow^\Delta \langle v_x, \delta_1 \rangle \quad \sigma' = \delta_1 \triangleright \sigma \quad a_x = \text{alloc}(x)}{\delta_x = \text{extend}(\sigma', a_x, v_x) \quad \langle e_2, \rho[x \mapsto a_x], \delta_x \triangleright \sigma' \rangle \Downarrow^\Delta \langle v, \delta_2 \rangle}{\langle \text{let } x = e_1 \text{ in } e_2, \rho, \sigma \rangle \Downarrow^\Delta \langle v, \delta_2 \triangleright \delta_x \triangleright \delta_1 \rangle} \quad \text{(E-LET)}$$

$$\frac{a_x = \rho(x) \quad v_x = \mathcal{A}(ae, \rho, \sigma)}{\delta_x = \text{update}(\sigma, a_x, v_x) \quad \langle e, \rho, \delta_x \triangleright \sigma \rangle \Downarrow^\Delta \langle v, \delta \rangle}{\langle \text{set } x := ae \text{ then } e, \rho, \sigma \rangle \Downarrow^\Delta \langle v, \delta \triangleright \delta_x \rangle} \quad \text{(E-SET)}$$

When evaluating an atomic expression (E-ATOM), the store is not modified, and hence the empty delta store [] is returned. When evaluating an application (E-APP), the store is first extended with a binding for the argument (represented by δ_x), and afterwards also potentially modified during the evaluation of the function body (represented by δ). The resulting delta store is therefore $\delta \triangleright \delta_x$. Similarly, when evaluating a let expression (E-LET), the resulting delta store composes the changes made by the evaluation of the right-hand side expression e_1, the binding of the variable x, and the evaluation of the body e_2. When evaluating a variable assignment (E-SET), we compose the change of the update operation with the changes returned by the subsequent evaluation.

One can show that the abstract big-step semantics defined with ($\Downarrow^{\Delta}$) is equivalent to the semantics defined with ($\Downarrow$), as stated by Theorem 1.

Theorem 1. $\forall e, \rho, \sigma, \sigma', v : \langle e, \rho, \sigma \rangle \Downarrow \langle v, \sigma' \rangle \iff \exists \delta : \langle e, \rho, \sigma \rangle \Downarrow^{\Delta} \langle v, \delta \rangle \land \sigma' = \delta \triangleright \sigma.$

4 Integrating Abstract GC

We now make use of these new big-step semantics using delta stores to integrate abstract GC. By using delta stores (instead of returning the updated store), it is now safe to evaluate an expression using an input store that has been garbage collected without taking references from the continuation into account (i.e., they may be removed by the GC). The key insight is that the computed delta store can later be *replayed* on the original store that has not yet been garbage collected, and in which the bindings necessary for the continuation are still present.

To enable this process, we first introduce such a replay operation for delta stores in Sect. 4.1. Using this new operation, we then integrate abstract GC into the delta store semantics in Sect. 4.2 In Sect. 4.3, we show that the resulting form of abstract GC is not just equivalent, but in fact superior to the traditional form of abstract GC found in small-step abstract interpreters.

4.1 Replaying Delta Stores

A key ingredient to allow the integration of abstract GC into the big-step semantics is the *replay* operation. It transforms a delta store δ (which was computed using a store where bindings for the continuation may have been collected) into a delta store δ' that "restores" the bindings necessary for the continuation (found in the original store σ). That is, it simulates ("replays") the changes captured by δ on σ, computing the changes that would have occurred with respect to σ.

To illustrate the purpose of the replay operation, consider an abstract interpretation (with abstract GC) for the following Scheme program:

```
(define (make-adder n)
    (lambda (x) (+ x n)))
(let ((f1 (make-adder 1)))
    (let ((f2 (make-adder 2)))
        (f2 (f1 0))))
```

Assuming a context-insensitive allocation policy, the abstract interpreter will allocate the same address for the variable n (henceforth denoted as @n) in both calls to make-adder. The first call will return a delta store containing the binding @n -> 1. This binding can (temporarily) be garbage collected when evaluating the second call: while it is still necessary for the continuation of that call, its evaluation itself does not require this binding. The second call will therefore return a delta store containing the binding @n -> 2. However, after returning from the second call, we can not just continue evaluation using a store that binds @n to 2. That is, we first need to use the replay operation to restore the old binding as well, resulting in a store where @n is bound to the join of 1 and 2.

Formally, we define replay : Delta $\to$ Store $\to$ $\mathcal{P}$(Addr) $\to$ Delta as follows:

$$\mathsf{replay}(\delta, \sigma, A)(a) = \begin{cases} \delta(a) & \text{if } a \in dom(\delta) \land a \notin A \\ \langle v_\sigma \sqcup v_\delta, \mathsf{inc}(c_\sigma) \rangle & \text{if } a \in dom(\delta) \land a \in A \land c_\delta = 1 \\ \langle v_\sigma \sqcup v_\delta, \infty \rangle & \text{if } a \in dom(\delta) \land a \in A \land c_\delta = \infty \end{cases}$$

where $\langle v_\sigma, c_\sigma \rangle = \sigma(a)$ and $\langle v_\delta, c_\delta \rangle = \delta(a)$. Note that replaying a delta store preserves the domain it is defined over (i.e., $dom(\mathsf{replay}(\delta, \sigma, A)) = dom(\delta)$).

Function replay takes three arguments: the delta store δ to be replayed, the original store σ (on which δ is replayed), and a set A of all addresses in δ that were *allocated* (i.e., representing (abstractions of) new addresses) during the computation of δ. The case where an address a is not in A, but is present in δ implies that the change represents an update to an existing binding (since no new binding for a was allocated). That is, address a was not collected, and therefore replay does not need to restore the original binding of a in σ (as we know that this binding was still present when the update happened). In fact, preserving $\delta(a)$ *as is* is important to maintain strong updates. In the case where address a in δ may come from a new allocation (i.e., $a \in A$), we join the old value in $\sigma(a)$ with the updated one in $\delta(a)$ (as extend would have done for a new allocation on σ). When $c_\delta = 1$, we know that a was only allocated once, and hence we increase the abstract count in σ by 1 (using inc). When $c_\delta = \infty$, we know that a may have been allocated multiple times, so the abstract count becomes ∞.

4.2 Delta Store Semantics with Abstract GC

We now modify the big-step evaluation relation ($\Downarrow^\Delta$) to integrate abstract GC. In order to do so, we need to keep track of which addresses in δ may have been *allocated* and which may have been *updated*. Keeping track of a set of allocated addresses A is necessary to support the replay operation (cf. sup.). Keeping track of a set of updated addresses U is necessary to correctly collect garbage in the resulting delta store, which needs to maintain all bindings reachable from the resulting value *and* all existing bindings that were updated during the evaluation (in order to ensure that side effects that happened during evaluation are not lost). We add these two sets of addresses directly to the result of the evaluation:

$$res \in \mathsf{Result} = \mathsf{Val} \times \mathsf{Delta} \times \mathcal{P}(\mathsf{Addr}) \times \mathcal{P}(\mathsf{Addr})$$

Next, we adapt the evaluation rules to integrate abstract GC as follows:

- For each evaluation rule, we trivially construct both A and U as the set of addresses allocated (resp. updated) directly in that rule, combined with those allocated (resp. updated) in recursive evaluation steps.
- In the E-LET rule (the only evaluation rule for λ_{ANF} with a non-tail recursive evaluation step), we need to ensure that the delta store computed by the first recursive evaluation step is replayed, so that the bindings needed for the second recursive evaluation step are restored. All other recursive evaluation steps in the evaluation rules do not have an additional (implicit) continuation for which bindings need to be preserved, and therefore do not require their delta store to be replayed (doing so would unnecessarily add imprecision).
- Analogous to the integration of abstract GC into $(\Downarrow)$ (cf. Sect. 2.2), we add an evaluation relation $(\Downarrow_\Gamma^\Delta)$ with the following E-GC rule.

$$\frac{\begin{array}{c}\sigma_{\mathsf{gc}} = \sigma|_{\mathcal{R}_{(\leadsto_\sigma)}(\mathcal{T}_{\mathsf{Env}}(\rho))} \\ \langle e, \rho, \sigma_{\mathsf{gc}}\rangle \Downarrow^\Delta \langle v, \delta, A, U\rangle \\ \delta_{\mathsf{gc}} = \delta|_{\mathcal{R}_{(\leadsto_{\delta \triangleright \sigma_{\mathsf{gc}}})}(\mathcal{T}_{\mathsf{Val}}(v) \cup U_{\mathsf{gc}})} \\ A_{\mathsf{gc}} = A \cap dom(\delta_{\mathsf{gc}}) \qquad U_{\mathsf{gc}} = \{a \in U \mid \sigma_{\mathsf{gc}}(a) \neq \bot\}\end{array}}{\langle e, \rho, \sigma\rangle \Downarrow_\Gamma^\Delta \langle v, \delta_{\mathsf{gc}}, A_{\mathsf{gc}}, U_{\mathsf{gc}}\rangle} \quad \text{(E-GC)}$$

That is, rule E-GC collects garbage in both the input store σ as well as the output delta store δ (computing reachable addresses over $\delta \triangleright \sigma_{\mathsf{gc}}$, as bindings in the delta store δ may reference those in σ_{gc} and vice versa). It also restricts the sets of addresses A and U: A can be restricted by only keeping addresses that are actually in δ (removing garbage-collected allocations), and U can be restricted by only keeping addresses that have an existing binding in the store σ_{gc}. The crucial difference with the E-GC rule of $(\Downarrow_\Gamma)$ is that the stores are garbage collected using only the references from the environment (for σ) and the returned/updated values as the GC root set (for δ). References from the continuation, previously kept alive using ψ, now no longer need to be taken into account, leading to more garbage being collected and therefore amplifying the benefits of abstract GC. We subsequently replace $(\Downarrow^\Delta)$ with $(\Downarrow_\Gamma^\Delta)$ for all recursive evaluation steps, so that GC is applied at every step.

The resulting evaluation rules for $(\Downarrow^\Delta)$ are given below:

$$\frac{v = \mathcal{A}(ae, \rho, \sigma)}{\langle ae, \rho, \sigma \rangle \Downarrow^{\Delta} \langle v, [], \emptyset, \emptyset \rangle} \text{ (E-ATOM)}$$

$$\frac{\langle \lambda x.e, \rho' \rangle \in \mathcal{A}(f, \rho, \sigma) \quad a_x = \text{alloc}(x) \quad v_x = \mathcal{A}(ae, \rho, \sigma)}{\delta_x = \text{extend}(\sigma, a_x, v_x) \quad \langle e, \rho'[x \mapsto a_x], \delta_x \triangleright \sigma \rangle \Downarrow^{\Delta}_{\Gamma} \langle v, \delta, A, U \rangle}{\langle f(ae), \rho, \sigma \rangle \Downarrow^{\Delta} \langle v, \delta \triangleright \delta_x, \{a_x\} \cup A, U \rangle} \text{ (E-APP)}$$

$$\frac{\langle e_1, \rho, \sigma \rangle \Downarrow^{\Delta}_{\Gamma} \langle v_x, \delta_1, A_1, U_1 \rangle \quad \delta'_1 = \text{replay}(\delta_1, \sigma, A_1)}{\sigma' = \delta'_1 \triangleright \sigma \quad a_x = \text{alloc}(x) \quad \delta_x = \text{extend}(\sigma', a_x, v_x)}{\langle e_2, \rho[x \mapsto a_x], \delta_x \triangleright \sigma' \rangle \Downarrow^{\Delta}_{\Gamma} \langle v, \delta_2, A_2, U_2 \rangle}{\langle \text{let } x = e_1 \text{ in } e_2, \rho, \sigma \rangle \Downarrow^{\Delta} \langle v, \delta_2 \triangleright \delta_x \triangleright \delta'_1, A_1 \cup \{a_x\} \cup A_2, U_1 \cup U_2 \rangle} \text{ (E-LET)}$$

$$\frac{a_x = \rho(x) \quad v_x = \mathcal{A}(ae, \rho, \sigma)}{\delta_x = \text{update}(\sigma, a_x, v_x) \quad \langle e, \rho, \delta_x \triangleright \sigma \rangle \Downarrow^{\Delta}_{\Gamma} \langle v, \delta, A, U \rangle}{\langle \text{set } x := ae \text{ then } e, \rho, \sigma \rangle \Downarrow^{\Delta} \langle v, \delta \triangleright \delta_x, A, \{a_x\} \cup U \rangle} \text{ (E-SET)}$$

4.3 Comparison to Traditional Abstract GC

It is interesting to compare the impact of our formulation of abstract GC for DSS with the impact of existing "traditional" abstract GC, as pioneered by Might et al. for small-step abstract interpreters [21]. Intuitively, we have already established that abstract GC in ($\Downarrow^{\Delta}_{\Gamma}$) (cf. Sect. 4.2) can be more efficient than the abstract GC integrated into ($\Downarrow_{\Gamma}$) (cf. Sect. 2.2): being able to omit the continuation references ψ results in a smaller GC root set, leading to more garbage being collected, therefore amplifying the beneficial effects of abstract GC. We now show that the same reasoning also holds for a comparison with abstract GC in the small-step semantics (as presented in Sect. 2.1). That is, because of the improved efficiency of *stackless* abstract GC, the result obtained through a big-step evaluation using ($\Downarrow^{\Delta}_{\Gamma}$) is guaranteed to be at least as precise as the corresponding result obtained by a small-step abstract interpreter using ($\rightarrow_{\Gamma}$).

Theorem 2 states this claim more formally:

Theorem 2. $\forall e, \rho, \sigma, v, \delta, A, U, \sigma_k, a_k : \langle e, \rho, \sigma \rangle \Downarrow^{\Delta}_{\Gamma} \langle v, \delta, A, U \rangle \rightarrow \exists v', \sigma', \sigma_k' :$
$\langle ev(e, \rho), \sigma, \sigma_k, a_k \rangle \xrightarrow{*}_{\Gamma} \langle ap(v'), \sigma', \sigma_k', a_k \rangle \wedge v \sqsubseteq v'$.

That is, when an expression e evaluates to v (using an environment ρ and store σ), there exists at least one sequence of evaluation steps for the small-step abstract interpreter that evaluates the same expression e to a less precise (or equally precise) value v'. We can match the small-step state ς evaluating e with the state ς' holding its result v' by ensuring that $a_{k\varsigma} = a_{k\varsigma'}$ (i.e., when the abstract interpreter reaches the same continuation a_k again with a return value). A high-level sketch for the proof of Theorem 2 is given in the appendix, while the full proof (using the Rocq theorem prover) is part of the replication package.

5 Integrating Flow-Sensitive Store Widening

We now formulate a new form of store widening for the big-step semantics using delta stores. Without any form of store widening, a fixpoint computation over the evaluation relation of Sect. 4 might be expensive, or even in some cases not computable. The store widening we propose is similar to the traditional notion of flow sensitivity: it solves the scalability issues, while still allowing strong updates and a limited form of abstract GC. Moreover, it can be efficiently formulated for DSS, as we have previously shown that delta stores are also joinable (which is efficient because of their minimal representation).

Section 5.1 explains why store widening is necessary to ensure that program semantics remain computable. Next, Sect. 5.2 shows how the DSS evaluation relation can be modified to integrate such (flow-sensitive) store widening.

5.1 The Need for Store Widening

The program semantics for λ_ANF expressed in terms of the evaluation relation ($\Downarrow_\Gamma^A$) (cf. Sect. 4) are always computable. The reason for this is that one can easily show the relation ($\Downarrow_\Gamma^A$) to be finite, since both Config and Result are also finite. However, the relation can still grow very large, as the size of Store alone is in the order of $\mathcal{O}(|\mathsf{Val}|^{|\mathsf{Addr}|})$, potentially leading to many different input configurations that need to be evaluated. Even worse, in an extension of λ_ANF (for instance with numerical abstract domains), we may want to choose a set Val that is not necessarily finite. Clearly, in this case, the relation ($\Downarrow_\Gamma^A$) would also no longer be finite, and therefore potentially not computable (preventing decidability).

For instance, a common abstraction for numerical domains is a *constant propagation lattice*, for which the Hasse diagram is shown in Fig. 1. Such an abstract domain is no longer finite, but adheres to the *ascending chain condition* (ACC). The ACC states that every weakly ascending sequence of values (i.e., a sequence $(v_n)_{n \in \mathbb{N}}$ where $v_i \sqsubseteq v_{i+1}$) eventually converges to a stable value (i.e., $\exists n : \forall k \in \mathbb{N} : v_n = v_{n+k}$). Intuitively, such a lattice has a finite "height", so that we can only "go up" in the lattice a finite number of steps. It is reasonable to expect an analysis to be decidable when the abstract domain Val adheres to the ACC, even if it is infinite.

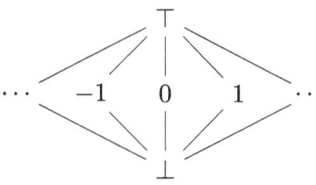

Fig. 1. Hasse diagram of a numerical constant propagation lattice.

Problem: Abstract GC Inhibits Convergence. Without abstract GC (and in the absence of strong updates), eval(e) would always be computable for any program e when Val adheres to the ACC (even when Val is otherwise infinite). The reason is that the store can only grow over a single execution trace (we say the sequence of stores is *monotonically increasing*), therefore eventually converging (as all values in the store converge, as guaranteed by the ACC). With abstract GC (and strong updates), this no longer holds. Bindings in the store can be removed (or strongly updated to a value that does not subsume the original one), and as such there is no guarantee of convergence in every trace. This requires us to make sure Val is finite in order to render eval(e) computable for any e.

We can easily illustrate this using the following Scheme program:

```
(letrec ((f (lambda (n) (f (+ n 1))))) (f 0))
```

We assume an abstract interpreter using a constant propagation lattice for the numerical domain (as depicted in Fig. 1) and a context-insensitive allocation policy (again writing @n for the address of variable n). The first call to f binds @n to 0. Without abstract GC, the next recursive call to f would extend that binding by joining the existing value with 1, resulting in a configuration where @n is bound to ⊤. Subsequent recursive steps would end up in the same configuration, therefore allowing the fixpoint algorithm to terminate. With abstract GC, the old binding of @n could be garbage collected before the store is extended for the next recursive call. As such, the second call would end up in a configuration where @n is bound to 2, the third one with @n bound to 3 and so on, resulting in an infinite number of configurations to evaluate.

Solution: Store Widening Recovers Convergence. The classical solution to ensure convergence for such domains is to introduce store widening [30]. Using store widening, stores of different configurations are joined together. Since a store is a finite mapping from addresses to values of the abstract domain Val, the ACC for Val implies the ACC for Store. Therefore, under the ACC, an infinite sequence of stores $\sigma_0, \sigma_1, \ldots$ from different congurations can be turned into a monotonically increasing sequence of stores $(\sigma'_n)_{n \in \mathbb{N}}$ where $\sigma'_0 = \sigma_0$ and $\sigma'_{i+1} = \sigma'_i \sqcup \sigma_{i+1}$, which is guaranteed to converge (to the stable value $\bigsqcup_{n \in \mathbb{N}} \sigma_i$) as $\sigma'_i \sqsubseteq \sigma'_{i+1}$ by design.

Traditionally, *global* store widening has been applied to both small-step (AAM-based) [30] and big-step (definitional) [2] abstract interpreters. Under global store widening, the stores of all configurations are joined in a single store. This results in a flow-insensitive analysis, as the abstract interpreter does not discern different stores at different program points. Unfortunately, global store widening renders both abstract GC and abstract counting completely useless: abstract GC is unable to collect any garbage (since it needs to keep everything that is reachable from any configuration/state), whereas strong updates are never applicable (since all abstract counts eventually become ∞ when the global store converges).

We can, however, choose a middle ground between purely local stores and global store widening. The store widening we propose for DSS in this section joins stores of configurations at the same program point. That is, the analysis keeps track of a single store per program point (being the join of all stores encountered at that program point). This corresponds to a flow-sensitive analysis. While less precise than local stores, it is known that flow sensitivity still allows for strong updates, and as we discuss in Sect. 5.2, a limited form of abstract GC.

5.2 Delta Store Semantics with Flow-Sensitive Store Widening

We now show how this form of flow-sensitive store widening can be integrated into the delta store semantics with abstract GC of Sect. 4. Doing so should ensure that the evaluation relation ($\Downarrow_T^A$) becomes finite (and therefore computable) whenever Val adheres to the ACC. This requires the following two modifications:

- We no longer keep the store directly as part of each configuration. That is, instead of having multiple configurations $\langle e, \rho, \sigma_i \rangle$ (i.e., with the same expression e and environment ρ but different stores σ_i), we now only have a single configuration $\langle e, \rho \rangle$, which gets associated with a single store $\bigsqcup_i \sigma_i$. As such, the definition of Config is updated as follows:

$$conf \in \mathsf{Config} = \mathsf{Exp} \times \mathsf{Env}$$

For a context-insensitive analysis, such a configuration effectively corresponds to a single program point[9]. To associate a single store with each configuration, we make use of a map $\Xi_{e_0} : \mathsf{Config} \to \mathsf{Store}$. The store $\Xi_{e_0}(conf)$ over-approximates the join of all stores σ_i that can occur at the configuration $conf$ (i.e., that previously were part of that configuration), where e_0 is the initial expression of the program[10]. We first define a relation (654$conf \subseteq \mathsf{Store} \times \mathsf{Config}$, where intuitively $\sigma \leadsto_{conf} conf'$ implies that σ potentially "flows to" $conf'$ during the evaluation of the configuration $conf$. We can then define $\Xi(conf)$ as the join of all (garbage-collected[11]) stores that flow to $conf$:

$$\Xi(\langle e, \rho \rangle) = \bigsqcup \{\sigma|_{\mathcal{R}_{(\leadsto\sigma)}(\mathcal{T}_{\mathsf{Env}}(\rho))} \mid \sigma \leadsto_{\langle e_0, [] \rangle} \langle e, \rho \rangle\}$$

- We ensure that the evaluation relation ($\Downarrow^A$) (and ($\Downarrow_T^A$)) become deterministic (i.e., they can be seen as functions $\mathsf{Config} \to \mathsf{Result}$). This is done by joining the results whenever there are multiple non-deterministic program paths.

Together, this suffices to show that ($\Downarrow_T^A$) becomes a finite relation: it is clear that by factoring out the store, Config becomes finite, and when ($\Downarrow_T^A$) is deterministic, only a single result $res \in \mathsf{Result}$ can be associated with each configuration. And

---

[9] Note that for a context-sensitive analysis, the context would be part of Config, and so the store would be shared per program point and context.
[10] For brevity, from this point on we drop the subscript and instead write Ξ for Ξ_{e_0}.
[11] Note that we apply garbage collection before joining the stores, which results in a more precise store compared to doing it the other way around.

although $(\leadsto)_{conf}$ is technically not finite (since an infinite number of stores can flow to a configuration *conf* when Val is infinite), $\Xi(conf)$ is computed as the join of all these stores, which is guaranteed to converge due to the ACC.

We now present the updated evaluation rules for $(\Downarrow^\Delta)$ and $(\Downarrow^\Delta_\Gamma)$, together with the derivation rules for the relation $(\leadsto)_{conf}$ (i.e., included in the same rules).

$$\frac{\sigma = \Xi(conf) \qquad v = \mathcal{A}(ae, \rho, \sigma)}{\underbrace{\langle ae, \rho \rangle \Downarrow^\Delta \langle v, [], \emptyset, \emptyset \rangle}_{conf}} \quad \text{(E-Atom)}$$

$$\frac{\begin{array}{c} \sigma = \Xi(conf) \qquad \langle \lambda x_i.e_i, \rho'_i \rangle \in \mathcal{A}(f, \rho, \sigma) \qquad v_x = \mathcal{A}(ae, \rho, \sigma) \\ a_i = \mathsf{alloc}(x_i) \qquad \delta_i = \mathsf{extend}(\sigma, a_i, v_x) \qquad \sigma_i = \delta_i \triangleright \sigma \\ \underbrace{\langle e_i, \rho'_i[x \mapsto a_i] \rangle \Downarrow^\Delta_\Gamma \langle v_i, \delta'_i, A_i, U_i \rangle}_{conf'} \qquad \sigma_r \leadsto_{conf'} conf_r \\ \hline v = \bigsqcup_i v_i \qquad \delta = \bigsqcup_{\sigma_i} \delta'_i \triangleright \delta_i \qquad A = \bigcup_i \{a_i\} \cup A_i \qquad U = \bigcup_i U_i \\ \sigma' \leadsto_{conf} conf' \qquad \sigma_r \leadsto_{conf} conf_r \qquad \underbrace{\langle f(ae), \rho \rangle \Downarrow^\Delta \langle v, \delta, A, U \rangle}_{conf} \end{array}} \quad \text{(E-App)}$$

$$\frac{\begin{array}{c} \sigma = \Xi(conf) \qquad \underbrace{\langle e_1, \rho \rangle \Downarrow^\Delta_\Gamma \langle v_x, \delta_1, A_1, U_1 \rangle}_{conf_1} \qquad \sigma_{r_1} \leadsto_{conf_1} conf_{r_1} \\ \delta'_1 = \mathsf{replay}(\delta_1, \sigma, A_1) \qquad \sigma' = \delta'_1 \triangleright \sigma \qquad a_x = \mathsf{alloc}(x) \qquad \delta_x = \mathsf{extend}(\sigma', a_x, v_x) \\ \sigma'' = \delta_x \triangleright \sigma' \qquad \underbrace{\langle e_2, \rho[x \mapsto a_x] \rangle \Downarrow^\Delta_\Gamma \langle v, \delta_2, A_2, U_2 \rangle}_{conf_2} \qquad \sigma_{r_2} \leadsto_{conf_2} conf_{r_2} \\ \sigma \leadsto_{conf} conf_1 \qquad \sigma'' \leadsto_{conf} conf_2 \qquad \sigma_{r_1} \leadsto_{conf} conf_{r_1} \qquad \sigma_{r_2} \leadsto_{conf} conf_{r_2} \\ \hline \underbrace{\langle \mathsf{let}\ x = e_1\ \mathsf{in}\ e_2, \rho \rangle \Downarrow^\Delta \langle v, \delta_2 \triangleright \delta_x \triangleright \delta'_1, A_1 \cup \{a_x\} \cup A_2, U_1 \cup U_2 \rangle}_{conf} \end{array}} \quad \text{(E-Let)}$$

$$\frac{\begin{array}{c} \sigma = \Xi(conf) \qquad a_x = \rho(x) \qquad v_x = \mathcal{A}(ae, \rho, \sigma) \qquad \delta_x = \mathsf{update}(\sigma, a_x, v_x) \\ \sigma' = \delta_x \triangleright \sigma \qquad \underbrace{\langle e, \rho \rangle \Downarrow^\Delta_\Gamma \langle v, \delta, A, U \rangle}_{conf'} \qquad \sigma_r \leadsto_{conf'} conf_r \\ \sigma' \leadsto_{conf} conf' \qquad \sigma_r \leadsto_{conf} conf_r \\ \hline \underbrace{\langle \mathsf{set}\ x := ae\ \mathsf{then}\ e, \rho \rangle \Downarrow^\Delta \langle v, \delta \triangleright \delta_x, A, \{a_x\} \cup U \rangle}_{conf} \end{array}} \quad \text{(E-Set)}$$

$$\frac{\begin{array}{c} \sigma_{\mathsf{gc}} = \Xi(conf) \qquad \langle e, \rho \rangle \Downarrow^\Delta \langle v, \delta, A \rangle \\ \delta_{\mathsf{gc}} = \delta|_{\mathcal{R}_{(\leadsto \delta \triangleright \sigma_{\mathsf{gc}})}(\mathcal{T}_{\mathsf{Val}}(v) \cup U_{\mathsf{gc}})} \\ A_{\mathsf{gc}} = A \cap dom(\delta_{\mathsf{gc}}) \qquad U_{\mathsf{gc}} = \{a \in U \mid \sigma_{\mathsf{gc}}(a) \neq \bot\} \\ \hline \underbrace{\langle e, \rho \rangle \Downarrow^\Delta_\Gamma \langle v, \delta_{\mathsf{gc}}, A_{\mathsf{gc}}, U_{\mathsf{gc}} \rangle}_{conf} \end{array}} \quad \text{(E-GC)}$$

The first modification is that since the store is no longer part of a configuration *conf*, we instead retrieve it as $\Xi(conf)$. Conversely, for every configuration *conf'* (reachable during the evaluation of *conf*) that normally would have included σ, we now instead derive that $\sigma \leadsto_{conf} conf'$. These derivations come both directly from the evaluation of the current configuration, as well as from recursive evaluations of other configurations. The second modification is that the E-App rule (the only evaluation rule for λ_{ANF} that faces non-determinism) now joins the results for each possible function that may be called. Doing so makes use of the join operator ($\sqcup_\sigma$) for delta stores to efficiently merge changes computed w.r.t. σ over multiple non-deterministic paths.

Note that computing ($\Downarrow_\Gamma^\Delta$) requires a fixpoint computation over both the relations ($\Downarrow_\Gamma^\Delta$) and ($\leadsto$)$_{conf}$. We again refer to the cache-based fixpoint algorithm presented by Darais et al. [2], which can be employed *mutatis mutandis* as one possible implementation for such a fixpoint computation.

Impact on Abstract GC. We recall that abstract GC offers three key advantages: (1) it avoids precision losses due to unnecessary joins (with garbage values), (2) it improves abstract counting by resetting abstract counts for collected addresses, and (3) it speeds up the fixpoint computation thanks to garbage irrelevance.

When using flow-sensitive ("per configuration") store widening, the precision improvements of (1) are largely negated. The reason is that addresses are usually identified by the program point they are allocated at, so that all values bound to an address end up joined in the same shared store associated with that program point (regardless of if it was collected before being allocated again[12]). In theory, some precision can still be gained from collecting garbage that arises from updates, since updates (unlike allocations) may occur at different program points.

The main precision benefit of abstract GC with flow-sensitive store widening comes from (2). With abstract GC, the abstract count of a collected address is reset to 0, so that it is increased to 1 when the address is allocated again. Store widening will only join (i.e., not necessarily increase) the abstract counts for all allocations of an address at its corresponding program point. Reclaiming garbage bindings before such allocations can therefore keep the count at 1 instead of ∞, increasing the potential for strong updates (and therefore precision).

Abstract GC is also useful in conjunction with flow-sensitive store widening because of (3). Specifically, garbage irrelevance makes the computation of Ξ more efficient, since the fixpoint iteration joining stores at the same program point together reaches a stable value more quickly when garbage bindings are removed. That is, the iteration does not have to continue until these garbage bindings converge to a stable value as well. In turn, this improves the convergence rate (and reduces memory consumption) for the fixpoint computation.

6 Evaluation

We have already formally shown that DSS with abstract GC always matches or improves upon the precision of traditional GC for a small-step abstract interpreter, using a mechanised proof implemented in the Rocq theorem prover (cf.

---

[12] Note that this assumes that allocations are differentiated using the same context sensitivity as configurations. For less precise allocators (e.g., a monovariant allocator in a context-sensitive analysis) – or when using trace partitioning [18] – the allocation of an address does not always end up widened in the same store. Therefore, it may be beneficial to reclaim previous occurrences of that address first, and such analysis designs can gain more precision when combining flow sensitivity with abstract GC.

Sect. 4.3). Likewise, we have discussed the impact of flow sensitivity for DSS, as well as its interaction with abstract GC (cf. Sect. 5.2). We now present an accompanying empirical evaluation, using our implementation in the MAF framework.[13] Both our implementation, as well as the mechanised Rocq proof for Theorem 2, are included as part of the replication package for this paper.

Specifically, we aim to answer the following research questions:

RQ1. How much precision is gained using a stackless form of abstract GC (as integrated for DSS in Sect. 4) compared to traditional abstract GC?

RQ2. What is the impact of flow-sensitive store widening (as discussed in Sect. 5) on the precision and scalability of DSS?

RQ3. What is the impact of abstract GC for flow-sensitive DSS?

Evaluation Setup. Our implementation in MAF extends the formalisations for λ_{ANF} to support a large subset of R5RS Scheme. As such, we are able to run our experiments using a benchmark suite of 15 Scheme programs: 9 from the Gabriel benchmarking suite [6][14] and 6 from the built-in benchmarking suite of MAF. Table 1 lists each Scheme program along with its size in LOC.

Table 1. Overview of the Scheme programs used as benchmarks, along with lines of code (LOC) for each benchmark. The Gabriel benchmarks are highlighted in **bold**.

Benchmark	LOC	Benchmark	LOC	Benchmark	LOC
boyer	593	**destruc**	65	matrix	648
browse	211	**diviter**	24	mceval	282
cpstak	24	**divrec**	19	regex	80
dderiv	83	**takl**	20	rsa	85
deriv	39	grid	35	**tak**	11

We compare different abstract interpreters in terms of precision and performance. For precision, we use the built-in precision measurement utilities of the MAF framework. These compare precision by first running the program using a concrete interpreter (multiple times to cover multiple program paths in non-deterministic programs), and subsequently measuring how many values in each abstract interpreter strictly over-approximate (i.e., are less precise than) the corresponding results of the concrete interpreter. A more precise analysis should therefore result in fewer over-approximations compared to a less precise one.

---

[13] Although we have not presented a formal proof for the soundness of DSS, we have validated this empirically using the automated soundness testing in MAF.

[14] We omitted the `ctak` benchmark and `triangl` benchmarks from the original Gabriel benchmarking suite. The `ctak` benchmark was removed due to its use of `call/cc` (which is not supported by the MAF framework, and also would not be trivial to integrate into DSS, since it breaks the context irrelevance of the semantics). The `triangl` benchmark was removed because it timed out for the concrete interpreter.

Unlike the minimal formalisations presented in this paper for λ_{ANF} (which only allow for limited allocation policies), our implementations do support various configurations for context sensitivity. We run our experiments using m-CFA [23] context sensitivity (which uses the top m stack frames as context) for varying values of m (where higher values of m may increase precision). For the abstract domain, we employ a constant propagation lattice (as depicted in Fig. 1, Sect. 5.1) as an abstraction for primitive domains in all experiments.

6.1 RQ1: The Precision Benefit of Stackless Abstract GC

Theorem 2 guarantees that the precision of DSS with abstract GC (i.e., using the evaluation relation $(\Downarrow_\Gamma^A)$) is always the same or better than that of an equivalent small-step abstract interpreter with abstract GC (i.e., using the transition relation $(\to_\Gamma)$). However, it does not guarantee that the precision is *strictly* better, nor does it tell us how much precision improvement can be expected.

In order to evaluate this empirically, we therefore compare precision with an equivalent implementation of AAM with abstract GC and abstract counting (also known as ΓCFA [21]). However, recall that such a small-step abstract interpreter may exhibit decreased precision compared to DSS for two reasons: the lack of stackless abstract GC and the lack of full stack precision (which DSS inherits from its foundation in abstract definitional interpreters). Since we are only interested in measuring the former, we have modified ΓCFA to instead use a fully precise continuation address allocator (specifically, the one from AAC [13]), so that it exhibits the same stack precision as DSS.

Table 2 compares the results for ΓCFA and DSS with abstract GC. Note that for benchmarks that timed out, we can use the partial results of the analysis in order to compute a *lower bound* for the number of over-approximations (as the result would only grow more imprecise as the analysis continues).

Comparison of Precision. The results confirm the claim stated by Theorem 2: in all benchmarks where both ΓCFA and DSS terminate, we have an equal (cpstak, regex) or lower (grid, rsa, tak) number of over-approximations for DSS. The context-insensitive (i.e., $m = 0$) analyses of the regex benchmark also show significant precision improvements for DSS: the analysis with ΓCFA times out with *at least* 34 over-approximations, and requires increased context sensitivity (i.e., $m \geq 1$) in order to achieve the same precision as a context-insensitive analysis with DSS. The improvements also hold when context sensitivity is increased for both abstract interpreters: for the dderiv benchmark with $m = 2$, ΓCFA has at least 11 over-approximations compared to exactly 7 in DSS. As we have modified ΓCFA with a fully precise continuation allocator, we can attribute these improvements to the stackless nature of abstract GC in DSS, which can reclaim more garbage compared to the abstract GC of ΓCFA.

We have also compared precision to the big-step abstract interpreter with abstract GC of Sect. 2.2, which is more similar to DSS but keeps track of a set of continuation addresses ψ. Our experiments show identical[15] precision results for

---

[15] Expect for the rsa benchmark due to a known, unrelated implementation difference.

Table 2. Comparison of the number of strict over-approximations (lower is better) and time taken between small-step ΓCFA and big-step DSS with (stackless) abstract GC. A time of ∞ indicates that the benchmark exceeded the time limit of 10 min; in this case, we report a lower bound for the number of over-approximations.

	$m=0$				$m=1$				$m=2$			
	ΓCFA		DSS		ΓCFA		DSS		ΓCFA		DSS	
	imprec	time	imprec	time	imprec	time	imprec	time	imprec	time	imprec	time
boyer	≥ 0	∞	≥ 0	∞	≥ 0	∞	≥ 0	∞	≥ 0	∞	≥ 0	∞
browse	≥ 5	∞	≥ 7	∞	≥ 0	∞	≥ 4	∞	≥ 7	∞	≥ 4	∞
cpstak	3	50 ms	3	26 ms	3	11 s	3	5 s	≥ 3	∞	≥ 0	∞
dderiv	≥ 28	∞	38	20 s	≥ 7	∞	7	1 s	≥ 11	∞	7	1 s
deriv	≥ 3	∞	3	1 s	≥ 3	∞	3	1 s	≥ 4	∞	3	1 s
destruc	≥ 8	∞	≥ 10	∞	≥ 8	∞	≥ 10	∞	≥ 3	∞	≥ 3	∞
diviter	≥ 4	∞	4	3 s	≥ 0	∞	4	3 s	≥ 0	∞	2	4 s
divrec	≥ 4	∞	4	3 s	≥ 0	∞	3	3 s	≥ 0	∞	3	3 s
takl	≥ 6	∞	6	1 s	≥ 3	∞	6	9 s	≥ 3	∞	6	4 m 48 s
grid	10	1m34s	7	200 ms	≥ 2	∞	7	167 ms	≥ 2	∞	7	390 ms
matrix	≥ 10	∞	≥ 10	∞	≥ 9	∞	≥ 10	∞	≥ 9	∞	≥ 10	∞
mceval	≥ 3	∞	≥ 3	∞	≥ 3	∞	≥ 3	∞	≥ 12	∞	13	36 s
regex	≥ 34	∞	0	92 ms	0	293 ms	0	95 ms	0	275 ms	0	100 ms
rsa	14	923 ms	7	75 ms	14	58 s	7	92 ms	≥ 14	∞	7	78 ms
tak	2	20 s	0	2 s	≥ 0	∞	0	1 s	≥ 0	∞	0	1 s

this interpreter as for ΓCFA (therefore omitted here for brevity). This confirms that the precision improvements for DSS in Table 2 indeed stem from being able to omit ψ from the GC root set (i.e., rendering the GC "stackless").

Comparison of Performance. Both ΓCFA and DSS time out for a significant number of benchmarks, showing poor scalability for both abstract interpreters. Timeouts are more frequent for ΓCFA. This can partially be explained by its use of the stack-precise AAC continuation allocator [13], which for the context-insensitive case (i.e., $m=0$) is known to raise analysis complexity from $\mathcal{O}(n^3)$ to $\mathcal{O}(n^8)$. Further performance improvements can also in part be explained by the increased precision of DSS: as precision increases, the abstract interpreter spends less time having to explore *spurious program paths* (i.e., execution paths that only exist due to excessive over-approximation of the program's control flow behaviour). This effect can also be observed for the same abstract interpreter by increasing context sensitivity (e.g., for the mceval benchmark with DSS).

6.2 RQ2: The Impact of Flow-Sensitive Store Widening

We now evaluate the impact of flow-sensitive store widening on both precision and scalability. For this purpose, we run the same experiments again, this time comparing a version of DSS without store widening (i.e., the $(\Downarrow_\Gamma^A)$ evaluation relation of Sect. 4) and a version of DSS with flow-sensitive store widening (i.e., using $(\Downarrow_{\tilde{\Gamma}}^A)$) as presented in Sect. 5). The results are shown in Table 3.

Table 3. Comparison of the number of strict over-approximations (lower is better) and time taken between DSS with and without flow-sensitive store widening (DSS-FS and DSS, resp.). A time of ∞ indicates that the benchmark exceeded the time limit of 10 min; in this case, we report a lower bound for the number of over-approximations.

	$m=0$				$m=1$				$m=2$			
	DSS		DSS-FS		DSS		DSS-FS		DSS		DSS-FS	
	imprec	time	imprec	time	imprec	time	imprec	time	imprec	time	imprec	time
boyer	≥ 0	∞	1251	9 m 46 s	≥ 0	∞	≥ 1236	∞	≥ 0	∞	≥ 48	∞
browse	≥ 7	∞	91	8 s	≥ 4	∞	88	22 s	≥ 4	∞	≥ 80	∞
cpstak	3	26 ms	3	9 ms	3	5 s	3	72 ms	≥ 0	∞	3	222 ms
dderiv	38	20 s	48	905 ms	7	1 s	46	2 s	7	1 s	38	5 s
deriv	3	1 s	29	517 ms	3	1 s	9	451 ms	3	1 s	8	787 ms
destruc	≥ 10	∞	15	610 ms	≥ 10	∞	15	738 ms	≥ 3	∞	13	1 s
diviter	4	3 s	6	1 s	4	3 s	6	2 s	2	4 s	4	2 s
divrec	4	3 s	4	2 s	3	3 s	4	2 s	3	3 s	4	2 s
takl	6	1 s	6	60 ms	6	9 s	6	143 ms	6	4 m 48 s	6	710 ms
grid	7	200 ms	12	106 ms	7	167 ms	12	212 ms	7	390 ms	10	237 ms
matrix	≥ 10	∞	180	8 s	≥ 10	∞	129	18 s	≥ 10	∞	128	1 m 27 s
mceval	≥ 3	∞	159	19 s	≥ 3	∞	157	2 m 02 s	13	36 s	≥ 157	∞
regex	0	92 ms	48	547 ms	0	95 ms	48	3 s	0	100 ms	48	7 s
rsa	7	75 ms	18	54 ms	7	92 ms	17	74 ms	7	78 ms	17	96 ms
tak	0	2 s	2	5 ms	0	1 s	2	19 ms	0	1 s	2	120 ms

Comparison of Precision. It is clear that store widening, even when applied per configuration, still greatly decreases precision compared to an equivalent abstract interpreter without any store widening. Across all benchmarks, DSS-FS has significantly more over-approximations compared to DSS. A key factor explaining these differences is that abstract GC no longer offers the same precision for DSS-FS as it did for DSS (we explore this further in RQ3). Instead, the analysis is now more reliant on increased context sensitivity in order to improve its precision.

Comparison of Performance. The key benefit of applying store widening is that it greatly improves the performance of the abstract interpreter (and therefore its scalability towards larger programs such as boyer, browse and mceval). Indeed, without widening, many programs fail to terminate for DSS, either because of an exponential explosion in the number of configurations to evaluate or because values in its (infinite) domain can never converge. In contrast, for DSS-FS, we only observe 4 timeouts in total, and in fact none for the context-insensitive variant (i.e., where $m = 0$). In other benchmarks (e.g., takl with $m = 2$), performance is improved by orders of magnitude. While the precision benefits of DSS without store widening are appealing, we therefore argue that *some* store widening (such as flow-sensitive store widening) is a must to analyze larger, real-world programs.

6.3 RQ3: The Impact of Abstract GC on Flow-Sensitive DSS

As discussed in Sect. 5.2, store widening limits the precision benefits of abstract GC. We can, however, expect it to have a positive impact on the performance of the analysis by reducing the number of iterations that are required for each flow-sensitive store to converge. We evaluate the impact of abstract GC in the setting of flow-sensitive store widening by comparing two versions of DSS-FS: one with and one without abstract GC. Table 4 shows the results.

Table 4. Comparison of the number of strict over-approximations (lower is better) and time taken between DSS-FS with and without abstract GC. A time of ∞ indicates that the benchmark exceeded the time limit of 10 min; in this case, we report a lower bound for the number of over-approximations.

	$m=0$				$m=1$				$m=2$			
	with GC		without GC		with GC		without GC		with GC		without GC	
	imprec	time	imprec	time	imprec	time	imprec	time	imprec	time	imprec	time
boyer	1251	9 m 46 s	1251	3 m 12 s	≥1236	∞	1249	6 m 13 s	≥48	∞	48	1 m 36 s
browse	91	8 s	98	2 s	88	22 s	88	8 s	≥80	∞	80	7 m 33 s
cpstak	3	9 ms	3	14 ms	3	72 ms	3	50 ms	3	222 ms	3	129 ms
dderiv	48	905 ms	48	379 ms	46	2 s	46	1 s	38	5 s	38	4 s
deriv	29	517 ms	29	223 ms	9	451 ms	9	288 ms	8	787 ms	8	453 ms
destruc	15	610 ms	15	449 ms	15	738 ms	15	743 ms	13	1 s	13	1 s
diviter	6	1 s	6	2 s	6	2 s	6	1 s	4	2 s	4	1 s
divrec	4	2 s	4	2 s	4	2 s	4	1 s	4	2 s	4	1 s
takl	6	60 ms	6	45 ms	6	143 ms	6	100 ms	6	710 ms	6	908 ms
grid	12	106 ms	12	185 ms	12	212 ms	12	301 ms	10	237 ms	10	374 ms
matrix	180	8 s	181	7 s	129	18 s	129	32 s	128	1 m 27 s	128	3 m 50 s
mceval	159	19 s	159	7 s	157	2 m 02 s	157	1 m 27 s	≥157	∞	≥151	∞
regex	48	547 ms	48	387 ms	48	3 s	48	3 s	48	7 s	48	12 s
rsa	18	54 ms	18	112 ms	17	74 ms	17	90 ms	17	96 ms	17	158 ms
tak	2	5 ms	2	6 ms	2	19 ms	2	28 ms	2	120 ms	2	323 ms

Comparison of Precision. As expected, abstract GC has very little impact on precision when employing flow-sensitive store widening. The only benchmarks that show some minor precision improvement are `browse` and `matrix`. The reasons for these limited precision improvements are discussed in Sect. 5.2. In summary, abstract GC's main precision benefit comes from updates (i.e., updates to mutable variables and mutable data structures). However, these may not occur frequently in our benchmarking suite: although Scheme is technically an imperative language, in practice it often encourages a more functional style, avoiding such side-effecting mutations. The benefits on DSS-FS with abstract GC may therefore be more pronounced for languages with programming styles that make frequent use of (field) assignments (such as Python or JavaScript).

Comparison of Performance. Both configurations achieve comparable performance results, with some benchmarks (such as `boyer`) showing a clear edge for DSS-FS without GC, and others (such as `matrix`) exhibiting better performance using DSS-FS with GC. The reason is that the integration of abstract GC impacts performance both positively and negatively.

The negative impact comes from the overhead that is associated with GC. In our implementation specifically, we use a tracing stop-and-copy GC applied at every evaluation step (in order to maximize the precision benefits); it is known that such a policy can potentially slow down an abstract interpreter by one or two orders of magnitude [29], and is therefore not recommended in practice.

Despite this significant overhead, the performance still holds up well compared to DSS-FS without abstract GC. This can be attributed to the positive impact of abstract GC on performance, as the stores at each program point converge faster without garbage. To measure this benefit without the technical overhead of abstract GC, we conducted a separate experiment measuring the number of iteration steps required for the fixpoint computation of the analysis. For instance, the `matrix` benchmark only requires 2448 iterations with GC compared to 3098 without, explaining its performance improvement. On average, for our experiments abstract GC decreases the number of iterations required by 27,8%.

7 Related Work

The benefits of abstract GC for the analysis of higher-order languages have long been recognised: early work by Jagannathan et al. [16] proposes a primitive (albeit inefficient) form of abstract GC in conjunction with abstract counting in order to improve the precision of must-alias analyses. Might et al. later pioneered the use of abstract GC (and abstract counting), as presented in this work, for small-step abstract interpreters constructed using the AAM approach [30] to abstract interpretation, referring to the resulting analysis as ΓCFA [21]. Their work shows that abstract GC offered order-of-magnitude improvements to both the precision and performance of abstract interpreters in this setting.

Later work made several efforts to integrate abstract GC into abstract interpreters that enjoy the benefits of pushdown control flow, such as the big-step abstract definitional interpreters of Darais et al. [2]. Abstract definitional interpreters are also the foundation of DSS. We have discussed the original integration of abstract GC into abstract definitional interpreters, and the shortcomings of this integration, in Sect. 2.2. Likewise, Earl et al. [4] show how abstract GC can be integrated into a pushdown flow analysis (aiming to reap the benefits of both). They formulate their approach as *stack introspection*: for every control point they approximate the set of continuation frames that could be on the stack, using their references as part of the root set to collect garbage. Similar to the suboptimal integration of abstract GC into abstract definitional interpreters, the resulting analysis no longer enjoys the context irrelevance of the original pushdown analysis, and does not achieve the same potential in precision improvements of abstract GC as the stackless form of abstract GC for DSS.

CFA2 [31] combines full stack precision with some form of abstract GC. It separates bindings on the stack from those on the heap. Stack bindings are automatically "garbage collected" as stack frames are popped; this is similar to how DSS can garbage collect (unreferenced) local variables (regardless of whether they are already allocated for the continuation) in a delta store upon returning. However, in CFA2, bindings may also escape to the heap, which is not GC'd.

The closest to our own work is the *heap fragment* semantics (HFAC) of Germane et al. [8,9]. Similar to how delta stores in DSS represent changes w.r.t. an original store, a heap fragment in HFAC only captures bindings relevant for the current evaluation. To our knowledge, HFAC is the only other existing formalism exhibiting all advantages of pushdown control flow and abstract GC, as listed in Sect. 1.1. We improve upon the work of [8] by adding support for abstract counting and collecting garbage in delta stores (whereas the technique presented in [8] only collected garbage for the input heap fragment). The authors of [9] point out the "formal weight" of HFAC, which significantly complicates the language semantics. Compared to their work, we present a novel and simpler formalism, capturing the essence of the mechanism that allows the integration of abstract GC. We also show how delta stores can be joined, and extend the formalism to incorporate a novel form of store widening that preserves flow sensitivity.

Monat et al. [24] also integrate abstract GC into a flow-sensitive analysis for Python (in the MOPSA framework). In contrast to our own work, their abstract garbage collector still includes continuation references as part of the GC root set, and therefore does not benefit from the precision improvements of "stackless" abstract GC. Similar to our own findings on RQ3 (cf. Sect. 6.3), they also report limited precision benefits when flow-sensitive widening is used, and argue that abstract GC is mainly useful to improve analysis performance and memory consumption. They also point out that abstract GC *may* improve precision due to its interaction with recency abstraction [1], similar to how we argued in Sect. 5 that it may improve precision due to its interaction with abstract counting.

We implemented abstract GC using a tracing stop-and-copy collector that is interleaved at every evaluation step. As observed by the results for RQ3 (cf. Sect. 6.3), this adds severe GC overhead (which for DSS-FS negates the performance benefits of abstract GC). Other frameworks [17,20,21] apply abstract GC less frequently to tame this overhead. Van Es et al. [29] propose replacing tracing abstract GC with abstract reference counting, which is automatically applied at every step without significant overhead. We leave the integration of such abstract reference counting into DSS open as future work.

The flow-sensitive store widening of Sect. 5 joins stores per control location (and context). Trace partitioning [18,25] can generalize this technique by using abstract traces to keep multiple stores at the same control location (but with different execution traces reaching that control location) separate. Keeping more stores separate improves precision, and may also increase the precision benefits of abstract GC (compared to what we observed in RQ3) as different values allocated at the same address may be joined in different stores (therefore making it useful to reclaim previous bindings at that address using abstract GC).

Germane et al. [7] distinguish between three different kinds of "control-flow sensitivity", so that an analysis is either *path-sensitive*, *flow-sensitive* or *flow-insensitive*. The second indeed corresponds to our own interpretation of flow sensitivity, as formulated for DSS with store widening in Sect. 5 (whereas the semantics of Sects. 2, 3 and 4 would be labelled as *path-sensitive*). Most existing abstract interpreters, based on AAM or abstract definitional interpreters, only consider using either entirely local stores (resulting in a path-sensitive analysis) or *globally* widened stores [2,12,30] (resulting in a flow-insensitive analysis) instead. Flow sensitivity has so far been more common in traditional data-flow analyses [14,15,26]. Interestingly, Oh et al. [27] suggest an *adaptive* approach to control-flow sensitivity, where different addresses are treated with different sensitivities (in their work, only handling them either flow-sensitively or flow-insensitively). For our own experiments, it is clear that the precision benefits of path sensitivity in combination with abstract GC are substantial, but impede analysis scalability when applied to all addresses. Applying their learning strategy for choosing between both control-flow sensitivities adaptively for each address could potentially bring together the benefits of both DSS and DSS-FS.

8 Conclusion

In this work, we have presented delta store semantics (DSS), a novel formulation for big-step abstract definitional interpreters where evaluation steps return a delta store to capture all changes made to the input store. Unlike regular stores, delta stores are more minimal (representing only changes), reusable (being able to be applied to or *replayed* for a (larger) store), composable and efficiently joinable. We have shown how these delta stores enable the integration of both abstract GC and a flow-sensitive variant of store widening into DSS.

When using DSS with abstract GC – without store widening – we not only achieve the full advantages of pushdown control flow and abstract GC, but also unlock an additional synergy between both that further increases the benefits of abstract GC. Specifically, we have shown both formally (using the Rocq theorem prover) and empirically (using our implementation in MAF) that this combination outperforms a small-step interpreter with abstract GC.

When using DSS with flow-sensitive store widening, our experiments confirm that DSS no longer faces the scalability issues that are inherent to the usage of local (path-sensitive) stores. Unlike global (flow-insensitive) store widening, we have shown that the resulting abstract interpreter still supports abstract counting (i.e., strong updates) and a limited form of abstract GC.

Acknowledgments. This work was partially supported by an Innoviris grant for the ECOPIPE project (Joint R&D 2022, grant number 2022-PS-JRDIC-8) and by the Research Foundation Flanders (FWO) (grant number 1187122N).

Disclosure of Interests. The authors have no competing interests to declare that are relevant to the content of this article.

Appendix

We can prove Theorem 2 using mutual induction on $(\Downarrow^\mathcal{A})$ and $(\Downarrow^\mathcal{A}_\Gamma)$. Doing so, however, first requires generalising this theorem in order to strengthen the induction hypothesis, resulting in Theorem 3.

Theorem 3. $\forall e, \rho, \sigma, v, \delta, A, U, \varsigma = \langle ev(e, \rho), \sigma_\varsigma, \sigma_{k_\varsigma}, a_k \rangle$,
$\mathcal{R}_\rho = \mathcal{R}_{(\leadsto_\sigma)}(\mathcal{T}_{\mathsf{Env}}(\rho)), \sigma_{gc} = \sigma|_{\mathcal{R}_\rho}, \mathcal{R}_v = \mathcal{R}_{(\leadsto_{\delta \triangleright \sigma_{gc}})}(\mathcal{T}_{\mathsf{Val}}(v))$:
$\mathcal{R}_k = \mathcal{R}_{(\leadsto_\varsigma)}(\{a_k\}), \sigma_{gc} = \sigma|_{\mathcal{R}_\rho}$:
$\langle e, \rho, \sigma \rangle \Downarrow^\mathcal{A}_\Gamma \langle v, \delta, A, U \rangle \land (\sigma_{gc} \sqsubseteq \sigma_\varsigma) \land (\Gamma(\varsigma) = \varsigma) \to \exists \varsigma' = \langle \boldsymbol{ap}(v'), \sigma_{\varsigma'}, \sigma_{k_{\varsigma'}}, a_k \rangle$:
$\varsigma \to^*_\Gamma \varsigma' \land (v \sqsubseteq v') \land (\sigma_{k_\varsigma} \sqsubseteq \sigma_{k_{\varsigma'}}) \land (\forall a \in dom(\delta) : \delta(a) \sqsubseteq \sigma_{\varsigma'}(a))$
$\land (\forall a \in \mathcal{R}_v \setminus dom(\delta) : \sigma_{gc}(a) \sqsubseteq \sigma_{\varsigma'}(a)) \land (\mathcal{R}_v \subseteq \mathcal{R}_{(\leadsto_{\sigma_{\varsigma'}})}(\mathcal{T}_{\mathsf{Val}}(vq')))$

The generalisation relaxes the precondition of the implication. That is, the big-step evaluation may use another store than the small-step one, as long as it is equal to or subsumed by the latter. This is necessary to ensure that the induction hypothesis can be applied in the E-LET case, since the second evaluation step may use a more precise store after continuing with a more precise result from the first evaluation step. Likewise, the generalisation strengthens the postconditions, which now for instance also ensure that the bindings in the resulting delta store are more precise than the corresponding bindings in the resulting store of the small-step evaluation. This is again necessary for the E-LET case, because the second recursive evaluation continues using the delta store produced by the first.

Theorem 2 can now be seen as a corollary of Theorem 3. We elide the proof of Theorem 3 here for brevity; instead, we have verified this property using a mechanised proof[16], implemented using the Rocq theorem prover.

References

1. Balakrishnan, G., Reps, T.: Recency-abstraction for heap-allocated storage. In: Yi, K. (ed.) SAS 2006. LNCS, vol. 4134, pp. 221–239. Springer, Heidelberg (2006). https://doi.org/10.1007/11823230_15

---

[16] For convenience, on a more standard version of λ_{ANF} without mutable variables.

2. Darais, D., Labich, N., Nguyen, P.C., Van Horn, D.: Abstracting definitional interpreters (functional pearl). Proc. ACM Program. Lang. **1**(ICFP), 12:1–12:25 (2017). https://doi.org/10.1145/3110256
3. Earl, C., Might, M., Van Horn, D.: Pushdown control-flow analysis of higher-order programs. In: The 2010 Workshop on Scheme and Functional Programming (2010)
4. Earl, C., Sergey, I., Might, M., Van Horn, D.: Introspective pushdown analysis of higher-order programs. In: ACM SIGPLAN International Conference on Functional Programming, ICFP'12, Copenhagen, Denmark, 9–15 September 2012, pp. 177–188. ACM (2012). https://doi.org/10.1145/2364527.2364576
5. Flanagan, C., Sabry, A., Duba, B.F., Felleisen, M.: The essence of compiling with continuations. In: Proceedings of the ACM SIGPLAN 1993 Conference on Programming Language Design and Implementation (PLDI), Albuquerque, New Mexico, USA, 23–25 June1993, pp. 237–247 (1993). https://doi.org/10.1145/155090.155113
6. Gabriel, R.P.: Performance and Evaluation of LISP Systems, vol. 263. MIT Press Cambridge, Massachusetts (1985). https://doi.org/10.7551/mitpress/5298.001.0001
7. Germane, K.: Full control-flow sensitivity for definitional interpreters. In: Giacobazzi, R., Gorla, A. (eds.) Static Analysis. SAS 2024. LNCS, vol. 14995, pp. 120–146. Springer, Cham (2024). https://doi.org/10.1007/978-3-031-74776-2_5
8. Germane, K., Adams, M.D.: Liberate abstract garbage collection from the stack by decomposing the heap. In: ESOP 2020. LNCS, vol. 12075, pp. 197–223. Springer, Cham (2020). https://doi.org/10.1007/978-3-030-44914-8_8
9. Germane, K., McCarthy, J.: Newly-single and loving it: improving higher-order must-alias analysis with heap fragments. Proc. ACM Program. Lang. **5**(ICFP), 1–28 (2021). https://doi.org/10.1145/3473601
10. Gilray, T., Adams, M.D., Might, M.: Allocation characterizes polyvariance: a unified methodology for polyvariant control-flow analysis. In: Proceedings of the 21st SIGPLAN International Conference on Functional Programming, ICFP 2016, Nara, Japan, 18–22 September 2016, pp. 407–420 (2016). https://doi.org/10.1145/2951913.2951936
11. Gilray, T., Lyde, S., Adams, M.D., Might, M., Van Horn, D.: Pushdown control-flow analysis for free. In: Proceedings of the 43rd Annual SIGPLAN-SIGACT Symposium on Principles of Programming Languages, POPL 2016, St. Petersburg, FL, USA, 20–22 January 2016, pp. 691–704. ACM (2016). https://doi.org/10.1145/2837614.2837631
12. Glaze, D.A., Labich, N., Might, M., Van Horn, D.: Optimizing abstract abstract machines. In: ACM SIGPLAN International Conference on Functional Programming, ICFP 2013, Boston, MA, USA, 25–27 September 2013, pp. 443–454. ACM (2013). https://doi.org/10.1145/2500365.2500604
13. Glaze, D.A., Van Horn, D.: Abstracting abstract control. In: Black, A.P., Tratt, L. (eds.) DLS 2014, Proceedings of the 10th ACM Symposium on Dynamic Languages, part of SPLASH 2014, Portland, OR, USA, October 20–24 2014, pp. 11–22. ACM (2014). https://doi.org/10.1145/2661088.2661098
14. Hardekopf, B., Lin, C.: Flow-sensitive pointer analysis for millions of lines of code. In: Proceedings of the CGO 2011, The 9th International Symposium on Code Generation and Optimization, Chamonix, France, 2–6 April 2011, pp. 289–298. IEEE Computer Society (2011). https://doi.org/10.1109/CGO.2011.5764696
15. Hind, M., Pioli, A.: Assessing the effects of flow-sensitivity on pointer alias analyses. In: Levi, G. (ed.) SAS 1998. LNCS, vol. 1503, pp. 57–81. Springer, Heidelberg (1998). https://doi.org/10.1007/3-540-49727-7_4

16. Jagannathan, S., Thiemann, P., Weeks, S., Wright, A.K.: Single and loving it: must-alias analysis for higher-order languages. In: MacQueen, D.B., Cardelli, L. (eds.) POPL 1998, Proceedings of the 25th ACM SIGPLAN-SIGACT Symposium on Principles of Programming Languages, San Diego, CA, USA, January 19–21 1998, pp. 329–341. ACM (1998). https://doi.org/10.1145/268946.268973
17. Jensen, S.H., Møller, A., Thiemann, P.: Type analysis for JavaScript. In: Palsberg, J., Su, Z. (eds.) SAS 2009. LNCS, vol. 5673, pp. 238–255. Springer, Heidelberg (2009). https://doi.org/10.1007/978-3-642-03237-0_17
18. Mauborgne, L., Rival, X.: Trace partitioning in abstract interpretation based static analyzers. In: Sagiv, M. (ed.) ESOP 2005. LNCS, vol. 3444, pp. 5–20. Springer, Heidelberg (2005). https://doi.org/10.1007/978-3-540-31987-0_2
19. Might, M.: Environment analysis of higher-order languages. Ph.D. thesis, Georgia Institute of Technology, Atlanta, GA, USA (2007). http://hdl.handle.net/1853/16289
20. Might, M.: Logic-flow analysis of higher-order programs. In: Proceedings of the 34th ACM SIGPLAN-SIGACT Symposium on Principles of Programming Languages, POPL2007, Nice, France, 17–19 January 2007, pp. 185–198 (2007). https://doi.org/10.1145/1190216.1190247
21. Might, M., Shivers, O.: Improving flow analyses via ΓCFA: abstract garbage collection and counting. In: Proceedings of the 11th ACM SIGPLAN International Conference on Functional Programming, ICFP 2006, Portland, Oregon, USA, 16–21 September 2006, pp. 13–25 (2006). https://doi.org/10.1145/1159803.1159807
22. Might, M., Shivers, O.: Exploiting reachability and cardinality in higher-order flow analysis. J. Funct. Program. **18**(5–6), 821–864 (2008). https://doi.org/10.1017/S0956796808006941
23. Might, M., Smaragdakis, Y., Van Horn, D.: Resolving and exploiting the k-CFA paradox: illuminating functional vs. object-oriented program analysis. In: Proceedings of the 2010 ACM SIGPLAN Conference on Programming Language Design and Implementation, PLDI 2010, Toronto, Ontario, Canada, 5–10 June 2010, pp. 305–315. ACM (2010). https://doi.org/10.1145/1806596.1806631
24. Monat, R., Ouadjaout, A., Miné, A.: Value and allocation sensitivity in static Python analyses. In: Proceedings of the 9th ACM SIGPLAN International Workshop on the State Of the Art in Program Analysis, SOAP@PLDI 2020, London, UK, 15 June 2020, pp. 8–13. ACM (2020). https://doi.org/10.1145/3394451.3397205
25. Monat, R., Ouadjaout, A., Miné, A.: Mopsa-C with trace partitioning and auto-suggestions (competition contribution). In: Gurfinkel, A., Heule, M. (eds.) TACAS 2025, Part III. LNCS, vol. 15698, pp. 229–235. Springer, Cham (2025). https://doi.org/10.1007/978-3-031-90660-2_17
26. Muth, R., Debray, S.K.: On the complexity of flow-sensitive dataflow analyses. In: POPL 2000, Proceedings of the 27th ACM SIGPLAN-SIGACT Symposium on Principles of Programming Languages, Boston, Massachusetts, USA, 19–21 January 2000, pp. 67–80. ACM (2000). https://doi.org/10.1145/325694.325704
27. Oh, H., Yang, H., Yi, K.: Learning a strategy for adapting a program analysis via Bayesian optimisation. In: Proceedings of the 2015 ACM SIGPLAN International Conference on Object-Oriented Programming, Systems, Languages, and Applications, OOPSLA 2015, pp. 572–588. ACM (2015). https://doi.org/10.1145/2814270.2814309
28. Reynolds, J.C.: Definitional interpreters for higher-order programming languages. High. Order Symb. Comput. **11**(4), 363–397 (1998). https://doi.org/10.1023/A:1010027404223

29. Van Es, N., Stiévenart, Q., De Roover, C.: Garbage-free abstract interpretation through abstract reference counting. In: 33rd European Conference on Object-Oriented Programming, ECOOP 2019, 15–19 July 2019, London, United Kingdom. LIPIcs, vol. 134, pp. 10:1–10:33. Schloss Dagstuhl - Leibniz-Zentrum für Informatik (2019). https://doi.org/10.4230/LIPIcs.ECOOP.2019.10
30. Van Horn, D., Might, M.: Abstracting abstract machines. In: Proceedings of the 15th ACM SIGPLAN International Conference on Functional programming, ICFP 2010, Baltimore, Maryland, USA, 27–29 September 2010, pp. 51–62 (2010). https://doi.org/10.1145/1863543.1863553
31. Vardoulakis, D., Shivers, O.: CFA2: a context-free approach to control-flow analysis. Log. Methods Comput. Sci. **7**(2) (2011). https://doi.org/10.2168/LMCS-7(2:3)2011

Author Index

B
Bae, Kyungmin 328

C
Campion, Marco 249
Chen, Weijun 62
Chihani, Zakaria 11
Chin, Wei-Ngan 90

D
Danvy, Olivier 1
De Roover, Coen 190, 357, 386
Drachsler-Cohen, Dana 221
Drewery, Alexandre 34
Dutta, Saikat 113

F
Foo, Darius 90
Fu, Yuxi 62

G
Gall, Tristan Le 11

H
Harif, Adi 278
Huang, Zixin 113

I
Itzhaky, Shachar 278

J
Jensen, Thomas P. 34

K
Katsura, Hiroyuki 305
Kobayashi, Naoki 305

L
Laurel, Jacob 113
Lee, Jaeseo 328
Lehmann, Julien 11
Lemesle, Augustin 11
Long, Huan 62

M
Mastroeni, Isabella 249
Misailovic, Sasa 113

N
Nagarakatte, Santosh 142
Narayana, Srinivas 142

P
Pichardie, David 34

S
Sakayori, Ken 305
Sato, Ryosuke 305
Shachnai, Matan 142
Song, Yahui 90
Stiévenart, Quentin 190

U
Urban, Caterina 249

V
Van Es, Noah 357, 386
Vandenbogaerde, Bram 190, 357, 386
Verbelen, Sarah 357
Vishwanathan, Harishankar 142

Y
Yao, Peisen 167
Yuviler, Tom 221

Z
Zheng, Junda 167

GPSR Compliance

The European Union's (EU) General Product Safety Regulation (GPSR) is a set of rules that requires consumer products to be safe and our obligations to ensure this.

If you have any concerns about our products, you can contact us on

ProductSafety@springernature.com

In case Publisher is established outside the EU, the EU authorized representative is:

Springer Nature Customer Service Center GmbH
Europaplatz 3
69115 Heidelberg, Germany

www.ingramcontent.com/pod-product-compliance
Lightning Source LLC
Chambersburg PA
CBHW070217211025

34312CB00021B/409